HANDBOOK OF
MARRIAGE
COUNSELING

HANDBOOK OF MARRIAGE COUNSELING

EDITED BY BEN N. ARD, JR.
AND CONSTANCE C. ARD

SCIENCE AND BEHAVIOR BOOKS, INC.
Palo Alto, California: 1969

Dedicated to

W. A. C.
and
M. M. A.

For support, encouragement, and backing over the years.

Fourth Printing, August 1972

Library of Congress Catalog Card 69-20467

ISBN 0-8314-0021-8

Contributors

Ard, Ben N., Jr., Ph.D. Professor of Counseling, San Francisco State College; Psychologist in private practice.

Ard, Constance C., M.A. Licensed Marriage, Family, and Child Counselor, San Francisco; Instructor, San Francisco State College.

Bach, George R., Ph.D. Director, Institute for Group Psychotherapy, Beverly Hills, California.

Bedford, Stewart, Ph.D. Psychologist, Chico, California.

Blinder, Martin G., M.D. Psychiatrist, San Francisco; Medical Director, Family Therapy Institute of Marin, San Rafael, California.

Blood, Robert O., Jr., Ph.D. Department of Sociology, University of Michigan.

Bowen, Murray, M.D. Clinical Professor in Psychiatry, Georgetown University Medical Center.

Dickinson, Charles H. Coordinator, Marriage Counseling Licensing Section, State Department of Professional and Vocational Standards, Sacramento, California.

Ellis, Albert, Ph.D. Executive Director, Institute for Rational Living, New York.

Gehrke (Luthman), Shirley, A.C.S.W., R.S.W. Co-Director, Family Therapy Institute of Marin, San Rafael, California.

Goodwin, Hilda M., D.S.W. Assistant Professor in Family Study in Psychiatry, University of Pennsylvania School of Medicine.

Harper, Robert A., Ph.D. Psychotherapist and Marriage Counselor, Washington, D. C. Past President, American Association of Marriage Counselors.

Hefner, Hugh M. Editor and Publisher of *PLAYBOY* magazine.

Hudson, Dorothy J., B.S. Family Counselor, Scottsdale, Arizona.

Hudson, John W. Ph.D. Professor of Sociology, Arizona State University.

Humphrey, Norman D., Ph.D. (Deceased) Formerly at Wayne State University.

Kerckhoff, Richard K. Ph.D. Department of Child Development and Family Life, Purdue University.

Kimber, J. A. Morris, Ph.D. (Deceased) Formerly Psychologist, Whittier, California.

Kirkendall, Lester A., Ph.D. Professor of Family Life, Oregon State University, Corvallis, Oregon.

Kirschenbaum, Martin, Ph.D. Co-Director, Family Therapy Institute of Marin, San Rafael, California.

Leslie, Gerald R., Ph.D. Chairman, Department of Sociology, University of Florida. Past President, American Association of Marriage Counselors.

Lyndon, Benjamin H., Professor, School of Social Welfare, State University of New York at Buffalo.

Lyndon, Clara B. Formerly Director, Counseling and Guidance Service, Merrill-Palmer Institute, Detroit.

Marsh, Donald C., Ph.D. Professor of Sociology, Wayne State University, Detroit.

Morgan, Owen, Ph.D. Director, Center for Family Life Studies, Arizona State University.

Moxom, James E., M.S.W. Psychological Services, Los Angeles.

Mudd, Emily H., Ph.D. Formerly Director, Marriage Council of Philadelphia.

Reiss, Ira L., Ph.D. Professor of Sociology, University of Iowa.

Rutledge, Aaron, L., Th.D. Director, Psychotherapy Program, Merrill-Palmer Institute, Detroit. Past President, American Association of Marriage Counselors.

Rydman, Edward J., Ph.D. Executive Director, American Association of Marriage Counselors.

Satir, Virginia, A.C.S.W. Family therapist; formerly Director of Training, Family Project, Mental Research Institute, Palo Alto, California.

Stern, Alfred, M.D. Gynecologist, Oakland, California.

Stokes, Walter R., M.D. Psychiatrist, Stuart, Florida.

Vincent, Clark E., Ph.D. Director, Behavioral Sciences Center, Bowman Gray School of Medicine, Wake Forest University, Winston-Salem, North Carolina.

Watson, Andrew S., M.D. Department of Psychiatry, University of Michigan.

Williams, John, M.A. Psychologist; Director, Northwest Branch, Institute for Rational Living, Seattle.

Wyden, Peter. Executive Editor, *Ladies Home Journal*.

Foreword

The multi-disciplinary field of psychotherapy, of which marriage counseling and family therapy is a very important part, is experiencing a phenomenally rapid growth. Within the past twenty-five years there have been several important changes which have helped to produce this growth. For example, there has been a profound shift from the authoritarian family in which the husband-father had the major control over his wife and children. Most of the family power, decision-making responsibility, and authority rested upon him, as did the responsibility for supporting his family economically. The shift from authoritarian to a more equalitarian family has profoundly affected the position of the head of the family as women have entered the economic marketplace in ever increasing numbers and especially as even larger numbers of mothers take their places in offices, assembly lines, and other occupations and professions. As women assume more important roles outside the home, so stresses, strains, and problems within the family relationships proliferate.

Little scientific evidence is in at this time, but there is concern expressed in some quarters that the growing rebellion of youth is a logical extension of the shift toward equalitarianism. In a new way and in ever-increasing numbers, the youth today are demanding a voice in education, marriage, sexual expression, and other significant areas of life. As women challenged the authority of man, so youth challenges the authority of the family and all other related social institutions.

These shifting patterns are related to, although not necessarily the cause of, some of the important problems which lead individuals and families to seek help from marriage and family counselors. The divorce rate, which tends to be higher in equalitarian families, is cited as a problem of our time. Increased juvenile delinquency and youth crime is another. The sexual revolution, reputed or factual, is popularly attributed to the "breakdown of the family." Some social observers have suggested that there are emerging new patterns and forms of marriage. On some college campuses there are "semester marriages" with no formal, legal, religious, or social approval. These are not unlike "trial marriages" of an earlier day, but they are occurring in far larger numbers. Premarital sexual relations are more prevalent and, apparently, are met with less social disapproval.

Many of the changes in the family and in marriage are due, among other things, to the influence of the mass media. Marshall McLuhan has

said "the family circle has widened. The worldpool of information father-
ed by electric media—movies, telstar, and flight—far surpasses any possible
influence mom and dad can now bring to bear. Character no longer is
shaped by only two earnest, fumbling experts. Now all the world's a
sage." He has suggested that ours is a time of crossing barriers and erasing
old categories. There is little question that children and youth of today
are far more aware of experiences and information from far beyond the
old boundaries of home, family, and church via television and radio. How
powerful are these electronic media in bringing about change? What inter-
generational and interfamily conflicts are generated by these everpresent
influences? These and related questions remain to be answered, but there
is little doubt about the fact that the influences are being felt most keenly
within the family.

We are living in a time of population explosion as well as information
explosion. The "baby boom" of just a few years ago has grown up to a
wave of young adults in the family formation period. This very large
portion of the total population, seeking education, jobs, mates, and personal achievement and fulfillment, and having learned that there are professionally qualified specialists in all areas of life, may be expected to turn
to the professional marriage counselor and family therapist when problems arise. The authoritarian father would "solve" his own problems while
the more equalitarian husband-father is more willing to ask the expert.

These trends have resulted in a significant increase in the need for
professionally trained marriage and family counselors. The public, in asking for help with marriage and family counseling, turned to the "helping
professions"—family doctors, clergymen, social workers, teachers, and
lawyers, who were not adequately prepared to handle such problems.
These professionals, not out of any specialized training in the complexities
of the dynamics of interpersonal interaction in marriage and the family,
but out of a genuine desire to be helpful, have provided succor. As this
need became more and more obvious, some of these professionals began
to specialize in marriage counseling. Out of this specialization during the
past twenty-five years have come some principles, concepts, tools, and
techniques which are the bases of the emerging profession.

Currently, marriage counseling, in its attempts to meet the increased
needs and expectations, has moved from the more typical individual and
conjoint therapy to family therapy. It has, in some places, begun to use
married couple group therapy with both spouses in the same group or in
separate groups. Some counseling has become group sensitivity training
for premarital or married couples. Weekend marathon group sessions are
being used by some counselors and therapists to accelerate the progress of
the therapeutic relationship. Obviously, the groups vary in intensity, techniques, theoretical orientation, or frame of reference. What is most
important is that the larger field of marriage counseling has transcended
its former boundaries and traditions.

With this book, Ben and Constance Ard have attempted to bring together in a comprehensive and coherent fashion, some of the most vital
papers to be found in the field. Out of the broad spectrum of marriage

counseling, they have formulated a carefully conceived frame of reference which will aid the scholar and the practitioner in his understanding of this developing field.

They have chosen some articles and papers that are classics. Still others are recent and vital statements of contemporary developments. They have not hesitated to include differences in approach, theory, and technique. What they have done is to call attention to the major techniques and issues, and they have, thereby, performed a most valuable service.

Edward J. Rydman, Ph.D.
Executive Director,
American Association of Marriage Counselors

Contents

Preface

The field of marriage counseling has "come of age," if we can argue from the fact that the American Association of Marriage Counselors celebrated its twenty-fifth centennial in 1967. An increasing number of professionals are now involved in marriage counseling, and there seems to be an increasing demand for marriage counseling across the country. Several states have passed laws pertaining to the certification or licensing of marriage counselors, and others are considering such laws. If all this can be said to show that marriage counseling is (or at least is becoming) a profession, with a scientific body of knowledge, some relevant theory, a code of ethics, and some specific techniques, then there would seem to be a need for a handbook of marriage counseling which would incorporate these basic elements in an easy-to-get-at reference work.

This is what we have attempted in this book. The articles in the *Handbook* represent a variety of points of view and are written by some of the outstanding professionals in the field. They have been purposefully selected to present provocative, controversial, contrasting points of view. We do not subscribe to the idea that a handbook must necessarily be dull, dry, or boring. We do not think the reader will find this book any of these. But the proof is in the pudding: check it out, read it, and see for yourself.

We are indebted to the many contributors to this volume for their articles and to the others in the field who have contributed the many books which have made the field what it is today. It has been our privilege to work with many of these contributors personally and to correspond with others. We hope that readers of this handbook, be they experienced counselors or beginners, will enjoy stimulating contacts with the ideas and the men and women in this field of marriage counseling.

If this handbook provides a ready reference for marriage counselors already practicing in the field and a stimulating introduction to the profession for the beginning counselor, it will have served its purpose.

San Francisco, California   Ben N. Ard, Jr.
1969   Constance C. Ard

Introduction

This handbook is intended as a fairly complete introduction to the field of marriage counseling. It obviously cannot contain *all* the pertinent knowledge about marriage counseling, but it does represent some of the basic knowledge, an overview of the field, something of its history and development, some of the philosophy and value problems in the field, some of the relevant theory, a sampling of some of the techniques used in the field, discussion of many of the problems faced by the marriage counselor, some of the laws pertaining to marriage counseling, the code of ethics of the national organization, and several articles dealing with practical help for the professional marriage counselor.

The articles are written by representatives of many professional fields, including psychologists, sociologists, psychiatrists, social workers, physicians, and other writers. The field of marriage counseling is truly interdisciplinary—that is one of its strengths. Sometimes practitioners who have had training in only one field (frequently from only one college or university, from teachers who only represented one point of view) end up with too narrow a view—thinking there is only one "right" way to do marriage counseling. If it accomplishes nothing else, this handbook is intended to stretch the minds of those who think that there is only one approach or one technique that needs to be applied in marriage counseling. The professional marriage counselor, just because he deals with people in an area where narrow-minded values frequently prevail (and are the causes of many of the marital problems he faces), particularly needs to have a broad, cross-cultural perspective if he is to be of optimal help to a variety of clients in our pluralistic, changing society.

In planning contents to be included in this volume, the editors conceived of marriage counseling in the broadest possible sense. It was defined as any counseling with one or more clients dealing with problems related to marriage, i.e., problems about getting married (premarital counseling); staying married; getting out of marriage; getting a divorce; sexual problems (premarital, marital, or extramarital); concerns about being a man (functioning as a man), husband, lover, father, friend; or as a woman, wife, lover, friend, mother. Consequently in the articles to be found in the following pages, the various contributors will deal with just these sorts of problems.

Some people have tried to distinguish "marriage counseling" as a separate specialty from psychotherapy; but in this handbook many of the authorities will not make this distinction, and so the reader will find in various of the articles the terms "marriage counseling" and "psycho-therapy" used interchangeably. We hope this will not bother the reader unnecessarily. Marriage counseling can be considered a special form of psychotherapy dealing particularly with the sorts of problems previously mentioned (marital, premarital, extramarital, sexual, etc.), using specific techniques geared to the nature of the problems encountered. If the term "psychotherapy" bothers some people (as it evidently does), what takes place can simply be called "marriage counseling," which to some people does not have such frightening overtones. So be it. We will leave it up to the professional marriage counselor to decide for himself just what labels he wishes to use. In this handbook, both terms will be used.

The handbook can be used in a variety of ways: as a textbook, to be read through critically and discussed; or as a reference work, to be kept handy on a nearby shelf in one's professional library for consultation when one wants to look up something about the code of ethics, the law, a different theoretical approach, or a new technique one may wish to try with a certain client or group of clients. Even if the answer to a particular question cannot be found in these pages, more frequently than not one can find a resource or a person to whom one can write for further information and help. We would hope that the indexes and appendices would prove of practical help to the counselor who wants to look up what might be available on a particular subject.

The handbook would also be of value to anyone outside the profession who wants to know something about marriage counseling; or to the layman who is concerned about some of the problems dealt with herein, is considering going to see a marriage counselor and wants to have some idea of what to expect, or is trying to do something on his own about adopting a new approach to some personal problem.

To each of the above readers, we say welcome to what we hope may prove a stimulating experience. We hope you find much to agree and disagree with in the following pages. If the handbook stretches your mind in some new ways, causes you to think in ways you have not thought before, it will have served a good purpose.

There will come a time, I know, when people will take delight in one another, when each will be a star to the other, and when each will listen to his fellow as to music. The free men will walk upon the earth, men great in their freedom. They will walk with open hearts, and the heart of each will be pure of envy and greed, and therefore all mankind will be without malice, and there will be nothing to divorce the heart from reason. Then life will be one great service to man! His figure will be raised to lofty heights—for to free men all heights are attainable.

Then we shall live in truth and freedom and in beauty, and those will be accounted the best who will the more widely embrace the world with their hearts, and whose love of it will be the profoundest; those will be the best who will be the freest; for in them is the greatest beauty. Then will life be great, and the people will be great who live that life.

MAXIM GORKY

Overview of Marriage Counseling

*... imperfect human beings can be of therapeutic assistance to
other imperfect human beings.*

CARL ROGERS

This first section serves as somewhat of an overview of marriage counseling—a broad look at the profession and the eclectic group of professional people who actually do marriage counseling. The highest of ideals have been held out for the marriage counselor; one might get the impression from reading some of the literature that he must be a super-human being, without flaw or imperfection. If marriage counselors need not be perfect but rather professional in their activities, what specifically does this mean?

Aaron Rutledge, in Chapter 1, discusses marriage counseling as a *profession* and as an *activity*. (Dr. Rutledge is particularly qualified to discuss these matters since he is a past president of the American Association of Marriage Counselors and heads one of the AAMC-approved training programs for marriage counselors at the Merrill-Palmer Institute in Detroit.) He makes a very basic point that the routine training of the established professions does not qualify persons as specialists in marriage relationships. Dr. Rutledge also gives us our first definition of marriage counseling and discusses the standards of the profession. This "classic" article was first published in 1955, so statements about legislation which were accurate then need to be checked against later legislation (cf. Chapter 42). Dr. Rutledge also suggests a plan for the training and certification of marriage counselors.

In the second chapter, Ben Ard discusses some of the assumptions which seem, implicitly, to underlie marriage counseling. In most cases these assumptions are of the broadest, most general sort, but not everyone in the field of marriage counseling would agree with each of them. These assumptions, then, may serve as ideas to be examined. Assumptions need to be explicit rather than implicit, and this article should, hopefully, stimulate thought and discussion about what the major goals and aims of marriage counseling are.

One assumption which some people in the field might differ with or question holds that there is a reality different from distorted perceptions (e.g., illusions, delusions, hallucinations, projections, fantasies, etc.). Some theoreticians deny that there is any objective reality and rely only on the

1

client's phenomenological field or subjective perceptions. The reader will have to decide for himself which assumption it is best to follow.

Another assumption which some might question is that the ultimate goal of marriage counseling is the optimal development of the *individual* client (rather than maintaining a marriage at all costs). Some marriage counselors might not agree with this individualistic approach. Again, each reader will have to decide for himself.

Chapter 3, by J. A. Morris Kimber, presents a factual study of just who has actually been doing marriage counseling in the United States in recent years. Kimber studied the telephone directories (specifically the yellow pages) in seventy-four cities throughout the United States to obtain his data.

Albert Ellis, in Chapter 4, presents a critical evaluation of marriage counseling. This "classic" article first appeared in the literature in 1956, so his statements and criticisms must be seen in the context of that time. Many of the criticisms still apply, however. Dr. Ellis deals with several important questions, such as, what kind of clients normally come for counseling? how deep-seated are the emotional disturbances or ineptness in interpersonal relations which they present? Dr. Ellis examines published cases to answer these questions. The distinction between "psychotherapy" and "counseling" is raised here, and we shall see it raised several times again throughout the handbook.

Another question Dr. Ellis explores is: what techniques of marriage counseling are usually employed (in the recently published cases)? He makes many critical points about the techniques used, and although the reader may disagree with some of the criticism, it should provoke thoughtful consideration of various ways of helping clients who seek help in marriage counseling.

CHAPTER 1

The Future of Marriage Counseling

Aaron L. Rutledge

Marriage counseling may be conceived of as a *profession* engaged in by people of many disciplines who have had specialized training, including clinical internship in handling marital problems. Marriage counseling may be thought of also as *an activity* carried on by people from various disciplines, with or without specialized training.

To argue that marriage counseling ought to be or ought not to be is not only conjecture but idle dreaming. The culture of which we are a part, with all of its family tension and unrest, is creating a growing need for skilled assistance in working at marital adjustment and growth. This same culture is now trying to satisfy this need by demanding marriage counseling and seeking to produce marriage counselors.

Major educational efforts are being made to teach people to seek help with marital problems; in colleges, in high schools, in churches and in lay groups. Popular media—press, radio, television, magazines and the movies—also have been used extensively.

The routine training of the established professions does not qualify persons as specialists in marriage relationships. The average physician is not prepared to deal adequately with marriage problems. Psychiatry as a whole does not attempt to do marriage counseling except in terms of one spouse. In most cases of marital conflict both mates are involved and to work with one alone may widen the breach in the relationship. At the least, working with only one spouse has major shortcomings in understanding and resolving marital problems. Clinical psychology is a good background for, and has much to contribute to, training in marriage counseling, but in itself does not provide adequate training. The same is true of social casework. The legal profession in general is ill-prepared to deal with emotional factors in marital conflict. The clergy see an overwhelming amount of marital stress, but most seminaries continue to offer inadequate training in this area, in spite of major progress in recent years.

Reprinted with permission of the author and the publisher from *The Merrill-Palmer Quarterly*, Summer, 1955.

MARRIAGE COUNSELING AS A PROFESSION

In each of the foregoing professions there are major exceptions, and from each group is emerging a small number of men and women who have been well trained, or are in training in marriage counseling. The American Association of Marriage Counselors, with a few more than a hundred members, is a very eclectic group, representing a great variety of disciplinary backgrounds, which is as it should be in marriage counseling.

In the meantime professional persons increasingly seek marriage counselors for their patients and clients. Attorneys, clergymen, and physicians are especially active in referring. An occasional group of physicians is employing a qualified marriage counselor to work exclusively with their patients, feeling that marital stress is a primary factor in the causation or aggravation of illness.

Supplemental education consisting of supervised training in handling cases is necessary to achieve professional status as a marriage counselor. There are few such professional persons but the number of individuals calling themselves marriage counselors is increasing rapidly.

What the public wants, it demands in one form or another. It will continue to want, demand, and get marriage counseling—either from professionals or from quacks. The professional person is called upon to respond to this need whether trained or untrained in marriage counseling.

The untrained, nonprofessional person who sets up practice as a marriage counselor poses another real problem. Among these will be well-meaning but misguided zealots who "just want to help people"; the "dabblers" who work out their own problems on others; and the charlatan who knows a good thing when he sees it and deliberately cashes in on the pain and anxiety of the client. A woman with eighth-grade education insisted upon being helped to get marriage counseling clients because "I just like to dabble in people's problems and it may as well pay off." One said, "I'm so interested in people; seem to know what they're thinking, why I do believe I'm psychotic." Another inquirer wrote: "Dear Sir, I want to be a marriage counselor. Will you please send me the material *in a hurry*." Unfortunately, there are places where certificates in marriage counseling can be obtained through correspondence courses.

There is a shortage of qualified marriage counselors, a lack of knowledge of recommended standards of training, and a total absence of means of creditation. For these reasons one of the unfortunate by-products of present educational efforts designed to stimulate people to seek help with marital problems is the creation of a fertile field for the incompetent and unscrupulous to exploit.

Competent marriage counselors compose a slowly growing and vital group which will continue to come from various disciplines, build upon these backgrounds through supervised training and experience, and become specialists in the vital area of man-woman relationships.

Marriage counselors do comprise a profession, and unless they establish themselves as such with adequate standards of training, experience, ethics, and regulations which become common knowledge, the public will continue to be at the mercy of the incompetent.

MARRIAGE COUNSELING AS AN ACTIVITY

Current developments indicate that the bulk of marriage counseling in the foreseeable future will be carried on as *an activity* by people from various disciplines with or without specialized training—from psychology, social work, medicine, the ministry, family life education, and guidance. Many of these professional people do satisfactory marriage counseling; others not only fail to help but are destructive forces in the lives of their clients. People keep going to these counselors and they do the best they can, with or without training. Even part-time marriage counseling should require certain standards, including a minimum of supervised casework. As an analogy, a doctor does not undertake a little surgery without specialized training.

While efforts are made to establish marriage counseling as a profession, it should never be forgotten that other basic disciplines have outstanding opportunities for marriage counseling, and their trainees should continue to function in this area when prepared to do so. Knowing one's limitations, being able to recognize symptoms and refer, are as essential here as in any area of maladjustment. Professional people are beginning to seek additional training and guidance in preparation for marriage counseling, and they would be glad to meet any standards established, if training opportunities were available.

WHAT IS MARRIAGE COUNSELING?

Marriage counseling begins when one or both members of a couple come to a counselor for help in resolving tension-producing difficulties. Marriage counseling is the process whereby professional skills and experience, within the context of an understanding and accepting face-to-face relationship, are brought to the assistance of spouses as they explore, evaluate, and clarify feelings and issues; as they seek to communicate verbally and emotionally; and as they learn to choose courses of action which will lead to some resolution of their problems. This can mean acceptance of facts which cannot be altered and/or growth of a more meaningful marriage relationship. It may mean the final dissolution of a marriage already destroyed, a situation which can only continue to damage the personalities involved. Such decisions are made by the counselees, not by the counselor.

The conflict may be rooted in a stunted or crippled personality and/or in the ignorance and misinformation of one or both members of the couple. On the other hand, it may lie in the nature of the relationship itself. Most often it is a multifaceted combination of both. When streams of communication within a marriage become dammed off, the backwaters of accumulated hurt feelings, misunderstanding, and resultant bitterness contaminate the spontaneous springs of love and relatedness.

The client (one or two) and the marriage counselor share in facilitating a better understanding of self, of the mate, and of the relationship. In concentrating upon each of the mates as persons, all the tools and techniques of individual counseling are needed. But marriage counseling must go further: increased understanding of the way he feels, and why, by one of a couple, becomes a stepping stone to gradual understanding of his mate's feelings, attitudes, desires, and deep-seated needs. The counselor who is also seeing the mate, or collaborating with someone who is, can be of inestimable help in the achievement of this second step. A third area of focus is the marriage relationship itself, which almost amounts to a third "person" to be counseled. These are distinct steps up the counseling ladder, but are areas in which there is simultaneous investigation and, hopefully, concomitant progress.

In some circles it has been assumed that marriage counseling requires less training and skill than personal counseling, since it is "merely concerned with the relationship." To the contrary, although a counselor first must be proficient with individuals, working with a marriage relationship requires additional knowledge and skills.

It is understandable that most members of the established professions are not prepared adequately to deal with marital problems. Individual dynamics acquire a new dimension when the role as a marriage partner is being encompassed. This examination of both marriage partners expands the already complicated procedure of counseling one person, and in a third realm of complication the counselor must recognize the unique mutuality inherent in the marriage relationship. The marriage counselor must work with inner-psychological factors, on the one hand, and with socio-psychological factors on the other hand. In focusing on the behavior patterns of *each*, he must also be able to concentrate on the interaction *between* spouses. Their dynamic relationship to each other brings about a "total" which is different from the individual capabilities and liabilities of the two people. The counselor becomes the third person in a triangular relationship, a helper to the wife and the husband, individually and together, in their decisions for change and growth or dissolution of the marriage. Thus, he becomes the target for projection and transference at a more intensive level than in most individual counseling. This requires a counselor who is strong enough, flexible enough, with enough training-experience not to permit his role with one spouse to be distorted by his relationship to the other. The situation is complicated further by the greater diversity of focus and of goals than is found in much individual counseling, since in working with a relationship the counselor is committed equally to the growth of each of the two persons and of their mutual relationship.

PROFESSIONAL STANDARDS

Existing standards for membership in the American Association of Marriage Counselors should be made public knowledge. The basic requirement is a doctoral degree or equivalent in some field which deals with human problems, such as psychology, sociology, theology, medicine, or law. In social work the graduate requirement is the master's degree. (It is questionable that this is adequate provision since some schools give a master's degree in social work for only one year of graduate study, while others have rigid and lengthy requirements.) In addition there must be several years' experience in which proficiency in marriage counseling has been demonstrated. For associate membership three such years of experience are requisite; for active membership, five years. The candidate must be sponsored by two active members who vouch for him professionally and personally. A committee is appointed to examine his qualifications, including how he handles cases, after which the membership votes upon his application.

Adequate time must be allowed through "grandfather" clauses for adaptation of those already in practice, but these standards should be revised upward to make mandatory supervised internship training and experience in handling marital problems as opportunities become available.

The foregoing would demand additional training facilities, especially at the internship level. (Present facilities for internship training in marriage counseling are the Marriage Council of Philadelphia; Marriage Counseling Service, The Menninger Foundation, Topeka, Kansas; and the Merrill-Palmer School, Detroit.) This in turn means that minimum standards of training, including qualifications for a training center, should be developed immediately. The AAMC has a committee working on these issues. Such an effort takes time but the need is urgent.

Another need would be formulation of a recommended preprofessional core of education, with perhaps a major in human development in marriage counseling, in some of the larger graduate schools, including schools of medicine and of theology. These candidates should be well grounded in one or more professional disciplines at the graduate level, with required work to form an adequate basis for internship training. The interdivisional programs in some of the leading graduate schools possess potential for preprofessional education in marriage counseling, although the curriculum might need to be supplemented by experience in an established clinical setting. Areas of graduate study for preprofessional education might include dynamics of personality development, theories of counseling and psychotherapy, the biological sciences, the dynamics of family living and theories of its development and function, psychosexual development and behavior, orientation to medical and psychiatric principles and practice training in research, and a workable knowledge of ethics, values, and philosophy. Such a background could be supplemented or intensified at needed points during the time of internship in the handling of cases, but most of it should be prerequisite.

Some long-term attention should be given to legislation providing for "privileged communication," since marriage counselors may become involved in court procedures. To date, no state gives such protection to marriage counselors as such. Only clergymen, physicians, and lawyers—in most states—have legal protection from compulsory testimony about a client. Obviously, legislation is not possible until qualification standards for marriage counselors have been established. The only hope, at present, is that a good many judges would, in the public interest, not permit such forced testimony.

Preparation of a plan for certification should be initiated as soon as possible. The American Association of Marriage Counselors has not fulfilled this need but it has served as a clearing house for inquiries about who is doing acceptable marriage counseling in any section of the country.

SUGGESTED PLAN FOR TRAINING AND CERTIFICATION

A plan for training and certification should be based upon careful evaluation of all existing factors and more than a prophetic glance into the future. It is inherent in the nature of any organization that first it just grows, later takes on maturity and demands status. The tendency then is to set standards so high that they would exclude the earlier members if they are forced to conform. AAMC has not been immune from this tendency; yet, that is the way a profession must develop if it and the public are to be protected.

Although the following plan is embryonic—possibly premature—it is presented with the belief that it is extremely important to stimulate further discussion and development in this vital area:

Select as candidates to become marriage counselors primarily those who have attained the doctorate, or equivalent, and who have functioned adequately in their professions for at least three years, part of which may have been concurrent with advanced training. Special emphasis should be placed upon degree of self-awareness and willingness to work toward a deeper self-understanding. The younger, recent graduate would not qualify for marriage counseling training; rather, he would begin in general clinical counseling and might be ready for major emphasis on marriage counseling by the end of his second year of internship. Give the candidates one year of intensive, supervised training in the actual handling of marriage counseling cases. Some then would function, with adequate supervision, quite effectively in an agency or in an institution, and the work experience would constitute additional internship or on-the-job training. The majority should have a second year of intensive supervision in marriage counseling within a counseling service, after which a few might be proficient enough to function adequately without supervision, counseling within an agency or school, provided adequate medical and psychiatric consultation were available.

Membership in AAMC would begin with student affiliation upon entrance into a recognized training center having on its staff at least one active member of the national organization. Three years of training in marriage counseling under supervision, plus other requirements, would qualify the trainee for associate membership. Very advanced persons who demonstrated outstanding ability during the training process would be given reasonable credit for pre-internship experience in marriage counseling.

Five years of such training-experience (making adequate allowance for other than marriage counseling supervision in the latter three years) would qualify an individual for active membership in AAMC. Then, only after passing an equivalent to a Board Examination in other professions, would the person be certified to enter private practice as a marriage counselor.

This procedure would place tremendous responsibility upon: (1) the training center, in the areas of selection, redirection of those better fitted for another field, training, and evaluation; (2) an examining board (AAMC appointed or otherwise), in setting levels of supervision and of consultation with respect to experience following the training period, and administering examinations and certification; (3) the aspiring marriage counselor, to practice within the agreed bounds; and, (4) professional persons doing marriage counseling as an activity, to obtain minimal blocks of training, including supervised experience, and to establish adequate consultation and/or supervisional relationships for the benefit of both themselves and their clients.

Good future standards, but what are the present minimum requirements?

CHAPTER 2

Assumptions Underlying
Marriage Counseling

Ben N. Ard, Jr.

Any growing science or profession, if it is to make sound progress, needs to question its basic assumptions and make them explicit rather than implicit. Assumptions influence procedures, techniques, methods, and ultimate goals, and for these reasons need to be brought out into the open and carefully scrutinized. This paper is offered as a preliminary discussion which the writer hopes will stimulate the thinking of anyone interested in this field.

There are several assumptions which can be seen as underlying marriage counseling. But before presenting some of them, it may clarify matters somewhat to state specifically just what marital maladjustment is understood to be in this context.

In the first place, marital maladjustment is frequently, but not necessarily always, one form of psychological maladjustment. Psychological maladjustment may be said to exist when the client denies to awareness various significant experiences or feelings, which consequently are not recognized and organized into his concept of himself, i.e., the gestalt of the self-structure (Rogers, 1951, p. 510). Potential guilt, tension, and/or anxiety arises from such a situation.

Healthy psychological adjustment may be said to exist, in these terms, when the concept of self is such that all the significant experiences and feelings of the client are, or may be, assimilated on a symbolic level into a consistent relationship with the concept of self (Rogers, 1951, p. 513). This psychological health or maturity, which is the framework within which the counselor sees the client, can be objectively determined, according to Erich Fromm. He says, "Man's main task in life is to give birth to himself, to become what he potentially is. The most important product of his effort is his own personality. One can judge objectively to what extent the person has succeeded in his task, to what degree he has realized his potentialities [Fromm, 1947, p. 237]." In other words, "A judgment that a person is destructive, greedy, jealous, envious is not different from a

Reprinted with the permission of the author and the publisher from *Marriage Counseling Quarterly*, 1967, *2*, 20–24.

physician's statement about a dysfunction of the heart or the lungs [Fromm, 1947, p. 236]."

If marital maladjustment brings the client to the marriage counselor, with what assumptions does the counselor enter into marriage counseling?

1. *Anxiety, tension, guilt feelings, or concern over the relationship is the* immediate *driving force that motivates clients to seek marriage counseling*. A subsidiary assumption here is that where such anxiety or tension is not sufficient to cause clients much difficulty or worry, they are not at that time ready to move into and through marriage counseling or psychotherapy of any kind.

Where this tension or anxiety is sufficient to motivate the client, it causes him to bring into consciousness (i.e., become aware of) more and more of his significant experiences and feelings. Once they are conscious, the concept of self is expanded so that they may be included as a part of a consistent, total self-concept.

2. *Marital maladjustments and problems can be alleviated or worked through by using certain specific methods, knowledge, and techniques*. This would seem to be the fundamental assumption under which marriage counseling as such has developed as a psychological service which may be distinguished from other psychological services such as psychiatry, casework, and various forms of psychotherapy (Ard, 1955; Cuber, 1948; Karpf, 1951; Mudd, 1951; Mudd & Preston, 1950).

3. *Most, but not all, of the ways of behaving which are adopted by the client are those which are consistent with his concept of self.* Lecky (1945) and Rogers (1951) have developed the ideas related to this concept, which seems helpful and necessary if we are to understand and explain much of the psychological behavior of clients.

4. *There is a* reality *which is different from distorted perceptions as illusions, hallucinations, delusions, projection, fantasy, etc*. A clear (i.e., objective) perception of reality cannot, of course, be gained by anyone if he has psychological blinders on. However, given proper conditions, better perceptions of reality are possible, at least in some cases.

This concept is necessary for any understanding of psychological illness. Freud has pointed this out (1924, Volume II, pp. 277–82). Erich Fromm (1947) states that "the person who has lost the capacity to perceive actuality is insane [p. 89]." In other words, "when a person sees objects which do not exist in reality but are entirely the product of his imagination, he has hallucinations; he interprets events in terms of his own feelings, without reference to, or at least without proper acknowledgement of, what goes on in reality [p. 89]. . . . The insane person is incapable of seeing reality as it is; he perceives reality only as a symbol and a reflection of his inner world [p. 90]."

Maslow (1950), in his study of psychologically healthy people, found that one characteristic common to these self-actualizing people was a more efficient perception of reality. In other words, the neurotic is not only emotionally sick—he is cognitively *wrong*. The importance of this finding can hardly be overestimated. As Maslow has pointed out, if health and neurosis are respectively correct and incorrect perceptions of reality, propositions of fact and propositions of value merge in this area; and in principle, value propositions should then be empirically demonstrable rather than merely matters of taste or exhortation. For those who have wrestled with this problem, it will be clear that we may have here a partial basis for a true science of values, and consequently of ethics, social relations, etc.

5. *It is one of the aims of marriage counseling (or psychotherapy in general) to help the client perceive reality more accurately.* That is, the aim is to strive for a high degree of correspondence between perception and reality. The psychologically healthy people studied by Maslow (1950) were far more apt to see what is "there," rather than their own wishes, hopes, fears, anxieties, their own theories and beliefs, or those of their cultural group.

This fifth concept implies a subsidiary assumption, namely that conscious acceptance of impulses, feelings, and perceptions greatly increases the possibility of conscious control, thus enabling more adequate (i.e., intelligent) behavior.

6. *The client has the capacity, in most instances, to resolve his own conflicts, given certain circumstances (i.e., in this instance, good therapeutic conditions).* Good therapeutic conditions means here, the helpful atmosphere which obtains in the good marriage counseling relationship.

7. *Through procedures and techniques used in marriage counseling, which establishes a good therapeutic atmosphere, the client is encouraged to communicate (i.e., verbalize) his feelings and experiences, and will thereby gradually bring more and more of his significant feelings and experiences into the realm of awareness.* In this regard it may be said that there is no sharp, clear dividing line between marriage counseling and psychotherapy. Marriage counseling shades into depth therapy in imperceptible degrees. Marriage counseling may include certain aspects or methods which are different from those seen in various kinds of psychotherapy (e.g., psychoanalysis and client-centered therapy), but marriage counseling also includes techniques and procedures which both these and other "schools" consider psychotherapy.

8. *There is a drive or tendency toward psychological health in most clients.* In other words, the organism has a basic tendency or striving to actualize (and therefore enhance) itself. In the majority of clients, the forward direction of growth is more powerful than the neurotic satisfactions of remaining immature and infantile. This drive moves the client in the direction of greater independence, self-responsibility, and autonomy (i.e., having all experiences available to consciousness). The client thus moves toward an increasing integration.

The best definition of what constitutes integration appears to be this statement that all the significant experiences and feelings are admissible to awareness through accurate symbolization, and organizable into one system which is internally consistent and which is, or is related to, the structure of the self (Rogers, 1951, pp. 513–14). The more that significant experiences and feelings are denied symbolization (i.e., awareness), or are given a distorted symbolization, the greater the likelihood that any new experience will be perceived as threatening, since there is a larger false structure to be maintained.

It is assumed, of course, that it is better to be mature than immature, psychologically healthy than unhealthy, spontaneous than rigid, relaxed than tense, etc. The client who satisfactorily completes marriage counseling (or psychotherapy) is more relaxed in being himself, more sure of himself, more realistic in his relationships. It is assumed that this is a good thing.

If the client is given the opportunity for a clear-cut choice between forward-moving and regressive behavior, this growth tendency will operate in most cases. This is why the counselor must help the client perceive accurately *all* the relevant factors in the situation. Unless experiences are adequately symbolized (i.e., verbalized), unless sufficiently accurate differentiations are made, the client may mistake regressive behavior for self-enhancing mature behavior.

These objectively derived standards for judging behavior in terms of psychological health come from the studies made by such men as Maslow (1950) and Fromm (1947). As the self-correcting science of human nature (psychology) gains better understanding of what mental health and psychological maturity are, we will have these qualities operationally defined.

9. *The optimal development of the individual's potentialities is the ultimate goal of marriage counseling.* From this statement it is obvious that marriage counseling cannot be interested in maintaining a marriage at all costs. This assumes by implication that divorce is sometimes a good thing. Fromm (1947) and Maslow (1950) have given the best descriptions of what we mean by the optimal development of the individual's potentialities.

10. *Marriage counseling is a good (i.e., worthwhile, helpful) thing.* All marriage counselors, it would seem, must make this assumption or they would not continue to offer the service.

All the above assumptions are interrelated. This is shown, for example, by the general tendency for clients to move in the direction of maturity *when the factors in the situation are clear.* This shows the function and necessity of the fourth assumption, regarding perceiving reality accurately. After the counselor has helped the client perceive reality more accurately, he relies on this tendency toward growth to move the client in the direction of maturity, mental health, psychological health, and well-being.

As the client perceives and accepts into his self-structure more of his significant feelings and experiences, he finds that he is replacing his previous value system, which was based so largely on introjections which have been distorted in their original perception and symbolization. These old values, based on distorted perceptions of reality, are replaced by new values, which are accepted because they are perceived as principles making for the self-actualization and enhancement of the person.

The greatest values for the enhancement of the person accrue when all experiences and all attitudes are permitted conscious symbolization, and when behavior becomes the meaningful and balanced satisfaction of *all* basic needs (these needs being available to consciousness). In other words, following marriage counseling (or psychotherapy), the individual is formulating his evaluations of experience on the basis of all the relevant data.

REFERENCES

Ard, B. N., Jr. Sex knowledge for the marriage counselor. *Merrill-Palmer Quarterly*, Winter 1955 *1*, 74–82.

Cuber, J. F. *Marriage counseling practice*. New York: Appleton-Century-Croft, 1948.

Freud, S. The loss of reality in neurosis and psychosis. *Collected Papers*. Vol. II. London: Hogarth Press, 1924. Pp. 277–282.

Fromm, E. *Man for himself*. New York: Rinehart, 1947.

Karpf, M. J. Some guiding principles in marriage counseling. *Marriage and Family Living*, Spring 1951. *13*, 49–51, 55.

Lecky, P. *Self-consistency: A theory of personality*. New York: Island Press, 1945.

Maslow, A. H. Self-actualizing people: A study of psychological health. *In* W. Wolff (Ed.), *Personality symposium No. 1*. New York: Grune & Stratton, 1950. Pp. 11-34

Mudd, E. H. *The practice of marriage counseling*. New York: Association Press, 1951.

Mudd, E. H. & Preston, M. G. The contemporary status of marriage counseling. *The Annals of the American Academy of Political and Social Science*, November 1950. *272*, 102–109.

Rogers, C. R. *Client-centered therapy*. Boston: Houghton Mifflin, 1951.

CHAPTER 3

Psychologists and Marriage Counselors in the United States

J. A. Morris Kimber

In February 1963 a study was published which took into consideration 1959–1960 classified telephone directory listings of marriage counselors, marriage counseling agencies, psychologists, and psychological agencies in twenty-three large cities of the United States (Kimber, 1963). Attention was called to the fact that clinical and counseling psychology had much in common with the growing profession of marriage counseling. It was felt that since this was the case, the new profession of marriage counseling deserved special attention by psychologists.

The present study is an expansion of the 1959–1960 survey. It differs from the former study in the following respects:

1. At least one city in each of the fifty states is included—the total number being seventy-four, more than three times the number listed in 1959–60. While the present study also gives attention to very large cities (200,000 or more), states having none of that size are represented by one of their largest.

2. The 1959–1960 study was made from classified telephone directory listings published over an eighteen-month period. The present survey is more concise in that it covers only twelve months, from February 1964 to January 1965. All directories except Boston, Honolulu, and Omaha are in the year 1964.

3. In the former study comparison of the growth of the two professions of marriage counseling and psychology was based on a longitudinal study of only one area as derived from data in the Los Angeles Central District Classified Directory. Comparison of the growth of the two professions in the present study is more complete in that it is based on (*a*) the increase or decrease of telephone directory listings of marriage counselors and psychologists in the twenty-three cities between 1959 and 1964; (*b*) the growth of the Los Angeles County Psychological Association (LACPA), and of the American Association of Marriage Counselors (AAMC) in the Los Angeles area; and (*c*) the increase in the membership

Reprinted with permission of the author and the publisher from *American Psychologist*, 1967, 22, 862–865.

of the two national organizations, the American Psychological Association (APA) and the AAMC.

Table 1 presents the findings of the 1964–65 survey. The cities italicized indicate those which were also studied in 1959–60. Whereas in the 1959–60 survey 291 marriage counselors and marriage counseling agencies were listed in the twenty-three cities, it is found that in those same twenty-three cities there are now 565 listed, an increase of 94 percent. In the former study 829 psychologists and psychological agencies appeared in the directories, while today there are 1,082, an increase of 31 percent. Although some of these eastern cities declined in population between 1959 and 1964, the population growth of the twenty-three cities together is 4 percent, as based on the 1960 United States census and the 1965 Rand McNally Atlas estimates.

TABLE 1

CLASSIFIED LISTINGS OF MARRIAGE COUNSELORS AND PSYCHOLOGISTS
IN THE YELLOW PAGES OF TELEPHONE DIRECTORIES:
FEBRUARY 1964 TO JANUARY 1965

City	Date of directory	Marriage counselors	Psychologists
1. Albuquerque, N. Mex.	Oct. 1964	8	9
2. Amarillo, Tex.	Nov. 1964	1	1
3. Anchorage, Alaska	1964	0	0
4. Atlanta, Ga.	Nov. 1964	9	26
5. Atlantic City, N.J.	July 1964	2	1
6. Baltimore, Md.	Oct. 1964	10	11
7. Billings, Mont.	Nov. 1964	4	0
8. Birmingham, Ala.	June 1964	5	2
9. Boise, Idaho	Dec. 1964	4	0
10. *Boston, Mass.*	Jan. 1965	28	25
11. Burlington, Vt.	June 1964	1	0
12. Cheyenne, Wyo.	Oct. 1964	1	0
13. *Chicago, Ill.*	1964	30	99
14. *Cincinnati, Ohio*	1964	3	10
15. Cleveland, Ohio	March 1964	26	45
16. Columbia, S.C.	Dec. 1964	2	1
17. *Dallas, Tex.*	Nov. 1964	16	28
18. *Denver, Colo.*	July 1964	28	34
19. Des Moines, Iowa	Oct. 1964	2	3
20. *Detroit, Mich.*	Sept. 1964	32	33
21. *Fort Worth, Tex.*	March 1964	6	5
22. Grand Forks, N.Dak.	June 1964	0	0
23. Greensboro, N.C.	Feb. 1964	3	2
24. Greenville, S.C.	July 1964	1	3
25. *Hartford, Conn.*	April 1964	6	9
26. *Honolulu, Hawaii*	Jan. 1965	6	9
27. *Houston, Tex.*	June 1964	12	29

Note. – Cities in italics are those studied in the previous article, Kimber 1963.

TABLE 1 (continued)

City	Date of directory	Marriage counselors	Psychologists
28. Huntington, W.Va.	Oct. 1964	3	2
29. Indianapolis, Ind.	Oct. 1964	7	8
30. Jackson, Miss.	Feb. 1964	1	2
31. Juneau, Alaska	July 1964	0	0
32. Kansas City, Mo.	Dec. 1964	14	24
33. Little Rock, Ark.	March 1964	1	0
34. *Los Angeles, Calif.*	Aug. 1964	99	158
35. Louisville, Ky.	Sept. 1964	2	3
36. Miami, Fla.	Sept. 1964	32	33
37. Milwaukee, Wis.	April 1964	6	21
38. *Minneapolis, Minn.*	1964	16	18
39. Muncie, Ind.	Aug. 1964	2	2
40. Nashua, N.H.	Feb. 1964	0	0
41. Nashville, Tenn.	April 1964	3	3
42. Newark, N.J.	Sept. 1964	13	30
43. New Orleans, La.	Dec. 1964	10	10
44. *New York, N.Y.* (4 boroughs)	1964	145	360
45. *Oakland-Berkeley, Calif.*	May 1964	13	23
46. Oklahoma City, Okla.	1964	5	6
47. Omaha, Neb.	Jan. 1965	2	1
48. *Philadelphia, Pa.*	Feb. 1964	30	62
49. Phoenix, Ariz.	1964	13	23
50. Pittsburgh, Pa.	Dec. 1964	11	10
51. Portland, Maine	July 1964	1	2
52. *Portland, Ore.*	Nov. 1964	13	20
53. *Providence, R.I.*	June 1964	2	5
54. Rapid City, S.Dak.	Nov. 1964	1	0
55. Reno, Nev.	May 1964	1	1
56. Richmond, Va.	Oct. 1964	2	6
57. Rochester, N.Y.	1964	4	15
58. Salt Lake City, Utah	June 1964	10	3
59. *San Francisco, Calif.*	Sept. 1964	11	41
60. *San Jose, Calif.*	Feb. 1964	14	27
61. *Seattle, Wash.*	March 1964	16	18
62. Sioux Falls, S.Dak.	Feb. 1964	1	1
63. Spartanburg, S.C.	June 1964	0	1
64. St. Louis, Mo.	May 1964	15	22
65. *St. Paul, Minn.*	Dec. 1964	13	15
66. Sumter, S.C.	Aug. 1964	0	1
67. Tampa, Fla.	Aug. 1964	10	12
68. Topeka, Kans.	Oct. 1964	1	1
69. Trenton, N.J.	Feb. 1964	7	7
70. *Tucson, Ariz.*	June 1964	7	4
71. *Washington, D.C.*	March 1964	19	50
72. Wichita, Kans.	June 1964	5	9
73. Wilmington, Del.	Oct. 1964	2	6
74. Winston-Salem, N.C.	July 1964	2	0
		831	1,451

The decline of listed psychologists and marriage counselors in certain cities, notably Los Angeles, apparently is to be accounted for not so much by legislation, as suggested in the previous study, as by suburbanization and the publication of large area classified directories, with less dependence on a central directory that is heavily weighted with "city limits" definition. For example, in Beverly Hills, a large and prosperous suburb of Los Angeles, the 1959 telephone directory yellow pages had eight listings of marriage counselors and 18 listings of psychologists which were found also in the 1959 Los Angeles yellow pages. In 1964 the suburb had 17 marriage counseling listings and 24 psychologist listings—increases of 113 percent and 33 percent, respectively. In addition, 25 percent of the 1959 Beverly Hills—Los Angeles marriage counseling listees dropped out of the 1964 Los Angeles telephone directory and 6 percent of the psychologists dropped out. These facts support the view that suburbanization is affecting these two professions. It is likely that similar changes also are taking place in the medical and other professions. And it is believed that this incipient situation will become more apparent in many large cities in future years.

In the present study a total of 831 marriage counselors and marriage counseling agencies were listed in the directories of the seventy-four cities, while 1,451 psychologists and psychological agencies appeared in the same yellow pages. In the former study the marriage counseling profession consisted of only about 35 percent of that of psychologists, while it now numbers almost 60 percent. The percentage increase of marriage counseling is probably due in part to the fact that it has virtually no regulation (except in California), while the profession of psychology is regulated by most states and closely scrutinized by professional colleagues. It is likely that many who are barred from practicing as psychologists are now announcing themselves as marriage counselors. In March 1965, 26 states had statutory licensing or certification of psychologists, while 17 states had nonstatutory certifying boards (Henderson & Hildreth, 1965). Thus some regulation of psychologists has taken place in 43 of the 50 states since the first legislation to certify psychologists was approved by the Connecticut legislature in 1945.

In contrast, only California has any regulation of marriage counselors (Kiplinger Service for Families, May 1965), its bill having been passed by the legislature in 1963, and amended in 1965. The law enables the Director of Professional and Vocational Standards to issue to qualified persons a license as a marriage, family, and child counselor. To qualify for a license an applicant must have "at least a master's degree in marriage counseling, in social work or in one of the behavioral sciences" obtained from an accredited college. And he must have "at least two years experience, of a character approved by the director." The license confers "the right to use the title, engage in the business, and advertise to the public that he is a Marriage, Family, and Child Counselor" (State of California, Marriage, Family, and Child Counselor Law, Business and Professions Code, 1963).

Thus the profession of marriage counseling is left relatively free and open to anyone, qualified or not, who wishes to call himself a marriage counselor and to set up a practice. The public is subject to this plight. However, one aid to good quality personnel is the requirement of high professional standards for membership in the national associations. A large number of psychologists are members of the APA, while a very small but increasing proportion of marriage counselors are members of the AAMC. The APA 1964 *Directory* lists over 22,000 members, while the AAMC 1964 Directory lists a total membership of 476.

Those who were listed under marriage counseling in the 1959 and the 1964 Los Angeles Classified Telephone Directory were studied to discover whether they belonged to either the APA or the AAMC. This survey was pursued on the assumption that membership in these organizations would indicate a degree of professional quality. It was found that 24 percent of those listed as marriage counselors in the 1959 telephone directory were in the 1959 APA Directory, whereas 39 percent of marriage counselors were so listed in 1964—an increase of 69 percent. In addition, only 2 percent were listed in the 1959 AAMC Directory, compared to 28 percent in 1964. In 1959 2 percent were members of both the APA and the AAMC, while in 1964 14 percent were members of both organizations.

In addition, a local organization, the Los Angeles County Psychological Association, which also requires high professional standards, shows an increase in its membership of 64 percent in the five-year period to 1965. Similarly, the membership of AAMC in the Los Angeles County area has increased 118 percent in the same period (Southern California Association of Marriage Counselors, 1965). Thus, in the Los Angeles area the number of professional-quality personnel in the professions of marriage counseling and psychology is rapidly increasing.

Similarly, it is noted that there has been an increase of psychologists in the marriage counseling profession across the United States, as shown by the increase in the number of psychologists in the AAMC. In the 1959 directory of the AAMC, 20 percent were also members of APA. In the 1964 directory 24 percent or almost one-quarter of the entire membership of AAMC were members of APA. This fact is of special interest in view of the 150 percent increase in the AAMC membership in the five-year period. The APA membership itself had increased approximately 26 percent in the same period.

In the 1959–60 study it was stated that psychologists and marriage counselors tended to be located in the same geographical areas. In the current study of seventy-four cities there is a positive correlation of .92 between listings of marriage counselors and psychologists, which is similar to the .88 positive correlation in the former study of fewer cities.

SUMMARY AND CONCLUSIONS

Evidence is accumulating that the private practice of psychology and of marriage counseling is on the increase throughout the United States.

Moreover, the number of psychologists in the marriage counseling profession is increasing. There is a high positive correlation between the number of psychologists and the number of marriage counselors practicing in major cities. The practice of psychology has been regulated in many states, while the practice of marriage counseling is still relatively unregulated. However, there is now a growing trend both for self- and public regulation of marriage counseling as indicated by the increasing membership in AAMC and the recent attempts at licensing.

Previous attention was called to the fact that "Whoever the marriage counselors of the United States are, it seems clear that few of them claim to be psychologists [Kimber, 1963]." Facts listed above indicate a change in this respect. Other alterations on the part of psychology also have a bearing on earlier observations (Kimber, 1959). For example, although there is no marriage counseling division of APA, there now exists an Academy of Psychologists in Marriage Counseling made up of APA members. Also since the previous observations were made, there have been postdoctoral institutes on marriage and family relations. Furthermore, a large and active group of APA members—Psychologists Interested in the Advancement of Psychotherapy (PIAP)—has come into existence and has been found useful to those who maintain that marriage counseling is substantially "a type of psychotherapy" (Harper, 1957).

It would appear, however, that two earlier proposals still deserve attention (Kimber, 1959).

1. There is no diploma offered by the American Board of Examiners in Professional Psychology (ABEPP) in marriage counseling. Neither is a diploma offered for specialization in psychotherapy—a discipline which is the main part of marriage counseling.

2. The bulk of courses pertaining to the subject of marriage and the family still appear to be in university departments other than that of psychology. This situation reminds one of the statement of the majority of physicians, viz., that most of their patients suffer from emotional, rather than organic conditions. Yet many medical schools still ignore this problem and do not furnish the young physician with a proportionate amount of training in how to deal with emotional problems. Unfortunately, in the same way, psychologists may admit that most adult emotional problems deal with marriage and the family, although their profession still provides inadequate training in "psychotherapeutic marriage counseling" (Kimber, 1961). Thus psychology departments are not furnishing adequate specialized training in an area which many clinical psychologists face daily.

Since psychology and marriage counseling have much in common, it still behooves psychology to keep in close touch with this growing profession and all that it claims to offer.

REFERENCES

American Association of Marriage Counselors. *American Association of Marriage Counselors directory*. Madison, N. J.: AAMC, 1959.

American Association of Marriage Counselors. *American Association of Marriage Counselors directory*. Madison, N. J.: AAMC, 1964.

American Psychological Assocation. *American Psychological Association directory*. Washington, D. C.: APA, 1959.

American Psychological Association. *American Psychological Association directory*. Washington, D. C.: APA, 1964.

Harper, R. A. Should marriage counseling become a full-fledged specialty? In C. E. Vincent, *Readings in marriage counseling*. New York: Crowell, 1957. Pp. 464–468.

Henderson, N. B., & Hildreth, J. D. Certification, licensing, and the movement of psychologists from state to state. *American Psychologist*, 1965, *20*, 418–421.

Kimber, J. A. M. The science and the profession of psychology in the area of family relations and marriage counseling. *American Psychologist*, 1959, *14*, 699–700.

Kimber, J. A. M. An introduction to the marriage counselor and his work. *Psychological Reports*, 1961, *8*, 71–75.

Kimber, J. A. M. Marriage counselors and psychologists in the United States. *American Psychologist*, 1963, *18*, 108–109.

Kiplinger Service for Families. When a marriage is in trouble . . . *Changing Times*, 1965, *19*(5), 43–45.

Los Angeles County Psychological Association. *Los Angeles County Psychological Association directory*. Los Angeles: LACPA, 1964.

Rand McNally and Company. Places of 20,000 or more, 1965 table. *Rand McNally commercial atlas and marketing guide*. (96th ed.) San Francisco: Rand McNally, 1965. Pp. 36–37.

Southern California Association of Marriage Counselors. *Southern California Association of Marriage Counselors directory*. Downey, Calif.: SCAMC, 1965.

State of California, Marriage, Family and Child Counselor Law, *Business and Professions Code*, Sections 17800 to 17847, (1963).

CHAPTER 4

A Critical Evaluation of
Marriage Counseling

Albert Ellis

To evaluate marriage counseling, as it is presently practiced in this country, in a straightforward manner is a difficult thing to do: for the simple reason that it is not easy to determine just what our marriage counselors are actually doing when the doors to their inner sanctums are closed and they are left alone with their clients and their consciences. Up until very recently, detailed reports of marriage counseling cases were a great rarity in the professional literature; and even today they are not too common.

The American publication which includes by far the most material on marriage counseling, and which, until November, 1953, had a special section sponsored by the American Association of Marriage Counselors, is *Marriage and Family Living*. A search of the files of this publication reveals that only since 1951, when Gladys Groves took over the editorship of the journal, have lengthy case reports of counseling cases been published in *Marriage and Family Living*; and, to date, six such cases have appeared. It may prove rewarding, in evaluating contemporary marriage counseling, to survey some of the aspects of these published cases.

The first questions that may be raised in regard to marriage counseling practice are: What kind of clients normally come for counseling; and how deep-seated are the emotional disturbances, or ineptness in interpersonal relations, with which they come to counseling? In the first case published in *Marriage and Family Living*, Dr. Walter Stokes' (1959) case of a married virgin, the counselor tells us that "it will be clear to anyone with psychiatric experience that Mrs. M. presented much more than a simple physical problem and that the mere supplying of authentic sex information could not have sufficed for her needs. Her main difficulty may properly be called psychiatric." In the second case, presented by Margaret Fitzsimmons (1951), the counselor notes that "although this marriage is a neurotic one, Mrs. K. appears to be a woman of fair ego strengths which are weakened during this stressful period. She appears to be a woman of normal personality with the neurotic trait of some masochism; she has

Reprinted with permission of the author and the publisher from *Marriage and Family Living*, February 1956, pp. 65–71.

22

anxiety arising from both the reality dangers to her husband's career and from the internal stresses of the marriage."

In the third case, Dr. Maurice J. Karpf (1951) wonders whether there is a "neurotic element in the girl's makeup, which prompted her to seek an alliance with a Negro," but doubts that she is seriously neurotic. In the fourth case, also one of Dr. Karpf's (1952), the counselor concludes that the client "does show evidence of a neurotic tendency."

In the fifth case, again presented by Dr. Karpf (1952), the counselor notes that "of the three cases in this series, this woman presents the most serious neurotic factors. She is dominated by fears, conflicts, hesitations, ambivalences, frustrations, and other neurotic manifestations." In the sixth case, counseled by Dr. Robert A. Harper (1952), the counselor finds that the female client shows sufficient neurotic symptoms, including "insomnia, slight hand tremor, strong guilt feelings about mother and deceased father, frequent crying, and omnipresent anxiety," to make a psychiatric referral appear desirable and that the male client shows "deep-seated insecurities and hostilities," and also is a good candidate for psychiatric referral.

It would appear, then, that of the seven individuals whose counseling is reported in detail in these six published cases, the counselors feel that five are clearly neurotic and the other two have some distinct neurotic symptoms and may be considered borderline cases.

Since there is a possibility that published cases of marriage counseling, because the authors are eager to present interesting material, may include more emotionally disturbed clients than would be found in the run-of-the-mill marriage counseling case, the writer decided to check his own records for comparable material. Accordingly, ten consecutive cases seen this year were examined.

In case No. 1, the husband was found to be a chronic alcoholic, inordinately tied to his dead mother, who had suffered two previous "nervous breakdowns"; and the wife was a reckless spendthrift who could not make any serious move in life without consulting her parents and sister. In case No. 2 the husband was an exceptionally immature individual who ran away from all family responsibilities; and the wife was a rigid, compulsive, fanatically righteous individual who was completely frigid. In case No. 3 the wife appeared to be a reasonably adequate person; but the husband was seclusive, antisocial, and interested only in making and saving money. In case No. 4 the girl was a borderline schizophrenic who had recently undergone shock treatment; and the fellow was a thoroughly disorganized individual who hadn't the self-confidence to try to do any of the things he wanted to do in life, and who hated himself thoroughly for not trying. In case No. 5 the wife was exceptionally insecure and super-sensitive because of early difficulties in her own family; and the husband was equally sensitive and insecure and kept deliberately lying to his wife, and giving her reasons to think that he was unfaithful when he actually was not, in order to get back at her for imagined wrongs.

In case No. 6 the husband was an individual with good ego-strength but the wife was a continually bungling, inadequate individual who has failed in school, socially, and in her work because she identified closely with an equally inadequate father. In case No. 7 the girl was over-attached to her own family and got her main life satisfaction from mothering a brood of grown-up relatives; while her fiance unconsciously or consciously engaged in almost all his major activities, including his plans for marriage, to spite his father and his older brother and to show them that he was superior to them. In case No. 8 the wife was completely subservient to her father and mother and slavishly forced herself and her husband to carry out religious rituals in which she did not believe but which her parents insisted that she carry on; and the husband was a love-hungry, outwardly ingratiating person who did everything his wife's way, but who finally built up so much underlying hostility toward her that he had several extramarital affairs with women whom he did not particularly like. In case No. 9 the fiance had been a weak-willed boy who was working far below his intellectual capacity, but who had recently, with the aid of intensive psychotherapy, been becoming stronger and more confident; but his fiancee, a very brilliant girl, was working far below her potential level, was failing badly in school, and was doing everything possible to disrupt their relationship although she said that she was eager to marry him. In case No. 10 the husband was a serious paranoid schizophrenic who insisted that his wife was going around telling people about his previous hospitalizations; and the wife was a thoroughly self-centered, sexually frigid woman who frankly loathed her husband but stayed with him mainly because she did not want to return to work.

It can readily be seen that out of the twenty individuals involved in these cases, all of whom came for routine marriage counseling and most of whom fully expected all their problems to be solved in a few counseling sessions, at least seventeen, or eighty-five percent, were distinctly childish, parent-tied, inadequate, neurotic or psychotic persons whose premarital or marital problems were intimately related to their emotional disturbances. Evidently, the kind of maladjusted counselee who is depicted in the cases published in the recent literature is not exceptional but is fairly typical of those seen in regular marriage practice.

In view of this fact, it should come as no surprise, then, that the cases reported in the literature are far from being one-shot affairs, but normally include a number of sessions which seems to be more consonant with the term "psychotherapy" than "counseling." Thus, Dr. Stokes seems to have seen his married virgin for at least twenty-six sessions. Margaret Fitzsimmons had at least ten interviews with her counselee. Dr. Karpf seems to have had at least seven sessions with his first case, nine with his second case, and six with his third (and "unsuccessful") case. Dr. Harper saw his couple twelve times before marriage, and apparently several times after they were married. This, again, checks with the writer's experience, since I find that most of my own marriage counseling cases are seen from six to ten times, while a sizable minority are seen from fifteen to thirty times.

The next question that arises is: What techniques of marriage counseling are usually employed in the recently published cases? Here the answer seems to be that although the giving of information is fairly frequent in the reported cases, the piloting of the counselees through their interpersonal problems, and toward a higher level of self-understanding and self-acceptance, is the main technique employed in virtually all the cases we are considering. Dr. Stokes (1951) frankly calls his own technique "a specially adapted kind of psychotherapy." Margaret Fitzsimmons (1951) states that in her cases "psychological support and clarification were utilized. Mrs. K developed self-awareness and some self-understanding. . . ." Dr. Karpf (1951, 1952), like Mrs. Fitzsimmons, insists that his three cases were all treated on a conscious level and that marriage counseling does not require deep therapy or extensive psychoanalytic probing. However, Dr. Karpf obviously tries to give his clients much more self-understanding than factual information and uses the latter mainly to bring out the former; he titles his cases, "Marriage Counseling and Psychotherapy," and he agrees with Dr. Robert W. Laidlaw's (1952) comment that "marriage counseling is a type of short-term, conscious-level psychotherapy." Dr. Harper (1952) employs the terms "therapy" and "therapeutic approach" throughout his paper, makes it clear that he only saw his clients because they resisted psychiatric referral, and frankly states that his main goal was to enable the clients to achieve better insight into themselves as well as into their relations with each other.

The writer (1953), from his own marriage counseling experience, can easily confirm the need for, and effectiveness of, the therapeutic approach employed in the recently published cases. That factual information, and particularly information in regard to sexual matters, often should be fully and frankly given to marriage counseling clients is a position that I certainly would not deny, and in favor of which I have more than once come out publicly. But factual information alone, even in those cases where both partners are reasonably well-adjusted and stable individuals, is frequently not enough and must be supplemented by serious efforts to enable the counselees to understand better (a) their own basic experiences, feelings, desires, anxieties, and inadequacies; (b) the general character structure of their potential or actual mates; and (c) some of the inevitable results, dangers, and possibilities for marital and personal growth that may be expected to result from the interaction between (a) and (b).

To sum up the facts of marriage counseling thus far surveyed in this paper: It would appear, on the basis of recently published cases of marital counseling, as well as on the basis of the writer's own counseling experience, that a great many of the individuals who come for counseling are more or less emotionally disturbed individuals, that their problems cannot be handled adequately in merely two or three sessions, and that, call it what we may, some form of psychotherapy, or the helping of these counselees to understand their personal and interpersonal selves, is necessary for even a partially satisfactory resolution of their problems. The only serious disagreement among the marriage counselors who have recently published cases and the discussants of these cases seems to be, not whether marriage counseling involves psychotherapy, but whether it necessitates psychotherapy of an intensive, prolonged, and unconscious-probing nature.

It seems to me that much of the apparent disagreement in this connection is actually of a semantic nature, and depends on the definitions we give to the terms "intensive psychotherapy" and performing psychotherapy on an "unconscious" level. According to orthodox Freudian doctrine, psychotherapy cannot possibly be intensive unless it is carried on for scores, and often hundreds, of sessions. According to this same doctrine, psychotherapy cannot get at unconscious levels of thinking and feeling unless it is not only prolonged, but employs specific techniques like free association, the analytic couch, and the interpretation of dreams. As a clinical psychologist who has had considerable experience in psychoanalysis, psychoanalytic psychotherapy, and marriage counseling, I would seriously question both these orthodox Freudian assumptions.

That psychotherapy, in order to be intensive, must normally be *somewhat* prolonged, is doubtlessly true. Even here, however, I have seen instances, in both my own practice and that of some of my psychotherapeutic associates, where psychotherapy of only three or four hours' duration was intensive enough to change, and change radically, the entire life of a patient. Just recently, for example, after but three sessions of face-to-face psychotherapy, one of my patients stopped his exclusive homosexual activity of many years' standing, began going with girls for the first time in his life, and at the same time carried through a drastic change in his vocational outlook and plans. Granting, however, that these very brief psychotherapeutic contacts can rarely be too intensive or effective, somewhat longer contacts, of from ten to twenty hours, can, and often are, just as "intensive" as are much longer periods of psychotherapy. Indeed, it has been no novelty in my professional career to have patients who had had up to two years of "intensive" analysis with an orthodox analyst tell me that they have gone much deeper into themselves and gained considerably more self understanding and insight in ten or twenty sessions in which I have been quite directive, probing, and interpretive than they did in several hundred less directive sessions of free associations.

Which brings me to the second point: namely, that getting at clients' unconscious processes need not necessarily be a matter of using the specific techniques of free association, dream analysis, and other orthodox psychoanalytic procedures. Making the counselee's unconscious motivation conscious simply means, in plain English, making him aware of drives, feelings, and actions of which he was previously not aware but which nonetheless importantly affected his behavior. But allowing him freely to associate for many analytic hours, and then finally showing him how his unconscious thoughts and feelings are revealed in his associations, is only *one* method of making him aware of his underlying motivations—and, I submit, often an uneconomic and woefully inefficient method.

Dr. Karpf, for example, in discussing Mrs. Fitzsimmons' case presentation, notes that "although the statement is made that 'the treatment was on a conscious level,' there seems, nevertheless, to be a search for unconscious motivation." In this, Dr. Karpf seems, to the present writer, to be correct. But in Dr. Karpf's own case of a Jewish girl who was considering marrying a Catholic boy, we are told that when Dr. Karpf presented to her the facts of the Catholic attitude toward intermarriage, she began to feel certain that her boyfriend would not break with his parents or abandon his Church, and that he was not meeting her half way as she had met him in being willing to turn from her family and her religious traditions. When Dr. Karpf suggested to her that it might be better for her to give her boyfriend an opportunity to decide for himself what his views would be, we are told that "she said with considerable bitterness that she now realizes that his decision was never in question although she had been too blind or too ignorant to recognize it." Subsequently discussion with her boyfriend proved that she was right in this surmise.

This means, now, that merely by presenting some facts to his client, and showing her what the Catholic attitude on intermarriage actually was, Dr. Karpf—according to his own description—enabled her to realize, or to be conscious of, an attitude of her boyfriend and her own reaction to this attitude, about which she had previously been quite ignorant or unconscious. Dr. Karpf, therefore, although presumably working on a purely conscious level with his client, has enabled her to be conscious of both her boyfriend's and her own attitudes and feelings of which she was previously semiconscious or unconscious.

Let us take another illustration from my own marriage counseling practice. I am now having a series of interviews with a couple who, for the last five years of their marriage, have been bitterly bickering because each claims that the other is overattached to his or her parents while he or she merely has normal filial or sororal love. To date, I have spent two sessions with each of them; and already both are ready to admit that not only are their mates overattached to his or her parents, but that they themselves are almost equally overattached. Yet, only a few days ago neither was conscious of his or her own parental dependency. How, without any employment whatever of free association, dream analysis, or other depth-centered techniques which we commonly employ in psychoanalysis, did I manage to make conscious the unconscious leanings of both these spouses? Simply by asking them for the facts of their actual behavior toward their parents and then pointing out to them the discrepancy between these facts and their interpretations of them. Thus, although the husband at first stated and honestly believed, that he "hardly ever" saw his parents and was in fact guilty about not seeing them more often, he was induced to catalog his recent visits to them and soon had to admit that he saw them many times each month; and although the wife at first claimed that her mother had very little influence over her, it was not difficult to show her that, in point of fact, she ran to her mother immediately for approval for almost everything she did.

Similarly, in both my marriage counseling and psychotherapy cases, I am continually helping to make conscious to clients and patients thoughts, feelings, and actions, of both themselves and of others who are importantly related to them, of which they were previously unaware or unconscious. And similarly, I believe, do all good marriage counselors, without perhaps ever resorting to specific techniques of depth-centered therapy which are employed in psychoanalysis, continually clarify to their clients these clients' underlying, semiconscious, or unconscious feelings. Even the most passive and nondirective, as well as the most fact-minded and information-giving counselors, give some measure of insight to their clients: else it is difficult to see how there would be any movement at all in counseling cases. And if insight is not merely another name for a person's awareness of his own thoughts and feelings about which he was previously unaware, or unconscious, then I do not know what it is.

It has been pointed out by one of the readers of this paper that the term "unconscious" has two uses: (a) to denote any material which is not conscious: that is, of which the client or patient is not fully aware; and (b) to represent (in the more strict Freudian sense) that part of the mental content which has been repressed (as distinguished from that which has been consciously suppressed) or has never been conscious because it would arouse the same degree of anxiety if it became conscious as would repressed material. This is a valid distinction; and it should certainly be recognized that not all unconscious material can easily be brought to light by a marriage counselor or psychotherapist, since there are often strong patient or client resistances to unearthing and recognizing such material. In some cases, where there are deep-seated psychological blocks against the individual's recognizing repressed material, the use of specialized psychotherapeutic techniques of free association, dream analysis, hypnotism, and so on, are necessary.

It would be my contention, however, that even deeply repressed, strongly affective unconscious material can often be brought to the surface by what many orthodox analysts would call non-psychoanalytic confrontation methods. One of my premarital counseling clients, for example, who has had great difficulty in urinating in public, was seen on a face-to-face interview basis; and during the second session it was pointed out to him that there were probably one or two main reasons for his urinating difficulties: fear and/or rebelliousness. He freely admitted fears in this connection but at first stoutly denied any major rebellious tendencies.

The client was then confronted with several facts from his own case history which indicated that he had been distinctly rebellious in certain important ways. He thought about these facts for a few minutes; admitted that he must have often been rebellious, particularly toward his parents; and *then*, suddenly, came up with a memory he had not recalled for many years. At the age of five and a half, after fleeing Nazi Germany with his parents and coming to New York City, he had felt very angry toward his mother for forcing him to go outside to play with other children whose language he did not speak and who seemed to be hostile to him. He began urinating behind the radiator in his room and telling his parents that the radiator was leaking. He felt great satisfaction in thus cleverly defying his mother. But he apparently became so guilty about this, particularly when he was finally discovered and his parents were quite kind and understanding, that he repressed the memory of this incident and only recovered it years later during his second counseling session. In the meantime, his guilt was unconsciously displayed through his symptom of having difficulty in urinating in public—which disappeared soon after this session.

Here, then, is an instance of what appears to be a clearcut case of a repressed, affect-laden unconscious thought that was brought to light by a different kind of confrontation than is usually achieved through free association, dream analysis, hypnosis, or similar depth-centered psychotherapeutic techniques. It is my hypothesis that repressed feelings of this type, as well as other kinds of unconscious thoughts and feelings, are often brought to consciousness by the usual marriage counseling techniques—whether or not the counselor is fully aware that this is what he is doing.

This review of recently published marriage counseling cases, then, leads to the following conclusions: (1) Most marriage counselors are, whether they know it or not, seeing clients who are often basically childish, inadequate, emotionally disturbed individuals. (2) Effective marriage counseling normally cannot be done in a few sessions but preferably requires a half dozen or more sessions with most clients, and a considerably larger number with some. (3) The best kind of marriage counseling that is now being done usually involves relatively short-term psychotherapy in a face-to-face situation. This psychotherapy, although it is not designed to be too intensive or specifically to probe unconscious thoughts and feelings, in point of fact is often more intensive and probing than it seems to be on the surface.

If this analysis of the current marriage counseling literature and of my own counseling cases is correct, then it would appear to have far-reaching implications for the field of marriage counseling in general and for the training of marriage counselors in particular. For if many or most of us are actually doing psychotherapy, it would certainly seem desirable that we fully recognize that this is what we are doing and that we have no illusions to the contrary. It may well be that, for various good or bad reasons, many members of the public are willing to go to someone who is called a "marriage counselor" rather than someone who is called a "psychotherapist." It may also be true that many reasonably well-adjusted individuals who do not need intensive psychotherapy could well benefit by several marriage counseling or premarital counseling sessions. These may be good reasons for continuing to say that we do "marriage counseling" instead of "psychotherapy." But it is still most important that, whatever the public may prefer to call us, we ourselves realize that we often, and perhaps almost invariably, do psychotherapy, albeit a special kind of psychotherapy that many orthodox analysts would hesitate to acknowledge as such. Unless we face this fact squarely, our marriage counseling effectiveness is likely to be minimal; and the heritage that we pass on to counselors in training is likely to be of dubious value to them, to their potential clients, and to the entire marriage counseling profession.

REFERENCES

Ellis, A. Marriage counseling with couples indicating sexual incompatibility. *Marriage and Family Living*, 1953, *15*, 53–59.

Fitzsimmons, M. Collaborative treatment in a marriage problem. *Marriage and Family Living*, 1951, *13*, 52–55.

Harper, R. A. A premarital case with two years' marital follow-up. *Marriage and Family Living*, 1952, *14*, 133–149.

Karpf, M. J. Marriage counseling and psychotherapy. *Marriage and Family Living*, 1951, *13*, 169–178.

Karpf, M. J. Premarital counseling and psychotherapy, two cases. *Marriage and Family Living*, 1952, *14*, 56–73.

Laidlaw, R. W. Discussion of Dr. Karpf's Premarital counseling and psychotherapy: Two cases. *Marriage and Family Living*, 1952, *14*, 66–67.

Stokes, W. R. A marriage counseling case: The married virgin. *Marriage and Family Living*, 1951, *13*, 29–34.

The Place of Philosophy and Values in Marriage Counseling

The first principle of sex education and marriage counseling gives attitudes precedence over anatomies.

ROBERT L. DICKINSON

In the quotation introducing this section, one of the early leaders in the field, Robert L. Dickinson, gives precedence to attitudes over anatomies, in both sex education and marriage counseling. This points up the need of carefully examining the place of "philosophy" and "values" in the profession of marriage counseling. Therefore this section includes a wide variety of points of view regarding philosophy and values toward marriage, family living, love, aggression, the "new morality" and even including the "*Playboy* philosophy."

Marsh and Humphrey, in Chapter 5, discuss the question: what is the character of the boundaries within which "successful marital adjustment" occurs? Middle-class conventions seem to these authors to be the boundaries. Is conformity to middle-class conventions really the goal toward which marriage counselors should work? Are marriage counselors just trying to build more WASP's (i.e., people with conventional, middle-class, white, Anglo-Saxon, Protestant values)? Marsh and Humphrey raise the very basic question: how can marriage counseling (which is supposed to be an application of scientific principles, in addition to being an art) properly function when its major orientation is toward the mores of the conventional institutional family? Is middle-class morality the truly appropriate point of departure for all "marriage problem phenomena"? Does the baseline from which "success" in marriage is determined need to be that of middle-class morality and conventionality?

Chapter 6, by a professional husband-wife team, Lyndon and Lyndon, presents a description of the area in which family life counseling (i.e., counseling on the premarital, marital, and parental levels) operates—namely, for whom and how it functions, and what it requires of the counselor, whatever his basic professional dscipline. The Lyndons discuss the "consumer" of counseling (the normal, the anxious, the seriously disturbed); the meaning of counseling (including "therapy" and education), both individual and group; the limitations of the counselor; and finally the minimal requisites of the counselor.

Ben Ard, in Chapter 7, discusses the many and varied attitudes toward love and aggression in our culture and specifically deals with the perils of loving. "Love" is not all "peaches and cream," it would seem, nor is it all candlelight, roses, dances, perfume, and candy. These attitudes toward love (and its opposite, aggression) influence why men and women have the continuing "battle between the sexes," and influence how they relate to each other in and outside of marriage. The attitudes toward "romantic love" expressed in this article would be disagreed with by many people. Each reader is urged to think through the implications of the various views expressed about "romantic love" and come to his own conclusions, after having considered all the relevant data. Do counselors have to be able to distinguish between "sick" and "healthy" love?

In Chapter 8, John Hudson discusses value issues in marital counseling from at least four points of view: (a) the field of marriage counseling; (b) the definition of a marriage counselor; (c) the orientation and training of the marriage counselor; (d) specific problems in the field of marriage counseling. Among the issues Hudson raises are: Should the marriage counselor limit himself to those marriage problems which are principally of a conscious or situational nature, or should he deal with problems involving personality disturbances and emotional conflicts which may involve the unconscious? Should marriage counseling have as one of its central values "adjustment"? And should the marriage counselor ever recommend divorce?

In Chapter 9 Robert A. Harper looks critically at some of the general issues of morality in marriage counseling, particular expressions of which are encountered in actual counseling circumstances. The three broad areas of moral issues are divorce, parenthood, and sex. The reader will have to resolve for himself whether or not he agrees with Harper that the basic moral issue in marriage counseling is to help clients free themselves from a stagnant and unrealistic morality which blocks progress in love. Dr. Harper also makes some very important distinctions in this chapter between what is *moral, nonmoral, immoral, unmoral*, and *amoral*, and suggests that the marriage counselor should be *nonmoral*.

Stewart Bedford discusses the "new morality" and marriage counseling in Chapter 10. How can a marriage counselor help individuals and couples make decisions regarding moral issues when the very term "moral" seems to be in a state of flux? Bedford takes the position that the marriage counselor needs to develop a framework for understanding (and hopefully accepting) the variations in moral codes that he is likely to encounter among his clientele. Perhaps most professionals would agree with the need for "understanding," but some might question the value of "accepting" all variations in moral codes. Bedford also discusses a value dilemma in a case involving artificial insemination.

In Chapter 11 we have a presentation of a philosophy that has been very influential among many members of the younger generation (particularly among the college educated), namely the *Playboy* philosophy as espoused by Hugh Hefner, editor and publisher of *Playboy* magazine. Young people today are developing new ideas toward themselves, marriage, sex, and man-woman relations in general. These excerpts from the *Playboy* philosophy are a frank statement of a new point of view, differing sharply from the traditional puritanical point of view which underlies many peoples' beliefs about these matters. If young people are developing new philosophies, marriage counselors need to know about them.

CHAPTER 5

Value Congeries and Marriage Counseling

Donald Chard Marsh and Norman D. Humphrey

What is the character of the boundaries within which "successful marital adjustment" occurs? The major underlying assumption of the typical marriage counselor appears to be that the best that can be done for a person "in trouble" is to aid him to be better able to bear the restrictions which middle-class society and culture impose upon him. The boundaries, in short, appear to be middle-class conventions, and success in marriage consists of conformity to them.

This also seems to be the verdict indicated by "objective research." Norman S. Hayner (1948) has derived a number of tentative conclusions drawn from the literature of marriage research. He indicates, among other things, that the longer the period of acquaintance, the better are the chances for a happy marriage. Companionship is a better basis for a stable relationship than romantic love; emotional maturity, rather than chronological age. Certain specific personality characteristics are associated with happiness in marriage. Optimists, those who are not dominant, those who are neither neurotic nor self-sufficient, and the like, are types that make good marriage partners. For happiness in marriage, personality needs should gear into each other. But dissimilarity of customs, religious background, and the like increase the risk of marital failure. While marriage problems center in the dynamic areas of sex, sex itself is secondary in import to personality factors in determining success of marriages. Occupations with small personal mobility and large impingements of social control are favorably associated with happiness in marriage. If both parents love their children, they provide a basis of emotional security for the children and for themselves.

From one perspective such materials would seem to add up to the fact that conformity to positive values of the middle class, to middle-class virtue, makes for happiness, or success, in marriage. But what of psychological factors? The literature also abounds in statements that cases of marital maladjustment can usually be traced to such factors as "emotional

Reprinted with permission of the authors and the publisher from *Journal of Marriage and the Family*, 1953, *15*, 28–34.

immaturity" on the part of one or both of the partners. The basic cause of such immaturity is felt to lie primarily in the person, who sometimes is also regarded as the consequence of the impress of his own parents' immaturity upon him. Psychological factors are thus often regarded as primary and causal. But, from another view, the "maladjustment" is manifestly relevant to certain cultural norms which are rarely questioned, let alone highlighted in the equation. Such an arrangement of conceptions is of questionable validity, for it makes the psychological factors primary, and themselves productive of states of tension, when by another construction, it is the cultural standard (normally, middle-class Protestant American morality, and more especially, virtue), which is the prime productive agent; and the so-called unhappiness and maladjustment, the psychological components, the actual consequence. As Jeurgen Ruesch, a psychiatrist, has noted, middle-class American culture is the "core culture":

> The American culture . . . can be described as that culture which is represented by the lower middle class, composed of people of Anglo-Saxon descent and of Protestant religion. It is the core culture . . . [which] set the cultural standards for the . . . country. All . . . immigrants were compelled to adapt to these standards. Public opinion in America is largely an expression of this core culture. We find it in novels, on the radio, in newspapers, public speeches and in the opinion of the man on the street [1948, pp. 126–127].

Certainly Mexican family organization, for example, and the culture it maintains, elicits different bases for "happiness" and "maladjustment" than those found in the United States. The question of the boundaries of successful marital adjustment devolves then, in part, into what is properly the independent, and what the dependent, variable: psychological make-up or cultural standard.

Yet, almost all of the adjustment-in-marriage studies, including those predicting adjustment, show relationships between what, in effect, is adherence to conventional standards of the middle class, and so-called success in marriage. Indeed, it would be very surprising if conventional middle-class persons, who were "well-adjusted," did not find themselves (or were not rated by friends) as correspondingly happy in their conventionalized states. To be unhappy would be to be "out-of-role," and the whole conditioning process would have gone for nought. But how adequate a criterion, except of conventionality, is a statement of happiness? As Erich Fromm (1949) has indicated: "What, for instance, do we know about the happiness of people in our culture? True enough, many people would answer in a public opinion poll that they were happy because that is what a self-respecting citizen is supposed to feel [p. 9] ."

"Happiness" continues to be employed, however, as the criterion of success in marriage prediction, and as the major goal of the marriage counselor and client. To be sure, some criterion of success is necessary. But a criterion which would escape the endless circle of conventionality might be preferable and more useful. Much of the marriage prediction material appears to be measuring, scaling, and correlating several aspects of the same phenomenon. A piece of middle-class conventionality is correlated with a part of adherence to the same morality; in effect with itself.

Emotional maturity (which is popularly indexed by the control of affect, in such forms as not exhibiting temper, inhibiting jealousy without manifest "projection," and the like) is also correlated with success in marriage. But what passes for "emotional maturity" is often simply adult middle-class moral excellence. A highly conventional middle-class person possesses much middle-class virtue. Hence "becoming mature" and being indoctrinated with middle-class morality, as they are utilized in the literature, are virtually the same thing. As Ruesch (1948) notes, "In the lower class, where expression of anger is permitted, and where non-conformance and rebellion are sanctioned by class ideals, there exist other means of expressing conflicts [than by physical symptom formation] [p. 124]."

Kingsley Davis (1938) has long since demonstrated some of the relationships between the mental hygiene movement and the class structure. C. Wright Mills (1943) has noted that the professional ideology of the social pathologists stems in part from their social origins and the values of their collective middle-class mentalities. Norton Springer (1938) indicates that middle-class children tend to be better adjusted emotionally than children on lower rungs of the status scale. Springer found that children who come from middle-class families make more satisfactory behavior adjustments than those who derive from a poor general social level. The latter indicate more maladjustment and undesirable personal characteristics. He feels that emotional stability is closely related to the general social status of the individual.

One may raise the question as to whether measures of emotional stability, like measures of happiness in marriage, do not, at the same time, largely measure middle-class morality, rather than scientific findings of an objective character. Because of the widespread use by marriage counselors of the findings of "objective studies," some of their assumptions and the implications for theory and for practice must be examined.

The change which has been underway for the past fifty years in American family culture (from the Burgess perspective as distinguished from Sorokin-Zimmerman viewpoint) has been that generally characterized as the movement from an institutionalized form to one understandable in terms of the central theme of companionship. While the stability of the companionship type of relationship depends upon strong interpersonal relations, the stability of the conventional type of family depended upon such things as gossip, mores, public opinion, and the like. Granted that there are still institutional aspects to the companionship type, and that there were companionship elements in the institutional family, it is nonetheless useful to treat the two types more or less as opposites. Most family counseling today, however, appears to be pointed toward the conventional family rather than toward the companionship relationship, and counseling invokes sanction from "objective" materials bearing on that somewhat anachronistic organization.

This situation gives rise to the question as to how a marriage counselor can deal with a problem situation deriving from conflicts in the area of strong interpersonal relations. In short, while counseling is supposed to be an application of scientific principles, in addition to being an art, how can it properly function when its major orientation is toward the mores of the conventional institutional family? There is certainly a basic unreality in regarding idealized middle-class morality as the truly appropriate point of departure for all marriage problem phenomena, even though such conventionality may be bolstered by findings of so-called objective studies.

Persons in trouble normally need some other standard imposed upon them than that which has been largely responsible for their "problem situation." It is almost notorious knowledge that relief for the guilt-ridden alcoholic cannot derive from his knowledge of the actuarial tables on the "vice" of alcoholism, or from moral invocation to reform.

Under these circumstances what sort of "definition of the situation" (Volkart, 1951) is appropriate to the marriage counselor? The research investigator, and consequently the marriage counselor, has in large degree come to the point where he is faced with the fact that success-in-marriage is what success-in-marriage predictions predict. While this position may be tenable "operationally," it is manifestly untenable from anything but a naive operational viewpoint. Such a question also requires something more than the trite answer that the situation must be defined on a "case-to-case basis." The definition of the situation has significance not only for marriage counseling, but also for American social science. For implicitly the counselor's definition of the situation also concerns itself with whether social scientific marriage prediction and analysis deal even with the American sociocultural whole, or whether they are to limit their generalizations only to the plane of reference of the idealized morality of a single status grouping, which findings in turn it imposes on the totality of its materials.

Does the baseline from which "success" in marriage is determined need to be that of middle-class morality and conventionality? Even within the American status structure there are other bases from which the data of the marriage counselors' "generalized other" may be drawn. (This extension of the term "generalized other" derives from the discussion in Mead, 1934.) The family, for that matter even the *good* family, might conceivably be something quite different from the middle-class conventional family.

Many persons in our society basically and ordinarily identify with "unconventional" subcultures. To be sure, some of these subcultures move in the direction of fulfilling personal sense satisfactions, rather than developing stable social relations. Other "deviant" relationships become quite stable. But it is with just such problems that the marriage counselor frequently must deal. The actuarial materials on happiness in these areas today do not exist.

A social segment in every metropolitan area, for example, works in downtown offices and shops and tends to find its sex partners, and to evolve stable social relationships, through association developed in downtown bars. How significant are factors such as residential propinquity or church attendance for success in the companionship type of marriage derived from these groupings? Such persons, participating as they do in a greater variety of subcultures than conventional middle-class persons, appear to be capable of much "multivalence." They consequently are able to emphasize one tradition and its dominant values in one circumstance, and a quite contrary tradition in another, without notable inner conflict, and with the several sets of values quite real and significant for adjustment to stable sex roles. Were the marriage counselor to define this situation with the criteria of middle-class conventionality in judging problems and probabilities for success in such unions, he would tend to do scientific violence to an equivalent reality. It would, however, be analogous to the case workers doing relief work early in the Depression, who asked themselves what there was in clients' psychological make-ups which prevented them from getting employment.

The instruments developed for the actuarial prediction of success in marriage never take into account such common phenomena in American married life as the "phantom lover." The phantom lover performs all sorts of services, including the sex act, in such fashion that amazing "happiness" accrues to some women, and he is rarely matched by, unless he is imaginatively combined with, his "surrogate," the actual husband. Middle-class morality does not countenance the existence of such a fantasy. It therefore never finds its way into the instrument from which predictive tables are derived. In view of the tendency toward homogamy in actual unions, and the tables indicating improbability for success the greater the discrepancy in cultural and religious background of mates, it would be interesting to determine the extent to which phantom lovers are of other ethnic and religious backgrounds.

The problem faced by the marriage counselor is thus, from a scientific viewpoint, at least twofold. The marriage bond and family relationship may not always be adequately defined in terms of what *ought to be* from the viewpoint of middle-class conventionality. And the counselor has little of an actuarial sort to guide him for other forms of relationship. He may even lack scepticism of the utility of his own values, which a knowledge of cultural relativity potentially could give him.

Under the circumstances how much "scientific" education for marriage is feasible? As Willard Waller (1951) said some years ago, "Various 'educational' programs have been devised in order to promote better family life. Many such programs are definitely harmful, since their effect is merely to strengthen the existing mores and to accentuate the conflicts of persons unable to live within the mores. . . . Where such educational programs are based upon the scientific study of the family, and the possibility of changing mores instead of conforming the individual to them is not excluded, they may be helpful [pp. 600–601]."

Programs of education for marriage, and marriage counseling as a field, obviously need now to recognize, as social case work in part has come to recognize in the past ten years, that something other than the standards of middle-class conventionality may be imposed on clients and students, and that success in marriage will have to be defined in terms of the several cultural traditions of the persons addressed. The areas of the "generalized other" must be examined until the most usual and tolerable locus of the person is determined.

Without a broad exploration of the anthropological literature bearing on the variety of fulfillments of personality needs, at least the lesson of Freud's rather obvious dictum, that the illicit sex relationship of the lower-class girl living on the ground floor of the Vienna apartment house will have quite different significance for her than the equivalent experience of her middle-class counterpart on the second story, must be taken into account. Cultural tradition molds sex roles and marital difficulties and, for that matter, marital counseling. But marital counseling potentially could escape it.

REFERENCES

Burgess, E. W., & Cottrell, L. S. The prediction of adjustment in marriage. *American Sociological Review*, 1936, *1*, 737–751.

Christensen, H. T. Family size as a factor in the marital adjustment of college couples. *American Sociological Review*, 1952, *17*, 306–312.

Davis, K. Mental hygiene and the class structure. *Psychiatry* 1938, *1*, 63.

Fromm, E. Psychoanalytic characterology and its application to the understanding of culture. *In* S. Stansfeld Sargent & Marian W. Smith (Eds.), *Culture and personality*. New York: The Viking Fund, 1949.

Hayner, N. S. The sociologist views mariage problems. *Sociology and Social Research* 1948, *33*, 20–24.

Mead, G. H. *Mind, self and society*. Pp. 154ff. Ed. by C. W. Morris. Chicago: University of Chicago Press, 1934.

Mills, C. W. The professional ideology of social pathologists. *American Journal of Sociology* 1943, *49*, 165–180.

Ruesch, J. Social technique, social status and social change in illness. *In* C. Kluckhohn & H. A. Murray (Ed.) *Personality in nature, society and culture*. New York: Alfred A. Knopf, 1948. Pp. 126–127.

Springer, N. Influence of general social status on the emotional stability of children. *Journal of Genetic Psychology*, 1938, *53*, 321–327.

Volkart, E. (Ed.) *Social behavior and personality: Contributions of W. I. Thomas to theory and social research*. New York: Social Science Research Council, 1951.

Waller, W. *The family: A dynamic interpretation*. Rev. by Reuben Hill. New York: Dryden Press, 1951.

CHAPTER 6

Counseling for Family Living

Clara B. Lyndon and Benjamin H. Lyndon

For many years professional attempts of all kinds have been made to meet problems of family life. More recently there has been an articulate demand for an increase in such services offered by both agencies and individual practitioners. To meet this request, people from many associated disciplines have moved into the area of counseling. The sociologist has progressed from a study of "The Family" to a consideration of a particular family. The psychologist, beginning with the tools for mental measurement and definition of personality structure, now thinks of applying his knowledge to the treatment of personality disorders. The social worker is concerned no longer only with manipulating the environment, but has also turned to techniques for easing inner stress and strain. We might make similar comment about others who function as counselors: the physicians, ministers, educators, etc. Counseling has become a cloak of many colors; its connotations may vary with the background of the individual counselor. However, if we think of counseling in terms of the needs of the applicant, we must find some generic base, common to any counseling situation regardless of the individual counselor's background. This generic base is found in the dynamics of human behavior.

Since family-life counseling is a function which uses a professional team of many skills, it is the purpose of this paper to attempt to describe the area within which it operates, for whom, how, and what is required of the counselor whatever his basic professional discipline.

As this field has developed, there has arisen a classification system based on categories of service rather than one based upon personality difficulty. These areas of operation have been counseling on the pre-marital, marital, preparental, and parental levels—a progression which parallels family development. Included too should be those problems not directly related to either marriage or the family, if such can be said to exist. However, whatever the grouping, even the most superficial scrutiny of problems of family living reduces them to the human being under emotional stress, so that basically our concern must be for the people who come seeking help. The "family" problems are in themselves not diagnostic entities separable in differentiated treatment, but rather are an expres-

Reprinted with permission of the authors and the publisher from the *American Journal of Orthopsychiatry*, 1951, *21*, 612–620.

sion of the personalities involved operating on one of the aforementioned
levels.

The "Consumer" of Counseling

The "consumers" of counseling service fall into three general, loosely
delineated categories: the normal, the anxious, and the seriously disturbed.

1. *The normal.* Here is an individual reacting with uncertainty to
some real, current or anticipated change in his life situation. Perhaps out
of ignorance, perhaps with a background of mild, universal insecurity, he
seeks out a counselor for assistance. He may gravitate to a group situation
advertised as a mental hygiene program or as "preparation" classes. Or,
when aware of such resources and financially able, he requests service of a
social agency or an individual practitioner. He usually brings with him the
uneasiness of anticipation. His is the quest for the definite—the answer to
a question—he has an awareness of a lack of knowledge.

The questions of individuals in the "normal" category are many and
varied, related to the particular experience they are facing—they reveal
some fearfulness but not usually of too deep-seated a nature. From those
contemplating marriage, there may be requests for sexual information,
questions regarding length of engagement, premarital sex relations, contraceptives, etc. Parents show some apprehension about handling a first
child, or about what to do when the first sibling arrives. Frequently these
people can find reassurance in learning that others have had the same
questions, that they are not alone in their concern.

Included in this category are those who, while usually fairly stable,
become anxious under the impact of some especially threatening situation.

Mrs. A came to the office to ask for advice on how to work out the
relationship between Johnny, her adopted son, and her own child Alice.
She had not been aware of any particular problem until friends began to
question her as to what she planned to do. She then began to feel that
perhaps she had not been doing the right thing.

After ten years of marriage the A's had thought that they were
doomed to childlessness. They adopted Johnny when he was two weeks
old. A year later Mrs. A became pregnant. She laughed and said, "It never
fails, does it?" Johnny is now five, Alice is three, and Mrs. A is expecting
another child in a few months. When they thought that Johnny would
understand, they explained to him that he was adopted and that they had
picked him out because they wanted a baby—who was their choice. Now
Mrs. A finds herself in a quandary. If she sticks to this explanation that
they chose Johnny, will Alice feel unwanted because they did not choose
her? She is concerned too about how each of them will react to the
coming child.

The counselor asked Mrs. A for some further information about each
of the children, and for most of the hour Mrs. A spoke very freely about
both of them. She seemed to delight in telling little anecdotes about them,

chuckled with amusement on occasion, and beamed with pride as she described how charming each one was in his own way. From her description one got no impression of any overt behavior difficulty in either of the children nor of any behavior which might indicate emotional disturbance. She seemed to dwell on indications that Johnny was a bright child, and the counselor thought that she might have some anxiety about his antecedents and his intellectual capacity. Mrs. A was therefore asked whether it would be of any help to her for Johnny to be given a psychological examination. She looked a little startled for a moment, said that she had not thought of it, and that, while it would be interesting to satisfy her normal curiosity about how he—"or Alice for that matter"—performed, she did not see any particular reason for it. She seemed entirely comfortable in her response.

There was some general discussion about the feelings of adopted children, in which Mrs. A showed a keen sensitivity and awareness of how they might feel. In response to her particular question, it was suggested that she might, at the appropriate time, tell both of the children that there were two ways that parents had babies. One was by choosing them as she had chosen Johnny, and the other was by giving birth to them. (She has already made some attempt to answer each child's questions about how babies are born.) Mrs. A thought this might be a very workable idea. She repeated that she had not considered that she had a problem until some of her friends disturbed her equilibrium by their questions. She smiled and said that as she looked at things now, she did not really think she did have a problem.

The interview was terminated with Mrs. A's comment that she appreciated the opportunity to talk and the counselor's invitation for her to renew the contact at any time in the future that she felt it might be of any value. No further appointments were made at this time since there did not seem to be any particular need.

Miss O and Mr. P were referred to a private practitioner by Miss O's older sister, who paid for the service. The two applicants were engaged to be married, the wedding date having been set. Miss O's parents were dead, and the older sister, who lived out of town, felt that premarital counseling would give the girl an opportunity to discuss any problems she might have. In a sense the counselor was asked to serve *in loco parentis*. Both Miss O and Mr. P were seen together first; then each was interviewed separately; and, finally, both were seen again in two final contacts.

In the first interview the girl related quickly while the man was initially tense and uncertain. They discussed their individual backgrounds, their relationship with each other, and some of their concerns about finances, continuation of education, the wife's working, and family responsibilities. By the end of this session it was obvious that each related to the counselor as an understanding father.

In the individual interviews the fact came out that they had unsuccessfully attempted intercourse. Each was concerned about this in his own way. The woman felt that she couldn't participate even though she was "passionate" because she had been taught it was "bad." She was also fearful because his penis seemed "so large," and hostile because in their attempts he had had premature ejaculations.

He revealed previous successful sexual relations with other girls and was concerned about his fiancée's passivity. It was to this fact that he attributed his premature ejaculations. He asked for specific advice as to how he must approach her "because she is a virgin."

Recognizing the possibility of deeper underlying meaning to these anxieties, the counselor still felt that a good deal could be offered in his "father" role and set the limited goal of education and support of essentially normal strengths. With each the sexual physiology of both sexes was discussed in simplest terms, misconceptions were pointed out and explained, and feelings about this were handled. She was referred to a competent gynecologist for specific medical advice on birth control procedures. His technique for the wedding night and subsequently was gone into with him.

In the final joint conferences the counselor helped them to discuss openly the fears they had been withholding from each other, what these meant and what might be done about them. The meaning of the marriage relationship in all of its implications was also reviewed. The counselor's final impression was that mutual understanding and a greater security in the relationship had developed.

2. *The anxious.* This individual appears with a configuration of some neurotic symptomatology. This may range from generalized feelings of uneasiness, vague fears, and mild somatic complaints to a clear-cut diagnosis of neurosis. In all, the manifestations of anxiety are evident, either directly or through the defenses set up to combat the anxiety. The composite life history of this group reveals an insecure and frequently inadequate childhood with considerable strength in the ability to overcome frequently serious handicaps. The pattern is repeated in many areas of their functioning—school, work, marriage, parent-child relationships. The man who keeps himself in a mediocre job because he doubts his own capacity to advance may also be the man who shies away from marriage, makes and breaks engagements, or becomes the "henpecked" husband and the uncertain father (if he doesn't reject fatherhood entirely).

Mr. Q is an attractive, intelligent man of 35, whose question of the counselor is, "What kind of girl should I marry?" He has had a number of contacts with a "psychologist," has been given a number of "personality inventories," and has been told that he has a number of aptitudes, should be successful in business, etc. He has read innumerable books on psychology, but is still left with feelings of doubt about himself. His further conversation reveals that he has been engaged to be married four times, and each time has broken the engagement—on one occasion only a few days before the wedding date, with the reason given to the girl that she was too good for him. He is at present interested in a young woman, and as he describes the relationship one can see the seeds of difficulty already being planted.

He is the only son in a family of six children and expresses the feeling that his trouble has always been "too many women." He spent considerable time describing early childhood experiences and the feelings of frustration and inadequacy he had had. At present he holds a good executive position, but plans to make a change because he doesn't think he can "make a go of it" (despite the evidence of the aptitude tests). When he became comfortable enough with the counselor, he said there was something else that bothered him a lot—an inhibition of urinary function (for which no organic basis has been found).

In view of the obvious indications of neurotic functioning, the counselor devoted his efforts toward helping Mr. Q see that an answer to his question about "what kind of girl I should marry" would not meet his need. He attained some insight into the fact that he himself seemed unable to sustain a relationship with a young woman, and on this basis referral for psychotherapy was made.

3. *The seriously disturbed.* These are the relationship-disabled, those obviously ill psychologically, intellectually or physically, or in any combination of these. Emotionally they may range from the severe neuroses to psychopathy or psychosis; their mental capacities from feeblemindedness to genius; their physical capacity from health to severe illness and handicap. This group brings to the counselor all of the distortions of an incapacity to relate except in extremes. Frequently they are thrust unwillingly into asking for help. Often they are propelled by the very mechanism which is self-defeating. It is frequently outside the realm of the counselor to attempt treatment of the seriously disturbed; what is important is that the proper resources be found for them, if this is possible.

Mr. and Mrs. R were referred to the agency by the domestic relations court, following Mrs. R's application for divorce. This was a more or less routine referral of a couple having marital difficulty.

Diagnostic interviews with Mr. and Mrs. R gave evidence of the fact that Mrs. R was a seriously disturbed, possibly psychotic woman and that the "marital difficulty" grew out of her paranoid condition. Mr. R was completely bewildered by some of her behavior, protested that he loved his wife and did not want a divorce. He expressed some concern in regard to the five small children in the home, who were sometimes very much frightened by their mother's bizarre actions.

In view of the indications of severe disturbance in Mrs. R, arrangements were made for psychiatric consultation. The case was discussed with the psychiatrist first and a diagnostic interview for Mrs. R was then planned. Mr. R was also seen once by the psychiatrist, who confirmed the counselor's diagnostic impressions and discussed the diagnosis with Mr. R.

Subsequent contacts with Mr. R, which covered a period of several months, were centered around interpretation of mental illness to him and helping him in planning for the necessary hospitalization of his wife, and for the care of the young children.

The Meaning of Counseling. In one way or another each of the individuals described seeks an answer to his problem. He may register in a publicized group or class which seems even remotely related to his concern. On the other hand, he may turn to a friend, a member of his family, an ethical private practitioner or a recognized professional agency. Frequently participation in a group is a prelude to seeking individual help, and, as in the case of group therapy, personal counseling may precede group activity.

Whenever he turns to an ethical person or agency, he is entitled to a guarantee that his personal integrity will be preserved in a professional relationship that has meaning in terms of his problem. It is no easy task to make such a guarantee. Our state of knowledge of human behavior has not advanced to the point of perfection, but within the limits of what we know as counselors for family living this much we can offer: *a meaningful professional relationship in which an effort is made to provide education, support, or therapy in terms of the needs of the person requesting the service and within the limits of the skill of the counselor and of the setting within which he operates.* This definition of counseling needs further clarification as it relates to both individual and group treatment.

Individual Counseling. Person-to-person counseling is inevitably based on the environment of the counselor-client relationship (Sterba, 1948; Groves, 1947). It is "meaningful" in terms of the psychological role created for the counselor by his client, a creation predicated on the life history of the client and reflecting the way he has related to important persons in his own past. It has meaning for diagnosis, that is, helping the counselor understand the person asking for help. It has meaning for treatment, for it is upon understanding how the client relates that therapeutic goals are set. The applicant, of course, must recognize the problem and accept the goal.

The relationship is the area within which *education*, the filling in of intellectual gaps of knowledge, is provided. It is because the counselor assumes for the client the position of the parental authority and the teacher-expert that the knowledge offered takes on not only intellectual meaning, but has the potential for emotional acceptance and incorporation.

It is the feeling exchanged between the counselor and client that makes it possible for the counselor to *support* the client's decisions and help him to make sound choices for himself. The relationship gives meaning to this process, for it provides for the uncertain person an ally at a time when he cannot cope with uncertainty by himself. At the same time, it has within it the implication that help now may make it possible for the client to be independent in the future.

For purposes of this discussion, therapy encompasses the area of emotional reeducation and the development of insight. The patient is helped through the process of reliving relationship experiences in his own past which were disastrous to his normal growth. In this process we can see how important the role of the counselor must be and how the meaning of the relationship is the *sine qua non* of treatment. The same implications are inevitably true where they form the basis for the client's development of emotional insight through living the experience, having its real meaning interpreted to him, and finally incorporating this understanding as part of his own personality structure.

Group Counseling. This type of counseling is even more complex than that which takes place in the one-to-one relationship; and at our present stage of knowledge even less is known about it. On the surface there appear to be some similarities, although it is certain that there are many more differences.*

It is clear that the counselor-group relationship is extremely important. In this sense each member of the group responds to the counselor in terms of his own individual psychology. This reaction, however, is colored and further complicated by responses to other members of the group. It is also influenced by their relationship to the counselor, which they express unconsciously through body reaction and both consciously and unconsciously through verbal response in the form of questions or comments. Counselor-directed questions are frequently an indication of the significance of this relationship. For example, the male counselor may be asked what he thinks about (1) men's extreme interest in sex, (2) women's working, (3) men who make perverted sexual demands, (4) the amount of a woman's personal allowance, etc. The woman counselor, of course, finds other types of queries directed at her which also point up the meaning of that relationship. What does *she* think of (1) women's disinterest in sex, (2) the working mother, (3) the travail of childbirth, (4) the amount of a woman's personal allowance, etc.?

Motives for entering a group differ greatly. We know of one excited mother in a group on parent-child relationships who pleaded that the course be continued or repeated; otherwise she "would have to spend Monday evenings at home with those three brats." However, as a matter of empiric observation, it is largely the more normal type of personality who appears in the nonselected group. Fortunately, it is for this group that the counselor-group relationship has the most significance as a basis for the educative process. As for the other two categories, the anxious and the seriously disturbed, there is some question as to whether they can benefit from this type of experience. Its value to them appears somewhat dubious, except as it may provide them with a stepping-off place from which to seek the supportive and therapeutic help they really need. The possibility of group therapy for these persons is not being discounted. However, work in this area has to date been so scattered and limited in scope as to require that evaluation of its potentials be withheld.

Some of the reasons why the group is less effective on an intensive level are inherent in the process itself. Some of these are as follows:

1. Group composition varies and therefore needs vary. In any group not selected diagnostically there will be found a large proportion of normal persons, a reasonably large number of the anxious, and a few seriously disturbed.

---

*Even the techniques which group counseling encompasses are manifold. Currently in use are lectures (with or without audio-visual aids), lecture-discussion, discussion only, and group therapy which may combine any of the foregoing. It is not our intention to discuss these techniques.

2. Group size may vary in extremes and in some instances, such as publicized courses or classes, numerical limits are beyond the control of the counselor.

3. The purpose of group meetings is usually defined in advance and this goal must be maintained within rather rigid limits.

4. Duration of the counseling service is usually predetermined by factors other than group need, ranging from one "buck-shot" lecture to an indeterminate number which is based on availability of counselors, space, amount of fees paid, etc.

5. Group intrarelationship is an uncertain factor for each individual within it; it may be therapeutic for one individual and anxiety-stimulating for another.

6. Groups do not provide opportunity for handling individual anxieties except as these concerns may be universalized by the counselor, or "treated" by comments of other group members.

7. Group situations require the availability of individual counseling as needed to meet specific requests for help from members of the group.

From the above it can be seen that the function of the group counselor is an involved one, which requires not only the awareness of the meaning of individual relationship, but also of the significance of group intrarelationship. We hold no brief that this is a simple process. On the contrary, we believe that it remains a challengingly complex one.

Limitations of the Counselor. Our definition included the concept that service can only be offered in terms of "the limits of the skill of the counselor." This is more important than may appear at a cursory glance, since it also involves by implication an understanding of "the needs of the person requesting the service." It can easily be seen that a nonmedical counselor queried about the meaning of an organic symptom and the ways, if any, of correcting it would be outside of his area of competence if he tried to answer the question. In more subtle emotional problems the same understanding of professional limitations must be shown. Some counselors by training are able to offer educative help; others may be able to combine that and supportive assistance; still others can offer therapy. But it is not necessarily true that just because a person brings a problem, *ipso facto* that particular counselor can treat it. One thing that an applicant can expect, however, is that the counselor should have a sound capacity for diagnosis.

As a matter of observation, it may be stated that too frequently counselors step out of their technical bounds and try to give help they are not competent to offer. A thoroughly qualified sociologist is not necessarily an able psychologist, or therapist—nor is an analyst always the best person to give service in the social milieu.

Minimal Requisites of the Counselor. Implicit in the counseling process is the concept that the process is a unified one, divisible only into specialized types such as parental, premarital, marital, etc., in terms of settings which offer such specific services. With this as our frame of reference let us examine the essentials of knowledge, attitudes, and skills that a counselor must have regardless of his basic professional competence.

Of *knowledge* little need be said. Certainly, there would be uniform agreement that culture, with all of its meaning to the family, the process of human development, the dynamics of behavior, anatomy, and physiology, and the meaning of illness are minimal areas of knowledge essential for any counselor. However, no amount of specific learning is in itself sufficient for the task. Much more important are basic attitudes and highly developed skills.

In our opinion there are two types of *attitudes* without which no individual can counsel another. The first of these relates to the client and may simply be stated as the philosophy that each man has the right to live his own life, on his own terms, in his own way as long as his way is not injurious to others. We cannot subscribe to the concept of one counselor that "the first goal proposed (in marriage counseling) is that the marriage counselor should seek to keep the family unit intact" and that "the second goal proposed for the marriage counselor is that his criterion for a successful marital adjustment be that his client not only remain married, but also that he plans, realistically, to have children." The comments presuppose a judgmental attitude which is unwarranted because it is based on arbitrary standards set by the counselor in terms of his own evaluation of the situation. There is no recognition of the basic needs of the client, nor of the fact that under any standards there are some marriages in our culture which are destructive to one or both partners and others in which the presence of children is contraindicated in terms of the personalities of the marriage partners.

The second attitude of importance is that toward self. Insight with its accompanying humility is an essential to knowing what one can do and how much should be done. The relationship between counselor and client is a two-way process. Just as the applicant has feelings about the therapist which come from his life history, so is the reverse equally true, and for the same psychological reasons. It is an emotional framework within which all of us react to each other. The counselor, however, has a responsibility to be aware of, and concerned with, the phenomenon, for the degree of objectivity on the part of the professional is dependent upon his understanding it. Lack of such awareness may distort the relationship and inevitably confuse the treatment process.

Finally, the *skills* of the counselor must be highly developed, involving, as they do, the transmission of knowledge, limited by self-awareness, through the interview or group relationship to the client. To say that one must know how to interview or conduct a group session is not enough. The counselor must always be aware of his relationship to his client or clients and know consciously how to use it to meet their needs. To operate without this awareness and skill is to negate the existence of oneself as a counselor.

REFERENCES

Groves, C. The counseling process. *Marriage and Family Living*, 1947, *9*, 75–78.

Lottier, S. Marriage counseling: Goals and techniques. *Marriage and Family Living*, Summer 1947, *9*, No. 3.

Sterba, Lyndon, & Katz. Transference in casework. New York: Family Service Association of America, 1948.

CHAPTER 7

Love and Aggression:
The Perils of Loving

Ben N. Ard, Jr.

One of the major tasks ahead for us in our society today is making the world safe for love. That is, we need to cut down on the aggression which is so frequently involved in love relationships. As Abraham Maslow (1954) has said, "We *must* understand love; we must be able to teach it, to create it, to predict it, or else the world is lost to hostility and to suspicion [p. 236]."

If we are to understand the etiology of love clearly, then we need to know the causes of love, how it starts, how it grows and is sustained, how it flowers, and how it dies. We need to know what factors help love to develop and what factors hinder the development of love.

Love is a very basic part of the human condition, as we know from cross-cultural studies of love. Such studies also show us that there are many different kinds of love, and not all of the various kinds of love are good—some kinds of love are very self-defeating.

The background from which I shall view love and aggression is that of a psychologist, sexologist, and marriage counselor. (I have been a psychologist in the student health service of a university in the Midwest as well as having a private practice in San Francisco.) I have seen the consequences of various mixtures of love and aggression in many people's lives.

During the following discussion, then, I shall be talking about *love* and *aggression*, two concepts which are very difficult to talk about with clarity unless we define our terms rather carefully. The concept of love has been treated so extensively in both poetry and prose that we shall have to delimit ourselves if we are to make any reasonable progress in our discussion.

Presented at the University of California, Davis campus, symposium on "The Etiology of Love," February 13, 1968.

That delightful poetess, Dorthy Parker, once penned four lines which pretty well sum up the matter:

TWO VOLUME NOVEL

The sun's gone dim, and
The moon's turned black;
For I loved him, and
He didn't love back.

Dorothy Parker. In the *Viking Portable Library*, p. 355

Dorothy Parker spoke in her poem about the crux of the matter I wish to discuss: the love of a maid for a man, and vice versa. So we shall leave to others the discussion of all other kinds of love, such as love of nature, love of God, love of old wine, tasty food, or stimulating books.

Therefore, I shall primarily be discussing the concept of love which deals with the feelings and ideas obtaining between men and women which involve some sexual connotations. (We shall leave so-called Platonic love to others to discuss.) I shall concentrate mostly on love between the sexes; in colloquial parlance that is sometimes referred to as "the battle between the sexes."

As has been pointed out by Dr. Albert Ellis, (1963)

> Many males in our culture are so thwarted by our sex codes and become so sex-hungry that they begin to see females only as sex objects and to depreciate any nonsexual attributes that they may have. In their turn, millions of our women become so resentful of the fact that the men's interest in them is almost primarily sexual that they become misanthropic and after a while find it almost impossible to love any man [p. 208].

These are some of the reasons why the battle between the sexes can be so bitter. As Ellis also stated,

> Again largely because of our different ways of raising males and females, the former are usually mainly obsessed with having premarital and adulterous affairs, while the latter are intent on confining their sex relations to monogamous marriage. This means that the sex goals of men and women are quite different in many instances, and that the men begin to resent the women for not, as they say in the vernacular, "putting out," while the women resent the men for being sexually exploitative and for not being as interested in marrying as they are [p. 208].

What does it really mean when one person says to another: "I love you"? It obviously means many different things to different people in various situations. Meerloo (1952) has described some of the different meanings as follows:

> Sometimes it means: "I desire you" or "I want you sexually." It may mean: "I hope you love me" or "I hope that I will be able to love you." Often it means: "It may be that a love relationship can develop between us." . . . Often it is a wish for emotional exchange: "I want your admiration in exchange for mine" or "I give my love in exchange for some passion" or . . . "I admire some of your qualities." A declaration of love is mostly a request: "I desire you" or "I

want you to gratify me" or "I want your protection" . . . or "I want to exploit your loveliness."

Sometimes it is the need for security . . . for parental treatment. . . . It may be self-sacrifice and a masochistic wish for dependency. However, it may also be a full affirmation of the other, taking the responsibility for mutual exchange of feelings. . . . [It may be] wish, desire, submission, conquest; it is never the word itself that tells the real meaning . . . [p. 83].

Heterosexual love, then, as I shall mean it in this context, is a reasonably strong or intense attachment, involvement, or favorable attitude, to say the least, between a male and a female. (Cf. Ellis, 1958, p. 160.)

What I shall mean in this context by *aggression* is the tendency of a person to do something harmful to another person or to himself. As used here, the word *hostility* might be considered a synonym. As Leon Saul (1956) has noted,

Many people like to believe that hostility is inherited, and therefore should be dismissed as something about which nothing, for the present at least, can be done. Others believe, falsely, that hostility is a strength, that without it men and women would be left defenseless in a world all too ready to attack and exploit the weak [p. 5].

In this sophisticated, psychological age, when Freud's ideas (understood or not, right or wrong) are accepted by perhaps most of the educated set, we need to look at Freud's concepts most critically, since they are seemingly accepted without question by too many so-called educated people. (Cf. Suttie, 1935.)

For example, Freud held that "the tendency toward aggression is an innate, independent, instinctual disposition in man and that it constitutes the most powerful obstacle to culture [Saul, 1956, p. 8]." I shall present a minority opinion that aggression or hostility is a disease to be cured and prevented like cancer, tuberculosis, or smallpox. (Cf. Saul, 1956, p. 8.)

Now, having suggested that not all of Freud's ideas are correct, let it be acknowledged that Freud and other psychoanalysts have given us some insights as to why we humans act the way we do in our relations with one another, particularly where these relations involve love and sex. For example, an English psychoanalyst, Melanie Klein (1964) has pointed out:

The reason why some people have so strong a need for general praise and approval lies in their need for evidence that they are lovable, worthy of love. This feeling arises from the unconscious fear of being incapable of loving others sufficiently or truly, and particularly of not being able to master aggressive impulses towards others: they dread being a danger to the loved one [pp. 62–63].

Melanie Klein has also noted that hatred

leads to our establishing frightening figures in our minds, and then we are apt to endow other people with unpleasant and malevolent qualities. Incidently, such an attitude of mind has an actual effect in making other people unpleasant and suspicious towards us, while a friendly and trusting attitude on our part is apt to call forth trust and benevolence from others [p. 115].

That the road to love is not always smooth is a part of our folklore.

Many of our most famous stories of the greatest loves have ended in mutilation, separation, and/or death for the lovers—e.g., Abelard and Heloise, Romeo and Juliet, Tristan and Isolde. (Then, perhaps, one may recall from American folklore what happened to Frankie and Johnnie.)

Wisdom about the perils of loving is available in unsuspected places. For example, in one of the famous blues songs sung by Joe Turner, entitled "Cherry Red," Joe says,

> I ain't never loved,
> And I hope I never will,
> 'Cause the loving proposition
> 'Gonna get somebody killed.

Part of the perils of loving, I should like to suggest, arise from the *romantic concepts* which are so common in our culture but which lead to unrealistic and false expectations, and therefore to subsequent disillusionment. These false romantic notions must inevitably cause disillusionment because of the frustration of the romantic, over-idealized *expectations*. But if one takes a more rational, realistic attitude toward love, then one can face even the end of that love as no catastrophe. As an illustration of this latter kind of attitude I am recommending, consider these lines from a sonnet:

> "Well, I have lost you; and I lost you fairly;
> In my own way, and with my full consent.
> Say what you will, kings in a tumbrel rarely
> Went to their deaths more proud than this one went.
> Some nights of apprehension and hot weeping
> I will confess; but that's permitted me;
> Day dried my eyes; I was not one for keeping
> Rubbed in a cage a wing that would be free.
> If I had loved you less or played you slyly
> I might have held you for a summer more,
> But at the cost of words I value highly,
> And no such summer as the one before.
> Should I outlive this anguish—and men do—
> I shall have only good to say of you."

Edna St. Vincent Millay, in *Collected Sonnets*, p. 116

Young men are, in general, less likely to be romantic than young women in our culture, but young men also build up unduly high hopes about the young women they love. Sometimes when these young women merely look at other men, they get beat up, along with the "other man."

Attempts to justify such aggressive behavior can frequently be reduced to the unquestioned assumptions about jealousy as a natural, normal, expected response—even an indication of "real, true, deep love" (Ard, 1967c)! Here again is an illustration of the detrimental aspects of the conventional, romantic concepts of love which are still very much in evidence in our culture to this day.

These conventional notions about romantic love are fed and nurtured by Hollywood movies, romantic novels, romantic magazines and television shows, as well as many parents (with other, ulterior, motives).

But romantic concepts of love originated many years ago, under the influence of the Christians. "Not until the Christian era, however, did the idea of romantic love, as we know it, put in its appearance [Farnham, 1953, p. 180]."

> Romantic love, as it appears in the Middle Ages, was not directed at first toward women with whom the lover could have either legitimate or illegitimate sexual relations; it was directed toward women of the highest respectability who were separated from their romantic lovers by insuperable barriers of morality and convention [Krich, 1960, p. 11].

Our romantic concepts of love have arisen, then, because our religious teachings have defined sex outside of lifelong, monogamous marriage as sinful, dirty, and wrong.

Donald Day (1954), in his history of the evolution of love between the sexes over sixty centuries, concluded:

> There is little doubt that the United States is still in a stage of extreme reaction to fantastic puritanism. The country has not yet finished its "fling" and may not as long as the "sterile" panderers of spirituality continue as they have for thousands of years to set themselves up as arbiters of nature's most powerful force—sex [p. 517].

What can be done to encourage good, healthy, sex-love relationships between men and women, in a society with such strange, mixed-up notions about sex and love? Some things can be done:

> By changing some of our more idiotic sex customs, as well as by learning to live sanely with them while they are still unchanged, we can significantly reduce the hate-creating aspects of sex while notably increasing its love-enhancing aspects. . . . In our own sexually inhibited society, there is some evidence that sexual blocking—even when it causes considerable hostility between the sexes . . . —also may foment a particular kind of romantic or obsessive-compulsive love. Romantic love . . . has its clearcut disadvantages, and is not necessarily a particularly good harbinger of mature, marital love [Ellis, 1963, pp. 205, 207].

That love and sex are frequently mixed up with aggression and hostility is known to most people. I would only like to document this fact for those people who still tend to look at the etiology of love through rose-colored glasses. One cannot study the consequences of love between the sexes without also touching on rape, violence, beatings, sadism, masochism, and murder. Pick up practically any newspaper on any day. The facts are available for anyone to see.

"Do you know that in New York City, a woman is raped every four and a half hours? [Herb Caen, San Francisco *Chronicle*, December 28, 1967]" Think about that. One response to that statement was: "She must be the happiest woman in the world."

Of course, many women have certain expectations about sex which involve some aggression. Some women seem to want to be raped, in effect.

Rape has even been defined as "assault with a friendly weapon [in the film *Waterhole Number Three*]."

Also in the San Francisco *Chronicle* for December 28, 1967, was a report of a slaughter over a wedding. In Istanbul a twenty-three–year–old youth allegedly killed his fiancée and eight members of her family after an argument about their wedding date.

On page one of the same paper was the report of the disenchantment of a battered bride in Mexico City. It took the young bride only a few hours—and three beatings—to decide she was disillusioned with marriage. Three hours after the wedding, at the wedding reception, the husband administered her first beating, in front of the guests, as a sign of married bliss. A donnybrook ensued. The police broke it up only to have another free-for-all break out again after the party resumed. After the third time around, the young wife went to the hospital suffering multiple bruises. So, one may really see, there are indeed perils involved in loving.

I would contend that aggression is essentially learned as the result of frustration, but it is also learned as "acceptable behavior," particularly in certain males in certain subcultures. The mass media help teach people that aggression is an acceptable form of behavior, even "manly."

Berkowitz (1962, p. xiii), in his studies of aggression, suggested that frequent portrayals of hostility in the mass media can affect the audience's attitude toward aggression, and that under certain specified conditions the portrayed violence may *evoke* as well as *shape* hostile responses. There seems to be a greater likelihood that media violence will increase the probability of subsequent aggression rather than provide a cathartic lessening of hostile energies.

How can one check out the possibilities of aggression in one's partner? There are no guaranteed ways of ruling out the possibility of aggression in any love relationship, but there are some possible hints in some recent research.

Drinking alcohol is frequently a release for aggressive tendencies in people who already possess strong aggressive inclinations. Observing the prospective partner under the influence of alcohol might not be a bad idea.

Humor preference in cartoons could be a measuring stick for determining these aggressive impulses, too, as has been demonstrated by Professor Hetherington of the University of Wisconsin (San Francisco *Chronicle*, December 22, 1967). Cartoons depicting aggression seem funnier to people with inhibited aggressive tendencies than to people lacking these impulses. So check out the prospective partner regarding what seems funny in aggressive cartoons.

That ideas about love between the sexes are changing should be no surprise to anyone in our culture who is the slightest bit aware of what is happening (Ard, 1967a). There is much discussion of the so-called "new morality" (Aiken, 1968).

If we can summarize these observations of moralists in the younger generation, we can say that "the new moralists are more 'cool' toward sex than their elders [Aiken, 1968, p. 70]." What does this mean (for those who aren't "hip")? It means, for one thing, that the young people who live by this "new morality" have fewer rules about sexual immorality.

> Furthermore, the young are less disposed than their elders to confuse questions of manners with questions of morals, questions of conventional rudeness or incivility with questions of immorality. And since questions of etiquette interest them little or not at all, they tend to be less full of resentments, less disposed to take umbrage, less exposed to affronts, to conventional jealousy, to the whole emotional paraphernalia of conventional sexual relations [Aiken, 1968, p. 70].

The new attitudes toward sex and love are developing among several subgroups in our society, not merely among the hippies or flower children. There is a type of affection-oriented permissiveness that has been developing among the new middle classes, particularly within the professional occupational groups (Reiss, 1967, p. 178).

As Aiken (1968) has pointed out, "Perhaps the most disturbing attitude among some of the new moralists is a pervasive failure of discrimination . . . [p. 70] ." I would like to urge upon you the basic idea that if a person wants to avoid some of the perils of loving, one of the first principles he or she will have to learn well is to *discriminate* in the choice of partners.

One of the things about which one needs to be very perceptive in one's choice of partner is the amount of *dominance* he has, i.e., the degree to which he will tend to try to dominate in the relationship. Maslow (1963) has found in his studies that "people who are secure show no sadism-masochism at all, nor do they seek to dominate or be dominated . . . [p. 108] ."

In a study of male sex aggression among college undergraduates, Kanin (1967) found that the most sexually aggressive males, although the most "successful" among their peers in terms of frequency, also tend to be sexually the most *dissatisfied*. Again it is the *expectations* which seem to explain these findings. "Exploitation of the female for erotic gratification permeates the entire approach of the aggressive male [p. 431] ." Corroborative evidence along these lines is also offered by Kirkendall (1961) in his study of premarital intercourse among college males.

Kanin's (1967) study might lead one to conclude that many aggressive males seek a high frequency of sexual outlet because of the influence of their *peers* (the significant other males' evaluations) rather than from the satisfaction gained from sexual relations per se. The "stud" self-concept does not seem to pay off in much real sexual satisfaction for the aggressive male, no matter how much of a ladies' man he considers himself to be.

Mate selection, which in our culture usually assumes some sort of love to be a factor, has been "explained" by the various scientists who study such matters through such theories as homogamy, heterogamy, complementarity, values, role theory, and psychoanalytic theory.

Homogamy means, briefly, that people tend to choose partners with traits *similar* to their own.

Heterogamy means, briefly, that people tend to choose partners with traits *different* from their own.

Complementarity means that the traits or needs of the partners dovetail, e.g., a sadist marrying a masochist.

The point about *values* is that people tend to marry partners with similar values.

Role theory explains why, for example, women are more likely to "marry up" (above their role or social class) than men are.

The *psychoanalytic theory* explains choice influenced by unconscious factors, e.g., unresolved oedipal complexes, etc.

Notions about romantic love influence what sorts of partners are chosen. And, as is well known, "The romantic orientation of females is noticeably different from that of males [Kephart, 1967, p. 470]." It has been said that women want love, and use sex to get it, while men want sex, and talk of love to get it. This is obviously an oversimplification and an overgeneralization, but there would seem to be an element of truth in it. Some women, of course, do not have the conventional romantic orientation, even some who write sonnets about love. Consider this sonnet by Edna St. Vincent Millay:

> I shall forget you presently, my dear,
> So make the most of this your little day,
> Your little month, your little half a year,
> Ere I forget, or die, or move away,
> And we are done forever; by and by
> I shall forget you, as I said, but now,
> If you entreat me with your loveliest lie,
> I shall protest you with my favorite vow.
> I would indeed that love were longer lived,
> And oaths were not so brittle as they are,
> But so it is, and nature has contrived
> To struggle on without a break thus far,
> Whether or not we find what we are seeking
> Is idle, biologically speaking.

In Collected Sonnets, p. 11

However, Edna, one must agree, was a most unusual woman. Not very many women in our culture would take such a view of their love relationships.

In a study of some of the correlates of romantic love among college students, Kephart (1967) found that the young people he studied *invariably* described their *current* experience as *love* rather than *infatuation*, the latter term usually being used in the *past* tense. This finding perhaps illustrates the absurd lengths to which many people in our culture go to maintain the illusions of romantic love, no matter how illogical or impossible it is, on the face of it.

Many problems result from the conventional views of man-woman relations in our culture.

> The kind of monogamous, monopolistic sex relations that we value in our society encourages members of both sexes to become insecure about winning

and retaining the exclusive affections and sex favors of the individuals in whom they are interested. Consequently, lovers and married partners tend to become exceptionally jealous of their loved ones for presumably causing them to be so jealous and insecure [Ellis, 1963, p. 209].

The *romantic* concept of love, the idea that there is a "one and only love" for each person (aren't such marriages "made in heaven"?) is obviously *not* in accord with the scientific facts. I have elsewhere (Ard, 1967a) referred to this concept of romantic love as the "needle in the haystack" theory.

A less self-defeating approach—a more rational, hopeful, and scientific approach—would at least open up the possibility that one may love more than one person in a, hopefully, long lifetime (and without feeling guilty about it, or being accused of being "promiscuous"). What men and women will seek in their sexual partners will, of course, vary from person to person, and at different points in their life (Ard, 1967b). Men, on the whole, do seem to be more concerned, relatively speaking, about their partner's physical appearance (Kephart, 1967).

If we ask what is the fundamental reason people seek love relationships, other than the obvious reason of desire for sexual satisfaction (which, by the way, is perfectly natural, normal, and desirable), it might be said that the fundamental desire is for *understanding*. As Nathaniel Branden (1967) has pointed out, "It is not blind 'acceptance' that a normal person desires, nor unconditional 'love,' but *understanding* [p. 7]."

What are some of the conclusions that one can draw about the etiology of love and the relationship of love and aggression, in order to cut down on some of the perils of loving?

Melanie Klein (1964) in her book *Love, Hate and Reparation*, concluded that "the more true satisfaction we experience, the less do we resent deprivations. . . . Then we are actually capable of accepting love and goodness from others and of giving love to others; and again receiving more in return [p. 118]." Another very basic point, overlooked by many (with the exception of Erich Fromm), is that "a good relation to ourselves is a condition for love, tolerance and wisdom towards others [p. 119]." Melanie Klein has also pointed out that

> if love has not been smothered under resentment, grievances and hatred, but has been firmly established in the mind, trust in other people and belief in one's own goodness are like a rock which withstands the blows of circumstance. . . . If we have become able, . . . to clear our feelings to some extent towards our parents of grievances, and have forgiven them for the frustrations we had to bear, then we can be at peace with ourselves and are able to love others in the true sense of the word [p. 119].

Finally, we need to distinguish between *sick* and *healthy* love. Some of the main characteristics of the person who loves in a healthy fashion are as follows: (Because of the nature of the English language, I have to say "he," but I am just underlining my reminder that "he" refers to either male or female.)

He is unusually accepting and understanding of his partner's failings and lapses; but he does not permit her to step on or walk all over him. He desires a considerable degree of companionship with his beloved; but he is not desperately lonely and miserable without her. He is willing to compromise with the desires of and to make distinct sacrifices for his mate or his child; but refrains from being a love slave or surrendering his basic individuality. He *dislikes* his loved one's unresponsiveness or unfairness to him; but never connects this with his personal worth and severely hurts himself by it. He is seriously involved with his beloved, but has much room for fun, merriment, and gaiety with her. He is saddened by the departure or death of those he loves, but does not go into a deep, prolonged period of depression because of their loss. He is *interdependent* with rather than totally independent or thoroughly dependent on his love partner. . . .

He becomes attached to another person because he *likes* and *enjoys* loving, and not because he has to compensate for some terrible feelings of inadequacy or worthlessness of his own. He is *eager* but not over-anxious to enter a love relationship [Ellis, 1963, p. 23].

What sort of society do we need in order to have the right sort of sex-love relationships? Albert Ellis (1963) has offered some suggestions:

It is possible, however, for a civilized society to arrange sex-love relationships so that hatred stemming from sex drives would be reduced while love which results from sexuality would be enhanced. In general, such a society would have to be enormously more liberal than ours. . . . Because of their lessened frustration, restriction, inhibition, and inadequacy, the inhabitants of a sexually liberal community are much less likely to hate themselves and their potential or actual sexual partners than are those of a highly restrictive community [pp. 210-211].

Insofar as these observations make sense, we can all work toward that kind of society wherein there would be less aggression and more love.

REFERENCES

Aiken, H. D. The new morals. *Harper's*, February, 1968.
Ard, B. N. Do as I do, be as I am: the bruising conflict. In S. M. Farber & R. H. L. Wilson (Eds.) *Sex education and the teenager*. Berkeley: Diablo Press, 1967. Pp. 78–88. (a)
Ard, B. N. Gray hair for the teen-age father. In S. M. Farber & R. H. L Wilson (Eds.) *Teenage marriage and divorce*. Berkeley: Diablo Press, 1967. Pp. 95–104. (b)
Ard, B. N. How to avoid destructive jealousy. *Sexology* Dec. 1967, *34*, 346–348. (c)
Berkowitz, L. *Aggression*. New York: McGraw-Hill, 1962.
Branden, N. Self-esteem and romantic love. *The Objectivist* December 1967, *6*, 1–8.
Day, D. *The evolution of love*. New York: Dial, 1954.
Ellis, A. On the myths about love. In A. Ellis, *Sex without guilt*. New York: Lyle Stuart, 1958. Pp. 159–167.
Ellis, A. *If this be sexual heresy*. New York: Lyle Stuart, 1963. Pp. 204–221.
Farnham, M. F. Sexual love—woman toward man. In A. Montagu (Ed.), *The meaning of love*. New York: Julian Press, 1953. Pp. 179–221.
Kanin, E. J. An examination of sexual aggression as a response to sexual frustration. *Journal of Marriage and the Family*, Aug. 1967, *29*, 428–433.
Kephart, W. M. Some correlates of romantic love. *Journal of Marriage and the Family*, Aug. 1967, *29*, 470–474.
Kirkendall, L. A. *Premarital intercourse and interpersonal relationships*. New York: Julian, 1961.
Klein, M. & Riviere, J. *Love, hate and reparation*. New York: Norton, 1964.
Krich, A. M. (Ed.) The anatomy of love. New York: Dell, 1960.

Maslow, A. H. *Motivation and personality*. New York: Harper, 1954.

Maslow, A. H. Self-esteem (dominance-feeling) and sexuality in women. In M. F. DeMartino (Ed.) *Sexual behavior and personality characteristics*. New York: Citadel, 1963. Pp. 71–112.

Meerloo, J. A. M. *Conversation and communication*. New York: International Universities, 1952.

Millay, E. St. Vt. *Collected sonnets*. New York: Harper, 1941.

Montagu, A. (Ed.) *The meaning of love*. New York: Julian 1953.

Parker, D. *The Viking portable library*. New York: Viking, 1944.

Reiss, I. L. *The social context of premarital sexual permissiveness*. New York: Holt, Rinehart & Winston, 1967.

Saul, L. J. *The hostile mind*. New York: Random House, 1956.

Suttie, I. D. *The origins of love and hate*. London: Kegan Paul, 1935.

CHAPTER 8

Value Issues in Marital Counseling

John W. Hudson

A consideration of the value issues in the field of marriage counseling must include looking at the problem from at least four points of view: (*a*) the field of marriage counseling; (*b*) the definition of a marriage counselor; (*c*) the orientation and training of the marriage counselor; (*d*) specific problems in the field of marriage counseling. In this chapter I will attempt to deal with each of these areas and some of their value implications in some detail, with the hope of raising questions which will encourage further inquiry by the reader.

The forces which converged to bring about the formalization of the field of marriage counseling included: (*a*) the marriage education movement, with its emphasis on getting to know the prospective marital partner and understanding the personality factors necessary for marital success; (*b*) the sex education movement and the research in animal and human sexual behavior; (*c*) the increased complexity of modern, urban living. Many individuals, including teachers, ministers and physicians, had been engaged in marriage counseling as the direct result of the requests of the groups with which they were working.

"A particularly important development in the field of marriage counseling in the United States was the organization in 1942 of the American Association of Marriage Counselors, the first national group to recognize marriage counseling as a distinct social and scientific discipline [Stone, 1957]." In its early years the American Association of Marriage Counselors met with the hope of meeting more effectively the needs of those seeking their help. Marriage counseling was viewed principally as a specialized field designated to deal with problems which were primarily on the conscious level. Cuber (2), in his article "Functions of the Marriage Counselor," lists the four functions of the marriage counselor as: (*a*) the advice-giving function (the giving of information, sometimes technical and sometimes lay); (*b*) the decisional function (assisting the client in making a decision); (*c*) the definitional function (if some act comes to be defined as "bad," "sinful," or "indecent," and then, somehow, one commits that act, he may acquire a serious maladjustment); (*d*) reorganization of be-

Reprinted with permission of the author and the publisher from H. L. Silverman (Ed.), *Marital Counseling*. Springfield, Ill.: Charles C Thomas, 1967. Pp. 164–176.

havior (this type of case frequently grows out of the preceding type and becomes possible only when the client has already partly defined the given behavior as wrong or inexpedient but cannot break the old "habit" by mere volition alone). Clark Vincent, commenting on Cuber's article, points out that the marriage counselor performing functions (*a*) and (*b*) would define marriage counseling in a manner different from the counselor performing primarily the function in the fourth category. Cuber set forth what was then, and continues to be, one of the major value and philosophical issues in the field of marriage counseling—the value issue concerning whether the marriage counselor should limit himself to those marriage problems which are principally of a conscious or situational nature or whether he will deal with problems involving personality disturbances and emotional conflicts which may involve the unconscious. The lines here are fairly well delineated. They seem to arise from whether a marriage counselor can be effective in many of the situations with which he is confronted without going into what has historically been the province of the psychologist and psychiatrist. Marriage counselors themselves are divided on this question. Each side has its vociferous spokesmen.

Laidlaw (1957), then chief of psychiatry at Roosevelt Hospital, New York, and past president of the American Association of Marriage Counselors, gave his point of view at the 1949 meeting of the American Psychiatric Association:

> Marriage counseling is a form of short-term psychotherapy dealing with interpersonal relationships, in which problems relating to marriage are the central factor . . . it is an approach carried out essentially at a conscious level. . . . If, as therapy progresses, unconscious factors are discovered which necessitate long and involved psychotherapeutic techniques, the case ceases to be in the field of marriage counseling.

Foster (1950), formerly director of the marriage counseling service and training program, Department of Social Applications, the Menninger Foundation, stated in 1950: "Marriage counseling is primarily and essentially an educational job."

The New York Academy of Sciences, recognizing the need for clarification of the fields of psychotherapy and counseling, established five commissions to explore the subject. The following statement is relevant here:

> We can express the difference in emphasis, then, by saying that counseling looks more often toward the interpretation and development of the personality in the relations characteristic of specific role-problems while psychotherapy looks more often toward the reinterpretation and reorganization of malignant conflictual elements within the personality through the relation with the therapist [Perry, 1955].

As recently as 1957, marriage counseling was placed by Mace in the general category of one of "the services which help the individual, at the conscious level, to achieve a better understanding of himself and of his destiny. This broad category includes all functionally directed education—teaching, preaching, and propaganda. It also includes all counseling in the generally understood meaning of the word."

In *Marriage Counseling: A Casebook*, edited for the American Association of Marriage Counselors, the authors state:

> The marriage counselor can best make his important contribution by equipping himself to function not as a pseudo-psychiatrist or analyst, but as one who has made a special study of the problems and interpersonal relationships of family life: the bonds, loyalties, and conflicts; the loves, rivalries, and hostilities; the need for identification and dependence, on the one hand, and the conflicting desire for independence, on the other; the wish for security and the urge for adventure; in brief, the stresses and strains involved in membership in a marriage and a family, and the psychosocial factors and influences of such membership on the personality [pp. 40–41].

The authors of the *Casebook* define marriage counseling:

> Marriage Counseling may be defined as the process through which a professionally trained counselor assists a person or persons to resolve the problems that trouble them in their interpersonal relationships. The focus is on the relationship between the two persons in marriage, rather than, as in psychiatric therapy, the reorganization of the personality structure of the individual.

Throughout the literature there are also individuals who point out: (*a*) that marriage counseling is a form of psychotherapy; (*b*) that the effective marriage counselor needs to be able to recognize and differentiate between psychotic and neurotic problems; (*c*) that many of the difficulties within marriages are the result of personality conflicts within or between marriage partners; (*d*) that the marriage counselor will be dealing with problems of the unconscious as well as the conscious, and at times will be involved in efforts at basic personality reorganization. Spokesmen for the marriage counselor's functioning as a psychotherapist have become more outspoken as the profession has developed.

Stokes (1959), psychiatrist and marriage counselor, in his discussion of an article entitled "The Orientation and Focus of Marriage Counseling," states:

> Marriage counseling is a form of individual psychotherapy in which there is a special concern with the ways in which marriage partners interact with each other. . . . Although I deeply believe in marriage counseling as a worthy and needed profession, I would reject the idea that my primary interest is really counseling in marriage. It so happens that marriage is the chief proving-ground of emotional maturity, as well as the arena in which the parent-child relationship so critically affects the emotional development of human beings. Therefore it is in marriage that the symptoms of emotional immaturity and neurosis most strikingly appear. . . . Thus I see the marriage counselor of the future as primarily a student of the human life cycle, with emphasis upon its emotional aspects. He will be a therapist concerned with the application of his knowledge to all members of the family, at every age [p. 25].

Rutledge (1963), director of marriage counseling and psychotherapy training at the Merrill-Palmer Institute and former president of the American Association of Marriage Counselors, has long been a champion of the idea that marriage counseling represents the most advanced and highly technical form of all psychotherapies. Commenting in *Marriage and Family Living*, Rutledge says:

> It is deceptive to believe that the marriage counselor does not deal with the unconscious just because he does not intend to. Clients bring themselves, including their unconscious motivation, to the counseling hour, whether they come for personal problems or because of marital difficulties. This certainly means the counselor should have a basic understanding of, and be able to recognize, evidences of the unconscious in the daily married life and in the counseling session [p.28].

Whitlock (1961), in a discussion of "The Use of Dreams in Premarital Counseling" went a step further in his opinion of the counselor's dealing with the unconscious:

> (1) The use of dreams in counseling and therapeutic contacts is a legitimate function for many specialists in human behavior, not just for the psychiatrist or psychoanalyst, as has often been claimed. (2) This automatically underlines the fact that, whether or not they know it, all counselors are dealing with unconscious material [p. 260].

Ellis (1962), in his discussion of the use of rational-emotive psychotherapy as a technique for use in marriage counseling, states:

> Very possibly, most of these troubled individuals should come for intensive psychotherapy rather than for "counseling," but the fact is that they do not. It therefore behooves the counselor, and especially the marriage counselor, to be enough of a trained and experienced therapist to be able to deal adequately with the individuals who come to him for help . . .

Albert (1963), in his article in *Marriage and Family Living*, adds a significant note in his conclusions:

> But it does appear highly worthwhile to urge that universities and other training centers require that marriage counselors-in-training receive a thorough grounding in motivation, personality development, abnormal psychology and diagnostics, as well as a working knowledge of psychoanalytic theory (including, perhaps, not only Freudian concepts but also such more recent approaches as those of Sullivan, Reich, Rogers and the Neo-Behaviorists). This would be in addition to courses in the specific area of marriage counseling, and such other relevant subjects as family dynamics and the sociology of the family.

Obviously, a marriage counselor with the type of training that Albert is recommending is not going to limit himself to advice-giving and dealing with only conscious, reality-oriented problems. The philosophical and value question of the role of the marriage counselor is at present unclear. The field of marriage counseling and its practitioners are faced with the value question of whether marriage counseling is to remain primarily an educational, advice-giving, reality-oriented service for "normal" people or whether it is to be a profession of highly trained, competent therapists prepared to deal with a wide variety of marriage problems, including those which have their roots in individual personality disturbances.

Marriage counseling from its inception has been a multidisciplinary profession. Among others, the disciplines have included psychology, sociology, medicine, social work, law, and religion. Each profession has been adamant in insisting upon the importance of its own special contribution to the field of marriage counseling. We find the psychologist frequently emphasizing psychological factors; the physician emphasizing physiological factors; the minister, spiritual factors; the sociologist, cultural factors; etc. Although specialized internships and training in marriage counseling may reduce these tendencies, it is usually not difficult to spot the principal theoretical bias of the marriage counselor. Undoubtedly, one of the major factors which contributes to a counselor's theoretical bias is the lack of a systematic theoretical structure for marriage counseling.

Related to the theoretical bias of the counselor are the methods and techniques of counseling and psychotherapy that he employs. We find individual marriage counselors who are identified with the Freudian approach, the Rogerian approach, Ellis's approach to psychotherapy, as well as with many others. Initially, most psychotherapeutic approaches were designed to be used in working with an individual client; consequently, they must be modified when applied to the interpersonal marital situation.

It is not the purpose of this chapter to analyze the underlying value assumptions of various theoretical approaches. It should be clear to the reader that a marriage counselor operating from a Freudian frame of reference, with its emphasis on instincts, drives, repressions, and unconscious conflicts, is going to reflect a different set of values than the therapist who operates from a Rogerian point of view. Marriage counselors who utilize Rogers' system will turn more to their own thoughts and attitudes. Rogerians hold to the value that the thoughts and feelings the therapist has toward the client are the most crucial antecedents to effective therapist behavior. Rogerians assume that "if the therapist holds the 'right attitude,' if he has a fundamental faith in the patient, the appropriate statements and expressive gestures by the therapist will follow [Ford & Urban, 1963]." If the marriage counselor subscribes to the theoretical position of Ellis's rational-emotive therapy, he will take a more active and direct role than either of the counselors described in the preceding therapeutic approaches. It is clear that the choice of personality theory and the method and techniques for the marriage counselor are not based solely on an objective analysis. His choice reflects his own conscious and unconscious values and biases.

Most schools of psychotherapy agree that the ideal theoretical model describes the counselor as one who: (a) takes a serious interest in the client and gives him his undivided attention: (b) does not respond or react to either the client's affectionate or hostile feelings; (c) does not pass moral judgment; (d) maintains neutrality both affectively and intellectually; (e) keeps his own emotional life separate from that of the client's; and (f) keeps his own biases and predilections out of the counseling situation. Obviously, as all ideal models are theoretical, it is highly doubtful that any counselor can measure up to the foregoing list. There is also

the question of whether the counselor who holds rigidly to these standards can be effective.

The marriage counselor is a product of his culture and, as such, reflects his own values in the counseling relationship (whether he is aware of
it or not). It is important, for both theoretical and therapeutic reasons, for
the marriage counselor to be cognizant of his values and how they operate
in the therapy. If the marriage counselor risks revealing himself from
behind the professional shroud of the passive, reflecting, nonjudgmental
mummy, it is inevitable that he will express his values, attitudes, and
opinions on a wide variety of subjects. This is particularly true when
working with married couples, as the basis for much marital disharmony
lies not only in the neurotic pattern of the individuals involved but in
their philosophical and value conflicts. The philosophical and value conflicts of husbands and wives arise frequently from their different sociocultural backgrounds. The marriage counselor first must face the fact that he
is a human being and, as such, holds values. Second, if he is going to be
effective in his counseling, much of his therapy with couples is going to
involve the exploration and discussion of values, including many of the
therapist's. Third, the counselor will consciously or unconsciously communicate his own values, and it may as well be done openly. Fourth, the
more open the counselor is regarding his own values, the freer and more
spontaneous the counseling can be.

A factor which influences the value position of the marriage counselor
is that marriage counseling has tended to be problem-oriented and has
directed its attention principally to the resolution of conflict situations.
Although it is not explicitly stated, it is clear from reading the literature in
the field of marriage counseling that one of the central values is that of
adjustment.

This concept is not unique to the field of marriage counseling, but is
particularly significant for the marriage counselor because he is frequently
working with two or more individuals. In many cases the marriage counselor cannot hold equally to the value of the integrity of both individuals
where adjustment is the value. It makes a difference whether one is talking
about adjustment in terms of the integration of self or adjustment in
terms of the compromising of self for the value of others. The value of
adjustment seems to have been adopted by many marriage counselors.
Where adjustment means the acquisition of new knowledge or skills which
will further facilitate the growth and development of an individual, it may
be appropriate; but where adjustment means the compromising of self-
values for the values of others for the sake of a marriage or family, the
value is dubious.

Green (1946) states; "Therapists who advocate any specific type of
adjustment are prone to sociological naivete. The institutional bases of
their own specific values are shifting ground so rapidly in modern society
that it is a rare combination of value and structure that is itself in adjustment." The conflict between self-values and the values of others is many
times erroneously thought to be resolved by the marriage counselor by
shifting the focusing of the counseling from the individual to the institu-

tion of marriage. Adjustment may become an end in itself without regard to the individual. The "well-adjusted" person is all too frequently seen as the individual who adapts himself to any situation, person, or marriage for the sake of avoiding personal or social disorganization. When the focus is shifted from individual values to the institutional values of marriage and family, it may implicitly or explicitly convey to the client that there is a value which transcends his personal wishes or desires. This may represent an unconscious rejection, on the part of the marriage counselor, of divorce as an acceptable solution to marital discord.

It is important for the marriage counselor to be aware of his position on the value issue of divorce. Much harm can be done to an individual by the counselor who insists that the only satisfactory solution to marital conflict is adjustment and reconciliation. He is apt to find himself in the position of contributing to far greater personal and family disorganization by his unrelenting value stand. An obvious case is the situation involving the married couple where one of the partners finds the marriage relationship to be no longer meaningful and wishes a divorce so that he can pursue his own personal interests. This picture may be further complicated where there are children. If the counselor is committed solely to the values of marriage and the family, he is apt to violate the integrity of the individual wishing to get out of the marriage, viewing his behavior as neurotic, disturbed, or immature.

Although the professional code of ethics of the American Association of Marriage Counselors does not state saving marriages as one of the goals of marriage counseling, the individual counselor may nevertheless find himself in this position, as the result of his own personal values or those which are imposed upon him by the agency for which he works or by the client who seeks his help. Because the marriage counselor is working within an interactional system—that is, the relationship between husband and wife, as well as other family members—he may be less able to disregard the effects of one individual's behavior on another.

One of the clearest statements of the value issue of divorce is made by Stokes in the February 1959, issue of *Marriage and Family Living*:

> I have small concern with the preservation of the marriage as such. My primary focus is upon the dignity and satisfactions of the individual spouses and only secondarily upon the sociological values associated with the marriage. I cannot conceive of accomplishing enduringly successful marriage counseling upon any other terms.
>
> I suspect that because marriage has been for so long entrenched as a religious sacrament, many marriage counselors still feel impelled to preserve marriage at any cost. . . . I often have a feeling that too much emphasis upon the sociological factors and values of marriage is just a rationalized hangover from the ancient mystical concept of marriage as an inviolable sacrament [p. 25].

Rutledge (1963), in his article, "Should the Marriage Counselor Ever Recommend Divorce?" says:

> If a marital diagnosis reveals that continued marriage of a couple not only promises nothing in the way of a healthy relationship but points to marked personality destruction for one or both, it is the marriage counselor's responsi-

bility to underline this prognosis. To be sure, one of the couple must make the decision to separate or not to separate, to divorce or not to divorce. But the counselor may be derelict in some cases unless he gives his professional opinion of the advisability of ending, with as little hurt as possible, a relationship that can bring only continued destruction of personality.

Barrier discusses Rutledge's article, quoting Section 14 of the proposed Code of Ethics of the American Association of Marriage Counselors which states:

> While the Marriage Counselor will feel satisfaction in the strengthening of a marriage, he should not feel obliged to urge that the married partners continue to live together at all costs. There are situations in which all resources fail, and in which continued living together may be severely damaging to one or several persons. In such event it is the duty of the Counselor to assess the facts as he sees them. However, the actual decision concerning separation or divorce is a responsibility that must be assumed by the client, and this should be made clear to him. If separation or divorce is decided upon, it is the continuing responsibility of the Counselor to give further support and counsel during a period of readjustment, if that appears to be wanted and needed, as it often is.

Barrier concludes her discussion of Rutledge's article with the statement: "It is not the role of the marriage counselor to recommend dissolution of the marriage [p. 325]."

In the thirteen years that I was affiliated with the Marriage Counseling Service and Psychotherapy Training Center of the Merrill-Palmer Institute, I was repeatedly struck with the infrequency with which divorce was recommended as a solution to an unsatisfactory marriage. With the system of courtship and mate selection that is used in our culture, it would seem that a certain percentage of individuals seeking the services of marriage counselors would be poorly mated and that, unless the counselor were committed solely to the values of adjustment or the sacredness of the marriage relationship, divorce would more frequently be recommended.

Related to the counselor's value system is the setting in which the counseling takes place, and this may influence the investment that the marriage counselor makes in the individual client. If he is in private practice, the selection of clients is more apt to be based on values reflecting his own financial welfare, professional status, prestige, and personal and therapeutic biases than if he operates in an agency setting where his salary is fixed. In an agency the size of his case load, the clients, and his preferences for particular types of marriage counseling problems may not be given consideration. The counselor working in an agency may find himself under more direct supervision, and his personal investment in his clients may not be as great. If the counseling is part-time and an adjunct to his primary responsibility, it will have an effect on the relationship between the marriage counselor and his client. The college teacher who does counseling as an outgrowth of his teaching is faced with different value issues than the minister who does counseling as part of his pastoral functions.

The teacher is frequently faced with the value dilemma of separating the roles of the critical evaluation and judgment of academic performance from the accepting, nonjudgmental role of counselor. The minister may find himself caught in a value dilemma arising out of theological precepts and religious convictions. When his theological precepts and religious convictions clash with the reality situations of his counselees, the minister may have to sacrifice either religious values or secular values.

Fees are one of the major value dilemmas for the marriage counselor. The problem of fee-setting is one which many counselors would prefer to avoid. In agencies it is frequently handled by administrative decision, but for the private practitioner there is no neat, ready-made solution. In discussions with many marriage counselors (both those working in an agency setting and those in private practice), I wonder at their inability to face this issue squarely. The amount of uncollected fees frequently equals the sum of a few years' annual collections. The counselor who has difficulty in setting and collecting his fees has many "valid" explanations. He may rationalize his failure to deal realistically with the issue on vague therapeutic grounds. He may set his fees low because of doubt about his own adequacy, or he may set his fees arbitrarily high on the sole assumption that if an individual is unwilling to pay a high fee, he is not sufficiently motivated to get help. There is little doubt that money has a variety of meanings to individuals, including marriage counselors, but it is an integral part of the counselor-client relationship and, as such, must be dealt with realistically. The arbitrary setting of fees without regard to the financial situation of the client, excessively large uncollected fees, refusal to see an individual at a reduced fee—all reflect value conflicts of the marriage counselor.

The sources of the marriage counselor's referrals pose value questions which cannot be dismissed casually. The marriage counselor may find himself being cast in the role of a clearing house for lawyers, courts, and physicians. He may find himself being used by other professional persons who are attempting to avoid their responsibility in helping their clients to face crucial issues. Under certain conditions referral to a marriage counselor may be a form of coercion. The coercion may be by a spouse, lawyer, physician, or other professional. Care must be taken by the counselor not to impose his value of counseling on the person. It is important to know the terms under which the client presents himself to prevent being caught in a power struggle. A value dilemma may arise if a client has been under some other therapist's care prior to his coming to his present counselor. If one uses the simple interpretation that this is a form of resistance or hostility on the part of the client toward his previous therapist, the value issue is resolved. It may be that the client is resistant or hostile, but there are other valid reasons for changing therapists. Among other valid reasons for changing therapists include: (a) inability to establish rapport with previous therapist; (b) fees of previous therapist prohibitive; (c) transportation to and from previous therapist inaccessible; (d) time of appointments inconvenient or not feasible for client; (e) previous therapist's theoretical and psychotherapeutic techniques unacceptable to client; and (f) incompetency of previous therapist. Care must be taken at all times to insure the rights of the client to choose his therapist.

Depending upon the particular state in the United States, or upon professional affiliations of the marriage counselor, he may or may not have privileged communication. The issue of privileged communication is being clarified for the marriage counselor in many states which have certi-fication or licensing acts. Although this handles the technical problem, it does not handle certain value issues that arise in marriage counseling. Because of the unique position the marriage counselor occupies, he frequently becomes apprised of information which may seriously affect a marital relationship. In most situations he is committed to the confidentiality of interview material given by each spouse. Situations arise where he might be able to facilitate the relationship or help to avert unnecessary complications if he were to divulge information given in confidence. Where privileged communication does not exist, it is important to inform the client in order to avoid future complications or legal involvement.

SUMMARY

Part of the reason for the formation of the American Association of Marriage Counselors and for its rapid growth arose from one of the assumptions of analytic therapy which had generalized itself into almost all psychotherapies. The assumption is that effective therapy can take place only in those situations where the relationship between the therapist and the client is not encumbered or complicated by contacts with any other members of the client's family. This position has been carried to ridiculous lengths by some therapists, including the refusal to talk to or see any other member of the family, even when permission has been granted to the therapist by the client. Some of the pioneer marriage counselors recognized that the interaction of husbands and wives frequently brought about problems which could be resolved only by a therapeutic approach to the couple rather than to an individual.

In recent years there has been an increasing recognition on the part of marriage counselors that values are both implicitly and explicitly operative in the counseling relationship. The very notion of counseling implies a value system. The particular theoretical orientation of the practitioner carries with it certain value assumptions. The circumstances under which the therapy occurs may denote certain value considerations which are functioning for both therapist and client. The value issues with which marriage counselors are faced become increasingly complex when the therapy involves a married couple.

The value position of the marriage counselor is probably more complex than that of any other individuals working in the helping professions. This comes about partly as a result of: (a) confusion in the minds of the individuals seeking the services of the marriage counselor regarding the role of the marriage counselor; (b) the orientation or capacity in which the marriage counselor functions; (c) the particular theoretical framework of counseling to which the marriage counselor subscribes; and (d) the source of referral. One of the best methods a marriage counselor may employ in examining his own values is the careful questioning of the underlying assumptions he makes to support his diagnosis of the individuals he is seeing. Psychological jargon and diagnostic categories are all too frequently rationalizations for more fundamental personal values on the part of the counselor. Whenever a marriage counselor finds himself viewing all marital conflict as the result of immaturities, neurotic patterns, personality disorders, or psychopathology, he is probably deluding himself regarding his own objectivity and value positions. Marriage counseling has adapted the methods and techniques of individual psychotherapy and has principally relied on existing theories of personality development. As a consequence, the marriage counselor must frequently force the problems arising out of marital interaction into theoretical systems which were originally constructed to explain individual behavior. The methods and techniques of therapy which he employs are likewise those originally designed for application to individuals.

With the implementation of standards of training and the establishment of training centers the professional marriage counselor is coming into his own.

Marriage counseling is evolving from an educational advice-giving, conscious, reality-oriented service to a scientific, highly specialized form of psychotherapy. The prestige of the profession is reflected in the increased number of individuals now referring to themselves as marriage counselors with psychological or sociological backgrounds, rather than as "psychologists or sociologists who do marriage counseling."

The further growth of the profession will hinge on the effectiveness with which we marriage counselors can deal with value issues, not only those of the client but, more importantly, our own.

REFERENCES

Albert, G. Advanced psychological training for marriage counselors—luxury or necessity? *Marriage and Family Living*, 1963, *25*, 181–184.

Cuber, J. F. Functions of the marriage counselor. *Journal of Marriage and Family Living*, 1945, 7, 3–5.

Ehrlich, D. & Wiener, D. N. The measurement of values in psychotherapeutic settings. *Journal of General Psychology*, 1961, *64*,, 359–372.

Ellis, A. Reason and emotion in psychotherapy. New York: Lyle Stuart, 1962.

Ford, D. H. & Urban, H. B. *Systems of psychotherapy*. New York: Wiley, 1963.

Foster, R. G. Marriage counseling in a psychiatric setting. *Marriage and Family Living*, 1950, *12*, 41–43.

Ginsburg, S. W. Values and the psychiatrist. *American Journal of Orthopsychiatry*, 1950, *20*, 466–478.

Green, A. W. Social values and psychotherapy. *Journal of Personality*, 1946, *14*, 198–228.

Greene, B. (Ed.) *The psychotherapies of marital disharmony*. New York: Free Press, 1965.

Laidlaw, R. W. The psychiatrist as marriage counselor. In C. E. Vincent (Ed.) *Readings in marriage counseling*. New York: Crowell, 1957. p. 52–61.

Leslie, G., Neubeck, G., Greene, K., Hill, T. & Luckey, E. Who are your untreatables? *Marriage and Family Living*, 1960, *22*, 333–341.

Mace, D. R. What is a marriage counselor? In C. E. Vincent (Ed.) *Readings in marriage counseling*. New York: Crowell, 1957. p. 29–35.

Mudd, E., Karpf, M. J., Stone, A. & Nelson, J. F. (Ed.) *Marriage counseling: A casebook*. New York: Assn. Pr., 1958.

Mudd, E. H. The practice of marriage counseling. New York: Assn. Pr., 1951.

Perry, W. G. On the relation of psychotherapy and counseling. *Annals of the New York Academy of Sciences*, 1955, *63*, 319–432.

Rutledge, A. L. Should the marriage counselor ever recommend divorce? *Marriage and Family Living*, 1963, *25*, 319-326.

Schofield, W. Psychotherapy: *The purchase of friendship*. Englewood Cliffs: Prentice-Hall, 1964.

Stone, A. Marriage education and marriage counseling in the United States. In C. E. Vincent (Ed.): *Readings in marriage counseling*. New York: Crowell, 1957, p. 12-19.

Stroup, A. L. & Glasser, P. The orientation and focus of marriage counseling. *Marriage and Family Living*, 1959, *21*, 20-25.

Whitlock, G. E. The use of dreams in premarital counseling. *Marriage and Family Living*, 1961, *23*, 258-263.

CHAPTER 9

Moral Issues in Marital Counseling

Robert A. Harper

Moral issues in marital counseling are usually most effectively dealt with by transforming them into nonmoral issues. Does this mean, then, that the marital counselor contributes to the undermining of morals in marriage? No, it means only that we must spend some time at the outset of this chapter in defining the terms we shall use in trying to understand moral issues in marital counseling.

Morality is that quality of behavior that makes it right or wrong. *Morals* is a term which refers to the alleged rightness or wrongness of specific standards or of concrete behavior. When we label certain behavior of an individual or group as *moral*, we are judging it to be in accord with a code of conduct with which the individual or the group is identified.

One of the difficulties in contemporary American society, composed of persons from widely varying cultural backgrounds, is that morality is a very complicated matter. It is difficult or impossible for the marital counselor who serves a heterogeneous group of clients to be a *moralist*—that is, a student and teacher of morals, one who moralizes. So to function he would have to be an expert on the widely varying moral codes of the persons who consult him. Moralists usually must confine themselves to their own particular constituency: the rabbi of an Orthodox temple may be in a sound position to give moral advice to Orthodox Jews, but his moral counsel may not be well received by Reformed or Conservative Jews, let alone gentiles; the minister of Missouri Synod Lutherans does not pass muster as a moralist for even other brands of Lutherans; and so on. Obviously, a marriage counselor cannot wear all sorts of moralistic cloaks for persons of various religions, nationalities, social classes, and other groups of varying moralities.

Even if it were possible, however, for a marriage counselor to be the expert defender of all the multitudinous varieties of moral codes, it would not be desirable. For the greatest effectiveness of help in marital counseling, we would contend, the atmosphere is not desirably moral, immoral, unmoral or amoral, but *nonmoral*. Let's look at the important distinctions in these terms.

Reprinted with permission of the author and the publisher from H. L. Silverman (Ed.), *Marital Counseling*. Springfield, Ill.: Charles C. Thomas, 1967. Pp.325–335.

We have already discussed *moral* marriage counseling. *Immoral* marital counseling would carry the meaning of recommending that individuals violate whatever moral codes to which they subscribe. This is obviously as difficult (and more undesirable) for the marital counselor as trying to be a positive moralist.

Unmoral marital counseling would be the kind provided by a person who lacks understanding of morality. The fact that the marital counselor can function most effectively by not being a moralist does not mean he lacks understanding of the nature and importance of morality in human behavior, nor that he lacks sympathetic understanding of moral conflicts of his clients.

Amoral marriage counseling would be the sort in which the counselor would advocate or function in accordance with a doctrine that exhalts the right of persons to disregard moral codes of all kinds. This would be the Nietzschean superman type of counseling, a type which, so far as we know, has never been advocated by any sane professional person.

Nonmoral marital counseling, however, simply contends that the criteria of right and wrong are not appropriately or helpfully applied to the problems presented in the counseling setting. A request the writer has heard many hundreds of times from couples in marital counseling is: "Just tell us which of us is right and which of us is wrong." And the appropriate answer invariably is that there is no right side or wrong side in marital disagreement—just *different* sides.

Why is this nonmoral position so important? The practical reason is that in marital counseling we are looking for *solutions* to problems. *Differences* between couples can, with the help of the counselor, be understood, reduced, compromised, and sometimes even removed. But so long as we look for right and wrong, we remain stymied by moral judgments rather than problem solutions. When the husband and wife, along with the marriage counselor, try to understand rather than judge, differences can usually be dealt with effectively.

It is important for the reader to realize that the very nature of a moral judgment is such that there is nothing to be understood: the matter is either right or wrong, and the person is either being good or bad. Negative moral judgments toward others come out in the form of contempt, condescension, scorn, ridicule, and even horror and loathing; and toward oneself in the form of guilt, shame, defensiveness, and inferiority feelings. Positive moral judgments toward others are expressed in uncritical admiration, fawning, idealization of character traits, and flattering judgmental generalizations; toward oneself in smugness, conceit, or pride.

Both negative and positive moral judgments, then, are obviously not to be encouraged in a situation where a marriage has encountered problems. Such feelings as those we have just listed block understanding of the ongoing process in marriage and prevent husband, wife, and counselor from working out daring and imaginative ways of improving the relationship.

Because marriage counseling is no place for making moral judgments does not mean, however, that there are not many moral issues to be dealt with in the process of counseling. If the counselor does not moralize, how can he help with these issues? He can encourage the clients to engage in rational evaluation, realistic appraisal, and critical conceptual thinking, instead of looking for moral edicts which cover their problems.

In actual counseling situations, such rationality and realism must be geared to the specific situations faced by the particular couple with whom the counselor is working. It should be of some value for us in this chapter, however, to look critically at some of the general issues of morality, particular expressions of which are encountered in actual counseling circumstances. As we do so, we shall be able to observe some of the differences in perspective between this method and one based on uncritical moralizing about the same issues.

The reader's attention is called at this point to the understanding that the questions raised and the assertions made about moral issues in the rest of this chapter are to be taken as stimulating to his critical conceptual thinking. They are not to be considered new moral dogma, but a challenge to develop creative, flexible, reality-oriented attitudes about some of the moral issues which occur in many contemporary marriages.

The three broad areas of moral issues that we shall now consider are divorce, parenthood, and sex. These are probably the three foremost clusters of long-standing moral judgments which have beclouded critical conceptual thinking about marriage.

DIVORCE

Although the morality about divorce is gradually changing in many subgroups of our society, a large percentage of Americans have been indoctrinated from a very early age in home, school, church, and various other settings to feel that any person who gets a divorce is a failure and a sinner. To their conditioning regarding failure and sin are added a jungle of legal technicalities and outright humiliations for many of the hundreds of thousands of American couples who seek divorce each year. When, then, some of these men and women indicate anxiety, confusion, and other emotional disturbances, the moralists like to point to such symptoms as proof of their thesis that divorce is automatically and inevitably a terrible thing.

Obviously, the marriage counselor's role is to help people to think through whether or not divorce is for them a more desirable course of action than a continuation of their particular marital relationship. It is relevant, then, to ask ourselves if, from a nonmoralistic point of view, divorce must be inherently "a terrible thing."

A rational study of divorce would seem to suggest that divorce might be thought of as an essential component of democracy. Just as there should be, in a democracy, no major abridgements of freedom of speech, assembly, and worship (including, as some moralists like to forget, freedom *not* to worship), just as there should be no attempt to prevent a person from *responsibly* taking and quitting a job rather than remaining forever in his first job, so, a critical conceptual judgment would seem to

tell us, there should be no interference with a person's *responsibly* entering or leaving a marriage, rather than remaining forever in his first
marriage.

All human freedoms are subject to irresponsible misuse, and divorce is
certainly no exception. In the hands of the irresponsible, divorce can be
cruel, exploitative, tragic. In the hands of the responsible, divorce can be
humane, kind, spirit-freeing. No one wants to abolish or drastically curtail
the use of automobiles because they can produce tragedy in the hands of
the irresponsible. Some can be prevented from using automobiles because
they are permanently too irresponsible; others can be educated to use
them responsibly. Most people can probably be educated to use both
marriage and divorce responsibly. This is one of the marriage counselor's
functions.

It is sometimes contended that divorce is always irresponsible for a
couple who has children. If moralistic attitudes are put aside, however, it
is difficult to find a marriage which, on realistic grounds, should be maintained strictly *because* of children. When two people have reached a point
where their marriage has for them lost all possible positive value and is
steadily accumulating negative values, what of a constructive nature is
likely to accrue for children by the maintenance of that marriage?

Many moralists point to statistics about delinquency and broken
homes. There are a number of fallacies concealed in such statistics, but the
fact most relevant here is that when two people have decided that their
marriage is dead and that they will stay married *only* for the children, that
home is already broken in an emotional sense. There is no evidence to
support the assertion that it is the physical parting of the parents that
hurts the children. Or, put differently, there is no evidence that emotionally estranged parents who stay physically in the same house for the
sake of their children really do their children any favor.

Faced with the moral issue of impending divorce with children
involved, the marriage counselor can often help the couple to remove or
reduce some of the undesirable effects of the earlier emotional break in
the marriage and to protect the children from some of the unnecessary
consequences of the physical break of separation and divorce. To help in
this way, the marital counselor will have many specific things to work out
with the couple regarding their particular children, but certain general
understandings can also be helpful.

One helpful understanding is that we have been so propagandized by
the picture of children who are mourning their departed parents that we
often overlook certain counterbalancing pieces of reality. For example,
children are very conservative, for they are—reasonably enough for chronological children—quite insecure in the world. Hence, they tend to
oppose anything that strikes them as a threat to their security systems, as
a major change in the status quo. If Daddy has been little more to the
children than an emotional stranger seen only briefly on weekends or
holidays, they will nevertheless fight bitterly, forlornly, tragically, to
retain his fleetingly familiar presence. But once Daddy is gone, even if he
has been a more constructive influence than the father just described,

children quickly adjust to life without father. They adjust *unless* Mother indicates (and perhaps Daddy, too, in the course of his visits with them) that something horrible has happened. "This is a terrible, terrible tragedy," say the parental emotional messages.

Children are, of course, excellent emotional mirrors. It is probable that we could reinforce in our children the feeling that *any* kind of change in the status quo is tragic, calamitous, unbelievably awful, providing we gave them the same sort of treatment we often do on the matter of divorce. Most of us, by way of illustration, have seen children temporarily indicate every bit as much disturbance over some such situation as a rip in a teddy bear as over a parent's departure from the home. The main difference is that they do not get the same reinforcement of their feelings of great tragedy from the adults around them on ripped teddy bears as they do on broken marriages. Hence, teddy-bear tragedies tend to be transitory, and parental divorce tragedies tend to get lasting reinforcement not only from their parents, but from neighbors, teachers, clergymen, and others.

Marriage counselors can do a great deal, then, even in the unfortunate situations where emotional divorce has already occurred, in helping parents to overcome some of the emotional damage they have already done to their children, and in helping them to avoid doing additional damage with separation and divorce. Responsibly and intelligently planned divorce need not be terrible and tragic, even when children are involved.

PARENTHOOD

Even in the face of the ever-more-threatening problems associated with excessive world population, and with tremendous deficiencies in the genetic quality and environmental training of high percentages of human beings born year by year, moral myths about parenthood go relatively unchallenged in our society. To stimulate critical thinking about the usually unquestioned points of view about parenthood, the marriage counselor must sometimes strongly state radically different views. The following assertions are beliefs held tentatively by the writer (subject to correction by much-needed research), but they are made in the form of rather unqualified assertions for the sake of clarity, readability, and, hopefully, startling challenge to prevailing prejudices about parenthood.

1. The only time reproduction is truly desirable for the children, for the married couple, and for the general society is when: (*a*) the husband and wife are considerably above average in such traits as mental and physical health, intelligence, emotional and social maturity, and creative and adaptive skills; (*b*) the marriage is a happy one; and (*c*) both the husband and wife not only want children in a sentimental sense, but are eager to make parenthood a main enterprise in their lives, and include in their eagerness a realization that this task means a lot of hard study, hard work, and sacrifice of many other satisfactions. While some of these parental traits are not easily determined by existing evaluative methods, just the setting up of even roughly determined standards of the sort

described would help to combat the moral myth that parenthood is a process to be entered into by the relatively stupid, ignorant, and undedicated.

2. Very few people meet all three of the foregoing criteria (*a*), (*b*) and (*c*). There is a fair number of healthy, intelligent, mature, creative, adaptive people who are quite successful in business or professional activities but think that marriage and parenthood can be successfully pursued as an avocation to which they give little time and attention and for which they have little or no preparation. The facts are that, in order to be even moderately successful in marriage and parenthood, under contemporary social circumstances, a great deal of time and energy and skill are required. Often indifference, at worst, or unskilled goodwill, at best, are all basically competent people offer family life; they have already given most of their available time, energy, and talent to out-of-home careers.

3. The minority of couples who do fairly well in fulfilling the standards mentioned are likely to have their happy marriages made happier by children. In fact, for this minority, the joyful labors of parenthood probably bring as deep a sense of creative achievement as is available in life.

4. Under present-day social conditions, ancient conceptions about *duties* or *rights* about having children are quite inappropriate. "Be fruitful and multiply" is exceedingly poor advice with increasingly excessive world overpopulation and accompanying problems. Concerning the matter of *duty*, married couples who choose not to have children are being much more dutiful citizens in the light of contemporary realities than those who do have children. The former are at least not adding to the overall weight of population or of the social and psychological problems which tend to arise from duty-inspired offspring. As for any *rights* that genetically, sociologically, and psychologically unqualified people may have to enter parenthood, these are privileges which have been socially granted and which may be socially removed. All individual rights are subject to the limitations set by the welfare of the society to which the individual belongs. And the welfare of the world society—that is, of all mankind—it becomes increasingly clear, depends upon drastic reduction in quantity and improvement in quality of population.

5. Just from their own vantage points, happy couples who do not prepare themselves seriously and well for the hard work and real sacrifices of parenthood are often in grave danger of having their previously sound marriages undermined by the arrival of children and the accompanying increase in life's stresses. Couples who have consulted the writer as a marriage counselor not infrequently mention that their troubles either began with, or were markedly increased by, the arrival of children.

6. Even more definitely, couples who were already quite unhappy prior to children are likely to find that the additional burdens of parenthood bankrupt their marriage and broaden and intensify their unhappiness.

7. Many of the people who urge married couples to have children and try to make them feel guilty if they do not are actually resentful of the

freedom and enjoyment of life indicated by some childless couples. "I am tied down with a life I find difficult and not very enjoyable with children (doing my duty); why shouldn't you be likewise?" are the thoughts which often lie behind the spoken "Nothing like children to make life worthwhile." Such propagandists for reproduction are malefactors, not benefactors, of the couples, of children thus reproduced, and of mankind in general.

Such observations as the seven just made are apt to be judged as very radical and misanthropic by some persons, but any less severe approach to the responsibilities of parenthoood seems to the writer to disregard current social reality. Realistic perceptions of existing world circumstances add up to the generalization that whenever parenthood is an involuntary function and/or one for which the individual is grossly unsuited, ill effects are very likely to ensue for all parties concerned.

Both the matter of desire and competency for parenthood are, however, relative. No parent is wholeheartedly happy about his role as a parent, and certainly no parent is perfectly equipped for the responsibilities of parenthood. But surely people who are functioning as parents predominantly contrary to their wishes and skills do injustice to themselves, their children, and their society.

There is a condition which accompanies some brain injuries and diseases psychiatrically referred to as *anosognosia*, the denial of illness. A patient with anosognosia may be paralyzed in his right arm, for example, and yet stoutly deny the existence of the paralysis. He apparently so reorganizes his perception that he is able to "remove" the paralyzed limb from his field of perceived reality. He is afraid to face the reality of paralysis; he feels comfortable in denying reality.

The denial of the difficulties, the burdens, the displeasures of parenthood (or, at least, the denial of their very formidable nature), we would suggest, involves much the same psychological process as the denial of illness in the brain-injured. This might be considered an instance of *moral anosognosia*. Many people are afraid to face the unhappy realities of parenthood; they feel more comfortable in denying these realities, in believing the myth that having children is a sure route to happiness and the good life.

SEX

The traditional moral outlook on sex, of course, is more irrational than that on any other single topic with which the marriage counselor has to deal. In critically rethinking some of the moral issues connected with sex, the reader will find in the following assertions about sex an outlook that differs radically from the conventional ones.

1. Realistic evidence seems to point to the desirability not only of fully educating children about sex, but of making contraceptive and prophylactic information and equipment completely available to all persons who reach the age of possible fertility. The writer does not mean making it discreetly possible for the young person of more than average

intelligence to worm such information and equipment out of the sexual black market. He means that it would be desirable to encourage young people to procure contraceptive and prophylactic knowledge and equipment. It is difficult to see what other purpose unwanted pregnancies and venereal disease serve in our society today than to punish or threaten to punish people who sexually function contrary to the ancient superstitions which constitute our premarital moral code.

It is undoubtedly true that some of the more guilt-ridden and faint-hearted youth are deterred by fear of pregnancy, of venereal disease, and of the alleged wrath of a vindictive Jehovah from engaging in premarital sexual intercourse. But they then often pay the lifetime price of anxiety and guilt about even marital sex, which seems a peculiar reward for touted virtue. Other costs of the deterrence program on young people who proceed with premarital sex are such things as: untreated venereal disease which fans out in a wide circle of infection; illegitimate children; guilt-ridden, resentment-filled shotgun marriages; sojourns in humiliating, morality-dripping homes for unwed mothers; illegal abortions; and a number of other priceless products of puritanism. It is only because we keep reciting rigidly to ourselves the moral ditty about the catastrophic nature of premarital coitus that we cannot even clearly see, let alone do anything constructive about, our completely unnecessary, utterly idiotic premarital sexual morality.

2. The writer thinks it would be desirable to educate young people frankly in how to use sex as an important part of their skills in interpersonal relations. The suggestion here made is not only to stop teaching them that premarital sexual intercourse is bad, but to teach them how to exercise their own critical faculties about deciding under what sorts of circumstances and with what sorts of partners it is likely to be functionally desirable for all parties concerned. We should try to educate them to develop the kind of maturity and experience and the kind of love and understanding of themselves and others to work out their widely varying self-guides for sex functioning along with other kinds of social functioning. The writer would trust young people, thus educated, to have considerably superior judgment in such matters to the second-hand judgments that come to them from the ready-made codes of moralists.

3. If we take a critical and rational look at abortion, here, too, we shall emerge with different ideas than the moralistic one that "to take a human life is always bad." We shall question, first of all, whether the life to be taken may be correctly considered human in light of what we know in modern sociopsychological terms regarding the postnatal development of human nature out of interpersonal relations. We shall ask, further, what is most desirable for all parties concerned in a specific situation: the potential human being, the mother, the father, and other people directly involved?

Under such changed approaches to abortion, our answer would at times be, if we were thinking instead of moralizing, that the greatest practical desirability would be to destroy the embryo or fetus. At other times, let it develop. But we would be humanizing the concept of therapeutic abortion to take into account the social and psychological, not just the physical, consequences of both continued and interrupted pregnancies.

Such a view of abortion, moralists say, would bring about loss of respect for human life. The writer believes it would do quite the contrary, in other words, increase respect for human life and for every human representative of that general life. Entrance into human life would become less the product of unhappy chance and increasingly the product of man's well-worked-out plans, his best critical judgment.

4. A sex ethic should be constructed solely for the welfare of living and future human beings and not to please our ancestors or any assumed supernatural beings or functions. What Moses, Jesus of Nazareth, Freud, and other respected figures from the past had to say should be taken into account for any leads they may provide us, but their points of view should be subjected to the same rational inspection as any other points of view. And any scientific evidence available (which in a sexually rational environment would become increasingly so) should take precedence over opinion from any source.

5. A rational sex ethic would be based on principles that derive from our knowledge of psychological, sociological, and biological facets of human behavior, and would not concern itself with moral edicts or mystical or spiritual observations. Since our present empirical observations, including the growing clinical information of motivations outside the individual's conscious attention, are still crude and relatively unsifted, our sex values need to be particularly tentative and flexible, subject to change as we acquire new knowledge about human behavior and as social conditions alter human needs.

6. Our system of values for sex would in no way unfairly discriminate against males or females. It would be basically the same for both sexes with differences, if any, designed strictly for the necessary protection of the males or females.

7. The system of values would likewise obviously exclude any other type of discrimination, such as that of race, creed, religion, color, or socioeconomic status.

8. A rational sex code would likewise not discriminate against children and adolescents except in instances where their welfare is demonstrably involved, where their sex-love activities need to be limited for the actual protection of *their* health and well-being, and *not* for the protection of adult moral prejudice.

9. A realistic system of values regarding sex must take into account the fact that reproduction is a natural, though fortunately relatively infrequent, result of human sexual activity. Marriage and family laws under such a system would be primarily concerned with the encouragement and enforcement of proper care and protection of children, rather than with the hemming-in of adults with rules which do not bear on anyone's welfare.

10. Such a system of values would be based on the biopsychological fact that sex is fun for human beings. Nature has provided the healthy

male and female with sexual dynamisms, which, unless restrained and perverted by social conditioning, provide the user with great pleasure. Probably more consistently enjoyable sensations proceed from the relatively unhampered erotic relationship of a man and a woman than from any other life activity. Any system of values which fails to take into account the outstanding fact that sex is pleasurable will be unrealistic, irrational, and contrary to human welfare (much of our conventional sex morality is testimony to this point).

11. The kind of system of values we have been discussing would view as criminal and legally punishable only those forms of sex activities in which one individual forces his attentions on an unwilling participant, willfully harms another, annoys others with his activities, or takes advantage of a minor. Other sexual deviations than these, however neurotic, should be considered eccentricities or illnesses, not crimes.

12. Finally, a system of values for sex, along with those for parenthood and divorce which we barely touched upon, must be woven into an all-encompassing system of values which helps each individual toward increasing fulfillment of his various capacities, especially his capacity to love. Mature love means the development of concern, understanding, esteem, and responsibility for all human beings, including oneself. No one achieves such love perfectly, but our efforts urgently need to be directed toward helping more individuals to progress in loving themselves and others.

The basic moral issue in marriage counseling is to help clients to free themselves from a stagnant and unrealistic morality which blocks progress in love. Many self-styled God-fearing people in our various social groups are also thought-fearing, love-fearing, science-fearing, and life-fearing people.

Although the social system of the West contains in many respects the same destructive components as the social system of the Communist East, we are still permitted greater individual freedom and nonconformity. It is still possible, although difficult, for persons who have feelings of concern, understanding, esteem, and responsibility for the human race to use opportunities within such institutions as the school, the home, the church, industry, labor, and government to foster the growth of love and care and their necessary companion, critical conceptual judgment.

As marriage counselors we have not only opportunities but profound responsibilities to stimulate ourselves, our clients, and others with whom we relate to question, to think, to examine the reality of our social life—including the marriage and family mores to which we have so stubbornly, so unthinkingly, so compulsively locked ourselves in what may well be a death embrace. These moral matters take priority, in the writer's opinion, over many of the other issues with which we have concerned ourselves as marriage counselors, for these matters are near the core of our continued existence as a civilization.

CHAPTER 10

The "New Morality" and Marriage Counseling

Stewart Bedford

How can a marriage counselor help individuals and couples make decisions regarding moral issues when the very term "moral" seems to be in a state of flux? How can a marriage counselor help clients face moral decisions in a time when there are such ideas as "the new morality?" As a start toward answering these questions, I would suggest a careful and rational look at some of the issues and questions involved.

To me, "the new morality" is an effort to redefine ground rules of living that can apply to the new territories being mapped out by the advances currently being made in the fields of science, industry, marketing, and communications. The marriage counselor, working in today's society, needs to be aware of these changes and the resulting implications for the various moral codes held by his clients. Understanding these changes could make it easier to help his clients maintain identity and perspective while also accepting the fact that they are first of all human beings, and second, that they are members of a complex society.

I believe that the human being is a creature with a limited repertoire of instinctual behavior patterns, but nontheless a biological being with basic, biological needs and drives. I am assuming that these drives and needs are natural and inherent, and therefore neither bad nor good per se—just there, and part of the creature called man.

Since we, as human beings, do not have extensive instinctive patterns of behavior, we are dependent on creating and learning patterns of behavior that help us adapt to changing and diversified environments. In fact, some people believe that one unique characteristic of man has been his creativeness and ingenuity in adapting to environmental change. We are inventors, innovators, and improvisors. We have fantasy and imagination. We have the power to be creative, and as a result we have created at least a part of the environment in which we live.

Our ingenuity has produced the automobile with rapid and mass travel—and smog, and highway congestion, and freeways, and the necessity for developing a maze of legal rules and regulations for driving.

Our medical scientists have brought many deadly diseases under control—to a point that "death control" makes it imperative that we take a new look at our opinion on "birth control."

Other scientists have extended our maps of space to new and fantastic dimensions and have taken more than preliminary steps to add the dimension of space to man's immediate environment. As a result we as individuals have had to fit our fantasies about God being "up there" to "out there" to "just where?"

Paleontology, anthropology, and archeology, with a big assist from atomic physicists, have pushed the date of man's origin back hundreds of thousands of years, while fellow scientists in the biological and chemical fields have come extremely close to the creation of life itself.

Behavioral scientists have done extensive work in mapping the mind, motivation, and behavior of man and have shown us among other things that we are not entirely conscious of all motivating factors and thinking involved in our reactions and behavior.

Biological scientists have developed "the pill," artificial insemination, and the ability to implant a fertilized ovum from one female to the womb of another.

The pill has allowed women one more degree of freedom, and artificial insemination and ovum-implanting have raised intricate and yet unanswered legal questions of parental rights and identity.

Other scientists and teams of scientists have clearly shown that we as human beings could conceivably control and direct our future evolutionary changes. Scientists (and others) have suggested that in the future, we as human beings: consider requiring governmental permission for conceiving children; establish semen banks with stock taken from our great men; establish deep-freeze storage for some individuals who die from currently incurable disease so that their lives could be restored at some time in the future; that we utilize suspended animation to send space travelers far into outer space to inhabit other planets.

These changes and projected changes wrought by science and industry make it imperative that we as human beings take a very careful look at our framework for making moral decisions—for the decisions related to these changes involve moral as well as scientific issues.

We as human beings would be well advised to consider the fact that we are apparently writing scientific and industrial change with one hand while with the other hand we are writing such statements as "the earth is flat and square, and on each corner sit giant storks that deliver new human beings already clothed." We would also be well advised to listen to the feedback we get from our young adults which says, "You, Dad, are the one that is square, and in each corner of your squareness there are lies and myths that tell us that we can trust no one older than ourselves."

The marriage counselor would be well advised to understand the effects of scientific change on moral decisions if he is going to be effective in helping his clients integrate their moral decisions with a rapidly changing environment.

To help his clients, the marriage counselor needs to develop a framework for understanding (and hopefully accepting) the variations in moral codes that he is likely to encounter in his clientele. Here, it would be helpful for him to learn to differentiate between moral codes and laws that are based on moral codes. The difference between moral codes and moral laws is essential in helping clients understand and define alternatives when the clients are faced with moral decisions. The marriage counselor, in understanding the difference between moral codes and moral laws, would then be in a better position to help his clients predict and understand the consequences related to various alternatives open to them in decisions with moral implications.

Moral codes in this context would be defined as rules developed by individuals or groups of individuals to encompass their own philosophies and/or religious beliefs.

Laws based on moral codes—*moral laws*—would be defined as governmental rules that incorporate the moral codes of some individuals or groups of individuals.

Recognizing these differences (particularly where harm to others and the infringement of the rights of others *is not involved*) is essential in helping clients understand their reactions and anticipated reactions to their decisions relating to moral codes and moral laws.

For the violation of the moral code, the client (whether a couple or an individual) might anticipate expulsion from the group that made the rule. This would then involve the loss of privileges and benefits from remaining in good standing in the group and whatever this meant to the client.

If the client violated a moral law, he might anticipate some governmental penalty in addition to being penalized by his group. The difference here would be important in terms of helping the client define his apprehension in terms of reality factors.

It would follow, then, that the marriage counselor needs to be aware of another facet of "the new morality," namely, the gradual attempt that is being made in the United States today to eliminate moral code from civil law. Moral laws dealing with sexual behavior would be of primary concern to the marriage counselor.

In the United States today state laws are the principal laws dealing with sexual behavior (where harm to others and the infringement of the rights of others is not involved) between consenting and competent adults. Almost without exception, these state laws have grown out of English common law. English common law in turn, was based on ancient, Judeo-Christian moral codes.

History tells us that the United States was the first nation to organize its government by a written constitution. The Constitution and the Bill of Rights were written by our founding fathers who had ample evidence of the dangers of governmentally dictated religions. These founding fathers wrote into the Constitution and Bill of Rights the principle of separation of church and state. In this respect, our founding fathers helped define a part of the framework of this "new morality" currently being defined in changes developing today.

CASE ILLUSTRATION

In way of illustration of some of these ideas in the context of marriage counseling, let us assume that we are counseling a couple who has been unable to have a child by natural means. They have had medical consultation and know that: the woman is fertile; the man is sterile but capable of having sexual relations; artificial insemination would in all probability result in a successful pregnancy if the sperm of a man other than the woman's mate were used.

The couple are active members in a religious group that classifies artificial insemination as adultery. The religious group classifies adultery as a serious enough sin that it requires expulsion from the group and the foregoing of all the privileges, including entrance to the promised land in the hereafter.

To complicate matters (we didn't really expect a simple case did we?), the couple live in a state that allows artificial insemination even though there is a law against adultery on the books.

To further complicate matters, the mates are both young, healthy, financially sound, and they both love children as well as each other. Both individuals want very much to have a child, and they both prefer one that would be at least "part theirs" as compared to one that they might adopt while still remaining in good standing in their church.

This is clearly a dilemma with both scientific and moral implications. Both parties are apprehensive and have guilt from even thinking about the possibilities. How can we as mature and rational marriage counselors help them see as many aspects of their dilemma as possible so that they can make as rationally sound a decision as possible?

Using some of the framework discussed, I would try and help them outline as many alternate solutions as they could in considering ways out of their dilemma. I would also try to get them to anticipate what they would think to themselves, or in a sense, what they would tell themselves about the consequences of the various alternatives (Ellis, 1962). I would point out to them that scientific advancement had made it possible to have alternatives open to them that were not available at the time the religious restrictions were formulated by past religious leaders. I would point out that from a legal standpoint they would probably not be violating any state criminal laws, although some questions might be raised in the future if either of them wanted out of the relationship. I would make a strong suggestion that they seek legal counsel regarding these legal questions, again to help them have the best information to aid them in making their decision. I would try to have them come up with their definitions of some of the terms (such as *adultery*) as they considered semantic and theoretical discrepancies. I would also try to have them define what their particular brand of religion meant to them and what being expelled from the religion would mean. I would try to help them differentiate between rational and irrational apprehension by helping them see and define differences between practical (reality-oriented) and theological implications of the various alternatives open to them. In short, I would try to help them evaluate the information available to them, including the information that they were giving to themselves in their own interpretations of their dilemma.

I would feel that the framework of the new morality would offer them new degrees of freedom to make their decision on the basis of the knowledge available to them today as well as the knowledge available to them from yesterday. As a marriage counselor, I would feel that this would be beneficial to them, to their progeny, and to society in general.

REFERENCES

Ellis, A. *Reason and emotion in psychotherapy*. New York: Lyle Stuart, 1962.

CHAPTER 11

Excerpts from the *Playboy* Philosophy

Hugh M. Hefner

"... *PLAYBOY'S* aims and outlook have been given considerable comment in the press, particularly in the journals of social, philosophical, and religious opinion, and have become a popular topic of conversation at cocktail parties around the country. . . . We have decided to state our own editorial credo here.

"What is this 'particular point of view,' then, that *PLAYBOY* shares with its readers? *What is a Playboy?* . . . He can be many things, provided he possesses a certain *point of view*. He must see life not as a vale of tears, but as a happy time; he must take joy in his work, without regarding it as the end and all of living; he must be an alert man, an aware man, a man of taste, a man sensitive to pleasure, a man who—without acquiring the stigma of the voluptuary or dilettante—can live life to the hilt. This is the sort of man we mean when we use the word *playboy* [December, 1962]. . . ."

"A major part of *PLAYBOY'S* spectacular success is directly attributable to our being a part of the new generation, understanding it, and publishing a magazine with an editorial point of view that our generation can relate to [December, 1962]. . . .

"The opposition to *PLAYBOY* is prompted by the significant element of puritanism that still exists in the United States. *PLAYBOY* offends some people, and makes others uneasy, because they think of sex as something either so sacred or so profane that it has to be hidden away in a dark room; they object to sex being frankly depicted or described in public [December, 1964]. . . .

"*PLAYBOY* is editorially interested in precisely those aspects of life that the Puritan was most against: sex, first and foremost, of course. But also our more general emphasis on pleasure and play; as well as the notion that the accumulation of material possessions can be a positive addition to the other interests in life. . . .

"If we were not sexually oriented, there would be no criticism. It is our positive approach to sex that distresses some people. . . .

"Since one of the things *PLAYBOY* is especially concerned about is the depersonalizing influence of our entire society, and considerable

---

editorial attention is given to the problem of establishing individual identity, through sex and as many other avenues of expression as may be available in a more permissive society, it is wrong to suggest that we favor depersonalized sex. Not unless, by depersonalized sex, we are referring to any and all sexual activity that does not include extensive involvement, commitments, and obligations. In this sense, it is true, to the extent that the magazine emphasizes the pleasures rather than the problems of sex, and focuses on that period of life in which real personal involvement is not yet desirable—a time of transition into maturity, prior to accepting the responsibilities of marriage and family.

"I certainly think that personal sex is preferable to impersonal sex, because it includes the greatest emotional rewards; but I can see no logical justification for opposing the latter, unless it is irresponsible, exploitive, coercive or in some way hurts one of the individuals involved. . . .

". . . we are among the most outspoken advocates of a more healthy, open, and positive outlook on sex. We treat it with humor, which helps to take the onus off it; we place our emphasis on approval rather than negation; and we attempt to treat sex in as attractive and appealing light as possible [December, 1964] . . . ."

"Kinsey found 'premarital sex statistically increased a woman's chances of getting married and of making a success of her marriage.' . . . Kinsey found 'considerable evidence' that sexual experience prior to marriage contributed 'to the effectiveness of the sexual relations after marriage' [July, 1963] . . . .

"The simple act of sex performed prior to marriage does not, per se, increase the chances of a successful marriage, of course. It is the attitudes that lead to the act that will determine how well a person adjusts both to sex and to marriage. There is a good deal more to sex than just the learned physical techniques (although the techniques themselves are largely underrated in our society and a majority of adults live out their lives with only the most rudimentary knowledge of this most vital of all human activities). Sex is often a profound emotional experience. No dearer, more intimate, more personal act is possible between two human beings. Sex is, at its best, an expression of love and adoration. But this is not to say that sex is, or should be, limited to love alone. Love and sex are certainly not synonymous, and while they may often be closely interrelated, the one is not necessarily dependent upon the other. Sex can be one of the most profound and rewarding elements in the adventure of living; if we recognize it as not necessarily limited to procreation, then we should also acknowledge openly that it is not necessarily limited to love either. Sex exists—with and without love—and in both forms it does far more good than harm. The attempts at its suppression, however, are almost universally harmful, both to the individuals involved and to society as a whole.

"This is not an endorsement of promiscuity or an argument favoring loveless sex—being a rather romantic fellow ourself, we favor our sex mixed with emotion. But we recognize that sex without love exists; that it is not, in itself, evil; and that it may sometimes serve a definitely worthwhile end.

"We are opposed to wholly selfish sex, but we are opposed to any human relationship that is entirely self-oriented—that takes all and gives nothing in return. We also believe that any such totally self-serving association is self-destructive. Only by remaining open, and vulnerable, can a person experience the full joy and satisfaction of human experience. That he must also, thereby, know some of the sorrow and pain of this world is without question, but that, too, is a part of the adventure of living. The alternative—closing oneself off from experience and sensation and knowledge—is to be only half alive. The ultimate invulnerability is death itself.

"This is not at odds with what we have previously expressed about the need for a greater *enlightened self-interest* in society. Too many people today live out their entire existence in a group, of a group, and for a group—never attempting to explore their own individuality, never discovering who or what they are, or might be. Searching out one's own identity and purpose, taking real pleasure in being a person, establishing a basis for true self-respect—these are the essence of living.

"We believe that life can be a greater pleasure if it is lived with some style and grace and comfort and beauty, but we do not believe that these are the all of it. It is possible to become so caught up in the trappings—both the form and the accouterments of living—that the real satisfactions become lost. Each man—and woman—should try to know himself, as well as the world around him, and take real pride in that knowledge. . . .

". . . if we truly respect ourselves, it is impossible not to respect our fellow man as well. . . .

"What we believe in, first and foremost, is the individual—and his right to *be* an individual [July, 1963]."

"It is our view that man is a rational being and while his heredity and environment play a major role in setting the pattern of his life, he possesses the ability to reason and the capacity for choice, not granted to lower animals, whose response to life is instinctually predetermined. The use, or lack, of use, of his rational mind, is, itself, a choice, and we favor a society in which the emphasis is placed upon the use of reason—a society that recognizes man's responsibility for his actions. . . .

"We believe in a moral and law-abiding society, but one in which the morality and the laws are based upon logic and reason rather than mysticism or religious dogma. . . .

"We believe that a society that emphasizes the individual and his freedom, is based upon reason, and has happiness as its aim is an ideal society and the one to be strived for. . . .

"This, then, is the foundation of our philosophy—an emphasis on the importance of the individual and his freedom; the view that man's personal self-interest is natural and good, and it can be channeled, through reason, to the benefit of the individual and his society; the belief that morality should be based upon reason; the conviction that society should exist as man's servant, not as his master; the idea that the purpose in man's life should be found in the full living of life itself and the individual pursuit of happiness [December, 1963]."

Theoretical Issues and Viewpoints

> *. . . I am distressed at the manner in which small caliber minds immediately accept a theory—almost any theory—as a dogma of truth.*
>
> CARL ROGERS

Marriage counseling has been considered by Manus (1966) as a technique in search of a theory. He has taken the position that although marriage counseling has developed out of a social need, it has not yet developed a consistent theoretical underpinning for its service. According to Manus, marriage counseling operates all the way from a near-theoretical approach to an inferential post hoc explanation. Neurotic interaction, social casework theory, communication theory, and symbolic interaction and role theory have all been involved to provide the rationale of marital counseling, according to Manus. But, he maintains, no attempt to integrate or verify these theories on empirical grounds is available.

Stroup and Glasser (1959) had been earlier critics of the orientation and focus of marriage counseling, and Manus (1966) has stated that since the publication of the Stroup and Glasser article, there has been little significant movement toward a coherent theoretical orientation in marriage counseling [p. 453). After reading through this handbook, the reader will have to decide whether or not he agrees with these critics of the lack of theory in marriage counseling.

The following section deals specifically with several different theoretical approaches to marriage counseling. Following this section is still another section on conjoint marriage counseling (Section IV), which has developed particular theoretical approaches of its own. Of course, group marriage counseling (Section V) has particular theoretical concepts arising from the nature of its parameters. In a sense, the whole handbook is sprinkled with various theoretical approaches to the different sorts of problems in marital, premarital, sexual, and other areas. But in the following section several outstanding authorities discuss in depth a variety of theoretical issues and viewpoints.

Hilda M. Goodwin and Emily H. Mudd, in Chapter 12, discuss various indications for marriage counseling, along with some of its methods and goals. Specifically, these authors examine the values sought in contemporary marriage, the basic concepts in counseling practice, the definition of marriage counseling, the goals of marriage counseling, the indications for marriage counseling, the structure and process of counseling, desirable gains in marriage counseling, and the future of marriage counseling.

In Chapter 13, Robert A. Harper discusses marriage counseling as rational, process-oriented psychotherapy. This theoretical orientation is basically compatible with Alfred Adler's "Individual Psychology," and has been influenced by the ideas of Albert Ellis. Dr. Harper makes a strong case for considering marriage counseling as psychotherapy. In fact, he states bluntly that marriage counseling *is* psychotherapy.

Among the many provocative and original ideas in the Harper chapter is the point that humor functions as a catalyst for communication. Harper also introduces the controversial concept of *reality* as a necessary part of any effective psychotherapy.

Ben Ard, in Chapter 14, discusses a rational approach to marriage counseling, spelling out some of the basic ideas of a provocative new approach, the rational approach of Albert Ellis. "RT," or rational therapy, is presented as a new approach to marriage counseling which deserves consideration, despite the fact that it introduces some controversial techniques and methods, such as vigorously attacking the irrational, unquestioned philosophical assumptions or ideas of the clients. Other new ideas of RT are the techniques of confrontation, confutation, de-indoctrination, and re-education, as well as a rather unique contribution, "homework assignments." Although many of these ideas may appear too radical to some readers, each of them can well be considered as a possible tool in the marriage counselor's armamentarium.

In Chapter 15, Aaron Rutledge discusses male and female roles in marriage counseling. Are there some particular problems in marriage counseling which should be handled by a female? By a male? By both a male and a female working together as a professional team?

In Chapter 16, Constance C. Ard discusses a frequently overlooked matter of fundamental importance in marriage counseling: the role of nonverbal communication. So much of the literature in the field of marriage counseling deals with verbal communication, interpretation, and the like that marriage counselors need to be aware of the added information they can make use of in the nonverbal communication evidenced by their clients.

Murray Bowen discusses in Chapter 17 the use of family theory in clinical practice—the current status and possible future of the family movement, his own theoretical and clinical orientation, family theory, and the clinical use of family psychotherapy.

REFERENCES

Manus, G. I. Marriage counseling: A technique in search of a theory. *Journal of Marriage and the Family*, 1966, *28*, 449–453.

Stroup, A. L., & Glasser, P. The orientation and focus of marriage counseling. *Marriage and Family Living*, 1959, *21*, 20–24.

CHAPTER 12

Marriage Counseling: Methods and Goals

Hilda M. Goodwin and Emily H. Mudd

The term "marriage counseling" has, over the years, been used to describe a wide variety of activities. Today the problem of defining what is meant by marriage counseling becomes a first essential of any discussion. Not only is there no clear definition of what constitutes a marriage except in the legal and religious sense, but there are no clear-cut or agreed-upon factors essential to a satisfying marriage for all individuals in our multi-pronged, rapidly changing society (Womble, 1966). Thus, one finds many different theoretical formulations, methods, and goals as the bases for a therapeutic approach to a troubled relationship between husband and wife. These varied approaches include "Haley's Marriage Therapy [Haley, 196?]," the psychodynamic approach to the individual problems of husband and wife (Greene, 1965), "role theory (Stein, 1959)," the transactional approach of Grinker (1961) and associates, and the sundry methods of working with a marriage reported by members of the interdisciplinary American Association of Marriage Counselors (Mudd, Karpf, Stone, & Nelson, 1958). At times the ideas advanced by these various theoretical formulations restate established principles of therapy or counseling without identifying them as such, and essentially offer new perspectives rather than new principles or facts.

In addition to the theoretical and conceptual differences, we find many variations in the structure of marriage counseling. Some counselors prefer to see only one member of a marriage, having the other partner work with someone else; others may see one partner primarily and the other spouse occasionally; still others may decide to work with the partners in individual and occasional joint interviews; others may prefer only joint interviews with the two spouses. More recently, group marriage counseling, involving either one spouse or at times both spouses, further complicates and enriches the picture.

Many similar problems are presented in therapy of the whole family. Even the question of how one defines the family unit is a moot one

Reprinted with permission of the authors and the publisher from *Comprehensive Psychiatry*, 1966, 7, 450–462.

(Christensen, 1964). Does one conceive of it empirically to at times involve an apparent outsider who is in reality a functional part of the family group, or do we hold to the theoretical unit of the nuclear family? There are many variables in considering any one of these family units. A family unit changes with time and has a different structure, a different function, different boundaries, and the members have different psychological needs, depending upon where the family is in the life cycle. This is also true of marriage, which, as Otto Pollak has indicated (Pollak, 1965), has many varied psychological orientations, functions, and kinds of reciprocal relationships between the spouses. Thus, in considering any specific marriage, it becomes essential to consider the psychological factors, the ego strength of the partners, the sexual factors, the economic factors, and the situational factors. In addition, the particular function of the marriage at the time help is sought, the past experiences of each spouse, and the nature and areas of current disfunctioning are essential factors for consideration.

We would define marriage as a partnership between two individuals which carries with it commitment, not only to each other, but to the third entity of the marriage, the marital relationship. This partnership, hopefully, will offer each spouse certain specific satisfactions and values (Mace & Mace, 1960). A primary satisfaction sought in many of today's marriages is the meeting of each partner's emotional and affectional needs— the fulfillment of which every individual seems to strive for, to be the most beloved or the most important adult to some one other person. Beyond this, marriage offers satisfaction for sexual desires and activities within a relationship that carries religious, social, and cultural acceptance, thus alleviating feelings of guilt and anxiety in this vital area of living. A third value consists of a way of life, recognized by the community, which is distinctly different from that enjoyed by a single person or by individuals living in other kinds of liaisons. The fourth value is a stable situation in which to work and plan *with someone* toward future living, having a companion with whom one may grow old and share disappointments, dissatisfactions, and frustrations as they are met in day-to-day living. An additional satisfaction for many couples is the projection of life into the future through their children. This carries an ongoingness in living that, in this day and age, may not be so readily available either through a religious philosophy or other media. However, it is our impression that many marriages today tend to remain stable only as the partners are able to offer at least minimal gratifications of each one's emotional needs. It is when either spouse begins to feel that his or her emotional needs are not met, and the rewards of marriage are not sufficient, that frustration, rejection, and conflicts emerge.

BASIC CONCEPTS IN COUNSELING PRACTICE

One of the basic concepts that determine both theoretical formulations and methods of working with marriage partners is related to balance within the reciprocal marital interaction. So long as there is an adequate dovetailing of each partner's needs and acceptable patterns of reciprocity in meeting them, the union seems to remain stable. We do not mean to imply that the marital partners are in any sense divorced from the larger environment, nor that there cannot be problems concerning children, in-laws, money, sexual adjustment, etc., arising within the marriage. However, it has become evident in our years of clinical experience that when there is a fundamentally positive reciprocal base for meeting each other's emotional needs, the capacity for problem-solving within the family remains high.

It is generally recognized that each partner carries into marriage many unresolved needs from childhood, and may attempt to have these satisfied by the spouse. However, it is not the type of need that is definitive, but whether the needs of the partners coincide and result in mutuality in emotional support and affection as the central components of the relationship. Thus, every marriage should be approached by the counselor as a unique organization of two individuals who have brought certain specific needs and desires to the situation, certain concepts of the marital roles of each, certain methods of communication, certain reciprocity in the sharing of responsibility, and varying degrees of commitment to the union.

Many people seeking assistance comment about difficulties in communication. It soon becomes apparent that part of the difficulty is not necessarily in the lack of verbal ability, but in the fact that the words used carry within them not a "dictionary meaning," but the meaning of the experiences behind the words to the person who is using them. This was illustrated vividly in a group of graduate "trainees" when a Protestant theologian spoke with great reverence of the word "cross" at Easter and of the redemption significance it had for him. A Jewish theologian in the same group listened and then replied that this word held a far different meaning for him. He explained that during his boyhood in a ghetto in Europe the marching of a group of Christians toward the ghetto and the infliction of severe punishment on the members of the Jewish race were symbolized for him by the cross the group carried as it came toward the ghetto (Goodwin, 1964). This same use of words to carry the emotional meaning of experience is part of the communication problems within any marriage situation. In a similar way idiosyncrasies of behavior, social manners, dress, tones of voice, and recognition of ceremonies communicate the meaning of the experiences behind them along with the present response.

The term "counseling" has been used to describe a variety of activities over the years and therefore carries different connotations to persons of different professional and experiential backgrounds. As the term "counseling" is used in this article, it is regarded as a learned art in which a professionally trained person has acquired certain basic knowledges, attitudes, and skills and has integrated these into a disciplined capacity to use himself therapeutically with individuals or couples seeking help with intrapersonal or interpersonal problems of adjustment. Their basic knowledges would include an understanding of physiological and personality growth, of psychodynamic theory, of cultural and ethnic factors as they affect the unique marital partners, of role interaction, of relationship theory, and of counseling skills and process. An understanding of the many facets in marriage—including the affectional, sexual, economic, ethical, and religious—is important (Goodwin & Mudd, 1964).

All of these factors bring important influences to bear on the behavior of both spouses and of the counselor as they relate to each other, and all influence the type, degree, and success of communication between the three. As the counselor deals in verbal and nonverbal communication, he will need to be expert in understanding language as it is related to thinking, feeling, and behavior, and he will need to be aware that the language which is characteristic of his own social position may facilitate or handicap the understanding he is attempting to achieve with his clients. It is also important that the counselor be related to the psychological processes involving circular transactions between the partners and between himself and the partners.

Marriage counseling differs from individual counseling in that the focus is upon the marital relationship and the circular interaction between the partners rather than on the specific intrapsychic forces within the individual partners. At times, as indicated by the process and content, a counselor may work with an individual on his intrapsychic difficulties as they relate to a particular area of difficulty in the marriage, with the focus moving back and forth between childhood needs and patterns of relating as they were developed in the past and are inappropriate in the current marital situation (Goodwin, 1957).

We would define complementarity of roles to mean that each person automatically acts in conformity with the role that he is expected to assume by the partner, and the disequilibrium occurs when for some reason or another this complementarity is disturbed, and the expectations of each from the other are disappointed, with the resultant tension, anxiety, and frustration occurring. Spiegel (1957) defines role as "a bold directed pattern or sequence of acts tailored by the cultural process for the transactions a person may carry out in a social group or situation [p. 1]." When role complementarity is established, the marriage presents stability and harmony, and is conducive to further work toward unifying the marital relationship.

GOALS OF MARRIAGE COUNSELING

Recognizing the complementary nature of the needs and patterns of behavior of the two marital partners as they are reflected in the reciprocal marital interaction, one of the essential goals of marriage counseling is to help the troubled partners come to some understanding of the interlocking and intermeshing nature of their problems. Through a compassionate and empathetic relationship with a marriage counselor, the partners are helped to some awareness of the ways in which their own feelings, attitudes, demands, expectations, patterns of relating, and responses affect this circular interaction. A second goal may be to help the partners come to terms with the satisfaction that may be realistically possible in adult life within the specific existential situation of their marriage.

The basic goal in marriage counseling is, therefore, not to effect any drastic change in the personality structure of either partner, but to help each to perceive his own reality, the reality of the partner, and that of the marriage more clearly. Where possible, counseling would assist each spouse to shift in his demands and patterns of relating sufficiently so that each may achieve at least minimal satisfactions and rewards within their particular marriage. In some instances counseling may help the couple clarify their inability to effect a satisfactory adjustment in this marriage, and a decision to seek psychiatric help for basically crippling personality characteristics may be made and referral effected for one or both partners. In certain instances a decision to terminate the marriage may be constructive and may be the final choice of one or both spouses.

The degree of change and the depth to which it may occur depends upon the individual's personality structure, its flexibility, the person's other assets, and the motivation to change. In some situations a very slight shift in each partner may permit the other spouse to receive sufficient gratifications out of the relationship to effect a satisfactory modification in the marital balance. In other situations in which the individuals exhibit greater flexibility in coping with change, are more open to their own and others' feelings, and have some capacity for genuine feeling communication, considerable growth toward maturity and toward a mutually supporting marital balance may occur.

There are a variety of sources in the United States where marriage counseling can be found. Among these are the member agencies of the Family Service Association of America, church-associated clinics, independent organizations, university services, as well as facilities offered in the private practice of psychiatrists, psychologists, social workers, teachers, ministers, and lawyers. Marriage Council of Philadelphia offers a clearly defined service, that is, psychologically oriented counseling help, either premarital or postmarital, to couples who are experiencing difficulties within their relationship (Mudd, 1951). With the current dissemination of knowledge on personality and on interpersonal dynamics, and with the mass media emphasizing the desirability of securing psychological help for troubled marriages, application for marriage counseling defines, to a degree, where the marital partners place their problems and where they are willing to begin to work on them. For those couples who perceive their difficulties as lying within the relationship, marriage counseling help is indicated. If there is pronounced intrapsychic illness in either or both partners, a referral for psychiatric care is indicated.

Marital conflict may begin at any stage of a marriage; in some situations it may precede the actual marriage ceremony. Today, with the increased number of situations in which pregnancy may precede the marital ceremony, conflicts may exist prior to, or from the date of, marriage. These may be engendered by the couple's feeling of loss of choice (although this may be denied in various ways), by the insecurity this loss creates concerning the partner's feelings about the spouse and the marriage, and by the necessity for changes in plans and for the assumption of responsibilities for which neither partner was prepared. For these and other unready couples, there are a number of life tasks to be accomplished before a unity and mutuality in marriage can be achieved. Each partner may need help in separating from the parents, in achieving a sense of personal identity, in understanding and accepting the roles of husband and wife, and in developing an identity as a married couple. In such situations marital counseling can often facilitate a couple's growth toward maturity and a mutually satisfying marital realtionship.

Another indication of the need for help with a marriage relationship may be found in the couple who are experiencing difficulty in "communication." Broken down, this usually means that the differences or conflicts have been denied. Each partner has suppressed his angry or negative feelings and has withdrawn more and more from the relationship. When this occurs, satisfactions and gratifications diminish until the accumulation of irritations and resentments break into the open and threaten the marriage. At such a period couples may seek help. More recently we are finding an increase in applications from couples approaching retirement and the ending of active life (Mudd, Mitchell, & Taubin, 1965). Old conflicts and difficulties tend to be exacerbated as life fears increase, and, as a result, a heavier demand for security and reassurance is placed on the partner. These couples utilize short-term individual and joint marital counseling very effectively.

Marital counseling is also sought by those individuals, either or both of whom have already obtained individual psychiatric help with some abatement of their own personal discomfort, but without observable improvement in the marital relationship. In other instances one marriage partner may be involved in individual therapy, with the result that the other partner feels isolated and confused concerning changes in the spouse which result in modifications in the marital interaction. The isolated spouse may, under such circumstances, seek marital counseling for himself, or this may be suggested by the psychiatrist. We have found that it is helpful to such partners to be involved together in a marital counseling group. Other couples for whom group marital counseling may be the treatment of choice are those individuals who experience little anxiety concerning their own adjustment, shift very slowly or not at all in individual counseling or therapy, but are unhappy in their marriage, and tend to almost totally project blame and responsibility for the difficulties and the necessity for change onto the spouse. We have found group marital counseling an effective method for working with such situations (Linden, Goodwin, & Resnik, 1966).

STRUCTURE AND PROCESS OF COUNSELING

Within our conceptual framework, we see marital difficulty arising, as indicated earlier, out of the reciprocal interaction of the two unique human beings who are the marital partners and who create in the process a third entity, the marital relationship, with its rewards and gratifications, its frustrations and hostilities. Thus, the essential center of interest in counseling with a marital pair is on the reciprocal dynamics of the marital relationship and what each partner puts into this, rather than specifically on the intrapersonal conflicts of each. However, the concept of "marital relationship," like most labels for human behavior, does not imply a continued or a consistent state of being, but a relationship which changes from day to day. At best, marital partners are intimately related to each other occasionally and at certain points in time, rather than with continuous awareness as many couples seem to expect.

There are inevitable periods when either spouse, engaged in the problems and tasks of daily living, needs to be to a degree disengaged. There is, however, a guideline that can be useful to beginning counselors—that is, the relative degree of mutuality there is in a relationship. Mutuality as used here would imply a recognition by each of the separateness as well as of the unity of the partner, and that he or she has responsibilities, wants, and needs of his own which coexist with those of the marriage. Each can perceive the other as a separate person and have concern and caring for the partner rather than expecting him or her to exist solely as an extension of himself or for his own satisfaction. This may be contrasted with the inordinately self-centered persons who have little or no ability to perceive the other as a separate individual but who expect an idealized happiness to be created for them by the spouse, who supposedly exists solely for them and for their satisfaction. Any failure of the spouse to meet the needs of such partner is considered as selfish and hostile.

The average couple will fall toward the middle of a continuum from a mutual capacity for caring and concern for each other to the other end of the scale where there is self-centeredness and inability to relate to another person or his needs. It thus follows that, in working with any couple, one has to take into consideration the specific individuals, the kind of reciprocal interaction flowing back and forth between them, and what possible solution one can work toward with this particular couple. The specific partners, their personality structures, dynamics, interrelationship, and chronicity of difficulties do determine, to a degree, the process and goal of counseling. In 66 percent of cases served at Marriage Council, follow-up contacts four years later indicated that the situation for which assistance had been sought had been resolved or modified (Ballard & Mudd, 1957). In certain cases a constructive goal can be to help the partners recognize that this union cannot give them or their children the kind of satisfactions desired. Support of their choice toward separation is seen as more desirable than a continuing destructive relationship between them. In other cases the goal may be to help either one or both partners accept the need for individual psychiatric help. This happens in approximately 10 percent of Marriage Council's cases.

Marriage Council has, over the years, offered individual counseling to marital partners and within the past several years has offered group marriage counseling to certain selected couples. Throughout, it has been the agency's philosophy to make every effort to work with both partners, and through experience over the years we have found it more helpful to have the same counselor work with the two marital partners. This enables the counselor to experience, directly and intuitively, nuances in feeling and behavior within individual and joint interviews that are not possible when two counselors see the spouses separately. In individual counseling each partner is seen on a weekly basis for approximately fifty minutes, and joint as well as individual interviews are held in initial contacts and as indicated thereafter by the process of counseling. In other situations, where it seems that group counseling might be a more efficient way of working with the couple, this is suggested and the couple is assigned to a group totaling not more than six couples, led by a man and a woman as co-counselors.

Of central importance to working with marriages are the personality and characteristics of the counselor, his orientation, and his basic background knowledge. It is important that the counselor be a person with capacity for depth in relationship. In our method of approach, capacity to form a relationship not only to one person, but to the two partners as a marital pair, is essential. This includes keeping as a basic concern the couple's interrelationship with each other without becoming over-identified with either one. It has been our experience that technical training and knowledge is not adequate in working with marital relationship problems. It is a definite advantage for the counselor, to whom a couple can relate and with whom they can work honestly and sincerely on their difficulties, to have had a certain amount of life experience which helps him in attaining perspective on the couple's situation. The counselor needs to see himself as an enabler using his knowledge and skill in the process of helping the partners to clarify the source of their difficulties, rather than as an authoritative person with a definite concept of what every marriage must be. Since marriage is a factor in every counselor's life, either through his parental situation or in his own life experience, the problem of over-identification with one spouse or the other is a difficult one. It is important, therefore, that the counselor be aware of his own attitudes and philosophy toward marriage, and be willing and able to examine his own part in the counseling process actively and continuously as he works with marriage problems.

In individual counseling, as the process moves beyond the initial stage of identifying the problems, of determining when they began and how the couple has tried to handle them, part of the focus is on helping the partners clarify what it is they want in marriage. Are their goals realistic or unrealistic? Is what they desire possible in an adult relationship, or is this an inappropriate need brought over from childhood that cannot be met realistically in a marriage? (Glasser, 1965).

The attempt is made in counseling to help the couple reduce the intensity of the conflict by verbalization, by helping the clients to deal with their feelings of hostility and guilt, and by strengthening their self-esteem, thus reducing their need for holding to rigid defenses. As the couple becomes related to the counselor as an empathetic, responsible adult who cares what happens to his clients, each client is helped to look at his own pattern of relating and behavior, and to determine how this affects the marital interaction. Gradually the client comes to see the other partner and the self more realistically. Inevitably, each member of a marital pair comes to counseling feeling that the change needs to be in the other partner. It relieves both guilt and anxiety to help them understand during the early interviews that the primary difficulty lies not in either person, but in the circular interaction that takes place between them—the failure of each to meet in a way that is satisfying for the other the kinds of needs and wants that each has (Sullivan, 1950).

Joint interviews are useful in helping clients to connect with their circular interaction. During the joint interview the interaction of the couple in its destructive phases may be demonstrated, and the counselor takes responsibility for enabling the partners to evaluate what has been occurring between them and the effect it has had on each. As each spouse is able to see the part each has played in their joint difficulties and to express angers, frustrations, and resentments, hostility is reduced and more positive feelings, hopefully, may begin to emerge. Essentially the counselor has both a therapeutic and a re-educational function as he helps the couple see the ways in which they behave destructively and find other more constructive types of reacting.

As stated earlier, the process may involve many variations, depending upon the character structure and capacity of the partners. In certain situations an ego-supportive and reality-oriented approach by the counselor may be the treatment of choice. "Borderline" clients, or clients suffering from various degrees of ego defect, constitute a large proportion of the clients who come today to social agencies for help with problems of interpersonal difficulties. Invariably the problem is perceived as a situational or interpersonal one, with little awareness of the part played by intrapsychic difficulties. Since these clients are struggling with a high degree of ambivalence, are apprehensive, distrustful of relationship, and have frequently been disappointed in prior attempts to secure therapeutic help, the management of the counselor-client relationship assumes great importance.

Our approach at the Division of Family Study* and Marriage Council* is based on a nurturing relationship with an active reaching out and interest in helping the partners and a genuine responsiveness to the feelings of each. Because of the weak ego strength of many clients, focus within interviews is kept on solving the current reality and relationship problems with which the client is struggling, and efforts are directed toward improving ego strength and functioning. Effort is directed toward helping these clients to know more clearly what they feel, and to connect their ways of behaving with the response they receive. There is a different use of techniques; that is, the counselor names and "talks to" *feeling* rather than working toward helping the client understand the *why* of the feelings he experiences. It is equally important to help these clients develop more

---

*Division of Family Study in Psychiatry, University of Pennsylvania School of Medicine; and Marriage Council of Philadelphia.—*Editors*

accurate perception of reality and more skill in reality testing. The counselor in these situations, without implication of criticism, helps the partners to review conflicts and incidents step by step, tentatively raising
questions concerning each partner's perception of the incident, other
possible interpretations of it, and the way it may have been perceived by
the other. Movement will be slow, but small gains in constructive ego
functioning may shift the balance in the marriage and set in motion a
more positive spiral of interaction, which in turn often effects constructively other interactional relationships of the client (Parad & Miller,
1963).

In 1958 group marriage counseling, involving four to six married
couples (eight to twelve individuals) in the same group, was instituted at
Marriage Council, and has continued to be one method in the treatment of
certain types of marital difficulty: for example, couples where one or
both are "acting out" their difficulties; couples where one or both partners are unaware or afraid of feeling; couples where one partner views self
as the victim and the spouse as the offender; couples where one or both
has had prior individual counseling or psychiatric therapy, with perhaps
some personal gain, but no perceptible improvement in the marriage;
couples where there is extreme use of projection and denial as major
defenses; and marriages in which a partner is an excessive drinker (Linden
et al., 1966).

Focus in groups, as in our individual counseling, is on the reciprocal
interaction between the partners, rather than on the individual's intrapsychic conflicts. Content of group discussions may vary within wide
limits, and is often characterized by excursions into past individual or
marital history as related to each person's current marital difficulties.
However, the ongoing focus and central theme is on the reality of the
day-to-day, interspouse relationship, individual striving, role expectations,
obvious psychological defenses, and conflicts as seen in the marriage. Each
partner's characteristic pattern for satisfying his own needs, as well as
modes of response to the demands of the spouse, emerge in the group
process.

Groups are led by male and female co-counselors who carry in the role
of counselors certain responsibilities. These include maintaining the focus
of group effort on the interrelationship between marital partners, creating
a group "climate" of acceptance, developing a group orientation through
mutual trust and the factor of universalization. This process is conducive
to expression of both positive and negative feelings and attitudes. It
stimulates and supports group interaction rather than communications
directed toward the co-therapists. The group members are thus enabled to
respond to each other intellectually and affectively. The co-counselors
assist the group to recognize distorted feelings, warped attitudes, specialized behavior, and ideational content through clarification, paraphrasing,
and simplification. They aid the development of group process through
the support of individuals or of their comments. They assist participants
in identifying and dealing with either positive or negative feelings toward
the co-counselors which have their roots in the past and are inappropriate

in relation to the present situation. In these various processes the marital partners become aware of their neurotic interlocking patterns of need and response.

As indicated earlier, there is no effort in our approach to work deeply on the intrapsychic problems or conflicts of any individual partner, but instead to help them become aware of the way in which their own wants, needs, and patterns of relating affect their marital relationship. Through this approach the major changes that may occur will be in the circular interaction between the husband and wife, and collaterally, after this first step occurs, changes are often apparent in other relationships of each partner: to their children, their parents, their business associates. However, changes may be carried to considerable depth, depending upon the partner's personality and capacity.

In situations where marriages have benefited, there will be better communication with more honesty and more directness, less hostility, less actual conflicts; and when conflict arises, each partner will tend to examine his or her own part in it more quickly, and the conflict will then be resolved within a shorter time. Couples will have found a better way of talking about and resolving their problems. Some change in their concept of their own and their spouse's role and more realistic perception of the partner and of his wants and needs and of the individual self occurs. Defenses of denial and projection are used less extensively, and there is an acceptance of more responsibility for self-discipline and control of own behavior with greater tolerance for both the self and the spouse in the human quality of their interaction. As each learns a little more about the self and the partner, there tends to be a reawakening of the earlier, more positive relationship, and some conviction about the other's care and concern is revived.

It seems of considerable significance that the changes described in the way in which partners hopefully will handle their daily relationships after counseling are almost identical with the processes of problem-solving and conflict resolutions reported by one hundred couples who consider their marriage and family relationships successful and whose communities concurred in this estimate. Apparently healthy couples, whose reciprocal interaction is mutually satisfactory, have spontaneously arrived at these processes as realistically practical and constructive.

THE FUTURE OF MARRIAGE COUNSELING

Marriage counseling has become one aspect of the day-by-day work of professional persons from a variety of backgrounds, primarily social work, psychology, the ministry, medicine, and education. Since the first services in marriage counseling were initiated in the United States in 1931, among those interested there has been a gradually increasing exchange of data based on experience. Articles and books, and more recently a systematic review of cases from members of the American Association of Marriage Counselors, have been published. Some forty-one cases in which there was follow-up contact after the close of the case were reported in *Marriage*

Counseling: A Casebook, edited by a committee of the association. After analyzing these cases, the conclusions of the committee as formulated in 1958 still seem pertinent to further developments in this specialization (Mudd et al., 1958).

> When the Committee undertook to prepare this casebook there was no evidence available as to whether or not there were common denominators between theory and practice in the field of marriage counseling. Nor was it known how specifically any school of psychological thought might affect or differentiate methods and techniques employed by counselors with their clients. The close relationship between some of the more general principles and procedures in marriage counseling, on the one hand, as stated in Chapter 2 ("Principles, Processes, and Techniques of Marriage Counseling") and, on the other, the methods actually used by marriage counselors in practice as presented in the case material seem to have important implications for the present status of marriage counseling as well as for the future development of this field. The high degree of correlation between these general principles and the case material indicates that although the field is relatively new, there has already been developed a considerable amount of generally accepted practice, whether such practice is consciously related to formulated theory or not.

The world of 1966, and specifically the conflictual involvements within the United States and internationally, focus increasingly on the problems of human beings caught in a culture pervaded by scientific discoveries and technological innovations (Lee, 1966). It is almost a platitude to reiterate that "the conduct of human affairs, in contrast to progress in science and technology, has suffered from reliance upon generalities, superstitions, fallacies, and prejudices. There is all too little pertinent research concerning man's relation to his fellows and few guides to aid in the attainment of creative, cooperative, and mutually constructive interaction (Mudd, 1966). Marriage counseling can serve as a beginning guide.

Marriage counseling deals with the most intimate interpersonal relations of men and women. It also deals with one of the smallest social systems in which the dynamics of interpersonal conflict resolution can be observed and studied. It furnishes data as yet little explored or utilized in careful research. It is now incumbent upon man to learn how his own behavior with his fellow man can be modified to accommodate to the exigencies of tomorrow.

On the basis of our counseling experience, we suggest that conflict resolution in various groups might benefit from the use of the conceptual framework and the processes of the counseling session: the unpressured, unaccusing atmosphere, the give and take, the catharsis, the perspective, and the support of efforts at new and mutually acceptable behavior and interaction.

REFERENCES

Ballard, R. G. & Mudd, E. H. Some theoretical and practical problems in evaluating effectiveness of counseling. *Social Casework*, 1957, 10.

Christensen, H. T. (Ed.) *Handbook of marriage and the family*. Chicago: Rand McNally, 1964. Chap. 22.

Glasser, W. *Reality therapy*. New York: Harper & Row, 1965. Chap. I.

Goodwin, H. M. The nature and use of the tri-dimensional relationship in the process of marriage counseling. Unpublished doctoral dissertation, Univ. of Pa., 1957.

Goodwin, H. M. Marriage counseling and the minister. *J. Religion Health*, 1964, *3*, 1.

Goodwin, H. M. & Mudd, E. H. Concepts of marital diagnosis and therapy as developed at the Division of Family Study, Department of Psychiatry, School of Medicine, Univ. of Pa. In E. M. Nash, L. Jessner, & D. W. Abse (Eds.), *Marriage counseling in medical practice*. Chapel Hill: Univ. of North Carolina, 1964.

Greene, B. L. (Ed.) *The psychotherapies of marital disharmony*. Glencoe, Ill.: Free Press, 1965.

Grinker, R. R., et al. *Psychiatric social work—A transactional casebook*. New York: Basic Books, 1961.

Haley, J. Marriage therapy. *Arch. Gen. Psychiat.*, 1963, *8*, 213-234.

Johnson, D. *Marriage counseling: Theory and practice*. Englewood Cliffs, N. J.: Prentice-Hall, 1961.

Klemer, R. H. *Counseling in marital and sexual problems*. Baltimore, Md.: Williams & Wilkins, 1965.

Lee, A. McC. *Multi-valent man*. New York: George Braziller Publisher, 1966.

Linden, M., Goodwin, H. & Resnik, H. Group psychotherapy of couples in marriage counseling. Paper presented at Annual Meeting of the American Psychiatric Association, May 13, 1966, Atlantic City, N. J.

Mace, D. & Mace, V. *Marriage East and West*. New York: Doubleday & Co., 1960, Chap. 2.

Mudd, E. H. *The practice of marriage counseling*. New York: Association Press, 1961.

Mudd, E. H. Conflict and conflict resolution in families. In S. Mudd (Ed.), Conflict resolution and world education. Vol. III. The Hague, Netherlands: World Academy of Art and Science, 1966.

Mudd, E. H., Karpf, M. J., Stone, A., & Nelson, J. F. (Eds.) *Marriage counseling: A casebook*. New York: Association Press, 1958.

Mudd, E. H., Mitchell, H. E., & Taubin, S. R. Leisure and retirement. In *Success in family living*, New York: Association Press, 1956. p. 192-209.

Parad, H. J., & Miller, R. R. *Ego-oriented casework*. New York: Family Service Association of America, 1963. Chaps. 2, 7-9.

Pollak, O. Sociological and psychoanalytic concepts in family diagnosis. In L. Green (Ed.) *The psychotherapies of marital disharmony*. Glencoe, Ill.: Free Press, 1965. Chap. II.

Satir, V. *Conjoint family therapy: A guide to theory and technique*. Palo Alto, Calif.: Science and Behavior Books, 1964.

Spiegal, J. P. The resolution of role conflict within the family. *Psychiatry*, 1957, *20*, 1.

Stein, H. D. Sociocultural concepts in casework practice. Smith College Studies in Social Work, Feb. 1959. p. 63-75.

Sullivan H. S. Psychiatry: introduction to the study of interpersonal relations. In *A study of interpersonal relations*. P. Mullahy (Ed.), New York: Hermitage Press, 1950. p. 98-121.

Womble, D. L. Preparing for marriage tomorrow, in *Foundations for marriage and family relations*. New York: Macmillan, 1966. p. 523-548.

CHAPTER 13

Marriage Counseling as Rational Process-Oriented Psychotherapy

Robert A. Harper

The ideas presented in this paper derive mainly from the writer's own clinical experience and theoretical eclecticism (Harper, 1959c). They appear to be basically compatible with Individual Psychology as developed by Alfred Adler (1956) and as applied to many contemporary therapeutic problems and situations by those who follow in his tradition (Adler & Deutsch, 1959). Specific formulation of the writer's clinical point of view has been considerably influenced by professional association with Albert Ellis (with whom he is currently collaborating on a major work in rational psychotherapy). As Ellis (1957) has pointed out, Individual Psychology and rational psychotherapy have many points of fundamental similarity.

Marriage counseling is more often than not conceived of as an activity different from psychotherapy and as not falling under the jurisdiction of either psychology or psychiatry (Kimber, 1959; Vincent, 1957). Its major trend to date has been greatly influenced by sociologists and nonpsychiatric physicians who, for the most part, represent marriage counseling as relatively superficial treatment of marital relationship problems of so-called normal persons and, hence, not calling for the knowledge or training of the psychotherapist. Stokes (1949, 1954), Ellis (1956, 1958), Laidlaw (1950), and Harper (1953, 1958a, 1958b, 1959a, 1959b) have been the most consistent and outspoken proponents of an opposing point of view, namely, that marriage counseling *is* psychotherapy. As the present writer (Harper, 1953) has stated, the contention that marriage counseling is *not* psychotherapy

> leads one to wonder if [this contention] may not be a rationalization of the psychotherapeutically untrained, for actual marriage counseling seems to be effective or ineffective to the extent that it penetrates and leads to the revision of the *personal dynamics and value systems of individual clients*. While special knowledge of marital relationships and general knowledge of related sociological phenomena appear essential, it is difficult to see how the marriage counseling process itself is basically anything other than a type of psychotherapy [p. 338].

Reprinted with permission of the author and the publisher from the *Journal of Individual Psychology*, 1960, *16*, 192–207.

Based on this clinical conviction, then, the terms "psychotherapy" and "counseling" are to be considered synonyms in this paper. If "marriage psychotherapy" did not seem too awkward, the term "counseling" would have been dispensed with.

MAJOR PROCESSES ON WHICH THERAPY FOCUSES

Let us begin with the "process-oriented" aspect of our concept of psychotherapy as applied to patients who have marriage-focused presenting problems. English and English (1958) present a variety of definitions of *process*. The basic one is that process is

> a change or a changing in an object or organism in which a consistent quality or direction can be discerned. A process is always in some sense active; something is happening. It contrasts with the structure or form of organization of what changes, which structure is conceived to be relatively static despite process change.

Process-oriented marriage counseling, then, directs its attention to the quality and direction of the changing activity, the dynamic behavior, and the life styles of the individuals who make up a marriage relationship. Although the writer recognizes, of course, that individual and interactional behavior must take place within certain anatomical and social structures, he regards these structures as realistic limitations for such behavior and not the major focus of the counselor's interest and attention. Such social structures, for example, as the marriage and family institutions, government, the school, or the church, interest the process-oriented therapist in *their influence on human processes and life styles* and not as valuable objects in and of themselves. He must take these institutionalized relationships importantly into account in his psychotherapeutic work; but his therapy is centered on the *functioning persons*, not the marriage or other relationship forms in which they participate and by which they are affected.

This may seem like belaboring the obvious. But, as already indicated, it seems currently necessary to distinguish as pointedly as possible this point of view from the "relationship treatment trend" in the amorphous field of marriage counseling.

Rationality. The chief process toward which marriage counseling can be directed in an inner-force–encouraging, block-removing, reconstructive therapeutic way is the rational process: the thinking, reality-perceiving and reality-understanding, the creative, the problem-facing and problem-handling process. Examples of how the rational process gets stalemated in man's nonrational culture, and some of the counter-socializing the present therapist undertakes in helping his patients to utilize more fully their rational abilities, will be dealt with below. Right now let us try to justify rationality's number one position.

Since love often gets top billing as a human process, especially when we are thinking about marriage, it may seem radical to state that the problem-facing and problem-handling process is more important. As Erich

Fromm (1947) brings out most clearly, deep, mature, broadly humanistic, outgoing love for another cannot be achieved by the individual until he has come truly to love himself. Self-love and self-esteem, as Fromm points out, are achieved mainly through the individual's experience of productiveness. And this experience in the adult human being, the present writer contends, is largely a by-product of the growing use of his rational process: creative thinking and practical problem-solving.

This elevation of the effectively functioning human mind to a position of primacy as a process is not just whimsy on the author's part. Such unwhimsical biologists as Julian Huxley (1948) and Nobel-Prize winning H. J. Muller (1958) assure us that man spearheads continuing organic evolution (so far as this planet is concerned) by his dynamic culture, his continuing ability to change and grow and learn, his questing intelligence, his flexible nonspecialization as an animal, his ability to perceive and deal rationally with reality-in-transition. Man, with his genetically unrigidified and unspecialized behavior patterns, is alone among the earthly animals prepared to make any major onward moves with the evolving universe. He will soon be capable, in fact, of leaving his particular planet and, perhaps in another decade or two, the planetary system of his particular star.

Man achieves this status as the spearhead of continuing evolution by utilizing the cerebrum-centered processes that distinguish him so dramatically from his closest earthly relatives. It is, therefore, the major satisfaction of his distinct humanness—an outstanding experience of the joyful process of self-fulfillment—whenever man regularly thinks creatively and acts upon the results of that thinking. If, with a fair degree of consistency, a particular human animal has a sense of utilization of his major cerebral processes, of facing and thinking creatively about and acting rationally toward reality, *that* person will have a sense of self-esteem, of happiness, and of self-love. Only then, as the writer sees it, is a human being a creature capable of the more distinctly human form of mature and realistic love called for in deep and abiding relationships.

Love. Marriage, like life, is a problem process, and ignored troubles simply grow into bigger and often unmanageable ones. Until the couple, then, just like the individual himself, is able to face and to handle with relative effectiveness the problems of married life, neither deep and lasting happiness nor deep and lasting love will be forthcoming from that life. The love herein referred to (as distinguished from the childish sentiment glorified in the opiates of our culture) is the process whereby the emotionally mature and secure individual identifies himself with another, the love object, in a way that makes that other *almost* as dear, as cared for, as valuable, as interesting, as enjoyable as himself. It is the opinion of the writer that to try to make the loved one *more*—or even *as*—precious as oneself is unrealistic self-delusion. *Almost*, it would appear, is the correct word.

Love, like any other process, can be used to corrupt and can itself be corrupted. One way it is corrupted is as a phoney sort of canned product—the outer shell of affection, the mechanical form of love. People go through the motions. They may temporarily fool themselves as well as others, but they do not contribute to the actual process of loving until they have the self-esteem, the self-confidence, the reduction of anxiety and guilt and shame, that enable them securely to participate in spontaneous love-making with an adult of the other sex. It is as a part of the process of mature love, that the process of sex is so important for the marriage counselor to understand and to communicate to his clients.

Sexual functioning, as one means of love expression, can also be corrupted into some kind of canned product. It can be contaminated by "spiritualizing": guilt and shame can be wrapped into some high-sounding theological package that can take all the *fun* out of the sex process and leave it a pallid, dead product. Love-making can also be "academicized." Much of the marriage manual teaching about sex helps to make it an academic product, e.g., by focusing attention on the mechanics of the sexual act rather than on the joyful process of erotic activity.

Sex as joy-love experience is exceedingly difficult to communicate to patients, most of whom have developed prudish and pornographic attitudes. Some of the change in attitude can be achieved through direct, head-on sexual reconditioning of the couple, and some through indirectly improving the couple's ability to communicate effectively and affectionately in nonsexual areas of marriage (Harper, 1958a). Just as effective individual problem-facing-and-handling is the outstanding means for achieving and maintaining self-love, so effective communication (deep and meaningful transmitting of thoughts and feelings directed toward problem-solving) is the major method of achieving and maintaining marital love.

Humor. In addition to the creative problem-managing process and the love-sex process, we shall consider the process of humor, which functions as a catalyst for communication.

The humor referred to is the spontaneous type, not a contrived variety. Nothing is more deadly to marriage or to marriage counseling than the canned jokes or the frozen platitudinous witticisms passed off by the ha-ha-I'm-a-card spouse and the chuckle-chuckle-I'm-real-droll counselor. Process humor usually does not even sound funny when repeated because it is alertly geared to the ongoing changes of the relationship in which it occurs.

Humor can, of course, be used negatively, either as hostile attack or retreating defense, in both marriage and marriage counseling. For humor to be used as a constructive process, it must be shared by the participants in an interaction. One way for a spouse or a counselor to achieve mutually experienced humor with the marital partner or the client is for the initiator of the humor to make himself the object. This too, can be tricky, for it is important that the humor be neither out of character nor in any way self-depreciating. The joke is on me (a real part of me); I laugh spontaneously with you; but I lose no self-esteem while doing so.

The great value of humor is not only that it makes the problem-handling process in marriage and in psychotherapy more pleasurable, but, by reducing anxiety and hostility, it makes for clearer perception of problems and for greater likelihood of finding satisfactory ways of dealing with them. It also helps to open the channels for the adult type of love. Much of the writer's marriage counseling is, therefore, tempered by the anxiety-and-hostility-reducing type of positive humor. It is directed toward challenging the husband and wife, as individuals and as a couple, to become aware of themselves as potentially capable, loving, lovable, problem-perceiving, and problem-handling persons.

RATIONAL THERAPY FOR IRRATIONAL BEHAVIOR

Our culture not only leads us mistakenly to focus a great deal of our attention on structure, content, and products, instead of on function, direction, and process. We are also conditioned by this same culture to develop clouded perceptions and irrational conceptions of the realities with which we are faced in social living. It is toward these cultural confusions of reality that a major portion of the writer's approach is directly pointed.

Contrast with client-centered therapy. By way of introductory contrast for the rationality-directed part of this approach, it seems appropriate to look for a moment at another form of therapy which is process-oriented, namely, client-centered or nondirective therapy. According to Rogers (1951), personal feelings are primary, are the fundamental core of the individual's self. Rational, process-oriented psychotherapists believe, on the other hand, that this emphasis on the emotions disregards the most important evolutionary development of the human animal: the over-powering potentialities of the ego or executive functions of his cerebrum. The writer does not contend that the healthy human animal does not have some strictly prehuman reactions, but he maintains that *many* of man's emotions are directly controlled by his thinking. If his thinking is irrational, his emotions will be disordered or, better, reality-disoriented. If his thinking is rational, his emotions will be effectively and realistically related to the demands being made on him as a functioning organism.

Direct handling of irrational beliefs. Much of the time of a rational, process-oriented therapist, then, as distinguished from a nondirective one, will be spent, quite directively, toward helping the patient to recognize and alter the irrational patterns of thinking that are causing much of the disruption in his own emotions and, along with the irrational beliefs of his spouse, the disruption of his marital relations. The marriage counselor needs to listen to and observe both the husband and the wife (sometimes separately and sometimes together), but then he needs to formulate and communicate concrete recommendations for change. The therapist needs to make specific assignments of experiments, in thought and action, to be carried out between therapy sessions (homework). These assigned changes need to be practiced at times in the counseling situation as well. An inhibited, masochistic wife, for example, may need to play the role of being self-assertive with the acceptance and guidance of the counselor, before she is prepared to stand up to, and communicate directly with, her husband. The overly aggressive wife, on the other hand, may need to face the test of learning how to relate in an equalitarian way to the therapist, who plays the role of the hostilely withdrawing husband, before she is able to deal adequately with her aggressive attitudes in the actual marital situation. But what these disturbed husbands and wives need most of the time, is instruction in *thinking*, and hence feeling and acting, rationally and realistically.

A considerable portion of the present therapist's time, then, is spent in helping patients to overcome some of their irrational, traditional, (often) downright stupid patterns of thinking about life in general and about themselves, their mates, and their marriages in particular. Every patient the writer has ever seen has had his own unique elements of irrationality; but many primitive and childish ideas are practically universal in our culture.

IRRATIONAL BELIEFS AND THERAPEUTIC COUNTER-BELIEFS

Illustrations will now be presented of these near-universals of irrationality which apply particularly to marriage and family situations. Following each example, the therapist offers (in greatly condensed form) the kind of counter-belief with which he attempts to recondition these people toward a greater degree of rationality. Such rational counter-propaganda (necessary to offset the propaganda of irrationality with which the patient has been conditioned and keeps reconditioning himself) is in each instance, of course, geared to the specific social situation and personality traits of the individual patient.

Irrational belief No. 1. It is absolutely essential for my mate to love and respect me, no matter how stupidly, boringly, or annoyingly I behave, and, if he (or she) does not, then we do not have real and true and deep and lasting love in our marriage and things are positively calamitous.

Rational counter-belief. It is enjoyable (but not necessary) to be loved and approved by one's mate a good portion of the time, but it becomes catastrophic *not* to be, *only* if one tells himself it is. If you avoid thinking: "Oh, dear, isn't this horrible that my mate does not currently love or approve me?" and think instead: "I wonder how I can function in this situation, so that *I* will more approve of *myself*," it is likely that, incidentally, your mate will have more love and esteem for you. but even if the spouse continues to be uncooperative in the situation, *you*, now thinking and functioning more realistically, will be happier.

Irrational belief No. 2. If my spouse and I loved each other truly at the time of marriage, then the love would be everlasting and our relationship positively wonderful. Conversely, if serious problems arise and persist, then we did not love each other enough, obviously, or things like this would never have happened.

Rational counter-belief. Love is a learned process, and, like any other form of learned reaction or interaction, it grows stronger with reinforcing experience and weaker with inhibition or disuse. The initial degree of love is quite unrelated to the nature and intensity of problems that will arise in the marriage. Love, steadily nurtured, will help to provide a desirable setting in which to develop the skills of communication necessary to manage marital problems, but will in no way protect the couple from the problems, or serve to substitute for the skills.

Irrational belief No. 3. Other people, especially my spouse, do things to me emotionally. "My husband doesn't make me happy;" "my wife angers me;" "he depresses me;" "if my wife wouldn't say stupid things to my friends, then I wouldn't get upset with her."

Rational counter-belief. Each person makes his own emotions. When your spouse calls you some undesirable name, for example, *that* does not hurt or upset or anger you. It is your *intervening evaluation* which makes you hurt or upset or angry. You evaluate (that is, "say to yourself") something like: "Isn't this awful, dreadful, despicable, etc., that this heel of a spouse—for whom I have done countless wonderful and self-sacrificing things—has the unloving and unappreciative gall to say that to me?" And *that* is what produces the negative emotions. You can change the emotional response by changing your evaluation. You can, with persistent practice, learn to say to yourself such things as: "So what? So he thinks I am a dirty name. Does this need to ruin *my* day? Isn't this mainly *his* problem? If it is also partly something for me to concern myself about, I'll ask him to discuss his complaint in calm, non-abusive tones either now or later." Or: "He seems to feel strongly about something (identified or unidentified). I think I'll disregard his name-calling and try calmly to find out what's annoying him."

Irrational belief No. 4. Certain things are unquestionably catastrophic, undeniably immoral, unthinkably intolerable, and rigidly inviolable. Hence, any discussion of these matters, or consideration of alternative approaches to problems connected with them, is impossible. Only a scum and a bum would do such a thing as this. He's a scum and a bum, so I am through with him.

Rational counter-belief. Yes, this is the nature of moral righteousness. You have been brought up to think that certain things are absolutely right and others absolutely wrong, and so it is indeed difficult (but *not* impossible, with help) for you to learn to exercise your critical conceptual judgment. Because you have been brought up on this childish nonsense is no reason for you to continue to believe it. Only if you *insist* on retaining these beliefs will they indefinitely remain as obstacles to your thinking, feeling, and acting realistically. This spouse of yours has done this undesirable, uncooperative, unhelpful thing (be it adultery, theft, wife-beating, child-rejecting, or whatever). It *may* be that this is so permanently characteristic of him, so symptomatic of a basic character disorder, that you will decide to separate from him. But let's make this judgment after a critical and rational inspection of the facts and after a calm and logical discussion with him.

Irrational belief No. 5. She hit me, so I hit her. Or: he lost his temper and called my mother an old bag, and so I felt I had a perfect right to let him know that his own sister is just a plain tramp. Or: she deliberately poured the liquor down the sink, so I took a pair of scissors and cut up all her evening gowns. I'd do it again, too, because I believe in an eye for an eye.

Rational counter-belief. Neurosis is essentially stupid behavior in a basically nonstupid person. When your spouse becomes neurotic, starts doing and saying stupid things, you not only aggravate *his* neurosis by reacting as you do, but you become equally, or perhaps more, stupid in *your* thoughts and feelings and actions. The only effective way out of a neurotic situation is for the respondent to be *less* neurotic—that is, *more rational*—than the initiator of the neurotic pattern. If instead of evaluating your spouse's neurotic words and actions as terrible, awful, etc., you say to yourself: "Keep your head, old friend. Be as nonstupid as possible. Find out what's eating this person rather than trying to imitate or excel his neurotic performance"—if you do this, you will be contributing to the reduction of neurosis in your marriage. At the very least, you can learn (with practice) to say: "So here he goes again. This is *his* idiotic merry-go-round; I'm not taking a ride to get the brass ring he's holding out to me."

Irrational belief No. 6. I don't *deserve* what is happening to me. Other people's children don't have four diseases in a row. Other people's husbands don't bet the rent money on the horses. *Why* must this happen to me? What have I done to *deserve* this?

Rational counter-belief. Reality at any present instant of time is inexorable. The past and the present cannot be altered. All we can work with is a future that will become a new present. It is quite likely that, in some instances, your past actions have been contributing factors to your present difficulties. Your friends and neighbors *may* have fewer misfortunes than you, or they may simply conceal their different sorts of problems from you. They may have been wiser or simply more fortunate than you. But the only reality you can work with is your own. You only distrust yourself and reduce your ability to deal with your problems by making inaccurate comparisons with your misperceptions of other people's realities. Your situation can undoubtedly be improved; certainly your attitude toward it can be. In any event, improvement is more apt to derive from rationally conceived action than by bemoaning a mythical dispensation of injustice. Let us look at the facts to see how we can most effectively deal with them.

CONCLUSION

Thus goes rational process-oriented marriage counseling. Both by word and example, the therapist stresses the fundamental importance (in life in general and in marriage in particular) of the processes of problem-facing-and-handling, love, and humor. Much of the therapeutic hour is devoted to combating irrational beliefs which block the patient from thinking rationally, loving, and enjoying life. The therapist then suggests effective alternatives in thought and action for the patient to practice between therapeutic sessions.

Does such marriage counseling work? In many instances, it is quite successful because it helps each party to the marriage to function in a basically less neurotic way. In a relatively few instances, these methods fail, and the writer then turns to other procedures (Harper, 1959b). He believes with Glad (1959) that different therapeutic techniques and values work with varying success both because of differing personalities of therapists and differing personalities of patients. For this therapist, however, it is seldom necessary to reach therapeutic "east" by sailing emotional "west." It is usually possible to fly directly "east" to what the writer considers the major cause of most of his patients' difficulties: patterns of irrational thought.

REFERENCES

Adler, A. *The individual psychology of Alfred Adler*. New York: Basic Books, 1956.
Adler, K. A., & Deutsch, Danica (Eds.) *Essays in individual psychology*. New York: Grove Press, 1959.
Ellis, A. A critical evaluation of marriage counseling. *Marriage and Family Living*, 1956, *18*, 65–71.
Ellis, A. Rational psychotherapy and individual psychology. *Journal of Individual Psychology*, 1957, *13*, 38–44.
Ellis, A. Neurotic interaction between marital partners. *Journal of counseling Psychology*, 1958, *5*, 24–28.
English, H. B., & English, Ava C. *A comprehensive dictionary of psychological and psychoanalytic terms*. New York: Longmans, Green, 1958.
Fromm, E. *Man for himself*. New York: Rinehart, 1947.
Glad, D. D. *Operational values in psychotherapy*. New York: Oxford University Press, 1959.
Harper, R. A. Should marriage counseling become a full-fledged speciality? *Marriage and Family Living*, 1953, *15*, 338–340.
Harper, R. A. Communication problems in marriage and marriage counseling. *Marriage and Family Living*, 1958, *20*, 107–112. (a)
Harper, R. A. Neurotic interactions among counselors. *Journal of counseling Psychology*, 1958, *5*, 33–38. (b)
Harper, R. A. Marriage counseling and the mores: A critique. *Marriage and Family Living*, 1959, *21*, 13–19. (a)
Harper, R. A. *Psychoanalysis and psychotherapy: 36 systems*. Englewood Cliffs, N. J.: Prentice-Hall, 1959. (b)
Harper, R. A. The responsibilities of parenthood: A marriage counselor's view. *Eugenics Quarterly*, 1959, *6*, 8–13. (c)
Huxley, J. *Man in the modern world*. New York: Mentor, 1948.
Kimber, J. A. M. The science and the profession of psychology in the area of family relations and marriage counseling. *American Psychologist*, 1959, *14*, 699–700.
Laidlaw, R. W. The psychiatrist as marriage counselor. *American Journal of Psychiatry*, 1950, *106*, 732–736.
Muller, H. J. *Science for humanity*. Yellow Springs, Ohio: American Humanist Association, 1958 (mimeographed).
Rogers, C. R. *Client-centered therapy*. Boston: Houghton Mifflin, 1951.
Stokes, W. R. Psychiatric insights in marriage counseling. *Marriage and Family Living*, 1949, *11*, 69–70.
Stokes, W. R., & Harper, R. A. The doctor as marriage counselor. *Medical Annals D. C.*, 1954, *23*, 670–672.
Vincent, C. E. (Ed.) *Readings in marriage counseling*. New York: Crowell, 1957.

CHAPTER 14

A Rational Approach to Marriage Counseling

Ben N. Ard, Jr.

Mark Twain, that perceptive observer of human beings, once said, "We all do no end of *feeling* and mistake it for thinking [*Life*, 1966, p. 16]." Throughout the history of counseling and psychotherapy, from Sigmund Freud to Carl Rogers, the major emphasis has been on the client's irrational impulses and *feelings*, rather than on what they *think*. There is a new approach in counseling and psychotherapy which goes against this trend.

One of the most provocative, challenging, and controversial approaches to marriage counseling that has been developed in recent years is the *rational* approach of Albert Ellis, a psychologist and marriage counselor who is Executive Director of the Institute for Rational Living in New York City.

In considering the kinds of problems marital partners face, we may divide the reasons for unhappy marriages into roughly two main causes: one, real imcompatibility between the spouses; or two, neurotic disturbances on the part of either or both the husband and wife which make them think and act in such a manner that there *appear* to be fundamental incompatibilities between them (Ellis & Harper, 1961a).

By *incompatibility* is meant truly irreconcilable differences in the basic attitudes, ideas, and interests of the marital partners. The main remedies here consist essentially of striving for mutual interests. This is often quite difficult and sometimes the differences are irreconcilable. Then the realistic alternative is divorce (Ellis & Harper, 1961a). A rational approach in this latter instance is for the marriage counselor to help his clients get through the divorce without unnecessary feelings of bitterness, resentment, failure, and guilt.

But what is a rational approach to marriage counseling for those couples who do not have irreconcilable differences but rather neurotic disturbances which are affecting their marriages?

Presented at the California State Marriage Counseling Association Convention/Symposium at Carmel, California, September 10, 1966.

Rational therapy (often called "RT" for short) is well fitted for counseling with individuals who do not believe that they are emotionally disturbed but who know that they are not functioning adequately in some specific area of life, such as their marriage. Possibly most of these troubled individuals should come for intensive, long-term psychotherapy rather than for marriage counseling, but the fact is that they do not (cf. Harper, 1960). It therefore behooves the marriage counselor to be enough of a trained and experienced therapist to be able to deal adequately with the individuals who come to him for help (Ellis, 1956). If he learns and practices the essentials of RT, he will be well prepared in this regard (Ellis, 1962).

Most couples who come for marriage counseling are victims of what has been fairly aptly called "neurotic interaction" in marriage (Ellis, 1958). Such neurotics are individuals who are not intrinsically stupid and inept—but who *needlessly* suffer from intense and sustained anxiety, hostility, guilt, or depression. Neurotic interaction in marriage arises when a theoretically capable husband and wife actually behave in an irrational, marriage-defeating way with each other. If the theses of RT are correct, then marital neurotic interaction arises from *unrealistic* and *irrational ideas, beliefs*, or *value systems* on the part of one or both of the marriage partners; and it is these beliefs and value systems which must be concertedly *challenged* if neurotic interaction is to cease.

What are some of these basic irrational ideas or beliefs that are common among clients of marriage counselors? One of the main irrational beliefs that people use to upset themselves with is the notion that it is a *dire necessity* for an adult human being to be *approved* or *loved* by almost all the significant other people he encounters; that it is most important what *others* think of him instead of what *he* thinks of himself. The ancient Greek philosopher Epictetus once gave us some words of wisdom that are perhaps relevant here: "If any one trusted your body to the first man he met, you would be indignant, but yet you trust your mind to the chance comer, and allow it to be disturbed and confounded if he revile you; are you not ashamed to do so? [quoted in Oates, 1940, p. 475]."

Applied to marriage, this irrational idea means the neurotic individual firmly believes that, no matter how he behaves, his mate, just because she *is* his mate, *should* love him; that if she does not respect him, life is a catastrophe; and that her main role as a wife is to help, aid, and succor *him*, rather than to be an individual in her own right.

The second major irrational belief which most neurotics in our society seem to hold is that a human being should or must be perfectly competent, adequate, talented, and intelligent—and is utterly *worthless* if he is incompetent in any significant way.

A third irrational assumption of the majority of neurotics is that they should severely *blame* themselves and others for mistakes and wrongdoings; and that punishing themselves or others will help prevent future mistakes. The concept of sin runs very deep in our culture. Many people are very upset by the behavior of other people. We need to return once again to the wisdom of Epictetus: "For no one shall harm you, without your consent; you will only be harmed, when you think you are harmed [Oates, 1940, p. 476]."

A fourth irrational assumption which underlies and causes emotional disturbance is the notion that it is horrible, terrible, and catastrophic when things are not the way one would like them to be; and that one should not have to put off present pleasures for future gains.

A fifth and final irrational belief which we shall consider here is the mythical supposition that most human unhappiness is *externally* caused or forced on one by the outside people and events; and that one has virtually no control over one's emotions and cannot help feeling badly on many occasions. Actually, of course, virtually all human unhappiness is *self-*caused and results from unjustified assumptions and internalized sentences stemming from these assumptions, such as some of the beliefs we have just been outlining. Another Stoic philosopher, Marcus Aurelius, has put the matter most succinctly, with regard to this last irrational idea: "If thou art pained by any external thing, it is not this thing that disturbs thee, but thy own judgment about it. And it is in thy power to wipe out this judgment now [Oates, 1940, p. 550]."

It is a staunch contention of Albert Ellis, then, that a seriously neurotic individual possesses, almost by definition, a set of basic postulates which are distinctly unrealistic, biased, and illogical (Ellis, 1957).

If what has been said so far is reasonably accurate, then the solution to the problem of treating neurotic interaction in marriage would appear to be fairly obvious (Ellis & Harper, 1961a). If neurotics have basically irrational assumptions or value systems, and if these assumptions lead them to interact self-defeatingly with their mates, then the marriage counselor's function is to tackle not the problem of the marriage, nor of the neurotic interaction that exists between the marital partners, but rather the problem of the irrational ideas or beliefs that *cause* this neurosis. This consists largely of showing each of the marital partners who is neurotically interacting (*a*) that he has some basic irrational assumptions; (*b*) precisely what these assumptions are; (*c*) how they originally arose; (*d*) how they currently are being sustained by continual unconscious self-indoctrination; and (*e*) how they can be replaced with much more rational, less self-defeating philosophies (cf. Ellis & Harper, 1961b).

In the rational approach to marriage counseling (as opposed to other approaches), there is an attempt to help the disturbed individuals acquire three levels of insight (Ellis, 1962). Insight Number 1 is the usual kind of understanding that the Freudians make much of: namely, the individual's seeing that his *present* actions have a *prior* or *antecedent cause*.

An additional and unique contribution of RT, however, is that rational therapy does not stop there but goes on to further insights. That is, Insight Number 2: namely, the understanding that the irrational ideas acquired by the individual in his past life are *still existent*, and that they largely exist today because *he himself keeps reindoctrinating himself* with these ideas, consciously or unconsciously.

And finally, Insight Number 3 is the full understanding by the disturbed individual that *he simply has got to change his erroneous and illogical thinking.* Unless the client, after acquiring Insights Number 1 and 2, fully sees and accepts the fact that for him to get better *there is no other way* than his forcefully and consistently attacking his early-acquired and still heartily held irrational ideas, he will definitely not overcome his emotional disturbance.

The rational therapist, then, adds to the marriage counselor's other methods the more direct techniques of confrontation, confutation, de-indoctrination, and reeducation as well as a rather unique contribution known as "homework assignments." In assigning "homework," the counselor tries to encourage, persuade, and impel clients to *do* the things they are afraid of (e.g., *risking* rejection) in order to *see* more concretely that these things are not actually fearsome. As Epictetus has stated, "Remember that foul words or blows in themselves are not outrage, but your judgment that they are so. So when any one makes you angry, know that it is your own thought that has angered you [Oates, 1940, pp. 472–473]."

More concretely, in applying RT to marriage counseling, each spouse is shown that his disturbed behavior arises largely from underlying unrealistic beliefs; that these beliefs may have originally been learned from early familial and other environmental influences but that they are now being maintained by *internal verbalizations*; that his marriage partner, in consequence, is rarely the real cause of his problems; that he himself is actually now creating and perpetuating these problems, that only by learning carefully to observe, to question, to think about, and to reformulate his basic assumptions can he hope to understand his mate and himself and to stop being unilaterally and interactionally neurotic.

Whenever marriage counseling clients can be induced to *work* at changing their underlying neurosis-creating assumptions, significant personality changes ensue, and their interactions with their mates, families, or other intimate associates almost always improve. More specifically, this work usually consists of: (1) fully facing the fact that they themselves are doing something wrong, however mistaken their intimates may *also* be; (2) seeing clearly that behind their neurotic mistakes and inefficiencies there invariably are important irrational, unrealistic philosophic *assumptions*; (3) vigorously and continually *challenging* and *questioning* these assumptions by critically examining them and by actively doing deeds that prove they are unfounded (i.e., homework assignments); (4) making due allowances for the intrinsic differences and frustrations of certain human relationships such as monogamous marriage; (5) learning to keep their mouths shut when one of their close associates is clearly behaving badly, or else to objectively and *unblamefully* point out the other's mistakes while constructively trying to show him or her how to correct them in the future; and (6) above all, continually keeping in mind the fact that a relationship *is* a relationship, that it rarely can spontaneously progress in a supersmooth manner, and that it must often be actively worked at to recreate and maintain the honest affection with which it often starts (Ellis, 1966).

While the ideas of Albert Ellis are considered heretical by many in the field of marriage counseling who have emphasized the importance of *expressing feelings* rather than *thinking rationally*, we may turn one final time to the ancient Greek philosopher of Stoicism, Epictetus, who as usual gets to the crux of the matter very quickly: "What disturbs men's minds is not events but their judgments on events. . . . And so when we are hindered, or disturbed, or distressed, let us never lay the blame on others, but on ourselves, that is, on our own judgments. To accuse others for one's own misfortunes is a sign of want of education; to accuse oneself shows that one's education has begun; to accuse neither oneself nor others shows that one's education is complete [Oates, 1940, p. 469] ."

Put in simple A-B-C terms, it is rarely the external stimulus situation, A, which gives rise directly to an emotional reaction, C. Rather, it is almost always B—the individual's beliefs regarding, attitudes toward, or interpretation of, A—which actually lead to his reaction, C.

Our job as marriage counselors, then, is to help clients see for themselves that it is necessary for them to work on the B step, their assumptions or internalized sentences, rather than railing at the external situation, A, or wallowing in their own miseries at C. If we can get our clients to work on their assumptions and challenge their self-defeating values, they can develop more rational and therefore more self-satisfying philosophies and lives.

REFERENCES

Ellis, A. A critical evaluation of marriage counseling. *Marriage and Family Living*, 1956, *18*, 65–71.
Ellis, A. *How to live with a neurotic*. New York: Crown, 1957.
Ellis, A. Neurotic interaction between marital partners. *Journal of Counseling Psychology*, 1958, *5*, 24–28.
Ellis, A. A rational approach to marital problems. In A. Ellis, *Reason and Emotion in Psychotherapy*. New York: Lyle Stuart, 1962. Pp. 206–222.
Ellis, A. The nature of disturbed marital interaction. *Rational Living*, 1965, *1*, 22–26.
Ellis, A. & Harper, R. A. *A guide to rational living*. Englewood Cliffs, N. J.: Prentice-Hall, 1961(b).
Ellis, A. & Harper, R. A. *Creative marriage*. New York: Lyle Stuart, 1961(a). Also available in a Tower paperback, retitled *The marriage bed*.
Harper, R. A. Marriage counseling as a rational process-oriented psychotherapy. *Journal of Individual Psychology*, 1960, *16*, 192–207.
Oates, W. J. (Ed.). *The Stoic and Epicurean philosophers*. New York: Random House, 1940.

CHAPTER 15

Male and Female Roles in Marriage Counseling

Aaron L. Rutledge

In no other relationship do the two-sided needs of humanity—i.e., the need for individuality and the need for nearness through relationship—find such opportunities for fulfillment and for threat as is present in modern marriage. The way this drama of need is lived out will be vitally related to the role perception of husband and wife.

Once men were men and women were women and both were glad of it, or so the popular songs would have it. It seemed enough for the dictionary to define *male* as the sex "which begets young" and *masculine* as denoting that which is opposite to female, especially vigor, strength, and independence. *Female* described that sex which "conceives and brings forth young," and *feminine* delineated those qualities which are opposite to male; i.e., those deeper, more tender, more gracious qualities.

Today the picture is not so clear. Separately and collectively, the many social forces making for the revolution and evolution in the American family scene during the last half-century have torn down the distinctions in male and female roles. In the emancipation of women the only way many knew to become "equal" was to become "male." Usurpation of the male role became the goal of the day, not true self-determination. Thus history has witnessed a few generations of lost women who have in turn helped produce generations of inadequate males. Slowly, some women are finding their way out of this morass into an awareness of selfhood that permits the flexibility to find one's way through the varied and cyclic course of life. More slowly, men are beginning to rediscover themselves and become more adequate mates and fathers of children.

But the sources of confusion have not been put to rest. For thousands of youth the stereotype of the patriarchal family is taught at one level, the highly distorted democratic ideal at another, and what is practiced may be hardly recognizable from the viewpoint of either. The conflict between these positions, within the individual and between the couple, comes to fruition in the marital stress or apathy which leads to the counselor's office.

Reprinted with permission of the author and the publisher from *Pastoral Psychology*, October, 1962.

Let us examine a few of the ways in which perceptions of what is male and female influence marriage relationships, especially as seen in the re-enactment of sibling and parent-child conflicts, in contrast with adult man-woman relationships.

I. *Sex against sex, or sibling rivalry.* Along with learned stereotypes of what is male and female, together with the fact of conflicting and overlapping stereotypes, an individual may react as if men and women were different kinds of creatures, either to be avoided or used as pawns in life's struggle. This can amount to the worst aspects of extreme sibling rivalry in a marriage, with sides chosen along sexual lines.

These stereotyped expectations, full of inconsistencies, become the major tools whereby two immature adults put on costumes and enter into the contest of marriage to see who can get the most out of it, with little ability to live spontaneously or to share. When children are born to such a spurious union, they become further sibling competitors in the juvenile tug of war for "my way, my rights, my pleasure, my, my . . . mine."

Example: A wife is highly offended that her husband has a girl friend. She misses the contest-oriented life which they once enjoyed. Early in marriage she changed jobs repeatedly to keep a salary larger than his. He traded cars to keep a flashier model than hers. She excelled at polo, but he continued to fall off the horse. Then it was swimming. She outdistanced him and became the rescuer when he almost drowned. He couldn't hit a barn with a scatter gun, whereas she scared him to death clipping cigarets from his lips at ten paces with a pistol. It does not make sense to her that he has surrendered in despair and spends hours just holding a woman's hands listening to music.

The *punching-bag marriage* is based on the philosophy, or rather, con-ditioned reflex, that those of one sex are superior creatures, should get their rights, punish when these are challenged or neglected, and administer additional beatings just to keep the inferior one in line. In the middle-class families where physical violence is taboo, verbal or emotional assaults may be perfected to an art. This demands a somewhat masochistic mate or one who is conditioned to expect and endure the mistreatment, if not "enjoy" it.

In this master-slave relationship in which one exists to serve the other, we see women in the ascendant position as often as men. A common occurrence just before such a couple comes for counseling is that these roles have shifted or been seriously challenged.

II. *The pseudo-therapeutic marriage*, or the reform-based relationship, is another expression of counterfeit marriage. The extent to which some human beings need to remake things is astounding. Some refinish old furniture, some overhaul automobiles, and some get married. This recon-struction may be assumed to be either a male or a female prerogative, although it tends to be generalized. He is going to remake her personal habits or housekeeping. She is going to change his drinking habits, religion, or smell. This phenomenon is seen in many marriages of quite sophisticated people, particularly in its "therapeutic" expression.

When democracy or equality is the ideal, each one may set about to change the other through "understanding and love," but to change him nevertheless. Their primary motivation in coming for counseling is the desire to find another method which will guarantee to change the mate. Such an experimental attitude usually fails because of essential nonpartici-pation in the marriage relationship as a committed adult.

Example: A professional man brings his wife, saying: "I married a Ph.D. becuase I wanted intellectual companionship. She's a bore—prattling about babies, cooking, and the neighborhood. . ." "No! I don't want her to work. I want her to take classes, read intellectual material—higher criticism, semantics, cybernetics . . ." "No. I don't want counseling for myself. You work with her; see me occasionally to tell me what you have learned that I can use to change her."

III. *The parentified marriage*. The central task of growing up is to find one's identity as a human being. This can force the child into trying on various stereotypes of male and female in order to gain from the parents the emotional sustenance so necessary to preserving himself as an entity, however segmentalized or crippled it may leave him.

In the absence of a warm relationship between two adults which would manifest itself in every facet of life, including the sexual, the child is likely to become aware of, and identify with, only the *parental* aspects of being adult. This can lead to a "parentified" type of marriage in which the roles are those of a pseudo child-parent relationship. One of the couple, needing to be an adult through "parenting" another, chooses (or is chosen by) a mate who needs to preserve the only "role" he knows, that of a child. These dynamics become endlessly complicated in that one who fits into either of these patterns is likely to have unconscious needs to play the opposite role. This means that even in a neurotic way the mates cannot be adequate for each other. These marriages make possible a socially acceptable survival, but such child's play is a poor substitute for relatively unencumbered and spontaneous interaction of two "whole" adults. A few common situations illustrate the phenomena.

The *mother-son marriage* is a common expression of the parentified relationship. This is the woman who as a girl saw or experienced only the mothering type of femininity. Mother's affectional and sex life, her relating as a total adult, were absent, hidden, or danger-fraught. As a result the girl was conditioned to express her adulthood only through being a mother, desiring both to emulate and to displace her own mother. Mar-riage becomes a chance for her to get a family for whom she can be a mother. She chooses a man who has to be a boy or needs primarily to be mothered. And there are many such candidates, products of unhappy marriages of crippled men and women. The male child of an unhappy woman is particularly vulnerable, catching the hatred she has for self and for husband because of her unhappy lot.

There may be enough drive toward healthy relations and enough desire to get away from the slavery to his own mother, to push such a youth toward marriage. Yet he has to marry a mother figure, not an adequate, total female.

Many such marriages seem to work quite well for months or even years, depending upon the degree to which the two sets of needs complement each other. A shift in need patterns brings acute conflict. Typically, this woman seeks help because her once fine husband has become a terrible husband. He is drinking, refusing to come home at night, gambling, or "running around." In an oversimplified way, this is what has happened. The marriage was "good" because she served well as the mother he needed, at the same time finding her chief satisfaction in that process. But she has become either such a poor mother that he must rebel or such a good mother that he has grown. When little boys grow, the next step is adolescence and adolescent rebellion. Now he is "sowing wild oats." Good mother to her little-boy husband, she cannot tolerate being a mother-wife to an adolescent-husband. She tightens the reins and he kicks over the traces all the more.

This dilemma, perhaps forcing into consciousness for the first time some of her unrealized potential as a woman, leads to further stress in the marriage. In other marriages, through the process of daily living, the wife grows into a more complete woman and then finds herself endlessly frustrated because the husband cannot shift roles and become an adequate adult male lover and companion.

These marriage types are commonly described as "neurotic complementarity." One person, feeling inadequate and incomplete, unable to live a whole life, finds another who can complement or complete the syndrome of personality need. A woman with strong repressed needs to rebel against what she perceives as the strictures of femaleness, chooses a man who becomes alcoholic, has affairs, or is sexually perverted. She may protest this male freedom or failure and yet wear the robe of female martyrdom with agonizing pride. The fact that she is living out vicariously the repressed side of her crippled self often becomes evident when, through counseling, he begins to make rapid changes toward health. She protests that counseling is making him worse, or she has an affair, begins to drink excessively, or to use drugs, or becomes mentally ill.

Of course, this whole picture may be seen with the wife as the actor-outer and the husband the martyred member of the conspiracy in neurotic living, in which one is the hell-raiser and the other the protector of home, ideals, mores, religious ideals or law, but who, in reality, is just as sick.

IV. *Marriage as adult self-fulfillment.* The complementarity of marriage is by no means limited to the neurotic or crippled components of personality. The basic biology of life is a complementarity of male and female. Such pairing of opposites to gain greater fulfillment permeates the entire life of man. Similarities in appearance, race, religion, education, and social class, although slowly breaking down, have tended to be the rule. However, it becomes increasingly evident that at the emotional level it may be the differentness of the other person, promising to meet unfulfilled personality needs, which really leads to marriage. This is the reciprocity of healthy nearness, two distinct individuals simultaneously making the life of self and of the loved other more complete through spontaneous giving, receiving, and relating. (See Winch's theory of *complementarity*, Jung's concept of *anima* and *animus*, and Rutledge's concept of *nearness*.)

Our culture will not return to clearly defined roles for men and women. Rather, there will be less and less distinction between what is male activity and what is female activity. But, as people become healthier specimens of human nature, the absence of rigid distinctions in function will make less and less difference, and greater flexibility will lead to more creative self-fulfillment through marriage.

ROLE IDENTIFICATION OF THE COUNSELOR

It may be redundant to say that counselors are only human, but an honest attempt should be made by each professional to locate himself and his marriage in the above preview of the kinds of dynamics with which he must work. Psychotherapeutic assistance for the counselor often is indicated, and would speed the process of self-understanding in almost every case. To be blind to these factors in himself, to live a haloed existence as mate and as counselor, is certain to result in client injury if not personal involvement that will threaten his career.

I. *How are responses determined by the counselor's own gender?* It is difficult to say whether the relation between the counselor's biological gender and his responses (whether verbal or emotional) is superficial or fundamental. It is a fact that he is male, or she is female. Yet, if the counselor is fairly healthy and aware of self, responses are less likely to be basically altered by the fact of gender. However, the effect of attitudes and feelings about the fact of gender are crucial. The counselor may have such fixed notions of what is expected in male or female behavior that he judges the client accordingly. Even if he controls himself to the point of saying nothing, his reaction will have registered upon the client. The effect may be essentially the same whether he feels judgmental or just becomes tense because the experience has activated his own sore spots about the "maleness" or "femaleness" within his own personality.

Circumstances can aggravate this problem. For instance, most of the marriage counseling done by a pastor will be requested initially by wives. There are more women than men actively involved in church activities. This loyalty naturally gives the pastor a deep appreciation of women, and may add up to a somewhat solicitous interest in their welfare. This can be quite complicated if, as many clergymen and other counselors do, he neglects his own wife under the guise of serving God, the Church, and Humanity. He can project upon the client's husband his own guilt, as well as hostility, because of his religious apathy. Thus the counselor's total attitude is colored by the preconceptions of an errant male. The husband's experiencing of this as rejection reinforces his own beliefs that his story won't be appreciated and he refuses to return for more of the same. Counselors with problem wives—whether naggers, frigid, or sexual actor-outers—may reject problem behavior of women to such an extent that the female client is repulsed, or guilt elements and other isolated factors are blown up out of proportion.

II. *How is this communicated to the client?* Distorted conceptions of what is male and female in general, and the counselor's biases in particular, may be verbalized to the client. "Most men are that way, you know." "Women have to be the understanding ones, you know." However, of much greater concern are the subtle ways in which the artifacts of male-female evolution are reinforced through stereotyped attitudes unconsciously applied.

Communication of attitudes and feelings is effected through all the senses, not merely verbal exchange. Verbal communication becomes heavily laden with the symbolic, and what is not said may become more powerful than that which is put into words. Stereotyped reactions in an emotionally charged atmosphere may be reinforced by symbolic expressions and by nonverbal messages through bodily tensions, emanations, and movements.

III. *The client's use of role perceptions.* A client may misuse the counselor's own conceptions of himself as male or female. Similarly the client may misuse the counselor's role as perceived by the client. Confusion is compounded when both sets of perceptions are serious distortions of reality.

A counselor may perceive of himself as the great father and protector of mankind. A client who needs to be protected may fall into an incapacitating dependency upon such strength, and cast the counselor in the role of father or mother. Contrariwise, another person may be repelled because this threatens to expose the dependency needs which are being fought and repressed. Whereas the perception of the counselor as an aggressive male lover may drive one woman away, it will seduce another into an erotically tinged *affaire de thérapie* and lead to further alienation from the husband.

The female counselor who has an undue need to "mother" clients will attract some and drive away others. The web of possessiveness, solicitousness, and unnecessary assumption of responsibility for the client can entrap many crippled personalities. When the health within the client begins to assert itself it is difficult for that counselor to let go and extend the freedom necessary to grow.

The ersatz masculinity or femininity of a counselor may repel or fascinate a client, either one to his detriment. One woman refused to return to a counselor after three sessions. She thought him "sincere and no doubt well-trained, but he's more nervous than I am. He either chain smokes or drinks coffee throughout the sessions, or drums incessantly on the desk." Further exploration of her feelings revealed: "He is uncomfortable as a man in the presence of a woman. I don't think he likes being a male."

Other clients, with greater need to distort and reinforce stereotype identifications will adopt the mannerisms, habits, language, and beliefs of the counselor's reactive way of life. Often this intensifies marital conflict because the mate cannot change to meet the new role, and is made increasingly uncomfortable by invidious comparisons to the counselor.

The counselor who is an ineffectual representative of his own gender is particularly at a disadvantage with a client with homosexual tendencies. He threatens to remind the latent or unhappy overt homosexual client of his own inadequacy and pain at a deeper level than can be faced. Or, the

confirmed homosexual sees through the counselor and approaches counseling with attitudes of disdain, exploitation, or homosexual love.

COUNSELOR-CLIENT IDENTIFICATION

Thus far we have been describing the neurotic transference and countertransference of the counseling relationship, along with the intricate
involvements of male-female role perceptions. Actually, whether the counselor is male or female is relatively insignificant in helping most clients. A
healthy counselor can experience a wide range of human emotions,
thoughts, and feelings. Contrary to stereotypical thinking, the ability to
express or understand aggression, strength and courage; or gentleness,
tenderness, and love; or scorn, guilt, and hatred are not gender based.
They are human and equally available within men and women.

The first level of experiencing a counselor may well be at the "transference" level; i.e., the client imputes to the professional what he expects,
both positively and negatively, based upon past experiences. He needs
either to lean on, or to fight, an authority figure, so he casts counselor in
the role of father or mother. He needs to work out unresolved feelings
about siblings, so he sees the counselor as brother or sister in either the
"palsy-walsy" or competitive sense. Religious terminology—father, padre,
brother, sister, mother, etc.—provides the pastoral counselor ready-made
vehicles through which unresolved conflicts can be worked through to
healthier concepts of self. The concept of "doctor" serves a somewhat
similar function.

A client may be concerned at first with the sex of the counselor. For a
while he may identify so strongly as to desire to be of the counselor's sex,
or to be like him in other ways, or he may react to the opposite extreme.
But such role concepts and expectations are merely symptomatic of
deeper needs. These needs are always twofold: at one level, he wants to
play-act a habitual role with someone who will accept it, or to be given a
more effective part to play in the drama of marriage—in three easy lessons.
But at another level the need is to discover the birthright sold for a mess
of role-playing pottage, and become the fulfilled person one was meant to
be. It is here that the counselor's *being* speaks louder than what he says,
cutting through the babble of client confusion, and calling forth the
unrealized potential as a human.

As the client gains insight through *being accepted as he is*, with all his
shortcomings, he has conflicting urges to defend what he is and to become
different. At first this may mean becoming like the counselor—a particularly difficult time in marriage counseling. The client of the same sex as
the counselor may become so "therapeutic" in aping the counselor as to
make life intolerable for the spouse. The client of the opposite sex to the
counselor can find a perfect escape from the pain of personal understanding and growth: "My counselor accepts me as I am, why can't my husband?" "Why can't my husband be like my counselor? So patient, kind,
understanding, so male!" Such thoughts further contaminate the marriage
as the counselor becomes the "other person" in the marriage triangle.

Although this fantasy can be used as an aid to counseling, it must be guided skillfully. Many a counselor meets the challenge of his life as he tries to navigate the ship of therapy between the Charybdis of the client's surging emotional and sexual needs on the one hand, and the Scylla of his own unmet needs on the other.

Back to our individual client who is now trying to become like his counselor. The next cycle of counseling is to help him clarify this need to change, to see it as the desire to become his own unrealized self, not a carbon copy of anyone else. He should be aided in identifying with the counselor, not as a person, but as a representative of the process of becoming, growing, and living effectively.

Whatever the route followed in getting there, most successful marriage counseling goes through the steps of each person's unraveling and becoming able to use insight in these areas: experiencing, although not necessarily understanding, a real person through the relationship with the counselor; gaining some basic understanding of what oneself is like, a little of why, and some beginning acceptance of responsibility for the past and the future; understanding of the mate's feelings and reactions, and giving him some right to be what he is and to feel what he feels; gaining some insight into the nature of the marriage relationship, the interactive process. Then, and usually only then, does the marriage show genuine improvement.

CHAPTER 16

The Role of Nonverbal Communication in Marriage Counseling

Constance C. Ard

Human beings are verbal animals. Even when they are not talking, they are more than likely thinking to themselves in sentences (Ellis, 1962; Ellis & Harper, 1961). So much of human behavior involves verbal interaction that it is easy to overlook the importance of *nonverbal* communication.

The scope of nonverbal modes of communication would include or involve any physical movement or gesture of any portion of the body—facial expressions, glances of the eyes, hand and arm movements, the manner in which an individual sits or walks, and what he expresses as he does these things (Bell, 1886; Spencer, 1910; Allport & Vernon, 1933; Birdwhistell, 1953; Barbara, 1956; Davitz, 1961; Dittman, 1962; Satir, 1964; Ekman, 1964, 1965; Rosenfeld, 1965; Wachtel, 1967). The tone of voice, how one touches another, the manner and style of dress, and the texture of skin around the eyes suggest additional modes of nonverbal communication. All personal mannerisms help to express how the individual feels towards himself, people, and life. In other words, his projection of self-worth and the values he holds may be indicated by his nonverbal communication. Many facets which an individual uses for means of nonverbal communication can be controlled—that is, if he is aware he is communicating nonverbally. Others cannot be controlled that easily. The latter could include a person's facial expressions and the eyes.

> Above all, the therapist must regard behavior and action as baselines of reality and must consider words—including his own—as secondary. If discrepancies arise between talking and doing, action always speaks louder than words. Once the patient has learned to observe action and to base his conclusions upon actions rather than words, he has a basis on which to function [Ruesch, 1963, p. 135].

There is a flaw here, however, in the implied suggestion to accept actions at face value, for there is no suggestion that the therapist verbally

Ard, C. C. Use of nonverbal communication in marriage counseling. *Marriage Counseling Quarterly*, 1968–69, 3–4, 32–45.

and logically "checks out" the nonverbal behavior or actions. Merely accepting the apparent meaning of nonverbal behavior could lead to misperception and projection. Nonverbal communication tends to be less guarded than verbal communication. This is accentuated and reinforced through our training in verbal communication, whereas nonverbal communication is generally disregarded or even discouraged (Beckman, 1963). Because of our careful censorship and control in the use of language, our true ideas and feelings can be camouflaged. Therefore, nonverbal behavior tends to be the more reliable form of communication (i.e., more likely to express one's "true" feelings or thoughts).

Professor Jerome Bruner of Harvard suggests that too much emphasis is placed on verbal communication: ". . . verbalization is not the only way people learn or know [Middleman, 1968, p. 80] ."

Hall (1959) suggests that the "counseling interview is primarily vocal communication between two people. Not what the person says, but how he says it—his intonation, rate of speech, and other expressive behavior—are the chief sources of information for the interview [p. 148] ."

I once had a client who could not (or preferred not to) look at people when they talked. She related that she could not concentrate as well. She also had the tendency not to "get involved" or want to care about others. "People-watching" was enjoyable for this client, but seldom did she look at people who were talking. She had had very little practice in how to handle and cope with people, men and women alike, who wanted to get close to her emotionally. During several interviews, her nonverbal communication was more clear and unguarded than her verbal communication. Part of her "homework" during the week was to practice looking at her boyfriend as he spoke to her, then "check out" her own thoughts and reactions about what she was hearing and observing from him. After several months of listening to and observing significant others, including her boyfriend, she was able to act more comfortably with the increased personalism of these relationships.

Each of us brings his own unique background of experiences to an interpretation of nonverbal cues (Wendt, 1962). This is why it is so important to check out these nonverbal cues by any means (e.g., stop assuming and start asking, check out one's perceptions with others, etc.). Satir (1964) suggested that feelings could be related to facts by asking for specific examples or documentation of each nonverbal behavior the client is referring to. For example, "the therapist can ask the client for data which help to support his perceptions: 'How do you know she doesn't care what you do?' or 'What does he do that makes you feel he is mean?' [p. 170] ." She goes on to say that "the nonverbal is a less clear or explicit communication, so it requires greater attention [p. 78] ."

It is interesting to note that nonverbal forms of communication are an infant's first means of expression. As the child begins to grow and "mature," nonverbal communication still persists; but due to our cultural demands, verbal communication moves into the spotlight. When nonverbal communication is placed in a secondary position, not only is a child's skill hampered in the area of communication, but his personality growth may be affected by diminishing his sensitivity to the natural and social environment, his ability to think critically, and his potential for creativity (Beckman, 1963). As we continue up the path of "maturity," many adults develop a sort of mask, behind which they conceal their true feelings and thoughts. Over the years the mask tends to become one with smaller holes, which can narrow the vision of the beholder.

A possible reason why some individuals may tend to overlook or not be aware of nonverbal communication is its covert nature. With friends and acquaintances we may disagree with a statement that has been made, but seldom do we comment about facial expressions, smiles, etc. Within the counseling arena, however, incongruent nonverbal communication should be questioned in a similar fashion to illogical verbalizations.

Ethnic and class groups differ both in the primary modes of nonverbal behavior and in the extent of their reliance upon nonverbal communication.

William Webster (1967) has observed that when counseling with adult Spanish-Americans and Negroes, the "hands and arms are very important adjuncts to the ability to communicate effectively [p. 1]," whereas counselors possessing middle-class standards generally do not use their hands or arms to communicate to any great extent.

Rowe, Brooks, and Watson (1960) suggest that people unfamiliar with American Indian gesture language are able to understand, through gestures alone, what is being communicated.

Chagall has said, "In mixed company, women practice a sort of visual shorthand, which later, they will laboriously and at great length decode in the company of other women."

Delaney (1968) suggests that "there is no mystical construct necessary for the understanding of emotions communicated by facial expression, hand gestures, and feet and body movements. This communicative ability to express oneself without the use of words is common to all men, cutting across cultural ties [p. 315]." (Cf. Vinacke, 1949; Vinacke & Fong, 1955.)

Other research (Ekman, 1965) on nonverbal behavior suggests that the direction of an individual's motives are indicated through facial expressions while manifestations of intensity of motivation can be observed in the gestures of the lower body. Arthur Rogers (1968) provides an illustration which was made possible through the use of a videotape:

> A young woman viewed herself on a videotape—with the sound turned off. Her gestures were alternately wide open, with hands extended to people, and closed off and restricted (all within the course of a few minutes of speech). Here gestures epitomized her central concern at the time. "That's it," she said. . . . "I don't know whether to be open or closed" [p. 39].

The use of the video tape when counseling with married couples presents a vast source of the "here and now" behaviors and verbalizations.

One can record the nonverbal as well as the verbal then immediately playback the information and "check it out" with the client. (See also Chapter 48, "Information-Gathering Techniques of Value in Marriage Counseling.")

NONVERBAL COMMUNICATION IN THE COUNSELING SESSION

How and why is nonverbal communication an important aspect in marriage, family, and child counseling? In the pages to follow I will describe the relationship of this introductory material to the counseling task. Illustrations have been drawn from the experience of colleagues as well as from my own clients and research.

When a new client comes to the office for marriage counseling, a handshake usually takes place. The handshake between the marriage counselor and his client is an indicator of some nonverbal communication. This was illustrated in an episode in the comic strip *Peanuts* (Schultz, 1966): Lucy is playing the role of the psychiatrist, whose help costs in this instance, 5 cents. (Don't let the cost fool you!) She has her hand extended to her client, good ole Charlie Brown, who asks, "What are you doing?" Lucy responds, "I want to shake your hand. . . . A doctor sometimes can tell a lot about a patient merely by shaking his hand. . . ." They shake hands. Lucy remarks: "Mercy, I can't believe it." "What's the matter?" asks Charlie. Lucy continues, "It's fantastic! I never would have believed it. The things you can learn about someone just by shaking his hand!" Charlie asks, "What's the matter?" Lucy responds, "I can't tell you. . . . This is one of those things that can never be discussed with a patient! It's much better that you don't know. Actually, I still can't believe it. I just can't believe it. . . ." As Lucy walks away Charlie is left standing, responding with his mouth wide open, "AAUGH!"

I suggest that as a counselor one *must* share these insights because they can be valuable in helping clients better understand their own behavior.

Let us consider some case illustrations of how married couples react to, or function with, nonverbal communication. One couple seen for marriage counseling devoted much talk to the areas of affection and making love. There were complaints that the husband was more affectionate before marriage than after; that he "stroked" his mate more while courting and "whispered sweet nothings in her ear"; but now that he has her "hooked," he can "relax". And she had assumed that after they were married and had a child, certain of his annoying behaviors would change—they did not, they were just more frequent.

Throughout the period of counseling I saw this couple together several times and observed that *nonverbal* cues were being exchanged. They usually sat apart from each other. When one partner did not like something the mate said, sharp glances of the eyes and a general tightness of the body would follow. I asked them if they were aware of this nonverbal behavior and how it seemed to reinforce what they were saying verbally. At times they were aware of it, but they did not "check it out." They reported just feeling "hotter under the collar." In fact, one reaction of the husband was to light another cigarette and look down or away from his wife while he continued to speak. We proceeded to work on what each person expected from the other in terms of *nonverbal* affection and reinforcement, as well as *what* they were saying to each other and *how* they were saying it.

Another couple was experiencing a different kind of communication difficulty. This couple communicated more on the nonverbal level than on the verbal. At times, they caused each other psychological hurts, as each neglected to check-out the messages that were received. Other times one partner would take a change in the tone of voice of the spouse as a personal affront, while the sender of the message would be unaware of a tone change. This couple was given a "homework" task of answering a nonverbal worksheet which caused them to stop and analyze how they were interacting, as well as how they interacted with their children. After several sessions and several weeks of working daily on their given home-work, they began to improve in their accuracy of both nonverbal and verbal communications. This helped to foster a freer, healthier relation-ship. They were instructed also to "stop assuming and start asking," which became easier with practice.

In the two examples cited, it was evident to the counselor that there was a great deal of nonverbal exchange, but the couples were unaware of it or did not check out what meanings they were perceiving. It appears to me, that in addition to various "homework" assignments which can help the couple learn how to communicate (on all levels) more congruently, the use of the video tape also could help the couples increase their aware-ness of the multiple channels of their communication. The video tape provides an immediate and accurate feedback which can be rerun as often as necessary.

Alger and Hogan (1967) suggest that by viewing videotape playbacks married couples can develop an "increased awareness of the activities and feelings of both marital partners [p. 1426]." This procedure would help them to become more aware of the many different messages they are sending. For example "one husband asked that the tape be stopped and said to his wife, 'You know, when you were talking there, I was feeling very tender and concerned and loving toward you, and yet as I see myself on the TV, I see that no one would ever know I was feeling that way by my bland look.' His wife then spoke, and as she did, tears were in their eyes. 'I didn't feel your caring then, but I feel it now' [Alger & Hogan, 1967, p. 1427]." This example illustrates how the nonverbal and verbal messages sometimes do not complement one another. By each person's becoming more attentive to his spouse's total communication or to the relationship between the nonverbal and verbal communication, errors are less likely to occur, and the partners can become more congruent if they continue to practice and work on their new knowledge.

Carl Rogers (1961) offers some food for thought regarding the ability to recognize congruence and incongruence within individuals, which could be applied to the marital situation:

With some individuals we realize that in most areas this person not only consciously means exactly what he says, but that his deepest feelings also match what he is expressing, whether it is anger or competitiveness or affection or cooperativeness. . . . Obviously, then, different individuals differ in their degree of congruence, and the same individual differs at different moments in degree of congruence, depending on what he is experiencing and whether he can accept this experience in his awareness, or must defend himself against it [p. 342].

Problems regarding "body language" between spouses come up quite often in sexual relations. Communicating through touch is often related to love-making. Mating is, according to Frank (1958),

tactile communication, reinforced and elaborated by motor activities and language, by concomitant stimulation, visual, auditory, olfactory, gustatory, and the deeper muscle senses, combined to provide an organic-personality relationship which may be one of the most intense human experiences . . . [p. 61].

Frank's theory of "tactile communication," in summary, suggests that "the skin functions as the organ of communication—both as a receptor and transmitter of messages. . . . In many interpersonal relations, tactile language functions most effectively and communicates more fully than vocal language [p. 35]."

Frank also states that "the elementary sexual process of the human organism may be transformed and focused into an interpersonal love relationship with an identified person to whom each is seeking to communicate, *using sex not for procreation . . . but as another language*, for interpersonal communication [p. 61]."

One particular couple I saw was faced with such a situation. The husband, in this case, had been approached by another woman desiring to have sex with him. There had been available opportunities for this new twosome to go to bed, but they stopped at the heavy petting stage. The wife knew about the other woman; in fact they were friends. There was no desire on either the husband's or the other woman's part to have sex relations for procreative reasons, only to partake in another form of communication.

Another example of a breakdown in nonverbal communication between partners appeared in the couple who had been married for twenty years. When questioned by the marriage counselor, the husband was unable to report whether or not his wife ever had had orgasm. This is a strong indicator of going-through-the-mechanical-motions of sex, but never being aware of, or "tuned in" to, the many nonverbal cues or indications present in the love-making experience.

To help illustrate a few of the tactual difficulties some people experience, perhaps Rollo May's (1966) statement would be appropriate:

It is a strange fact in our society that what goes into building a relationship—the sharing of tastes, fantasies, dreams, hopes for the future, and fears from the past—seems to make people more shy and vulnerable than going to bed with each other. They are more wary of the tenderness that goes with psychological and spiritual nakedness than they are of physical nakedness in sexual intimacy [p. 21].

NONVERBAL COMMUNICATION IN CHILDREN

Children tend to use nonverbal communication automatically until adults interfere or fail to respond. Most children are very adept at communicating and reading nonverbal communication.

Much has been written discussing therapy with children. Moreno (1946), Moustakus (1953), and Axline (1947) are a few who have written about, and worked with, children in play therapy. Play therapy gives the child an opportunity to act what he is thinking and feeling in the "here and now."

It would be helpful when working with children in play therapy to have intermittent periods for verbal discussion of some of the child's nonverbal behavior, to describe it and perhaps interpret together its meaning and use. Beier (1966) has suggested that children may use facial expressions, gestures, and silences to express their emotions. Also valuable within the child's communicative framework are his toys. Children learn rather quickly that certain behaviors will elicit certain adult responses, including specific uses of toys.

Examples of how a child might communicate two different messages would be his verbal expression of warmth toward a person while his body was very tight and rigid; his saying everything is fine while he's sobbing; saying that he does not have a stomach ache while he is clutching at his stomach; and when questioned regarding a fight with a boy at school, giving a verbal response "no" about his involvement while his facial expressions say "yes" he was involved and his voice pitch changes. When a child's nonverbal and verbal communications are in conflict, they call for further checking out by the receivers.

Nonverbal communication can be said, then, to have a prime position in the family structure of interaction. How might a greater awareness of nonverbal communication help the members of a family unit? There are several ways. It can help parents to understand their children and spouses to understand one another by providing an additional avenue of communication. Attention to nonverbal communication may help family members understand nonfamily persons better (e.g., friends, people with different cultural backgrounds, etc.). Even though children are frequently ahead of adults in understanding nonverbal communication, children can still benefit from being helped to "read" siblings' and parents' nonverbal behavior more accurately. Attention to one's own nonverbal communication may help each individual family member to understand himself better, especially those messages he is communicating to others without awareness. In so far as family members can improve their skills at understanding nonverbal communication, they will probably increase their ability to get their wants, needs, and desires met more adequately, inside the family as well as outside. They probably would be more creative and more spontaneous in their nonverbal reactions, so the quality of their interpersonal relations in general should increase due to the increased variety of their behaviors.

Adults who use nonverbal communication often seem unaware of doing so. They seem to be poor at interpreting cues of their own because they are unaware of other adults' nonverbal communication. Some use this ability easily and readily with children but not with other adults. It is as if they do not have the time or patience to do so with adults. The family counseling setting can provide an excellent opportunity for family members to learn how to recognize the various types of messages they are sending. It would also provide family members the opportunity to learn how to "check-out" certain nonverbal messages, instead of falling into the "over-psychologizing" trap. There may not be some deep, dark, negative reason for a person's behavior—Freud notwithstanding—and reading interpretation *into* behavior can be a serious mistake.

Modes of nonverbal communication in a family group probably allow adults to teach children indirectly what to believe and how to behave. Beier (1966), in dissecting the "anatomy of a message," distinguishes between a "persuasive" message, in which "the sender codes his message in full awareness of what he is doing," and an "evoking" message. Beier goes on to say, "Repeated persuasive messages will create certain value systems in the child without his ever becoming aware of where he learned these values [p. 12]."

Satir (1964) explains how the counselor can relate silence to covert controls: The counselor says, "I saw you looking at mother. Were you thinking she didn't want you to speak? Maybe you think if you speak you'll get clobbered. We'll have to find out what makes it so unsafe to talk [p. 167]."

When the counselor is working with a family unit, video tape is again valuable. More than likely the family members are unaware of the discrepancy between their nonverbal and verbal communications. The video tape can record these discrepant responses, and then be replayed, dissected, and clarified by the family members. It would provide them with a close and immediate look at *what* and *how* they are saying something and how other members of the family react—nonverbally as well as verbally. Hopefully, this will help sharpen each person's awareness of his unique behaviors and how he functions within his family. If adults and children alike can learn how to express appropriately what they think and feel, even on controversial issues or in once taboo areas, then the nonverbal communication would be a means to support the growth of creative, spontaneous, healthy interpersonal behavior.

A QUESTIONNAIRE ON NONVERBAL CUES

I prepared a list of questions regarding nonverbal cues and responses, which was sent to parents but elicited very little response. This indicated to me that many parents are not aware of these nonverbal cues. This questionnaire has been given as a homework task to couples who are having communication difficulties. My goal is that by pondering the questions and searching for answers, the couple will show a valuable carry-over into their personal interactions. The questions are:

What differences have you noted in your individual children's abilities to "read" you nonverbally? How do you as parents interpret or "check out" this nonverbal communication?

In what manner does your child interpret or "check out" nonverbal communication? Does he/she experiment, try different behavior?

Can you tell your child's inner feelings from the way he/she sits in your lap, or leans against you, or touches you (i.e., interacts nonverbally)? Are these messages the same for each child (if there is more than one)? Do they change over time?

Before your child learned to talk, what were some of the best indications that he/she gave to you of his/her desires, feelings, wishes, and needs?

In what ways do children communicate nonverbally among themselves? Are they better at this than adults?

What part of your child's or spouse's body most clearly gives away (i.e., nonverbally) their innermost state?

What changes in nonverbal communication have you noticed in your children as they progress from infancy, through childhood, adolescence, and into maturity?

What are the first signs you notice in your spouse or children that foretell "trouble ahead"?

Can you recall an instance when you received two conflicting messages— one verbal, one nonverbal? Which is a more reliable indicator of the sender's inner state? Why or how do you know?

Do any members of your family (spouse or children) tend to give nonverbal cues to their psychological state (for example, a visible build-up of tension) before they reveal it to you verbally? How do you know?

Are there any nonverbal signs by which you are able to understand your spouse better? Please describe them.

Can you describe an instance of a nonverbal cue which told you a different message than the verbal message that your spouse was giving to you at the time?

What signs does your spouse evince (other than verbal communication) which are "dead give-a-ways" of his/her inner state (e.g., wiggle feet; pull ear; drum on table)? What do these signs mean?

Do you and your spouse have any nonverbal cues or signals which you use to communicate in situations where you do not want other people to catch your meaning (e.g., at parties, in front of children, etc.)?

Parents, and children alike need to sharpen their level of awareness as to what they are saying, both with their words and with their body language. If more attention were devoted to this within the family unit, fewer breakdowns in communication would be presented to the marriage and family counselor. The assistance of the counselor in teaching the family how to look more carefully and listen more thoroughly to the body and verbal exchanges could be indeed an enriching and growing experience.

Just as a painting is more than the sum of its physical ingredients, so true meaning is often found only in the Gestalt of a total communicative action; that is, in the combined effect of its words, sounds and movements, but not in the communication significance of any single element by itself [Knapp, 1963, p. 153].

In the process of evaluating ourselves and our relationships to the world about us, we tend to rely on words rather than facts. The healthier and the more aware a person is, the more accurate a map he creates of himself, and the more he "knows himself," as he is and not as he feels he should be. A map can never represent all of its territory; one's self-evaluation in and of itself omits certain details of one's actual self—we never know ourselves completely [Barbara, 1956, p. 289].

Our work as counselors, psychologists, psychiatrists and physicians working with couples, families, and children needs a closer examination. What are *we* saying, and how are *we* saying it?

REFERENCES

Alger, I. & Hogan, P. The use of videotape recordings in conjoint marital therapy. *American Journal of Psychiatry* May, 1967, *73*, 1425–1430.

Allport, & Vernon, P. *Studies in expressive movement.* New York: Macmillan, 1933.

Axline, Virginia. *Play Therapy.* New York: Houghton Mifflin, 1947.

Barbara, D. A. The value of nonverbal communication in personality understanding. *Journal of Nervous and Mental Disease* 1956, *123*, 286–291.

Beckman, D. R. The fifth language arts: non-verbal communication. *Elementary English*, February 1963.

Beier, E. G. *The silent language of psychotherapy.* Chicago: Aldine, 1966.

Bell C. *Anatomy and philosophy of expression as connected with the fine arts.* (7th ed.) London: G. Bell & Sons, 1886.

Birdwhistell, R. *Introduction to kinesics.* Louisville, Kentucky: University of Louisville Press, 1953.

Davitz, F. & Davitz, J. L. Nonverbal vocal communication of feeling. *Journal of Communication*, June 1961, *11*, 81–86.

Delaney, D. J. Sensitization to non-verbal communications. *Counselor Education and Supervision* Spring, 1968, *7*, 315–316.

Dittman, A. T. The relationship between body movements and moods in interviews. *Journal of Consulting Psychology*, 1962, *26*, 480.

Ekman, P. Body position, facial expression and verbal behavior during interviews. *Journal of Abnormal and Social Psychology*, 1964, *68*, 295–301.

Ekman, P. Communication through nonverbal behavior: a source of information about interpersonal relationship. In S. S. Tomkins & C. B. Izard (Eds.), *Affect, cognition and personality.* New York: Springer Press, 1965. Pp. 390–442.

Ellis, A. *Reason and emotion in psychotherapy.* New York: Lyle Stuart, 1962.

Ellis, A. & Harper, R. *A guide to rational living.* Englewood Cliffs, New Jersey, 1961.

Frank, L. Tactile Communication. *ETC.,* Autumn, 1958, *16*, 31–79.

Fretz, B. Postural movements in a counseling dyad. *Journal of Counseling Psychology*, 1966, *13*, No. 3.

Hall, E. *The silent language.* Conn.: Fawcett, 1959.

Knapp, P. *Expression of the emotions in man.* New York: International University Press, 1963.

May, R. An antidote for the new puritanism. *Saturday Review*, March 26, 1966.

Middleman, R. R. *The non-verbal method in working with groups.* New York: Association Press, 1968.

Moreno, J. L. *Psychodrama.* New York: Beacon House, 1946.

Moustakas, C. E. *Children in play therapy.* New York: McGraw-Hill, 1953.

Rogers, A. H. Videotape feedback in group psychotherapy. *Psychotherapy: Theory, Research and Practice*, Winter, 1968, *5*, 37–39 (1).

Rogers, C. *On becoming a person.* Boston: Houghton Mifflin, 1961.

Rosenfeld, H. Gestural and verbal communication of interpersonal affect. Paper read at Midwestern Psychological Association meetings, 1965.

Rowe, F., Brooks, S., & Watson, B. Communication through gestures. *American Annual of the Deaf*, 1960, *105*, 232–237.

Ruesch, J. The Role of communication in therapeutic transactions. *The Journal of Communication*, September, 1963.

Satir, V. *Conjoint family therapy: a guide to theory and technique.* Palo Alto, Calif.: Science and Behavior Books, 1964.

Schultz. *Peanuts*. San Francisco *Chronicle* (United Feature Syndicate, Inc.), November 6, 1966.

Spencer, H. *Principles of psychology*. Vol. 2. New York and London: Appleton Press, 1910.

Vinacke, W. E. The judgment of facial expression by three national-racial groups in Hawaii: I. Caucasian faces. *Journal of Personality*, June, 1949, *17*, 407–429.

Vinacke, W. E., & Fong, R. W. The judgment of facial expressions by three national-racial groups in Hawaii: II. Oriental Faces. *Journal of Social Psychology*, May, 1955, *41*, 185–195.

Wachtel, P. L. An approach to the study of body language in psychotherapy. *Psychotherapy: Theory, Research and Practice*, August, 1967, *4*, 97–100 (3).

Webster, W. Gestures in Counseling. *Newsletter of the California Counseling and Guidance Association*, February, 1967, *7*, 1–3 (3).

Wendt, P. R. The language of pictures. In S. I. Hayakawa (Ed.), *The use and misuse of language*. Greenwich, Conn.: Premier Book, 1962.

CHAPTER 17

The Use of Family Theory
in Clinical Practice

Murray Bowen

In little more than one decade, family psychiatry has evolved from the relative unknown to a position of recognized importance on the psychiatric scene. The term "family therapy," or some variation of it, is known to the informed lay person. What is the origin and current status of the "family movement"? I believe it is a "movement," which I shall attempt to convey in this paper. Since there is disagreement even among leaders of the family movement about some of the critical theoretical and therapeutic issues, any attempt to explain or describe the family movement will represent the bias and viewpoint of the author. In this paper I shall present some of my ideas about circumstances that gave rise to the family movement and some ideas about the current status and future potential of the movement. The main body of the paper will be a presentation of my own theoretical orientation, which provides a blueprint for the clinical use of family psychotherapy.

I believe that the family movement began in the early and mid-1950's and that it grew out of an effort to find more effective treatment methods for the more severe emotional problems. In a broad sense, I believe it developed as an extension of psychoanalysis, which had finally achieved general acceptance as a treatment method during the 1930's. Psychoanalysis provided useful concepts and procedures for the mass need of World War II, and a "new" era in psychiatry began. Within the course of a few years psychiatry became a hopeful, promising specialty for thousands of young physicians. Membership in the American Psychiatric Association increased from 3,684 in 1945 to 8,534 in 1955. Psychoanalytic theory had explanations for the total range of emotional problems, but standard psychoanalytic treatment techniques were not effective with the more severe emotional problems. Eager young psychiatrists began experimenting with numerous variations in the treatment method. I believe the study of the family was one of these new areas of interest.

Reprinted with permission of the author and the publisher from *Comprehensive Psychiatry*, 1966, 7, 345–374.

There are those who say the family movement is not new and that it goes back twenty-five years or more. There is some evidence to support the thesis that current family emphasis evolved slowly as the early psychoanalytic formulations about the family were put into clinical practice. In 1909 Freud (1949) reported the treatment of "Little Hans," in which he worked with the father instead of the child. In 1921 Flugel (1960) published his well-known book, *The Psycho-analytic Study of the Family*. There was the development of child analysis and the beginning of the child guidance movement, in which it became standard procedure for a social worker or second therapist to work with parents in addition to the primary-psychotherapy with the child. Later, the child guidance principles were adapted to work with adults, both in inpatient and outpatient settings, in which a social worker or second therapist worked with relatives to supplement the primary psychotherapy with the patient. With these early theoretical and clinical awarenesses of the importance of the family, there is accuracy to the statement that "family" is not new. However, I believe that the current family direction is sufficiently important, new, and different to be viewed as a movement. I shall review some of the theoretical and clinical issues that seem important in this development.

Psychoanalytic theory was formulated from a detailed study of the individual patient. Concepts about the family were derived more from the patient's perceptions than from direct observation of the family. From this theoretical position, the focus was on the patient and the family was outside the immediate field of theoretical and therapeutic interest. Individual theory was built on a medical model with its concepts of etiology, the diagnosis of pathology in the patient, and treatment of the sickness in the individual. Also inherent in the model are the subtle implications that the patient is the helpless victim of a disease or malevolent forces outside his control. A conceptual dilemma was posed when the most important person in a patient's life was considered to be the cause of his illness, and pathogenic to him. Psychiatrists were aware that the model did not quite fit, and there were attempts to tone down the implicit starkness of the concepts, but the basic model remained. For instance, the concept of the unconscious postulated that the parent could be unconsciously hurtful while trying to help the child. This was different from what it would be if the hurt had been intentional or an irresponsible act of omission, but it still left the parent as "pathogenic." There were efforts to modify diagnostic labels, and there were even suggestions that labels be discarded, but a *patient* requires a *diagnosis* for his *illness* and psychiatry still operates with a medical model.

One of the most significant developments in the family movement, which distinguishes it from previous "family" work, is a change in the basic treatment process. Since the beginning of psychoanalysis, the analysis and resolution of the transference has been viewed as the primary therapeutic force for the treatment of emotional illness. Though modified by different "schools," the "therapeutic relationship" is the basic therapeutic modality used by most psychiatrists. The confidential, personal, and private nature of the relationship is considered essential for good therapy. Over the years there have been methods, rules, and even laws to guard this privacy. Since the beginning of the child guidance movement there have been efforts to involve the family in "treatment," but the "therapeutic" patient-therapist relationship was protected against intrusion and the family assigned secondary importance. Among those who initiated the current family movement were psychiatrists who, in addition to the patient's dilemma, began to pay more attention to the family side of the problem.

I believe the current family movement was started by several different investigators, each working independently, who began with either a theoretical or a clinical notion that the family was important. As the focus shifted from the individual to the family, each was confronted with the dilemma of describing and conceptualizing the family relationship system. Individual theory did not have a conceptual model for a relationship system. Each investigator was "on his own" in conceptualizing his observations. One of the interesting developments has been the way investigators first conceptualized the system and the ways these concepts have been modified in the past ten years. There were terms for the distortion and rigidity, the reciprocal functioning, and the "interlocking," "binding," "stuck togetherness" of the system. The following illustrates some of the terms used by a few of the early investigators. Lidz and Fleck (1957) used the concept "schism and skew," and Wynne and his co-workers (1958) used the concept "pseudomutuality." Ackerman, one of the earliest workers in the field, presented a conceptual model in his 1956 paper, "Interlocking Pathology in Family Relationships." He also developed a therapeutic method which he calls "family therapy," which might be described as observing, demonstrating, and interpreting the "interlocking" to the family as it occurs in the family sessions. Jackson and his co-workers (Bateson, Jackson, Haley & Weakland, 1956) used a different model with the concept of the "double bind." As I perceived his original position, he used communication theory to account for the relationship system and individual theory to account for functioning in the individual. His "conjoint family therapy," which I interpret as the joining of individuals in family therapy, would be consistent with his conceptual scheme. I conceived of a preexisting emotional "stuck-togetherness," the "undifferentiated family ego mass," and developed a therapeutic method for which I have used the term "family psychotherapy," which is designed to help individuals differentiate themselves from the "mass." Other investigators used a spectrum of slightly different terms to describe and conceptualize the same family phenomenon. As the years pass, the original concepts tend to be less "different."

CURRENT STATUS AND POSSIBLE FUTURE OF
THE FAMILY MOVEMENT

The family movement is currently in what I have called a "healthy, unstructured state of chaos." The early investigators arrived at "family therapy" after preliminary clinical investigation and research. There may have been one exception to this general statement, recounted by Bell (1961), one of the earliest workers in the field. He misinterpreted a statement about psychotherapy for the family, following which he worked out his own plan to begin seeing family members together. After the idea of "family therapy" was introduced, the number of family therapists began to multiply each year. Most went directly into family therapy from their orientation in individual theory. Group therapists modified group therapy for work with families. As a result, the term "family therapy" is being used to refer to such a variety of different methods, procedures, and techniques that the term is meaningless without further description or definition. I consider this "healthy," because once a therapist begins seeing multiple family members together, he is confronted with new clinical phenomena not explained by individual theory, he finds that many previous concepts have become superfluous, and he is forced to find new theoretical concepts and new therapeutic techniques. The increasing number of family conferences become forums for discussion of experiences and acquiring new ways to conceptualize the family phenomenon.

A high percentage of therapists are using the term "family" to designate therapy methods in which two or more generations (usually parents and children) attend the sessions together, the term "marital therapy" when two spouses are seen together, and "individual therapy" when only one family member is seen by the therapist. The one most widely held concept of "family therapy," both within the profession and by the public, is that of entire families (usually parents and children) meeting together with the therapist while the family acquires the ability to verbalize and communicate thoughts and feelings to each other, with the therapist sitting alongside to facilitate the process and to make observations and interpretations. This I have called "family group therapy." In my experience, this can be amazingly effective as a short-term process for improving family communication. Even a slight improvement in communication can produce dramatic shifts in the feeling system, and even a period of exhilaration. I have not been able to use this as a long-term method for resolving underlying problems.

Although the family movement may continue to focus on "therapy" for many years to come, I believe the greatest contribution of "family" will come from the theoretical. I think the family movement rests on solid ground, that we have hardly scratched the surface in family research, and that "family" will grow in importance with each passing generation. The study of the family provides a completely new order of theoretical models for thinking about man and his relationship to nature and the universe. Man's family is a *system* which I believe follows the laws of natural systems. I believe knowledge about the family system may provide the pathway for getting beyond static concepts and into the functional concepts of systems. I believe that family can provide answers to the medical model dilemma of psychiatry, that family concepts may eventually become the basis for a new and different theory about emotional illness, and this in turn will make its contribution to medical science and practice.

THEORETICAL AND CLINICAL ORIENTATION OF THE AUTHOR

The primary goal of this presentation is to describe a specific theoretical and therapeutic system in which family theory serves as a blueprint for the therapist in doing family psychotherapy and also as a useful theoretical framework for a variety of clinical problems. A family orientation is so different from the familiar individual orientation that it has to be experienced to be appreciated. It is difficult for a person who thinks in terms of individual theory, and who has not had clinical experience with families, to "hear" family concepts. Some are better able to hear abstract theoretical ideas while others hear simple clinical examples. The first part of this section is designed as a bridge between individual and family orientations. To provide a variety of bridges, it will include a spectrum of clinical observations, broad abstract ideas, theoretical concepts, and some of my experiences as I shifted from an individual to a family frame of reference.

My family experience covers twelve years and over ten thousand hours of observing families in family psychotherapy. For the first five years of family practice I also did some individual psychotherapy, and I had a few patients in psychoanalysis. The term "family psychotherapy" was reserved for the process when two or more family members were seen together. The technical effort was to analyze the already existing emotional process between the family members and toward keeping myself emotionally disengaged, which I called "staying out of the transference." This will be discussed later. During those years I used the term "individual psychotherapy" for the process when only one family person was seen. I had not dealt with my own emotional functioning sufficiently nor developed techniques to avoid a transference, and there was the "either-or" distinction between family and individual psychotherapy. I considered it *family* when the emotional process could be contained within the family, and *individual* when this was not possible. During those years, another evolutionary process was taking place. After having spent thousands of hours sitting with families, it became increasingly impossible to see a single person without "seeing" his total family sitting like phantoms alongside him. This perception of one person as a segment of the larger family system had governed the way I thought about, and responded to, the individual, and it had changed my basic approach to psychotherapy. For the past seven years my practice has been devoted entirely to "family" psychotherapy, although about one-third of the hours are spent with only one member of a family. The volume of clinical experience has been in private practice where an average clinical load of forty families are seen with a maximum of thirty hours per week. In past years only a few families have been seen more than once a week, and an increasing number do as well with less frequent appointments. It has been difficult to communicate the notion of avoiding a transference and "family" psychotherapy with only one family member. It is my hope that this can be better clarified in this paper.

A number of facets of the human phenomenon come into view in observing family members together that are obscured with any composite of individual interviews. Any person who exposes himself to daily observations of families as they relate to, and interact with, each other is confronted with a whole new world of clinical data that do not fit individual conceptual models. I use the terms "relate to" and "interact with" because these are a few of the inadequate terms that have been used to describe the family phenomenon. Actually, family members are *being*, and *doing*, and *acting*, and *interacting*, and *transacting*, and *communicating*, and *pretending*, and *posturing* in such a variety of ways that structure and order are hard to see. There is something wrong with any single term that has been used. To this point, family research has gone toward selecting certain areas for detailed, controlled study. In 1957 one of my research associates (Dysinger) did a study called "The Action Dialogue in an Intense Relationship," which was an attempt to blank out words and do a coherent "dialogue" from one period of gross action between a mother and daughter. Birdwhistell (1952) and Scheflen (1964) have made a significant contribution in their precise definition of "kinesics," "body language" system, automatic in all relationships. One of the popular areas for study has been "communication," which on the simplest level is verbal communication. There have been the linguistic studies and the different communications that are conveyed by nuances in tone of voice, inflection, and ways of speaking—communications that each person learns in infancy and uses without "knowing" he knows it. Bateson, Jackson, and co-workers (Bateson, *et al.*, 1956), from analysis of verbal communication, developed their concept of the "double bind," which has to do with conflicting messages in the same statement. There is also the area of nonverbal communication and extrasensory perception, which operates with fair accuracy in some families. There is an advantage in using terms such as "communication" or "transactional" system in that each lends itself to more precise research analysis. The disadvantage is in the narrowness of the concept and the necessity of using a broad interpretation of the concept. For instance, under "communication" theory it becomes necessary to assume the full range of verbal, action, nonverbal, extrasensory, and feeling communication, plus other modalities such as a visceral response in one family member to anxiety or a mood shift in another. However one approaches the family, each investigator has to choose his own way of conceptualizing the family phenomenon.

One striking group of clinical patterns, present to some degree in all families, will provide a brief view of the family relationship system. These follow the general pattern of the family process that diagnoses, classifies, and assigns characteristics to certain family members. Observations may prove reasonably consistent, periodically consistent, or inconsistent with the family pronouncements about the situation. The "family projection process" by which a family problem is transmitted to one family member by years of nagging pronouncements, and then fixed there with a diagnosis, has been discussed in detail in another paper (Bowen, 1959). Family assignments that overvalue are as unrealistic as those that devalue, though the ones that devalue are more likely to come within the province of the psychiatrist. The diagnosed one may resist the family pronouncement and precipitate a family debate; or he may alternately resist and accept; or he may invite it, at which time the assigned characteristic becomes an operational *fact*. Family debates on subjects such as "rejection," "love," and "hostility" will force the therapist to reevaluate his own use of such terms. As I see "rejection," it is one of the most useful mechanisms for maintaining equilibrium in a relationship system. It goes on constantly between people, usually unmentioned. At one point in the family process someone makes a fuss about "rejection" and the debate starts. At a point when rejection is present throughout the family, the one who claims "rejection" is usually more rejecting of the other, rather than the obverse being true. Positive statements about the presence or absence of "love," with reactions and counterreactions, can occupy the scene while there is no objective evidence of change in "love" within the family. Whatever love *is*, it is factual that many family members react strongly to statements about it. The misuse and overuse of the concept "hostility" is another in the same category. The same can apply to terms such as "masculine," "feminine," "aggressive," "passive," "homosexual," and "alcoholic."

The use of the term "alcoholic" provides a good example. In one family, two generations of descendants referred to a grandfather as alcoholic. He had been successful and fairly responsible except to his wife, who was a very anxious woman. He found reason to stay away from her and he did drink moderately. The wife's label was accepted by the children and transmitted to the grandchildren. A recent consultation with another family illustrates another aspect of the problem. A wife had presented the details of her husband's alcoholism. I asked for the husband's view of the problem. He agreed he had a real drinking problem. When asked how much he drank, he flared with, "Listen Buster! When I tell you I have a drinking problem, I mean it!" When asked how many days he had lost from work because of drinking, he said, "One! But I really hung one on that time." It can be grossly inaccurate to assign *fact* to statements such as, "He was an alcoholic." It can be accurate and also convey a *fact* about the relationship system if such statements are heard as, "One family member *said* another was an alcoholic." This applies to the entire spectrum of terms used in the family relationship system.

I would like to present the concept of the family as a system. For the moment I shall not attempt to say what kind of system. There is no single word or term that would be accurate without further qualification, and qualification would distort the *system* concept. The family *is* a system in that a change in one part of the system is followed by compensatory change in other parts of the system. I prefer to think of the family as a variety of systems and subsystems. Systems function at all levels of efficiency from optimum functioning to total dysfunction and failure. It is necessary also to think in terms of overfunction, which can range from compensated overfunction to decompensated overfunction. An example of this would be the tachycardia (overfunctioning heart) of an athlete in strenuous physical activity, to tachycardia that precedes total heart failure and death. The functioning of any system is dependent on the functioning of the larger systems of which it is a part, and also on its subsystems. On a broad level, the solar system is a subsystem of the larger system, the universe. The molecule is one of the smallest defined subsystems. On another level, the process of evolution is a system that operates slowly over long periods of time. There is sufficient knowledge about evolution to recognize the general patterns of its function, but there is much less knowledge about the larger systems of which evolution is a subsystem. We can look back and make postulations about the factors that influenced past evolutionary change, but our lack of knowledge about the larger systems reduces us to guessing about the future course of evolution.

From observing families I have attempted to define and conceptualize some of the larger and smaller family functioning patterns as they repeat and repeat, and as old patterns tone down and new ones become more prominent. The research started with schizophrenia in which one family member was in a state of total dysfunction and collapse, and the patterns so intense they could not be missed, but it required work with the entire range of human dysfunction to see the patterns in broader perspective. One of the most important aspects of family dysfunction is an equal degree of overfunction in another part of the family system. It is factual that dysfunctioning and overfunctioning exist together. On one level this is a smooth-working, flexible, reciprocating mechanism, in which one member automatically overfunctions to compensate for the dysfunction of the other, who is temporarily ill. Then there are the more chronic and fixed states of overfunctioning and dysfunction in which flexibility is lost. An example would be the dominating (overfunctioning) mother and passive father. The overfunctioning one routinely sees this as necessary to compensate for the poor functioning of the other. This might be valid in the case of temporary illness in one spouse, but in the chronic states there is evidence that the dysfunction appears later to compensate for overfunction in the other. However it develops, the overfunction–dysfunction is a reciprocating mechanism. In previous papers (Bowen, 1959, 1960) I called this the "overadequate-inadequate reciprocity." Symptoms develop when the dysfunction approaches nonfunctioning. Families often do not seek help until flexibility of the system is lost and the functioning of one member is severely impaired. When the mechanism advances beyond a certain point, anxiety drives the mechanism toward panic and rapid increase in both overfunction and dysfunction. The increased pressure can "jam the circuits" of the disabled one into paralyzed collapse. Even at this point, recovery can begin with the slightest decrease of the overfunctioning, or a slight decrease in the dysfunction.

Some of the main functional patterns observed in families have been formulated into component concepts that comprise the family theory of emotional illness. It would be more accurate to say "family dysfunction." The broad family patterns of emotional illness are also present in physical illness and social dysfunction such as irresponsible behavior and delinquency. The component concepts (subsystems) are among those I believe to be the most critical variables in human dysfunction. Symptoms in any part of the family are viewed as evidence of dysfunction, whether the symptoms be emotional, physical, conflictual, or social. There have been most promising results from the effort to view all emotional symptoms as evidence of family dysfunction rather than as intrapsychic phenomena.

The "therapist" also fits into this concept of the family as a system. This is a combination theoretical-therapeutic system in which theory determines therapy, and observations from therapy can in turn modify the theory. The original design, reported in another paper (Bowen, 1961), has been continued, although both the theory and therapy have been constantly modified. From the early days of the research there was increasing emotional detachment from the families. The more one observes families, the easier it is to detach from the narrow conceptual boundaries of individual theory; and the more one detaches from individual theory, the easier it is to see family patterns. The early family psychotherapy was predominantly observational, with questions to elicit more information about the observations. Over the years, "research" families have done better in family psychotherapy than those for whom the primary goal was "therapy." This helped establish a kind of orientation which has made all families into "research" families. It has been my experience that the more a therapist learns about a family, the more the family learns about itself; and the more the family learns, the more the therapist learns, in a cycle which continues. In the observational process with early families, some were able to restore family functioning without much "therapeutic intervention." The most successful families followed remarkably consistent courses in accomplishing this. Thereafter, it was possible to "intervene" and tell new families about successes and failures of former families and to save the new families endless hours and months of trial-and-error experimentation. In broad terms, the therapist became a kind of "expert" in understanding family systems and an "engineer" in helping the family restore itself to functioning equilibrium.

The overall goal was to help family members become "system experts" who could know the family system so well that the family could readjust itself without the help of an outside expert, if and when the family system was again stressed. It is optimum when the family system can begin a shift toward recovery with the important members of the family attending the hours. There were those in which the family became "worse" during the therapy, the "helpless one" becoming more helpless in response to the overfunctioning of the other. Some would struggle through this period and then move toward recovery; others would terminate. In these situations, it was found to be more profitable to work with one side of the reciprocity until the family was able to work together without increasing the "bind." It is far easier for the overfunctioning one to "tone down" the overfunctioning than for the poorly functioning one to "pull up." If the overfunctioning one is motivated, I see this one alone for a period of "family" psychotherapy in which the goal is to free the immobilized system and restore enough flexibility for the family to work together. From my orientation, a theoretical system that "thinks" in terms of family and works toward improving the family system *is* family psychotherapy.

With this theoretical-therapeutic system, there is always the initial problem of the therapist establishing the orientation of the system. Most families are referred with a diagnosis for the dysfunction. They think in terms of the medical model and expect that the therapist is going to change the diagnosed family member, or the parents may expect the therapist to show or tell them how to change the child without understanding and modifying their part in the family system. With many families, it is surprisingly easy for the therapist to establish this family orientation in which he stands alongside to help them understand and take steps to modify the system. To help establish this orientation, I avoid the diagnosis of any family member and other medical model concepts such as "sick" or "patient." I persistently oppose the tendency of the family to view me as a "therapist." Instead, I work toward establishing myself as a "consultant" in family problems for the initial interviews, and as a "supervisor" of the family effort for the long-term process. When the therapist allows himself to become a "healer" or "repairman," the family goes into dysfunction to wait for the therapist to accomplish his work.

From this discussion of the family as a system, I have avoided saying what kind of a "system." The family *is* a number of different kinds of systems. It can accurately be designated a social system, a cultural system, a games system, a communication system, a biological system, or any of several other designations. For the purposes of this theoretical-therapeutic system, I think of the family as a combination of "emotional" and "relationship" systems. The term "emotional" refers to the force that motivates the system and "relationship" to the ways it is expressed. Under relationship would be subsumed communication, interaction and other relationship modalities.

There were some basic assumptions about man and the nature of emotional illness, partially formulated before the family research, that governed the theoretical thinking and the choice of the various theoretical concepts, including the notion of an "emotional" system. Man is viewed as an evolutionary assemblage of cells who has arrived at his present state from hundreds of millions of years of evolutionary adaptation and maladaptation, and who is evolving on to other changes. In this sense, man is related directly to all living matter. In choosing theoretical concepts, an attempt was made to keep them in harmony with man as a protoplasmic being. Man is different from other animals in the size of his brain and his ability to reason and think. With his intellectual ability he has devoted major effort to emphasizing his uniqueness and the "differences" that set him apart from other forms of life, and he has devoted comparatively little effort to understanding his relatedness to other forms of life. A basic premise is that what man thinks about himself, and what he says about himself, are different in many important ways from what he *is*. Emotional illness is seen as a disorder of man's emotional system, and man's emotional system is seen as basically related to man's protoplasmic being. I view emotional illness as a much deeper phenomenon than that conceptualized by current psychological theory. There are emotional mechanisms as automatic as a reflex and that occur as predictably as the force that causes the sunflower to keep its face toward the sun. I believe that the laws that govern man's emotional functioning are as orderly as those that govern other natural systems and that the difficulty in understanding the system is governed more by man's reasoning that denies its existence than by the complexity of the system. In the literature there are discrepant views about the definition of, and the relatedness between, *emotion* and *feelings*. Operationally I regard an *emotional* system as something deep that is in contact with cellular and somatic processes, and a *feeling* system as a bridge that is in contact with parts of the emotional system on one side and with the intellectual system on the other. In clinical practice, I have made a clear distinction between feelings, which have to do with subjective awareness, and opinions, which have to do with logic and reasoning of the intellectual system. The degree to which people say, "I feel that . . ." when they mean, "I believe that . . ." is so commonplace that many use the words synonymously. However valid the ideas behind the selection of these concepts, they did play a major part in the choice of concepts.

An attempt has been made to keep terminology as simple and descriptive as possible. Several factors have governed this. The effort to think of the family as a fluid, ever-changing functional system was impaired by the use of the static, fixed concepts conveyed by much of conventional psychiatric terminology. Early in family research, the loose use of psychiatric terms, such as "depressed," "hysterical," and "compulsive," interfered with accurate description and communication. An effort was made to prohibit the use of psychiatric jargon within the research staff and to use simple descriptive words. This was a worthwhile discipline. It is difficult to communicate with colleagues without using familiar terms. An effort was made to bridge this gap by the sparing use of familiar terms. In the early years I worked toward some kind of correlation of family concepts with psychoanalytic theory. In writing and professional communication, the use of certain familiar terms would evoke vigorous discussion about the proper definition and use of terms. When the discussions went beyond productive exchanges of views and into nonproductive cyclical debates that consumed both time and energy, I elected to describe the family phenomenon in terms that did not stir up debates, to advance the research as far as possible, and to leave integration of individual and family concepts for some future generation. Although there are inaccuracies in the use of the term "family psychotherapy," I have retained it as the best working compromise between the theory and the practice, and for describing it to the professions to which it is related.

THE FAMILY THEORY

The central concept in this theory is the "undifferentiated family ego mass." This is a conglomerate emotional oneness that exists in all levels of intensity—from the family in which it is most intense, to the family in which it is almost imperceptible. The symbiotic relationship between a mother and child is an example of a fragment of one of the most intense versions. The father is equally involved with the mother and child, and other children are involved with varying lesser degrees of intensity. The basic notion to be conveyed at this moment is that of an emotional process that shifts about within the nuclear family (father, mother, and children) ego mass in definite patterns of emotional responsiveness. The degree to which any one family member may be involved depends on his basic level of involvement in the family ego mass. The number of family members involved depends on the intensity of the process and the functional state of individual relationships to the central "mass" at that moment. In periods of stress, the process can involve the entire nuclear family, a whole spectrum of more peripheral family members, and even nonrelatives and representatives of social agencies, clinics, schools, and courts. In periods of calm, the process can remain relatively contained within a small segment of the family, such as the symbiotic relationship in which the emotional process plays back and forth between mother and child, with the father isolated from the intense twosome.

The term "undifferentiated family ego mass" has been more utilitarian than accurate. Precisely defined, the four words do not belong together, but this term has been the most effective of all in communicating the concept so that others might "hear." Also, the four words, each conveying an essential part of the concept, have provided latitude in theoretical extension of the idea. Clinically, the best examples of the relationship system within the undifferentiated family ego mass are conveyed by the more intense versions of it, such as the symbiotic relationship or the "folie a deux" phenomenon. The emotional closeness can be so intense that family members know each other's feelings, thoughts, fantasies, and dreams. The relationships are cyclical. There is one phase of calm, comfortable closeness. This can shift to anxious, uncomfortable overcloseness with the incorporation of the "self" of one by the "self" of the other. Then there is the phase of distant hostile rejection in which the two can literally repel each other. In some families, the relationship can cycle through the phases at frequent intervals. In other families the cycle can stay relatively fixed for long periods, such as the angry rejection phase in which two people can repulse each other for years, or for life. In the rejection phase, each can retreat into a similar emotional involvement with another family member or with certain other people outside the family. Within the family emotional system, the emotional tensions shift about in an orderly series of emotional alliances and rejections. The basic building block of any emotional system is the triangle. In calm periods, two members of the triangle have a comfortable emotional alliance, and the third, in the unfavored "outsider" position, moves either toward winning the favor of one of the others or toward rejection, which may be planned as winning favor. In tension situations, the "outsider" is in the favored position and both of the emotionally overinvolved ones will predictably make efforts to involve the third in the conflict. When tension increases, it will involve increasing outside members, the emotional circuits running on a series of interlocking emotional triangles. In the least involved situations, the emotional process shifts about in a subtle process of emotional responsiveness, which might be compared to an emotional chain reaction. These mechanisms can be defined in the later stages of family psychotherapy, in which it is possible to analyze the family emotional system. For instance, a smile in one family member might initiate an action response in another, and this initiate a reverie about a dream in another, which is followed by a "change the subject" joke in another.

There are three major theoretical concepts in the theory. The first has to do with the degree of "differentiation of self" in a person. The opposite of differentiation is the degree of "undifferentiation" or "ego fusion." An attempt has been made to classify all levels of human functioning on a single continuum. At one end of the scale is the most intense version of the undifferentiated family ego mass in which "undifferentiation" and "ego fusion" dominate the field and there is little "differentiation of self." The symbiotic relationship and the "folie a deux" phenomenon are examples of clinical states with intense ego fusion. At the other end of the scale the "differentiation of self" dominates the field, and there is little overt evidence of ego fusion. People at this end of the scale represent the highest levels of human functioning. Another concept has to do with the relationship system *within* the nuclear family ego mass and the *outside* emotional forces from the extended family emotional system and from the emotional systems of work and social situations that influence the course of the process within the family ego mass. Important in this concept is the "family projection process," by which parental problems are transmitted to their children. The patterns of this process have been incorporated into a third concept, which deals with the multigenerational interlocking of emotional fields and parental transmission of varying degrees of "maturity" or "immaturity" over multiple generations. For practical purposes, the term "family ego mass" refers to the nuclear family which includes the father, mother, and children of the present and future generations. The term "extended family" refers to the entire network of living relatives, though in the everyday clinical situation this usually refers to the three-generation system involving grandparents, parents, and children. The term "emotional field.' refers to the emotional process in any area being considered at the moment.

The Differentiation of Self Scale is an attempt to conceptualize all human functioning on the same continuum. This theory does not have a concept of "normal." It has been relatively easy to define "normal" measurements for all areas of man's physical functioning, but attempts to establish a "normal" for emotional functioning have been elusive. As a baseline for this theoretical system, a detailed profile of "complete differentiation of self," which would be equivalent to complete emotional maturity, has been assigned a value of 100 on a scale from 0 to 100. The lowest level of "no self," or the highest level of "undifferentiation," is at the bottom of the scale. Some of the broad general characteristics of people at the various levels of the scale will be presented.

People in the lowest quarter of the scale (0 to 25) are those with the most intense degree of "ego fusion" and with little "differentiation of self." They live in a "feeling" world, if they are not so miserable that they have lost the capacity to "feel." They are dependent on the feelings of

those about them. So much of life energy goes into maintaining the relationship system about them—into "loving" or "being loved" or reaction
against the failure to get love, or into getting more comfortable—that
there is no life energy for anything else. They cannot differentiate between a "feeling" system and an "intellectual" system. Major life decisions are based on what "feels" right or simply on getting comfortable.
They are incapable of using the "differentiated *I*" (I am—I believe—I will
do—I will not do) in their relationships with others. Their use of "I" is
confined to the narcissistic, "I want—I am hurt—I want my rights." They
grew up as dependent appendages of their parental ego masses and in their
life course they attempt to find other dependent attachments from which
they can borrow enough strength to function. Some are able to maintain a
sufficient system of dependent attachments to function through life without symptoms. This is more possible for those in the upper part of this
group. A "no self" who is sufficiently adept at pleasing his boss might be
considered a better employee than if he had some "self." This scale has
nothing to do with diagnostic categories. All in the group have tenuous
adjustments, they are easily stressed into emotional disequilibrium, and
dysfunction can be long or permanent. The group includes those who
manage marginal adjustments and those whose efforts failed. At the extreme lower end are those who cannot exist outside the protective walls of
an institution. It includes the "dead enders" of society, many of the lower
socioeconomic group, and those from higher socioeconomic groups with
intense ego fusions. I would see the hard core schizophrenic person at 10
or below on the scale, and his parents at no more than 20. In family
psychotherapy, I have yet to see a person in this group attain a higher
"basic" level of differentiation of self. Many attain reasonable alleviation
of symptoms, but life energy goes into getting comfortable. If they can
gain some symptom relief and a dependent attachment from which they
can borrow strength, they are satisfied with the result.

People in the second quarter of the scale (25 to 50) are those with less
intense ego fusions and with either a poorly defined self or a budding
capacity to differentiate a self. This has to be in general terms because a
person in the 30 range has many of the characteristics of "lower scale"
people, and those between 40 and 50 have more characteristics of a higher
scale. This scale provides an opportunity to describe "feeling" people.
From 50 down it is increasingly a *feeling* world except for those at the
extreme lower end who can be too miserable to feel. A typical *feeling*
person is one who is responsive to emotional harmony or disharmony
about him. Feelings can soar to heights with praise or approval or be
dashed to nothingness by disapproval. So much life energy goes into "loving" and seeking "love" and approval that there is little energy left for
self-determined, goal-directed activity. Important life decisions are based
on what feels right. Success in business or professional pursuits is determined more by approval from superiors and from the relationship system
than the inherent value of their work. People in this group do have some
awareness of opinions and beliefs from the intellectual system but the
budding "self" is usually so fused with feelings that it is expressed in

dogmatic authoritativeness, in the compliance of a disciple, or in the opposition of a rebel. A conviction can be so fused with feeling that it becomes a "cause." In the lower part of this group are some fairly typical "no selfs." They are transilient personalities who, lacking beliefs and convictions of their own, adapt quickly to the prevailing ideology. They usually go along with the system that best complements their emotional system. To avoid upsetting the emotional system, they use outside authority to support their position in life. They may use cultural values, religion, philosophy, the law, rule books, science, the physician, or other such sources. Instead of using the "I believe" of the more differentiated person, they may say, "Science has shown . . ." and it is possible to take science, or religion, or philosophy out of context and "prove" anything. It is misleading to correlate this scale with clinical categories, but people in the lower part of this segment of the scale, under stress, will develop transient psychotic episodes, delinquency problems, and other symptoms of that intensity. Those in the upper range of the scale will develop neurotic problems. The main difference between this segment and the lower quarter of the scale is that these people have some capacity for the differentiation of selfs. I have had a few families in the 25 to 30 range who have gone on to fairly high levels of differentiation. It is a situation of *possibility* but *low probability*. Most in this range will lose motivation when the emotional equilibrium is restored and symptoms disappear. The *probability* for differentiation is much higher in the 35 to 50 range.

People in the third quarter of the scale (50 to 75) are those with higher levels of differentiation and much lower degrees of ego fusions. Those in this group have fairly well-defined opinions and beliefs on most essential issues, but pressure for conformity is great and under sufficient stress they can compromise principle and make feeling decisions rather than risk the displeasure of others by standing on their convictions. They often remain silent and avoid stating opinions that might put them out of step with the crowd and disturb the emotional equilibrium. People in this group have more energy for goal-directed activity and less energy tied up in keeping the emotional system in equilibrium. Under sufficient stress they can develop fairly severe emotional or physical symptoms, but symptoms are more episodic and recovery is much faster.

People in the upper quarter of the scale (75 to 100) are those I have never seen in my clinical work and that I rarely meet in social and professional relationships. In considering the overall scale, it is essentially impossible for anyone to have *all* the characteristics I would assign to 100. In this group I shall consider those that fall in the 85 to 95 range which will include most of the characteristics of a "differentiated" person. These are principle-oriented, goal-directed people who have many of the qualities that have been called "inner directed." They begin "growing away" from their parents in infancy. They are always sure of their beliefs and convictions but are never dogmatic or fixed in thinking. They can hear and evaluate the viewpoints of others and discard old beliefs in favor of new. They are sufficiently secure within themselves that functioning is not affected by either praise or criticism from others. They can respect the self and the identity of another without becoming critical or becoming emotionally involved in trying to modify the life course of another. They assume total responsibility for self and are sure of their responsibility for family and society. They are realistically aware of their dependence on their fellowman. With the ability to keep emotional functioning contained within the boundaries of self, they are free to move about in any relationship system and engage in a whole spectrum of intense relationships without a "need" for the other that can impair functioning. The "other" in such a relationship does not feel "used." They marry spouses with equal levels of differentiation. With each a well-defined self, there are no questions or doubts about masculinity and femininity. Each can respect the self and identity of the other. They can maintain well-defined selfs and engage in intense emotional relationships at the same time. They are free to relax ego boundaries for the pleasurable sharing of "selfs" in sexuality or other intense emotional experience without reservation and with the full assurance that either can disengage from this kind of emotional fusion and proceed on a self-directed course at will.

These brief characterizations of broad segments of the scale will convey an overall view of the theoretical system that conceives all human functioning on the same continuum. The scale has to do with *basic* levels of differentiation. Another important aspect has to do with *functional* levels of differentiation which is so marked in the lower half of the scale that the concept of *basic* levels can be misleading. The more intense the degree of ego fusion, the more the "borrowing" and "lending" and "giving" and "sharing" of self within the family ego mass. The more the shifting of "strength" within the ego mass, the more likely the marked discrepancies in functional levels of self. The occasional brief shifts are striking. One of the best examples of this is that of the regressed schizophrenic person who pulls up to resourceful functioning when his parents are sick, only to fall back when they have recovered. Other shifts are so fixed that people wonder how one spouse so strong would marry another so weak. A striking example of this is the overadequate husband who might function well in his work at perhaps 55 on strength from a wife housebound with phobias, excessive drinking, or arthritis and a functioning level of 15. In this situation, the basic level would be about 35. Fluctuations in the upper half of the scale are present but less marked, and it is easier to estimate basic levels. People high on the scale have almost no functional shifts. Other characteristics apply to the entire scale. The lower the person on the scale, the more he holds onto religious dogma, cultural values, superstition, and outmoded beliefs, and the less able he is to discard the rigidly held ideas. The lower a person on the scale, the more he makes a "federal case" of rejection, lack of love, and injustice, and the more he demands recompense for his hurts. The lower he is on the scale, the more he holds the other responsible for his self and happiness. The lower he is on the scale, the more intense the ego fusions, and the more extreme the mechanisms such as emotional distance, isolation, conflict, violence, and physical illness to control the emotion of "too much closeness." The more intense the ego fusions, the higher the incidence of being in touch with the intrapsychic of the other, and the greater the chance that he can intuitively know what the other thinks and feels. In general, the lower the person on the scale, the more the impairment in meaningful communication.

Relationship System in the Nuclear Family Ego Mass

An example of a marriage with spouses in the 30 to 35 range will convey an idea of several concepts in this theoretical system. As children, both spouses were dependently attached to parents. After adolescence, in an effort to function autonomously, they either denied the dependence while still living at home, or they used separation and physical distance to achieve autonomy. Both can function relatively well as long as they keep relationships distant or casual. Both are vulnerable to the closeness of an intense emotional relationship. Both long for closeness but both are "allergic" to it. The marriage for each duplicates essential characteristics of former ego masses. They fuse together into a "new family ego mass" with obliteration of ego boundaries and incorporation of the two "pseudo selfs" into a "common self." Each uses mechanisms previously used in their families of origin in dealing with the other. For instance, the one who ran away from his own family will tend to run away in the marriage. The most common mechanism is the use of sufficient emotional distance for each to function with a reasonable level of "pseudo self." The future course of this new family ego mass will depend on a spectrum of mechanisms that operate *within* the family ego mass, and others that operate *outside* in their relationships within the extended family system.

Within the family ego mass, spouses use three major mechanisms to control the intensity of the ego fusion: (1) *Marital conflict* in which each spouse fights for an equal share of the common self and neither gives in to the other. (2) *Dysfunction in one spouse.* A common pattern is a brief period of conflict followed by one spouse's reluctantly "giving in" to relieve the conflict. Both spouses usually see self as "giving in," but there is one who does more of it. In another pattern, one spouse volunteers to be the "no self" in support of the other on whom they become dependent. The spouse who "loses self" in this mechanism may come to function at such a low level that they become candidates for physical, emotional, or social illness. There are some marriages that continue for years with one functioning well and the other chronically ill. (3) *Transmission of the problem to one or more children.* This is one of the most common mechanisms for dealing with family ego mass problems. There are a few families in which ego mass problems are relatively contained within one of the three areas. There are a few with severe marital conflict but no impairment of either spouse and no transmission to the children. There are also a few with no marital conflict, no dysfunction in either spouse and in which the entire weight of the marital problem goes into one child. There may be no significant symptoms until after adolescence, when the child collapses in psychotic dysfunction or other dysfunction of comparable degree. In most families, the problem between the spouses will be "spread" to all three areas. The few families in which the problem remains con-

tained in one area are important theoretically. The fact that there are
some families with intense marital conflict and no impairment of children
is evidence that marital conflict does not, within itself, cause problems in
children. The fact that serious impairment of children can develop in
calm, harmonious marriages is further evidence that impairment of children can occur without conflict. The degree of the problem between the
spouses can be assigned quantitative measures. The system operates as if
there is a certain amount of "immaturity" to be absorbed by the system.
Large quantities of this may be "bound" by serious dysfunction in one
family member. One chronically ill parent can be a kind of "protection"
against serious impairment of children. In the area of transmission to
children, the family projection process focuses on certain children and
leaves others relatively uninvolved. There are, of course, families in which
the "quantity" of immaturity is so great that there is maximum marital
conflict, severe dysfunction in one spouse, maximum involvement of children, conflict with families of origin, and still free-floating "immaturity."

The mechanisms that operate *outside* the nuclear family ego mass are
important in determining the course and intensity of the process *within*
the nuclear family. When there is a significant degree of ego fusion, there
is also a borrowing and sharing of ego strength between the nuclear family
and the family of origin. In periods of stress the nuclear family can be
stabilized by emotional contact with a family of origin, just as the nuclear
family can also be disturbed by stress in the family of origin. In general,
the intensity of the process in a nuclear family is attenuated by active
contacts with the families of origin. There is one striking pattern illustrated by the following example: The father separated himself from his
family when he left for college. There was no further contact except
infrequent, brief visits and occasional letters and Christmas cards. He married a wife who maintained close contact with her family, including frequent exchanges of letters and gifts, regular family reunions, and visits
with scattered members of the clan. Five out of six of the father's siblings
followed the same pattern of separating from the family of origin. The
mother was one of five siblings, all of whom married spouses who were
brought into the emotional orbit of her family. This pattern is so common
that I have called these *exploding* and *cohesive* families. The spouse who
separates from his family of origin does not resolve the emotional attachment. The old relationship remains "latent" and can be revived with emotional contact. Through the "active" relationship with the cohesive family, the nuclear family system is responsive to emotional events within the
cohesive extended family. There are other nuclear families in which both
spouses detach themselves from families of origin. In these the spouses are
usually much more dependent on each other, and the emotional process in
the family tends to be more intense. The average family in which both
spouses are emotionally separated from families of origin tend to become
more invested in the emotional systems of work and social situations. An
example is a family in which the principal outside emotional tie was the
father's long-term emotional dependence on his boss at work. Within
weeks after the sudden death of the father's boss, a teen-aged son was in

serious dysfunction with a behavior problem. A brief period of "family" psychotherapy with the father alone restored the family emotional equilibrium sufficiently for the parents to work productively together toward resolution of the parental interdependence. Knowledge of the relationship patterns in the extended family system is important in understanding the overall problem and in devising a family psychotherapy program.

Multigenerational Transmission Process

One of the important concepts of this theoretical system is the pattern that emerges over the generations as parents transmit varying levels of their immaturity to their children. In most families the parents transmit part of their immaturity to one or more children. To illustrate this multigenerational pattern in its most graphic and extreme form, I shall start with parents with an average level of differentiation and assume that in each generation the parents project a major portion of their immaturity to only one child, thereby creating maximum impairment in one child in each generation. I shall also assume that in each generation one child grows up relatively outside the emotional demands and pressures of the family ego mass and attains the highest level of differentiation possible in that situation. It would be essentially impossible for this pattern to occur generation after generation, but it does illustrate the pattern. The example starts with parents at 50 on the scale. They have three children. The most involved child emerges at 35 on the scale, much lower than the basic level of the parents and a fairly maximum degree of impairment for one generation. Another child emerges with 50, the same basic level of the parents. A third grows up relatively outside the problems of the family ego mass and emerges with a level of 60, much higher than the parents. In considering the child at 35 who marries a spouse in the 35 range, the personality characteristics of this marriage would vary according to the way this family ego mass handles its problems. A maximum projection family would have a calm marriage and almost total preoccupation with the health, welfare, and achievement of the most involved child, who could emerge with a level as low as 20. They could have another who grew up outside the family ego mass with a level of 45, much higher than the parents. To have two children, one at 20 and another at 45, is hardly probable. The child at 20 is already in the danger zone and vulnerable to a whole spectrum of human problems. In his early years he might be an overachiever in school, and then in the postadolescent years go into an emotional collapse. With special help he might eventually finish school, spend a few aimless years, and then find a spouse whose "needs" for another are as great as his. At this level of ego fusion the problems are too great to be contained in one area. They will probably have a variety of marital, health, and social problems, and the problem will be too great for projection to only one child. They might have one child at 10, another at 15, and another who grows up outside the family mass to a level of 30, much above the basic level of the parents. The ones at 10 and 15 are good candidates for total functional collapse into states such as schizophrenia or criminal behavior. This illustrates former statements that it requires at least three generations for a person to acquire the level of "no self" for a later collapse into schizophrenia. In the average situation the immaturity would progress at a much slower rate. Also, in every generation there are children who progress up the scale, and in the average family the upward progression is much slower than illustrated in this example.

It is emphasized that the scale level figures used in the preceding examples are to illustrate the broad principles of the theoretical system. The shift in functional levels in the lower half of the scale is so responsive to such a variety of hour-to-hour and week-to-week shifts, through good years and bad, that approximate levels can be established only after having awareness of the particular variables most operative over a period of time for a given family. It is the general level and the pattern that are most important in the clinical situation. The levels in the multigenerational concept are strictly schematic and for illustrative purposes only. The postulations for this concept were derived from historical material covering three to four generations on approximately 100 families, and ten or more generations on eight families.

There is one other theoretical concept that I have combined with my own work that is used with every family in psychotherapy. These are the personality profiles of the various sibling positions as presented by Toman in *Family Constellation* (Toman, 1961). I consider his work one of the significant contributions to family knowledge in recent years. He presents the thesis that personality characteristics are determined by the sibling position and the family constellation in which one grows up. I have found his personality profiles to be remarkably accurate, especially for people in the mid-scale range of my Differentiation of Self Scale. Of course, he did his study on "normal" families and made no attempt to estimate other variables. He also did not consider the personality alterations of the child who was the object of the family projection process. An example of the shift is a family of two daughters. The older, the one most involved in the family emotional system, emerged with the profile of a younger "baby." The younger daughter, who was less involved in the emotional system with the parents, emerged with more of the characteristics of an older daughter. Most of his profiles contain a mixture of the adult and the infantile characteristics. The higher a person on the scale, the more the adult qualities predominate; the obverse is also true.

CLINICAL USE OF FAMILY PSYCHOTHERAPY

I hope that the theoretical concepts help the reader think more in terms of family systems rather than diagnostic categories and individual dynamics. Each point in the theory has application in clinical evaluation and in family psychotherapy. This section will be presented in three main parts: (1) survey of the family fields, (2) the process of "differentiation of self" in family psychotherapy, and (3) family psychotherapy principles and techniques.

Survey of the Family Fields

This is a term used to designate a family "evaluation" process used in the initial interview with every family I see. It is designed to get a volume of factual information in a brief time. The information is used with the family theory for a formulation about the overall patterns of functioning in the family ego mass for at least two generations. The formulation is used in planning the psychotherapy. Initially, it required a number of hours to get this information. With practice, and the careful structuring of the interview, and an average uncomplicated family, it is possible to do a survey adequately for planning the psychotherapy in one hour. This is different from the kind of "evaluation" in which the therapist may spend several hours with all family members together to observe the workings of the family relationship system. In the training of young therapists, considerable experience in observing multiple family members together is essential. It is not possible to *know* a family without direct clinical observation, and it is not advisable to work with segments of families until one has a working knowledge of the whole. For the average family, the initial interview is with both parents, who can usually provide more information than one. In addition, it provides a working view of the marital relationship. If there is evidence that marital discord might interfere with the fact-gathering, I often ask to see the one parent who has the most knowledge about the family. Some interesting developments come from this. Most families seek help when there is dysfunction in one or more of the three main stress areas of the nuclear family system: (1) marital conflict, (2) dysfunction in a spouse, or (3) dysfunction in a child. To illustrate this survey, I shall use a family referred for a behavior problem in a teen-aged child.

In surveying the family fields, I first want to know about the functioning in the nuclear family field, and then how the functioning of the extended family field intergears with the nuclear field. A good starting point is a chronological review of the symptom development in the teen-aged child, with specific dates and circumstances at the time of each symptom eruption. Many symptomatic eruptions can be timed exactly with other events in the nuclear and extended family fields. The parents might report the child first played hooky from school "in the eighth grade," but it would convey much about the family system if one knew the day he played hooky was the day his maternal grandmother was hospitalized for tests for a feared cancer. Information about feeling and fantasy systems of other family members on that day would be helpful if it could be obtained.

The second area of investigation is the functioning of the parental ego mass since marriage. This emotional unit has its own system of internal dynamics that change as it moves through the years. The internal system also responds to the emotional fields of the extended families and to the reality stresses of life. The goal is to get a brief chronological view of the internal system as it has interresponded with outside forces. This might be compared to two constantly changing magnetic fields that influence each other. The internal functioning is influenced by events such as closeness or distance and emotional contact with extended families, changes in residence, the purchase of a home, and occupational success or failure. Major events that influence both emotional fields are births within the central ego mass and serious illness or death in the extended family. Functioning within the ego mass can be estimated with a few questions about stress areas, which are marital conflict, illness or other dysfunction, and projection to a child. A change in stress symptoms might be related to internal dynamics or external events. The dates of changes are important. A change from a calm to a conflictual relationship might be explained by the wife as "the time I began to stand up to him," when it would in fact be timed exactly with a disturbance in an extended family.

Important ego mass changes accompany the birth of children. The birth of the first child changes the family from a two-person to a three-person system. At an important event such as this, it is desirable to do a "fix" on the entire family system, including place, date, ages of each person in the household and the functioning of each, and a check on the realities in the extended families. It is desirable to get readings on the feeling-fantasy systems of various family members at stress points, if this is possible. A check on the family projection process is often easy by asking about the mother's fantasy system before and after the birth of the child. If it is a significant projection process, her worries and concerns have fixed on the child since the pregnancy, her relationship with this one has been "different," she has long worried about it, and she is eager to talk about it. An intense, long-term, projection process is evidence of a deeper and more serious problem in the child. A projection process that started later, perhaps following the death of an important family member, is much less serious and much easier handled in family psychotherapy. A projection process, usually between mother and child, *changes* the internal functioning of the family system. This much psychic energy from mother to child will change the psychic energy system in the family. It might serve to reduce marital conflict, but it might also disturb the husband to the point he would start spending longer hours at work, or he might begin drinking, or have an affair, or become emotionally closer to his parents. This survey is followed to the onset of symptoms in the child for which there are already nodal points that may be connected with dates and events in the parental relationship. The survey provides a picture of general functioning levels, responsiveness to stress, and evidence about the flexibility or rigidity of the entire system. It also provides a notion about the more adaptive spouse, who is usually the more passive. The adaptive one is much more than one who "gives in" on a controlled surface level. This involves the entire fantasy, feeling, and action system. A spouse who develops physical symptoms in response to an emotional field is in a "cell to cell" adaptiveness that is deep.

The next area of investigation is the two extended family fields, in either order the therapist chooses. This is similar to the nuclear family survey except it focuses on overall patterns. Exact dates, ages, and places are very important. The occupation of the grandfather and a note about the marital relationship and the health of each grandparent provides key clues to that family ego mass. Information about each sibling includes birth order, exact dates of birth, occupation, place of residence, a few words about spouse and children, a note about overall life course, and frequency and nature of contact with other family members. From this brief information, which can be obtained in five or ten minutes, it is possible to assemble a fairly accurate working notion about the family ego mass, and how the nuclear parent functioned in the group. Siblings who do best are usually least involved in the family emotional system. Those who do poorly are usually most involved. Distance from other family members and quality of emotional contacts with family provide clues about the way the person handles all emotional relationships and whether this tends toward an "exploding" or "cohesive" family. A high incidence of physical illness often occurs in those with low levels of differentiation of self. The sibling position is one of the most important bits of information. This, plus the general level of family functioning, makes it possible to postulate a reasonably accurate personality profile to be checked later. In general, a life style developed in the family of origin will operate in the nuclear family and also in family psychotherapy.

Surveys of the family fields follow the same pattern for other problems, except for different emphases. Certain areas may require detailed exploration. It is always helpful to go back as many generations as possible. The overall goal is to follow the total family through time with a focus on related events in interlocking fields. The lower the general level of differentiation in a family, the greater the frequency and intensity of the related events. A secondary dividend of a family field survey is the family's beginning intellectual awareness of related events. The family emotional system operates always to obscure and misremember and to treat such events as coincidental. Family replies to an effort to get specific dates might go, "That was when he was about . . . 11 or 12 years old," and, "He must have been in the fifth grade," or, "It was about five or six years ago." It requires persistent questioning and mathematical computation to get specific information. The obscuring process is illustrated by a family in family psychotherapy. Ten days after the wife returned from her mother's funeral, her daughter developed nephritis. Some weeks later the wife was insisting that the daughter's illness preceded her mother's death. The husband's memory and my notes were accurate. In theoretical thinking, I have never been willing to postulate causality or go beyond noting that such events have a striking time sequence. I believe it may have to do with man's denial of dependence on his fellowman. I avoid glib dynamic speculations and record the family explanations as, "The family member said . . ." I have never been able to use the related events early in psychotherapy. Early in family psychotherapy there was the temptation to show this to the family after the initial interview. Some families found reason to never return. My goal is to keep asking questions and let the calendar "speak" when others are able to "hear."

The family field survey is primarily for the therapist in knowing the family and how it operates, and in planning the psychotherapy. If the symptoms develop slowly in the nuclear family, it is likely to be the product of a slow buildup in the nuclear family. If the symptoms develop more quickly, the situation deserves a thorough exploration for disturbance in the extended family. If it is a response to the extended family, it can be regarded as an "acute" situation and it is fairly easy to restore the family functioning. The following is an example of multiple acute problems following a disturbance in the extended family.

A 40-year-old woman was referred for a depression for which hospitalization had been suggested. Her husband belonged to a "cohesive" family of six siblings, all of whom lived within a few hundred miles of their parents. Two months before, his 65-year-old mother had a radical mastectomy of breast cancer. Two weeks after the operation, one of the husband's sisters had a serious automobile accident which required months of hospitalization. Six weeks after the operation, one of the husband's brothers had a son arrested for a series of delinquent acts, the first of which had occurred two weeks after the operation. After an initial interview with the depressed wife alone, the husband and wife were seen together. A few hours with the process focused on feelings about the mother brought rapid relief of the depression and set the stage for long-term family psychotherapy with both together.

The Process of Differentiation of a Self

The basic effort of this therapeutic system is to help *individual* family members toward a higher level of differentiation of self. An emotional system operates with a delicately balanced equilibrium in which each devotes a certain amount of being and self to the welfare and well-being of the others. In a state of disequilibrium, the family system operates automatically to restore the former togetherness equilibrium, though this be at the expense of some. When an individual moves toward a higher level of differentiation of self, it disturbs the equilibrium and the togetherness forces oppose with vigor. In larger emotional systems, an individual may seek an ally or group to help oppose the forces of the system, only to find self in a new undifferentiated oneness with his allies (even a sect or minority group within the larger system) from which it is harder to differentiate than from the original oneness. Any successful effort toward differentiation is for the individual alone. Some of the forces that oppose the "differentiation of self" will be described later. When the individual can maintain his "differentiation" stand in spite of opposition, the family later applauds.

One of the important concepts in this theoretical system has to do with "triangles." It was not included with the other concepts because it has more to do with therapy than the basic theory. The basic building block of any emotional system is the "triangle." When emotional tension in a two-person system exceeds a certain level, it "triangles" a third person, permitting the tension to shift about within the triangle. Any two in the original triangle can add a new triangle. An emotional system is composed of a series of interlocking triangles. The emotional tension system can shift to any of the old preestablished circuits. It is a clinical fact that the original two-person tension system will resolve itself automatically when contained within a three-person system, one of whom remains emotionally detached. This will be discussed under "detriangling the triangle."

From experience with this therapeutic system, there are two main avenues toward a higher level of "differentiation of self." (1) The optimum is differentiation of a self *from* one's spouse, as a cooperative effort, in the presence of a potential "triangle" (therapist) who can remain emotionally detached. To me, this is the "magic" of family psychotherapy. They must be sufficiently involved with each other to stand the stress of "differentiation" and sufficiently uncomfortable to motivate the effort. One, and then the other, moves forward in small steps until motivation stops. (2) Start the differentiation alone, under the guidance of a supervisor, as a preliminary step to the main effort of differentiating a self *from* the important other person. This second avenue is a model for family psychotherapy with one family member. A third avenue is less effective: (3) the entire process under the guidance of a supervisor who coaches from the sidelines. Direct use of the "triangle" is lost, the process is generally slower, and the chances of an impasse are greater. As a general comment about "differentiation," the highest level of differentiation that is possible for a family is the highest level that any family member can attain and maintain against the emotional opposition of the family unit in which he lives.

Family Psychotherapy Principles and Technique

My optimum approach to any family problem, whether marital conflict, dysfunction in a spouse, or dysfunction in a child, is to start with husband and wife together and to continue with both for the entire period of family psychotherapy. In most families, this "optimum" course is not possible. Some 30 to 40 percent of "family" hours are spent with one family member, mostly for situations in which one spouse is antagonistic or poorly motivated, or when progress with both is too slow. The method of helping one family member to "differentiate a self" will be discussed later. The method of working with the two parents evolved from several years of experience in which both parents and symptomatic child (usually postadolescent behavior and neurotic problems) attended all sessions together. An average course would continue a year or more. Family communication improved, symptoms disappeared, and the families would terminate, much pleased with the result. There was no basic change in the pattern of the parental relationship, postulated to be fundamental in the origin of the problem. On the premise that the entire family system would change if the parental relationship changed, I began asking such parents to leave the child at home and to focus on their own problems. These have been the most satisfying results in my experience. Many of the children who initiated the family effort were never seen, and others were seen only once. The parents who achieved the best results would continue about four years at once a week for a total of 175 to 200 hours with better results than could be achieved with any other psychotherapeutic method in my experience. The children were usually symptom free in a few weeks or months, and changes have gone far beyond the nuclear family into the extended family system. The time has been so consistently in the four-year range that I believe it might require this amount of time for significant differentiation of self. Some people can spend a lifetime without defining themselves on numerous life issues. I am now experimenting with less frequent appointments to reduce the total amount of time.

The basic process of working with husbands and wives together has remained very much the same over the years with some different emphases and modifications in theoretical concepts. In the past I stressed the communication of feelings and the analysis of the unconscious through dreams. More recently, it has been a process of watching the step-by-step process of externalizing and separating out their fantasy, feeling, thinking systems. It is a process of knowing one's own self, and also the self of the other. There have been comments such as, "I never knew you had such thoughts!" and the counterresponse, "I never dared tell anyone before, most especially *you*!"

The following is an example of two small "differentiation" steps with the emotional response of the other. One wife, after many hours of private thinking, announced, "I have decided to take all the thought, time, and energy that I have devoted to trying to make you happy and to put it into trying to make myself into a more responsible woman and mother. Nothing I tried really worked anyway. I have thought it out and I have a plan." The husband reacted with the usual emotional reaction to an "I" position by the other. He was angry and hurt. He ended with, "If I had realized it would come to this after fifteen years, I can tell you one thing, there never would have been a wedding!" Within a week he was happy with his "new" wife. Some weeks later, after much thinking by the husband, he announced, "I have been trying to think through my responsibilities to my family and to work. I have never been clear about this. If I worked overtime, I felt I was neglecting my family. If I spent extra time with the family, I would feel I was neglecting my work. Here is my plan." The wife reacted with emotion about his real selfish lack of concern finally showing its true color. Within a week that had subsided.

As spouses change in relation to each other, they disturb the emotional equilibrium in families of origin where there are the same emotional reactions and resolutions as between themselves. Most of these spouses have become the most responsible and respected in both extended family systems. The emotional opposition to change also occurs in social and work emotional systems. The main point to be communicated here is that a change in "self" disturbs the emotional equilibrium and evokes emotional opposing forces in all interlocking emotional systems. If two spouses can make the primary changes in relation to each other, it is relatively easy to deal with the other systems.

One of the most important processes in this method of psychotherapy is the therapist's continuing attention to defining his "self" to the families. This begins from the first contact, which defines this theoretical and therapeutic system and its differences from others. It proceeds in almost every session around all kinds of life issues. Of importance are the "action" stands which have to do with "what I will do and will not do." I believe a therapist is in a poor position to ask a family to do something he does not do. When the family goes slowly at defining self, I begin to wonder if there is some vague, ambiguous area of importance about which I failed to define myself.

At this point, I shall describe *family* psychotherapy with one family member. The basic notion of this has to do with finding a way to start some change in the deadlocked family; with finding a way to get into contact with family resourcefulness and strength, and to get out of contact with the sickness morass; and with getting some differentiation to rise out of the family quagmire. Actually, if it is possible to get some differentiation started in one family member, it can loosen up the entire family system. Communication of this idea has been difficult. To those who use a medical model and consider the therapeutic relationship the basic healing force in emotional illness, the idea is erroneous. I have used several different concepts in trying to write about the idea and a number of different angles in trying to teach it. There are those who heard it as "treating the healthiest family member instead of the patient, on the grounds that the healthiest is more capable of modifying behavior." This is an accurate description of the goal, but it uses a "health" concept in the place of "sickness," which is still a medical model. A therapist who attempts to "treat" the healthiest with his medical orientation could either drive him away or make him into a "patient."

The conflictual marriage provides one of the best examples of working with one spouse. This is a clinical situation in which the emotional system is already fairly well locked in dysfunction before the partners seek help. A fair level of overt conflict is "normal," and it has to reach a relative state of dysfunction before they seek help. The marriage began with an almost idyllic model in which each devoted a high percentage of "self" to the happiness and well-being of the other. This I have called a "fraudulent" emotional contract, in which it was realistically impossible for either to live up to the agreement. With this arrangement, the functioning of self *is* dependent on the other and, in that sense, any failure in happiness or functioning *is* the fault of the other, The emotional investment in each other continues, only it shifts into negative energy that accuses, indicts, and diagnoses. I believe the conflictual marriage is an enduring one because of the energy investment. The amount of *thinking* time that goes into the other is probably greater than calm marriages. With the intensity of emotional interdependence and the ability to utilize conflict, the conflictual spouses usually do not seek help until adaptive mechanisms are jammed. In a high percentage of conflictual marriages, I see one spouse alone for a few months to a year before calm working together is possible. Choice about the one to see first is easy when one is motivated and the other antagonistic. It is a little different when both are seen together and the repetitious "accuse the other—excuse self" continues in the interview. If they have any capacity to stop the cycle and look at the pattern, I continue with both together. If a vigorous effort to help them contain the cycle is not successful, I say that I consider this cyclical and nonproductive, that I am not willing to spend time this way, and that I want to see the healthiest, best-integrated one alone for a period of time to help this one gain some objectivity and emotional control. A request for the "healthiest" establishes a different orientation and changes their long-term diagnosing, "You are the sick one who needs a psychiatrist." I do not see spouses alternately. It invites "triangling," neither really works at the problem, each expects the other to do it, and each tends to justify self to the therapist. My "I" stands, all based on experience, are in terms of what I will do and will not do, and are never in terms of "what is best."

Since the process of working with one family member alone is similar in all situations, I shall describe the effort with the conflictual spouse in some detail. The early sessions go into a detailed communication of an orientation with the use of clinical examples and a blackboard for diagrams. In broad terms, the concept is one of withdrawing psychic energy from the other and investing it in the poorly defined ego boundaries. It involves the idea of "getting off the back" of the other (by reducing the "other-directed" thinking, verbal and action energy which is designed to attack and change the other) and directing that energy to the changing of self. The changing of "self" involves finding a way to listen to the attacks of the other without responding, of finding a way to live with "what is" without trying to change it, of defining one's own beliefs and convictions without attacking those of the other, and in observing the part that self plays in the situation. Much time is devoted to establishing the therapist's self in relation to the one spouse. These ideas are passed along for their possible use in defining a "self." He is told that others have found some of them helpful; that the effort will fail if he tries them without incorporating them into "self" as his own beliefs; that he would be unrealistic to try something he could not really believe in; and it will be his responsibility to find other ideas and principles if these do not fit with his own "self." He is assigned the task of becoming "research observer" and told that a major part of each hour will go into his report on his efforts to see self. I tell him about the predictable stages he can expect if his efforts are successful in defining "self" and containing the critical actions, words, and thoughts that have been trying to direct the life of his spouse. If he is successful at this, the first reaction will be a version of, "You are mean, selfish, and vicious; you do not understand, you do not love, and you are trying to hurt the other." When he can listen to the expected attack without reacting, a milestone will have been passed. Then he can expect a withdrawal from the other which emphasizes, "To heck with you. I do not need you." This will be the most difficult stage. He might get depressed and confused and develop a whole spectrum of physical symptoms. This is the reaction of one's psyche and soma as it cries out for the old dependence and togetherness. If he can live with the symptoms without reacting, he can expect the other to make a new and different bid for affection on a higher level of maturity. It is usually not many days after that before the other spouse asks to take the therapy hour, and often not many hours before they can finally work together.

The life style of this low level of "differentiation" is the investment of psychic energy in the "self" of another. When this happens in the therapy, it is transference. A goal of this therapy is to help the other person make a research project out of life. It is as important to keep "self" contained with the therapist as the other spouse. If the person understands the life-goal nature of the effort, and that progress will slow down or stop with energy invested in the "self" of the therapist, he is in a better position to help keep the energy focused on the goal. If progress does stop, the family psychotherapy is shifted to a similar effort with the other spouse. It is not possible to use this "differentiation of a self" approach with two spouses. It results in intense "triangling."

Work with one sick spouse depends on the problem and which one seeks help. If the well one seeks help, the "sick" one is near collapse. With these I work toward avoiding a relationship with the sick side of the family, and work toward relating to the well one about his problems with the sick one. Some of these families achieve remarkable symptom relief with a few appointments, but these people are not motivated for more than symptom relief. When the "sick" one seeks help, I maintain a detached, "Let's examine this and understand your part in the family problem." The cells of the "sick" spouse literally go into dysfunction in the presence of the other spouse, especially in those with severe introjective and somatic dysfunctions. If the other spouse is brought in too early, the therapy effort may terminate within a few hours. A goal is to propose "family" early and wait until the "self" of the sick one can operate in the presence of the other without going into dysfunction. There have been some excellent long-term results which include about six months with the sick one and some two years with both. Problems such as impotence and frigidity belong more in the area of relationship functioning. These can usually be converted to "family" within a few hours and the response has been good. Impotence often disappears within a few weeks and frigidity is rarely mentioned after a few months. Most of these go on with long-term family therapy for two years or more.

The problem of the "triangled" child presents one of the most difficult problems in family psychotherapy. From the initial family survey can come a fair estimate of the intensity of the process. If it is not too severe, the parents can focus on their own problems immediately, they almost forget about the child and, suddenly, he is symptom free. Even with severe "triangling," I do a "trial run" with both parents together to test the flexibility in the parental relationship. In the severe "triangling" or projection of the parental problem to the child, the parents are not able to leave the child out of their feelings, thoughts, and actions. There are the less severe versions in which parents try hard to work on their problem but the relationship between them is dull and lifeless. Life and self are invested in the child. The "gut reaction," in which a parent's "insides tie into knots" in response to discomfort in the child, is common. After several years of symptom-relieving methods, including working with various combinations of family members, I began what I have called "detriangling the triangle." This is too complex for brief discussion but it involves helping one parent to establish an "I" position and to "differentiate a self" in the relationship *with the child*. If there is another "magic" in family psychotherapy, it is the family response when one parent can begin to "differentiate a self" from the amorphous "we-ness" of the intense undifferentiated family ego mass. One bit of clearly defined "self" in this sea of amorphousness can bring a period of amazing calm. The calm may quickly shift to other issues, but the family *is* different. The other parent and child fuse together into a more intense oneness that alternately attacks and pleads with the "differentiating parent" to rejoin the oneness. If the differentiating one can maintain a reasonable "I" for even a few days, there is an automatic decrease in the intensity of the attachment between the other two and a permanent decrease in the intensity of the triangle. The second step involves a similar effort by the other parent to "differentiate a self." Now the parental relationship has come a little more to life. Then there is another cycle with each parent separately, and then still more life and zest between the parents. Differentiation proceeds slowly at this level of ego fusion, but there have been a few of these families that have gone on to reasonable levels of differentiation.

There are several other configurations of family psychotherapy with one family member, but this provides a brief description of the basic principles. It is used when the family system is so stalled that efforts to work with the multiple family members increase the dysfunction, or when work with multiple members reaches a cyclical impasse. The effort is to help one family member to a higher level of functioning which, if possible, can restore function to the family system.

REFERENCES

Ackerman, N. Interlocking pathology in family relationships. In S. Rado & G. E. Daniels (Eds.), *Changing concepts in psychoanalytic medicine*. New York: Grune & Stratton, 1956.

Bateson, G., Jackson D., Haley, J., & Weakland, J. Toward a theory of schizophrenia. *Behav. Sci.*, 1956, *1*, 251–264.

Bell, J. E. Family group therapy, Public Health Monograph 64, 1961.

Birdwhistell, R. *Introduction to kinesics*. Louisville, Ky.: University of Louisville Press, 1952.

Bowen, M. Family relationships in schizophrenia. In Auerback (Ed.), *Schizophrenia–An Integrated Approach*. New York: Ronald Press, 1959.

Bowen, M. A family concept of schizophrenia. In D. Jackson (Ed.), *The Etiology of Schizophrenia*. New York: Basic Books, 1960.

Bowen, M. Family psychotherapy. *Amer. J. Orthopsychiat.*, 1961, *30*, 40–60.

Bowen, M. Family psychotherapy with schizophrenia in the hospital and in private practice. In I. Boszormenyi-Nagy & J. L. Framo (Eds.), *Intensive family therapy*. New York: Harper & Row, 1965.

Dysinger, R. The action dialogue in an intense relationship. Paper read at Annual Meeting, American Psychiatric Association, Chicago, 1957.

Flugel, J. C. *The Psycho-analytic study of the family*. London: Hogarth Press, 10th Impr., 1960.

Freud, S. Analysis of a phobia in a five year old boy. In *Collected papers*. Vol. III. London: Hogarth Press, 1949.

Lidz, T., Cornelison, A., Fleck, S., & Terry, D. The intrafamilial environment of the schizophrenic patient: II. Marital schism and marital skew. *American Journal of Psychiatry*, 1957, *114*, 241–248.

Scheflen, A. The significance of posture in communication systems. *Psychiatry*, 1964, *26*, 316–331.

Toman, W. *Family constellation*. New York: Spring Publishing Co., 1961.

Wynne, L., Rykoff, I., Day, J., & Hirsch, S. Pseudo-mutuality in family relations of schizophrenics. *Psychiatry*, 1958, *21*, 205–220.

Conjoint Marriage Counseling

Before I built a wall, I'd ask to know
What I was walling in or walling out
And to whom I was likely to give offense.
Something there is that doesn't love a wall
That wants it down.

ROBERT FROST, "MENDING WALL"

During its early years, marriage counseling placed considerable emphasis on seeing individual spouses separately, although there has long been a practice of seeing both spouses together at times. Some theoreticians would claim that marriage counselors have generally failed to develop the potential inherent in joint interviewing, while family therapists have made increasing use of it.

Members of the various helping professions are developing a body of theory and approaches which might be called "conjoint marriage counseling." However it is labeled, conjoint marriage counseling is seen differently by different practitioners. In this section, four representatives of four different professions (a sociologist, a social worker, a psychologist, and a psychiatrist) discuss different aspects of this recent trend in counseling.

Gerald R. Leslie, a sociologist, describes conjoint therapy in marriage counseling in Chapter 18. Leslie states that conjoint therapy aids in the identification and working through of distortions, helps hold transference and countertransference in check, quickly brings marital conflicts into the open and into counseling sessions, and emphasizes current relationship problems. Leslie concludes, however, that conjoint therapy is not a panacea and is probably inappropriate with some clients and problems.

In Chapters 19 and 20, Virginia Satir, a social worker and author of the book *Conjoint Family Therapy* (1967), discusses the concepts of therapy and the role and technique of the therapist and conjoint marital therapy. Satir bases her approach on communication theory as previously developed by such men as Ruesch, Bateson, and Jackson.

Ben Ard replies in Chapter 21 with a critique of communication theory in marriage counseling. Several basic questions are raised, including a critical examination of some of the basic assumptions of communication theory. Will all marriages improve if marriage counselors help their clients "communicate" better (or more)? In Ard's view, improving communication alone may not necessarily maintain a marriage, or even improve it. Unquestioned values, expectations, premises, and assumptions need to be critically examined for their consequences, he suggests, and fatalistic determinism is not helpful to clients who have developed pathological ways of interacting. *What* is communicated may be more important than *how* it is communicated.

Finally, in Chapter 22, Andrew Watson, a psychiatrist, states the premises about the marriage relationship, then the strategic and practical goals. of a conjoint treatment of marriage partners are described. The dynamics of transference-countertransference are conceptualized and techniques of interpretation are set forth. Despite Watson's statement that it is not yet possible to specify contraindications for conjoint counseling, each professional marriage counselor will want to think through very carefully the implications of this fast-growing approach.

CHAPTER 18

Conjoint Therapy
in Marriage Counseling

Gerald R. Leslie

The term "conjoint therapy" has been popularized more by family therapists than by marriage counselors. After a long period of failure to appreciate fully the potential inherent in joint interview techniques, it appears
that conjoint therapy may become a major approach to marriage counseling in the relatively near future.

It is ironic that marriage counseling and family therapy should have
developed along such separate but parallel lines. Both are twenty years
old, plus or minus a few years. Both developed rather quietly as far as the
outside world was concerned. And both had terrific impact upon the small
group of "insiders" who called themselves, respectively, family therapists
and marriage counselors. Some members of both groups, it might be
added, have seen themselves as doing the ultimate in pioneering work in
counseling and psychotherapy. If their claim is granted, the further plau-
dit may be added that modesty has not always been one of their primary
virtues.

THE DEVELOPMENT OF FAMILY THERAPY

If the author sees it adequately, family therapy developed largely
within psychiatry. Some child psychiatrists, particularly, were moving in
the direction of family therapy during the 1940's (Burlingham, 1951).
Therapy with children often revealed that the child's difficulties reflected
emotional problems in the mother, or, more radically, conflict between
the parents. The analytic taboo against the therapist's having contact with
other members of the patient's family was not as strong in child psychiatry, and therapy with the child often led to therapy with the mother.
While some psychiatrists religiously referred other family members to different therapists, some began to experiment with, and to see virtue in,
having the same therapist work concurrently on different aspects of a
family's problems. Eventually, this led some therapists to seeing whole
families in joint-interview situations (Shellow, 1963).

Reprinted with permission of the author and the publisher from *Journal of Marriage and the
Family*, 1964, *26*, 65–71.

Other psychiatrists working specifically with schizophrenic children were moving in the same direction (Bowen, 1960). They began to work with schizophrenic families. Scattered groups over the country developed their own approaches to family therapy, often unaware that others were proceeding along similar lines. First there were guarded conversations at professional meetings, then formal papers on family therapy, and subsequently the family therapy "movement" appeared full-blown and in print.

Some of the developments in psychiatry toward family therapy do not fall neatly into the two patterns described so far. The best known work outside these two groups probably is that of Nathan Ackerman (1958). Ackerman made the jump from individual to family therapy earlier and more aggressively than most. Other psychiatrists working in a variety of settings groped through stages such as the concurrent analysis of married couples and the stereoscopic technique (Martin, 1953) toward analysis of the family neurosis (Grotjahn, 1960).

As radical as these developments appeared to many psychiatrists, a sociologist-observer sees in them at least two other things. One is that, in spite of the drastic shift in definition of the diagnostic and treatment unit, there remains a strong emphasis upon a biologically based concept of illness, and analysis of the interaction between family members tends to be structured in terms of "cure" of the ill members (Parsons & Fox, 1952). Psychiatrists do operate as physicians, with the result that both organic problems and psychopathology are more conspicuous among their patients than among the clients of many nonmedical therapists.

The second striking thing is the conspicuousness of what sociologists and anthropologists call simultaneous invention (Ogburn, 1926). Pioneers in therapy methods, as evidenced by the fact that there were so many of them working relatively independently of one another, appear very much to have been products of their time.

THE DEVELOPMENT OF MARRIAGE COUNSELING

Not only were there convergences toward family therapy within psychiatry, but the parallel movement called marriage counseling was developing at the same time. In some respects, marriage counseling was ahead of its psychiatric counterpart, but in other respects, it gradually fell behind.

During its early years marriage counseling probably was unique in the degree of its focus upon relationships. It came into existence to treat relationship problems rather than personal problems (Leslie, 1965). Diagnosis and treatment planning involved two persons *and* a relationship. For a while, there was an attempt to adapt the old bio-medical model to marital conflict, and people wrote and spoke of "sick" marriages. This model was so inappropriate, however, that it soon was discarded for a more broadly applicable one.

Marriage counselors came to view marital interaction as constituting a social system (Parsons, 1951). In this framework, the person is no longer the basic unit of analysis, and less priority is assigned to personality factors. Both personality and relationships are conceived as entities, each being composed of simpler elements or systems and each having dynamics of its own, such that neither is completely reducible to the other. These systems are interpenetrating, of course. Social systems are composed of roles; and conversely, roles, as configurations of behavior, are components of personality.

As a system the marital relationship is viewed as having unique properties resulting from the impingement of two personalities upon one another in a particular social context. The relationship possesses dynamic force in its own right and influences the way in which personality is manifested. A man who has neurotic difficulties, for example, may or may not give malignant expression to those difficulties depending upon the kind of woman he marries and the resulting relationship between them. Moreover, to "cure" his neurosis may upset the relationship between the partners to the point where either or both manifest symptoms more disabling than the original ones. Marital diagnosis involves making integrated appraisals of both partners and the relationship so that treatment of the partners may be coordinated and gains in one area of personal or marital functioning used to reinforce gains in other areas of living.

From the beginning marriage counselors typically worked concurrently with both partners to a relationship. The early marriage-counseling literature is replete with assertions of the advantages inherent in such a procedure. Though social workers had long assigned one worker to entire families, the emerging family therapists generally had not reached this point.

Curiously, however, marriage counselors failed to see the full potential in having the same counselor work with different members of the family. This failure is reflected in the traditional marriage-counseling approach to the use of joint interviews. The literature stresses the usefulness of initial joint interviews for diagnostic purposes and then generally urges their discontinuance until counseling is nearing its terminal stages (Skidmore & Garrett, 1955). The impression is created that more systematic use of joint interviews is apt to be unproductive and to bog down in quarreling and recrimination.

Thus, even while marriage counselors were trumpeting the uniqueness and advantages of their approach, they lagged in developing it. The emerging family therapists, to whom the idea of conjoint therapy originally was anathema, were more creative. For approximately the past ten years, marriage counselors have been gradually awakening to the fact that someone has stolen their thunder. Gradually, they are now exploring the marriage counseling use of conjoint therapy. The thesis of this paper is that the implications of conjoint therapy for marriage counseling are considerable and that most of the limitations on such use are yet unknown.

CONJOINT THERAPY IN MARRIAGE COUNSELING

The term conjoint therapy is not precise. Its essence is the systematic use of joint interviews in which the counselor simultaneously interviews two or more persons, usually the marital partners. In purest form conjoint therapy involves *all* interviews being conducted as joint interviews, with neither partner being seen in individual sessions. The author and his colleagues have been doing some experimentation with this pure form of conjoint therapy and are finding it feasible in a small proportion of cases. Occasional couples whose problems are acute rather than chronic, who focus consistently on a particular problem area, and who are both motivated to strengthen their relationship by working out their problems appear to be good risks for pure conjoint therapy.

In this experiment, most of the counselors most of the time prefer to do some individual interviewing of the partners early in counseling. At these individual sessions, excessive hostility to the other partner is drained off through catharsis, "privileged" communication permits the revelation of attitudes and behavior that would not be revealed with the partner present, and thorough diagnostic study of each of the two partners is done. When the counselor believes that the couple can work productively in joint sessions, conjoint therapy becomes the sole or major technique for most of the counseling process. The joint interviews become the major vehicle for insight development, and further individual interviews are used only when anxiety in one of the partners mounts to the point of interfering with progress in the joint interviews.

The experimenters have not yet determined whether the alleged advantages in this combination of joint and individual sessions are really advantages to the clients. Few would question the legitimacy of the cathartic and personality-assessment functions of the individual interviews, but there is some doubt about the need of counselors to "know the whole story" through the revelation of material that is not to be shared with the partner. That counselors feel more comfortable when they know more about the clients may partly reflect the counselor's discomfort in working with the unfamiliar new technique of conjoint therapy. A less charitable interpretation would stress the elements of psychological voyeurism inherent in marriage counseling (Grotjahn, 1960) and indicate that the counselor's need to know is not necessarily consistent with his clients' welfare. More experience with conjoint therapy should illuminate this question, but in the meantime experience indicates that some individual interviews mixed with more frequent joint interviews may be the most widely applicable form of conjoint therapy.

Finally, conjoint therapy shades off into traditional marriage-counseling technique when joint interviews become occasionally interspersed among individual interviews. For purposes of this paper, the term conjoint therapy will be used to refer to the first two patterns only.

Effects upon the Counseling Process

Much has been written about the psychotherapeutic process. The intention of this paper is not, however, to survey or analyze that literature. Suffice it to say that, through accretion and reinforcement, a body of principles has become widely accepted without those principles having been subjected to controlled empirical test. The following discussion of effects of conjoint therapy upon marriage counseling process is of the same order. To persons with comparable backgrounds of training and experience, it should make sense or at least provide thought for discussion. To determined unbelievers, none of that which follows can be adequately proven.

The identification of distortions. In marriage counseling, as in psychotherapy generally, clients present themselves to the counselor in ways that involve considerable distortion. The identification and working through of these distortions is an involved problem even when the clients are essentially healthy, and it may be prolonged where there is much pathology.

Many clients distort consciously and perhaps willfully. Virtually all clients—indeed, all people—have done many things of which they are not proud and which they do not wish to reveal to others. Desiring and needing acceptance from the counselor, they conceal information that might threaten that acceptance. Even when clients are able to avoid the temptation of deliberate concealment, they are prone to present themselves in one-sided, biased fashion. No matter how hard they try to be objective, they are too immersed in their conflicts to see themselves in adequate perspective. It is common in marriage counseling to hear the same relationship described by husband and wife in such different terms that the counselor must force himself to realize that the clients are talking about one another. And finally, of course, there are distortions that derive from repression. These may be mere fragments, or they may be systematic and comprehensive. Obviously, they present the greatest difficulty.

Individual psychotherapy may proceed for months without the therapist being able to break through the barriers presented by these distortions. It is the author's experience that in conjoint therapy such distortions tend to be fewer and less extreme and that clients cling to them less tenaciously. When one counselor is seeing both partners, and when, at least part of the time, they are being seen in joint sessions, there is less possibility of, and less need for, concealment. Each partner is forced to hear descriptions and interpretations of his behavior that differ from his own. Furthermore, the rapport that develops between each client and the counselor is not based upon such a partial, favorable revelation of self. The clients confirm directly that the counselor can accept them in spite of the things that they wish to conceal.

Just as surely, the unwitting distortions of each partner are quickly revealed. Whether these are merely problems of perspective or whether they result from repression, neither partner can escape at least the fact that distortion is occurring. To the likely criticism that such rapid confrontation is apt to result in even more serious symptoms, the author can only reply that he has not usually found it so. Ackerman's (1958) observation that so-called family secrets, allegedly very dangerous, are neither very secret nor especially dangerous is pertinent here.

The situation in traditional marriage counseling practice when the counselor must lengthily unravel and work through distortions with each partner before bringing them together is largely cut short. What might otherwise take months is frequently accomplished in a very few sessions.

Moreover, the counselor in conjoint therapy is not placed in the position of having constantly to restructure his relationship with each of the partners.

The handling of transference and countertransference. The author uses the terms transference and countertransference very broadly. The transference neurosis of classical psychoanalysis is included but extended to embrace all distortions of the counselor-client relationship. As with distortions in the clients' productions discussed above, transference distortions may occur at different levels, ranging along a continuum, perhaps, from the mildest sort of personalizing of the relationship to the full-blown transference neurosis.

Some degree and some form of transference is exceedingly common in marriage counseling. On the other hand, permitting the development of an integrated transference neurosis is not necessary for the satisfactory resolution of much marital conflict, and the working through of such a relationship unnecessarily lengthens the counseling process. Marital conflict does not usually derive directly from unresolved pre-oedipal situations, and the conscious problem-solving abilities of most marriage-counseling clients are considerable.

Even in conventional marriage-counseling practice, incipient transference reactions tend to be held in check because the participation of the other spouse discourages the development of a "private world" between counselor and client. In conjoint therapy the physical presence of the other partner is an even more effective deterrent. Each spouse's tendencies to maneuver the counselor into private roles run head up against the counselor's relationship with the other partner. Thus too much regression is discouraged, and the partners are encouraged to work on their problem at more current relationship levels. Where the counselor still becomes a parent surrogate, he is more likely to become a joint parent and to reinforce the relationship between the partners.

With some marriage-counseling clients, transference becomes pronounced even in conjoint therapy. The interplay between counselor and two clients occasionally gets exceedingly complicated. Traditionally-oriented therapists to the contrary notwithstanding, this writer finds that most counselors handle these multiple transference situations about as well as they handle other transference problems. The added burden of having to work through distortions with both partners is at least partly offset by the lower probability of the counselor becoming unwittingly caught up in either pattern of distortion. Not only do many common forms of transference become very obvious to the counselor doing conjoint therapy, but many common forms of countertransference are quickly identified as well.

The drawing-out of conflict. A third effect of the systematic use of conjoint therapy in marriage counseling is to bring the marital conflict into the open and into the counseling sessions. Herein lies both a major advantage of conjoint therapy and a major source of resistance to its use by some counselors.

Marriage counselors long have recognized that when hostile spouses are seen jointly, they are apt to begin to fight. Conventional practice is based upon the assumptions that if the clients are permitted to fight, their relationship will deteriorate and the counselor will lose control of the counseling sessions, and that, as he loses control, he loses his ability to aid the clients. Two of these assumptions may be challenged, and the third may be shown to have little to do with conjoint therapy *per se*.

It is true that many couples in joint session will fight. It does not follow, however, that the fighting need produce deterioration of the marital relationship. For the question is not whether the couple will fight, but only whether they will fight in the presence of the counselor. They have been fighting at home and will continue to do so. Moreover, while the deteriorating effect of the conflict upon their relationship is what brings them into counseling, the ability of most couples to tolerate prolonged, severe conflict should not be overlooked. They are both afraid of their conflict, and they are accustomed to living with it. When a counselor excludes that conflict from the counseling sessions, he may inadvertently heighten the clients' fears. On the other hand, when the counselor can accept the conflict without alarm, the effects of the conflict upon the partners tend to become less malignant.

There is no good reason why conflict in the counseling sessions should cause the counselor to lose control. The counselor permits the expression of other feelings without losing control because he does not become embroiled in those feelings. But when clients begin to fight, they may trigger both anxiety and hostility in the counselor. Counselors themselves may be rather controlled people to whom outbursts of direct hostility are threatening and whose own tendencies to respond in kind, or perhaps to withdraw, are uncomfortably close to the surface. When this happens or when the resulting anxiety is communicated to the clients, the counselor may indeed lose control of the sessions and the confidence of the spouses. But this is a counselor problem, not a characteristic of conjoint therapy as such. Not only do many counselors quickly become comfortable with conflict in the counseling sessions, but they learn to use it to advantage.

Direct alteration of interaction. Whereas under conventional marriage-counseling procedure there may be prolonged inconsistency between the behavior of clients in the counseling sessions and their behavior in relation to one another outside the sessions, conjoint therapy admits the counselor directly to current squabbles. When the partners find that the counselor can empathize with each of them without taking sides, they can become more objective about both the partner and themselves. Each can be helped to make tentative gestures toward a less hurtful pattern of interaction and find that the other partner reciprocates. This process, in time, becomes cumulative and circular. Gradually, the couple can be led out of conflict according to dynamics analogous to those which led them into it originally.

The partner's interaction during the sessions provides a model for interaction between sessions. Each partner becomes, with the counselor, a kind of co-therapist working throughout the week. Because both partners are involved, alliances within the triad are avoided. More of the responsibility for solving their problems is shifted to the clients, where it belongs. Less dependence upon the counselor is encouraged, and eventually less weaning away from the counselor is required.

Focus on current relationships. A final distinguishing feature of conjoint marriage counseling, and one that has been implied above, is the emphasis it places on current relationships. The term "current" does not connote momentary, ephemeral, or trivial here. Roughly, it marks off the period from the time of marriage forward. Spouses seen together do not receive great encouragement to relive their early family experiences. The emphasis is upon what hurts them as a pair. They will, naturally, ferret out the bases for their conflicts both in what has occurred between them and in the fund of experience which each partner brought into the marriage. They will develop insight into the effects of childhood experience, but the emphasis is upon the contribution of childhood experience to the marital conflict and not upon early frustration or personality impairment as such.

By implication, personality reconstruction is not a primary goal in marriage counseling. Most couples become more comfortable with their own dynamics, with those of the partner, and with the common product. That change is inherent in this process is obvious. There is no sharp line between marriage counseling and reconstructive therapy. But there are differences of degree and emphasis. The point is simply that with a marriage counseling emphasis, conjoint therapy has many advantages that are just beginning to be appreciated.

Limitations in the Use of Conjoint Therapy

Limited successes with conjoint therapy should not blind its users to its limitations. The temptation is there, but to portray conjoint therapy as a panacea will only bring discredit upon it and delay its taking its proper place in the therapeutic arsenal. Unfortunately, the full limitations upon the use of conjoint therapy are not yet known. There follow some suggestions regarding these limitations based upon the author's own experience.

Lack of counselor preparedness. Most professional marriage counselors received their training in the tradition of individual psychotherapy which emphasized the exclusiveness of the counselor-client relationship and which stressed the alleged dangers involved in becoming entangled in the clients' conflicts. Consequently, few of them have much skill in the conduct of joint interviews, and their first efforts along these lines frequently result in disappointment. The resulting threat to professional self-concept encourages the rejection of the technique rather than acknowledgment of the need to develop new skills.

Beyond this, conjoint therapy is inherently more demanding upon the counselor. He must respond continuously and rapidly to an exceedingly broad range of stimuli. He must almost simultaneously hear, accept, and reflect the communications of both partners; he must protect each partner; and he must continuously support the relationship. It is demanding work for which some counselors may not be suited.

There also may be limitations upon the number of such interviews that any counselor can successfully complete in the course of a working day.

Lack of client preparedness. Clients as well as counselors have problems. Some client problems undoubtedly make the systematic use of joint interviews inadvisable.

Among marriage-counseling clients, the problem of motivation is important. If it is true that marriage-counseling clients "hurt less," on the average, than psychiatric patients and sometimes have to be "coaxed" to work concertedly on their problems, the more rapid confrontation inherent in conjoint therapy may tend to drive some of them out of counseling. Since the prognosis for such clients is not usually good, it may be asked whether this is really a disadvantage.

There is a more subtle problem related to the nature of the clients' motivations. It may be assumed that a disproportionate number of persons who seek out a marriage counselor need to work out their difficulties within the context of marriage. But some marriage-counseling clients come specifically seeking support for the dissolution of an intolerable relationship. At various levels of consciousness, these motives may be mixed and confused. Clients who are committed to separation may only be handicapped by joint sessions. Those whose motivations need to be worked through and clarified may be worked with far more efficiently in individual sessions.

There are also forms of client maladjustment that militate against the use of conjoint therapy. How many such patterns there are and how severe the illness must be are not yet known. Two examples recur in the author's own practice. Not surprisingly, clients in whom there are integrated paranoid features tend to interpret the conjoint situation as conspiratorial. Whether these delusions could eventually be worked through in conjoint therapy is less relevant than the fact that whatever advantages ordinarily accrue to conjoint therapy are lost in this instance.

Similarly, clients who have suffered such severe early deprivation that they are seriously crippled emotionally cannot participate actively in conjoint therapy any more than they can in individual therapy. When such persons are brought into conjoint therapy with hostile partners, the overwhelming need for protection of the disabled spouse blocks the development of the desired cumulative circular interaction.

CONCLUSION

This has not been a comprehensive discussion of conjoint therapy in marriage counseling. Such would require a substantial monograph rather than a brief article. Moreover, most of the pages for that monograph could not yet be written. The message of this article is really very simple. Marriage counselors have been slow to recognize the congruence of conjoint therapy with their basic orientation to counseling. Experiments with it indicate that it perhaps has more advantages for counselors than for the psychiatrists who originated it. Fascination with a new technique, however, should not obscure the fact that psychotherapy is a wondrously complex process which persistently defies universal solutions.

REFERENCES

Ackerman, N. *The psychodynamics of family life*. New York: Basic Books, 1958.

Bowen, M. Family psychotherapy. *American Journal of Orthopsychiatry*, 1961, *31*, 40–60.

Burlingham, Present trends in handling the mother-child relationship during the therapeutic process. *The Psychoanalytic Study of the Child*, 1951, *5*, 31–37.

Can one partner be successfully counseled without the other? *Marriage and Family Living*, February 1953, *15*, 59–64.

Grotjahn, M, *Psychoanalysis and the family neurosis*. New York: W. W. Norton, 1960.

Haley, J. Observation of the family of the schizophrenic. *American Journal of Orthopsychiatry*, 1960, *30*, 460–467.

Leslie, G. R. The field of marriage counseling. In Christensen, H. (Ed.), Handbook on marriage and the family. New York: Rand-McNally, 1965.

Martin, P., & Bird, W. An approach to the psychotherapy of marriage partners. *Psychiatry*. May 1953, *16*, 123–127.

Mittelman, B. The concurrent analysis of married couples. *The Psychoanalytic Quarterly*. April 1948, *17*, 182–197.

Ogburn, W. F. The great man vs. social forces. *Social Forces*, December 1926, *5*, 225–231.

Parsons, T. *The social system*. Glencoe, Ill.: The Free Press, 1951.

Parsons, T., & Fox, R. Illness, therapy, and the modern urban American family. *Journal of Social Issues*, 1952, *8*, 31–44.

Shellow, R. S., Brown, B. S., & Osberg, J. W. Family group therapy in retrospect: Four years and sixty families. *Family Process*, March 1963, *1*, 52–67.

Skidmore, R., & Garett, H. The joint interview in marriage counseling. *Marriage and Family Living*, November 1955, *17*, 349–354.

CHAPTER 19

Family Communication
and Conjoint Family Therapy

Virginia Satir

1. In this chapter, I should like to state in a general way some ideas about psychic health and illness in order to show their relevance to the interactional approach of family therapy. I also want to present my own picture of what a family therapist is and does, since he becomes, to an important degree, a model for his patients' subsequent behavior.

   I am not trying to present a "philosophy of therapy." These ideas appear to me as working tools, helpful in organizing my own way of handling therapy, or as a conceptual core around which therapeutic growths may be structured, rather than as a system of thought possessing value in and for itself.

2. The most important concept in therapy, because it is a touchstone for all the rest, is that of *maturation*.

   a. This is the state in which a given human being is fully in charge of himself.
   b. A mature person is one who, having attained his majority, is able to make choices and decisions based on accurate perceptions about himself, others, and the context in which he finds himself; who acknowledges these choices and decisions as being his; and who accepts responsibility for their outcomes.

3. The patterns of behaving that characterize a mature person we call functional because they enable him to deal in a relatively competent and precise way with the world in which he lives. Such a person will—

   a. manifest himself clearly to others.

Reprinted with permission of the author and the publisher from Virginia Satir, *Conjoint Family Therapy* (rev. ed.). Palo Alto, Calif.: Science and Behavior Books, 1967.

    b. be in touch with signals from his internal self, thus letting himself know openly what he thinks and feels.

    c. be able to see and hear what is outside himself as differentiated from himself and as different from anything else.

    d. behave toward another person as someone separate from himself and unique.

    e. treat the presence of different-ness as an opportunity to learn and explore rather than as a threat or a signal for conflict.

    f. deal with persons and situations in their context, in terms of "how it is" rather than how he wishes it were or expects it to be.

    g. accept responsibility for what he feels, thinks, hears and sees, rather than denying it or attributing it to others.

    h. have techniques for openly negotiating the giving, receiving and checking of meaning between himself and others.*

4. We call an individual dysfunctional when he has not learned to communicate properly. Since he does not manifest a means of perceiving and interpreting himself accurately, or interpreting accurately messages from the outside, the assumptions on which he bases his actions will be faulty and his efforts to adapt to reality will be confused and inappropriate.

    a. As we have seen, the individual's communication problems are rooted in the complex area of family behavior in which he lived as a child. The adults in the family provide the blueprint by which the child grows from infancy to maturity.

    b. If the male and female who were his survival figures did not manage jointly, if their messages to each other and the child were unclear and contradictory, he himself will learn to communicate in an unclear and contradictory way.

5. A dysfunctional person will manifest himself incongruently, that is, he will deliver conflicting messages, via different levels of communication and using different signals.

    a. As an example, let us take the behavior of the parents of a disturbed child during their first interview with the therapist. When the therapist asks what seems to be the trouble, they practically deny that there is any.

        M: Well, I don't know. I think financial problems more than anything . . . outside of that, we're a very close family.

        F: We do everything together. I mean, we hate to leave the kids. When we go someplace, we take the kids with us. As

---

*This description of maturity emphasizes social and communication skills rather than the acquisition of knowledge and recognized achievement, which in my view derive from the first two.

far as doing things together as a family, we always try to do that at least once a week, say on Sundays, Sunday afternoon, why we always try to get the kids together and take them out for a ride to the park or something like that.

b. In words, they imply that there is no reason why they should be in a therapist's office. But their actual presence there, and the agreement they have already made to enter therapy, amount to an admission of the contrary. And the father presents a further contradiction when he reduces his claim that the family does "everything" together to a statement about the rides they take on Sunday afternoons.

6. In addition, a dysfunctional individual will be unable to adapt his interpretations to the present context.

a. He will tend to see the "here and now" through labels which have been indelibly fixed in his mind during the early part of his life when all messages had survival significance. Each subsequent use of the label will strengthen its reality.
b. Therefore, it is conceivable that he will impose on the present that which fits the past, or that which he expects from the future, thus negating the opportunity to gain a perspective on the past or realistically shape the future.
   —For example, a school-age girl was brought into therapy because she was acting strangely and talking in riddles. When the mother was asked, "When did you notice that your child was not developing as she should?" she replied, "Well, she was a seven-month baby, and she was in an incubator for six weeks." The child's present and past difficulties were thus connected in a very illogical fashion.*
   —Later she said that after she brought the baby home from the hospital, "She wouldn't give me any reaction, just as though she couldn't hear. And I'd take her around and hold her next to me, and she wouldn't pay any attention, and I know it upset me, and I asked the doctor and he said it was nothing, she was just being stubborn—that's one thing that sort of stuck in my mind with her."
   —By using the word "stubborn" for the baby's indifference, the mother has given the baby a label that does not suit the context of babyhood. It implies that the child can be held accountable for willfully refusing to return the mother's love. Later on, the

---

*The communication aspects of this situation Jackson has labeled "past-present switches." Thus, the answer to the therapist's question, "How out of all the millions of people in the world did you two find each other?" may be as useful in family diagnosis as psychological testing. This question allows the spouses to describe their present relationship under cover of talking about the past. For further examples of this phenomenon, see Watzlawick's *An Anthology of Human Communication* (1964).

mother applies the same explanation to the child's strange behavior.

—By using the label "stubborn," and by implying in her first statement that the child's difficulties have a physical cause, the mother is able to absolve herself of blame; in fact, she has a double coverage. It is hard for such a mother to see her child's present problems objectively because she has already imposed her own interpretation on them.

7. Finally, a dysfunctional individual will not be able to perform the most important function of good communication: "checking out" his perceptions to see whether they tally with the situation as it really is or with the intended meaning of another. When two people are neither of them able to check out their meanings with each other, the result may resemble a comedy of errors—with a tragic ending. Here is one possible misunderstanding between a husband and a wife:

> *Report*: W: "He always yells." H: "I don't yell."

> *Explanation*: W: "I don't do things to suit him." H: "I don't do things to suit her."

> *Interpretation*: W: "He doesn't care about me." H: "She doesn't care about me."

> *Conclusion*: W: "I will leave him." H: "I will leave her."

> *Manifestation*: Wife uses invectives, voice is loud and shrill, eyes blaze, muscles stand out on base of neck, mouth is open, nostrils are distended, uses excessive movements. Husband says nothing, keeps eyes lowered, mouth tight, body constricted.

> *Outcome*: Wife visits divorce lawyer. Husband files a countersuit.

8. Difficulty in communicating is closely linked to an individual's self-concept, that is, his self-image and self-esteem.

   a. His parents may not only have given him inadequate models for *methods* of communication, but the *content* of their messages to him may have been devaluating.
   b. In order to form his self-image, the child has a demanding task. He must integrate messages from both parents (separately and together) telling him what to do with aspects of living like dependency, authority, sexuality and coding or labeling (cognition).
   c. If the parents' own attitudes are uncertain, or if they disagree with each other, the messages the child takes will be equally confused. The child will try to integrate what cannot be integrated, on the

basis of inconsistent and insufficient data. Failing, he will end up
with an incomplete picture of himself and low self-esteem.

d. In addition, the child's parents may depreciate his self-esteem
more directly. He looks to them to validate his steps in growth; if
these are not acknowledged at the time they occur, or if they are
acknowledged with concomitant messages of disgust, disapproval,
embarrassment, indifference or pain, the child's self-esteem will
naturally suffer.

9. Low self-esteem leads to dysfunctional communication:

a. When there is a conflict of interests. Any relationship presupposes
a commitment to a joint outcome, an agreement that each partner
will give up a little of his own interests in order to reach a wider
benefit for both.
   —This outcome is the best objective reality that can be arrived at
   in terms of what is possible, what is feasible, what fits the best
   all the way around.
   —The process used for reaching this outcome depends on the self-
   concepts of the persons engaged in it. If their self-esteem is low,
   so that any sacrifice of self seems intolerable, it is likely that the
   process will be based on some form of deciding "who is right,"
   "who will win," "who is most loved," "who will get made." I
   call this the "war syndrome."
   —If a person operates by means of this war syndrome, it is inevitable that his ability to seek objective information and arrive at
   objective conclusions as to what fits will be greatly impaired.
b. Dysfunction in communication will also follow when the individual is unable to handle different-ness.
   —An individual who has not achieved an independent selfhood will
   often take any evidence of different-ness in someone he is close
   to as an insult or a sign of being unloved.
   —This is because he is intensely dependent on the other person to
   increase his feelings of worth and to validate his self-image. Any
   reminder that the other is, after all, a separate being, capable of
   faithlessness and desertion, fills him with fear and distrust.
   —Some couples express their objections to each other's different-
   ness freely and loudly (the "teeter-totter syndrome"), but
   others, less secure in this area, prefer to pretend that different-
   ness does not exist.
   —With such couples, communication becomes *covert*. Any message
   which might call attention to the self as a private agent, with
   likes and dislikes, desires and displeasures of its own, is suppressed or changed. Wishes and decisions are presented as if they
   emanated from anywhere but inside the speaker himself; statements are disguised as symbolic utterances; messages are left
   incomplete or even not expressed at all, with the sender relying
   on mental telepathy to get them across. For example, a couple

‑okk

who overtly behaved as if they had absolutely no problems responded in therapy to the "How did you meet?" question as follows:

H: "Well, we were raised in the same neighborhood."

W: "Not exactly the same neighborhood" (*laughs*).

This slight modification on the wife's part presaged many revelations of serious division between them.

10. Thus far we have been talking about dysfunctional behavior rather than the symptom that calls attention to it. What is the connection between them?

    a. Dysfunctional behavior is, as we have seen, related to feelings of low self-esteem. It is, in fact, a defense against the perception of them. Defenses, in turn, are ways which enable the person with low self-esteem to function *without* a symptom. To the person himself and to the outward world, there may appear to be nothing wrong.

    b. But if he is threatened by some event of survival significance, some happening which says to him, "You do not count; you are not lovable; you are nothing," the defense may prove unequal to the task of shielding him, and a symptom will take its place.

    c. Usually it is only then that the individual and his community will notice that he is "ill" and that he will admit a need for help.

11. How, then, do we define therapy?

    a. If illness is seen to derive from inadequate methods of communication (by which we mean all interactional behavior), it follows that therapy will be seen as an attempt to improve these methods. The emphasis will be on correcting discrepancies in communication and teaching ways to achieve more fitting joint outcomes.

    b. This approach to therapy depends on three primary beliefs about human nature:

      —First, that every individual is geared to survival, growth, and getting close to others and that all behavior expresses these aims, no matter how distorted it may look. Even an extremely disturbed person will be fundamentally on the side of the therapist.

      —Second, that what society calls sick, crazy, stupid, or bad behavior is really an attempt on the part of the afflicted person to signal the presence of trouble and call for help. In that sense, it may not be so sick, crazy, stupid, or bad after all.

      —Third, that human beings are limited only by the extent of their knowledge, their ways of understanding themselves and their ability to "check out" with others. Thought and feeling are inextricably bound together; the individual need not be a prisoner of his feelings but can use the cognitive component of his feeling to free himself. This is the basis for assuming that a human being can learn what he doesn't know and can change ways of commenting and understanding that don't fit.

12. This brings us to a discussion of the role of the therapist. How will he act? What picture will he have of himself?

   a. Perhaps the best way that he can see himself is as a *resource person*. He is not omnipotent. He is not God, parent or judge. The knotty question for all therapists is how to be an expert without appearing to the patient to be all-powerful, omniscient, or presuming to know always what is right and wrong.
   b. The therapist does have a special advantage in being able to study the patient's family situation as an experienced observer, while remaining outside it, above the power struggle, so to speak. Like a camera with a wide-angle lens, he can see things from the position of each person present and act as a representative of each. He sees transactions, as well as the individuals involved, and thus has a unique viewpoint.
   c. Because of this, the family can place their trust in him as an "official observer," one who can report impartially on what he sees and hears. Above all, he can report on what the family cannot see and cannot report on.

13. The therapist must also see himself as a *model of communication*.

   a. First of all, he must take care to be aware of his own prejudices and unconscious assumptions so as not to fall into the trap he warns others about, that of suiting reality to himself. His lack of fear in revealing himself may be the first experience the family has had with clear communication.
   b. In addition, the way he interprets and structures the action of therapy from the start is the first step in introducing the family to new techniques in communication.
   c. Here is an example of how the therapist clarifies the process of interaction for a family:

   Th: (*to husband*) I notice your brow is wrinkled, Ralph. Does that mean you are angry at this moment?

   H: I did not know that my brow was wrinkled.

   Th: Sometimes a person looks or sounds in a way of which he is not aware. As far as you can tell, what were you thinking and feeling just now?

H: I was thinking over what she [his wife] said.

Th: What thing that she said were you thinking about?

H: When she said that when she was talking so loud, she wished I would tell her.

Th: What were you thinking about that?

H: I never thought about telling her. I thought she would get mad.

Th: Ah, then maybe that wrinkle meant you were puzzled because your wife was hoping you would do something and you did not know she had this hope. Do you suppose that by your wrinkled brow you were signalling that you were puzzled?

H: Yeh, I guess so.

Th: As far as you know, have you ever been in that same spot before, that is, where you were puzzled by something Alice said or did?

H: Hell, yes, lots of times.

Th: Have you ever told Alice you were puzzled when you were?

W: He never says anything.

Th: (*smiling, to Alice*) Just a minute, Alice, let me hear what Ralph's idea is of what he does. Ralph, how do you think you have let Alice know when you are puzzled?

H: I think she knows.

Th: Well, let's see. Suppose you ask Alice if she knows.

H: This is silly.

Th: (*smiling*) I suppose it might seem so in this situation, because Alice is right here and certainly has heard what your question is. She knows what it is. I have the suspicion, though, that neither you nor Alice are very sure about what the other expects, and I think you have not developed ways to find out. Alice, let's go back to when I commented on Ralph's wrinkled brow. Did you happen to notice it, too?

W: (*complaining*) Yes, he always looks like that.

Th: What kind of a message did you get from that wrinkled brow?

W: He don't want to be here. He don't care. He never talks. Just looks at television or he isn't home.

Th: I'm curious. Do you mean that when Ralph has a wrinkled brow that you take this as Ralph's way of saying, "I don't love you, Alice. I don't care about you, Alice."?

W: (*exasperated and tearfully*) I don't know.

Th: Well, maybe the two of you have not yet worked out crystal-clear ways of giving your love and value messages to each other. Everyone needs crystal-clear ways of giving their value messages. (*to son*) What do you know, Jim, about how you give your value messages to your parents?

S: I don't know what you mean.

Th: Well, how do you let your mother, for instance, know that you like her, when you are feeling that way. Everyone feels different ways at different times. When you are feeling glad your mother is around, how do you let her know?

S: I do what she tells me to do. Work and stuff.

Th: I see, so when you do your work at home, you mean this for a message to your mother that you're glad she is around.

S: Not exactly.

Th: You mean you are giving a different message then. Well, Alice, did you take this message from Jim to be a love message? (*to Jim*) What do you do to give your father a message that you like him?

S: (*after a pause*) I can't think of nothin'.

Th: Let me put it another way. What do you know crystal-clear that you could do that would bring a smile to your father's face?

S: I could get better grades in school.

Th: Let's check this out and see if you are perceiving clearly. Do you, Alice, get a love message from Jim when he works around the house?

W: I s'pose—he doesn't do very much.

Th: So from where you sit, Alice, you don't get many love messages from Jim. Tell me, Alice, does Jim have any other ways that he might not now be thinking about that he has that say to you that he is glad you are around?

W: (*softly*) The other day he told me I looked nice.

Th: What about you, Ralph, does Jim perceive correctly that if he got better grades you would smile?

H: I don't imagine I will be smiling for some time.

Th: I hear that you don't think he is getting good grades, but would you smile if he did?

H: Sure, hell, I would be glad.

Th: As you think about it, how do you suppose you would show it?

W: You never know if you ever please him.

Th: We have already discovered that you and Ralph have not yet developed crystal-clear ways of showing value feelings toward one another. Maybe you, Alice, are now observing this between Jim and Ralph. What do you think, Ralph? Do you suppose it would be hard for Jim to find out when he has pleased you?

14. The therapist will not only exemplify what he means by clear communication, but he will teach his patients how to achieve it themselves.

   a. He will spell out the rules for communication accurately. In particular, he will emphasize the necessity for checking out meaning *given* with meaning *received*. He will see that the patient keeps in mind the following complicated set of mirror images:
   —Self's idea (how I see me).
   —Self's idea of other (how I see you).
   —Self's idea of other's idea of self (how I see you seeing me).
   —Self's idea of other's idea of self's idea of other (how I see you seeing me seeing you).

Only if a person is able to check back and forth across the lines of communication, can he be sure that he has completed a clear exchange.

  b. The therapist will help the patient to be aware of messages that are incongruent, confused or covert.

  c. At the same time, the therapist will show the patient how to check on invalid assumptions that are used as fact. He knows that members of dysfunctional families are afraid to question each other to find out what each really means. They seem to say to each other: "I can't let you know what I see and hear and think and feel or you will drop dead, attack or desert me." As a result, each operates from his assumptions, which he takes from the other person's manifestations and thereupon treats as fact. The therapist uses various questions to ferret out these invalid assumptions, such as:

      "What did you say? What did you hear me say?"

      "What did you see or hear that led you to make that conclusion?"

      "What message did you intend to get across?"

      "If I had been there, what would I have seen or heard?"

      "How do you know? How can you find out?"

      "You look calm, but how do you feel in the stomach?"

  d. Like any good teacher, the therapist will try to be crystal-clear.
    —He will repeat, restate and emphasize his own observations, sometimes to the point of seeming repetitious and simple. He will do the same with observations made by members of the family.
    —He will also be careful to give his reasons for arriving at any conclusion. If the patient is baffled by some statement of the therapist's and does not know the reasoning behind it, this will only increase his feelings of powerlessness.

15. The therapist will be aware of the many possibilities of interaction in therapy.

  a. In the therapeutic situation, the presence of the therapist adds as many dyads (two-person systems) as there are people in the family, since he relates to each member. The therapist, like the other people present, operates as a member of various dyads but also as the observer of other dyads. These shifts of position could be confusing to him and to the family. If, for example, he has taken someone's part, he should clearly state he is doing so.

b. The therapist clarifies the nature of interchanges made during therapy, but he has to select those that are representative since he can't possibly keep up with everything that is said. Luckily, family sequences are apt to be redundant, so one clarification may serve a number of exchanges.

c. Here is an illustration of the way the therapist isolates and underlines each exchange.

—When the therapist states, "When you, Ralph, said you were angry, I noticed that you, Alice, had a frown on your face," this is an example of the therapist reporting himself as a monad ("I *see* you, Alice; I *hear* you, Ralph"), and reporting to Ralph and Alice as monads (the use of the word *you*, followed by the specific name). Then, by the therapist's use of the word *when*, he establishes that there is a connection between the husband's report and the wife's report, thus validating the presence of an interaction.

—If the therapist then turns to the oldest son, Jim, and says, "What do you, Jim, make of what just happened between your mother and father?" the therapist is establishing Jim as an observer, since family members may forget that they monitor each other's behavior.

—When Jim answers, everyone knows what his perception is. If it turns out that Jim's report does not fit what either Alice or Ralph intended, then there is an opportunity to find out what was intended, what was picked up by Jim, and why he interpreted it that way.

16. Labeling an illness is a part of therapy that a therapist must approach with particular care.

a. A therapist, when he deals with a patient, is confronting a person who has been labeled by others or by himself as having emotional, physical or social disorders. To the non-therapeutic observer, the behavior which signals the presence of a disorder is usually labeled "stupid," "crazy," "sick" or "bad."

b. The therapist will use other labels, like "mentally defective," "underachieving," "schizophrenic," "manic-depressive," "psychosomatic," "sociopathic." These are labels used by clinicians to describe behavior which is seen to be deviant: deviant from the rest of the person's character, deviant from the expectations of others, and deviant from the context in which the person finds himself.

c. The observations made by clinicians over the years have been brought together under a standardized labeling system called the "psychiatric nomenclature." It is a method of shorthand used by clinicians to describe deviant behavior.

d. These labels often presuppose an exact duplication of all the individuals so labeled. Over the years, each of the labels has been given an identity, with prognosis and treatment implications based on the dimensions of that identity.

e. If a therapist has labeled a person "schizophrenic," for instance, he may have based his prognosis of that person on his ideas about schizophrenia, rather than on an observation of a person who, among other labels like "human being," "Jim," "husband," "father," "chemist," has the label "schizophrenic."

f. But neither the clinician or any other person has the right to treat him only in terms of the label "schizophrenic" while losing sight of him as a total human being. No label is infallible, because no diagnosis is, but by identifying the person with the label, the therapist shuts his mind to the possibility of different interpretations which different evidence might point to.

g. The therapist must say to his patient, in effect: You are behaving now with behavior which I, as a clinician, label "schizophrenia." But this label only applies *at this time, in this place*, and *in this context*. Future times, places and contexts may show something quite different.

17. Let us close this discussion of the role of the therapist with a look at some of the specific advantages family therapy will have compared to individual or group therapy.

a. In family therapy, the therapist will have a greater opportunity to observe objectvely. In individual therapy, since there are only two people, the therapist is part of the interaction. It is hard for him to be impartial. In addition, he must sift out the patient's own reactions and feelings from those which might be a response to clues from the therapist himself.

b. The family therapist will be able to get firsthand knowledge of the patient in two important areas.
   —By observing the individual in his family, the therapist can see where he is in terms of his present level of growth.
   —By observing a child in the family group, the therapist can find out how his functioning came to be handicapped. He can see for himself how the husband and wife relate to each other and how they relate to the child.
   —This kind of firsthand knowledge is not possible in individual therapy, or even in group therapy, where the individual is with members of his peer group and the kind of interaction that can be studied is limited to this single aspect.

18. As a therapist, I have found certain concepts useful, somewhat like measuring tools, in determining the nature and extent of dysfunction in a family.

a. I make an analysis of the techniques used by each member of the family for *handling the presence of different-ness*. A person's reaction to different-ness is an index to his ability to adapt to growth and change. It also indicates what attitudes he will have toward other members of his family, and whether he will be able to express these attitudes directly or not.

—The members of any family need to have ways to find out about and make room for their different-ness. This requires that each can report directly what he perceives about himself and the other, to himself and to the other.

—Example: Janet misses her hatpin. She must say, "I need my hatpin (clear), which I am telling you, Betty, about, (direct), and it is the hatpin that I use for the only black hat I have (specific)." Not: "Why don't you leave my hat alone?" or "Isn't there something you want to tell me?" or going into Betty's room and turning things upsidedown (unclear, indirect, and unspecific).

—As I have said before, when one of the partners in a marriage is confronted with a different-ness in the other that he did not expect, or that he did not know about, it is important that he treat this as an opportunity to explore and to understand rather than as a signal for war.

—If the techniques for handling different-ness are based on determining who is right (war), or pretending that the different-ness does not exist (denial), then there is a potential for pathological behavior on the part of any member of the family, but particularly the children.

b. I make what I call a *role function analysis* to find out whether the members of a family are covertly playing roles different from those which their position in the family demands that they play.

—If two people have entered a marriage with the hope of extending the self, each is in effect put in charge of the other, thus creating a kind of mutual parasitic relationship.

—This relationship will eventually be translated into something that looks like a parent-child relationship. The adults, labeled "husband" and "wife," may in reality be functioning as mother and son, father and daughter, or as siblings, to the confusion of the rest of the family and, ultimately, themselves.

—Here is an oversimplified example of the way things might go in such a family:

Suppose Mary takes over the role of sole parent, with Joe acting the part of her child. Joe then takes the part of a brother to their two children, John and Patty, and becomes a rival with them for their mother's affections. To handle his rivalry and prove his place, he may start drinking excessively, or he may bury himself in his work in order to avoid coming home. Mary, deserted, may turn to John in such a way as to make him feel he must take his father's place. Wishing to do so but in reality unable to, John may become delinquent, turning against his mother and choosing someone on the outside. Or he may accept his mother's invitation, which would be to give up being male and become homosexual. Patty may regress or remain infantile to keep her place. Joe may get ulcers. Mary may become psychotic.

—These are only some of the possibilities for disturbance in a family that has become dislocated by incongruent role-playing.

c. I make a *self-manifestation analysis* for each member of a family. If what a person says does not fit with the way he looks, sounds and acts, or if he reports his wishes and feelings as belonging to someone else or as coming from somewhere else, I know that he will not be able to produce reliable clues for any other person interacting with him. When such behavior, which I call *"manifesting incongruency,"* is present in the members of a family to any large degree, there will be a potential for development of pathology.

d. In order to find out how the early life of each member of a family has affected his present ways of behaving, I make what I call a *model analysis.*

—This means that I try to discover who the models were (or are) that influenced each family member in his early life; who gave him messages about the presence and desirability of growth; who gave him the blueprint from which he learned to evaluate and act on new experience; who showed him how to become close to others.

—Because these messages have survival significance, the ways in which they are given will automatically determine the way the individual interprets later messages from other adults, who may not be survival-connected but who may be invested with survival significance, like spouses, in-laws or bosses.*

19. The ideas in this chapter have been discussed out of the context of ongoing therapy, where they belong. In the next chapter, I hope to show more specifically how I, as a therapist, incorporate them into the action of therapy.

REFERENCES

Watzlawick, P. *An anthology of human communication.* Palo Alto, Calif.: Science and Behavior Books, 1964.

---

*While there are obvious connections between this theory and both the analytic concept of transference and the Sullivanian concept of parataxic distortion, there are also differences. In particular, instead of inferring from the transference the probable nature of the individual's early environment, I use the information about his past to evaluate the survival significance of his current messages.

CHAPTER 20

Techniques of Conjoint
Family Therapy

Virginia Satir

1. The therapist must first create a setting in which people can, perhaps
   for the first time, take the risk of looking clearly and objectively at
   themselves and their actions.

   a. He must concentrate on giving them confidence, reducing their
      fears, and making them comfortable and hopeful about the
      therapy process.
   b. He must show that he has direction, that he is going somewhere.
      His patients come to him because he is an expert, so he must
      accept the label and be comfortable in his role.
   c. Above all, he must show patients that he can structure his ques-
      tions in order to find out what both he and they need to know.

2. The patient is afraid. He doesn't dare ask about what he doesn't
   know; he feels little, alone, and frightened.

   a. He suffers from the Crystal Ball Syndrome: "I'm supposed to
      know. But I am little and can't ask. Yet I am big and omniscient; I
      can guess. You, the therapist, should be able to guess too."
   b. He suffers from the Fragility Syndrome: "If I ask, the other
      person will fall apart. If I ask, I will get an answer that will make
      me fall apart."
   c. He suffers from Fear of the Unknown. Pieces of the past are
      missing or can't be looked at. This or that is forbidden territory.
   d. He doesn't know what it is he doesn't know; he feels hopeless. He
      has been operating from insufficient information for a long time.
      He feels that there is no point in continuing the struggle.
   e. He can't ask about what he doesn't know; he feels helpless. Sick
      people can't be direct about what they want. They can tell about
      what hurts, not about what is wrong.

Reprinted with permission of the author and the publisher from Virginia Satir, *Conjoint Family Therapy* (rev. ed). Palo Alto, Calif.: Science and Behavior Books, 1967.

f. He fears that therapist will lie to him; he feels suspicious. He assumes that others know and won't tell; that others see and hear everything. ("Ma always knew when I was in the cookie jar. So others know what is inside of me.")

3. The therapist is not afraid.

    a. He does dare to ask questions, and the way he frames them helps the patient to be less afraid as well.
  —The therapist asks what the patient can answer, so that the patient feels competent and productive.
  —The therapist engages the patient in a history-taking procedure to bring out details of family life. This makes the patient feel he knows things the therapist doesn't know, that he has something to contribute. (Patients get very involved in building this factual history of their own past. They argue with each other about the facts, correct the therapist, and so forth.)
  —The therapist asks questions which the patient can emotionally handle at the time, so the patient can feel he is in control.

    b. The therapist doesn't know what it is he doesn't know, but he knows how to find out and how to check on his knowledge.
  —The therapist does not assume anything. He must not think he knows more than he does. All he can assume is that there is a body before him; it is breathing; it is a male or a female of certain age.
  —If the therapist operates from assumptions without checking on them, he is often wrong. He must question his patients constantly:

        "Does she like being beaten, or not?"

        "Did they ever get to the movies?"

        "What does 'Well, sort of' mean?"

  —He must question his own assumptions too. Does their coming late to the appointment mean they are "resisting" or not? (There is a story about a man accused by the therapist of "resisting" therapy because he arrived late for the therapy hour. Later the therapist discovered the man had been held up by a serious accident on the freeway.)

    c. The therapist can ask about what he doesn't know; he knows how to get facts.
  —Facts about planning processes: "Did you get to the movies as you planned?" or, "Did you ever get the bread on the table?"
  —Facts which reveal loopholes in planning. For instance, the mother complains that her children don't do chores. The therapist finds by questioning that she never tells them what to do; all the instructions are in her head.

—Facts about perceptions of self and other: "How did you expect he would react?" or, "What did you assume she thought?"

—Facts about perceptions of roles and models: "Who does what in your house?" or, "How did your dad handle money?"

—Facts about communication techniques:

"You weren't sure what he meant? What was it about his behavior that made you uncertain?"

"What did you say to him? What did you say back to her?"

"Did the words coming out of his mouth match the look on his face?"

"Did you try to get your point across? How? Then what did you do?"

—Facts about how members express sexual feelings and act out. The therapist doesn't give double-level messages to patients to the effect that he really wants to hear about these subjects more than any other. His questions concern everyday living, *including* sex activities and periods of acting out. When discussing sexual material, the therapist does so in an open, concrete, matter-of-fact way. He treats this subject like any other. He says: "What way is it?" not, "Who is to blame?"; "How does that go?" not, "Why don't you respond?"

d. The therapist does not fear the patient is lying to him; he is not suspicious. He realizes the patient is not deliberately withholding information or misrepresenting it. He is responding to a vague fear of blame and low self-worth.

4. The therapist shows the patient how he looks to others.

a. The therapist rises above the cultural prohibition against telling others how they manifest themselves:

"Your nose is bleeding."

"Your slip is showing."

"You seem to want to be friends with him but you don't act the way you say you feel."

"You seem to want to succeed but you act as though you might be afraid to try."

b. The therapist realizes that people are grateful to be told how they manifest themselves.

"We all need three-way mirrors. Yet we assume that others see in us what we feel we are manifesting."

> "We can give information if we do it in such a tone that our good will is clear. Clarity of intent gets across if our words, face, tone of voice, are all of a piece."

But such information must also be given in an appropriate context, in an appropriate relationship. The telling must not be overdone, and good things must be told too. For example, a husband had a glob of something on his shoe. He and his wife sat through a whole therapy session with me. Finally the wife mentioned it to her husband. He asked her why she hadn't told him, and she said she didn't want to embarrass him or hurt him. Also, she thought he knew about it. He was angry that she hadn't told him. Even though the news we get from others may be uncomfortable, we prefer that to not knowing the impression we give.

c. The therapist can also put the tape recorder to good use. Playing back tapes of previous conversations (which were openly recorded, of course) can be a good way of showing people how they sound and look to others, as well as making it easier for patient and therapist to study the interactions of therapy. In addition, the positive moves of patients can be pointed out to them while playing back tapes.

5. When the therapist asks for and gives information, he does so in a matter-of-fact, nonjudgmental, light, congruent way.

   a. The therapist verbally recreates situations in order to collect facts. He has a flair for acceptance and imagination:

      Th: Now let me see. There was no bread. What did you do for bread that night?

      W: Well, we didn't have any.

      Th: Well, then you didn't get enough to eat. Now let's take a look at what you were trying to do. You wanted food on the table and it wasn't there. And you thought Harry was going to bring it. Your husband is telling you that you don't keep him informed, and you are telling him he doesn't care what happens in the house, what happens to you. Let's see where this all started. Here you are, Harry, coming in the door wondering if dinner's cooked. And your wife is thinking, "We don't have any bread . . ."

   b. By showing he is easy about giving and receiving information, the therapist makes it easier for the patient to do so.
     —I can ask—so can you.
     —I can give information—so can you.
     —I can receive information—so can you.

—I can give a clear message—so can you.

(But the therapist must beware of the inappropriate light touch. One time a trainee-therapist sat with a smile on her face while a patient was telling her about very painful material. The trainee's consultant-observer pointed this out to her after the session was over. She was unaware that she was doing this, and said she guessed she always smiled when things were painful to cover up what she was feeling inside. The therapist must be congruent in his behavior.)

6. The therapist builds self-esteem.

   a. The therapist makes constant "I value you" comments along the way:

      "You're a responsible person."

      "You have feelings too, you know."

      "You can want things for yourself, can't you?"

   b. The therapist labels assets. The patient is like a grocery store after an earthquake, with unlabeled goods lying all around. The therapist takes a tally for the patient; what is in stock, how it might be sold. The therapist says:

      "You showed you could do that quite well."

      "You never allowed yourself to develop that, did you?"

   c. The therapist asks the patient questions he can answer.
   d. The therapist emphasizes that he and his patients are equals in learning.
     —By asking questions, he tells his patients: "You contribute to what I know." (Family members check each other on facts and this should be encouraged.)
     —He admits that he can make mistakes: "I goofed on that. I'm sorry," or, "I forgot. It was careless of me. I should have remembered."
     —By his actions, he tells his patients, "I share what I know." The therapist shares as much of his assumptions and knowledge as he can, but at the right time and in an appropriate manner.
   e. The therapist includes himself as a person whose meaning can be checked on: "I will try to be perfectly clear. You check me if you don't follow me."
   f. The therapist takes the family's history and notes past achievements.
   g. The therapist begins to accentuate the idea of good intentions but bad communication:

"I think Mother and Dad very much want to get across their messages, but somehow something seems to stand in their way."

"In this family I see everyone wanting to report on what they see and hear and on what they wish for, but somehow behaving as though others won't hear."

"There is no lack of good intentions, good wishes in this family. But somehow everyone seems to have trouble making these wishes clear."

"I don't think for a minute that anyone in this family wants to give pain to others. But when comments are made, they always seem to come out in the form of accusations."

"Why is it that members of this family don't seem able to give open reports to each other on what they see and hear?"

h. The therapist asks each family member what he can do that brings pleasure to another member:

"What can you do, Joe, that you know ahead of time will bring pleasure to Mary?" (and vice versa)

"What can you do, Johnny, that will bring big smiles to Mother's face?"

By these questions the therapist not only further delineates family rules, but he helps each member to see himself as others see him. Maybe Johnny says (about his father): "I can't do anything to please him." Maybe Joe says (about what he thinks his wife wants of him): "Just bring in the money." Maybe Mary says (about what Joe wants of her): "Just keep him fed."

i. The therapist is human, clear, direct. Love is not enough. The therapist works for maximum adaptability by helping the family to feel they are likeable. He raises their capacity to give and minimizes their sensitivities to painful subjects, thereby decreasing the necessity for defenses.

7. The therapist decreases threat by setting the rules of interaction.

a. The therapist sees to it that all are present: "We need your reaction, experience, on this," or, "Only you can tell us what you saw and heard."

b. He makes it clear that no one is to interrupt others:

"You're all talking at once. I can't hear."

"I guess Johnny will have to speak for five minutes, then Patty can speak for five minutes."

"You're hurting my eardrums."

c. He emphasizes that no one may act out or make it impossible to converse during the session:

"I have to hear in order to do my work."

"You got your point across. Now let's get to work."

"No wonder you have not been able to work this out. Nobody is listening to anybody else."

"Now I know how deeply you feel about this. There's no further need to show me."

"When you can talk in an adult manner, then come back and we'll get to work. Until then we will have to terminate therapy."

d. He makes sure that no one is allowed to speak for anybody else:

"When you speak, speak for yourself only."

"Let Johnny speak for himself. You can't be an authority on Johnny."

"Have you ever crawled inside another's skin and looked at a thought? You can't do it. Neither can I. We have to check."

"You can collect evidence on his behavior and on what he says and see if they fit. You can then ask about it. But only he can explain why his messages didn't fit."

"Did you ever *ask* what he meant by what he said? Or did you just guess?"

e. He tries to make everyone speak out clearly so he can be heard.

f. He makes direct requests to people to speak up:

"I'm a little deaf. Not very deaf, but a little deaf. You're going to have to speak up."

"We don't want to miss what you have to say."

"Maybe you feel that what you have to say isn't important."

g. He kids:

"Cat get your tongue?"

"Know the language?"

"You need practice in exercising that lower lip."

h. He relates silence to covert controls:

"I saw you looking at Mother. Were you thinking she didn't want you to speak?"

"Maybe you think if you speak you'll get clobbered."

"We'll have to find out what makes it so unsafe to talk."

8. The therapist decreases threat by the way he structures the interviews:

a. The therapist announces that therapy is aiming toward a concrete goal and will have a definite end.
   —At the very beginning he sets boundaries: "This is not going to be an open-end process, one which may drag on indefinitely. The total number of interviews within which we shall try to work will be . . ."
   —He may also set more limited deadlines: "At the end of five sessions, we shall re-evaluate to see what has been accomplished, where we need to go."

b. The therapist plans the interviews so that the family will understand that he sees them as a *family* and is not taking anyone's side.
   —He may begin therapy by seeing the two mates, the "architects" of the family, or he may see the whole family together. But whenever he starts with a new family, he wants to see them all together at least once, even when the children are too young to enter therapy, in order to understand the operation of the family and what each person's place in it is.
   —He never sees the I. P.* and his parents alone, as this would only reinforce the common assumption that the I. P. is the root of the family's trouble.
   —He never sees any unit other than the parents alone before he and the family are clear on the whole family's way of operating. Doing so before this understanding is reached may make the therapist appear to be in a coalition with certain family members, or getting privileged data which may be kept from other members. The therapist must guard against any actions which might be taken by the family as a message about "who is to blame," "who is loved most," "who is sick," etc.
   —After the operation of the family is made explicit to the therapist and the family, he can see individuals on a basis understood by everyone to pertain to some work relating to a marital pair, an individual, the sibling unit, and so forth.
   —The therapist singles out units when it seems practical or feasible. Sometimes family members are away for business or camp and seeing the separated units comes about naturally. If he sees anyone separately, it is always with the idea of reporting back to the family group what he and they have "discovered."

___
*Identified Patient.

9. The therapist decreases threat by reducing the need for defenses.

    a. In my opinion, the dysfunctional family operates within a reign of terror, with all members fearing they will be hurt and all members fearing they will hurt others. All comments are taken as attacks on self-esteem. Therefore, the therapist must reduce terror. Defenses, as I see them, are simply ways of enhancing self-esteem and defending against attacks on self-esteem. So the therapist does not have to "destroy" defenses in order to produce change. He exerts all his efforts to reducing terror, reducing the necessity for defenses.

    b. The therapist asks each family member what he can do that brings anger from another member:

> "What can you do which you know, as sure as sure, will make Dad blow his cork?"

> "What can you do, Mary, that will make Joe especially mad?"

Such questions further delineate family rules and prohibitions. They help family members make covert rules overt. They also continue to decrease fears about showing anger.

    c. The therapist interprets anger as hurt:

> "Well, as far as I am concerned, when a person looks angry, this simply means he feels pain inside. In some way he feels his self-esteem is in danger."

> "We will have to work out ways so that you can all give clear messages without feeling you will hurt other people's feelings."

> "Dad may look angry but he is really feeling some kind of pain and hurt. He will have to give a clearer message about his pain, so that others will know what is going on inside him."

    d. The therapist acknowledges anger as a defense and deals with the hurt:

> H: It's all I can do to keep from killing you!

> W: You're a mean old man!

> Th: Now I know how deeply disappointed you both are. Things have turned out so differently from what you hoped. Let's see what happened which has prevented the two of you from having joy and pleasure in your lives.

    e. The therapist shows that pain and the forbidden are all right to look at:

"Did you see your parents' pain? Were you able to relieve it?"

"So your dad had a wooden leg. You couldn't talk about that, could you? That was painful for your family to talk about. Why?"

"So Roger was adopted. Did you know this, Roger? What did Mother tell you about it? Why weren't you able, Mother, to tell Roger this?"

f. The therapist burlesques basic fears in the family:

"Mother and Dad won't drop dead if you simply comment on what you see and hear."

"You must think that Mother and Dad are pretty fragile creatures. They look like pretty strong people to me."

"You seem to act, Mary, as if Joe will fall apart if you simply report on what you have observed."

By burlesquing, or by painting the picture ad absurdum, the therapist helps decrease overprotective feelings and feelings of omnipotence, thus further reducing the need for defenses.

10. The therapist decreases threat by handling loaded material with care.

a. He handles loaded material by careful timing, going from least-loaded to most-loaded.
—He goes from a history of the past, how couples first met, what they saw in each other, to the present interaction.
—He starts with a discussion about the parents of origin and leads on to a discussion about the present parents.
—The timing of questions is done by the order in which they are asked during the history-taking:

"What did your parents do for fun?"

"How were your parents different from each other?"

"Were your parents able to disagree?"

"How did your parents disagree?"

"What do *you* do for fun?" etc.

b. The therapist switches to less loaded material when things get hot.
—To one subject rather than another (this depends on what in the family is the most loaded material).
—To the past rather than the present: "How did money-handling go in your family when you were a kid?"

c. The therapist handles loaded material by generalizing what one expects to see in families:

> "It is not unusual for families to hurt, have pain, have problems, fight."

> "When one person in a family is hurting (or angry, or frightened) all are feeling the same way."

> "When one person in a family is hurting, all share a responsibility in that hurt."

d. The therapist handles loaded material by relating feelings to facts.
  —He asks for specificity, examples, documentation: "He beats you sometimes? How often?" or, "He sort of cheats? What do you mean?"
  —He asks about data that patients use to support their perceptions: "How do you know she doesn't care what you do?" or, "What does he do that makes you feel he is mean?"
  —But he does not ignore the real things to which patients are responding. He must be careful not to analyze a perception without checking it out against reality.
  —Neither does he wallow in feeling or allow others to do so. He must also keep from analyzing feelings separate from the context of interaction.

e. He handles loaded material by using his own personal idiom.
  —He uses slang: "Dad hit the ceiling then, huh?" or, "I guess the fur flew then."
  —He uses profanity, vulgarity: "All right. So he acted like a bastard that time," or, "You must have been mad as hell."
  —He avoids pedantic words and psychiatric jargon. He uses "self-esteem" instead of "poor sex identity"; "count" and "valued" instead of "acceptable"; "lovable" instead of "loved," etc.

f. He handles loaded material by translating hostile behavior and feelings:

> "So you felt unlovable."

> "So you felt attacked."

> "So what came out of your mouth didn't match the pain inside. How come?"

g. He handles loaded material by preventing closure on episodes and complaints (besides, he often has insufficient data from which to evaluate what feelings are about): "As we go along this will become clearer," or, "We can learn more about that."

11. Let us now move forward to seeing how the therapist re-educates patients for adulthood, for accountability.

a. The patient constantly gives clues that he does not feel accountable:

"I can't do it." (I am little, insignificant.)

"They won't let me do it." (Others are bigger than I am. I am a victim.)

"You made me do it." (I fix accountability in you.)

"Yes, I do it, but can't help it. I don't know why." (I fix accountability inside me, but I am not related to myself.)

"I did it because I was drunk (amnesic, crazy)." (I was not me.)

"I didn't mean to do it." (I was not me.)

"I did it because I love you." (Blackmail Syndrome.)

b. The therapist uses certain techniques for restoring the patient's feeling of accountability.
—He reminds the patient of his ability to be in charge of himself:

"Who eats for you?"

"Who goes to the toilet for you?"

"You can decide, you know."

"You don't have to rob yourself, you know." (To a patient who wants to quit school.)

"How did it happen, if you didn't mean to do it?"

"Others can't see your inside wish. They can only see the outward behavior which gives a clue to the wish. You have to make your wishes clear."

"You invested that person with authority over you. Why did you give your authority away?"

"You made an agreement with him that he would control you. Does this have to go on?"

"What stands between you and your ability to control Mary?"

—The therapist checks back always on pronouns to see who did what to whom. Schizophrenics, for instance, never say exactly who did what. They say: "Children shouldn't do such and such." The therapist pins the patient down: "You mean Johnnie?" The therapist makes the patient's covert accusations overt so that they can be dealt with and so that he can check if the pronouns are accurately placed.
—The therapist deals with tattletalers:

S: (*to mother*) I'm going to tell on you.

Th: Now I think you want to get Ma in trouble. Does this happen at home? How come you parents are in a position where your kids can get one of you in trouble?

* * * * * * *

M: My husband drinks.

Th: (*turns attention to what wife can report on herself*) Do *you* drink?

* * * * * * *

D: (*discrepancy watcher*) He gets ten cents. I only get five cents.

Th: You want to make sure you get your share of things. That you don't get robbed or left out.

—The therapist deals with spokesmen:

> "How does it happen that you have to be a spokesman for Johnny? He can speak for himself. Let's ask him about this."

> "Does this go on at home? People speaking for other people? How do you suppose this came to be?"

—The therapist deals with acting-out of children. He doesn't turn to the parents; he asks the child, "How come?" He reminds the child that he has a choice about his behavior. He isn't a victim. He can influence his environment.

c. The patient-therapist relationship itself highlights problems of accountability.
    —The patient behaves in a certain way. He acts as if he is stuck with that behavior, can't help it. If the therapist, too, treats this behavior as separate from the person, he is saying to the patient, "I expect you to have no controls." So he highlights the behavior as belonging to the person, and he sets up behavior treatment goals.
    —The patient expects the therapist to be a great white father or mother from whom all things flow. He expects the therapist to take charge. The therapist does take charge, but does not treat the patient like a child or expect him to behave like one. He treats the patient like an adult and expects him to behave like an adult. He does not violate the adult label.

—The therapist is not indispensable to the patient, though he may need to think he is. He is not like the parent of the schizophrenic who says: "You can't feed yourself. You need me to live." So he doesn't give to patients in a "feeding" and "draining" kind of way. He only makes it possible for them to give to themselves and get from other family members.

12. The therapist helps the patient to see how past models influence his expectations and behavior.

   a. He reminds patients that they are acting from past models:

   "I would expect you to be worried about that. As you said, your dad never . . ."

   "Your mother handled money that way. How *could* you have learned other ways?"

   "Now it sounds to me as if you are giving the same kind of message to him that you saw your mother give to your dad. Yet you didn't like the way your mother and father handled things and are struggling hard to do it differently. Let's see what may be standing in your way."

   b. The therapist openly challenges expectations: "Do you really believe that all children should be beholden to their parents?"
   c. The therapist reminds patients that they married each other for the very qualities about which they are now complaining. "Now this is what you said you liked about your wife. I wonder why you don't like it now?"
   d. The therapist highlights expectations by completing communication:

   Th: (*to Johnny*) Do you like spinach?

   S: No.

   Th: Did you know your mother thought you did like spinach?

   S: No, but I didn't want to hurt her feelings.

   Th: (*to mother*) Did you ever ask him if he liked spinach?

   M: No, I thought all men did. Pa did.

   e. The therapist highlights expectations by exaggerating them: "*Your* Pa did it, so *naturally* all men do it!"

13. The therapist delineates roles and functions.

    a. The therapist recognizes roles himself, in addressing and treating a family.

       —He calls couples "Mother" and "Dad" when referring to them as parents and by their first names when referring to them as individuals or as husband and wife.

       —In history-taking, the therapist includes members in a relevant order. He takes the father first, as head of the house, and next, the mother. He then takes the oldest sib first, saying to the younger ones: "Wait a minute. You haven't arrived yet. You haven't been born!"

    b. The therapist questions patients about their roles:

> "You wear three hats—individual, marital, parental. I can see the parental, but where are the other two?"
>
> "Before marriage you were Miss So-and-So. What happened to her?"
>
> "Why do you have to get permission?"
>
> "Are you Daddy's wife?"

    c. The therapist can teach explicitly about roles. He lists three roles on the blackboard: individual, marital, parental. He does this so that patients will see that they have a choice as to how they will treat each other. If the therapist makes patients aware of how they are responding and shows them other ways to respond, they can then choose among these ways. Creativity in living is having a wider choice of alternatives.

14. The therapist completes gaps in communication and interprets messages.

    a. The therapist separates the relationship part of a message from its content. Patients usually confuse the two and talk about relationships in "content" terms:

       —"This coffee is no good" is a patient's way of saying, "You are no good."

       —"Glasses get dirty" is a schizophrenic's way of saying, "You can't see straight."

    b. The therapist separates comments about the self from comments about others. Patients usually confuse the two, and can't figure out which part of an interchange tells them something about the speaker and which part is addressed to them.

       —"I'm tired" can be a statement about the speaker's fatigue. It can also be a question: "You too?" It can also be a request: "Help me!"

—So when the patient tells the therapist what B said, the therapist asks what the patient got out of B's message.

c. The therapist points out significant discrepancies in communication:

> F: I feel fine.

> Th: You look awful. How come you say you feel fine when you look awful. Can't you allow yourself to feel like hell?

* * * * * * *

> F: (to child, whose symptom is related to the father's delinquent behavior) Be good and I'll be back soon.

> Th: (to father) I think there were two parts to that message which perhaps confused her. You said to be good very loud and clear, but you did not tell her where you were going and when you would be back. Did the second message come through equally loud and clear?

d. The therapist spells out nonverbal communication:

> Th: (to Johnny) You looked to your mother first, before answering. I wonder if you feel you have to get permission to speak.

> Th: (To Patty, who takes her father's hand during an argument between her mother and father) Are you telling your dad that you sympathize with him?

* * * * * * *

> Th: (in reference to seating pattern) You all act as though you would like to get as far away from him [me, her] as possible.

e. The therapist spells out "double-level" messages:

> D: (to mother) May I go to school?

> M: (to daughter) When I was a little girl, I never had an education.

> Th: (to mother) Now your daughter asked you if she could go to school and I'm wondering if she got an answer from you. Should she go to school or shouldn't she?

15. In general, here are my criteria for terminating treatment.

   a. Treatment is completed:
     —When family members can complete transactions, check, ask.
     —When they can interpret hostility.
     —When they can see how others see them.
     —When they can see how they see themselves.
     —When one member can tell another how he manifests himself.
     —When one member can tell another what he hopes, fears, and expects from him.
     —When they can disagree.
     —When they can make choices.
     —When they can learn through practice.
     —When they can free themselves from harmful effects of past models.
     —When they can give a clear message, that is, be congruent in their behavior, with a minimum of difference between feelings and communication, and with a minimum of hidden messages.

   b. Another set of criteria for terminating treatment is when the adult male and female as husband and wife can:
     —*Be direct*, using the first person "I" and following with statements or questions which:

Criticize	Find fault
Evaluate	Report annoyance
Acknowledge an observation	Identify being puzzled

     —*Be delineated*, by using language which clearly shows "I am me" and "You are you." "I am separate and apart from you and I acknowledge my own attributes as belonging to me. You are you, separate and apart from me, and I acknowledge your attributes as belonging to you."
     —*Be clear*, by using questions and statements which reflect directness and the capacity to get knowledge of someone else's statements, directions, or intentions, in order to accomplish an outcome.

   c. In short, treatment is completed when everyone in the therapy setting can use the first person "I" followed by an active verb and ending with a direct object.

Harold R. Harrell

CHAPTER 21

Communication Theory in Marriage Counseling: A Critique

Ben N. Ard, Jr.

Faulty communication (frequently, lack of communication) would seem to be one of the major reasons why so many families do not function at their optimal level. Counseling with married couples, as well as with parents and children, has led many people in the various helping professions to the general conclusion that lack of effective communication lies at the root of many a family's problems (cf. Ruesch & Bateson, 1951; Satir, 1964; Watzlawick, Beavin, & Jackson, 1967). Thus faulty communication can justifiably be labeled "the rock on which families founder."

By communication I mean any messages conveyed in whatever way from one person to another. Communication does not refer, thus, to verbal, explicit, and intentional transmission of messages alone; the concept of communication is intended to cover here, as in other discussions in the field (cf. Ruesch & Bateson, 1951, pp. 5–6), all those processes by which people influence one another—verbal and nonverbal, explicit and implicit, clear and unclear, intentional and unintentional, aware and unaware, pathological and healthy.

There would seem to be little doubt that communication difficulties lie at the heart of many a family's problems. Most workers in the helping professions could probably agree on this basic point. Where disagreements might begin to appear, however, is on how professionals can best be of help in working with families with problems.

What communication problems (quarrels, for example) frequently turn out to be are disagreements about the nature of the relationship involved, rather than conflicts over the specific content or apparent messages being communicated. As Watzlawick, Beavin, & Jackson (1967) have found,

> . . . it seems that the more spontaneous and 'healthy' a relationship, the more the relationship aspect of communication recedes into the background. Conversely, "sick" relationships are characterized by a constant struggle about the nature of the relationship, with the content aspect of communication becoming less and less important [p. 52].

Presented at the National Council on Family Relations' annual conference, August 17, 1967, at the San Francisco Hilton Hotel.

213

Communication difficulties in families frequently began before the family in question was even a functioning unit. Communication gets off to a bad start during the dating period: expectations of what each *assumes* will be the "proper" behavior of the other are rarely ever explicitly spelled out. As one moves through dating, the engagement period, and into marriage (with its marital roles and, later on, parental roles), these expectations change (often, again, without being explicitly discussed). As Don Jackson (1965) has observed,

> Couples . . . who engage in wondrously varied behavioral ploys during courtship, undoubtedly achieve considerable economy after a while in terms of what is open to dispute, and how it is to be disputed. Consequently they seem . . . to have excluded wide areas of behavior from their interactional repertoire and never quibble further about them [p. 13].

Some of this is perhaps good, but some of the results may turn out later on to be detrimental to the marriage. For example, a couple during courtship may discover that they have differences regarding their respective views and values concerning religion. But, as often happens in our culture, these religious differences may not prove very detrimental during the courtship phase. Because the girl, for example, may want so badly to get married, she may "conveniently overlook" the differences regarding religion. In an attempt to avoid facing a very touchy issue, the couple may avoid all discussion of their basic values in this area. Yet when children come along and questions must be decided about their religious training, then it is frequently too late to find out that there are basic, fundamental differences in values which cannot be resolved.

To turn to another illustration, one couple married and only later found out that they differed in a very fundamental way about race questions. He was a segregationist while she was an integrationist, and they lived in a southern town where the election of the sheriff turned on just this issue. They tried seemingly endless communication on this issue to no avail; neither could change the other. So they agreed that this subject was never to be a topic for dinner table conversation because it ruined too many dinners. In other words, they did not communicate any more about race relations. But they agreed that each had the right to go out and work for the election of his respective candidate for sheriff.

Ruesch and Bateson (1951) have maintained that the definition of a relationship depends not merely upon the skeleton of events which make up the interaction but also upon the way the individuals concerned see and interpret those events. "This seeing or interpretation can be regarded as the application of a set of propositions about the world or the self whose validity depends upon the subject's belief in them [p. 220]." For example, "if each comes to believe in the hostility of the other, that hostility is real to this extent and to the extent that each acts upon its belief [p. 222]."

But we need to avoid the phenomenological trap this sort of theorizing can lead us into, if we are to be of most help to clients with such problems. The fact that a husband feels he has justification for jealousy does not tell us in fact whether or not the wife has done anything to justify his jealous reaction. Feelings are not enough to base one's actions on; one needs still to check the reality involved, not merely one's feelings. *Reality* is a "bad word" to many in the helping professions today, but I am suggesting that we counselors need to get that concept back into our thinking, if we are to be of more effective help to clients.

With the recent emphasis on communication as the most important, if not the key, factor in marriage counseling, joint conferences with both partners in a marriage are sometimes thought to clear up misunderstandings stemming from lack of communication. But the joint conference can become the means of further separating spouses instead of bringing them together. Husband and wife may make wild accusations and say cutting things to each other. Once these things are said in the presence of a third party, even a professional person, they tend to become fixed and to take on a different significance and value. A joint conference can provide an ideal opportunity for both parties to say things to punish and hurt each other which neither will forget because of the presence of a third party (cf. Mudd et al, 1958, p. 52).

Much of the therapeutic help that has been heretofore offered to families has been based (implicitly, at least) on the assumption that if spouses can become fully aware of the communication pattern they are caught in, this "insight" will "cure" the problem. However, even when both spouses are evidently fully aware of their pattern, this awareness does not help them in the least to do something about it (cf. Watzlawick et al, 1967, p. 87). The prevailing emphasis on nondirectiveness or permissiveness has held up therapeutic progress. Clients have to be encouraged, persuaded (even directed!) to *do* something about the pattern in which they appear to be caught (cf. Ellis, 1966).

There is an assumption among many people in the family life field that "there is no difficulty that enough love will not conquer." But love alone is not enough, and will not conquer all difficulties.

An analogous assumption seems to be implied in recent communication theory, namely, that "there is no difficulty that enough communication will not conquer." But communication alone, no matter how effective, will not conquer all difficulties, either.

Improving communication, in and of itself, will not always maintain a marriage. Too much uncritical reliance on the assumptions of recent communication theory, including this basic one, will not necessarily provide the best therapy for husbands, wives, and families in need of help.

As an illustration of the absurd lengths to which couples can go in non-communication, one married couple I know have eaten steaks cooked rare for many years—each spouse *assuming*, without checking, that the other preferred his steak cooked that way. Frequently where there is lack of communication, there are *unquestioned assumptions* that need to be looked into—in this instance the assumption that a "proper" spouse will defer to the other and eat his food the way the other prefers. (Self-sacrifice is a very basic unquestioned value in our middle-class culture.)

My own research study of married couples who were followed through twenty years of marriage indicated, among other things, that even those couples who maintained their marriages over twenty years had problems communicating with each other about such simple matters as their desired frequency of intercourse (Ard, 1962). The husbands consistently *under-estimated* their wives' preferred frequency of intercourse, while the wives consistently *overestimated* their husbands' preferred frequency.

Turning to relations between parents and children, there is a serious and apparently growing communication gap between generations; of late this seems to be particularly so regarding drugs and sex. Many young people seem to be operating on the unquestioned principle of protecting their parents from uncomfortable truths (i.e., truths which the youth assume would make their parents uncomfortable). This principle of protecting others from uncomfortable truths, whether it be between parents and children or between spouses, is a very shaky basis on which to maintain an effective relationship.

The unquestioned assumption underlying much of this "spare the parents uncomfortable truths" sort of thinking is the middle-class cultural premise that we should bend over backwards never to "hurt" those who love us or gave birth to us. But to hide behind that "honor thy father and mother" bit and on that basis to refuse ever to discuss our basic differences with our parents or children surely is self-defeating.

When a parent who has not resolved all of his own sexual problems suspects his youngsters of having sexual thoughts or indulging in sexual behavior which he defines as "sinful," it frequently arouses too many anxious feelings which he may try to pacify (often unknowingly) by clamping down tighter controls on the young, or by blindly denying the evidence before his eyes of his youngsters' sexual maturity (Ard, 1967a).

As a further commentary on the sad state of communication within American marriages, I would like to relate the reaction to a recent paper I presented at a conference on "Teen-age Marriage and Divorce" (Ard, 1967b). I suggested many things, but the one thing all the newspapers picked up was one suggestion to the teenage husband, to wit: "Now that you have married the girl, try to make friends with her." I was only suggesting that too many young men marry girls with whom they are passionately involved but with whom they are not really friends.

This evidently startling idea was picked up out of all the other things that were said and played up by editors and headline writers across the nation. The attention this idea received is a commentary upon either the editors and headline writers and/or the said state of communication in our American marriages.

Much of the recent interest in communication theory has, understandably, emphasized verbal communication. But *nonverbal* communication needs attention as well, for several reasons. For one thing in early childhood the primary tools of communication are nonverbal. Long before a child communicates verbally, he functions on the basis of communication skills which are chiefly nonverbal. Much of the most significant communication throughout life remains at a nonverbal level. Too much of what in the past has been assumed to be "intuition" or some "sixth sense" has really been just very perceptive nonverbal communication. Sherlock Holmes can teach us more in this regard than a passel of mystical seers.

Perhaps an illustration of how nonverbal communication works would clarify matters here. If a wife notices a pained expression flicker across her husband's face during dinner table conversation, she might assume that he was expressing (nonverbally) a negativy reaction to the topic or situation being discussed. And she might be right. But there is a possible danger here, if she does not check out her assumption: her husband may merely be having gas pains. If so, she would have been "over-psychologizing," and that can get people into deeper trouble very quickly!

In the recent study of communication the emphasis has been on the *how* of interaction rather than the *why*. So we get extensive studies of "communication systems" (families?) which go into the matter as if they were studying computers, using terms such as "feedback loops" and "input-output systems." The proverbial man from Mars could observe a computer system and possibly figure out *how* it works, but he still would not know *why*, which is a different sort of question entirely. I hope research in this field of family communication, in its great surge of interest in the *how*, never forgets the importance of also asking *why* (cf. Watzlawick et al, 1967, pp. 130–131).

There seems to have developed, in recent communication theory, a tendency to "explain" pathological behavior—for example, that resulting from a double-bind pattern, where messages are paradoxically contradictory—as the *only* thing the persons involved could do. Schizophrenic behavior is all that can be expected from a child reared in a double-binding schizophrenic family, it would seem, according to the theory. The schizophrenic behavior (communication pattern) is seen as "appropriate" (cf. Watzlawick et al, 1967, pp. 212–213, 217).

This sort of theorizing would seem to be a fatal flaw, a self-defeating trap, a fatalistic determinism in the very field (counseling and psychotherapy) where the possibility of promoting better ways of responding is our only justification for existence as a profession. If the faulty communication was "all that the identified patient could do under the particular circumstances," then it would seem difficult to help him see that in the future (after counseling or psychotherapy) there would be another alternative, a better way of reacting, when in contact with schizophrenic people who do give out contradictory messages.

If families are not to founder on the rock of faulty communication, they need to become more aware of their problems in communication. As Watzlawick et al (1967) have put it,

> What we can observe in virtually all these cases of pathological communication is that they are vicious circles that cannot be broken unless and until communication itself becomes the subject of communication, in other words, until the communicants are able to metacommunicate [p. 95].

We need to get family members to check their premises (cf. Branden, 1966), to question their definitions, to challenge their assumptions (cf. Ellis, 1966), and to look into the objective validity and consequences of their basic values.

Unfortunately, too much of the professional help provided for families in trouble does not seriously question the cultural premises or values which are at the base of many apparent "communication" problems. Too often the typical American counselor or therapist permits the client to make some minor movements away from the cultural premises (through the counselor's "permissiveness") but *ultimately* helps the client to *adjust to* the cultural premises. As Ruesch and Bateson (1951) have put it, "Though on the surface it looks as if the patient had moved away from the cultural premises by talking about feelings and thoughts, he is in reality finally adjusting to the surroundings in which he lives [p. 133]." In another passage Ruesch and Bateson state that "the American therapist's aim is to socialize the patient. This is done by making the patient accept the fact that the group acts as a censor of his action [p. 167]."

If clearing up communication problems leads to a forthright facing of value conflicts, then this is, indeed, a step in the right direction. But we must follow through if there is a difference in assumed values and get the participants to challenge and question their values, if these values are the conventional ones in our culture, which are self-defeating and largely definitional.

Because values have been seen by many in the helping professions as "off limits" (i.e., the professional is supposed to be "neutral" or not to deal with the client's values), we have avoided dealing with the basic problem underlying communication difficulties: differences in basic values (which are rarely examined or questioned, even when they are self-defeating). Ellis and Harper (1961a, 1961b) have provided some helpful suggestions on just what sort of values these frequently are in our culture, as well as some ways of helping the client eliminate his reliance upon them.

Values are even more basic than mere communication, and in a sense, logically prior to communication. If conflicts in a family are assumed to be due to a lack of communication (which is often true), or due to faulty communication (also often true), we may still be led down a blind alley by assuming that if we merely improve the communication in the family we have solved the problem. The most effective communication can lead to the break-up of a family because the basic values are ultimately in conflict. We need to get at the basic values of people in conflict, whether they be spouses or parents and children, and see if these values need to be changed or not, rather than merely going along with those conventional values that are assumed without question by most people in our culture, including the helping professions, who should know better. (cf. Maslow, 1959).

In conclusion, if families are not to founder on the rock of faulty communication, counseling and psychotherapy should get beyond merely improving communication within the family (important as that will always continue to be) and get at the basic values involved in family conflicts. Families and individuals often integrate their lives on levels that are not ultimately satisfactory but which only give the *illusion* of well-being (cf. Browning & Peters, 1966, p. 189). It is the counselor's professional responsibility to see these hidden, assumed values and to warn families and individuals of their possible consequences.

BIBLIOGRAPHY

Ard, B. Sexual behavior and attitudes of marital partners. Unpublished doctoral dissertation. Ann Arbor: University of Michigan, 1962.

Ard, B. Do as I do, be as I am: The bruising conflict. In S. M. Farber & R. H. L. Wilson (Eds.), *Sex education and the teenager*. Berkeley: Diablo Press, 1967. Pp. 78–88. (a)

Ard, B. Gray hair for the teenage father. In S. M. Farber & R. H. L. Wilson (Eds.), *Teenage marriage and divorce*. Berkeley: Diablo Press, 1967). Pp. 95–104. (b)

Branden, N. Psychotherapy and the objectivist ethics. In B. Ard (Ed.) *Counseling and psychotherapy: Classics on theories and issues*. Palo Alto: Science and Behavior Books, 1966. Pp. 251–269.

Browning, R. L., & Peters, H. J. On the philosophical neutrality of counselors. In B. Ard (Ed.), *Counseling and psychotherapy: Classics on theories and issues*. Palo Alto: Science and Behavior Books, 1966. Pp. 187–195.

Ellis, A. The essence of rational therapy. In B. Ard (Ed.), *Counseling and psychotherapy: Classics on theories and issues*. Palo Alto: Science and Behavior Books, 1966. Pp. 94–113.

Ellis, A. & Harper, R. A. *Creative marriage*. New York: Lyle Stuart, 1961. (a)

Ellis, A., & Harper, R. A. *A guide to rational living*. Englewood Cliffs, N. J.: Prentice-Hall, 1961. (b)

Jackson, D. D. The study of the family. *Family Process*, 1965, *4*, 1–20.

Maslow, A. H. (Ed.) *New knowledge in human values*. New York: Harper, 1959.

Mudd, E., et al (Eds.) *Marriage counseling: A casebook*. New York: Association Press, 1958.

Ruesch, J., & Bateson, G. *Communication*. New York: Norton, 1951.

Satir, V. *Conjoint family therapy*. Palo Alto: Science & Behavior Books, 1964.

Watzlawick, P., Beavin, J. H., Jackson, D. D. *Pragmatics of Human Communication*. New York: Norton, 1967.

CHAPTER 22

The Conjoint Psychotherapy of Married Partners

Andrew S. Watson

Since the appearance in 1956 of Eisenstein's *Neurotic Interaction in Marriage*, publication of papers and books on the treatment of family and marriage problems has mounted. While for many years social workers and others have done "marriage counseling," psychiatrists only recently have started to work actively in this field, or at least to report their work in publication (Grotjahn, 1959, pp. 90–104). The impact of psychoanalytic theory and practice on the concepts and techniques of psychotherapy has tended to focus on the treatment of individual patients and has aimed at altering intrapsychic as well as external adaptation through manipulation of the psychological process. This has brought excellent therapeutic results in certain categories of patients, but many others have not been treated or their treatment has failed. Frequently this has been accounted for by judging them as "untreatable," or by deciding that the psychotherapeutic method was poorly applied. It appears that many of these conclusions were arrived at largely by assumption, since there is not only little objective data to support such a view, but also increasing evidence to the contrary.[1] Clearly, adaptive potential and versatility seem to be consistently underestimated by professionals.[2] Likewise, the literature reveals that there is good reason to search further for causes of family disruption using the psychodynamic concept of homeostasis as a launching point (Bell, 1961, pp. 4–5, 48–52; Jackson, 1959, pp. 122–141; and Bowen, 1961, pp. 40–60). In this paper, I will endeavor to explain and conceptualize my recent treatment efforts with family and marriage problems.

---

[1]For example, studies of the placebo effect demonstrate that even very "sick" psychotics have considerable capacity to improve with nothing more than the increased attention paid them in the context of research operations (Frank, pp. 65–74).

[2]See the work of Berlien on military adjustment.

Reprinted with permission of the author and the publisher from the *American Journal of Orthopsychiatry*, 1963, *33*, 912–922.

Several specific premises regarding the nature of marital unions will be utilized but not explicitly substantiated here. They are:

1. That marriage partners choose each other for highly specific, conscious and unconscious reasons. This selection represents the summation and gratification of normal and appropriate goals, as well as various neurotic and symbolic needs that must be met either intrapsychically or socially (Ackerman, 1958, pp. 148–149; Bell, 1961, pp. 4–5, 48–52; and Sherman, 1961).

2. Both partners enter into a mutually "satisfying" interlocking homeostatic balance (Basamania, 1961, p. 22, and Jackson, 1959, pp. 129–145). Despite external appearances to the contrary, they reach a state of psychological equilibrium that "gratifies" both mature and neurotic needs for both partners (Kubie, 1956). One of the treatment objectives in this kind of therapy will be to elucidate the details of this interlocking system, in order to open up the possibility for a different and more appropriate adjustment between them.

3. This homeostatic relationship may also be viewed as a mutually shared communication system involving many verbal as well as nonverbal communication devices (Grotjahn, 1960; Jackson, Riskin, & Satir, 1961). Therefore much characterological interchange will take place, and this will lead inevitably to the necessity for emphasizing the interpretation of character manifestations in this form of treatment.[3]

4. Any therapeutic disruption in the psychological homeostasis of one partner in the marriage will inevitably force upon all other members in the family an alteration in their psychological adjustments. For this reason, it appears that often the most efficient way to impinge upon the interlocking adjustment of the partners is to have both participate in the insight-producing process. This would simultaneously tend to bring about revised homoeostatic techniques for each. The family anxiety level may be kept closer to optimal limits than often occurs when individuals are treated separately and only one member has opportunity for, and access to, insight-producing experience (Ackerman, 1961, pp. 61–64).

These, then, are the premises on which this form of treatment is based. In addition, all the basic hypotheses of psychodynamic theory are utilized and woven into the treatment situation.

TECHNIQUE

There have been several recent papers describing the treatment of marriage partners in various kinds of combinations and with various goals. For example, Ackerman (1958) used "interpretive family treatment," while Hambidge (1959) used "simultaneous analysis of marriage partners" to designate such procedures. Greene (1960) describes "concurrent analysis," and Martin and Bird (1959) describe "concurrent psychotherapy," but in neither case are both partners present at the same time. Geist and

---

[3]As Reich puts it, *how* material is stated is as important as *what* is said, and is the focus for interpreting character defenses.

Gerber (1960) as caseworkers shying away from the word "therapy," call their technique "joint interviewing," as does Sherman (1959). Carroll (1960, pp. 57–62) employs "family unit therapy."

Since none of these adequately designated an insight-producing psychotherapy focused on interpretation of transferences and carried on by a single therapist with both partners simultaneously present, I sought a new designation.

The meanings of the word "conjoint" seemed to satisfy the above requirement. No sooner had the expression "conjoint treatment of marital partners" been coined, when the excellent paper, "Conjoint Family Treatment," by Jackson and Weakland (1961) appeared in print. Correspondence with Jackson revealed that this term had been used in an earlier paper (1959, pp. 122), which I had not yet seen.

In conjoint psychotherapy, both marriage partners are seen together, and the strategic goal of the interpretive process is to work through the central neurotic distortions of their interlocking adaptive and communication systems. This involves interpretation of the multiple transferences, utilizing all the traditional psychoanalytic concepts of personality dynamics. Because of the more complex transaction in these sessions, several specific procedures are followed.

It will be clear to all sophisticated in the theory of psychotherapy that there is an extremely complex interlocking system of transference-countertransference operations present in a therapeutic setting where three individuals participate. Because of this fact, it is essential at the very beginning of treatment to understand thoroughly the characteristics and etiology of each partner's psychological participation.

When the decision has been made to treat a couple conjointly, both parties will be interviewed separately for two or three sessions in order to obtain a thorough anamnesis and diagnostic formulation. Following the suggestion of Saul, an effort is made to isolate and formulate the core psychodynamic forces operating in each spouse and relate them to precise etiological data. Early memories are obtained; family backgrounds are explored with emphasis on recollections and thoughts about significant family members; dreams and other specific historical details needed to develop the diagnostic formulation are collected. By the time these interviews are concluded, the therapist should be able to make at least a well-educated guess about the meaning of the various communications that will be present during the course of treatment. Just as the significance of communications becomes more clear as individual psychotherapy progresses, so they will become more meaningful in the course of conjoint treatment.

Some may leap to the assumption that patients in this kind of treatment setting will not talk freely about the details of their fantasy life, but this has not proved true. It is my impression that freedom to communicate in such treatment is more often than not a function of the therapist's comfort and countertransference than it is of the patient's inhibition. As Ackerman (1958) has stated, "These so-called secrets turn out not to be real secrets at all. Far more often they are common family knowledge surrounded by a tacit conspiracy of silence [p. ix] ." I share this view, and when the basis for the conspiracy is worked through, the participants have no further need to avoid free discussion or free association.

As the exploratory sessions with each partner are drawing to a close, it is usually in order to make some general statement to each about specific adaptive techniques that appear to create their difficulty. Then, when both are brought back into the conjoint setting, they will have some anticipation about their own contribution to the marriage problems.

As in all psychotherapy, conjoint treatment starts where the patients want it to start. They may or may not talk about themselves, their children, or a multitude of other problems. Material is not judged "good" or "bad" but as communication relating to the significant problems or resistances. Associations are interpreted in the same way as they are in any other form of psychotherapy. However, one factor controls the interpretive choice made at any given time: *All interpretations will focus on those aspects of the material and dynamics that relate to the process of communication between the spouses.* In other words, in selecting which of several alternative interpretations to make, the therapist will choose the one that is related dynamically to the cause of the communication distortion in the marriage. Material mainly relevant to only one partner will not be interpreted.[4]

As material is brought up by one or the other partner and its meaning is interpreted in the presence of both, it helps the listening or observing spouse to impersonalize communications and progressively see them as a function of his partner's psychic problem. This distance-producing measure facilitates improvement in the ego's perceptive capacity, progressively decreases the narcissistic identifications between the partners, and thereby improves their capacity to communicate rationally and resolve mutual problems more objectively. For example, if psychological closeness is ego-threatening to a husband, any demonstration of closeness and intimacy by his wife will cause him to withdraw and she will usually interpret this as personal rejection. When this maneuver manifests itself and is interpreted in treatment, the husband can learn to understand why he "needs" to withdraw. At the same time, the wife is learning why she views such reactions as personal and, progressively, how to objectify the meaning of the withdrawal.

Another important aspect of this technique is that the therapist must observe strict strategic neutrality. He will interpret objectively whatever he sees in the behavior of both spouses, and from time to time will focus his attention on one more than the other. Over the course of treatment, however, he will not ally with one party more than with the other. This is especially important in the beginning phases of treatment, and it is essential to establish this fact clearly to both participants. For the first several hours, this necessitates shifting interpretive focus back and forth between

---

[4] This focus is concurred in by Bell (1961, pp. 4–5), Carroll (1960, p. 60), Ackerman (1961, pp. 65–66,), Jackson & Weakland (pp. 36–38) and others.

the partners, so that hours end with each receiving approximately equal attention from the therapist. Interpretation should also balance in terms of their positive and negative implications to the partners.

After setting forth to both partners the psychological premises stated above, the therapist then encourages the unfolding of the marital problems. Usually this happens quickly and in very vivid form. As in all transference-oriented treatment, it is possible to see at first hand the nature of the psychological participation of both partners. The therapist need not speculate about what has happened at home, since he may directly observe the interaction between them, as well as their individual transferences to him. Especially in the early phases of treatment, this is excellent material to focus upon, since it gives patients insight into the goals of treatment, provides them with sufficient gratification to offset some of the anxiety this technique produces, and thereby creates "hope" that the treatment will be worthwhile. Such an attitude is a crucial element for effective therapy (Carroll, 1960, p. 59; Chance, 1959, pp. 151–154).

One of the principal tactical advantages of this kind of treatment lies in the fact that it is possible to make an interpretation to one spouse, though its main impact is directed toward the other one. If there is strong resistance or ego vulnerability in one, a correlated interpretation can be made to the other spouse, thus turning the interlocking nature of the marital neurosis to therapeutic advantage. For example, if there is a provocative-masochistic tendency in one, coupled with sadistic-criticalness in the other, either side of this emotional axis may be interpreted. Both hear the interpretation and perceive it in terms of their own dynamics. If they have a psychological need to do so, they may, temporarily at least, be permitted to view this as "the other person's problem." Such displacement-potential is useful for regulating the timing of interpretations, while permitting the therapist to deal with current pertinent material. This considerably increases therapeutic flexibility.

This approach stirs up active psychological participation in the couple, with mounting anxiety usually related closely to the emotional stalemate that brought them to therapy. It is important to give reassurance during the early stages, while they are in the process of discovering their own powers to sustain such discomfort. The therapist, during his early experience with this form of treatment, will likewise reverberate to the patient's anxiety, until he too finds that it is possible to carry out and control such therapy. Ultimately, his calmness and comfort in participating in this process, more than anything else, provide patients with the will to explore and accept what had been frightening in the past and had always caused avoidance and reinforced repression (Bowen, 1961, p. 56).

Another characteristic of this technique is the degree of participation in the process by the therapist. In most one-to-one psychotherapy, the therapist can remain essentially passive, only occasionally making interpretive or confronting remarks. In conjoint treatment, where interpretation often centers upon some character manifestation, the "action" is fast-moving and the therapist will by necessity bring himself more into view (Ackerman, 1961, pp. 63–64; Jackson & Weakland, 1961, pp. 38–39).

Also, as interpretations are made, he may "lend" his identity by way of references to personal experiences that serve to underscore his awareness of the problems as well as his belief that they may be resolved. This can be analogized to the ego support rendered by parents to their children as they encourage the annexational identifications that press them forward in their exploration and mastery of reality. Though this kind of support is more specific and tangible in conjoint treatment, it is certainly present at least by implication in the most classical psychoanalytic process. In fact, one might say that one of the criteria for psychoanalysis is the capacity on the part of the patient to perceive this fact. If patients cannot, some alternative approach must be taken (Erickson, 1956).

From the supervisory observation of residents utilizing this kind of therapy, it is clear that there are many "styles" in which it can be conducted. However, in comparison with other forms of therapy carried out by the same resident, there is likely to be much more activity exhibited in conjoint treatment. Needless to say, this has countertransference implications. For example, it has been stated that many who practice psychotherapy do so in order to participate vicariously in the emotional life of others (Szasz, 1956; Wheelis, 1956). The essentially passive relationship of the therapist to his patient in most kinds of psychotherapy permits such participation while retaining relative noninvolvement. To whatever degree this need is present in a given therapist, he will be strongly disinclined to utilize such procedures as conjoint therapy. The corollary probably is also true, that the more actively inclined will find this method holds special attraction. (In assaying any psychotherapeutic process, it is obviously important to take into account the therapist's conscious and unconscious attitudes about "how" and "what" therapy "will work" (Frank, 1961, pp. 114–141).

Once this treatment technique has been elected, it should be the dominant therapeutic mode, at least until the interlocking psychological problems of the couple have been resolved. However, on occasion one spouse may try to use the therapeutic situation to act out neurotically, in a way that would create individual problems and disrupt the timing of the therapeutic process. Such maneuvers should be blocked promptly by the therapist through interpretation. If such acting out cannot be checked within the conjoint sessions, there is reason to see that spouse individually sufficiently often (usually one to three sessions) to clarify and obviate the motives for such masochistic moves. Any reactions stirred up in the partner *not* seen alone must be dealt with actively, and occasionally he, or she, too must be seen alone in order to retain balance.

After the conjoint sessions have been reinstituted, the material that came out in the individual meetings can usually be worked slowly into the discussions. Sometimes these separate sessions turn out to have been flanking moves to avoid a conjoint issue. In such a case it must be so interpreted to the partners, and the therapist should view the separation as a tactical miscalculation.[5] At other times enormously valuable material

---

[5] Some therapists such as Bell (pp. 24–28) would refuse altogether to see one family member alone. This has not been a problem in our work.

emerges which, when dealt with conjointly, moves therapy forward precipitously because of the therapist's deepened understanding and the patients' added insight.

TECHNICAL PROBLEMS

The main problems arising in conjoint treatment are the product of the more complex transference-countertransference reactions. Clearly, conjoint therapy should not be undertaken unless the therapist can comprehend quickly what is going on in the sessions and can think freely about the material in precise psychodynamic terms. So much occurs during the conjoint sessions that the therapist has no time to pause and reflect at length before dealing with the material. Neither can he sit by and wait for multiple confirmations of the psychodynamic theme before he decides to make an interpretation. To do so puts him far behind the affectively significant events, and he may never come abreast of the significant transactions. While there will be much reiteration of material, the same timing problem will always exist.

Obviously there are two sets of transferences, as well as two sets of countertransferences (I say "sets" deliberately, to reflect the overdetermined imago present in any individual's repetition-compulsion). Because of the presence of both marital partners and the more realistic presentation of problems, there is an increased risk of the therapist's unconsciously identifying with one or the other spouse. However, by being aware of this hazard and through more active involvement in the therapeutic process, there is greater opportunity for empathic identification and a quicker grasp of the problems unfolding before and with him. Under these circumstances it is neither possible nor effective to have long periods of silence nor to avoid finding answers to specific reality problems. This does not mean that the goal is simply to gratify. Rather, the exploration for answers is carried on in a way that impinges dynamically on the neurotic process of the couple. The *act* of mutual exploration is contrived to clarify the defensive maneuvers of each spouse in such a way as to increase insight and maturation even as a problem is being solved (Grotjahn, 1959, pp. 100–101). Obviously this is different from the kind of communication used in more typical psychotherapeutic interpretation. It appears, however, that its dynamic effect is similar. Defensive distortions are forced into sight where their current implications can be subjected to reality testing and possible revision.

Another common countertransference anxiety in conjoint treatment arises when the partners begin to make threatening remarks about getting a divorce, or some other offer to act out. Because both partners are present to witness the intense affect unleashed, and because it may readily be interpreted as more than mere transference, the therapist is likely to wonder if he may not have a tiger by the tail. These occasions may be turned to good therapeutic advantage, but only if the therapist is comfortable in taking them up and working them through. He may very easily assume that he has been the cause of such an upset. While this is obviously not true, the physical presence of both partners with their emotional reactions to the therapeutic situation makes this distortion easy to believe.

The therapist is also likely to react with deep concern to other kinds of highly charged material as it emerges and creates the specter of serious trouble between the partners. As noted above, such material is not truly secret, and its revelation presents an opportunity to clarify issues that have too long been hidden just deeply enough to prevent resolution and yet cause marriage difficulties. To date, there have been no instances in which truly damaging material has arisen. Rather, it has been confirmed that the information was "known" by both parties beforehand.

TECHNICAL ADVANTAGES

Though it is often stated that the psychotherapist presents no value judgments to his patients, I do not accept this view. For example, whenever it is decided that there has been a neurotic distortion such as projection, a value judgment about reality has been made and, along with it, an estimate of the degree of distortion. All this is inferred from what the patient has said, which places a large analytical task upon the therapist. Though he does have access to transference reactions with which to check out impressions of extra-therapy behavior, there is always the possibility of error due to observational bias, as well as the likelihood that some reactions to the therapist will be different in kind from those to other persons in the environment. In conjoint therapy there is the immediate advantage of direct observation of the participants in the family problem. This facilitates more objective evaluation of the partners' behavior and limits the need to judge distortion from more indirect data. This frees the therapist's energy to deal with the complexity of the process, and well offsets the disadvantages arising from the increased distortion potential caused by the complicated interaction.

Another marked advantage of this technique results from the pressure it places on the couple to re-examine their reality testing. When an interpretation is made to one spouse, the other has the opportunity to hear it, remember it, and reintroduce it, during the interim between therapeutic sessions. This provides the therapist with a working assistant for each of the partners, who will constantly reinforce the interpretation he makes during therapy sessions. While there is a possibility and even a probability that interpretations will be used for nontherapeutic purposes, the general summation effect is reinforcement of, and mounting pressure toward, increased reality testing by both spouses. In most individual psychotherapy there is a strong tendency for the patient to leave the hour and fall back into archaic patterns of problem-solving and old ego defenses. Ever so slowly the therapist breaks into the automaticity of the defense system, to bring about broadening of the reality-testing and subsequent improvement in the patient's capacity to synthesize and manipulate current experience. The speed with which conjoint therapy improves reality-testing is a distinct advantage. There is, in addition, the marked ego satisfaction that comes from the fact that both spouses are participating jointly in the solution of common problems. Here there is no untreated spouse to build up fantasies of being conspired against by the therapist (Ackerman, 1961, pp. 57, 64; Ackerman, 1959, p. 111; Brodey, 1959). Instead, there is the clear opportunity to work with the partner and share in the resolution of difficulties. Thus one of the principal problems in treating a married person may be avoided.

Another advantage in conjoint treatment is that insights are gained in the very context from which problems arise. This removes much of the need to translate from transference back to reality, since reality and transference are close together in time and content and therefore more accessible to perception and learning. Such contextual analysis appears to enhance markedly the speed of such learning, even while maintaining the advantages of individual treatment to ferret out and clarify neurotic distortions. This avoids vicarious guilt in one partner for gaining something the other is not getting, and facilitates the forging of a new ego ideal that can be held jointly by both (Ackerman, 1959, pp. 115–116).

The final advantage I would like to comment on is economic. There is ample evidence that the decision of *who* gets psychotherapy depends to a large extent on economic status (Chance, 1959, Ch. 7; Hollingshead & Redlich, 1958). Obviously, if the multiple parties to a marriage problem may be successfully and simultaneously treated, the saving of professional time will have at least two immediate and practical reverberations for this group of patients:

1. Therapy will become at least twice as available, which is important in the face of an absolute shortage of treatment personnel.

2. The cost of treatment to such a couple may be halved, which can extend the availability of treatment to many who cannot now afford it.

There are other economic effects in conjoint treatment. Several writers have commented on the speed with which this process works, and I concur fully with such observations (Bell, 1961, pp. 49–50; Bowen, 1961, pp. 57–58). Psychodynamic elements that ordinarily take months to raise to awareness sufficient for their being re-examined and reality-tested emerge and are effectively altered in a matter of four or five sessions. While these new insights are not fully integrated in such a short time, the improved adaptation that re-evaluation of attitudes and feelings carries with it begins and gains momentum. Patients can then return to their own reality-testing and experience-gathering with a likelihood for continued maturation.[6] This accelerated process, if the passage of time demonstrates that gains are maintained, will result in much saving of expensive professional time as well as many direct and indirect economic and social gains for patients.

---

[6]It seems appropriate here to quote part of a footnote from Freud's Rat-man case:

"It was impossible to unravel this tissue of phantasy thread by thread; the therapeutic success of the treatment was precisely what stood in the way of this. *The patient recovered, and his ordinary life began to assert its claims: there were many tasks before him, which he had already neglected for too long, and which were incompatible with a continuation of the treatment.* I am not to be blamed, therefore, for this gap in the analysis. The scientific results of psychoanalysis are at present only a by-product of its therapeutic aims, and for that reason *it is often just in those cases where treatment fails that most discoveries are made.*" (Italics added.)

INDICATIONS

To discuss indications for conjoint therapy at length would be premature. However, there are several specific situations in which they seem clear-cut:

1. In those family relationships where the commonly held distortions are so gross and so reality-disruptive that speed in checking family disintegration is a critical factor, conjoint treatment seems to offer an ideal way in which to slow down the destructive neurotic process and provide a chance to resolve at least the surface problems before they destroy the marriage, and often the children.

2. This technique is especially well suited to cases in which the problems are largely of an acting-out, characterological nature. It helps greatly in "trapping" these maneuvers where they can be seen, interpreted, and attached to some of the underlying neurotic dynamisms and affects. This makes it very useful in just that type of case in which the parties are "poorly motivated" and "not ready" for treatment. Once they are seen in this therapeutic setting, they may very quickly be led to "discover" reasons and feelings to justify continuing.

Various writers have proposed narrower indications than these, such as the presence of children, and the absence of psychosis. I myself have not felt these limits to be necessary, and successful treatment has been carried on outside of them.

The question arises as to how far conjoint treatment can be carried. The answer to this is not yet clear, since various cases have proceeded (and are proceeding) to the handling of all levels of psychopathology from superficial to deep. It does appear, however, that when the focus of psychological emphasis shifts away from elements of mutual emotional cathexis to the partners, if further therapy is needed it should move to individual sessions. There is reason to believe that one should not leap too quickly to this alternative, since it is clear that even dreams and fantasies among marriage partners have a high degree of mutuality. These facts seem to indicate that there will be far-reaching therapeutic potential for conjoint psychotherapy.

Contraindications

As with the discussion of indications, it is not yet possible to set forth any specific contraindications. Couples have been treated who were grossly psychotic or involved in the weirdest varieties of reality difficulties, as well as more run-of-the-mill and superficial problems. If reality is not too far out of hand, it appears possible to utilize this kind of treatment advantageously. Neither have any situations arisen in which it was felt that this method was "dangerous." The question of contraindication, then, must also remain open until further experience has been accumulated.

Conjoint psychotherapy of marriage partners seems to hold promise as a means for therapeutically intervening in many problems that have formerly defied success. The principal bar to utilization may rest more in countertransference problems than it does with difficulties experienced by patients. Its main prerequisite is the capacity to understand psychodynamic events with facility so that therapeutic interventions may be made promptly and in the context of the early appearance of material. To date, a precise statement of indications and contraindications may not be made.

REFERENCES

Ackerman, N. W. *The psychodynamics of family life*. New York: Basic Books, 1958.
Ackerman, N. W. The psychoanalytic approach to the family. In J.. H. Masserman (Ed.), *Individual and familial dyanmics*. New York: Grune & Stratton, 1959.
Ackerman, N. W. A dynamic frame for the clinical approach to family conflict. In *Exploring the base for family therapy*. New York: Family Service Association of America, 1961.
Basamania, B. W. The emotional life of the family: Inferences for social casework. *American Journal of Orthopsychiatry*, 1961, *31*, No. 1, 74–86.
Bell, J. E. Family group therapy. Public Health Monogr. No. 64, Washington, D. C.: U. S. Government Printing Office, 1961.
Berlien, I. C. Psychiatric aspects of military manpower conservation. *Journal American Psychiatric Association*, 1954, *111*, No. 3, 91–99.
Bowen, M. Family psychotherapy. *American Journal of Orthopsychiatry*. 1961, *31*, No. 1, 40–60.
Brodey, W. M. Some family operations and schizophrenia. *Archives of General Psychiatry*, 1959, *1*, 388–389.
Carroll, E. J. Treatment of the family as a unit. *Pennsylvania Medical Journal*, 1960, *63*, No. 1, 56–72.
Chance, E. *Families in treatment*. New York: Basic Books, 1959.
Eisenstein, V. W. Neurotic interaction in marriage. New York: Basic Books, 1956.
Erikson, E. The problem of ego identity. *Journal of American Psychoanalytic Association*, 1956.
Frank, J. D. *Persuasion and healing*. Baltimore, Md.: Johns Hopkins Press, 1961.
Freud, S. A case of obsessional neurosis. In *Collected Papers*, Vol. 3. London: Hogarth Press, 1950.
Friend, M. R. The historical development of family diagnosis. *Social Service Review*, 1960, *34*, 11–12.
Geist, J., & Gerber, N. Joint interviewing: A treatment technique with marital partners. *Social Casework*, 1960, *41*, No. 2, 76–83.
Greene, B. L. Marital disharmony: Concurrent analysis of husband and wife. *Diseases of the Nervous System*, 1960, *21*, No. 2, 73–78.
Grotjahn, M. Analytic family therapy: A survey of trends in research and practice. In J. H. Masserman (Ed.), *Individual and familial dynamics*. New York: Grune & Stratton, 1959.
Grotjahn, M. *Psychoanalysis and the family neurosis*. New York: W. W. Norton, 1960.
Hambridge, G. The simultaneous psychoanalysis of marriage partners. Paper read at meeting of the American Psychoanalytic Association, Philadelphia, 1959.
Hollingshead, A. B., & Redlich, F. C. *Social class and mental illness*. New York: John Wiley & Sons, 1958.
Jackson, D. D. Family interaction, family homeostasis and some implications for conjoint family psychotherapy. In J. H. Masserman (Ed.), *Individual and familial dynamics*. New York: Grune & Stratton, 1959.
Jackson, D.D., & Weakland, J. H. Conjoint family treatment. *Psychiatry*, 1961, *24*, Suppl. 2, 30–45.
Jackson, D. D., Riskin, J., & Satir, V. A method of analysis of a family interview. *Archives of General Psychiatry*, 1961, *5*, 322–324.
Kubie, L. S. Psychoanalysis and marriage. In V. Eisenstein (Ed.), *Neurotic interaction in marriage*. New York: Basic Books, 1956.
Martin, P., & Bird, H. W. A marriage pattern: The "lovesick" wife and the "cold sick" husband. *Psychiatry*, 1959, *22*, 246.
Menninger, K. Hope. *American Journal of Psychiatry*, 1959, *116*, 481–491.
Reich, W. *Character analysis*. New York: Orgone Institute Press, 1949.
Saul, L. J. The psychoanalytic diagnostic interview. *Psychoanalytic Quarterly*, 1957, *26*, No. 1, 76–90.
Sherman, S. N. Joint interviews in casework practice. *Social Work*, 1959, *4*, No. 2, 20–28.
Sherman, S. N. Concept of the family in casework theory. In *Exploring the base for family therapy*. New York: Family Service Association of America, 1961.
Szasz, T. On the experiences of the analyst in the psychoanalytic situation. *Journal of American Psychoanalytic Association*, 1956, *4*, 204–208.
Wheelis, A. The vocational hazards of psychoanalysis. *International Journal of Psychoanalysis*, 1956, *36*, 171–184.

Group Marriage Counseling

> *No man is an island, entire of itself;*
> *Every man is a piece of the continent,*
> *a part of the main;*
> *If a clod be washed away by the sea,*
> *Europe is the less,*
> *as well as if a promontory were,*
> *as well as if a manor of thy friends, or*
> *of thine own were;*
> *any man's death diminishes me,*
> *because I am involved in Mankind;*
> *and therefore never send to know*
> *for whom the bell tolls;*
> *it tolls for thee.*
>
> JOHN DONNE

In view of what appears to be a constantly increasing need for marriage counseling, and the apparent reality that there probably will never be enough competent, professionally trained marriage counselors to meet this pressing need, there would seem to be an obvious point in considering group marriage counseling as one alternative to serve the growing number of people who are having difficulties in marriage.

Obvious or not, group marriage counseling has not received the attention in the field one might expect under these circumstances. The first casebook on marriage counseling put out by the American Association of Marriage Counselors (Mudd et al, 1958) did not include anything on group marriage counseling. Neither did a recent compendium on *Marital Counseling* edited by Silverman (1967). The literature on group marriage counseling in the years between is relatively sparse, considering the seeming importance of an approach that offers to meet the needs of more people with fewer professional helpers than any other alternative.

Blinder and Kirschenbaum, in Chapter 23, provide a discussion of the technique of married couple group therapy and a brief review of some of the previous work in this highly valuable field. One can probably predict safely, without fear of contradiction, that what with the recent popularity of "encounter groups," sensitivity training groups, "T-groups," Synanon groups, and various other sorts of groups for the games people play, there will be an increasing interest in group marriage counseling.

CHAPTER 23

The Technique of Married Couple Group Therapy

Martin G. Blinder and Martin Kirschenbaum

In the past decade, a score of papers have appeared describing the experiences of various workers in treating married couples in groups. Most have been pleased with their experiment; a few have had serious reservations.

A review of the literature by Gottlieb and Pattison (1966) revealed that most objections to the treatment of married couples, within or outside a group setting, stemmed from unnecessarily narrow commitment to psychoanalytic theory rather than from pragmatic considerations. The more operational concerns of those with an interpersonal or transactional approach—namely, that such treatments might result in either inhibition of group process by defensive pairing of the spouses in an anxious coalition against attempts at exploration of their neurotic interaction, or contrariwise, the destruction of a marriage through premature dissolution of the neurotic ties binding the couple together, intensification of neurotic acting-out, or release of quantities of long repressed hostility incompatible with conjugal living—were not borne out in practice.

Leichter (1962) found that married couple group therapy enabled the spouse to serve as an auxiliary ego, expanded "the mate's ego capacity to deal with conflictual material," reduced the spouse's investment in maintaining his partner's pathology, and loosened the pathological symbiotic ties, resulting in the emergence of the marital partners as individuals.

Hastings and Runkle (1963) found that the resolution, within the group, of marriage neuroses initially used by the couple as resistance to therapy served to open new channels of communication and paved the way for amelioration of marital conflict at home.

Gottlieb and Pattison (1966) found that the group made possible mobilization of hope for marital rehabilitation; a permissive atmosphere for open scrutiny of supposedly hidden family "secrets"; recognition of angry outbursts for poorly executed and misperceived attempts at intimacy; provision of a model for healthy and constructive disagreement via open discussion of differences between cotherapists; acceptance of a measure of personal freedom and self-determination in the spouse (individuation) in place of defensive and unhappy symbiosis ("unity

Reprinted with permission of the authors and the publisher from *Archives of General Psychiatry*, 1967, *17*, 44–52.

identity"); disruption of marital games and parataxic distortions peculiar to a couple consequent to their crossmarital projection onto other group members who refuse to respond in the expected way; exposure to, and development of, alternative and more adaptive patterns of marital inter- action; replacement of irrelevant marital disputes by more direct, appro- priate, and constructive means for expression of painful intrapsychic conflicts; explicit rendering of nonverbal obstructions to clarify conflict; an increase in the capacity to grasp the spouse's thoughts and feelings ("correction of manifest communication distortion"); adoption of more realistic expectations of what narcissistic gratification marriage can and cannot provide ("correction of neurotic distortion"); and finally, recogni- tion (if not always a thorough working-through) of the multifaceted mani- festations of transference. While these workers focused primarily on neuroses manifested by marital disharmony, the effects of their thera- peutic techniques were profound in other areas of the patients' lives, with these areas providing an increasing portion of the grist for the group's mill.

Neubeck (1954), Perelman (1960), and Von Emde Boas (1962) are among the more enthusiastic of others who have found married couple group therapy an effective treatment modality. Blinder et al (1965) have reported encouraging experiences with groups consisting of seven to eight entire families.

RATIONALE

Marriage may be viewed as the purposeful, highly specific selection of a mate on the basis of various conscious and unconscious criteria, in the hope of gratifying the mature and neurotic needs of both partners. A marriage may be expected to disappoint its participants when many of the following exist reciprocally:

Perceptual distortions. "Mates in dysfunctional marital pairs see their spouses as they expect them to be rather than as they really are and treat them accordingly [Satir, 1965]." They may, for example, misperceive them as significant and conflictual persons in their past; they may persist in seeing their spouses in roles better fitting their own unexpressed hopes than the spouses' actual capabilities; they may attribute to their spouses many of their *own* unconscious attitudes which in turn are internaliza- tions of important childhood figures, or they may project onto the spouses those aspects of their own personality that rebel against these introjects. All of these leave to the misperceived and unsuspecting spouse the impossible task of resolving the residua of upheavals in his partner's parental home. Because communication between the partners is faulty, neither recognizes the part his misperceptions play in the conflicts that inevitably result.

Disturbances in communication. Partners may act upon unwarranted assumptions about each other's wishes or feelings, and are then hurt when the spouse acts contrary to expectations. They fail to correct their mis- apprehensions because (a) it has rarely occurred to them to check them out explicitly with the spouse; (b) they lack or are afraid to use the verbal techniques with which to do so; (c) they are more comfortable altering their perceptions to fit their expectations; (*d*) they fail to recognize or correctly interpret crucial nonverbal cues; and (*e*) messages they consider universally clear are, in fact, idiosyncratic to themselves.

Frustrated dependency needs. The inevitable failure of any marital union to meet lifelong narcissistic yearnings for all-absorbing, unconditional love often is reflected in the development of psychosomatic symptoms.

This failure may also result in states of chronic, irrational anger frequently punctuated by acute episodes of rage. Such may be a woman's response to her husband's efforts to meet his own dependency needs while seemingly ignoring hers; such may be the feelings of a man whose wife's very presence threatens his independence, thereby augmenting his dependency yearnings to an intolerable degree.

There may be rejection of a spouse upon whom despised dependency feelings have been projected. This is the mechanism that may lie behind a compulsive husband's intolerance of his wife's feminine emotionality, or a "phallic" wife's denigration of her husband's "failure to be a real man."

Alcohol abuse is another common consequence of frustration of dependency needs. Typically, a husband will struggle with unacceptable, unmet dependency yearnings, which are usually kept repressed because of the threat their recognition would constitute to his sense of masculinity, but which are permitted expression through episodes of total alcoholic helplessness, a helplessness mercifully kept from clear representation in consciousness by the fact of his intoxication. The alcoholic's spouse typically defends against recognition of *her* dependency by compensatory aggressive, controlling, domineering, and militantly abstinent behavior, which provides her a reassuring semblance of strength and independence, but also serves, self-defeatingly, to force her spouse to greater alcohol abuse and a proportionately reduced capacity to meet directly her dependent needs. Convinced by her own childhood experiences that no support or security may be had from an adult relationship with a man, and offering her husband scant opportunity to persuade her otherwise, she snatches what moments she can of a sense of mature womanhood by unconsciously acting to keep her husband a child. (The alcoholism-abstinence roles are easily exchanged in a married couple; the dynamics are then sex-reversed but otherwise identical.)

Threats to adaptive defenses. A functional marriage provides each partner a measure of security he cannot readily attain alone. Partners in a dysfunctional marriage, however, often inadvertently fail to support each other's defenses against anxiety because their self-esteem is so low that each is too desperately seeking relief for himself to notice the anxiety of the other; because each is unable to distinguish between behavior that buttresses the other's security system and that which may be perceived as a threat; because of the misbelief that what is helpful to one partner can only be obtained at the expense of the other; because the anxiety felt by one partner may be so severe as to cause him to distort, misuse, reject, and in other ways disqualify, (i.e., render ineffective) the help his spouse may willingly provide; or, because the partners feel compelled to obtain security from the knowledge that each can control the other, rather than from the unifying, pleasurable process of reaching mutually satisfying goals through cooperation and a sharing of skills.

Many pathological interactional forces making for a conflictual, unhappy marriage do not necessarily jeopardize its stability; indeed, neurotic bonds may at times be stronger than healthy ones. The marriage that seriously threatens the individual security system of its participants, however, is likely to be fragmented and short-lived.

Fears of the unfamiliar. There are those for whom the unpredictable, however painful, is relatively less discomforting than the unknown, whatever hope it may hold for the future. Accordingly, these people unconsciously select marriage partners with whom they can live out the same unresolved conflicts they have known in their childhood homes, and who embody introjects of the same elements that obstructed resolution of the parental conflict. Though they secretly hope this time for a different outcome, they continue in the old, familiar, but unproductive pattern. Should their first marriage dissolve, they would more often than not recreate it with other partners selected according to the same unconscious criteria, as in the case of the woman who marries and divorces a succession of alcoholics.

Obviously, the degree to which a spouse can play into his partner's basic conflicts depends somewhat on that partner's ability to blindly project onto the spouse what he wishes to see. Nevertheless, people tend to select repetitively and with uncanny accuracy spouses who do to some extent conform, or can be pressured into conforming, to their concept of what he or she must be like. One cannot long project a round picture on a square screen. For example, a woman chooses to marry a man she hopes will *not* treat her as her father did, but she expects from past experience that he, "being a man," *will*. Often, the husband does indeed behave like her father, because she either unconsciously selects him for that reason or acts to make him conform to her expectations. She can live with him, however unhappily, because she was trained to deal with this behavior as a child, perhaps by developing somatic complaints, perhaps by acting-out, or by withdrawal. She may complain vociferously about her husband's behavior and seek treatment for her own symptoms. When therapeutic pressure is applied, however, to change the homeostatic equilibrium from the level of her expectations to the level of her hopes—to the unfamiliar— she becomes anxiously aware of how much she prefers that the marriage continue in the old way, with both partners perpetuating a pattern already present in their parental homes, and now, to a greater or lesser extent, in their own. If at first present to a lesser extent, their overreactions to each other will soon make it a greater one.

In their efforts to maintain the familiar pathological equilibrium, spouses will sabotage their partners' attempts to remove the very symptoms that appear to cause so much dissension between them, lest this clear the field for exposure of their own pathology. (The man whose wife ceases to be frigid may suddenly find himself impotent; the woman whose husband's headaches no longer confine them to the house may for the first time be confronted with the fact of her own agoraphobia.) They will see in their spouses' attempts at healthy individuation a threat to their own autonomy, and set up elaborate family rules that suppress overt expression of innocent differences. They will be intolerant of the inevitable episodes of nonpathological regression so often prerequisite to subsequent spurts of growth or change in fixed attitudes. And, of course, the spouse's entrance into therapy for treatment of "his" or "her" problems seems quite acceptable until the spouse actually begins to change, and consequently, upset the couple's neurotic equilibrium.

Thus, conflictual marriages may occur between those who appear "good matches" as well as between those who do not. If the spouses are very much alike, they may still lash out at characteristics in the other despised in themselves, or they may attempt to preserve, to the detriment of the marriage, the other's nonadaptive defenses because of the protection they afford the apparently asymptomatic mate. If they are not alike, conflict usually arises not from the differences themselves, but from the threat these pose to self-esteem and established patterns of behavior, or from efforts to force the other into a more familiar mold.

CLINICAL ILLUSTRATIONS

These five interlocking motifs coalesce into a complex of reciprocal neurotic patterns that cause marital disharmony ranging from occasional sexual failure to divorce. The example that follows is the annotated and somewhat telescoped transcript of a "simple" exchange between Mr. and Mrs. C near the start of a married couple group session. Difficult, perhaps, to assimilate outside the context of the couple's history or the flow of the group, it nevertheless illustrates how these five patterns serve as a frame of reference for the couple's every transaction.

Mrs. C's harsh, overcritical parents have left her with a chronic sense of inadequacy. She characteristically projects this punitive introject of her parents onto her husband and consistently reacts with further loss of self-esteem to that which she misperceives as originating in him, as illustrated by her reply to Mr. C's first statement.

Mr. C: The roast didn't turn out as well tonight.

Mrs. C: I spent literally hours working on dinner, and all you have to say is I'm a bad cook.

In this example Mrs. C has made an incorrect assumption about her husband's attitude—an assumption she fails to check out. In point of fact, however, she has unconsciously selected in Mr. C a man who tends to be somewhat critical, as was her father, in the hope that this time there will be a better outcome—that she will win the man's unqualified affection and approval. Thus, although he is indeed a screen for his wife's projections, Mr. C is in "reality," somewhat demanding.

Mr. C: "I *don't* think you're a bad cook, but I *do* expect you to prepare a good meal without a lot of fuss.

Mrs. C: Well, I wouldn't need to "fuss" if you came home on time once in a while instead of wasting half the night at the bar with your cronies.

Mrs. C also projects onto her husband those aspects of her own personality that secretly rebel against her punitive introjects; and so, she chastises *him* for irresponsibility—irresponsibility conceived within her own mind but attributed to her spouse. She has also expressed a dependent need for her husband's attention and, in an idiosyncratic way, a wish that things be better between them.

Mr. C perceives her remarks as an attack on the self-assertiveness he may need to ward off despised feelings of dependency engendered by contact with his wife.

> Mr. C: Maybe I get a lot more out of spending the evening with Charlie instead of coming home to this every night. If only we could have a little peace in the house.

The husband has also sent an idiosyncratic message that he wants things to be better between them, but at this point, a suggestion that Mrs. C give up maladaptive but comfortably familiar behavior is not likely to meet acceptance. Now, in full rebellion against the real and fantasized demands of her husband, she rejects him completely.

> Mrs. C: Oh, why don't you eat out with them from now on?

Thus we see how a complex set of interactional distortions has transformed a mutually desired joint outcome (a pleasant, intimate meal together) into disappointment and pain for both partners.

PROCEDURES

Many of the methods used in individual, family, and traditional group therapy will serve the leader of a married couple group in good stead. There are, however, a number of techniques either unique to married couple group therapy or of special importance here. These are discussed in the sequence in which they are commonly used during the course of treatment. (Illustrative examples are drawn from one of the author's groups consisting of four couples (Anna and Alan A, Betty and Boris B, Carla and Courtney C, and Dora and Daniel D), here labeled alphabetically according to increasing age, ranging from the early 20's [Mr. and Mrs. A] to the late 50's [Mr. and Mrs. D].)

Four couples are usually selected for the group. There follows a series of four or five conjoint interviews with each couple separately so that the therapist can more quickly establish rapport and obtain diagnostic impressions. (Throughout the course of treatment patients are also seen alone, as necessary.) At the first group meeting the therapist has the patients introduce themselves; the method each member chooses to disseminate this simple information is often a harbinger of things to come.

The therapist then asks each couple their previous day's fears and fantasies as they contemplated coming to their first group session. This leads to an inquiry as to how each couple views the problems that impelled them to seek treatment. Care is taken not to *prematurely* force members, convinced that "their problem" consists entirely of the other spouse's symptoms, into accepting the therapist's concept that the ill partner is symptomatic for them both.

As soon as the couples start to feel comfortable about the group situation, the question of confidentiality, etc., one couple is chosen by the therapist for the group's initial focus. A relatively nonthreatening area of likely conflict, such as "getting Johnny to bed," "making out the budget," or "sitting down to eat" is used as a vehicle to begin exploring this couple's characteristic pattern of neurotic interaction. Such exploration becomes meaningful to the rest of the group as soon as the therapist begins to deal with some of the universal dynamics described in the preceding section, at which point the therapist may ask: "Has any other couple (or person) had an experience such as the one we just heard?"

In succeeding sessions the therapist notes and, where appropriate, comments on disturbed patterns of communication, distortions of perception, and erroneous assumptions. Whenever, for example, a spouse characteristically speaks for the other or reacts very strongly with anger, silence, or anxiety to another's seemingly innocent statements, the therapist intervenes and has the group examine the interaction.

In example 1, the therapist asks Betty B, whose husband Boris consistently speaks for her, to comment on her husband's assertions.

Example 1:

Boris: (*Referring to his wife*) It's a great struggle for her to come to this group. She always feels uncomfortable talking here.

Therapist: There is something in the group, Betty, that makes you uncomfortable?

Betty: Not particularly, Doctor, but if he doesn't get to speak everything on his mind he gets very antsy so I just sit and listen.

Therapist: Did you know that, Boris?

Boris: (*To wife*) She was always afraid to recite in class.

Betty: Oh, that was 15 years ago.

Therapist: Perhaps, Boris, there are other assumptions you have made about your wife—her silence and other habits—that bear checking out.

The group sessions provide many opportunities for the therapist to demonstrate how poorly the unverified assumptions of one partner coincide with the thoughts of the other. Gradually, the verbal spouse grows reluctant to speak for his more reticent mate (who soon becomes less reticent) and begins verifying his suppositions before making any authoritative statements.

When a spouse's reactions to his mate's seemingly innocent remarks seem inappropriately vehement, the therapist inquires as to what in his mate he was responding. His answer is then compared with the observations of the group, which may reveal an area of perceptual distortion in the responding mate or the unintended transmission of disqualifying nonverbal messages from the stimulus partner.

Example 2:

Courtney: I never saw a woman give so much to her kids as Carla.

Carla: Damn it, Court, will you lay off that? (*Silence. Carla sits sullenly; Courtney is crestfallen.*)

Therapist: Carla, I can see Courtney has really gotten to you, I wonder what he did that you were responding to?

Carla: He's just setting me up so when Joey [their son] disappears again for a week, I feel . . . (*starts to cry*).

Dora: It sounded to me, Carla, that Courtney was only trying to be nice.

Carla: I know that sarcastic grin.

Courtney: Sarcastic grin? I'm just being pleasant.

Boris: You did have a big grin on your face.

Therapist: When Courtney smiles, Carla, you think what he is saying is insincere? Or what?

Similarly, the therapist would actively intervene when a mate is noted to be constantly struggling to offer his spouse something she continually rejects. Such unhappy transactions are readily traced to the mate's misperception of what he thinks his spouse wants, setting the stage for his spouse's refusal of whatever he offers.

The therapist can use a particular couple's manner of speaking to stimulate other group members to examine their own verbal transactions. For example, some couples use pronouns in an idiosyncratic way which serves to hinder rather than facilitate communication. In the illustrative group, the therapist had frequent occasion to point out that Mr. and Mrs. B used "he" and "she" rather than "you" and "I" (as in example 1), whenever talking to the group about themselves, a form of address well suited to destroying intimacy and to the creation of false assumptions.

Mr. and Mrs. C had a somewhat different pronoun problem. Mrs. C typically would switch persons so frequently as to make her statements quite ambiguous, a communicative defect conducive to paranoid responses from her puzzled spouse.

Example 3:

Carla: (*To husband*) *You* ruined all of my plans, and then *he* storms out.

Mr. C is the subject of both angry phrases. His wife, however, has shifted her frame of reference in midsentence here, as she would often do when anxious. In this instance, the therapist intervened to reduce her anxiety and then suggested how she might make herself clearer.

The group also provides the therapist many opportunities to point out how partners send each other paralyzing double-bind messages, as in the case of the wife who repeatedly told her husband to bring her little gifts from time to time "without her asking"; or that of the husband who would demand that his wife "speak her mind freely," but would consistently compliment her effusively just before she spoke, effectively seal-ing-in any anger toward him that she might have wanted to express; or that of the wife who also begged for her spouse's full expression and then suddenly "felt faint" were he to say something she considered unkind.

Examination of these sorts of transactions brings the topic of "covert communication" into focus. By seeing how other couples disqualify verbal messages (as in the above examples), members of the group can under-stand how their own apparently innocent requests for or transmission of information can contain threats and other suppressive maneuvers aimed at the spouse. Once the group has given up preoccupation with the defense of one spouse or the other on the basis of mere explicit content and has begun to recognize disqualifying nonverbal cues, messages with multiple meanings, and other obstacles to clear and accurate transmission of intent, it is time for the major task of the married couple group therapist, "dis-crepancy analysis."

Discrepancy Analysis. Several family incongruencies lend themselves to group treatment. The first of these is that which occurs between what the partners *hope* to obtain from each other and what they have come to *expect*, either through bitter experience in their own home, current distorted perceptions, or their own subversive activities. A woman may hope for warmth and explicit expression of concern and affection from her husband, but has learned to expect only irritable indifference; for his part, there may be hopes for harmony and smiles of wifely contentment, but expectations of only complaints and criticism. Their mutual dis-appointment and subsequent attacks on the disappointing object (the offending spouse) are apparent in their arguments with each other and with other members of the group.

Dysfunctional couples will have arguments in most of the major areas of marital contact, such as raising children, spending money, achieving sexual gratification, etc., but these topics are merely vehicles for expres-sion of a basic discrepancy that transcends any operational differences of opinion. At an appropriate time the therapist can intervene and dissect out the primary recurrent discrepancy underlying most of these argu-ments. He can reveal to the couple and the group that they are not really talking about the budget, for example, but about unmet, deep-seated emotional needs; he can trace the historical roots of these needs and elicit similar experiences from other members of the group; finally, he can engage them in finding better ways to meet these needs than that of fruitless and largely irrelevant arguments.

Example 4:

Anna: Sometimes, as soon as Alan comes home, he walks past me right to the frige, takes a can of beer and goes upstairs to play the guitar. He doesn't say hello to me or Tommy, he doesn't ask how we are, or say how he is, he just goes upstairs and plays that thing all night as loud as he can.

Alan: I play it for about an hour, and I just play it loud enough to hear.

Anna: Oh, come on! Last night you played it so the house shook.

Alan: Well, you kept on bugging me.

Therapist: What do you mean by "bugging me," Alan?

Alan: She kept on coming up and giving me things to do.

Anna: I just asked you if you were coming down to dinner.

Alan: Yeah, come to dinner—and call Professor Roberts, and put a light bulb in the hallway. . . .

Therapist: Let's stop things for a second, Alan. First, I think this is the first we've heard, isn't it, of your being an avid musician?

Alan: (*Laughs*) I'm not actually, but nothing works better than that in cooling me off after ten hours in the drugstore. I'm so prickly I don't want to talk to anyone or be with anyone. . . .

Therapist: So then, playing is some sort of outlet for you—sort of makes you human again?

Alan: Yeah, if she'd just. . . .

Therapist: Well, let me hold things for just a second. Now Anna, if I understand you, by the time Alan gets home you've got quite a few things that have to get done.

Anna: Yes. Well, not really.

Alan: Oh boy!

Carla: Why are you so pissed off, Alan?

Courtney: He doesn't like to do a bunch of shit when he gets home, [after] working ten hours.

Therapist: Well, let's see if we can find out. Okay, Anna, you get upset with Alan because he plays the guitar instead of some other things?

Anna: It's just that I would like him to show once in a while that he knows he is married and has a wife and a son and a home. . . .

Alan: I know I've got them. I work hard enough. . . .

Anna: . . . he just walls himself off in the bedroom with that guitar.

Therapist: Walls himself off?

Anna: Like nobody else exists.

Therapist: Nobody else?

Alan: If I don't wall myself off, ten minutes after I start playing she is in there, telling me to do this or do that.

Dora: She just wants to see you, Alan.

Alan: I just as soon not be seen some nights—'til I unwind.

Therapist: Now, let me see if I understand; Anna, you don't object so much to the guitar as you do to the fact that it seems to exclude you and the family—which is really you again; and Alan, you want a little time to yourself to sort of settle down after your latest battle with the drugstore.

Alan: Yeah. I'm a lot nicer when I'm settled down, aren't I, Anna? (*Anna nods.*)

Therapist: So, Alan, you hope to settle down so you can make things go smoother with Anna, and Anna, you want to be with Alan in hopes that he will share things with you and make you feel more—more married?

The therapist has now isolated the hopes of both partners and can proceed to explore their expectations. In the example given, it came out that Anna's family had been deserted on three separate occasions by her father, the family broken up, and Anna placed several times in a foster home. She expected Alan to leave her, too, and interpreted his need to isolate himself briefly and work off his anger and frustration as a threat to the marriage. Alan, for his part, had spent his childhood meeting the incessant and arbitrary demands of his parents, particularly his mother, in whose shop he had worked since the age of 7. He characteristically anticipated that Anna also would make unreasonable demands upon him, in the name of family unity or "helping the weaker sex," and misinterpreted her requests for recognition accordingly. The therapist was able to use the A's to show the group how both partners hoped for a satisfying relationship but anticipated its ruin, one by loss of a spouse and the other by oppression.

In the next session, Dora and Daniel volunteered that they thought they had a similar quarrel each morning at breakfast. The group was able to discover that Dora hoped for warmth and affection before her husband left for work but expected rudeness, which she would often prophylactically ward off with criticism the moment her husband entered the room; Daniel also hoped for warmth and affection but expected only criticism, which he defended against by sullen withdrawal, regardless of his wife's mood.

The transactions of these couples were also examined for a discrepancy between *intent* and *performance*. Both couples intended to bring about a more harmonious marital relationship, but performed in such a way as to accomplish the opposite. Alan's attempts to prevent his tension from adversely affecting his wife served only to drive him further away. Dora and Daniel, too, strove for intimacy in a self-defeating manner.

In these situations, the therapist is able to detoxify the conflict by relabeling it as *an attempt to achieve intimacy* rather than a wish to inflict pain; once having accepted this relabeling, the couples are able to examine, nondefensively and without rancor, the effects of their present efforts, and explore alternative means which might be available for achieving their desired goals. Each participant's alternatively trying his old and then his new techniques for achieving an understanding with group members other than his spouse is often an enlightening experience.

The last, but probably most fundamental, discrepancy to be worked through is that existing between the partners' "survival myth" and "survival reality" (Gehrke & Kirchenbaum, 1967). Many marriages operate on the mutual assumption that open expression of conflict, the possession of feelings contrary to those of the spouse, or a desire for some measure of individual development independent of the spouse constitutes a withdrawal of love. Furthermore, the partners see any alteration in the marital equilibrium as a dire threat to their continued existence (the survival myth). They have never been taught, or have rejected, the survival reality, which is that a marriage is a union of two separate *individuals* who, though they frequently come to amicable agreement and compromise, nevertheless bring to the marriage different sets of values and a potential for different kinds of growth; that honest expression of these differences and the opportunity for independent growth are essential to a viable, healthy relationship; and that marriage is a unique, dynamic, and flexible interpersonal exchange subject to constant variation, many layered shifts, and the ebb and flow of feeling.

Betty and Boris, for example, maintained that they never argued, agreed on everything, and came to the group only to ensure that Betty would have a professional contact established should she have another "nervous breakdown." They were so protective of each other in their efforts to present a united front that they had effectively sealed themselves off from any other adult relationships outside of those forced upon them by membership in the group. When a group member would comment that it seemed in a particular instance that the B's did not really see eye to eye, they would become quite anxious and change the subject. Gradually, the therapist was able to reassure the B's that they indeed had each other, that they need not cling so tightly, that an occasional expression of "I" feelings did not mean the death of the "we" feelings. This interpretation was also helpful to Betty, providing her another example upon which to base her growing understanding that her husband's need for individual expression did not mean he was growing away from her.

The therapist next explores the parental roots of the group's dysfunctional behavior (*model analysis*). The extent to which the therapist may be active when using this technique is demonstrated in the following example.

Example 5:

During the tenth hour Anna began crying, whereupon Alan could be seen to pull away from her. In the process of examining this transaction with them, the therapist asked the following questions (replies are deleted for the sake of brevity).

"Alan, did you notice Anna was crying? What did it make you feel? What did you make of it? How did you arrive at that? Anna, did you notice Alan's response? What did it make you feel? What did you make of it? How did you arrive at that? What did you make of what Alan has said? What did you expect from Alan? Where did you learn what to expect from men?" (There followed a discussion of Anna's childhood and her feeling that only by tears could she give vent to her angry disappointment at her father's having left her alone.) "Alan, when Anna started crying, what did you want to do? I wonder how it comes about that you cannot do that? Anna, can you think of what might be getting in Alan's way?" (To group) "I'd be interested in some other responses to Anna's tears."

"Alan, someone you love is crying; you want to embrace her and cannot. I wonder if you expect a negative outcome if you should try and reach out to her? Has this happened to you before?" (There followed a discussion of Alan's childhood, with the group members as well as the therapist asking pertinent questions, in which Alan revealed that when all else failed, his mother would manipulate him to do her bidding by loud sobbing.) "Has anyone else in the group had a similar experience with his parents?"

The group was next asked what techniques Alan might try in order to achieve a more satisfying outcome (e.g., touching his wife, asking her what is bothering her, giving some clear sign of his concern). Having understood what is holding him back, he should be in a position to try other modes of behavior. Anna, too, aware now of the effect tears have on Alan, can with group support begin to look for other ways of having her needs met.

In all sessions the group is encouraged to comment when one spouse causes the other to turn away. Among the most frequently visible devices partners inadvertently use to destroy marital intimacy is that of role confusion. Couples frequently will misuse, in the group, the occupational roles they inappropriately impose upon their marriage. One woman, a teacher, lectured the group pedantically as she always had her husband; one man, a graduate student in psychology, was more of a therapist to his wife than a husband. Such interaction opens the door to exploration of "How comfortable are we in the role of wife and husband; Where did we learn the skills and how well did we learn them?"

A word about group resistances is in order at this point; a number occur repetitively in a married couple group. They make take the form of unspoken rules such as, "We can talk about feelings but we don't show our feelings here." The therapist can prevent the group from suddenly shifting focus away from a couple at a critical moment in favor of an intellectual discussion by demonstrating that the group will not fall apart if feelings come out, and that the therapist himself is not above showing what he feels inside.

In the same vein is the rule: "We never attack our parents." Inevitably, certain couples are assigned parental roles and are then vigorously protected by the group from honest examination of their conflicts. The therapist must demonstrate by his manner that objective inquiry into a couple's defense system is in no way an attack. A point must be made of supporting any group member who attempts to break these oppressive, upspoken rules. Other more general group resistances quite common to married couple therapy groups have been cheerfully catalogued by Berne (1966).

One modus operandi that stands out in examination of almost any group session is the therapist's persistent and deliberate relabeling of potentially destructive action according to its positive intent (e.g., Mrs. X's repeated "helpful" comments on her husband's driving are an attempt to make meaningful contact with him), in contrast to more psychoanalytic interpretations of intent which may often be negative (e.g., Mrs. X's repeated helpful comments about her husband's driving serve to cover the murderous impulses she has about him).

In married couple group therapy, positive interpretation of intent serves to turn the patient from defensive and fruitless justification of his dysfunctional goals to constructive participation in group process, through which he is freed to examine the effect of his behavior and to experiment with alternatives. Giving the spouses more benevolent views of their marital interaction liberates the psychic energy with which they may change. It is difficult to react in a blind, angry fashion to a stimulus no longer perceived as hostile. The therapist, it is hoped, is no Pollyanna, but a perceptive observer who struggles to seek the words that will enable his warring, stalemated patients to recognize the relatively benign wish lying behind the most misguided dysfunctional behavior.

SUMMARY

An interpersonal theory of disturbed marital interaction views marriage as the purposeful, highly specific selection of a mate on the basis of various conscious and unconscious criteria, in the hope of gratifying both the mature and neurotic needs of its participants, who can expect disappointment when there are many reciprocal perceptual distortions, disturbances in communication, frustrated dependency needs, threats to adaptive defenses, and fears of the unfamiliar. The therapy group obtains for its members a healthier marital equilibrium through correction of these perceptual and communicative errors, alleviation of reciprocal anxieties, analysis of discrepancies, and facilitation of intimacy. The therapist's persistently positive interpretation of intent serves to turn the patient from defensive and fruitless justification of his dysfunctional goals to constructive participation in group process, through which he is free to examine the effects of his behavior and experiment with alternatives.

REFERENCES

Berne, E. *Principles of group treatment.* New York: Oxford University Press, 1966.

Blinder, M. G., et al. "MCFT": Simultaneous treatment of several families. *American Journal of Psychotherapy*, 1965, *19*, 559–569.

Gehrke, S., & Kirschenbaum, M. Survival patterns in family conjoint therapy: Myth and reality. *Family Process*, 1967, *6*, 67–80.

Gottlieb, A., & Pattison, E. M. Married couples group psychotherapy. *Archives of General Psychiatry*, 1966, *14*, 143–152.

Hastings, P. R., & Runkle, R. L. An experimental group of married couples with severe problems. *International Journal of Group Psychotherapy*, 1963, *13*, 84–92.

Leichter, E. Group psychotherapy with married couples: Some characteristic treatment dynamics. *International Journal of Group Psychotherapy*, 1962, *12*, 154–163.

Neubeck, G. Factors affecting group therapy with married couples. *Marriage Family Living*, 1954, *16*, 216–220.

Perelman, J. L. Problems encountered in psychotherapy of married couples. *International Journal of Group Psychotherapy*, 1960, *10*, 136–142.

Satir, V. Conjoint marital therapy. In B. L. Green (Ed.), *The psychotherapies of marital disharmony.* New York: The Free Press, 1965.

Von Emde Boas, C. Intensive group psychotherapy with married couples. *International Journal of Group Psychotherapy*, 1962, *12*, 142–153.

Premarital Counseling

Keep your eyes wide open before marriage, half shut afterward.

BEN FRANKLIN

If marriages are to be better in the future than they have been in the past, education for marriage and premarital counseling would seem to be among the necessary steps. Many marriage counselors do premarital counseling and would like to do more, since prevention of marital difficulties may be more effectively handled in premarital counseling rather than in attempts at patching up a deteriorating marriage if not an already broken marriage.

In this section three sociologists and two psychologists discuss various aspects of premarital counseling and background information relevant to premarital counseling.

In Chapter 24, Albert Ellis, a psychologist and Executive Director of the Institute for Rational Living in New York City, discusses a rational approach to premarital counseling. Some of the questions that need to be dealt with in premarital counseling are such questions as: "Is my fiancée the right person for me?" "Should I have premarital sex relations?" "How can I find a suitable mate?" "How can I overcome my sexual incompetence or my homosexual leanings before I marry?"

Dr. Ellis discusses how these and other questions can be handled in premarital counseling according to the principles of "rational psychotherapy," which he and Dr. Robert A. Harper have been developing for the past several years. Dr. Ellis puts his ideas into a basic A-B-C schema which can be adopted and tried by any marriage counselor in his practice, or even put into practice by any interested person in his own private life. The theory and practice of rational psychotherapy are applied to two cases of individuals who were seen for premarital counseling.

In Chapter 25, Ira L. Reiss, a sociologist who has made extensive research inroads into how and why America's sex standards are changing, discusses the sexual "revolution" myth. He covers several important topics, including race differences and class differences, guilt feelings, the importance of responsibility, patterns of permissiveness, and a comprehensive theory to summarize his findings.

In Chapter 26, Lester A. Kirkendall, a psychologist, takes a courageous look at contraceptives for the unmarried. This is a controversial topic and one in which many people have conflicting views. Dr. Kirkendall gives the reader a chance to honestly examine and think about what some people would consider unthinkable. With the advent of the pill and the loop, the topic of contraceptives has received much more attention in all the mass media. Unmarried as well as married people will have to come to some decision regarding contraceptives. Kirkendall's article may provide a thoughtful and provocative first step into this difficult area.

In Chapter 27, Clark Vincent, an authority on sociological aspects of premarital and extramarital pregnancies, discusses counseling in such cases. Several topics are discussed, including cases involving unmarried mothers, counseling with the young unwed mother, counseling with the unwed's parents, whether there should be a marriage, decisions concerning the baby, unmarried fathers, married and divorced "unwed" mothers, the divorced unmarried mother, and, finally, maintaining the context in counseling with such cases. Dr. Vincent's remarks were originally addressed to an audience of physicians, but they can be profitably studied by any of the helping professions as well as anyone going through such experiences personally or with friends or family.

In Chapter 28, Owen Morgan, a psychologist, presents some points for premarital discussion in groups coming together for premarital counseling. Dr. Morgan has led many such discussions when he formerly worked at the Merrill-Palmer Institute in Detroit. Each person leading group discussions in premarital counseling may want to develop different topics and approaches, but Dr. Owen Morgan gives us some thought-provoking suggestions.

CHAPTER 24

A Rational Approach to
Premarital Counseling

Albert Ellis

People come for premarital counseling obviously because they have problems; and people with problems, as has been stressed by Ellis (1956),
Harper (1953, 1955), Laidlaw (1950), and Lawton (1958), can often best
be helped by some form of marriage counseling which not only presents a
solution to their present circumstances but also goes to the root of their
basic problem-creating disturbances. They need, in other words, some
type of psychotherapy.

Although I see a few clients for premarital counseling who have simple
questions to be answered, which can sometimes be resolved in one or two
sessions, the majority come for deeper and complicated reasons. Their
typical presenting questions are: "Is my fiancée the right person for me?"
"Should I be having premarital sex relations?" "How can I find a suitable
mate?" and "How can I overcome my sexual incompetence or my homosexual leanings before I marry?" These and similar questions usually
involve deep-seated personality characteristics or long-standing emotional
problems of the counselees.

When put in more dynamic terms, the real questions most individuals
who come for premarital counseling are asking themselves are: "Wouldn't
it be terrible if I were sexually or amatively rejected? or made a mistake in
my sex-love choice? or acted wrongly or wickedly in my premarital
affairs?" And: "Isn't it horribly unfair that the girl or fellow in whom I
am interested is unkind? or un-understanding? or overly-demanding? or
too selfish?"

In other words, the vast majority of premarital counselees are needlessly anxious and/or angry. They are woefully afraid of rejection,
incompetence, or wrongdoing during courtship or marriage; and they are
exceptionally angry or hostile because general or specific members of the
other sex do not behave exactly as they would like them to behave. Since,
according to the principles of rational psychotherapy which I and
Dr. Robert A. Harper have been developing for the past several years,

Reprinted with the permission of the author and the publisher from *Psychological Reports*,
1961, *8*, 333–338.

feelings of anxiety and resentment are almost always needlessly self-created, and inevitably do the individual who experiences them more harm than good, my psychotherapeutic approach to most premarital counselees is to show them as quickly as possible how to rid themselves of their fear and hostility, and thereby to solve their present and future courtship and marital difficulties.

The main theoretical construct and counseling technique which I employ in extirpating a client's shame and anger is the A-B-C theory of personality, which has been outlined in several articles and books (Ellis, 1957, 1958, 1960a; Ellis & Harper, 1960a, 1960b; Harper, 1960). This theory holds that it is rarely the stimulus, A, which gives rise to a human emotional reaction, C; rather, it is almost always B—the individual's system of beliefs regarding, attitudes toward, or interpretations of, A—which actually leads to his reaction, C.

Take, for example, premarital anxiety—which is usually the main presenting symptom of young people who come for counseling before marriage. I have recently been seeing a girl of twenty-five who, in spite of her keen desire to marry and have a family, has never been out on a date with a boy. She is reasonably good-looking and very well educated, and has had a good many opportunities to go with boys, because her entire family is concerned about her being dateless and will arrange dates for her on a moment's notice. But she always has found some excuse not to make appointments with boys, or else has made dates and then canceled them at the last minute. At the very few social affairs she has attended, she has latched on to her mother or some girl friend and has literally never left her side and never allowed herself to be alone with a male.

Although it is easy to give the girl's problem an impressive "psychodynamic" classification and to say that she is pregenitally fixated or has a severe dependency attachment to her mother, such labels, even if partially accurate, are incredibly unhelpful in getting her over her problem. Instead, she was simply helped to understand that her phobic reaction to males, at point C, could not possibly be caused by some noxious event or stimulus at point A (such as her once being rejected by a boy in whom she was interested); but that her own catastrophizing sentences at point B must be the real, current cause of her extreme fear of dating boys.

"What," I asked this client, "are you telling yourself at point B that makes you react so fearfully at point C?" At first, as is the case with many of my clients, she insisted that she wasn't telling herself anything at point B; or that, if she was, she couldn't say what she was telling herself. In my now distant past as a psychoanalyst, I used to take this kind of denial seriously, tell myself some of my own nonsense at point B to the effect that the patient was not yet ready for deep interpretation, and spend the next several months helping her avoid the main issue by demonstrating to her that she had some kind of an Electra complex which she was repressing and that she now, by long-winded processes of free association and dream analysis, had to dig up and face. Being, at the present stage in the game, a less naive and wiser psychotherapist, I now refuse to take a simple *no* for an answer and keep insisting that the client must on theoretical grounds be telling herself *something* at point B. Now what—and let's have no nonsense about this—is it?

My persistent questioning soon paid off. The client, on urging, found that she was telling herself that it would be perfectly awful if she went with boys and, like her two older sisters before her, was seduced sexually before marriage but (unlike these sisters) didn't actually marry her seducer. These internalized sentences, in their turn, were subheadings under her general philosophy, which held that marriage rather than sex was the only real good in life and that any girl who failed to achieve the marital state was thoroughly incompetent and worthless. Perversely enough, as happens in so many instances of neurosis, by overemphasizing the necessity of her marrying, my client literally drove herself into a state of panic which effectively prevented her from achieving the goal she most desired.

What was to be done to help this client? In my psychoanalytic days I would have encouraged her to transfer her love and marital needs toward me and then, interspersed with a great deal more free associational and dream analysis evocation and interpretation, I would have tried to show her that because I accepted her, she could fully accept herself and then presumably feel free to go off and marry some other male. Maybe, after a few thousand hours of analysis, this would have worked. Or maybe she would have become just as parasitically attached to me as she now was to her mother and would have finally, at the age of 65, realized that I was not going to marry her, and would have been pensioned off to a home for ex-analysands, which I sometimes fondly think of organizing.

Not being willing any longer to risk this dubiously fortuitous outcome of therapy, I very directly took this girl's major and minor irrational philosophies of life and directly challenged them until, after three months of counseling, she decided to give them up. More specifically, I vigorously attacked her notions that premarital sex relations are wicked and shameful; that marriage is the only good state of female existence; and that anyone who fails in a major goal, such as the goal of having a good relationship with a member of the other sex, is completely inept and valueless as a human being. I induced this client to believe, instead, that sex-love relations can be worthwhile in themselves, quite apart from marriage; that marrying may be a highly *preferable* but hardly a *necessary* goal for a female; and that failing in a given purpose is a normal part of human living and proves nothing whatever about one's essential worth.

In miracles or any other supernatural influences I passionately disbelieve. But the changes that took place in this patient concomitant with her reorganizing her sex-love and general philosophies of life were almost miraculous. It needed relatively little urging on my part to get her to make several dates with young males; she thoroughly enjoyed petting to orgasm with some of these partners; a few months later she entered into full sex-love relationship with one of them; and she is now engaged to be married to her lover. Moreover, although we rarely talked about some of the other important aspects of her life, she has also gone back to college, which she had left in despair because of her poor social life there, and is intent on becoming a nursery school teacher. Quite a constructive change, all told!

Let us consider another case of premarital counseling along rational psychotherapeutic lines. A 28-year-old male came for counseling because he kept becoming angry at his fiancée, ostensibly because she continually "unmanned" him by criticizing him in public. On questioning, he also admitted that he had never been fully potent with a female and had acute fears of whether he would succeed sexually with his fiancée after they were married. According to psychoanalytic interpretation, he was really not afraid of his fiancée's unmanning him in public, but of unmanning himself when he finally got into bed with his bride; and her so-called attacks on him were actually a projection of his own castration fears.

So I would have interpreted in my psychoanalytic youth. Fortunately, however, I had the good sense to call in this client's fiancée; and I quickly found that she was a querulous, negativistic woman and that she did, figuratively speaking, often castrate my client in public. Whereupon I quickly set about doing two nonpsychoanalytic and highly directive things. First, I talked the fiancée herself into becoming a counselee, even though she at first contended that there was nothing wrong with her, and that the entire problem was the result of her boyfriend's inconsiderateness and ineptitude. When I saw her for psychotherapy (in all, forty-eight sessions of individual and a year of group therapy, since she proved to be a rather difficult patient), I set about showing her that her anger, at point C, stemmed not from her boyfriend's inept behavior, at point A, but from her prejudiced and grandiose interpretations of this behavior at point B.

I showed this woman, in other words, that she kept saying to herself: (a) "John is doing these inept and inconsiderate things to me"; and (b) "He *shouldn't* be acting that way and is a no-good sonofagun for doing so." Instead, I insisted, she would do much better by saying to herself: (a) "John is doing these things, which I consider to be inept and inconsiderate to me"; and (b) "If I am correct (which I may or may not be), then *it would be much nicer* if he could be induced to stop acting this way; and I should be doing everything in my power to help him see what he is doing, without blaming him for his behavior, so that he changes his actions for the better."

When I convinced this client that no one is logically ever to blame for anything, and that people's errors and mistakes are to be accepted and condoned rather than excoriated if we are truly to be of help to them, she not only stopped berating her boyfriend in public but became a generally kinder and less disturbed individual in her own right (cf. Ellis, 1960b).

Meanwhile, to flashback to my original client in this pair, whom we left gnashing his teeth at his fiancée and shivering in his pajamas about the spectre of his sexual impotence, he proved to be a relatively easy convert to the cause of rational thinking. After sixteen sessions of highly directive counseling he was able to see that, whatever the verbal harshness of his intended bride, her words—at point A—could only hurt and anger him—at point C—if he kept telling himself sufficient nonsense about these words at point B.

Instead of what he had been telling himself at point B—namely, "That bitch is castrating me by her horrible public criticism, and she has no right to do that to poor weakly me"—he was induced to question the rationality of these internal verbalizations. After actively challenging his own unthinking assumptions—particularly, the assumptions (*a*) that his fiance'e's critical words *were* necessarily horribly hurtful; (*b*) that she *should not* keep repeating her criticism of him; and (*c*) that he *was* too weak to hear this criticism and not be able to take it in his stride—this client began to believe in and tell himself a radically different philosophy of sex-love relationships, namely: "There goes my poor darling again, making cracks at me because of her own disturbance. Now let me see if any of her points about me are correct; and, if so, let me try to change myself in those respects. But let me also try, in so far as she is mistaken about her estimates of me, to help her with her own problems, so that she doesn't need to keep being nasty to me in public." When this change in his internalized sentences was made, my client improved remarkably in his ability to take his fiance'e's criticism; and his hostility toward her largely vanished.

He was then also able to face the matter of his own impotence—which proved to be, as it so often does, a result of his worrying so greatly over the possibility of his failing that he actually tended to fail. When he was able to acquire a new sexual and general philosophy about failing, he became more than adequately potent.

In his new philosophy, instead of saying to himself: "If I fail sexually, it will be terrrible, and I will be totally unmanned," he began to say: "It is highly desirable, though not necessary, that I succeed in being potent; and in the event that I am impotent for the present, there are various extravaginal ways of satisfying my partner; so what's the great hassle?" Losing his acute fear of his fiance'e's publicly criticizing him, he helped her to be much less critical.

The main aspects of rational therapy which are usually applied to premarital counseling, then, include the counselee's being taught that it is *not* horrible for him to fail in his sex-love ventures; that there is no reason why his love partner *should* act the way he would like her to act; and that any intense unhappiness that he may experience in his premarital (or, later, marital) affairs almost invariably stems from his *own* self-repeated nonsense rather than his partner's attitudes or actions. Rational therapy, in these respects, directly forces the patient to accept reality, particularly in his relations with his sex-love partner.

REFERENCES

Ellis, A. A critical evaluation of marriage counseling. *Marriage and Family Living*, 1956, *18*, 65–71.

Ellis, A. Outcome of employing three techniques of psychotherapy. *Journal of Clinical Psychology*, 1957, *13*, 334–350.

Ellis, A. Neurotic interaction between marital partners. *Journal of Counseling Psychology*, 1958, *5*, 24–28. (a)

Ellis, A. Rational psychotherapy. *Journal of General Psychology*, 1958, *59*, 35–49. (b)

Ellis, A. Marriage counseling with demasculinizing wives and demasculinized husbands. *Marriage and Family Living*, 1960, *22*, 13–21. (a)

Ellis, A. There is no place for the concept of sin in psychotherapy. *Journal of Counseling Psychology*, 1960, *7*, 188–192. (b)

Ellis, A., & Harper, R. A. *Creative marriage*. New York: Lyle Stuart, 1961. (a)

Ellis, A., & Harper, R. A. *A guide to rational living*. Englewood Cliffs, N. J.: Prentice-Hall, 1961. (b)

Harper, R. A. Should marriage counseling become a full-fledged specialty? *Marriage and Family Living*, 1953, *15*, 338–340.

Harper, R. A. Failure in marriage counseling. *Marriage and Family Living*, 1955, *17*, 359–362.

Harper, R. A. A rational process-oriented approach to marriage counseling. *Journal of Family Welfare*, 1960, *6*, 1–10.

Laidlaw, R. W. The psychiatrist as marriage counselor. *American Journal of Psychiatry*, 1950, *106*, 732–736.

Lawton, G. Neurotic interaction between counselor and counselee. *Journal of Counseling Psychology*, 1958, *5*, 28–33.

CHAPTER 25

How and Why America's Sex
Standards Are Changing

Ira L. Reiss

The popular notion that America is undergoing a sexual "revolution" is a myth. The belief that our more permissive sexual code is a sign of a general breakdown of morality is also a myth. These two myths have arisen in part because we have so little reliable information about American sexual behavior. The enormous public interest in sex seems to have been matched by moralizing and reticence in scholarly research—a situation that has only recently begun to be corrected.

What *has* been happening recently is that our young people have been assuming more responsibility for their own sexual standards and behavior. The influence of their parents has been progressively declining. The greater independence given to the young has long been evident in other fields—employment, spending, and prestige, to name three. The parallel change in sexual-behavior patterns would have been evident if similar research had been made in this area. One also could have foreseen that those groups least subject to the demands of old orthodoxies, like religion, would emerge as the most sexually permissive of all—men in general, liberals, nonchurchgoers, Negroes, the highly educated.

In short, today's more permissive sexual standards represent not revolution but evolution, not anomie but normality.

My own research into current sexual behavior was directed primarily to the question, Why are some groups of people more sexually permissive than other groups? My study involved a representative sample of about 1,500 people, 21 and older, from all over the country; and about 1,200 high-school and college students, 16 to 22 years old, from three different states. On the pages that follow, I will first discuss some of the more important of my findings, then suggest seven general propositions that can be induced from these findings, and finally present a comprehensive theory about modern American sexual behavior.

Reprinted with permission of the author and the publisher from *Trans-action*, 1968, March, 26–32.

ARE RACE DIFFERENCES ROOTED IN CLASS?

A good many sociologists believe that most of the real differences between Negroes and whites are class differences—that if Negroes and whites from the same class were compared, any apparent differences would vanish. Thus, some critics of the Moynihan Report accused Daniel P. Moynihan of ignoring how much lower-class whites may resemble lower-class Negroes.

But my findings show that there are large variations in the way whites and Negroes *of precisely the same class* view premarital sexual permissiveness. Among the poor, for instance, only 32 percent of white males approve of intercourse before marriage under some circumstances—compared with 70 percent of Negro males. The variation is even more dramatic among lower-class females: 5 percent of whites compared with 33 percent of Negroes. Generally, high-school and college students of all classes were found to be more permissive than those in the adult sample. But even among students there were variations associated with race. (See Table I.)

TABLE I

PERCENT ACCEPTING PREMARITAL SEX

	Lower-class adults[*]	Lower-class students[**]
White men	32% of 202	56% of 96
Negro men	70% of 49	86% of 88
White women	5% of 221	17% of 109
Negro women	33% of 63	42% of 90

[*] From National Adult Sample
[**] From Five-School Student Sample

The difference between Negro and white acceptance of premarital intercourse is not due to any racial superiority or inferiority. All that this finding suggests is that we should be much more subtle in studying Negro-white differences, and not assume that variations in education, income, or occupation are enough to account for all these differences. The history of slavery, the depressing effects of discrimination and low status—all indicate that the Negro's entire cultural base may be different from the white's.

Another response to this finding on sexual attitudes can, of course, be disbelief. Do people really tell the truth about their sex lives? National studies have revealed that they do—women will actually talk more freely about their sex lives than about their husbands' incomes. And various validity checks indicate that they did in this case.

But people are not always consistent: They may not practice what they preach. So I decided to compare people's sexual attitudes with their actual sexual behavior. Table II indicates the degree of correspondence between attitudes and behavior in a sample of 248 unmarried, white, junior and senior college-students.

TABLE II

SEXUAL STANDARDS AND ACTUAL BEHAVIOR

Current Standard	Most Extreme Current Behavior			Number of Respondents
	Kissing	Petting	Coitus	
Kissing	64%	32%	4%	25
Petting	15%	78%	7%	139
Coitus	5%	31%	64%	84

Obviously, the students do not *always* act as they believe. But in the great majority of cases belief and action do coincide. For example, 64 percent of those who consider coitus acceptable are actually having coitus; only 7 percent of those who accept nothing beyond petting, and 4 percent of those who accept nothing beyond kissing, are having coitus. So it is fairly safe to conclude that, in this case, attitudes are good clues to behavior.

GUILT IS NO INHIBITOR

What about guilt feelings? Don't they block any transition toward more permissive sexual attitudes and behavior? Here the findings are quite unexpected. *Guilt feelings do not generally inhibit sexual behavior.* Eighty-seven percent of the women and 58 percent of the men said they had eventually come to accept sexual activities that had once made them feel guilty. (Some—largely males—had never felt guilty.) Seventy-eight percent had *never* desisted from any sexual activity that had made them feel guilty. Typically, a person will feel some guilt about his sexual behavior, but will continue his conduct until the guilt diminishes. Then he will move on to more advanced behavior—and new guilt feelings—until over that; and so on. People differed, mainly, in the sexual behavior they were willing to start, and in how quickly they moved on to more advanced forms.

The factor that most decisively motivated women to engage in coitus and to approve of coitus was the belief that they were in love. Of those who accepted coitus, 78 percent said they had been in love—compared with 60 percent of those who accepted only petting, and 40 percent of those who accepted only kissing. (Thus, parents who don't want their children to have sexual experiences but do want them to have "love" experiences are indirectly encouraging what they are trying to prevent.)

How do parents' beliefs influence their children's sexual attitudes and conduct?

Curiously enough, almost two-thirds of the students felt that their sexual standards were at least similar to those of their parents. This was as true for Negro males as for white females—although about 80 percent of the former accept premarital intercourse as against only about 20 percent of the latter. Perhaps these students are deluded, but perhaps they see through the "chastity" facade of their parents to the underlying similarities in attitude. It may be that the parents' views on independence, love, pleasure, responsibility, deferred gratification, conformity, and adventurousness are linked with the sexual attitudes of their children; that a similarity in these values implies a similarity in sexual beliefs. Probably these parental values, like religiousness, help determine which youngsters move quickly and with relatively little guilt through the various stages of sexual behavior. Religiousness, for the group of white students, is a particularly good index: Youngsters who rank high on church attendance rank low on premarital coitus, and are generally conservative.

Despite the fact that 63 to 68 percent of the students felt that their sexual standards were close to their parents' standards, a larger percentage felt that their standards were even closer to those of peers (77 percent) and to those of very close friends (89 percent). Thus, the conflict in views between peers and parents is not so sharp as might be expected. Then too, perhaps parents' values have a greater influence on their children's choice of friends than we usually acknowledge.

THE IMPORTANCE OF RESPONSIBILITY

This brings us to another key question. Are differences in sexual standards between parents and children due to changing cultural standards? Or are they due to their different roles in life—that is, to the difference between being young, and being parents responsible for the young? Were the parents of today that different when they courted?

My findings do show that older people tend to be less permissive about sex—but this difference is not very marked. What is significant is that childless couples—similar to couples with children of courtship age in every other respect, including age—are much more willing to accept premarital intercourse as standard (23 to 13 percent). Furthermore, parents tend to be *less* sexually permissive the *more* responsibility they have for young people. Now, if the primary cause of parent-child divergences in sexual standards is that cultural standards in general have been changing, then older people should, by and large, be strikingly more conservative about sex. They aren't. But since parents are more conservative about sex than nonparents of the same age, it would seem that the primary cause of parent-child divergences over sex is role and responsibility—the parents of today were *not* that different when courting.

Being responsible for others, incidentally, inhibits permissiveness even when the dependents are siblings. The first-born are far less likely to approve of premarital intercourse (39 percent) than are the youngest children (58 percent).

Another intriguing question is, How do parents feel about the sexual activities of their boy children—as opposed to their girl children? The answer depends upon the sex of the parent. The more daughters a white father has, the more strongly he feels about his standards—although his standards are no stricter than average. The more sons he has, the less strongly he feels about his beliefs. White mothers showed the reverse tendency, but much more weakly—the more sons, the stronger the mothers' insistence upon whatever standards they believe in. Perhaps white parents feel this way because of their unfamiliarity with the special sexual problems of a child of the opposite sex—combined with an increasing awareness of these problems.

What explains these differences in attitude between groups—differences between men and women as well as between Negroes and whites? Women are more committed to marriage than men, so girls become more committed to marriage, too, and to low-permissive parental values. The economic pressures on Negroes work to break up their families, and weaken commitment to marital values, so Negroes tend to be more permissive. Then, too, whites have a greater stake in the orthodox institution of marriage: more white married people than unmarried people reported that they were happy. Among Negroes, the pattern was reversed. But in discussing weak commitments to marriage, we are dealing with one of the "older" sources of sexual permissiveness.

The sources of the new American permissiveness are somewhat different. They include access to contraception; ways to combat venereal infection; and—quite as important—an intellectualized philosophy about the desirability of sex accompanying affection. "Respectable," college-educated people have integrated this new philosophy with their generally liberal attitudes about the family, politics, and religion. And this represents a new and more lasting support for sexual permissiveness, based on a positive philosophy rather than hedonism, despair, or desperation.

In my own study, I found that among the more permissive groups were those in which the fathers were professional men. This finding is important: it shows that the upper segments of our society, like the lower, have a highly permissive group in their midst—despite the neat picture described by some people of permissiveness steadily declining as one raises one's gaze toward the upper classes.

PATTERNS OF PERMISSIVENESS

All these findings, though seemingly diverse, actually fall into definite patterns, or clusters of relationships. These patterns can be expressed in seven basic propositions:

1. The *less* sexually permissive a group is, traditionally, the *greater* the likelihood that new social forces will cause its members to become more permissive.

Traditionally high-permissive groups, such as Negro men, were the least likely to have their sexual standards changed by social forces like church-attendance, love affairs, and romantic love. Traditionally low-

permissive groups, such as white females, showed the greatest sensitivity
to these social forces. In addition, the lower social classes are reported to
have a tradition of greater sexual permissiveness, so the finding that their
permissiveness is less sensitive to certain social forces fits this proposition.

2. The more liberal the group, the more likely that social forces will
help maintain high sexual permissiveness.

There was diverse support for this proposition. Students, upper-class
females in liberal settings, and urban dwellers have by and large accepted
more permissiveness than those in more conservative settings.

Indeed, liberalism in general seems to be yet another cause of the new
permissiveness in America. Thus, a group that was traditionally low-permissive regarding sex (the upper class), but that is liberal in such fields as
religion and politics, would be very likely to shift toward greater premarital permissiveness.

3. According to their ties to marital and family institutions, people
will differ in their sensitivity to social forces that affect permissiveness.

This proposition emphasizes, mainly, male-female differences in courting. Women have a stronger attachment to, and investment in, marriage,
childbearing, and family ties. This affects their courtship roles. There are
fundamental male-female differences in acceptance of permissiveness,
therefore, in line with differences in courtship role.

Romantic love led more women than men to become permissive (this
finding was particularly true if the woman was a faithful churchgoer).
Having a steady date affected women predominantly, and exclusiveness
was linked with permissiveness. Early dating and its link with permissiveness varied by race, but was far more commonly linked with permissiveness in men than in women. The number of steadies and the number of
times in love were associated with permissiveness for females, but were
curvilinear for males—that is, a man with no steadies, or a number of
steadies, tended to be more permissive than a man who had gone steady
only once.

Such male-female differences, however, are significant only for whites.
Among Negroes, male-female patterns in these areas are quite similar.

4. The higher the overall level of permissiveness in a group, the greater
the extent of equalitarianism within abstinence and double-standard subgroups.

Permissiveness is a measure not only of what a person will accept for
himself and his own sex, but of what behavior he is willing to allow the
opposite sex. Permissiveness, I found, tends to be associated with sexual
equalitarianism in one particular fashion: I found, strangely enough, that a
good way to measure the *general* permissiveness of a group is to measure
the equalitarianism of two subgroups—the abstinent, and believers in the
double-standard. (Nonequalitarianism in abstinence means, usually, petting is acceptable for men, but only kissing for women. Equalitarianism
within the double-standard means that intercourse is acceptable for
women when in love, for men anytime. The nonequalitarian double-standard considers all unmarried women's coitus wrong.) In a generally high-

permissive group (such as men), those adherents who do accept abstinence or the double-standard will be more equalitarian than will their counterparts in low-permissive groups (such as women). The implication is that the ethos of a high-permissive group encourages female sexuality and thereby also encourages equalitarianism throughout the group.

5. The potential for permissiveness derived from parents' values is a key determinant as to how rapidly, how much, and in what direction a person's premarital sexual standards and behavior change.

What distinguishes an individual's sexual behavior is not its starting point—white, college-educated females, for instance, almost always start only with kissing—but how far, how fast, and in what direction the individual is willing to go. The fact is that almost all sexual behavior is eventually repeated, and comes to be accepted. And a person's basic values encourage or discourage his willingness to try something new and possibly guilt-producing. Therefore, these basic values—derived, in large part, from parental teaching, direct or implicit—are keys to permissiveness.

Since the young often feel that their sex standards are similar to their parents', we can conclude that, consciously or not, high-permissive parents intellectually and emotionally breed high-permissive children.

6. A youth tends to see permissiveness as a continuous scale with his parents' standards at the low point, his peers' at the high point, and himself between but closer to his peers—and closest to those he considers his most intimate friends.

The findings indicate that those who consider their standards closer to parents' than to peers' are less permissive than the others. The most permissive within one group generally reported the greatest distance from parents, and greatest similarity to peers and friends. This does not contradict the previous proposition, since parents are on the continuum and exert enough influence so that their children don't go all the way to the opposite end. But it does indicate, and the data bear out, that parents are associated with relatively low permissiveness; that the courtship group is associated with relatively high permissiveness; and that the respondents felt closer to the latter. Older, more permissive students were less likely to give "parental guidance" as a reason for their standards.

7. Greater responsibility for other members of the family, and lesser participation in courtship, are both associated with low-permissiveness.

The only child, it was found, had the most permissive attitudes. Older children, generally, were less permissive than their younger brothers and sisters. The older children usually have greater responsibility for the young siblings; children without siblings have no such responsibilities at all.

The findings also showed that as the number of children, and their ages, increased, the parents' permissiveness decreased. Here again, apparently, parental responsibility grew, and the decline in permissiveness supports the proposition above.

On the other hand, as a young person gets more and more caught up in courtship, he is progressively freed from parental domination. He has less responsibility for others, and he becomes more permissive. The fact that students are more sexually liberal than many other groups must be due partly to their involvement in courtship, and to their distance from the family.

Thus a generational clash of some sort is almost inevitable. When children reach their late teens or early 20s, they also reach the peak of their permissiveness; their parents, at the same time, reach the nadir of theirs.

These findings show that both the family and courtship institutions are key determinants of whether a person accepts or rejects premarital sexuality. Even when young people have almost full independence in courtship, as they do in our system, they do not copulate at random. They display parental and family values by the association of sex with affection, by choice of partners, by equalitarianism, and so on.

However, parental influence must inevitably, to some extent, conflict with the pressures of courting, and the standards of the courting group. Young people are tempted by close association with attractive members of the opposite sex, usually without having any regular heterosexual outlet. Also, youth is a time for taking risks and having adventures. Therefore, the greater the freedom to react autonomously within the courtship group, the greater the tendency toward liberalized sexual behavior.

This autonomy has always been strong in America. Visitors in the 19th century were amazed at freedom of mate choice here, and the equalitarianism between sexes, at least as compared with Europe. The trend has grown.

Now, families are oriented toward the bearing and rearing of children —and for this, premarital sex is largely irrelevant. It becomes relevant only if it encourages marriages the parents want—but relevant negatively if it encourages births out of wedlock, or the "wrong," or no, marriages. Most societies tolerate intercourse between an engaged couple, for this doesn't seriously threaten the marital institution; and even prostitution gains some acceptance because it does not promote unacceptable marital unions. The conflict between the family and courtship systems depends on the extent to which each perceives the other as threatening its interests. My own findings indicate that this conflict is present, but not always as sharply as the popular press would have us believe.

Courtship pressures tend toward high-permissiveness; family pressures toward low-permissiveness. It follows that whatever promotes the child's independence from the family promotes high-permissiveness. For example, independence is an important element in the liberal position; a liberal setting, therefore, encourages sexual as well as other independence.

A COMPREHENSIVE THEORY

To summarize all these findings into one comprehensive theory runs the risk of oversimplifying—if the findings and thought that went into the theory are not kept clearly in mind. With this *caveat*, I think a fair theoretical summary of the meaning of the foregoing material would be: How much premarital sexual permissiveness is considered acceptable in a court-ship group varies directly with the independence of that group, and with the general permissiveness in the adult cultural environment.

In other words, when the social and cultural forces working on two groups are approximately the same, the differences in permissiveness are caused by differences in independence. But when independence is equal, differences come from differences in the socio-cultural setting.

There is, therefore, to repeat, no sexual revolution today. Increased premarital sexuality is not usually a result of breakdown of standards, but a particular, and different, type of organized system. To parents, more firmly identified with tradition—that is, with older systems—and with greater responsibilities toward the young, toward the family, and toward marriage, greater premarital sexuality seems deviant. But it is, neverthe-less, an integral part of society—their society.

In short, there has been a gradually increasing acceptance of, and overtness about, sexuality. The basic change is toward greater equalitarian-ism, greater female acceptance of permissiveness, and more open discus-sion. In the next decade, we can expect a step-up in the pace of this change.

The greater change, actually, is in sexual attitude, rather than in be-havior. If behavior has not altered in the last century as much as we might think, attitudes *have*—and attitudes and behavior seem closer today than for many generations. Judging by my findings, and the statements of my respondents, we can expect them to become closer still, and to proceed in tandem into a period of greater permissiveness, and even greater frankness. I do not, however, foresee extreme change in the years to come—such as full male-female equality. This is not possible unless male and female roles in the family are also equal, and men and women share equal responsibil-ity for child-rearing and family support.

SUGGESTED READINGS

The Encyclopedia of Sexual Behavior edited by Albert Ellis and Albert Albarbanel (New York City: Hawthorn Books, 1961). The most complete and authoritative source of its kind avail-able. Contains articles by approximately 100 authorities in the field.

Journal of Social Issues—"The Sexual Renaissance in America"—April 1966. Many of the key figures in this area have contributed to this special journal issue: Robert Bell, Jessie Bernard, Carlfred Broderick, Harold Christensen, Paul Gebhard, Lester Kirkendall, Roger Libby, Lee Rainwater, Ira L. Reiss, Robert Sherwin, and Clark Vincent.

The Sexual Behavior of Young People by Michael Schofield (Boston: Little, Brown and Co., 1965). A recent, carefully executed study of English teenagers with much fascinating information that can be compared with American studies.

CHAPTER 26

A Counselor Looks at Contraceptives for the Unmarried

Lester A. Kirkendall

In 1962 a book on thermonuclear warfare was published with the title, *Thinking about the Unthinkable* (Kahn, 1962). This might well serve as a subtitle for this article, for certainly in the area of sexual behavior "thinking about the unthinkable" has become our task.

While this discussion revolves around sex standards, changing sexual ethics represents only one turbulency in a rapidly changing world. Our age is one with many problems which are interrelated and interacting, and all of which have moral implications and aspects. Thus the rising demand that recognition of personal worth be based upon individual merit, as against status derived through birth or membership in some particular group, requires an alteration in racial relations with attendant alteration in moral concepts. The applications of technology which have resulted in an ever-increasing abundance of material goods, greater comforts and conveniences, better health and longer life have raised moral questions about how to utilize and distribute these benefits. The linkage of thermonuclear power to weapons of fearful destructiveness raises tremendous moral questions about how to deal with our hostile and aggressive impulses. The growing availability of leisure time, control of the reproductive processes, and changing concepts about the purpose and place of sex in life have raised a multitude of issues concerning the moral use of sex.

These changes and others are world-wide in scope. Practically no aspects of our lives are left untouched.

Neither did the current debate about sexual standards arise with the advent of "the pill." It has been developing for a long time, and the pill only serves as a convenient symbol around which to focus discussion. Furthermore, the debate involves much more than a simple, straight-line relationship between contraceptive methods and ethical conduct (Kirkendall & Ogg). The increased accessibility and effectiveness of contraceptive methods, changing sex roles, an increasing reliance on secular authority, the greatly decreased need to use sex always in the interest of reproduc-

This article is based on a paper entitled "Contraception and the Unmarried—Sense and Nonsense," presented at a conference on "The Pill and the Puritan Ethic," sponsored by the Faculty Program Center of San Francisco State College, February 10–12, 1967.

tion, and the greater openness with which sex is discussed in our society—these forces and others have, over a period of time, produced the problems and intensified their nature. There are even further complexities. Thus the title of this article is "A Counselor Looks at Contraceptives for the Unmarried," but how the questions relating to this issue will finally be resolved is tied to such complex matters as our beliefs as to what constitutes morality, what the nature of sex is, the character of male-female nature, and in what manner the sexes should relate to each other. Until we come to terms with these matters, all we can hope for in the sexual realm is contradiction, confusion, and trouble.

To focus on the moral issue is realistic, for our traditional concepts concerning morals baffle and impede all our efforts to arrive at more rational and constructive ways of dealing with human sexuality. If we could come to terms with the moral issue, a major accomplishment would have been achieved.

The first task in "thinking about the unthinkable" is to be starkly realistic. In the interest of realism, I wish first to set forth six premises upon which I am basing my discussion, and then note some of the forces which are bringing us to the inevitable confrontation with the issue of contraception and the unmarried. I hope this will aid in arriving at a point of mutual understanding, if not agreement.

1. *In dealing with sexual matters or with any human relationship, we are properly concerned with morals and standards.*

2. *Contraceptive information will surely become increasingly available.* At the present time it is available in printed form to anyone who has the money to purchase a paperback from a book stand. And those who haven't the money can stand behind the upright racks to read. Securing this information verbally still comes harder, but willingness to discuss contraceptive devices and practices openly is increasing, too.

3. *Contraceptive devices are presently available to the unmarried and will, without doubt, become increasingly accessible and effective.*

4. *Neither contraceptive information nor devices can be kept from those who want them, excepting perhaps the most ignorant, immature, and confused.*

5. *We have always had, and will continue to have, nonmarital sexual intercourse.* In fact, I would expect the amount might increase substantially in the future, particularly among those who have once been married but are later found among the divorced or widowed in middle or late life. The high rates of marital breakup and the marked degree of mobility in our society suggest, too, that postmarital and extramarital intercourse will increase significantly in the future.

6. *The sexual patterns of individuals are influenced much more profoundly by many other factors than contraceptive knowledge or the availability of contraceptives.* I have no convincing evidence that knowledge or ignorance of contraceptive devices has much to do with the sexual practices currently followed by an individual. Over a span of time and in combination with other factors, however, I do believe knowledge and availability of contraceptives will help influence standards.

Discussion almost invariably concentrates upon unmarried youth, rather than including the many middle-aged or elderly persons who are unmarried, and the divorced. This is, of course, a reflection of our culture's obsessive concern with premarital intercourse. But the problem of obtaining contraceptive information and devices is much less for these older, experienced individuals than it is for those who are younger, more naive, and relatively inexperienced. The latter are, therefore, in a very real sense the proper objects of our concern.

Considering the realities we face, I should like to propose a three-pronged program.

1. *Our first need is to strip away the hypocrisy and deceit with which we have surrounded sexual matters.* Our need is to recognize realistically what exists and what is happening. So far as contraception is concerned, this calls for an acknowledgment that devices are now available, and will continue to be, and are being used by many unmarried. Consideration of their use by the unmarried must be related to moral issues, sound medical and health practices, and educational programs. The moral issue cannot be approached in the traditional sense; rather it must be placed in the context of the quality of the relationship, the responsible expression of feeling, and the incorporation of sexuality into growing, developing relationships. This right must be acknowledged.

Many questions on specific details relating to this point will be raised. To many of them I shall have simply to reply that answers will come from the knowledge gained through the experiences of other cultures and from our own.

2. *Contraceptive information should be provided as an integral part of a broad sex education program which is itself contained within the context of learning about human growth and development, human relations, or family life.* Education about contraception needs always to be contained within such a framework. We need much more effective teaching than we now get in regard to all aspects of human sexuality, and information about contraception should be a part of such instruction.

3. *Effective advisory-counseling services need to be set up to which young people can go to discuss various kinds of human relations problems, including personal problems involving sex.* Few schools have the kind of service I envision, and in the present state of public thinking, few can. So far as counseling on sex matters is concerned, a special competence and capacity on the part of the counselors would be required. They would have to be objective and nonjudgmental, and have a climate of freedom which exists hardly anywhere in the public schools. Incidentally, such services should be available to all persons, not just young people.

In this connection I was interested in the "family planning clinics for the unmarried" which were being developed in London when I was there in August, 1965. There are now four such clinics in England. These clinics were planned specifically for the unmarried with the dissemination of contraceptive information and devices a major function. They were also prepared to do counseling and educational work concerning sex with their clients. This latter purpose should be a major one, and in any advisory service of this kind it probably will become a major function if the staff is alert to the needs of the clientele and prepared to do this kind of counseling.

The Netherland's organization, NVSH, which combines family planning and sex education functions, prescribes contraceptives for "engaged" couples. Denmark and Sweden very frankly include teaching about contraceptives as a part of their educational program, and communities provide openly for the dissemination of contraceptives without making marital status a requisite.

I mention these circumstances, for I wish to emphasize that developments elsewhere foreshadow what I earlier called the "inevitable confrontation." It is in fact already here. Our alternatives are to deal with the issues rationally, objectively, and within a *moral* context, or to maintain our *immoral* stance of hypocrisy and duplicity. This, in turn, leads to disastrous outcomes for innumerable young people and their families. Reiss (1966), looking at the same contradiction, phrases it another way. He says, "What we are deciding is which sources of contraceptive information we will promote and how important it is to us to make coitus safer— we are not deciding . . . whether or not there will be premarital coitus. There will be premarital coitus regardless of what decision we make on the dissemination of contraceptive information."

At this point we face at least four interesting contradictions, four strange illogics. These represent the "nonsense."

First is the serious lack of logic with which the subject is discussed. In England in 1965, I witnessed a television debate over the desirability of establishing a family planning clinic for the unmarried in Birmingham. As might have been expected, the reaction of some of the participants was highly emotional, and assertions were made that this was the equivalent of "condoning promiscuity." It was further predicted that the presence of such clinics would result in unwanted pregnancies ("there will be pregnant girls all over the place") and forced marriages. That these were the very evils the clinics hoped to combat was never acknowledged. Rationality was completely discarded; logic was tossed to the winds. This is typical of the kind of thinking we find on this emotionally highly charged subject.

A second illogical position has already been mentioned: the assumption that we have a choice of giving or not giving contraceptive information and devices to the unmarried. Even my good friend, Dr. Mary Calderone, Director of the Sex Information and Education Council of the United States (SIECUS), sometimes makes this assumption. In one article (1966) she asks, "How will you answer my first question: should contraception be made available to teenagers? I'll be frank and immodest and give you my own answer, which is *no*"

Here Dr. Calderone assumes that we have a choice in this matter. This is not the case, and neither she nor I can do anything about it. We can only choose, as she says, between alternatives:

> I would suggest to you that there are, in honesty, only two courses open to us:
> One is to throw up our hands, say sex is good for every one at every age, hand out the contraceptives, and go into our own bedrooms and close the doors.

> The alternative, of course, is more difficult, more painful, and much more work: it is to take stock of ourselves and our attitudes before we can answer, really answer, the questions (regarding contraception and teenagers) posed earlier... [pp. 38–39].

We not only make contraceptives quite available to males particularly (thus perpetuating the double standard), but we make them available in such a way as to bring youth into the transaction as full-fledged partners in the duplicity and hypocrisy with which we have surrounded sex. We could scarcely have done better at this if we had consciously and conscientiously planned for this result. Let me illustrate what I mean.

Americans are often critical of the "openness" which they understand to exist in the Scandinavian countries. During a visit to the family planning clinic in Stockholm in the fall of 1965, I saw a classroom which I was told was used for high school classes coming to the clinic to learn about contraceptive methods and devices. Also I understood that sometimes parents asked that their teenage youth come to the clinic for contraceptive information. I have mentioned this situation to American audiences and have had in return expressions of shock and strong disapproval. Americans see this as a flagrant "condoning of immorality," i.e., of premarital intercourse.

Let us contrast this "immorality" with our own. As I returned from Scandinavia in 1965, I drove across the United States from New York. In one of the states I traversed, I found in every filling station restroom from one to three condom vending machines. In one I found seven such machines. The purchaser could buy long or short condoms under several brand names.

Situations of this kind abound, but our concepts of morality and our sex attitudes require us to pretend they do not exist.

A third contradicttion arises from the fact that American youth are continually being extended both privileges and responsibilities which recognize their increased knowledge and social autonomy as compared to their parents' and grandparents' generations. Youth have been taught to ask questions, to search for answers based on evidence, to test solutions, and to seek new ones if the first ones do not work. We approve this state of mind in most areas, but are distressed with it when it comes to sex.

In the area of sex, however, we seem to wish to deny youth the right even to think about their sexuality, to say nothing of giving them control over it. Here we have chaotic confusion for everyone, especially youth. On one hand sex is portrayed as natural, fun, exciting, and glamorous; on the other, sex is dangerous, wrong, degrading, immature, and to be denied and repressed except in marriage. We ask denial of youth yet bombard them with erotic enticements and stimulation.

". . . our society, despite its skill in the techniques of communication, seems unable to deal in a forthright manner with the conflict we impose upon the adolescent. We do not sanction his overt sexuality, yet we have no alternative to propose [Health Tips, 1966]." The adult generation has, for the most part, been unable even to set up a meaningful, constructive dialogue with the younger generation. This would seem to be the most elementary requirement in dealing with our confusion, yet we are unable to do even this much. How much longer must this continue? How can we learn to deal with human sexuality more maturely?

A fourth illogic resides in our attitudes toward protection as they relate to sex in comparison with other aspects of living.

Anything we do in life has some risk involved in it. In all other areas of risk than sex (and apparently drug usage), we may seek to prevent certain behavior, but at the same time if the behavior occurs, we seek to minimize the risks by providing protections which reduce the hazards. Along with the reduction of hazards commonly goes detailed teaching designed to explain the situation and to help an individual weigh and evaluate threats. He is taught how to cope with the hazards if he chooses to accept them. But in the matter of sexual behavior we seek to reduce the risks by increasing the hazards, and also by refusing to weigh and evaluate them.

When youth drive automobiles, the risks may entail serious property damage, severe injury of one or many persons, and most serious of all, death. Here we enact legislation to keep immature and unsafe drivers off the road. But we also provide whatever safeguards we can. We build safety devices into the roads, make insurance policies available, put driver education into the schools, ask for periodic checkups on the autos—in short, we try to cut down on the hazards at the same time that we try to obtain responsible driving.

In body contact athletics such as hockey or football, where injuries are frequent and deaths do occur, we require physical examinations to insure proper conditioning, provide shields and pads which will buffer blows, provide a team physician; in short, we do all we can to insure safety while accepting the fact that risks are an inevitable aspect of participation.

When it comes to sex, what happens? Recently I was party to a discussion which centered around the development of an educational program for pregnant teenage girls in a home for unwed mothers. I found the board of directors split on the question of whether these girls should be given any contraceptive information. Apparently the division occurred over the moral issue. Undoubtedly the provision of contraceptive information was construed by some as "condoning premarital intercourse."

But was not the denial simply condoning more illegitimacy, more forced marriages, unwanted children, and abortions? Is not this clearly a situation in which the moral decision would be to provide both these girls and society badly needed protection against these likely outcomes?

A number of young people are extending the principle of protection against hazards to their sexual relationships on their own volition and in a rational systematic way. A number have discussed with me the study they have made of contraceptive procedures before they obtained contraceptive devices and initiated intercourse. More and more will probably follow this practice. I find still others who in frank discussion with one another have agreed upon extended sex play to the point of orgasm as their way of dealing with the threat of pregnancy. And, of course, many decide to forego sexual participation at either of these levels. They have made these decisions as a consequence of their own study and discussion. For these young people, those organizations such as schools and churches, those adults who refuse to discuss with them views concerning contraceptives and sexual practices and standards are simply becoming irrelevant (Hettlinger, 1966).

I have cited the educational programs of several other countries which have included contraceptive education. Actually we have been edging toward a similar position in the United States. I know of a few high schools in which contraception is discussed, but such instruction at the high school level is clearly not widespread.

At the college-university level the most widely quoted statement on the sexual dilemma is probably the report put out by the Group for the Advancement of Psychiatry (GAP, 1965). This report comments that the provision of contraceptive information or materials is not usually considered to be within the scope of the university health service. The report goes ahead to say:

> The broad, over-the-counter availability of contraceptive pills, diaphragms, condoms, and foams indicates the need for a reexamination of this position and suggests possible modification. . . . To those who might advocate dispensing contraceptive materials, we would say that this cannot be done routinely or casually. Prescription of contraceptive devices requires as much judgment as does any other medical decision. It should again be noted that many students will interpret the dispensation of contraceptive devices as sanction for their use.
>
> We believe, however, that silence is not the only alternative to dispensing diaphragms and pills. Providing contraceptive information in the college setting seems to us tenable and appropriate, either on an individual basis in response to requests or in the context of sex education. It is also proper that such resources provide information about the public health aspects of venereal disease. A decision to dispense contraceptive information but not contraceptive devices would be consistent with respect for the autonomy of the student and would place the responsibility for the use of the information in his own hands [pp. 134–135].

What must come, in my opinion, is what I have already suggested—a broad, thoroughly honest and frank discussion of sex in relation to all aspects of life. This instruction should be set firmly in a framework which assumes that in their sex life youth will be weighing, evaluating, and finally choosing among alternatives. Recognition must be given to the inevitability of some form of sexual expression throughout childhood and youth. It is with this that I am primarily concerned. The issue of contraceptive procedures as they relate to the unmarried can then be dealt with rationally and in the context of a meaningful view of sex and life.

Perhaps we could think our way through this morass with more assurance if we were more certain as to the forces and factors which motivate sexual behavior. We are prone to think that every situation in which intercourse might occur will be pressed to the hilt for just that outcome.

It also indicates the fear we have of the overwhelming and all-encompassing power of sex.

The expectation that students in coeducational dorms would engage in profligate intercourse if they had the opportunity has been the basis of much opposition to this innovation in our colleges and universities. And, of course, in these conditions intercourse has, does, and will occur, but it is also clear that under conditions of open recognition of feelings, of frank discussion of possible alternative behavior patterns, and an enlistment of the student's help in obtaining desirable living conditions, the abandon which is envisioned does not occur.

Let me share a portion of a personal letter written by Ken Jacob, advisor for a coeducational dormitory at the University of Washington.

> I am definitely in favor of coeducational residence halls as a means of increasing the potential for social, intellectual, and personal development. It seems natural that men and women should eat, talk, relax, and study together without inheriting all the pressure that we associate with a "date," i.e., what to wear, where to go, what to say, how to impress. As a result of men and women living in the same halls, much of the mystery about sex seems to disappear. These contacts seems to produce more relaxed, more honest and open relationships.
>
> We have men and women in the same wing and on the same floor with an unlocked door separating the two wings. When I go to conferences or when visitors note this arrangement, they are appalled and accuse us of irresponsibility. They feel we are asking for trouble because the physical arrangement makes it so easy for men and women to get together. But I am convinced there is no significant difference in the sexual behavior between a coeducational hall and a noncoeducational hall. The sexual behavior of the students is apparently controlled by factors other than the physical facilities; possibly peer group influence, fear of social ostracism, or their own ethical and moral beliefs.

Dr. Ira Reiss (1966), a recognized authority on sex standards says:

> Rubber condoms came in almost immediately after the vulcanization of rubber in the 1840's, and the female diaphragm came into use starting in the 1880's. These methods hardly seem to have produced immediate radical changes in premarital coital participation. The changes in sexual standards and behaviors in America during the eighteenth and nineteenth century seemed much more related to more basic parts of our social and cultural structure than to any available contraceptive techniques. As in so many other technological areas, the reception and use of an innovation depends on the values of the society. The attitudes of a society must be ready for a technological change to be accepted.
>
> On an individual level, I believe we have enough social scientific evidence to say that the basic values of an individual determine the use to which he will put new technical information, just as one may raise the basic question whether the development of a "pill" type cure for alcoholism (which is now being worked on) is likely, in and of itself, to make heavy drinking more attractive than it is now. I think the removal of the negative consequence of heavy drinking is likely mainly to encourage those who already have strong motivations in that direction [pp. 51–57].

I agree with the observations of Mr. Jacob and Dr. Reiss. I do not believe a policy of greater openness, more readiness to disseminate contraceptive information and devices to the unmarried in the context of a concern for their responsible use, would immediately result in reckless promiscuity, or that patterns of sexual behavior would be greatly and quickly changed. We often evoke visions of some disaster such as this when we are faced with change. Racial integration of schools and public facilities, it was predicted, would be followed by bloodshed and violence. While this did occur in some communities, there were others in which it did not. The experiences in the latter made it clear that when education for understanding took place, when openness and honesty characterized proceedings, and when there was a desire on the part of leaders to reach an honest and humane accommodation, disaster did not follow.

I do expect that in the future there will be an increasing number of unmarried youth who experience intercourse in affectional relationships. But I think this will happen quite independently of what is done with respect to openness about contraceptives. I also think that with the right kind of teaching about sex, sex roles, and personal responsibilities, and with a stabilization of family life (please note this last phrase), there may be a decline in the kind of irresponsible sexual expression which is presently the source of most of the evils about which we are concerned. I do believe, too, that many of the disasters which result from that kind of out-of-marriage intercourse, which will inevitably occur, can be averted by knowledge and use of contraceptives.

Acceptance of the suggestions I have offered could have further important consequences. It might relieve our intense preoccupation with premarital intercourse as the focal point of moral concern. If we could accomplish this, we could then begin to assess the significance of such immoralities as the double standard and other inequalities based simply upon the fact of sex membership; the misuse of sex in commercialization and the mass media; and the hypocrisy and dishonesty with which we have enveloped sex.

We should be able, too, to deal more effectively with other social problems as they relate to contraceptives. We have witnessed, and are still involved in, the battle as to whether unmarried women on welfare should have access to contraceptive information. When this was first attempted, public outcry forced a retraction of that policy. Nevertheless, there has been a gradual growth in the extent to which welfare agencies do dispense contraceptive devices, though public opinion probably remains strongly opposed to this.

The same condition exists with reference to the dissemination of contraceptives through college health services. Witness the outcry which arose some time ago when college authorities acknowledged that this was occurring at Pembroke. Yet as I move about the country, I hear that various colleges are following this policy on a *sub rosa* basis. I have talked with health service and private physicians who are giving prescriptions to "the pill" on request, without making any definitive inquiries as to marital status, but ostensibly to "regulate the menstrual cycle," and actually to get off the hook on which they find themselves.

In other words, our procedures are making hypocrites and deceivers out of more and more persons, including even professional people. What happens is that we reject a straightforward effort to work out a reasonable public policy, then we shut our eyes, turn around, and walk backward into the very practice which has just been renounced. I am not arguing that one view in these matters is all wrong, the other unqualifiedly right. But I am arguing that in the matter of sexual behavior and the development of public policies on contraception we need to be realistic and honest, reevaluate our traditional concepts, devise approaches and criteria for testing them, and ultimately come to some conclusions about the relative effectiveness of various procedures.

Time is too short to go into the relation between attitudes toward sex and public policy concerning contraceptives as they relate to population control, but Lee Rainwater (1965) has made it clear that a close relationship does exist. Efforts to do the most effective work in population control are hampered by ignorance and inhibited, hypocritical attitudes toward sex, and a resulting incapacity to teach either about sex or the use of contraceptive methods and devices.

The development of a reasoned, realistic attitude toward the existing and growing body of knowledge about contraception and its techniques is clearly connected with effective methods of dealing with a good number of the other problems we face.

But now I must turn to a major issue, namely to our concepts of morality. We have dwelt so long and with such intensity on premarital intercourse as the central moral concern that we have largely ignored other sexual immoralities in our culture—in fact, even other nonsexual immoralities. Our principal concern has focused on premarital penile-vaginal penetration. Virtue, or the lack of it, in youth is determined by counting how many have or have not had this experience. If we could go beyond this preoccupation, we might realize that the conception and birth of unwanted children to parents neither mature enough nor equipped to care for them is a far greater immorality. Yet we insist upon assuring the latter consequence upon the assumption that a lack of knowledge or inaccessibility of contraceptives will keep some penis from entering some vagina, and that this offsets all other evils.

Our neurotic fixation on premarital intercourse as the central issue in sexual morality was illustrated by an article by Robert Moskin in *Look* (November 15, 1966) on "Sweden's New Battle over Sex." From reading the article one would assume that the Swedish battle was entirely over premarital sex standards. No other aspect of sexual activity was discussed. The article itself mentioned a book, *Sex and Society in Sweden* by a Swedish author, Brigitta Linner (1967). The impression was left that this book dealt with premarital intercourse as the central moral issue. It so happened that in October of 1966, Random House, Mrs. Linner's publishers, had asked me to write a preface for the book. I had completed this just a few days before the article appeared. The major moral concern in Sweden, as Mrs. Linner sees it, is not premarital intercourse but how men and women may *relate* themselves honestly, responsibly, and with equality to their family, business, social, and civic roles. She discusses, for example, the possibility that in the case of divorce and the payment of alimony, the wife might, in the interest of fairness, have to pay alimony to the husband. That has occurred in Sweden. But scarcely a hint of equalitarian and responsible role adjustments as a moral issue appears in the article. News of a battle over premarital intercourse suits our preconceptions and our obsessive preoccupation. And it calls for us to maintain the fiction that youth can be frightened away from premarital intercourse if they know nothing of contraceptives.

We must rethink our concepts of sexual morality. Joseph Fletcher (1966) has written of the movement away from legalism and of the "situational ethics" approach. I find myself sympathetically allied with him, but making a somewhat different approach. However, Dr. Fletcher's feeling that it is necessary to move in the direction of dealing with morals on another basis than divine authority and revelation is shared by me and many others. Thus James H. Burtness (1966), of the Lutheran Theological Seminary in St. Paul, Minnesota, writes, "The shift from space to time and the shift from absolutes to situations is also a shift from a sex ethic centered in legal permission to one centered in relational responsibility." To this quotation could be added many others, which emphasize that our primary moral concern must be for responsible relationships rather than with an act itself.

We can deal with the issue of sexual morality in a constructive way only as we move away from our concentration on acts to a concern for "relational responsibility." Dr. Fletcher (1966) writes of the "law of love." I am in essential agreement with that, though I have been speaking in other terms. I can spell out my views more clearly when I speak of a concern for interpersonal relationships based upon genuineness and integrity, and provide specific illustrations from everyday experiences of what I mean.

But regardless of whether you accept Dr. Fletcher's terminology, that of Mr. Burtness, or mine, I nevertheless am sure of one thing: the time has passed when we can start and end our moral concern by focusing simply on an act which must be either accepted or renounced. We must be concerned with those attitudes, experiences, and that behavior which enable us to relate honestly and genuinely with one another and with all others, as human beings, capable of giving and receiving love.

We can and do get into all kinds of absurdities as a consequence of focusing on participation in, or renunciation of, the premarital sex act as the determinant of moral worth. The individual who has never had this experience is virtuous; the one who has had is immoral. In the January 1967 issue of *Cavalier* appeared an article entitled "The New Puritans of the Sexual Establishment" (Collier, 1967). In it I am described as "a small benign man, one of the important figures in the Sexual Establishment" who speaks liberally and seemingly in accepting terms, but who always winds up by saying *no* to premarital intercourse.

After my son, a university senior, read the article, he consoled me by putting his arm around me and saying, "Poor Pop! He can't win for losing. First he is that evil-minded advocate of free love who is leading all our youth to hell; then he's that mean old Puritan who won't let them have their fun."

And he is correct in that I have had both criticisms. This contradiction, however, becomes quite understandable when one remembers that the starting point and the focus of my concern is the development of interpersonal relationships based on genuine honesty, integrity, and respect. The starting point and focus of my critics is the premarital sex act. Those who feel it should never occur premaritally under any condition are disturbed that I don't spend my time condemning it. They see me as "an advocate of free love" and write the university president requesting my dismissal. Those who feel the act should occur quite without let or hindrance, see me as a "New Puritan," and they write for *Cavalier*.

Finally, new developments often bring with them subtle and unexpected consequences. Thus I think the widespread use of effective contraceptives will force us to a re-examination of the purpose and place of sex in our culture and in individual lives. The central, and in fact the only acceptable, use of sex has for ages been in the service of procreation. Any use of sex which did not include the possibility of reproduction has been regarded as unworthy—even sinful. This concept is implicit in those teachings of the Catholic Church concerning the natural and unnatural uses of sex.

But with a burgeoning population, the need for a widespread and fervent use of sexuality in the service of procreation has completely disappeared. An attempt to confine sexual expression entirely to procreative needs would curtail sexual expression most sharply. This is a curtailment very few persons would be willing to accept—or have accepted. At the same time the old insistence that this is the only proper use of sex is still strong.

It cannot remain strong, however, and future developments, of which the pill is only one, will force us to a thoroughgoing reassessment of the meaning and purpose of sex. How heavily shall the play–pleasure function be weighted? Can sex be used to develop warmth, cordiality, and love in relationships, within and outside of marriage? How can sex be used in improving communication and in developing unity? What can be the contributions of human sexuality beyond procreation, to the enrichment and fulfillment of individual potentialities and the strengthening of relationships? The increasing effectiveness of contraceptive procedures is making it necessary that we address ourselves to questions such as these.

The use of the pill makes the woman a conscious and premeditated participant in the sexual relationship. We have been told many times that girls did not wish to carry contraceptives or to participate in the use of contraceptive methods for the reason that they could no longer pretend that they were swept away by the passions of love. This attitude has been an integral part of the double standard. It cast the male in the role of the aggressor and the seducer; the female in the role of the innocent one swept away with passions of the moment. What will be the net effect of an increasing use of the pill? My guess is that the pretense and shame which went with the double standard will further deteriorate as more and more women turn to the pill.

This should be, in the long run, a benefit to women. They should be relieved of the need for pretense and dissembling. The behavior of both sexes could then be appraised fairly by the same standards. Instead of being faulted because they are women, women can be regarded and respected as individuals, having the same privileges and assuming the same obligations in relationships as men.

And how will this affect males? Traditionally, the man has been all too ready to shift responsibility for the decisions relating to the consequences of sexual associations to the female. The girl has been the one to draw the line; males have said, "Any girl can stop me any time she wants." The girl has been made the keeper of the morals. This attitude was well typified by one of the male subjects in my study *Premarital Intercourse and Interpersonal Relationships* (Kirkendall, 1966). He described a situation in which he and four other boys had picked up a girl, plied her with beer, then taken her to the woods and one after another copulated with her. This chap closed his comments about the incident with the observation, "She just didn't have any morals."

The point is that with women openly taking over the responsibility for contraceptive procedures, the male may be further freed for a carefree existence in sexual matters.

I am not asking the sexual experiences be laden with guilt or a somberness which denies the desirability of enjoyment, but I do feel that the heart of our sexual problem is male–female associations in which the responsibilities accompanying them are somewhere nearly equally distributed and equally accepted.

And consequence of eliminating pregnancy as a probable outcome of intercourse is that older persons, reared with the traditional attitudes of the early twentieth century, are being forced to a reassessment of their views about sexual standards. After all, the continual weakening of the threat of possible pregnancy as a motivating power requires reanalysis.

In my files is a letter from Richard Hettinger (1966), a well-known religious writer, himself an author in this field. He asks, "*Does* premarital intercourse have harmful effects upon the personalities of the people concerned and upon their capacity for mature relationships then or later—any more, for example, than heavy petting? Or is it in itself harmless, and only when virtually promiscuous, a symptom of a more basic disorder? In other words, are we old people against it just because we are jealous of the freedom and pleasure of the young?"

This is a question which realistic adults are having to face more and more as a consequence of the head-on collision between "the pill and the Puritan Ethic."

We have come to the point where the older generation has much to learn from the younger generation, not only about arithmetic and space travel, but about sex as well. They stand to learn both from what youth have read and studied about sex and from what they have learned from their experiences. We often speak of the abysmal ignorance of youth about sex, and in a certain sense and with respect to some aspects of sex this is true. But in the last decade our youth have grown up in an atmosphere in which a free access to sexual information and experience was definitely greater than was the case when their parents and/or grandparents were young. For them as youth an open and frankly expressed interest in sexuality as an aspect for study was looked upon askance. For today's youth this barrier is far, far weaker.

In my discussions with youth I have become aware, too, that the sexual experiences of those couples who are able to communicate freely, who have a sense of responsibility and feeling toward one another, and who approach their sexual relationships as equals is quite different from the double-standard, guilt-ridden, boy-loses-respect-for-girl sexual experiences so common in my college generation. This is extremely hard for many adults to understand.

The concern which is sometimes expressed over the sexual ignorance of youth is at least partially misplaced. The sexual ignorance of adults is also an important factor in the situation. But even this is not the focal point of my concern. My deep concern is the almost unbridgeable communication gap which exists between the generations, of which the knowledge differential is but one aspect. Until we can bridge this gap, I see little hope of the present generation of middle-aged and older adults being able to help the generation just coming into maturity. In a very real sense the perfection of contraceptive techniques which effectively remove the threat of pregnancy as a consequence of nonmarital intercourse may be the final test of whether effective cross-generational dialogue can be developed. The older generation must learn to discuss sex in a more open, more accepting way, rather than orienting all thinking toward threats. Either that or there will be no dialogue.

The perfection of contraceptives means that whether or not a sexual relationship will occur and what its consequences will be are much more than ever before in the realm of conscious, deliberate, serious, and purposeful choosing. Sex education, then, needs to become the kind of education which will contribute to wisdom, integrity, and humaneness in choice. This kind of education cannot be based simply upon the patterns of the past, but must take into realistic account the developments and conditions of the present. Members of the older generation cannot in this matter afford to be cultural dropouts.

The very ease with which sexual relationships can now be experienced may contribute to a strengthening of the sense of need for individual responsibility and integrity, and of the importance of finding and respecting a caring relationship.

Myron B. Bloy, Jr., (1966) provides us with a realistic challenge when he says, "We must stop simply wailing through the shambles of the past and learn to use our expanded freedom as the occasion for new growth towards our adulthood. This is clearly a highly bruited moment in history, for the only alternative to using our freedom for fresh maturation is to allow it to dissolve into mere anarchy—an end that many traditionalists actually seem to desire as they passively wring their hands over the present simply because it confounds so much of the past. Freedom is not simply our release from captivity, but, more fully, the occasion, the elbowroom, to lay hold of our destiny as men [p. 20] ."

If we are to meet this challenge we must accept as our goal a full and joyous life in which sex is an integral part, but subordinate to a deeper need—that of individual realization and meaningful relatedness to others. Sexual expression and its denial must be ordered in the interest of these larger goals. William Saroyan expressed it vividly in the play *The Time of Your Life*, when he wrote:

> In the time of your life, live—so there shall be no ugliness or death for yourself or for any life your life touches. . . . In the time of your life, live—so that in that wondrous time you shall not add to the misery and sorrow of the world, but shall smile to the infinite delight and mystery of it.

REFERENCES

Bloy, M. B., Jr. *Crisis of cultural change*. New York: Seabury Press, 1966.

Burtness, J. H. The new morality: Some bibliographical comment. *Dialog* Winter 1966, 5, 10–17.

Calderone, M. S. Contraception, teenagers and sexual responsibility. *The Journal of Sex Research* April 1966, 2, 37–40.

California Medical Association. Rx for health, growing up sexually. *Health Tips*, 1966.

Collier, J. L. The new Puritans of the sexual establishment. *Cavalier*, January 1967.

Fletcher, J. *Situation ethics*. Philadelphia: Westminster Press, 1966.

Group for the Advancement of Psychiatry (G.A.P.) *Sex and the college student*. New York: G.A.P., 1965.

Hettinger, R. The irrelevance of religion. In *Living with sex: The student's dilemma*. New York: Seabury Press, 1966.

Kahn, H. *Thinking about the unthinkable*. New York: Horizon Press, 1962.

Kirkendall, L. A. *Premarital intercourse and interpersonal relationships*. New York: Matrix House, 1966.

Kirkendall, L. A., & Ogg, E. *Sex and our society*. New York: Public Affairs Pamphlet No. 366.

Linner, B. *Sex and society in Sweden*. New York: Pantheon Books, 1967.

Moskin, R. J. Sweden's new battle over sex. *Look*, November 15, 1966.

Rainwater, L. *Family design*. Chicago: Aldine Press, 1965.

Reiss, I. Contraceptive information and morality. *The Journal of Sex Research*, April 1966, 2, 51–57.

Saroyan, W. *The time of your life* (A play).

Stanford Observer. Colleges and contraceptives: The physicians' dilemma. January 1967.

CHAPTER 27

Counseling Cases Involving Premarital and Extramarital Pregnancies

Clark E. Vincent

The physician who assumes the counseling role with patients having sexual problems or questions will need to keep in mind the social contexts out of which such problems and questions arise. This is especially true of counseling in cases of extramarital pregnancy, where the physician is quickly confronted with some of the contradictions in social attitudes concerning illicit sexual behavior.

The most persistent of these contradictions is to be found in the social practices and attitudes by which our society *inadvertently encourages, if not implicitly condones, the cause (illicit coition), and explicitly censures and condemns the result (illicit pregnancy).* I have illustrated this contradiction at length elsewhere (Vincent, 1961), and will only note here in passing that the physician is confronted directly by it in such cases as that of the mother who confidently brings her teen-age daughter in for a diaphragm fitting, but who subsequently and angrily brings that same daughter in with a premarital pregnancy.

The remainder of this chapter is an attempt to balance the physician's knowledge about the anatomic and physiologic aspects of sex with information concerning some of the social and emotional aspects. It is also an attempt to highlight several unique opportunities the physician has for counseling with different categories of unmarried mothers.

Physicians, more so than any other professional group, have long been aware that many of the commonly accepted stereotypes of unmarried mothers are erroneous. Prior to the late 1950's the predominant image of unmarried mothers was that they were poor, uneducated, very young and emotionally disturbed females. Such an image had been derived over the years from published accounts of premaritally pregnant females who had come to the attention of therapists and psychiatric social workers and/or who had been attended at a county hospital, maternity home or charity institution. The physician has attended these mothers, but he also has attended in private practice the upper and middle-class females in the

Reprinted with permission of the author and the publisher from R. H. Klemer (Ed.), *Counseling in Marital and Sexual Problems*. Baltimore: Williams and Wilkins, 1965. Pp. 149–160.

279

older age groups bearing children out of wedlock. Because of his exposure to a broad cross-section of unmarried mothers from all walks of life, the physician has been in a unique position to develop counseling techniques and procedures that are not limited to any one socioeconomic or age group of unmarried mothers.

COUNSELING WITH THE YOUNG UNWED MOTHER

If the physician is to be helpful in his counseling relationship with the unmarried mother, particularly the very young one, he will need to be very clear in his own mind and to make it clear to the young girl that *she* is the patient, not the parents who brought her into his office or the couple who may be waiting to adopt the child.

This distinction is undoubtedly not an easy one to make when the parents or the adoptive couple are paying the bill, but it is a crucial one if a bona fide counseling relationship is to be established with the unmarried mother.

The very young unwed mother who is brought to the physician by her parents is already in a very awkward and potentially rebellious position vis-à-vis her parents. When the physician fails to explicate to her and to her parents that she is the patient, she will tend to see him as only an extension or tool of her parents and his efforts to be of other than medical help to her will be quite unsuccessful.

The physician's failure to establish and maintain her status as the patient was the most frequently expressed criticism of the several hundred unwed mothers interviewed in my own study several years ago. (Vincent, 1961). Many felt the physician had simply been a tool in the hands of the parents or adopting couple. Some indicated this as the reason they never returned to a given physician after the initial visit to ascertain pregnancy. There is a very viable grapevine among single females who become pregnant and who pass the word very quickly concerning the kind of treatment received from given physicians—thus accounting, in part at least, for the fact that over a period of time certain physicians build up quite a clientele of unmarried mothers.

When the single girl comes alone for her initial visit to ascertain pregnancy, the physician has not only a unique opportunity, but also a responsibility, to make sure that she does not become "lost" until the onset of labor pains. For the health and welfare of both the unmarried mother and the child to be, it is important that the physician be able to communicate the importance of regular medical checkups and proper care during pregnancy. Too frequently, young females of inadequate means disappear after the visit to ascertain pregnancy and reappear only when the baby is about to be born. If proper care is to be provided for those females who do not become private patients, the physician will need to have and to impart accurate and up-to-date information about other resources in the community, and to follow through on referrals to such other resources.

Whether she becomes his private patient or never returns, her initial visit is a particularly impressionable experience for her. The very manner in which the physician confirms that she is indeed pregnant may very well be indelibly etched upon her mind and emotions, and thereby, for that moment, assign him the role of counselor—regardless of his desire or intent to have such a role. The manner and the words he uses to convey the information that she is pregnant need to be chosen carefully. Her anxiety and her needs at that moment may be such that an offhand remark or the most casual of comments may be interpreted either as complete approval of her sexual behavior or as utter rejection of both her and her behavior.

Some of the young unwed mothers with whom I have talked manifested all too clearly the failure of their parents to distinguish between the doer and the deed. Some parents reject both in so devastating a manner as to preclude ever being of future help to their daughters. Other parents are so accepting and "understanding" that they encourage their daughters to "con" themselves into believing that no mistake was made, thereby precluding the learning experience and dignity that can accrue from admitting one's mistakes and accepting responsibility for them.

The girls with whom I have talked indicated in a variety of ways their parents' failure to provide them with a learning experience. Some denied any self-responsibility and were quite convinced that their illicit pregnancies were entirely the fault of their male partners, or their parents who were either too rigid or too permissive. Others, who did assume some responsibility for their pregnancies, did not perceive them as mistakes but as inconveniences—inconveniences which were viewed as worthwhile by some girls because they received a parent financed sojourn to another state during the later months of pregnancy, and were able to provide a childless couple with an adopted baby. They were explicit in their belief that they would not have come by such a trip had they not become pregnant. They also reported that their younger sisters thought their parents would provide them a similar "fun" trip when they were older.

Counseling the Unwed's Parents

The confirmation of the young female's pregnancy is also a highly impressionable moment for her parents, and perhaps is the time when they are most likely to express to her those thoughts and judgments they will later regret having expressed with so much destructive hostility and bitterness. The physician can be of considerable help to parents at such a time by encouraging them to vent some of their anger and disappointment before talking with their daughter in the hope that their subsequent discussions with her will be more constructive than destructive. He may also be able to help them examine the degree to which their attitudes toward their daughter involve a projection or displacement of their own feelings of failure as parents.

Should There Be a Marriage?

The question of whether the young girl should marry the father of the child-to-be is almost inevitable. The young girl is less likely to ask it in the form of a question; more likely she will try to demonstrate adult status by

stating either that she does or she doesn't plan to marry the male involved—hoping, perhaps, that someone will question her statement. In
their haste to state their own pro or con position about marriage, the
parents may overlook her need to act as if she had already thought
through this decision; their arguments with her then influence her to
crystalize a decision she really wasn't ready to make. The physician can
help the parents to understand the girl's need to act as if everything had
been thought of and planned for, and can help both the girl and her
parents recognize that the fact of pregnancy is only one of many variables
to be considered in reaching a decision about marriage.

Decisions Concerning the Baby

Physicians attending unwed mothers in private practice are in a highly
strategic position to influence the mother's decisions about whether she
keeps or releases her baby, and which channels to use if the baby is to be
released for adoption. Such physicians are the primary source of information about adoption for the older, out of state unwed mothers, and are
the initial source of such information for many of the younger unwed
mothers of middle and high socioeconomic status. Unwed mothers in the
latter category usually obtain information initially from their parents who
frequently have derived their information from physicians rather than
social workers or adoption agency personnel. The strategic position of the
physician in influencing the mother's decisions about her baby (Vincent,
1961) imposes a responsibility to be informed and objective about various adoption procedures and agencies.

The following excerpts from three case histories illustrate unwed
mothers' differential interpretations and usages of adoption information
provided by physicians and social workers.

UNWED MOTHER A:

"I'm placing the baby for adoption. . . . Our family doctor recommended a
doctor here who could handle it very quietly. . . . I won't even see it, but that's
best. It's a closed chapter in my life. Besides, there are more people out here
wanting (to adopt) babies than they have, so I know it will get a good
home. . . . My parents would never forgive me if I didn't leave it here. They can
forgive me as long as no one finds out about why I'm here. . . . To bring the
baby home would make liars of them. . . . It would be unfair to the baby to
grow up with me and know that it was an illegitimate child. . . . If I kept the
baby I'd probably never be able to find a man who would marry me."

UNWED MOTHER B:

"I'm not going to lose my baby forever. My aunt and uncle out here will
keep it for me until I finish college. . . . I won't marry until I find a man who
will accept it as our child, but in the meantime it would only hinder my college
work if I kept the child with me and it will be better for the baby in the
meantime to be in a home with two people who love children as much as they
(aunt and uncle) do. . . . My doctor told me there were lots of opportunities to
give my baby to a couple who really wanted one and would give it all the love
it needed and the best home imaginable. But I know how I would feel when I
grew up if I found out that my own mother gave me up for adoption and

didn't want to raise me. . . . This way the baby will always know I did the best thing possible for it. . . . When she gets older I'll be able to explain that I loved her too much to give her away."

UNWED MOTHER C:
        "I planned when I left home to have the baby adopted, but I can't do it. . . . The social worker explained that it was my decision, but that I should feel they had enough people to choose from to be really able to select a good home. . . . Mother will be furious and Dad will probably disinherit me when I come back with the baby, since they gave clear instructions I was to have it adopted, but I can't do it. . . . What kind of a person would I be if I let someone else have my baby? What would the baby think of me when it grew up if it knew I deserted it for just anyone to have? . . . . I really think that after a while my parents will respect me more for keeping the baby, and what would a future husband think of me as a mother if he knew I gave my child away even if it wasn't his? [Vincent, 1961, pp. 216–17]."

On interpreting these statements, will some girls hate themselves later for giving their babies away? We have no way of knowing, given the paucity of follow-up studies, but such statements do illustrate the unwed mother's need for the most informed and competent counseling possible in making the extremely difficult decision about what to do with her baby and in implementing that decision.

The physician attending the unwed mother may or may not have another responsibility, depending on how he views the professional ethics involved. This possible responsibility pertains to those attitudes and wishes concerning the baby which the mother may express during delivery and/or while partially anesthetized. Should the physician share with other professional personnel who might be involved in helping the unwed mother, the feelings and attitudes expressed during delivery if such feelings and attitudes are strongly and consistently contraindicative of the already announced decision about the baby? Many, if not most, physicians may ignore, or perhaps compartmentalize, such expressions from the patient as being unrelated and irrelevant to their medical role. But does the professional ethic concerning the patient's confidences uttered during periods of extreme stress or while partially anesthetized always supercede consideration of the future welfare of both the mother and the child?

"UNMARRIED FATHERS"

The concentration upon the female in studies and public concern about illegitimacy tends to obscure the biologic fact that the male is half the cause. The readiness with which they take advantage of the protective anonymity and irresponsibility proffered by society and by unwed mothers may too easily deceive us into believing that unmarried fathers go merrily on their way without remorse or guilt. And although many such fathers are quick to assert either that they had no feelings of guilt and responsibility, or that they quickly resolved such feelings, they just as quickly supply explanations which suggest the contrary.

If he is married, the male may emphasize that the female involved preferred no help or further contact for fear of becoming known as the "other woman"; or he may excuse himself by expressing suspicions that his wife has previously been similarly involved. If single, he may readily cite the advice of the family physician and/or that of the girl's parents to the effect that it is to the advantage of all concerned to sever all ties, including any financial help that might imply future marital obligations. Valid and quasi-soothing as such types of reasons may be, they inwardly distress the male reared in a society where the masculine role is to protect, and not to be protected by, the female.

The fathers who do maintain contact with their illicit sex partners are further demasculinized when unable even to see, much less take pride in, their offspring. And although it might commonly be thought they have no interest in doing so, the comments, questions, and implicit wishes expressed to me by unmarried fathers lead me to believe that a sizable proportion of them do. Whether it be called the male ego, the deep-seated desire to create and produce, or the showing of virility, there is something in a man of all walks of life which exacts a price when he is denied identification with that which he has helped to create, even when the denial is of his own choosing.

There is another category of rationale which the unmarried father employs in convincing himself and others that he has no guilt or obligations. This consists of his derogatory evaluations of his sex partner. His mildest portrayal will include such statements as the following taken from case histories: "She was old enough to know what she was doing." "She encouraged it as much as I did." "She went into it with her eyes open." "She could have said *no*."

A far more disparaging picture is painted by other unmarried fathers, some of whom one suspects are struggling less successfully with their feelings of guilt and/or inadequacy; it is these descriptions which, over the years, have undoubtedly contributed to, and prolonged, the misleading and negative stereotyping of unwed mothers:

"Why should I think it's mine when I know half a dozen guys who've had her?"

"She asked for it, always teasing everybody in the office. If it hadn't been me, it would be someone else sooner or later."

"Why shouldn't she take the consequences? She got paid for it twice over in all the parties, trips, and good times and even clothes I bought her. She has a hell of a lot more now than when I met her."

It is true that the male does not have to endure the physical discomforts of nine months of pregnancy and the labor pains of birth. Nor does he have to face the censorious comments and stares of others and wrestle with the decision about whether to keep or to release the baby for adoption. In fact, the enormity of what the unmarried mother must face is such as to usually make us forget that the physical discomfort of pregnancy and the pain of birth may afford her a form of "punishment," a degree of atonement, unavailable to the unmarried father. Also, for some unmarried mothers there is a feeling of retribution derived from having supported the traditional concepts of motherhood; for example, courageously completing pregnancy even though afraid, away from loved ones and censured. And difficult as the decision may be, many unwed mothers experience a sense of at least partial retribution to society when their illicit pregnancies subsequently make it possible for childless couples to achieve the cherished goal of having a family.

My intent is not to minimize the lopsidedness with which the burdens of stigma, hardships, and responsibilities in illegitimacy are borne by females. Rather, it is to illustrate the extent to which we have ignored the counseling needs of the males involved. It is also to suggest that counseling with the unmarried mother may be facilitated when her sexual mate is also seen by the physician.

MARRIED AND DIVORCED "UNWED" MOTHERS

A counseling opportunity available more frequently to physicians than to any other professional group involves the married and the divorced "unwed" mothers. Census data do not differentiate among married, divorced and single unwed mothers; therefore, we have no way of knowing how many of the *estimated* 245,000 illicit births in the United States in 1962 were to divorced women or to married women impregnated by men other than their husbands. In fact, we have no way of knowing how many of the more than 4,000,000 births recorded as legitimate in 1962 were the result of extramarital intercourse.

We do know from census reports that in the twenty-year period from 1940 to 1960, the illegitimacy rate increased five times as much among women aged 25 to 29 (538 percent), as among those aged 15 to 19 (108 percent).

The higher rates and greater increases in illegitimacy among older women, as shown in Table 1, give us reason to suspect that extra- and postmarital intercourse may be responsible for a considerably greater proportion of illicit births than is commonly assumed. Adulterous illegiti-

TABLE 1

INCREASE OF ILLEGITIMACY RATE

Age of Unmarried Mother	Illegitimacy Rate*		Percentage of Increase
	1940	1960	
10–14	0.4	0.6	50%
15–19	7.4	15.3	108%
20–24	9.5	39.3	314%
25–29	7.2	45.9	538%
30–34	5.1	28.0	449%
35–39	3.4	14.4	323%
40–44	1.2	3.6	217%

*Number of illegitimate births per 1,000 unmarried females.

macy is easily concealed from official records, of course, and is probably only reported in the minority of cases. Thus, in the absence of census data breakdowns for *pre-, extra-,* and *post*marital pregnancies, we are left with very tentative information from only a few individual studies that have differentiated among these types of illicit pregnancies.

As shown by the following information from 1,062 "unwed" mothers, there was a higher proportion of divorced and married mothers among those attended and reported by physicians in private practice, than among those attended in maternity homes and a county hospital where they were reported by social caseworkers (Vincent, 1961). The fact that few studies are made of "unwed" mothers attended in private practice helps maintain the emphasis on the young, single, never married ones who go to maternity homes and county hospitals where studies are usually conducted.

TABLE 2

STUDY OF 1,062 UNWED MOTHERS

Marital Status of "Unwed" Mother	Reported by Physicians in Private Practice*	Reported by Social Caseworkers	
		Maternity Home†	County Hospital††
Single—never married	65%	82%	76%
Divorced or widowed	23%	11%	18%
Married	11%	4%	0%
No answer	1%	3%	6%
	100%	100%	100%

*Total number of cases −425.
†Total number of cases−265.
††Total number of cases−372.

The minimum attention given to adulterous and postmarital pregnancies is also consistent with society's tendency to emphasize only selected aspects of a given social problem in such a way that perspective is distorted, and other forms of that same social problem are obscured. But the fact remains that each year there are a conservatively estimated 45,000 to 75,000 divorced and married "unwed" mothers who are in potential need of counseling, and that physicians are the major contact with these females.

Perhaps the most striking question concerning adulterous pregnancies is: "Why does a married woman ever reveal that it was not her husband who impregnated her?" The answer in the case of those seeking counseling help is frequently that either the marriage is threatened because the husband knows, or the wife seeks help in resolving her own feelings and course of action without her husband's awareness of the problem. In the case of women who inform their physicians that their pregnancies are adulterous, the answer may be that they need at least one confidant and/or fear they will reveal such information anyway while under the effect of anesthesia during delivery.

In an effort to be of aid to physicians counseling divorced and married women involved in illicit pregnancies, I should like to share a few impressions based on questionnaire data from 256 such women, and on interview and counseling sessions with 35 such women.

The Divorced Unmarried Mother

The sexual caution of divorced women tends to be reduced by their desire to escape the socially stigmatized category of the divorcee as soon as possible, and by their openness in male-female conversation as learned while married. Not only is the divorcee frequently perceived by men as easy sex prey (as William Goode notes in *After Divorce*), but she herself may unintentionally foster such a view. Previously accompanied by her husband and protected by marriage, she became accustomed to open and frank discussions of sex in mixed groups; now she has to relearn some of the coyness that traditionally accompanies courtship. Without such coyness, and tacitly pressured by society and friends to prove via a successful marriage that it was not she who failed in the first marriage, her involvement with men tends to progress at a much faster and less cautious pace than even she recognizes—until she is pregnant and the man is no longer interested or returns to his wife.

An unknown proportion, perhaps the majority, of divorces involve a period of continued, somewhat sporadic, sexual intercourse between the ex-partners. In the cases of so-called "friendly" divorces, the continuation of coition is frequently regarded as mutually enjoyable, with no love or family obligations expected; and abortion may be a frequent solution when pregnancy occurs. Even when this solution is unavailable or unacceptable to the mother, she is reluctant to affix paternal responsibility on the former husband, in part perhaps because of her feeling that others would think her foolish for continuing sex relations with her ex-husband.

In cases where the divorce was not mutually desired, the wife may perceive intercourse as a potential means for reclaiming her husband. She may also, as one stated, "want a memory of him. . . . I hope it's a boy that looks just like him. . . . That way a part of him will always be with me." There is also the case of the ex-husband who desires a reconciliation and who, after considerable effort that often includes the argument of "for old times' sake," impregnates his ex-wife, only to find this makes her even more adamantly opposed to reconciliation.

MAINTAINING THE CONTEXT

One of the counseling needs common to a wide variety of cases involving premarital coition and illicit pregnancy is the need of the counselee to maintain an historical and contextual perspective of their sexual experience. Adult women may unceasingly condemn themselves by imposing adult judgments upon those sexual acts they experienced during adolescence. Married women may judge too harshly in retrospect their earlier "love" affairs involving coition with other men. Knowing now, at 35, the depth and quality of love they have for their husbands, they may continually reinforce guilt feelings about earlier sex unions with other men with whom they fell in love while single. It is not always easy to maintain the context within which a given event or experience took place years previously, but it is important to try to do so. This does not mean that all early or prior sexual experiences should be lightly excused. It does mean that the woman of 45 should not judge her experiences at 18 as if she at that time had the wisdom, judgment, and values she now has at 45.

The physician may frequently find opportunity to provide both ameliorative and treatment types of counseling in helping his patients maintain perspective concerning the context in which given sexual behavior occurred. The single female who has coition with a male during the time she thinks they are in love and are going to be married, may need help in remembering that at the time of their sex union the context was one of love and planning for marriage. Too often in those cases where the couple later fall apart and decide not to marry, the girl takes the sex experience out of the context in which it occurred and may either feel she has to proceed with the marriage to preserve her self-image as a nice girl, or may regard herself overly harshly as less worthy of her future husband as yet unmet.

The married woman impregnated during an affair with another male may also need help in maintaining the total context within which her affair took place. Her own guilt and self-condemnation may propel her to project too much blame on either herself or her husband and thereby reduce the chances for a strengthening of the marriage. Again, this is not to say she should completely absolve herself of any blame, but that the physician can help her understand the totality of events and circumstances that almost imperceptibly led to the illicit coition.

Physicians are already overworked and spread too thin, but the members of no other professional group have quite the same unique opportunities to become "significant others" in times of sexual crises. Physicians who are genuinely concerned about illegitimacy and the price it exacts from youth will find much to do: (1) in providing the community with a more accurate perspective of illegitimacy, (2) in reaffirming confidence in youth and in not being afraid to point up the adult and community contributions to illegitimacy, (3) in contagiously educating parents to cherish the individual without condoning his mistakes, and (4) in being sensitive to those young men and women who are desperately in need of a significant relationship and identification with at least one adult with whom they can discuss their own sexuality as a mental and physical health entity.

REFERENCES

Goode, W. *After divorce*. Glencoe, Illinois: The Free Press, 1956.

Vincent, C. E. *Unmarried Mothers*. New York: The Free Press of Glencoe, 1961.

Vincent, C. E. Divorced and married "unwed" mothers. *Sexology*, 1962, *28*, 674–679. (a)

Vincent, C. E. Spotlight on the unwed father. *Sexology*, 1962, *28*, 537–542. (b)

CHAPTER 28

Some Points for
Premarital Discussion

Owen Morgan

This chapter is prepared with the purpose in mind of passing on in written form some of the things I would hope to talk over with young people who seek premarital consultation. None of them are meant as the "pronouncements," which they might appear to be without any opportunity for discussing them together, but primarily as something to stimulate thinking and for people to use as they relate to the meanings which their own experiences have for the two of them. My hope would be that reading this might prompt young people to talk with some professional person—counselor, family life educator, clergyman, or physician—who is specifically trained in helping people as they move into marriage.

Ultimately, the discussion will deal with specific aspects of the sexual relationship in marriage. These are by no means necessarily the most important aspects; in fact, my own feeling is that, important as they are, they are secondary to the deeper meaning of marriage. People get married primarily because of the human quest for love, belonging, intimacy (in the general sense), the need to be needed—in other words, because of the desire to live significantly with someone they love. Even in cultures where there is a great deal of sexual freedom outside of marriage, people still do marry. Some one figured it up and concluded that less than one-tenth of one percent of the average couple's time is spent in any kind of direct sex play (although broader ramifications of sexuality certainly run through much of marriage). It is the meaning which a husband and wife have to each other in all aspects of their living together that determines the success of a marriage. Sometimes people forget this. For example, some writers have asserted that much marital difficulty stems from sexual maladjustment due to disparity in the size of sex organs. It is true that "bigness" and "littleness" have a lot to do with marital success, but it is the bigness or littleness of people as persons, and not that of physical anatomy, which is more likely to play the greater part in most cases.

You may wonder, then, why the sexual relationship in particular is given so much attention in this discussion. It is largely because there is less likelihood that people marrying have had a good opportunity for learning in a sensible way about this part of marriage, and especially because many couples are likely to have more difficulty learning to communicate with each other in this area. Also, each of the partners will be likely to have had more previous experience with other aspects of the marriage relationship, since scarcely anyone has lived in isolation. After all, marriage is primarily a human relationship—one which is more intimate, more permanent, more continuous, more rewarding, sometimes more frustrating and disappointing, but in very few ways entirely different from other kinds of relationships (sex and parenthood roles tending to be major exceptions). For example, there are many ways in which living with a roommate is similar to marriage, and in general one of the best indications for predicting the likelihood of success in marriage is the way each of the parties has been able to get along with the people he or she has lived with, played with, and worked with up to this time. This is, of course, barring any specifically warped attitudes or behavior patterns concerning the ways in which marriage *is* different, either in degree or kind.

Thus, human relations skills, attitudes, personality and behavior patterns constitute the basic equipment a person brings to marriage. Emotional maturity (bigness rather than littleness, being as concerned with the welfare and happiness of another as with your own, having given up childish ways and adopted those of an adult, not *having* to have your own way); adaptability or flexibility as contrasted with rigidity; having a purpose in life, hopefully somewhat similar to that of your mate; and the capacity to both give and receive love, warmth, and understanding—these are the keystones on which marriages stand or fall. Such human relations skills as the ability to communicate and talk out your feelings and thoughts, hopes and aspirations, problems and disappointments with each other in ways which are neither personally threatening nor defensive, are also mighty valuable assets. Obviously the ability to *listen* with understanding to each other is important, too. None of these behavior characteristics or skills can be acquired merely by will or resolution alone. They are much more basic than some of the other things we will talk about here. Sometimes it may be possible for a person or a couple, realizing their importance and the need to work to develop them, to do so in the process of being married and living together. Usually, though, habits, personality patterns, and ways of looking at life have been going in certain directions long before marriage enters the picture. There is no point in *blaming* anyone for lacking these qualities, for rare indeed is the person who is like he is just because he decided he would be that way. This does not mean that no one has any responsibility for his behavior, but understanding and basic acceptance constitute the atmosphere which fosters growth rather than blame or guilt. And it is not safe to rely on the marriage relationship to modify ways of behaving and responding. When a person recognizes a need for real growth, recognition of this need being an important first step, it is wise for him to talk and work with someone trained to give help of this kind.

It may well be that the most important factor of all in determining your qualification for marriage is the way you feel about being *you*—the degree to which you feel comfortable in your own skin.

There are some common misconceptions about marriage which we might stop to consider. The first concerns what happiness lies waiting for you in marriage, just lying there for you to stumble into. A couple finds in marriage pretty much just what they put into it—themselves—for their own personalities and the resulting relationships are the ingredients. Foolish indeed is the unhappy single person who concludes that all he needs to be happy is a trip to the altar. Another misconception is that love is all that counts. True, love is essential, but marriage isn't all "moonlight and four roses"; there is a lot of down-to-earth working together in the everyday realities of living. Besides, it is practically impossible to love each other all the time; there are times when every married couple gets fed up with each other, at least momentarily, just as almost all parents sometimes get fed up with their children (and vice versa)—clear to the ears. It is quite important to realize this, for many young people get hit over the head hard with it, both in marriage and in parenthood, and are likely to think it is because they are "bad" or "abnormal" people, not realizing that others experience the same thing. There are bound to be irritations, upsets, conflicts, disappointments, and frustrations. A successful marriage is not characterized by an absence of all conflict and difficulty, but rather by the ability to work through them.

Still another false assumption is that the honeymoon will be the best time of the marriage and sexual utopia—or any other kind. A further misconception is that you don't have to pay for what you get in marriage. There is a lot of give and take, and the person who isn't equipped or prepared to give up a lot for the very great potential satisfactions is in for a rude awakening, just as is the person who thinks there is something magic about a thirty-minute wedding ceremony which automatically assures everlasting satisfactions for the couple without any further effort on their part. In summary, marriage quite likely provides greater opportunity for the deepest satisfactions known to humans, but it quite likely provides greater disappointments and frustrations, too. In other words, it may well be true that the range of meaningful experiences is wider in marriage because the intensity and continuity of the relationship is greater.

Any new venture requires adjustments, and marriage is no exception. People should not expect to immediately shuck off their old habits of living as single individuals and start automatically to live as a married couple. Building a sense of "we-ness" along with "I-ness" is probably the most important task facing the couple. There are practical things to learn and to work out in this respect. For example, if a person is used to sleeping alone, sleeping with anyone else—man, woman, or beast—may take some getting used to. An instance has been reported of one brand new bridegroom who spent the latter part of his wedding night huddled up on the floor next to the radiator with his overcoat over him because there wasn't much else he could do after his wife stretched herself out diagonally across the bed, all wound up in the blankets. (Veteran husbands might have some suggestions here, but the bridegroom wouldn't even have considered them so few hours after the wedding ceremony!)

In planning the wedding and all the activities leading up to it, some thought can very wisely be given to the fact that utter exhaustion is not the best condition for launching wedded life.

A honeymoon which, regardless of its length, provides an element of unhurried relaxation and privacy is helpful in beginning this venture. It is a good idea to have done some planning ahead of time, but not so rigidly as to rule out flexibility. (It is, by the way, a good idea to let some responsible person know something of your likely whereabouts in case of an emergency at home.) The honeymoon and early stages of marriage might best be considered merely as a continuation of the "courtship plane," rather than assuming that this is to be the peak of marital bliss.

Popularly anyway, the honeymoon is thought of as having a large and important sexual component. Again, this is partly because it is more likely to be a new experience and one for which the couple has presumably been waiting. Even if there have been premarital sexual experiences, there can be more freedom and completeness now. Not that this is all the bride and groom have been waiting for, but in most of the other areas there is at least more of an overlap with previous experience. Of course, even without a premarital sexual relationship per se, there is still some overlap, unless we make an arbitrary and artificial distinction between sexual intercourse and all other forms of loving relating, including in most cases a certain amount of erotic play. Still, there would usually be *more* of a difference between what is *to be* experienced and what *has been* experienced during previous years of the person's life in the sexual area than in other realms.

Sex, like marriage, is essentially another kind of a *human relationship*, although physically more intimate than most others. (It should be noted here that it is entirely possible [a] for sexual intercourse to occur without any real relationship or psychological intimacy, and [b] for two people to be deeply and personally intimate without any sexual behavior at all.) My own definition runs something like this: "Sex is a good and delightful way for a couple to express their love for each other and to have fun together—and when they are ready (ideally, that is) to become parents. It is essentially another way of relating to, and communicating with, each other." In all aspects of this very human relationship, but even more particularly in sex, such qualities as love, consideration, understanding, patience, and mutuality are most significant. These qualities are much more important than specific knowledge about sexual anatomy or techniques. In the sexual relationship there is a potential for fulfillment and completion that is not likely to be duplicated elsewhere in life, and it is in the meaning which this holds for the particular couple, rather than physical sensations as such, that the core of the experience lies.

It is unreasonable to think that all couples can learn to relate sexually with utmost effectiveness in the early weeks of marriage. There may be an instinctual basis, but loving is partially an art, which requires the development of understandings and skills that can come only through experience over a period of time. Any universal expectation of sexual bliss during the honeymoon leaves the door wide open for disappointment. In fact, some couples may have relatively little success at first, but patience and a reasonable lack of haste and urgency are likely to pay dividends later. Being able to talk with each other and to help each other is especially important here. There is really no valid reason to think that the wedding night is a complete failure if either fatigue, miscalculated menstrual schedule, or what have you, happens to postpone for a brief time initiation of intercourse itself. Usually this wouldn't be the case, but in instances where it is, there's lots of time a-waitin'.

Presumably the bride and groom will have seen a physician for a general examination and premarital consultation. He has checked, along with other things, the condition of the hymen and taken steps to remedy or show the girl how to remedy the situation if such steps are needed. With the kind of life girls live now, the use of tampons, more frequent and earlier pelvic examinations, etc., many brides need no medical help here, though they have not had previous sexual experiences.

For most couples in this day and age, having a choice about when a pregnancy is to occur is important. This is another matter in which the physician's help should be sought. He is the one who can provide not only the prescription but also the education and guidance for the couple in the most effective use of whatever means of family planning they choose. In many metropolitan areas a local agency affiliated with the national Planned Parenthood organization provides excellent help for couples with family planning if they do not consult a private physician for this purpose. This consultation should take place at least several weeks before the time when sexual intercourse is begun. If the rhythm method is to be used, medical guidance is particularly important in order to maximize the reliability of this method, which even under medical supervision is by no means completely reliable.

In only an artificial way can the sexual part of marriage be separated from the rest of the relationship. It is an integral part of a whole network of relationships in the marriage. It is a very important part, but like any of the others, it needs to be viewed in the perspective of the total meaning which living and loving together have for any particular couple. Frequently, one or the other of two extreme points of view is encountered. The first would hold that sex is the crux of marriage and that almost everything that goes on rests on the sexual basis. The other would maintain that this aspect of marriage really hasn't much significance at all and that we should think as little of it as possible. Neither of these positions seems at all tenable. Marriages built on sexual attraction alone, unless the rest of the relationship grows, are likely to be shallow and hazardous. On the other hand, if sex has no significance, then men might just as well marry men and women marry women. When unfortunate negative attitudes and a too-often appalling lack of information don't distort the potentials of the sexual relationship, it can make marriage a more delightful and a more meaningful kind of life, adding zest to the experience of living together through the years. (In *The Happy Family*, by David Levy and Ruth Munroe, the chapter on "Sexual Satisfaction" depicts the variety of meanings which the sexual relationship can have.) Once again though, it is the satisfaction and meaning found in all aspects of living together which is the ultimate criterion for our marriages today, so no one particular area can be considered by itself. There have been marriages in which sexual activity was *in*voluntarily ruled out which were more satisfying to the partners than *some* in which it served as a major focal point. The ideal would seem to be making the most of *all* potential avenues of sharing, communication, and joy, including of course the sexual channels.

Just as attitudes concerning roles of men and women in general have been modified through the years, so have those about sexual relationships. Today there is more thought given to making them a more mutual kind of experience, as in other relationships. This is in contrast to traditional views which held that sex was something of an obligation for wives and a right for husbands. Women were not supposed to really find any pleasure in sex, but it was their duty to "submit" in order to satisfy their husbands. Actually, in recent years this pendulum may have swung too far in the opposite direction, with many articles in popular journals carrying the implication that husbands are usually "at fault" if their wives don't find some sort of ethereal and superhuman ecstasy.

The criterion for success in sexual living should be much the same as for the marriage in general—the satisfaction of the partners involved rather than merely the kind or intensity of sensations. Some people may think that a "democratic" type family, with a balance of power, mutual participation in decision-making, etc., is the only thing; but if some families prefer another sort and are happy with that, then more power to them (and less to anyone who tries to show them how miserable they are)! Since the relationship between expectations and fulfillment is important in determining "satisfaction" (e.g., when you expect a movie to be really out of this world and find it only mediocre, you are more disappointed than if it hadn't been given such a buildup), let's take a moment to discuss the reasonableness of expectations about marriage. What we say here is important for marriage in general, not just for some isolated segment of it.

It is difficult to avoid something of a dilemma here, for expectations can be either too high or too low. Not knowing anything about what to expect nor how to enhance the experience can detract from satisfactions, too. For example, to carry the analogy of a movie further, a person who had never experienced a movie before and had lttle idea of what to expect might go to a drive-in theater and see the film without knowing he was supposed to make use of any audio device. He might enjoy the *seeing* of the show, not realizing that it could have been even better. It might not be accurate to say that he was dissatisfied, yet we would likely agree that he was sort of missing the boat. On the other hand, if this person always expected to hear stereophonic sound or to have cool breezes blow on him when mountain scenes were shown, he might well be disappointed. Similarly, if wives are led to anticipate the earth trembling, stars quivering, bells playing heavenly tunes and the aforementioned indescribable ecstacy, they may feel cheated in their actual sexual experience and think they are unhappy in their marriages. Again our contention that happiness in marriage cannot be measured only in terms of physical sensations. On the other hand there is little valid reason to assume that eventually the sexual experiences can't be mutually enjoyable instead of just for one to enjoy and the other to tolerate. Even if the wife herself doesn't care whether she really gets involved and is relatively satisfied with nothing more than the feeling that, "It's so nice that I can provide satisfactions for my husband whom I love so much," there is still the husband's feeling to think about. If he is satisfied with this, too, then none of the rest of us has any business complaining, but *he* may prefer something besides sole satisfaction for himself. The average wife would probably find some satisfaction in just watching her husband enjoy a meal she had prepared. But wouldn't it be reasonable to think that the husband might enjoy the meal more if they ate together and both enjoyed it? This is what is meant by "mutuality," and it is likely to be fostered by the participation in, and enjoyment of, the sexual relationship (and others) by both parties. (A good reading reference here is the chapter "The Art of Loving" by Dr. Kenneth Walker in the book *Men: The Meaning and Variety of Their Sexual Experiences*, edited by A. M. Krich.)

Now that the idea of mutuality and enjoyment together of married life has been stressed, the following paragraphs are offered in the hope that they may contribute to these goals in the sexual relationships.

In the majority of cases the husband's sexual response, at least in the early years of marriage, will be "nearer the surface" and perhaps will be more readily called into play than the wife's. There is some question as to whether this is due to the nature of the two sexes or is related to the teachings of our culture. There is nothing at all "wrong" if this is reversed, but it is more usual to find it as stated. This means, for one thing, that the husband may initially be interested more often than his wife. It is a rare marriage indeed where the sexual desire of husband and wife fit exactly the same pattern. Again, in some cases the frequency of desire may be reversed, but usually the other way around, at least in the earlier stages of marriage. Kinsey found that males reached the peak of sexual desire in late teens or early twenties, females in late twenties or early thirties. Again one is led to wonder whether this is strictly physiological or may be due to a later sexual awakening for women in our culture. At any rate, one or the other will sometimes be initially interested in sex play at times when the partner's attention is on something else altogether. However, if both partners maintain what could be called an attitude of "receptivity," i.e., a willingness to get involved in love-making and to permit words, caresses, etc., which will enhance interest and arousal, it will usually be possible for both to be caught up in the "spirit of the game" with something other than apathy or indifference. The emphasis is not meant here to be just on physical love-making or mechanical techniques, but includes warmth, responsiveness, and love in a broader sense. One writer (English, 1953) stresses the importance of seeing the capacity in men for tender love instead of *just* a passionate desire.

Another important difference often found between male and female sexual response—and one closely related to that described above—is that in many cases the husband can initiate, engage in, and complete his sexual "cycle" much more quickly than can his wife. It was because of a failure to recognize this that wives often used to have little part in the sexual relationship other than merely providing satisfaction for their husbands. One person has described this in terms of an analogy with a mile race between the typical husband and wife—pointing out that unless the husband either gave his wife a head start or stopped to let her catch up, he would usually finish way ahead of her. In sexual terms the finishing would be the sexual climax or orgasm. Because of the physiology involved, it is practically impossible for the husband to undertake intercourse until he is sexually aroused and has the resulting erection. This situation does not necessarily hold true for the wife, inasmuch as it is at least physically possible for her to engage in intercourse without being aroused, just as it is possible for her to continue after a climax (though perhaps not so enjoyably as before). In fact, there may be times when a couple has intercourse wherein the wife doesn't really get involved at all, and this may be less disturbing for her than a situation wherein she becomes highly aroused but finds that her husband has finished and she is left "in mid-air." The latter point makes it important to realize that sex play is not limited to intercourse as such—especially to intercourse in one particular way—and that at particular times mutual satisfaction is more likely if couples are willing to vary their pattern.

This might be a good point at which to say something about the sexual climax, for it is around this phenomenon that much confusion and misinformation have been in evidence. Actually it would make more sense to talk in terms of *contentment* and *relaxation*, for these are better operational terms for the goal, especially if we add the term *satisfaction* to the other two. However, since so many people ask questions specifically about the nature and significance of the *climax*, the following information is given: In the male this comes at the point of ejaculation of the seminal fluid containing the sperm cells. In the female there is no corresponding ejaculation, and the climax is not at all essential for conception. Some women have been confused about this because they interpret the secretion of the lubricating substance within and at the entrance to the vagina during sexual excitement as an ejaculation.

In terms of the build-up of excitation or tension and its release, the orgasm could be likened to the release of the string on an archer's bow after it has been pulled tighter and tighter to the point where it is very taut, then suddenly released. This "release" is usually accompanied by pleasurable sensations and sometimes by rhythmic muscular contractions in the genital area, the experience being somewhat more general and diffuse in the female as compared with a more specifically genital focus in the male. It is very important to note that the experience varies tremendously from individual to individual, and from time to time with the same person. For some couples it may take several weeks, months, or maybe even years to acquire the experience, skills, and teamwork essential for the wife to reach this potential. In some cases she may never experience anything exactly of this nature and yet be very happily married and find considerable enjoyment in the sexual relationship. Everything else being equal, there seems a better chance that the enjoyment will be enhanced if both usually experience some sense of contentment and relaxation following their sex play; beyond this no further prescription should be given concerning the nature of the response for any particular couple or time. Unfortunately, husbands and wives have sometimes been led to believe that if both partners don't finish explosively and even at exactly the same moment, they are really missing the mark. Such might be the ultra-ideal, but it is not a reasonable or realistic expectation in many cases. The feeling of satisfaction and completion or relaxation of some sort may leave one or both partners in such a state of drowsiness that sleep is the natural aftermath. When this is the case, it should not be interpreted as a lack of love or caring. For other people the experience will lead to a period of closeness and loving which will be more directly expressed.

In striving for some sort of mutual participation and response, it is important for each partner to know what sorts of love-play are effective in arousing the other. (Note: Premaritally, *if* they are committed to limiting their physical intimacy, it is equally important to know this in terms of avoiding intense arousal.) In much literature there has been an emphasis on the husband's knowing how to arouse the wife, without much attention to what the wife can do to make it interesting for the husband. Beyond just the specific caresses, it is very important for both to sense each other's responsiveness to all kinds of cues. Monogamy does not need to be equated with monotony—despite popular misconceptions to the contrary—if husband and wife will make some effort and devote some attention to keep it from being so and if they avoid being so involved in other roles that they shove this potentially vital and enlivening part of their life into the closet of routine. Both should have not only the responsibility but the opportunity and privilege to make it otherwise. (See the chapter, "Being a Married Mistress" in *How to Be a Woman*, by Mary and Lawrence K. Frank, keeping in mind that the implications should hold for both.) Sex is not "something that one person does to another" or "a favor which the wife bestows on the husband" (or vice versa); it should be a delightful and fulfilling experience together.

In the human organism there are certain erogenous or sexually sensitive zones. Some are rather common to most of the species, but others are more individual; and it is for this reason that adequate communication between husband and wife is particularly important. Again, this is assuming that there is a backdrop of tender and devoted love in general and that love play or sex play is primarily another way of expressing this love for each other, even if there are times when the mood is frivolous or in some other way is not just a direct reflection of abiding love. In this chapter we are discussing persons, not machines or animals, and this should especially be kept in mind when we discuss anatomy, physiology, or techniques, lest we leave the impression that it is just a physical process. The passionate and partially animalistic element of sex should not be ruled out by any means, and an attempt to see it just in a spiritual sense may be questioned, for it is a combination of tenderness and wildness. The caution here is against a mechanistic, step one–step two, approach. Lips and tongue are usually sexually sensitive, and from there on, except for the more specifically erogenous areas common to most, there is the great individual variation suggested before. In the male, the glans or head of the penis is the most specific center. In women the breasts, particularly the nipples, are usually sensitive, although not always to the same extent from individual to individual; but the clitoris is the most sensitive organ for the majority of women. Unknown to many is the fact that this tiny organ is homologous to the male penis. In some respects it resembles a miniature penis, and in embryonic development it is this which develops into the penis in the male. In the female it remains largely imbedded or sheathed in tissue, with barely the head or glans protruding just at the point where the inner lips of the vulva come together. It is important for both husband and wife to be aware of this organ, for it is direct, though gentle stimulation of the protruding glans (head) which will be most effective in increasing most wives' sexual arousal. Some think that with greater maturity the vagina itself may become the center of sexual excitation, but at least in early marriage the clitoris usually has an important place in this function. The clitoris, like the penis, tends to become somewhat erect during sexual arousal.

When the woman reaches a certain point of arousal, the sexual parts will ordinarily be bathed in a lubricating or moistening secretion, much like saliva in consistency. Unless this secretion has taken place, even very gentle stimulation (fondling) of the clitoris or surrounding genital area may be irritating rather than pleasurable. In most cases the response to the general love-making and the whole atmosphere of anticipation will take care of sufficient arousal for the moistening to take place. In some cases, however, it is important for some other means of moistening to be used. Saliva is the most readily available substitute. Another possibility is a non-greasy material such as surgical jelly or hand lotion.

In all of this preparation for the sexual relationship, usually spoken of as "foreplay," husband and wife have equal opportunity for participation (with neither being more responsible than the other). Sometimes the playing is the end as well as the means. It would be most unfortunate to leave the impression that this is some sort of chore, the price to be paid for the final part of the experience. Couples who take delight in all aspects of this playing with, and responding to, each other, both broadly and specifically speaking, know the zest, the joy, and the meaning which it can add to marriage. This is only another way of saying that the true value of marriage is the love, understanding, affirmation, and appreciation which "this man and this woman" have for each other in this most intimate of human relationships.

SUGGESTED READING

Chesser, E. *Love without fear*. New York: Roy, 1947. (paperback: Signet Books, $.35).

Ellis, A. *The art and science of love*. New York: Lyle Stuart, 1960. (paperback: Dell Publishing Co., 1965, $.95)

Ellis, A. Myths About Sex Compatibility. *Sexology*, May 1962, *28*, 652–655.

English, O. S. Sexual love: Man for Woman. In E. M. Ashley Montagu (Ed.), *The meaning of love*. New York: Julian Press, 1953.

English, O. S. Sex adjustment in marriage. In Fishbein & Kennedy (Eds.), *Modern marriage and family living*. New York: Oxford University Press, 1957.

Fromm, E. *The art of loving*. New York: Harper, 1956. (paperback: Bantam Books, $.60).

Jourard, S. *Personal adjustment: An approach through the study of healthy personality*. New York: Macmillan, 1963. Revised edition: Chapter 9, Interpersonal Behavior and Healthy Personality; Chapter 10, Healthy Interpersonal Relationships; Chapter 11, Love and Healthy Personality; Chapter 12, Sex and Healthy Personality.

Kovinovky, N. Premarital medical examination. In C. Vincent (Ed.), *Readings in marriage and family counseling*. New York: Cromwell, 1957.

Levy, D., & Munroe, R. *The happy family*. New York: Knopf, 1938.

Lewin, S., & Gilmore, J. *Sex without fear*. New York: Medical Research Press, 1953.

McGinnis, T. *Your first year of marriage*. New York: Doubleday, 1967.

Montagu, A. *The meaning of love*. New York: Julian Press, 1953.

Overstreet, H., & Overstreet, B. *The mind goes forth*. New York: Norton, 1956.

Stone, A., & Stone, H. *A marriage manual*. New York: Simon & Schuster, 1952.

Street, R. *Modern sex techniques*. New York: Wehman, 1959. (paperback: Lancer Books, 1966, $.75).

Walker, K. The art of love. In A. M. Krich (Ed.), *Men: The meaning and variety of their sexual experience*. New York: Dell, 1954. (paperback).

Special Techniques in Marriage Counseling

He that will not be counseled cannot be helped.
THOMAS FULLER

Marriage counseling is a field where, because of the particular needs of the clients and the problems they face, special techniques have been developed by the various helping professions that are involved in marriage counseling. Some of these techniques are still controversial in the field but are included in this section so that both professionals and laymen may learn more about them in order to decide whether or not they want to consider using them in their professional or private lives.

In Chapter 29, two social workers, Shirley Gehrke and James Mòxom, focus on the marriage relationship itself and explain a method they have termed "relationship counseling." They discuss both diagnosis and treatment techniques for five diagnostic classifications: conflict in the area of masculine-feminine roles, the sado-masochistic conflict, the detached-demanding conflict, the oral-dependent conflict, and the neurotic illness conflict.

One of the most prevalent and recurring problems in marital relations is quarreling. George R. Bach and Peter Wyden, in Chapter 30, discuss marital fighting and offer some suggestions or rules for making these fights "pay off," as they say. Dr. Bach is a psychologist from Southern California and Director of the Institute of Group Psychotherapy; here he and Peter Wyden share with the reader some ideas about "constructive aggression" from their book *The Intimate Enemy* (1968).

Several very basic issues are raised by this article. Should marriage counselors encourage quarreling among clients who come for marriage counseling? Will the expression of aggression help or harm marriages? Is what is needed "training in marital fighting"? Do lovers and spouses who don't fight actually miss a great deal, as Bach and Wyden suggest?

There are professionals in the field who would disagree with Bach and Wyden, and say that marriage counselors need to help clients fight and quarrel *less*, to *reduce* hostility rather than encourage its expression. To find out the basic cause of expressed hostility and aggression, and to help clients reduce the frequency and heat of quarrels might seem to some professionals (and some marital partners) as a worthier goal. Each reader will have to come to his own conclusion on these matters. Professional ethics and personal values as well as one's theoretical and personal philosophy of life obviously enter into the final conclusion in these matters. The reader will also want to compare the point of view expressed by Bach and Wyden with those expressed by the authors of the other papers in this section.

Albert Ellis, in Chapter 31, discusses neurotic interaction between marital partners and what can be done about it. Ellis sets forth five common neuroticizing ideas which cause difficulty among marital partners: the dire need for love, perfectionism in achievement, a philosophy of blame and punishment, catastrophizing frustrations, and the belief that emotion is uncontrollable. He discusses the effect upon marriage of these neurotic irrationalisms, and presents a method of treating neuroticism in marriage—a rational approach—using a case illustration of this approach.

In Chapter 32, Robert O. Blood, Jr., a sociologist at the University of Michigan, presents some ideas on resolving family conflicts. He discusses the sources of family conflict (compulsion, intimacy, smallness, change) and some normative mechanisms for preventing family conflict through avoidance of probable sources of conflict, allocation of rights and duties to particular roles, and equality of treatment within the family. Dr. Blood also offers some instrumental mechanisms for resolving family conflicts, including increased facilities for family living, priority systems for the use of limited facilities, and enlargement of areas of autonomy. Finally, Dr. Blood discusses processes of resolving family conflict (including discussion, mediation, accommodation, and separation).

In Chapter 33, Aaron Rutledge discusses husband-wife conferences in the home as an aid to marriage counseling. Erik H. Erikson has also made use of home visits in his attempts to help families in trouble. Maybe marriage counselors need to consider something more than merely sitting back in their offices, waiting for clients to come in. We need not consider the practitioner's office as the only conceivable consultation room. This home conference idea of Rutledge's is, indeed, a radical, controversial, provocative suggestion but the idea is certainly still worthy of consideration.

John Williams, a psychologist in private practice in Seattle, offers in Chapter 34 a feedback technique for improved communication among married couples. This "stop-repeat-go" technique can be used in the marriage counselor's office during counseling sessions and also be assigned as "homework" between sessions. A case example provides a clear illustration of how this technique actually works.

CHAPTER 29

Diagnostic Classifications and Treatment Techniques in Marriage Counseling

Shirley Gehrke and James Moxom

In marital counseling, the approach used by many caseworkers has been to treat the individuals involved in terms of their respective neuroses, with change in the marital relationship coming as a byproduct of improved individual adjustment. This method really amounts to treating an individual who happens to have a marital problem rather than treating the marriage relationship itself. The same approach would be used whether the person, married or single, was requesting help about a problem in his job, school, marriage, or other relationships.

Such an approach undoubtedly has its merits and is in some cases one answer, in others the only answer. However, with this method, long-term treatment is often necessary before there is any improvement in the presenting marital problem. Many clients may not sustain treatment to this extent, because their request is for relief of conflict in the marriage and not reconstruction of their individual personality patterns.

We have focused our treatment approach on the marriage relationship itself, because we see a difference in treating an individual who has a marital problem and in treating the problem in the marital relationship. In explanation, it is our contention that people marry each other to have certain needs met through marriage, and as long as these needs are met, the marriage can be stable, even with an extreme degree of neurosis in one or both partners. When something happens to upset the balance in this mutually satisfying relationship, conflict results. To illustrate:

A equals the husband and his total personality adjustment.
B equals the wife and her total personality adjustment.
C equals the marriage relationship, which contains both A and B but also something different and apart, which is the result of the interaction of A and B and their effect on each other.

It is C on which we focus.

Reprinted with permission of the authors and the publisher from *Family Process*, 1962, *1*, 253–264.

In these situations, casework can be used to help restore the balance lost in the relationship without resolving the individual neuroses, and this is often really what the clients are requesting. It may happen that a person initially requesting marital counseling may decide to focus mainly on his problems as an individual rather than as a marriage partner. However, we then believe that help becomes something other than marital counseling.

The first principle in the use of this method is that the same caseworker must see both partners. Sharing a caseworker focuses attention on the binding factor in the marriage, the relationship between the partners. This focus becomes the first bridge in communication, sustaining the relationship until husband and wife gain some ability to communicate with understanding.

The use of one caseworker is reassuring to clients if they want the marriage. It demonstrates the caseworker's role of strengthening the relationship rather than separating the partners through assignment to two different caseworkers. If they do not want the marriage, this approach encourages a quick recognition of this fact, as it forces clients to try to get their needs met through each other, to recognize what each can expect from himself and his partner, and to make a choice as to whether or not he can tolerate the relationship on this basis.

We have chosen to term this method "relationship counseling." The first step is a joint interview unless one or both partners refuse. If they do, this has diagnostic implication in terms of the degree of their estrangement and inability to communicate. In this instance the first step is to help the clients reach the point where they can share a joint interview.

In the joint interview the caseworker recognizes certain facts with the clients:

1. They have reached an impasse, in having tried without success many different ways of handling their problems.
2. The purpose of counseling is to help them break through this impasse.
3. A third person is necessary to assist in bridging the gap by enabling meaningful communication through increased understanding of themselves and their effect on each other.
4. Therefore, the end result of counseling is that the third person is not needed.

The main purposes of the first interview are to familiarize the clients with the counseling method and to give them an opportunity for mutual commitment to an exploratory period of two or three interviews. This period enables them to learn how the caseworker functions so that they can judge whether this is the type of help they want and need. It affords the caseworker an opportunity to diagnose the problem and as much as possible to help the clients to diagnose it also. Another joint interview is offered at the end of the exploratory period. This allows clients to commit themselves to continuing treatment based on the diagnostic understanding that clients and caseworker have reached at that point and gives clients some indication of the length of time necessary for treatment. The use of structure in this manner acts out the caseworker's conviction of the mutual responsibility of husband and wife in solving a marital problem and allows each to be encouraged by the other's expressed willingness to expend effort in solving their problems.

An accurate diagnosis of the relationship problems as well as an appraisal of the individual strengths and weaknesses of the marital partners is important for the caseworker. To effect more immediate and accurate diagnosis, we have devised the following diagnostic classifications and treatment techniques, which we have successfully applied in "relationship counseling."

I. A CONFLICT IN THE AREA OF MASCULINE-FEMININE ROLES

A. Diagnosis

In this relationship, both are in conflict about being married and having a sexual partner because of doubt about their adequacy in their respective male and female roles. The result is that the wife acts more masculine and the husband acts more feminine than usual. The wife chooses a dependent, passive male who she feels is inferior and not demanding sexually. The man is generally withdrawn, inadequate and has a severely impaired ego. He may be alcoholic, enuretic or obese. He is sexually apathetic and makes infrequent demands. Almost without exception, the woman, although frigid, complains of insufficient sexual interest on the husband's part; and even though she doesn't enjoy sex, she is usually the aggressor, and the sex life is geared toward her needs. The roles are reversed here as in every other area.

This wife controls in order to be sure her own dependency needs are met, and the husband submits to maintain his dependency. This relationship frequently resembles that of mother-child, as she indulges him because she needs his passivity to maintain her semblance of independence and to prevent excessive demands being made on her as a woman. She has high expectations of herself and glories in her independence. As long as she tolerates her husband's "shortcomings," he is satisfied with the marriage. If the husband becomes ill or unemployed, she may go to great lengths to help out, but if this incapacity extends over a long period of time, she feels unloved and unprotected, and becomes excessively controlling in a more hostile, frantic way.

If she becomes too controlling or demanding, the husband becomes upset and withdraws, both to protect himself from her demands for more masculinity than he has and to maintain a semblance of independence. He may also both defend himself and retaliate by becoming critical of her in the area of her feminine identification. She is, of course, especially sensitive in this area, particularly with regard to her appearance. She feels unattractive and frequently does not make the most of her physical attributes—her attire may be masculine and she gives little attention to make-up or hair styling.

This couple gives the impression of a stable family group active in the community. The wife has a history of being active socially but mostly with groups. There is a striking absence of intimate relationships with either men or women. Her success in work or community activity masks her uncertainty about her desirability as a feminine woman and serves as a substitute for meaningful one-to-one relationships. She talks about wanting a "real man," meaning one of impervious strength and perfection; and she is always disappointed and castrating when her husband does not meet her expectations. She is in conflict because she is really frightened of very masculine men as she cannot control them. They threaten her shaky feminine identification, but she cannot appreciate the more passive male who is the only kind she could possibly marry. This relationship is characterized by many separations, violent arguments, and divorce.

B. Treatment

Movement in this relationship stems from the wife's ability to gain insight into her controlling ways and what this represents—her need to defend her femininity by aggressive masculine ways. This often is best done by going over incidents she brings to the interview in which she has exerted this control until she is able to recognize the pattern. Once she sees the pattern, she can give it up.

Goals are slight with the man because of his lack of ego strength, and he is seldom able to gain understanding of what is involved. He is often uncertain as to what the male role is, or does not have enough conviction about it to know in what ways to assert himself. The caseworker simply needs to support the strengths in the man and encourage any effort he makes toward self-expression. The wife, in giving up her controlling pattern, leaves a vacuum for him to enter. If she doesn't attack when he moves in, he will stay there. He moves as a result of the changes she makes. The caseworker makes a mistake if he gives the impression that the husband should try to push the wife out. Once the wife sees the results of her efforts, she is ready for continued change but is still critical. Then it is important to emphasize the positives in the relationship, pointing out the feminine or more attractive qualities in the wife to her husband, and helping her recognize the better qualities in her husband so that she can be more appreciative of her choice. When the caseworker establishes a good relationship with both, he can be more directive about this. In the continuing course of treatment, further elaboration on the wife's control pattern can often help her gain real insight into her need for this pattern.

II. THE SADO-MASOCHISTIC CONFLICT

A. Diagnosis

In this relationship the man uses marriage to express his hostile, rivalrous feelings toward women. She submits because her severely limited self-regard convinces her that this is the best she can do in a relationship and she doesn't deserve anything better.

He is aggressive, sadistic, and humiliating in his behavior toward her. She is dependent, submissive, and enduring, with great tolerance for his belittling treatment. However, she is also provocative and subtly hostile. Her helplessness and subtle hostility encourage excess in her husband's expression of feeling. The marriage is characterized by "living in conflict."

These people need each other, however, and will seldom terminate the relationship permanently. The wife is disorganized and often unable to pursue homemaking activities. The man is deeply insecure and hostile, finds it difficult to be magnanimous in marriage, nags and interferes even in the housework. The wife is given to hysterical outbursts, usually provoked by her husband, who needles and harangues her until she is completely unstrung. She plays into this to get release for her feelings and be punished for her hostile feelings toward him.

In the sexual relationship he is often rough, always the aggressor. She retaliates with frigidity and subtle castrating behavior such as disinterest, delaying tactics, tacit disparagement of husband's techniques, disgust, or martyr-like endurance. Often she compels him to adopt deviant measures to elicit sexual satisfaction from her. Her actions, plus his hostility to women, often provoke a potency problem on the part of the man.

He may disparage his wife by philandering, rationalizing that she is disinterested. He then disparages his paramour by leaving her for his wife and may use the same mechanism by leaving his wife for his mother. He deals with the marriage problem by blaming others and forcing his will in a demanding, depreciating manner. She is usually a patiently enduring martyr about the whole thing, or accepts all the blame in a self-depreciating manner.

B. Treatment

Most of the time, in these relationships, contact with an agency will be initiated by the wife because of difficulty with a child, or because she has reached even her masochistic limits in terms of the amount of punishment she can take. The husband will usually come also because he desires to establish more control and will gladly use help in doing this. If he initiates contact, as sometimes happens, it is because the marriage is threatened and he is seeking to re-establish controls. This man, more than any other type, needs this marriage. Therefore, when this couple comes for help, change has to be initiated by the wife because she has something to gain. Very often, the husband sees himself as assistant to the caseworker in gaining better understanding of the wife in order to bring about his own desired results.

With this couple, transference must be used in that the caseworker becomes the ideal parent—firm but warm, forgiving, noncondemning. It is necessary to clarify the limits of the caseworker and the casework process and to reaffirm these constantly. These partners will use the caseworker to attack each other. They frequently misinterpret what the caseworker says, have very little tolerance for each other, and want the caseworker to do things they feel they cannot do. It is necessary to constantly reaffirm focus, by recognizing that this problem has existed for years, that there are certain things the caseworker can and cannot do, the most important of which is that changes are made by them, not the caseworker. If limits are not firmly set, the couple will go in circles, get into heated arguments, constantly dredge up the past.

In addition to preventing manipulation by the clients, treatment involves firm support of the strengths of each partner. It is important to help the wife gain a more realistic view of herself, recognizing the part she plays in provoking punishing situations for herself, and to help modify her need to do this. She needs encouragement to seek recognition and satisfactions for herself without extreme guilt and self-depreciation. As she makes changes, it is necessary to establish a new balance in the marriage. In some instances, the husband may not be able to accept her as a more assertive person, and change may mean the dissolution of treatment or the marriage or both. In most instances, however, the change is not drastic and slight change may be reassuring to the husband as he can then get some of his dependency needs met by his wife. The sado-masochistic pattern is not discontinued. It is simply reduced in degree to a point where outbursts are fewer and less intense. The neurotic pattern is maintained but in a much more tolerable degree, allowing room for some healthier satisfactions. The result is greater stability and a more constructive balance in the marriage.

III. THE DETACHED-DEMANDING CONFLICT

A. *Diagnosis*

The partners in this relationship are markedly dependent. Each wants a parent who can meet his needs without demanding anything in return. The relationship is characterized by emotional detachment on the man's part and an intense open demand for love on the woman's part. Each is disappointed and disillusioned in his expectations of what the other can do.

The man appears the strong, silent type—sturdy, reliable, individualistic. His wife interprets his detached calm as emotional strength. She gets the father she needs, who generally works hard, provides an adequate living, and handles financial matters. However, he has nothing to give in a relationship except dependability, so that his wife is in conflict because she got what she wanted and finds it is not enough. Her own father was rejecting and inconsistent, and unconsciously she expects her husband to reject her also. Therefore, she demands constant proof of his love and acceptance, and he reacts to these demands with further withdrawal. Usually the women in these marriages are socially charming, vivacious, and effervescent. The husband misinterprets the wife's vivacity as independence, assuming she will require little from him. He has unrealistic attitudes about what a relationship is, marries a demanding woman because this is the only type who will take the trouble to hammer away at his protective shell long enough to involve him in a marriage. She has a need to prove she can win love from a man, and from past experience with her father, she is convinced it is necessary to demand and push if she wants to get it. The woman has usually been more active in bringing about the marriage. There is frequently a history of premarital relations and pregnancy. Both are asking for the same thing—unconditional love and approval—but express this need in different ways.

There is almost no giving in the relationship. Both are markedly sensitive to criticism and interpret the slightest expression of negative feeling on the part of the other as personal criticism even though it may obviously be directed at no one.

Early in the marriage the wife tries very hard. When she doesn't get the results she wants, she deteriorates rapidly. Housekeeping and child care become overwhelming burdens, and her work becomes disorganized. She is prone to hysterical outbursts far out of proportion to the stimuli, and frequent lack of emotional control. Her increasing disorganization frightens her husband, who withdraws even more or attacks critically. He may even withdraw physically in "socially acceptable" ways—working on hobbies, business trips, extra jobs, etc. This is a further and often unbearable threat to the wife's unmet dependency needs.

There is usually trouble from the beginning of the marriage as the normal stress and strains of marriage reveal the deep dependency needs of each partner.

B. Treatment

Treatment in this relationship, more than any other, must be geared toward direct handling of the extreme ambivalence on the part of the man. He is in conflict as to whether or not he really wants this or any other relationship. On one hand he sees relationships as demanding more than he is prepared to give. On the other hand he sees a lonely barren existence without people. It is necessary to face him directly with the choice. As this man often has the idea that demands will never end if he once lets go enough to give of himself, the caseworker can help him in his choice by presenting a more realistic picture of the amount of change necessary. Once he makes the decision to involve himself in treatment in an effort to save his marriage, the treatment goal is to help him relax and risk communication and giving of his feelings. It is necessary to point out that he has to make conscious efforts to give as it will not come naturally. Once a relationship is established with this man, the caseworker can often be quite directive as to what conscious effort the man might try.

By the time this couple get to the point of requesting treatment, he is getting more satisfaction outside of his home, and she is drawing more into the home with increasing hostility and panic. Housekeeping deteriorates, which infuriates the husband as he is often compulsive. Sexually, she becomes frigid. This woman feels undeserving and guilty about taking satisfactions. She needs help in recognizing that satisfactions are necessary and important to her but will not come just because she may deserve them. She needs help in recognizing her hostility and handling it more directly. Extremely important is an awareness on her part that her husband is never going to meet all her needs and that she will need to seek satisfactions in friends and community activities so that she will not need or expect so much from marriage.

The most difficult goal for this couple to achieve is communication with each other. They may show marked improvement, but this can be deceptive. They may be exerting conscious efforts toward change but be reporting back to the caseworker about any changes rather than discussing them with each other. They can achieve a better adjustment this way, but it won't last. It is necessary to point this out and help them develop incentive for effort from each other to sustain benefits rather than depending on the caseworker to do this. The goal of treatment is to help this couple achieve an emotional exchange which will help satisfy their dependency needs in the marriage. The prognosis is poorer in this group than others because often the man has little invested in the relationship, needs only a semblance of normality, and may not choose to do more. If the man really decides to involve himself in treatment, then the prognosis is good.

IV. THE ORAL-DEPENDENT CONFLICT

A. Diagnosis

In this relationship both partners are passive, dependent people striving for immature childish gratifications. There is a mutual attempt at domination resulting in stormy quarrels. Each exhibits "temper tantrums" frequently accompanied by physical violence on the part of both. This is not of a sadistic nature but resembles a sibling rivalry type of fighting. There is no emotional giving at all in these relationships. Neither has ever achieved a satisfactory adjustment on his own, away from parents. Therefore, both are still tied to parents and at the slightest provocation will run home.

The relationship is characterized by emotional emptiness and an intense longing for affection. Each wants complete victory over the other at any cost and because of strong dependency needs is alarmed at the prospect of losing the other. Each exhibits little interest in the well-being of his partner. The man frequently adopts activities generally associated with adolescence—motorcycle clubs, sports car racing, skin diving—preferring to be with "the boys." The wife bitterly complains about this although guilty of the same adolescent behavior.

They both feel like hurt, neglected children, become hostile to each other, exhibit irresponsible and unreliable behavior and look elsewhere for sympathy. Flight is characteristic—home to mother, retreat within self, desertion.

B. Treatment

In this relationship, there should be no attempt on the caseworker's part to change the situation. All this couple is requesting is the reestablishment of a tranquil balance without individual personality change. It is necessary to deal directly with the precipitating factor, which may involve environmental manipulation or, if no concrete action is possible, simply soothing the clients as you would excited animals until the crisis is past.

Because treatment goals are limited, contact should be short term for the purpose of handling the immediate problem, with the door left open for these clients to contact the caseworker when another crisis arises. There is no need or point in attempting to set up a sustained, long-term treatment plan. The prognosis is good if the caseworker remains with the environmental situation which precipitated the contact. Successful treatment is impossible if the caseworker gets involved with the oral dependency problem.

V. THE NEUROTIC ILLNESS CONFLICT

A. Diagnosis

In this relationship, the woman is helpless in manner, chronically ill, and expects her mate to be omnipotent and to relieve her suffering. Always disappointed, she expresses unconscious resentment through depression and exacerbation of symptoms. The considerate mate is patient and stays in the marriage because of his extreme sense of inadequacy. He is strengthened by the idea of helping a weaker one. He always fails, resulting in further loss of confidence. The sick person's tacit disappointment and criticism leads to intense resentment. The man's limited self-regard and inability to enjoy the good things in life cause him to handle his resentment by redoubling his efforts to meet his wife's needs.

B. Treatment

This relationship is not treatable on a marital counseling level even though the marital problem is apparent and at the root of whatever difficulty they are presenting.

It may appear that these categories are overlapping. It is true that a couple may seem to show characteristics of several of the categories, but it has been our experience, without exception, that these are surface similarities and that deeper probing reveals the basic conflict falls clearly in one of these areas and varies only in matter of degree, not type.

Within each classification, the degree of disturbance varies, but even so the same treatment applies. The degree simply determines the goals—the more extreme the degree, the more limited the goals. The greater the strengths evident, the greater the goals.

If the caseworker accurately evaluates the strengths and establishes appropriate goals, then help is possible for any who apply. If, as sometimes happens, one partner in the marriage wants to continue and the other does not, then help can be given but becomes counseling to a person with a marital problem rather than marital counseling per se. This needs to be spelled out with the client.

In all of these diagnostic classifications, joint interviews may be used intermittently in the following instances:
1. Contradictory stories from the husband and wife point out the need for clarification.

2. One or both express the desire to discontinue treatment.
3. A plateau is reached and there is no movement.
4. It seems advisable to pause for review and consensus of accomplishments to date and determination of future goals.
5. There is need to encourage greater communication; this is especially useful when the problem falls within classification IV.
6. A conclusion is reached in the treatment process; also for follow-up in one to six months after termination.

We have found that by focusing our diagnostic thinking and treatment goals on the marital relationship rather than the individuals, clients are involved in treatment much more quickly and sustain the treatment process to an appropriate termination. Treatment time usually lasts six to nine months. This means that there is no serious attempt to change the personality make-up of the individuals involved but simply to help them establish a marital balance.

In this article, we have presented a brief description of a marital counseling method with the diagnostic classifications and treatment techniques which we have used successfully. It is our expectation and hope that this presentation will stimulate questions and explorations which will further develop the body of knowledge in "relationship counseling."

CHAPTER 30

Marital Fighting: A Guide to Love

George R. Bach and Peter Wyden

In one of their public-opinion surveys some years ago the pollsters of the Louis Harris organization asked couples across the country, "Most of the time, what is the biggest single source of friction between you and your spouse?" The two main fight issues mentioned by husbands and wives were money spending and child-raising. However, as a close third they listed a variety of remarkably trivial-sounding complaints. Husbands objected to too much petty criticism from the wives. Wives complained because their husbands were too sloppy around the house.

One husband remarked: "My wife is always after me over nothing: clothes, cleaning up the yard, this and that. I stopped listening years ago."

This typical fight evader had elected to tune out on a vast amount of strategic intelligence about his marriage. But so, strangely enough, do most intimates who daily engage in epic battles about such matters as burning the toast, misplacing a car key, setting the clock, airing the dog, forgetting an errand, arriving late, arriving early, and so on and on.

There are four psychologically important reasons for this amnesia:

1. In the heat of battle, intimates cannot think as clearly as they usually do; or they may react to an angry voice like an ostrich sticking his head in the sand.

2. Shame represses memory. In the calm of dawn's early light it is easy to recognize the disproportion of the emotional stress that the partners experienced over such *apparent* trivialities. The embarrassment during the Monday-morning quarterbacking goes so deep that partners frequently apologize for each other ("Oh, he was so mad he didn't know what he was saying"). They may even seek escape in after-the-fact evasion ("I didn't mean it. Don't mind me. I was so mad I don't even remember what I said").

3. A trivial issue may be a decoy. It may be part of a broader—but usually not consciously schemed—battle plan. It may be an excuse to get angry just to scare the partner; or to make a big impression on him; or test the limits of the bond snap-line (how much anger can he take?). More likely, the trivial issue camouflages a signal that calls for sensitive decoding. Forgetting to run an errand may actually mean to a partner, "You

Reprinted with permission of the authors and the publisher from the *Ladies Home Journal*, September 1968, page 76.

don't interest me anymore"; telling an off-color story at a party may be interpreted as, "You deliberately try to humiliate me." These messages are often exaggerated by injustice-collectors. They lie in wait, prepared to seize upon any trivial act as proof of deeper villainy. To them, being seven minutes late to an appointment proves habitual neglect; talking to another woman at a party is taken as evidence of secret philandering.

4. The substance of the trivial issue itself really is trivial and therefore isn't worth remembering! Often it is so absurdly trivial that it would be downright embarrasing to remember having been so upset over "nothing."

Why, then, do intimates experience so much anguish when they fight over "trivia"? Why does a pair of pants turn into a "federal case"? Why do *strangers* often fight violently (perhaps even lethally) over important matters, but almost never over trivial ones? There are three explanations:

1. Intimates care deeply about each other, while strangers rarely do. Intimates are forever scanning each other for information about the "temper" or the "good" or "bad" nature of each other. They hold hypotheses about where they stand with each other and, like scientists, they like to check them out. This is an intuitive technique and a constructive one as long as it is not overdone in the exaggerated, vindictive manner of the people we call spouse-watchers, who silently gather evidence against their partners, much like peeping Toms or FBI agents.

2. The intensity of fighting over trivia is often the result of the cumulative effect of quietly "gunny-sacking" one's grievances instead of arguing them out. Between intimates and non-intimates alike, a minor disappointment is an equally trivial drop in the bucket of life's frustrations. The crucial difference is that the bucket into which intimates drop a trivial grievance is often already full. Any new stress, however small, will increase the reservoir of tensions until something has to spill over. Trivial bickering, therefore, functions as a safety valve in enduring intimate relationships. If trivia is dismissed often enough as "not worth having a fight about" and all minor frustrations are suppressed in the interests of domestic peace and harmony, there is eventually bound to be a major explosion, perhaps over trivia, perhaps over something far from trivial. In either event, there is bound to be too much heat and not enough light.

3. Between intimates, as the discerning reader will have gathered, trivia often is anything but trivial. It is a kind of emotional shorthand that intimates develop in the course of thrashing out an enduring relationship. With important exceptions, a specific fight over trivia can be a clue to a more basic underlying conflict. Only the apparent fight issue is trivial; the emotions it arouses are quite likely to be serious.

What serious message is being conveyed in the following seemingly absurd domestic tiff?

It is Friday morning. Sam Rhodes, a certified public accountant, is about to leave for work. His wife, Hope, is making the beds.

HE: I hope I can get away for a game of golf with Charlie tomorrow.

SHE: Why not? Let me help you get ready for it. Is there anything you need?

HE: Say, do you mind taking my golf pants to the cleaners this morning and have them done on the "one-day special"? I have to have them back tonight if I'm going to play tomorrow.

SHE: Sure. It'll be fun for you tomorrow. You always enjoy playing with Charlie.

HE: Be sure to have the pants back. They're the only ones I'm comfortable in.

SHE (annoyed): Why do you always worry about those silly things? Please leave everything like that to me. You should keep your mind free for the office.

Now it's Friday evening. Sam comes home after work. Hope is fixing dinner.

HE (cheerful): Hello, honey! Oh boy, am I glad this week is over! I sure look forward to a good game of golf tomorrow. Did the pants come back from the cleaners?

SHE (shocked): No.

HE (more alarmed than angry): Should I run down to get them? Maybe you better phone the cleaners so they don't close before I get there!

SHE (devastated): Oh, I'm so sorry, darling! I completely forgot to take them! Wasn't that stupid of me? I had to go shopping anyway, and I could have done it so easily. I even went by the cleaners this morning. I just forgot. I really am so sorry!

HE (very angry): That's great. In other words, you don't keep your promises. That's really irresponsible! You just don't care about me anymore. You just ruined my weekend. Thanks loads!

SHE (shouting): How can you say that! You know how much I love you! You're cruel! You hurt me very much by what you just said. (She cries.) I don't know why I put up with a selfish, ungrateful man like you!

Good fighters don't fan the flames of such a conflagration, as these contenders did, thereby setting off an appalling explosion that ruined their weekend; nor would they find it rewarding to pour water on the fire by resignedly accepting the wife's forgetfulness as "sloppy housekeeping." After they learned to level with each other in our fight training sessions, Sam and Hope took up the issue of the not-so-trivial pants again. Here is how it went the second time around:

HE (stating position and making demand): I hope you don't mind if I spend tomorrow with Charlie playing golf. If I'm going to play tomorrow, I need these pants cleaned today.

SHE (checking out): You really want to play golf tomorrow?

HE (confirming): Yes, I think it's a reasonable request, after a week's hard work. I want the exercise, and Charlie is fun to play with.

SHE (stating her position and making counter-demand): Well, it's reasonable *if* you would also spend some of your spare weekend time with me and the kids.

HE (checking out her proposal): Can I play golf with Charlie tomorrow if we do something together as a family Sunday?

SHE (leveling about what she's really after): Yes, I want you to take all of us to the beach and out to dinner. I think that's a reasonable distribution of your leisure time, don't you?

HE (pinpointing areas of agreement and disagreement): Well, to be perfectly honest, I prefer staying home Sundays and watching the ball game on TV to milling around on the beach or in restaurants.

SHE (probing): Under what conditions *would* you spend some time in family activities? Or can't you stand to go out with us? I know I like for us to go out and you like to stay home. Who is going to have his way?

HE (proposing conditions of agreement): Let's alternate between my way, your way and then develop a third way: a new way of spending family time that might be fun for all of us.

SHE (checking him out): In other words, every third weekend I have my way, and you will really cooperate?

HE (committing himself to a position for time being): Yes, but this weekend I want to play golf with Charlie on Saturday, watch baseball on Sunday—

SHE (interrupts): And take us out to dinner Sunday night! That's great, and I will have your golf pants clean and ready for your game tomorrow.

When this couple made a systematic, good-willed attempt to get to the bottom of the pants issue, they found that the pants could hardly have mattered less. The real issue was a conflict between the wife's and the husband's differing notions over how to spend their leisure time. Once they recognized the true issue, they could settle their differences by open negotiation.

On other occasions, the bone of contention may be less obvious. Suppose the husband tells his wife, "Why in hell can't you match the socks in my drawer?" This explosion may hide the dark husbandly suspicion that she is applying the strategy of deliberate "disorder" and is telling him, "You don't love me enough" or "You like to torture me" or even "I think you like me to depend on you just so you can let me down." She may indeed be using "disorder" to signal him, "I'm tired of you being a helpless little boy" or "I don't respect you for expecting me to do this; you should be beyond this sort of thing." More likely, the fight is really trivial. She is only signaling him, "I'm sick and tired of being your servant."

The only way to find out whether the socks issue is trivial or not is to ask for a formal fight engagement. The husband can then flush out the underlying trouble: "What is it, darling? Are you just trying to keep me irritated?" If the answer is that the wife has a maid complex, a solution can be sensibly negotiated. Perhaps she should have some paid help for a few hours a week. The husband should realize that this solution only reduces the source of the wife's irritation. It won't eliminate it. Now it is up to him to show his wife in new ways that she rates as a person with him, not just as a maid; that being a maid in the socks department doesn't make her a maid anywhere else.

Suppose the sock is on the other foot. Suppose the husband litters the house with socks, cigar stubs, newspapers and tools, and is then upset if the house is in disarray and tells his wife, "You're a lousy housekeeper!" Then it's up to the wife to do the decoding. Does it mean he feels she doesn't love him enough?

Chances are that the issue is not as serious: the husband is probably only signaling that coming home at night is no fun for him; that he had to take orders at the office all day and now wants to have somebody to boss around. Perhaps she should let him have this pleasure up to a reasonable point. At any rate, she shouldn't—as some frustrated housewives do—leave the vacuum cleaner and ironing board well displayed in the evening by way of demonstrating silently to him, "See, I'm doing my best!"

Actually, in investigating fights that break out when husbands come home from work at night, we found that many men get plenty of aggression release through conflicts on their jobs, while housewives only have the kids to yell at and usually feel guilty about getting too angry at them too often. It is rewarding for a husband in these cases to make adequate listening and sympathizing allowances for wifely carping about what a "terrible day" she had at home while he was having an interesting time with the fellows at the office.

Among major fight issues that are more serious than they appear and are therefore often erroneously downgraded as trivial are what we call nesting fights. Man is a territorial animal, and the maintenance of cooperative nesting behavior is an intricate art. If a wife says, "I'm sick of apartments, I want a house in the suburbs," she is probably not talking about real estate but about her image of herself and her joint image with her husband. Furniture fights ("I don't want wall-to-wall carpeting; I don't want our house to look like a hotel lobby!") also provide admirable illustrations of why nesting is a danger zone.

Each partner usually has his own taste in furniture. He is likely to be cagey about disclosing it. If his taste turns out to be tasteless, it becomes embarrassingly visible to the partner and even outsiders. He may therefore maneuver the partner into becoming responsible for a particular purchase; or at least try to make the partner co-responsible for getting an item he himself wouldn't quite have guts enough to get. The trouble is that most people's nesting image tends to be fuzzy. Also, most people tend to be error-phobic; instead of learning from a mistake, they prefer to avoid the experience and find a scapegoat for any ensuing problems. Finally, for many people such items as tables, lamps and (especially) pictures are really extensions of themselves. So furniture can become an adult security blanket that is sometimes more important than clothes—a fact that is well known to furniture salesmen.

Not infrequently, a ridiculously tiny annoyance becomes a conditional stimulus and serves to ignite a disproportionately serious conflict. This happens when a trivial point reminds a partner of a nontrivial issue that is gnawing at him. In such a case the trivia becomes a cue to him that the partnership is out of balance.

This is what happens in the fights for "optimal distance." Intelligent fighting regulates the intensity of intimate involvement by occasionally creating relief from it. It makes intimacy controllable. It enables partners to locate the optimal distance from each other—the range where each is close enough not to feel "left out," yet free to engage in his own thoughts and autonomous activities, uncontaminated by the other's encroachments.

Almost nobody realizes that some fights have no issue except: "Keep your distance!" These seemingly mysterious encounters often occur after love-making.

Many couples tell us that the morning after their love-making was particularly and mutually satisfying, a fight will break out over "nothing." Perhaps the husband gets up and can't find any clean underwear. Or the coffee is too weak. Or the kids are too noisy. Or the wife wishes out loud that he would say a pleasant word at breakfast, for once. Anyway, he gets furious. The wife becomes enraged. He growls. She blows up and reminds him that she not only made a special effort to make love nicely the night before; she had also lately done *this* for him and *that* for him and why does he have to be so ungrateful and ill-tempered?

This is one of a never-ending series of fights that helps partners to find and to reset their optimal range—the psychological distance from each other that makes them most comfortable. Unconsciously they designed the fight to find out how close an intimate can come without making the partner feel engulfed; and how far he can move away without making the partner feel rejected.

Once we had learned to interpret these fights correctly, we advised our trainees not to be too vexed by them. We also cautioned clients not to be envious when somebody said of another couple, "They're very close, you know." Optimal distance or, if you prefer, optimal closeness, is the ideal goal—not *extreme* closeness. Of course, what's optimal for one partner may be uncomfortable for the other. But this difference can be adjusted, and we teach trainees how to measure—and how to make up for—such a natural disparity.

One amusing but useful at-home exercise begins with the partners conversing while they face each other about 15 feet apart. As they continue to talk, Partner A walks up to Partner B until they make physical contact. Then Partner A slowly backs away until he reaches the right distance to make conversation comfortable for A. At that point A stops and the partners measure the distance between each other with a tape measure. The experiment is repeated with Partner B doing the walking and backing up. Almost invariably, the partners' distance preferences differ. These measurements, although inexact, suggest each partner's tolerance for closeness. The partner who requires more distance to be comfortable is the one who will be more likely to start fights for optimal distance.

"Don't come too close to me" is the message he is signaling.

Every intimate sends such a signal from time to time because true intimacy is a state of entwinement that occasionally proves exhausting. We advise couples to take this fatigue seriously and to study each other's limits.

We tell trainees to develop their own distancing techniques. If they are having a lot of optimal distance fights they may find it advisable to take a vacation with another couple to dilute intimate contacts; or they might vacation separately.

Usually, however, optimal-distance problems subside after periodic solitary self-confinement at home. We call those pauses "refueling." Some people establish a private music corner, where they listen to Beethoven or to The Beatles while they allow their recuperative forces to take hold. Others meditate over a book or a stamp collection. Our trainees know that when a partner puts up a sign (either figuratively or sometimes literally) that says, "Do not disturb—refueling!" nobody needs to feel guilty or angry. The refueling partner is only taking a break to make intimacy work better in the long run. According to the outmoded romantic model of marriage, it may not be "nice" to pull up one's drawbridge and withdraw into Fortress Me. In realistic intimacy, it is necessary and desirable as long as it is not misused as a cover-up for habitual withdrawal.

Sometimes it is fruitless to look for serious motives behind a trivial fight, because such motives may not exist at all. In such cases it may be destructive to dig into a partner with investigative questions. Indeed, the word "why?" is the most overused word in marriage. Much of the time nobody could uncover the real, way-deep-down answer to why a partner did something; and if anybody did find out, it might not help. Lively participation in the give-and-take of the here-and-now pays off best.

How can anybody know when a trivial fight doesn't need to be decoded for underlying causes? Our first suggestion is that students learn to recognize, and to ignore, the useless volcanic eruptions of the type of temper outburst that we call The Vesuvius. This is just blowing off steam—a spontaneous irrelevant sounding-off of free-floating hostility. It is an adult tantrum that does not involve a partner directly, although it is advisable to have an intimate on hand as an audience. A Vesuvius unleashed against no one and on the open street would lead to curious glances and conceivably to arrest on charges of disturbing the peace.

A beautiful Vesuvius was delivered by one husband who came home from work and yelled at his wife, à propos of nothing in particular, "If that S.O.B. Jones does it just once more, I'll punch him in the nose, and that goes for your Uncle Max, too!" (Nobody had mentioned Uncle Max for weeks; he functioned here only as a free-floating kitchen sink handy for throwing into the Vesuvius.)

The Vesuvius is never directed at anybody who is at the scene of the explosion or nearby. It never involves issues that are pending between partners. It doesn't deal with anything that the partner who is witnessing the Vesuvius could be expected to do anything about. And it evaporates as quickly as a puff of smoke. The best way to make certain that a Vesuvius is not, in fact, a bugle call to a serious fight is to listen sympathetically to a partner's outburst and to wait a bit for what happens next. In an authentic Vesuvius, nothing does.

One of our trainee husbands came home from work and found a written Vesuvius posted to the door. It was from his wife. It simply said,

"I've had it." The husband became quite upset. He started searching for his wife, and found her almost immediately at her girl friend's house next door. The women were having some drinks in the kitchen. When the husband appeared, his wife brightened up and said, "Hey, look who's here!" Her Vesuvius had blown up—and over.

The worst way to handle the Vesuvius is to take it at face value and "hook in." Suppose a husband suddenly shouts, "I'm going to take this lousy lawnmower and throw it into the swimming pool!" the trained wife would never say, "Yeah? You and who else, you pipsqueak?" She would wait for the squall to subside.

Trivia can also be dismissed as trivial when it becomes the subject of a fun fight. This is a fight without real issues, as when two puppies tease each other aggressively but without a bone. A gesture or inflection may be the giveaway as to whether a fight is for real or for fun. The husband may say, for example, "You *mean* it?" If the wife says, "Sure I *mean* it" in a certain way, both are likely to recognize that there is no issue.

Most fun fights, however, rage over pseudo-issues. Are the 1967 cars better than the 1968 cars? Did Adlai Stevenson lose the Presidency in 1952 because he wasn't married? Did the husband (or wife) miss the point of last night's movie? These are fun fights because nobody has a great stake in the outcome.

Fun fights have sensible functions. They help prevent boredom. They can entertain an audience. They may serve to get others—especially children—involved in a family activity ("What do you think, Jimmy?"). They may also provide vicarious exercise and release for everybody's natural aggressive proclivities; typically, such an exercise surfaces as what we call "good-willed sadism" in a game of wits.

The bridge table is a fine place for such a game because almost everybody enjoys a hostility-releasing laugh at somebody who is losing. Incidentally, our trainee couples are always urged to play *against* each other. This allows for a healthy aggression outlet and minimizes the far more cutting hostilities of a partnership situation. ("What's gotten *into* you? How *often* have I told you not to . . .")

Lovers and spouses who don't fight over "nothing" actually miss a great deal. Especially they miss out on the erotically rejuvenating powers of the revived courtship pattern where attraction and repulsion alternate in the familiar cycle of realistic romance: attraction-repulsion, counterattack-chasing, refusing-forgiving, calling back-resistance, surrender, etc. In general, the redundant sameness of rituals doesn't serve the cause of realistic leveling, but this is an exception. We found out the hard way that long-term intimates can ill afford to dismiss trivial fighting as something that is beneath them.

Exactly how does trivial fighting stimulate love? The cause-and-effect process operates because the aggressive chase and the assertive claim of the partner as "mine" are themselves a strong stimulus to the arousal and release of love emotions. Conversely, attraction wanes when couples no longer chase or claim each other because they take each other for granted.

Very True!

The security of belonging—and being spoken for—is enjoyed by stable couples at the price of a less intensive love-releasing experience. Contrary to folklore, both sexes like to chase and to be chased at various times, to seduce and be seduced, to claim and to be claimed. And the partner who is always available, always accommodating, robs himself and the pursuer of considerable pleasure—although there are times in an authentic intimate relationship when easy availability can become a comfortable insurance against sexual frustration.

It is fortunate that sometimes the very absence of major fight issues makes intimates "pick" fights. They may bicker to upset the marital applecart just to be sure there are no rotten apples in the load.

Trivial fighting, then, deserves encouragement as long as the issues are current, the style is spontaneous and neither partner attempts to be hurtful or depreciating.

CHAPTER 31

Neurotic Interaction between Marital Partners

Albert Ellis

A recent book, *Neurotic Interaction in Marriage* (Eisenstein, 1956), includes several interesting papers by eminent psychoanalytic therapists; but I could not find anywhere in its pages a simple, cogent definition of neurosis. A neurotic, to my way of thinking, is simply an individual who is theoretically capable of acting in an intelligent, flexible, self-constructive manner but who is actually behaving in an illogical, inflexible, self-defeating way. Neurosis does not consist merely of unintelligent or highly disorganized behavior. Some individuals who act in this way, such as mentally deficient or brain-damaged persons, are truly incapable of acting differently and are therefore defective rather than neurotic. But when a man or woman is capable of remaining undisturbed and flexible when faced with difficult situations and that person does not fulfill his or her own potentialities—then, I say, neurosis is evidenced. Or, stated more concretely, any individual who needlessly suffers from intense and sustained anxiety, hostility, guilt, or depression is neurotic.

If this definition of neurosis is reasonably accurate, then we can say that a husband or wife neurotically interacts in marriage when either, or especially both, of them becomes needlessly disturbed or disorganized, or suffers unnecessary anxiety, hostility, guilt, or depression in his or her relations with the other partner. Stated differently: neurotic interaction in marriage arises when a theoretically capable husband and wife actually behave in an irrational, marriage-defeating way with each other.

IRRATIONAL IDEAS OR BELIEFS CAUSING NEUROSIS

Human neurosis, as I have contended in several recent papers on the subject of rational psychotherapy (Ellis, 1956; Ellis, 1957a, 1957b, 1958, in press), invariably results from the individual's having illogical or irrational ideas, beliefs, assumptions, or philosophies. For if he is theoretically capable of acting in a non—self-defeating way, and he actually defeats

Reprinted with the permission of the author and the publisher from the *Journal of Counseling Psychology*, 1958, 5, 24–28.

himself and brings unnecessary anxiety and hostility into his relationships with himself and others, he must have some biased, unrealistic, irrational beliefs or value systems which block his potentially sane thinking, emoting, and behaving.

The Dire Need for Love

The first main neuroticizing idea I found in a study of the unrealistic beliefs of fifty-nine clients (Ellis, 1957a) was the notion that it is a dire necessity for an adult human being to be approved or loved by almost everyone for almost everything he does; that it is most important what others think of one instead of gaining one's own self-respect; and that it is better to depend on others than on oneself. Applied to marriage, this means that the neurotic individual firmly believes that, no matter how he behaves, his mate, just because she is his mate, should love him; that if she doesn't respect him, life is a horror; and that her main role as a wife is to help, aid, succor him, rather than to be an individual in her own right.

When both marriage partners believe this nonsense—believe that they must be loved, respected, and catered to by the other—they are not only asking for what is rarely accorded an individual in this grimly realistic world, but are asking for unmitigated devotion from another individual who, precisely because he demands this kind of devotion himself, is the least likely candidate to give it. Under such circumstances, a major marital holocaust is certain to occur.

Perfectionism in Achievement

The second major irrational belief which most neurotics in our culture seem to hold is that a human being should or must be perfectly competent, adequate, talented, and intelligent in all possible respects and is utterly worthless if he is incompetent in any way. When married, these neurotics tend to feel that, as mates and particularly as sex partners, they should be utterly successful in achieving. The wife therefore berates herself because she is not a perfect housewife, mother, and bedmate; and the husband because he is not an unexcelled provider and sex athlete. Then, becoming depressed because of their supposed inadequacies, both husband and wife either compulsively strive for perfection or hopelessly give up the battle and actually make themselves into poor spouses and lovers. Either of these maladjusted choices of behavior usually soon incenses the other mate, and another marital holocaust ensues.

A Philosophy of Blame and Punishment

A third irrational assumption of the majority of neurotics is that one should severely blame oneself and others for mistakes and wrongdoings; and that punishing oneself or others for errors will help prevent future mistakes. Married neurotics, in consequence, particularly tend to get upset by their mates' errors and stupidities, spend considerable time and energy trying to reform their spouses, and vainly try to help these spouses by sharply pointing out to them the error of their ways.

Because, as we previously noted, emotionally disturbed human beings

already have the tendency to blame themselves too much for their imperfections; because even healthy men and women tend to resist doing the
so-called "right" thing when they are roundly berated for doing the so-
called "wrong" one; and because criticized humans tend to focus compulsively on their wrongdoings rather than calmly face the problem of how
they may change their behavior—for many reasons such as these, one
partner's blaming another for this other's imperfections does immense
harm in just about one hundred percent of the cases. Even the counselor—who quite obviously is on his client's side—rarely can get away with
blaming an individual; and spouses—who were often wed in the first place
mainly because the bride or groom felt that he or she would not be
criticized by this spouse—can virtually never do anything but the gravest
harm to their relationships by criticizing their mates. But this is precisely
what most neurotics are driven, by their basically false philosophies of
living, to do.

Catastrophizing Frustrations

A fourth idiotic assumption which underlies and causes emotional
disturbance is the notion that it is terrible, horrible, and catastrophic
when things are not the way one would like them to be; that others
should make things easier for one, help with life's difficulties; and that
one should not have to put off present pleasures for future gains. In their
marriages, neurotics who consciously or unconsciously espouse this I-
cannot-stand-frustration system of values invariably get into serious difficulties. For marriage, of course, is an exceptionally frustrating situation in
many instances, involving considerable boredom, sacrifice, pleasure post-
ponement, doing what one's mate wants to do, and so on.

Neurotic individuals, consequently, bitterly resent their marriages and
their mates on numberless occasions; and, sooner or later, they clearly
show this resentment. Then, neurotically feeling that they are not loved or
are being frustrated in their desires, the spouses of these neurotics get in a
few or a few hundred counterlicks themselves, and the battle is again on.
The ultimate result can be a hellish marriage—or a divorce.

The Belief That Emotion Is Uncontrollable

A fifth and final irrational belief which we shall consider here—since
we do not have enough time at present to examine all those revealed in
the original study—is the mythical supposition that most human unhappiness is externally caused or forced on one by outside people and events
and that one has virtually no control over one's emotions and cannot help
feeling badly on many occasions. Actually, of course, virtually all human
unhappiness is self-caused and results from silly assumptions and internalized sentences stemming from these assumptions, such as some of the
beliefs which we have just been examining. But once a married individual
is convinced that his own unhappiness is externally caused, he inevitably
blames his mate and his mate's behavior for his own misery; and, once
again, he is in a marital stew. For the mate, especially if she is herself
neurotic, will contend (a) that she does not cause his unhappiness; and

that (*b*) he, instead, causes hers. Such silly beliefs, again, are the stuff of which separations are made.

EFFECT UPON MARRIAGE OF NEUROTIC IRRATIONALISMS

It is my staunch contention, then, that a seriously neurotic individual possesses, almost by definition, one might say, a set of basic postulates which are distinctly unrealistic, biased, and illogical. Consequently, such an individual will find it almost impossible to be too happy in an utterly realistic, everyday, down-to-earth relationship such as modern marriage usually is. Moreover, being unhappy, this mate will inevitably jump on his or her partner—who, if reasonably well adjusted, will tend to become fed up with the relationship and to want to escape from it; and, if reasonably neurotic, will return the spouse's resentful sallies in kind, thus leading to neurotic interaction in marriage.

No matter, therefore, how irrational the beliefs of one spouse may be, it takes a double neurosis to make for true neurotic marital interaction. Suppose, for example, a husband believes that he must inordinately be loved by his wife, no matter how he behaves toward her; that he must be competent in all possible respects; that he should blame others, especially his wife, for errors and mistakes; that he must never be frustrated; and that all his unhappiness is caused by his wife's behavior and other outside events. If the spouse of this severely neurotic husband had virtually no similar illogical beliefs of her own, she would quickly see that her husband was seriously disturbed, would not take his hostility toward herself with any resentment, and would either accept him the way he was, or would calmly try to see that he got professional help, or would quietly conclude that she did not want to remain married to such a disturbed individual and would divorce him. She would not, however, neurotically react to her husband herself, thus causing a mighty conflagration where there need only be a nasty, but still limited, flame.

A METHOD OF TREATING NEUROTICISM IN MARRIAGE

If what has thus far been said in this paper is reasonably accurate, then the solution to the problem of treating neurotic interaction in marriage would appear to be fairly obvious. If neurotics have basically irrational assumptions or value systems, and if these assumptions lead them to inter-act self-defeatingly with their mates, then the marriage counselor's function is to tackle the problem not of the marriage, nor of the neurotic interaction that exists between the marital partners, but of the irrational ideas or beliefs that cause this neurosis *a deux*. And this, as I have insisted in a previous paper (Ellis, 1956), and as Harper (1953) has also previously shown, can only be done by some form of intensive psychotherapy.

My own marriage counseling is part and parcel of the technique of rational psychotherapy which I have been developing in recent years. It consists largely of showing each of the marital partners who is neurotically interacting (a) that he has some basic irrational assumptions; (b) precisely what these assumptions are; (c) how they originally arose; (d) how they are currently being sustained by continual unconscious self-indoctrination; and (e) how they can be replaced with much more rational, less self-defeating philosophies. More concretely, each neurotic spouse is shown that his disturbed behavior can arise only from underlying unrealistic beliefs; that these beliefs may have originally been learned from early familial and other environmental influences but that they are now being maintained by internal verbalizations; that his marriage partner, in consequence, is never the real cause of his problems; that he himself is actually now causing and perpetuating these problems; and that only by learning carefully to observe, to question, to think about, and to reformulate his basic assumptions can he hope to understand his mate and himself, and to stop being unilaterally and interactionally neurotic.

A Case Example

Let me cite an illustrative case. A husband and wife who had been married for seven years recently came for marriage counseling because the wife was terribly disturbed about the husband's alleged affairs with other women, and the husband was "fed up" with his wife's complaints and general unhappiness, and thought it was useless going on. It was quickly evident that the wife was an extremely neurotic individual who believed that she had to be inordinately loved and protected; who hated herself thoroughly for her incompetency; who severely blamed everyone who did not love her unstintingly, especially her husband; and who felt that all her unhappiness was caused by her husband's lack of affection. The husband, at the same time, was a moderately disturbed individual who believed that his wife should be blamed for her mistakes, particularly the mistake of thinking he was having affairs with other women, when he was not; and also believed that it was unfair for his wife to criticize and sexually frustrate him when he was doing the best he could, under difficult circumstances, to help her.

In this case the somewhat unorthodox procedure of seeing both husband and wife together at all counseling sessions was employed—largely because I found this method to be time-saving, in that the main difficulties between the mates are quickly arrived at, and because I feel that the witnessing of one mate's emotional re-education by the other spouse may serve as a model and incentive for the second spouse's philosophic reformulations. The husband-wife-therapist group, in this sense, becomes something of a small-scale attempt at group therapy.

In any event, because the husband in this case was less seriously disturbed than the wife, his illogical assumptions were first brought to his attention and worked upon. He was shown that, in general, blame is an irrational feeling because it does neither the blamer nor his victim any good; and that, in particular, although many of his complaints about his wife's unrealistic jealousy and other disturbances might well have been justified, his criticizing her for this kind of behavior could only serve to make her worse rather than better—thus bringing more of the same kind of behavior down on his head. He was also shown that his assumption that his wife should not excoriate or sexually frustrate him was erroneous: why should disturbed individuals not act in precisely this kind of manner? He was led to see that even though his wife's actions were mistaken, two wrongs do not make a right—and his reaction to her behavior was equally mistaken, in that instead of getting the results he wanted, it was only helping make things worse. If he really wanted to help his wife—as he kept saying that he did—then he should, for the nonce, expect her to act badly, stop inciting himself to fury when she did so, and spend at least several weeks returning her anger and discontent with kindness and acceptance— thereby giving her leeway to tackle her own disturbances.

The husband, albeit with some backsliding at times, soon began to respond to this realistic approach to his wife's problems; and, in the meantime, her irrational assumptions were tackled by the therapist. She was shown how and why she originally acquired her dire need to be inordinately loved and protected—mainly because her mother had not given her the love she required as a child—and how necessarily self-defeating it was for her, as an adult, to continue to reinfect herself with this nonsensical belief. Her general philosophy of blaming herself and others was ruthlessly revealed to her and forthrightly attacked. She, like her husband, was shown just how such a philosophy is bound to alienate others, rather than win their approval or get them to do things in a different and presumably better manner. Finally, her notion that her un- happiness was caused by her husband's lack of affection was particularly brought to conscious awareness and exposed to the merciless light of rationality. She was shown over and over again how her unhappiness could only come from within, from her own attitudes toward external events such as her husband's lack of love, and that it could only be expunged by her facing her own integral part in creating it.

As the husband in this case started accepting his wife's neurosis more philosophically, she herself was more easily able to see, just because he was not goading and blaming her, that she was the creator of her own jealousies, self-hatred, and childish dependency. She began to observe in detail the sentences she kept telling herself to make herself unhappy. On one occasion, when the counselor was explaining to the husband how he kept goading his wife to admit she was wrong, ostensibly to help her think straight but actually to show how superior to her he was, she interrupted to say: "Yes, and I can see that I do exactly the same thing, too. I go out of my way to find things wrong with him, or to accuse him of going with other women, because I really feel that I'm so stupid and worthless, and I want to drag him down even below me." This, in the light of her previous defensiveness about her jealousies, was real progress. After a total of twenty-three joint sessions of counseling, the fate of the marriage of this couple was no longer in doubt, and they decided to go ahead with child- bearing and rearing, which they had previously avoided because of their mutual uncertainties. They also solved several other major problems which were not necessarily related to their marriage but which had previously proved serious obstacles to happy, unanxious living.

In conclusion: neurotic interaction in marriage results when an emotionally disturbed husband and wife think and act illogically, not only in their own right but with each other. If their individual and mutual neuroses are forthrightly attacked by uncovering, challenging, and working through, the fundamental irrational beliefs and assumptions which underlie their neurotic interaction can be replaced by self- and mutual understanding that is a prime prerequisite to lasting marital love.

BIBLIOGRAPHY

Eisenstein, V. W. (Ed.). *Neurotic interaction in marriage.* New York: Basic Books, 1956.
Ellis, A. A critical evaluation of marriage counseling. *Marriage and family living,* 1956, *18*, 65–71.
Ellis, A. Rational psychotherapy. *Journal of General Psychology,* 1958, *59*, 35–49.
Ellis, A. Outcome of employing three techniques of psychotherapy. *Journal of Clinical Psychology,* 1957, *13*, 344–350. (a)
Ellis, A. Rational psychotherapy and individual psychology. *Journal of Individual Psychology,* 1957, *13*, 38–44. (b)
Ellis, A. Hypnotherapy with borderline schizophrenics. *Journal of General Psychology,* in press.
Harper, R. A. Should marriage counseling become a full-fledged speciality? *Marriage and Family Living,* 1953, *15*, 338–340.

CHAPTER 32

Resolving Family Conflicts

Robert O. Blood, Jr.

Aside from the inner conflicts of the individual person, the family is the smallest arena within which conflict occurs. Since the scale of conflict is so much smaller than occurs between the great powers of the world, can the ways in which families resolve their conflicts ever apply to international conflict?

The present article deals primarily with the inherent characteristics of family conflict, some of them diametrically opposite to international conflict. Nevertheless, the study of small-scale conflict seems most likely to yield new hypotheses relevant to large-scale conflict if the family is studied on its own terms. Were we to limit ourselves to facets of obvious relevance, new ways of looking at international conflict might be missed. In any case, a general theory of conflict must eventually embrace all ranges of social systems, from the largest to the smallest. Hence family conflict has potential interest for its similarities with, and its differences from, large-scale conflict.

Conflict is a widespread and serious problem in the contemporary American family. Roughly, one marriage in every four ends in divorce, which is usually preceded, and often caused, by the failure of family members to avoid or solve their conflicts. Many additional families survive their periods of stress only at great cost to their physical and mental health. Many a husband's ulcers, a wife's headaches, and a child's nervous tics are traceable to domestic tension and warfare.

SOURCES OF FAMILY CONFLICT

How does it happen that conflict afflicts so many families? Families everywhere tend to have certain characteristics which lay them open to potential conflict.

Compulsion

For one thing, a family is not a voluntary organization (except for the husband and wife). Children do not choose their parents. When the going

---

Reprinted with permission of the author and the publisher from *Conflict Resolution*, 1960, 4, 209–219.

gets tough, they cannot resign their membership. Even the parents are under heavy pressure to stick with the group no matter what.

Such involuntary participation tends to intensify conflict, once it originates. Because they have to continue living in the same house year in and year out, family members can develop deep antipathies for one another. What began as a mere conflict of interest easily turns into emotional hatred through the accumulation of grievances between two family members. Once such hostility has arisen, conflict can become self-perpetuating.

Intimacy

The conflict potentialities inherent in the involuntary membership of the family are accentuated by the intimacy of contact within the family. In school or church or business, physical distance and social formality are maintained at some minimum level. Moreover, contact is restricted to a limited range of relationships, such as teacher-pupil, priest-parishioner, or boss-secretary. (This is what Talcott Parsons (1949) calls "functionally specific relationships.")

By contrast, relationships within the family are functionally diffuse. Family members lay all sorts of claims on one another for economic maintenance, recreational companionship, sexual responsiveness, sympathetic understanding, love and affection, etc. The comprehensiveness of these claims points to additional potential sources of conflict.

When conflict does occur within the family, it lacks the restraint imposed by concern for public opinion. If a man's home is his castle, it is also the place where his dungeons of despair are. A man who would never strike a woman in public finds his fury uncontrollable when goaded by a nagging wife behind closed doors. A child who would be patiently admonished in a public park needs a pillow in his pants for the same behavior at home. The very privacy which makes possible the most uninhibited embrace within the bedroom permits an equally uninhibited tonguelashing. Intimacy of contact, therefore, contributes to both the extensity and the intensity of conflict within the family.

Smallness

While families everywhere are characterized by compulsory membership and intimate contact, the American family's small number of children further magnifies the problem of conflict, especially between siblings. In a large family, one child's share of his mother's attention and affection is so limited that it matters little whether he has it or not. In a two-child family, however, one child can monopolize the parent simply by vanquishing his sole sibling. Under these circumstances sibling rivalry becomes acute.

Similarly, among three siblings, the inherent instability of the triad typically leads the two older children to battle for the pawn. Again limited size dictates who the potential enemy shall be, makes him highly visible in the small group, and leads to the development of long-term feuds.

Change

The above family features would not be so bad were it not for the rapidity with which the family situation changes. Given fixed ingredients, a stable equilibrium might be sought. But families change so fast that a moving equilibrium is the best that can be hoped for.

Families change rapidly in size. Census figures show that newlyweds typically have hardly more than a year in which to work out their marital relationship before it is altered by the nausea of pregnancy. Then the children come every two years—bing, bing, bing. A decade and half later they leave for college or its working-class equivalents with similar rapidity (Glick, 1955).

Meanwhile the family may have maintained the same size, but the needs of its members were rapidly changing. Every time a new child starts to crawl, to climb, to wander across the street, to go to school, to experience puberty, or to drive a car, the pattern of family living must be readjusted. The changing "developmental tasks" of growing individuals create corresponding "family developmental tasks." Even parents' needs change as, for example, when the mother loses her figure or the father fails to get the raise he expected. Since the American family specializes in personality development and personal need fulfilment, such individual changes tend to disrupt the family equilibrium.

Given so many potentialities for conflict, what mechanisms exist for preventing the total disruption of what is so often called the "basic unit" in society?

NORMATIVE MECHANISMS FOR PREVENTING FAMILY CONFLICT

No society can afford to turn its back on family conflict. The family is too indispensable a unit of social structure and too necessary a means for the transmission of culture to the oncoming generation to be allowed to fall apart.

Consequently, every society tends to develop patterned ways of inhibiting the emergence of conflict. With the passage of time, these mechanisms tend to acquire the force of norms. That is, social pressures are mobilized to increase the likelihood that these mechanisms will be utilized, and social sanctions are imposed on those who violate them.

Different preventive mechanisms are found in various societies, depending partly on the points at which their family system is especially vulnerable to conflict. The following analysis classifies particular taboos and requirements in broad categories of general interest.

1. *Avoidance of probable sources of conflict.* Many societies have devices for keeping apart potential or actual family members who otherwise would be likely to come into conflict with each other. By "potential family members" are meant couples who are not yet married. Societies have many ways of screening out those most predisposed to conflict. The traditional "publishing of the banns" allowed triple opportunities for

objections to be raised to an inappropriate partnership. The formal engagement notifies parents and friends of the couple's intentions, providing a last opportunity for pressures to be brought to bear in disapproved cases. Studies of broken engagements show that such pressures often successfully prevent what would presumably be conflict-laden marriages (Burgess & Wallin, 1953).

Studies of "mixed marriages" of many sorts show a greater incidence of conflict due to the contrasting cultural values, expectations, and behavior patterns of the partners (Landis, 1949). Church organizations mobilize their resources to discourage interfaith marriages, and informal social pressure tends to prevent heterogamous marriages across racial, national, or class boundaries. Although a majority of all mixed marriages succeeds, such social pressures presumably break up in advance those mixed marriages which would be least likely to succeed.

New preventive mechanisms in our society are marriage education and premarital counseling. An estimated 10 percent of American college students now take a course in preparation for marriage, one of the main purposes of which is to rationalize the process of mate selection through emphasizing numerous ways of testing compatibility (Bowman, 1949). Most such courses operate on the premise that young people are liable to contract incompatible marriages if they are not careful. Hence the chief value of compatibility testing is to detect which relationships are incompatible.

One of the main functions of premarital counseling, similarly, is to provide couples in doubt with an opportunity to look objectively at the conflicts already apparent in their relationships and to provide them with emotional support as they go through the process of deciding to avoid each other in the future.

Two legal moves designed to avoid domestic difficulties are almost universal among the fifty states. One of these is the five-day waiting period between the time of applying for a marriage license and the date of the wedding. This provides an opportunity for those intoxicated with wine or perfume to sober up and reconsider. Similarly, the age at which couples can marry without the blessing of their parents has been increased to eighteen for the bride and twenty-one for the groom. Since teen-age marriages have a conspicuously higher divorce rate, raising the minimum age probably reduces the number of marriages which get off to a bad start.

Once the marriage has been contracted, one of the widespread sources of difficulty is the in-law relationship. Since marriage involves a drastic shift in allegiance from parents to spouse, newlyweds often have ambivalent feelings which are reflected in inter-spousal jealousy and conflict. This marital tension makes its correspondingly difficult for couples to get along with their parents-in-law.

Our society reduces friction in this area by warning couples not to move in with their in-laws if they can possibly avoid doing so. Some societies prescribe even stricter avoidance by restricting or prohibiting social intercourse with the mother-in-law. Especially taboo is the familiarity of joking with the mother-in-law. Reserve and formality are frequently required. Sometimes complete avoidance is the rule—one must neither talk with nor even look at the mother-in-law.[1] Although there may be social losses, such mechanisms of avoidance effectively rule out the possibility of conflict between potentially hostile individuals.

2. *Allocation of rights and duties to particular roles.* A second way in which societies prevent conflict is by distributing the authority, privileges, and responsibilities of family members according to a fixed pattern. In so doing, these societies predetermine the outcome. In fact, they short-circuit the conflict process completely because they take the issue out of the area of legitimate controversy. Henceforth only in socially deviant families does conflict ever occur over the allocated matters. For example, the incest taboo allocates sexual privileges exclusively to the husband and wife. Murdock (1949) and other anthropologists believe that the reason why this allocation pattern is found universally is because it is essential to family harmony. It functions to prevent sexual jealousy and rivalry within the family which would exist if more than one member of the family were allowed access to the same sexual partner.

Similarly, authority in the family is seldom distributed evenly among family members or (vaguer yet) left to each new family to decide for itself. Almost every society centralizes legitimate power in one role, usually that of the father. This is not to say that the wife and children are necessarily excluded from consultation in the decision-making process. Indeed, consideration for the wishes of the members of his family may be enjoined on the patriarch. However, a patriarchal family system specifies that in a showdown—when husband and wife cannot agree on mutually exclusive alternatives—the husband's wishes should prevail. The beauty of this system lies not in male superiority but in the fact that a ready out is available from any deadlock which may arise. It could as easily be the wife (and is in a few societies). It is handy, however, to have a way of avoiding prolonged crises within the family.

Authority need not be allocated entirely to one role. Each partner may have certain areas of family living in which he has autonomous jurisdiction. For example, most Detroit husbands make the final decision about what car to buy, while the typical wife decides how much money to spend on food for the family.[2] Whenever people grow up expecting the husband or the wife to make decisions on their own in the "proper" areas, those areas are effectively removed from the domain of conflict.

Herein lies the problem of the democratic family. Whenever two or more family members believe they ought to share in making a certain decision, they have added another potential conflict to their portfolio. The American family has been drifting in the direction of a "companionship" ideology, which specifies that an increasing number of decisions should be made jointly. A good example is the family vacation, which 66 percent of all Detroit housewives report is planned fifty-fifty. In the

---

[1] Most of the cross-cultural examples in this paper are drawn from George P. Murdock (1949).

[2] All references to Detroit families are drawn from the writer's 1955 interview study of 731 housewives, a representative sample of the Detroit Metropolitan Area (Blood, 1960).

long run, mutual planning is likely to produce results which at least partly please both partners. And, according to our democratic philosophy, this is an improvement over the old system of fully pleasing one partner at the expense of the other.

But the process may be painful. The trend "from institution to companionship" has opened a whole Pandora's box of potential new conflicts. These do not necessarily materialize; under the classical patriarchate, they could not.

The blurring lines in the division of labor similarly open the way to more conflict. In a time when women did the dishes without question, dishwashing was not a topic for cartoons (symptoms of sore spots in any society). But as men and women alike begin to wonder whether and how much men should help out in the kitchen, a new area of controversy is added to the list. Thus a clearly defined division of labor, like a clear-cut allocation of authority, may be a social device for preventing conflict.

3. *Equality of treatment within the family.*. The allocation of authority to particular members of the family does not mean the right to wield it arbitrarily. Despotic power creates unrest within the body domestic just as much as in the body politic. To prevent such unrest, the centralization of authority must be coupled with a bill of rights for the weaker family members to protect them from discriminatory treatment.

The exercise of power within the family takes two forms: (1) influencing or forcing the individual to alter his behavior (either by doing something he does not want to do or by stopping what he would like to do) and (2) granting or withholding favors. Even though the ability to exercise both types of power may be vested primarily (or ultimately) in the father, it is well to remember that the mother is a powerful figure for her children, especially when they are small. Indeed, every member of the family has the power to grant or withhold his attention, love, and respect, regardless of how weak he may be in other respects. Therefore, when we speak of the necessity of equal treatment, we are not referring to the father alone.

How does equal treatment manifest itself in the family? The illustrations are endless. If Johnnie gets a story before he goes to bed, so must Jane. If he has to pick up the living-room floor, she has to be forced to do her share. If Tom gets to use the family car on Friday, then Dick has a right to it on Saturday. Children and parents alike recognize the justice of such claims and can appeal to the moral value of fair play to secure equality. Insofar as equality is achieved, conflict tends to be avoided.

The administrative problem is complicated, however, by the fact that siblings are rarely of the same age. As a result, the principle of equality cannot always mean uniformity of treatment at any particular time. If John stays up until nine o'clock, that does not mean Jane can—being two years younger, she must have extra sleep. Accepting such seeming discrepancies is not easy for younger children. However, parental emphasis on the idea that, "when you are ten years old, you will be able to stay up until nine o'clock, too" is often effective.

Age-graded equality is likely to prevent conflict especially well when the system for moving from one notch to the next is clearly understood by all concerned. For instance, if every child's allowance automatically increases a nickel on his birthday, the younger siblings can feel confident that they will receive their "just deserts" when the proper time comes.

In the light of what was said earlier about the conflict-preventing function of the incest taboo, it is apparent that the custom of polygyny presents very serious problems. Whenever there are several wives but only one husband, the danger of jealousy and conflict among the wives is very acute. It is not surprising, therefore, that polygynous societies have devised all three types of measures for preventing the outbreak of such conflict. (1) Avoidance is achieved by placing each wife and her children in a separate hut. (2) Authority over subsequent wives is usually allocated to the first wife—her position is thereby less threatened, and the loss of exclusive wifehood is offset by the addition of maid service. (3) More important for our present purposes is the common requirement that the man treat his wives equally, that he not play favorites among them. This often takes the form of requiring the husband to follow a strict schedule of rotation among his wives, spending an equal number of nights with each in turn. No society can effectively control the warmth or coolness with which he treats an unpopular wife; however, this merry-go-round rule at least spares her the humiliation of public knowledge of her husband's disfavor.

Equality of treatment is not an easy achievement, especially where intangibles like affection and attention are involved. Only the childless couple can completely avoid conflict from this source. As soon as the first child arrives, competition for the time and interest of the mother is created. Since she does not have enough time to go around, she must be prepared to say to her son, "I played with you last night, so tonight you should not object to my going out with your father." Even the child whose oedipal wishes have not been effectively resolved may accept such a statement if the norm of family equality has been adequately learned.

Avoidance, allocation, and equality—not separately but in combination—are the inventions which cross-cultural research shows to have been practical ways by which societies have prevented family conflict.

INSTRUMENTAL MECHANISMS FOR RESOLVING FAMILY CONFLICTS

Despite the existence of preventive mechanisms, and wherever those mechanisms do not exist, conflict occurs. The means of ending those conflicts seem far less often culturally prescribed. Rather there seem to be a number of optional procedures, in the United States at least, which are available to families as ways out of their dilemmas. These mechanisms are instrumental in the sense that they can be employed as means to achieve certain ends, if the family so desires.

1. *Increased facilities for family living*. When conflict results from scarce facilities, it is sometimes possible to satisfy both the conflicting parties by increasing the resources at the family's disposal. For example, sibling jealousy often originates from the mother's preoccupation with the new baby on her return from the hospital. An extra "mother" in the form of grandmother or nurse relieves the real mother of part of her work load so that she can give more attention to her displaced child.

Those societies with an extended family system have built-in grandmothers, aunts, and cousins who flexibly replace the mother when her attention is unavailable. Ethnographers report a general lack of sibling rivalry under this multiple mothering.

Conflict in the American home often centers around the use of scarce physical facilities. The current trends to a second car, a second television set, and a second telephone result not only in increased profits for the corresponding manufacturers but in decreased tension for family personnel who can now use parallel facilities simultaneously instead of having to compete for control of single channels. Similarly, the new-fangled recreation room provides the rest of the family with a retreat when daughter decides to throw a party in the living room, taking the tension off competition for "the only room in the house where I can entertain my friends."

2. *Priority systems for the use of limited facilities*. When enlargement of facilities is impossible, family conflict often becomes chronic. There is perpetual tension between family members, perennial jockeying for position, and fear that the competitor is getting ahead or taking advantage. Such feuding can often be seen among young children and is difficult to end by rational means. With older family members, war weariness may eventuate in a desire for peace at any price. Conflict may then be ended by facing the issues and arriving at decisions in some fashion or other.

The product of such decision-making is often a priority system governing the use of the scarce facility. If the bone of contention is the television set, a schedule for the whole week, born of a major showdown, may take the place of petty conflict "every hour on the hour." If the scarcity has been financial, the record of decisions takes the form of a budget. Here the mutual recriminations sparked by overdrawn bank accounts can be obviated by advance planning about where the money is to be spent.

The beauty of a budget, as of any other system, is that personal control ("I say you must") is replaced by impersonal control ("The budget says you must"). The process of agreeing on a budget is still liable to plenty of conflict, but, once formulated, a budget tends to divert attention from the hostile antagonist to the operational code.

3. *Enlargement of areas of autonomy*. Analogous in many ways to the method of effecting an absolute increase in the facilities available to family members is the chopping-up of existing facilities into smaller units, which can then be made available exclusively to different members of the family. This results in a relative increase in the facilities at the disposal of the individual without the necessity of securing the consent of other family members. Hence potential conflict is avoided. For example, some couples plague themselves with difficulty by trying to arrive at joint deci-

sions about the disposition of the scarce commodity of money. Worse yet, each partner may endlessly reproach the other for the petty expenditures he has already made. Such bickering can be ended by granting each partner an allowance to be spent as he sees fit without the necessity of accounting to the other for his whims and fancies. This innovation correspondingly restricts the area in which decision-making (and potential conflict) must occur to more critical areas of financial management.

The method of granting autonomy is not limited, however, to the use of scarce facilities. The problem of adolescent-parent conflict may be resolved by judicious increases in the amount of autonomy granted the teenager. Some parents clash head-on with their high-school sons and daughters in attempting to curb their adoption of the latest fads in dress and speech. Certainly, the easiest way out of this dilemma is to recognize that teenagers are old enough to decide for themselves what to wear and how to talk.

Similarly, conflict may result from undue stress on total-family activities. The mother who worries about finding recreation which both her four-year-old and her fourteen-year-old will enjoy may be troubling herself unduly, since almost anything she chooses evokes dissent from one child or the other. Autonomy under such circumstances need not mean a complete atomization of the family but simply a willingness of a subgroup within the family to enjoy singing nursery rhymes without feeling the necessity of compelling disinterested members to join.

4. *Safety valves for reducing tension between family members.* Insofar as conflict within the family is precipitated or accentuated by accumulated interpersonal resentment, various means are available for reducing the level of this tension. Vacations are one such resource. Of course, a family may find plenty of things to quarrel about on a vacation, but at least they are new issues. As far as the old problems are concerned, a change of scenery makes it possible to forget about them for a while; on return they may even have lost their power to provoke antagonism.

A change in personnel may be just as effective. Adding a pal or two for the morning play period may so restructure relationships within the sibling group that the old feuds are disrupted at least for the time being.

For some purposes, however, it is most effective to get away from the family group completely. One reason we speak of harried housewives but not of harried husbands is that wives (and especially mothers) are so often tied down to the four walls and the four faces of the home. The piling-up of petty irritations into peaks of tension results in perennial irritability and conflict-proneness. Then little issues provoke major crises because of the loading of accumulated tension.

Under these circumstances escape mechanisms are not childish but sensible. Getting out of the house produces a sense of relief. A television farce or romance produces the right kind of distraction. Even "going home to mama" may be useful, provided mama does not take daughter's troubles too seriously.

There may be corresponding value in masculine and children's expeditions. The husband's "night out with the boys" may be resented by his wife but is likely to result in a new look in marital relations. And the children need not always be on the receiving end for personnel changes but may find welcome escape from the network of conflict by visiting their friends in return.

There is also what the psychologists call "catharsis"—the reduction of tension through telling one's troubles to someone else. There is little doubt that "unloading" one's difficulties on someone else genuinely lightens the burden of conflict for most people. In so doing, it reduces the necessity for purposeless vindictiveness which prolongs the conflict. In effect, catharsis (like the other safety valves) helps to break the vicious circle of attack and retaliation which so often characterizes families with a long history of conflict.

The only problem involved in the use of catharsis is the selection of the target. Among the shoulders which might conveniently be cried on are those of the husband (provided he is not the antagonist in the conflict), the mother, and the neighbor. Providing a sympathetic ear for the spouse is one of the major steps in accomplishing what I like to call the "mental hygiene function" of marriage. Mothers and neighbors can usually be counted on to be sympathetic—but sometimes too much so, tending to jump into the conflict, too, starting a mobilization race on both sides.

Because of these dangers in lay friendships, couples in serious conflict sometimes find it useful to turn to a professional third party, for instance, a clergyman, doctor, or family counselor. These functionaries are accustomed to providing people with discreet opportunities for catharsis.

Whatever the specific safety valve opened, the reduction of the head of steam facilitates the tolerance of frustration and a patient approach to finding satisfactory solutions to the basic sources of conflict.

PROCESSES OF RESOLVING FAMILY CONFLICT

So far we have been ducking the main issue of what happens when two parties to a family conflict collide head-on. To treat this problem, it is necessary to assume that the two partners (for it is most often the husband and wife who find themselves in this position) think of each other as equals. Hence the problem cannot be solved by appeal to differential authority.

One obstacle to resolving family conflict is that it is often dyadic in nature. Hence voting is impossible. Or at least there is no way to break the inevitable tie. Some families have found that conflicts of limited importance can be settled by ordinary voting procedures—especially if there is an odd number of children in the family. But this easy way out is available at best during a small fraction of the total family life-cycle.

What, then, to do in case of a deadlock?

Discussion

The natural first step is to talk things over, to outline the various possible solutions, to weigh the pros and cons in an attempt to arrive at some sort of solution. This process of decision-making has been studied and analyzed too well elsewhere to need detailed treatment here (Blood, 1955). Suffice it to say that there are three major types of solutions which can be reached: (1) *consensus*—that is, mutual agreement by both partners that a vacation at the lake would be best for both of them; (2) *compromise*—one week at the lake and one week in the mountains so that both partners gain part and lose part of their objectives; (3) *concession*—two weeks in the mountains, not because the wife is convinced that that would be most enjoyable, but because she decides to end the conflict by dropping her own demands.

Most families solve most of their problems by such processes of communication followed by decision-making.

Mediation

Occasionally, couples need outside help in arriving at a decision. Here relatives and friends can seldom qualify because they are usually more closely aligned with one partner than the other. Hence professional personnel are almost the only resort.

The function of the third party in this case is seldom to take over the decision-making process. Rather he acts as a catalytic agent, enabling the couple to become more objective and more rational by his very presence. If conflict is serious and hostile feelings have accumulated, he may work with each partner separately for a long time. Only after self-insight and mutual empathy have been achieved might it be productive for the couple to be seen jointly. Meanwhile the couple may discover on their own that they have already acquired the ability to settle their conflict, aided by the new skills and understandings gained in counseling. Even when only one partner turns to a third party, the beneficial repercussions of the counselor's collaboration may be felt throughout the family.

Accommodation

In one sense, accommodation might be listed as a type of decision. More accurately, however, it represents the recognition of a failure to agree. In the classic phrase, we "agree to disagree" or to "live and let live." In the specific case of the summer vacation, this could mean separate vacations for husband and wife (though so much autonomy runs heavily counter to American mores).

It is not always possible for the parties to a family conflict to go their separate ways. If the issue at hand is the need for a new car, one either gets one or one does not. But if John likes to play tennis while Mary likes to go to concerts, Mary could accommodate herself to going it alone while John finds a different partner.

Essentially, accommodation involves adopting a philosophical attitude of resignation—coming to the conclusion that further attempts to influence the partner are just not worth the conflict they provoke. Hence expectations of mutuality are abandoned in favor of accepting the partner as he is.

Separation

If neither discussion, mediation, nor accommodation succeeds in set-
tling family conflict, the last resort is separation. In a sense, separation
does not really settle conflict at all, but it usually does end it. If the
antagonists are no longer within shooting distance of each other, their
attention is soon likely to be diverted from the point at issue.

The term "separation" is usually applied to husband and wife. If they
cannot live together in peace, few there are who would force them to go
on living in conflict. Even those groups who are most opposed to divorce
and remarriage recognize that separating the marriage partners is sometimes preferable to prolonging the agony.

Separation can also occur between parents and children. The military
academies of this country are populated by boys whose parents were
unable to arrive at peace treaties with them. And the older adolescent who
leaves home for college, job, or marriage sometimes only thus terminates
his or her revolutionary war.

Separation is the most drastic way out of family conflict, yet those
who have tried it often say that peaceful loneliness is an improvement
over perpetual conflict.   *that's a point!*

CONCLUSION

Returning now to the question of the similarities and differences between family conflict and conflict in other settings, it is apparent that the
sources of family conflict are largely distinctive. Families are uniquely
small and intimate. The structure and developmental tasks of the family
are transformed with unusual speed. Only in the involuntary nature of
world society is there a close analogy.

Much as the sources of conflict may differ between the family and the
world community, the mechanisms for preventing and resolving conflict
have more in common. International "mechanisms of avoidance" include
the United Nations Emergency Force sealing the border between Israel
and Egypt and the proposals for disengagement in Central Europe. The
"allocation of authority" to a world court and a world government would
alter the naked struggle of sovereign nations among themselves. "Equality
of treatment" is just as difficult a problem among nations differing in size,
wealth, and maturity as among children differing in age. However, the
admission of all nations to membership in the United Nations might
achieve minimal equality and bring excluded nations within the sphere of
authority of the international organization. Rotation systems in key international offices tend to reduce international jealousy.

"Increased facilities" for international living are provided through
economic development, reducing the envy of the "have" nations by the
have-nots. "Priority systems" for the use of limited facilities apply to such
international waterways as rivers and harbors on which multiple countries
depend. "Enlargement of areas of autonomy" reduces international conflict as colonial powers become independent. International "safety valves"

Family vs world conflict and resolving techniques

include the opportunities for catharsis provided by the open forum of the General Assembly and by smaller-scale talks at or below the summit.

Big-power rivalry between East and West is closely analogous to the conflict between husband and wife. Voting has little value when the conflicting parties perennially deadlock or veto each other. The focus under such circumstances must be on the same processes that enable families to resolve their deadlocks. Discussion through negotiation and diplomatic talks may lead to consensus, compromise, or concession internationally as well as familially. The General Secretary of the United Nations has increasingly become an international mediator, as have many of the smaller powers. Accommodation to the status quo has been the outcome of many an international crisis that for a time threatened to disturb the peace. But separation, in a shrinking world, is one process not open to national societies, for, much as they may dislike each other, they must go on forever living in the same international "house."

REFERENCES

Blood, R. O., Jr. *Anticipating your marriage*. Glencoe, Ill.: Free Press, 1955.

Blood, R. O., Jr., & Wolfe, D. M. *Husbands and wives: the dynamics of married living*. Glencoe, Ill.: Free Press, 1960.

Bowman, H. A. *Marriage Education in the Colleges*. New York: American Social Hygiene Association, 1949.

Burgess, E. W., & Wallin, P. *Engagement and Marriage*. Philadelphia: J. B. Lippincott, 1953.

Glick, P. The life cycle of the family. *Marriage and Family Living*, 1955, *17*, 3–9.

Landis, J. T. Marriages of mixed and non-mixed religious faith. *American Sociological Review*, 1949, *14*, 401–407.

Murdock, G. P. *Social structure*. New York: Macmillan Co., 1949.

Parsons, T. The social structure of the family. In R. N. Anshen (Ed.), *The family: its function and destiny*. New York: Harper & Bros., 1949.

CHAPTER 33

Husband-Wife Conferences in the Home

Aaron L. Rutledge

In his office in Iran everything usually went well for the thirty-year-old oil company employee, but at home the end of the day brought restlessness, sleepless nights, and mental torture. He felt that he deserved to die for he knew not what. His social life (that which was available) was uninteresting. His head ached incessantly. His back, his chest—any part of his anatomy was subject to aches and pains. Sometimes he desired his twenty-nine-year-old wife sexually, but often all desire left him for weeks, and even months.

The company doctor had found it impossible to help, except through sedation at periods of most acute stress. He recommended requesting an early furlough to the States, and suggested consultation with a psychiatrist in Boston.

The wife wondered if her failure to conceive was a factor in his disturbance. She believed that her sterility was of emotional origin, and also her failure to menstruate for several months, in spite of medical care.

There had been fun again, after two years of boredom, as they rediscovered the thrills of relaxation and sexual satisfaction on the freighter voyage home. But then, back in his parental home, there was renewed bickering and tension. The familiar chasm separated them again, and his symptoms reappeared. He remembered, resented, but then agreed to consult a psychiatrist as suggested by the company physician.

After listening for an hour, the psychiatrist said: "Your marriage is the cause of your trouble. If a man has love and acceptance waiting at the end of the day, returning home will be a refreshing experience. The fact that you tense up there means your home life is not adequate. You won't be well until you do something about it."

In the next quarrel he flared: "Well, that does it! Divorce is the answer! The marriage is no good, and I'll never be well so long as we live together!" The wife was shocked at this first hint that he wished to end the marriage. Later she reasoned: "I've tried everything I know to please you, even to forcing myself into different personality types to fit your

Reprinted with permission of the author and the publisher from *Marriage and Family Living*, 1962, *24*, 151–154.

ever-changing moods. Sure, I'm not pleasant to live with a great deal of the time now because I've crawled into a shell to keep from being rejected again. I can't take it like this either. If the psychiatrist feels our marriage is the cause of all this, let's go see the 'marriage doctor'." He laughed at the idea, but a few days later asked if she wanted to buy the double bed they had discussed to replace the company-owned twin beds.

They found the marriage counselor nearest her parental home, where the remainder of the vacation was to be spent. There was time to see each of them separately four times, and they were seen together in a final session. In these interviews saving the relationship had become their major goal. She had a better picture of her "shell," and he realized that there would be only unhappiness with any woman until he understood himself better.

He saw himself as an overprotected boy who had run away to early independence and self-sufficiency. A chain of events had led to exemption from armed service. His first major physical symptoms and anxiety attacks had grown out of unconscious assumption of responsibility, with its attendant guilt, for the death of a brother in action. Soon a promotion had doubled job responsibility, reactivating repressed feelings of inadequacy and dependent needs, but all ties with home had been cut and there was no one upon whom to lean. At this point the attractive army nurse showed up and they were married. She failed to relieve his anxiety; in fact, the added responsibility increased it. Resentment, escape from responsibility, and other needs found expression in chronic illness and unusual demands upon her for care. Her cooking, housekeeping, and talking were upsetting to him, and openly he compared her to his mother, who had warned him against marrying a person of a different religion.

Everything the wife knew as a nurse failed; she could not be mother and wife when he didn't know which he wanted. She offered all she had as a woman, to be rejected more often than accepted, and finally withdrew into a protective shell. The conferences helped tear away the shell, revealing the hurt little girl loved by no one, who had worked her way through nurses' training only to be imposed upon by selfish relatives. She had enlisted in the Army for unconscious as well as conscious reasons. When they met, his needs clicked with her need to be needed, and that was sufficient for a while. But she needed to be loved and cared for, too, and he could only receive and demand more; not so much a husband as a son. After a noble trial she had run away again; this time into herself.

With encouragement these new insights were shared, they began labeling residual childhood needs, recognizing personality strengths in themselves, and started responding to the wholesome needs of each other.

The short stay in the United States necessitated putting this couple on their own much too soon in terms of conventional counseling. Obviously, they would have profited by long-term therapy, but the only way to continue the process was by means of planned husband-wife conferences in the home with the follow-up assistance of the company doctor. In the final conference, together, they were given home conference instructions, the gist of which follows.

THE HOME CONFERENCE PLAN

Your relationship "got this way" through the action and reaction of two personalities, and together you can undo the damage and grow a meaningful relationship.

Ordinarily each of you would be seen separately for a longer time, working toward a progressive understanding of (1) yourself, (2) your mate, and (3) the marriage relationship; how each reacts, feels, behaves, and why. With hurt feelings and bitterness drained off and the total situation seen in better perspective, you would be expected to carry on most of the work on your own.

The suggestions being made to you now would be made even if we could work together for several months. You are an exception only in that you are to be on your own earlier than is usual.

Since a major barrier in your marriage is lack of understanding, and since understanding is dependent upon communication, the biggest single task is learning to express true feelings and attitudes toward each other and toward the relationship.

You have concluded that a satisfying marriage relationship must be equalitarian, with neither person being the boss nor the bossed. Your relationship will grow as the individuality of each is made secure and meaningful. The goal is neither to find fault nor to place blame, but to evaluate and understand. When disturbed feelings are buried inside, they grow and abcess; and yet when they burst out, there is hurt and confusion. The goal is to prevent both, by finding another way of handling feelings.

The following suggestions may seem rigid and arbitrary; but unless temporarily you go "by the book", you may find yourselves dropping out along the way, cutting it short, or developing the process in a one-sided manner.

Arrange two conference periods a week for several weeks. Set an hour—say 8:00 p.m., Tuesdays and Fridays—and permit only the gravest emergency to interfere, and even then use the next evening. In each conference—

1. Mrs. B. talks 20 minutes;
2. Mr. B. talks 20 minutes;
3. she has 10 minutes for questions to clarify feelings;
4. he has 10 minutes for questions to clarify feelings;
5. Conference ends on the hour.

At the next conference, he talks first, etc., alternating. Agree that if tempers flare, you will wait a few minutes, then begin again. If you cannot cool off, postpone the discussion until the next evening. Remember, you are giving each the right to express feelings, whatever they are, in an effort to understand. If either has harsh or confused feelings inside, they will do both of you less harm if brought into the open, with agreement not to nurse grudges.

Agree in advance not to raise voices, but feel both the right and the obligation to express your feelings frankly. When one is talking, the other will listen just as attentively as I have listened to each of you, and you will not interrupt the speaker. Talk about all the feelings you have discussed with me, but never quote me to each other or in any way try to pit me against the other. I am interested equally in you.

Devote the first two periods to "bad" feelings out of the past and present. During the second and subsequent weeks give one period to "bad" feelings and the next to "what's right with us," things you have enjoyed, liked about each other, and had fun doing together. Part of this latter period might well be given to planning the family life to allow for a balance of work, social and recreational interests, relaxation, and worship, although you go to separate churches.

Don't be in a hurry to change the content or frequency of these periods, but eventually you may have only one conference a week, and will give it to both "good" and "bad" feelings. You may want to retain this "family hour" long after you cease to need it for straightening out confused feelings. Every family could use at least an hour a week on serious sharing and planning. When children come along they can be incorporated into the discussions, giving them an early taste of real democratic living.

Some of the things to be discussed positively at these sessions would be your place in the community, sex, your religious beliefs and your individual places in your church, some outstanding issues of your way of life, etc. The primary goal is not to change the other, but to learn to communicate openly and freely all your feelings, with a view to understanding more fully each other, yourself, and your relationship. This can become the means of making marriage so meaningful that minor adjustments will begin to fall into place.

Between these conferences you may have hurt feelings. If one loses control, the other will listen until the tempest is over, and then calmly suggest: "We have a time to discuss such matters, so let's postpone this." The other well may respond: "Yes, now we will get busy at other things in order to get our minds off it until then."

If things pile up unbearably for either of you, back off into a corner and write out your thoughts just as if you were talking to me; seal the envelope, lay it aside for mailing to me, and walk off from it just as you walk out of my office. Later, in your conference, you can discuss it quietly and objectively with each other.

I am counting on your doing this in a wholehearted manner for the sake of each of you and your marriage. Here is a copy of these suggestions so that each of you may become thoroughly acquainted with the plan before you undertake it.

A follow up over several years has demonstrated the effectiveness of the plan for this couple, both in terms of a meaningful marriage and the clearing up of psychosomatic symptoms in both.

MODIFICATIONS

The aid to marriage counseling illustrated in this case has been used regularly with a variety of clients over the past twelve years, usually during the final phases of counseling. The possible modifications of the plan are limited only by the needs of the individuals and the insight and ingenuity of the counselor.

1. Some couples may need to attempt these discussions in the counselor's presence until they get accustomed to handling hurts together, although trying the procedure on their own with instructions is preferable for many from the beginning.

2. The amount and degree of structuring may vary, and the length of time before initial rigid requirements can be relaxed, will be determined by their progress in communication. It may be necessary to continue the controls to guarantee somewhat equal production and emotional release;

otherwise the conferences can deteriorate to the level of previously unsuccessful communication.

3. Discussion can be limited to specific problem areas. On the other hand, some couples might need to begin discussing subjects about which there is little stress, establishing a pattern of participation before moving into ego-involved areas. They might be temporarily limited to the past, or to contemporary events, until the counselor feels that the relationship can survive facing the real conflict areas.

4. Bibliotherapy may prove effective, either as a beginning place, or as a means of stimulating understanding of human motivation in general. Books or pamphlets with pertinent information may be used to advantage on prescription of the counselor.

5. Although the method has been illustrated in the context of a democratic marriage, it is equally applicable in other systems so long as respect for an individual is a vital value.

6. Many couples with little or no counseling assistance can adapt this to their own needs as a "do it yourself" way of facilitating healthy marital interaction.

LIMITATIONS AND PRECAUTIONS

1. At least an average level of maturity seems essential to this method, or certainly a fairly equal emotional balance, and some desire on the part of both to make the relationship work. There must be mutual acceptance of the method.

2. There could be destructive consequences with psychopathic personalities, or those subject to strong paranoid trends, deep depressions, or uncontrolled impulses or compulsions.

3. Enough time must be spent in individual therapy to drain off intensive hostilities if the process is not to degenerate into mere quarreling or even fisticuffs. Each must be helped to avoid using confidences revealed here as psychological weapons later in their experiences together.

4. The rigid structuring makes it seem artificial and unreal for a while.

5. Often one spouse refuses to verbalize, although willing to listen to the other. This can be a passive expression of hostility, saying, "See, it's you who has the bad feelings; it's your problem."

6. There is some risk of uncovering feelings difficult to control, or too severe for the other to accept, by shocking confessions or release of pent-up contempt.

7. Some tend to dwell too persistently upon old hurts, making the past an escape from or justification for the present.

8. Others tend to stop the process much too soon—"nothing more to discuss"—which leads to further piling up and renewed resistances and misunderstanding.

9. This procedure may strip bare a personality previously held together by various defense mechanisms, leading to serious emotional disturbance.

All of this is to say that the counselor uses the method by prescription based upon his diagnostic understanding of each personality and of the marriage relationship.

VALUES OF THE METHOD

1. Planned home conferences afford a further opportunity to ventilate pent-up feelings, can reduce the frequency of counseling interviews, and well may decrease the number of professional conferences necessary.

2. Re-living disturbing experiences a second time, after they have been excavated in counseling sessions, provides further clarification, assimilation, acceptance, and re-integration. Facing oneself where he lives—in the area and with the person where stress is felt—can facilitate integration and personal growth, and speed the healing of the relationship illness.

3. It can bring about growth in understanding of how the mate feels, and lead to increasing respect for him as a person. Understanding has a way of awakening dormant love in a previously embittered mate, and being understood is the most therapeutic of experiences.

4. It prevents the accumulation of feelings of anger, hate, fear, loathing, shame, resentment, and guilt which poison a relationship. It calls for facing up to hurtful experiences while fresh, rather than evasion or repression, while at the same time minimizing the need for destructive types of quarreling.

5. When only one of a couple is undergoing psychotherapy, the growth process may be one-sided, which can broaden the gap between the mates and lead to divorce. In such a case these husband-wife conferences in the home make the individual counseling process a mutually shared effort toward self-determination of their marriage relationship.

6. Improved communication, along with the development of honesty, frankness, and spontaneity in the conferences, spreads to daily life, affording a stimulating variety of responses to each other, and creating an environment more in keeping with reality. Long-term repression as a means of controlling dangerous feelings toward the mate often results in burying or overcontrolling *all* feelings, including love and affection. Only as one is permitted to express in words his "bad" feelings and have them accepted can he learn to "let go," giving wholesome feelings of affection, love, and tenderness a chance to develop and find expression.

7. A couple can be led to work over any or all major areas of their life together, resolving problems not acute enough to take to the counselor, and developing a more meaningful family image to guide them.

8. As new conflict areas emerge in daily life, and the couple find themselves confused in their own attempts at solution, private conferences with the counselor are made more specific and meaningful if they have been working according to this plan.

9. This puts the couple in a position of accepting responsibility for the major part of the adjustment process much earlier than is possible

otherwise, avoiding excessive dependence upon the counselor. Adjustment may be desirable as a temporary goal, but initiative and creativity, which must emerge from mutual efforts, are necessary to a growing meaningfulness in marriage.

10. Such conferences may provide the basis and motivation for continued regular discussions long after the presenting problem is resolved. This guarantees that subsequent hurtful experiences and feelings will be handled, rather than allowed to accumulate. Without regular conferences as part of the family plan, one might feel that an "incident" was not serious enough to call a special session. If regular sessions are being held, it is easy to handle the difficult occasion together. Often this is the means of reactivating the significance of previous individual therapy and marriage counseling sessions long after they have ceased, affording the insight necessary to resolving the new crisis. A regular family conference can provide the setting for week-by-week examination of family interests, whether legal, economic, spiritual, social, recreational, or otherwise. This becomes the working center into which each of the children can be drawn as he learns to participate in discussions, decisions, and the sharing of family—and hence life—responsibilities.

CHAPTER 34

Feedback Techniques in Marriage Counseling

John Williams

The husband stated that although he really enjoyed sex with his wife, he felt he could enjoy it more if she would just relax, would be willing to experiment with some new ways to achieve satisfaction, and could possibly challenge some of her overly strict ideas about sex with which her frigid mother had indoctrinated her during her childhood.

"All you ever think about is sex," Mary Rogers said through clenched teeth, her voice dripping with sarcasm. "Sex and fun and that damn bedroom. You just think I'm no good in sex, and you hate me. You've always blamed the failure of everything in this marriage on me. And especially about sex. It's all my fault. Oh, why did we ever . . ." she started crying and hid her face in her hands.

Jack Rogers tried to pat her hand, saying, "That's not what I'm trying to tell you, Dear. You don't understand."

His wife jerked her hand away and shouted at him, "Oh, just shut up. There you go again, blaming me and saying it's all my fault and that I never listen to you." She turned away from him, sitting back in the corner of the big easy chair in my office, dabbing at her eyes with a wadded piece of tissue and staring out the window, sniffing and sniveling and feeling very sorry for herself.

I thought to myself how many hundreds of couples I have heard go through this typical way of trying to communicate with each other. The Rogers, like the others, certainly had a lot to learn before they were going to be able to talk to each other, and to other people, in a sane, rational way.

I frequently use (as have many other therapists) a special form of communication practice with a couple like this which I call the "feedback" technique, or "stop-repeat-go" talking. I have found that, although the process is fairly laborious, when I can get couples to practice using it in my office and also to use it as homework during the week, some fairly dramatic results can be obtained quickly.

Ellis (1962; Ellis & Harper 1961a, 1961b) has frequently stated how important communication is, not only in the sexual sphere of a relationship but in a person's total adjustment to life. Most of the people I see really do not know how to say clearly what they are thinking and feeling—in addition to their having numerous neurotic motivations that cause them to block and be afraid of saying the wrong thing, to talk too much from anxiety, to say things to purposely cloud issues and confuse the other person, or to express hostility which generally breaks down any attempt at communication. Furthermore, most people are really very poor listeners. They "hear" with preconceived prejudices; they generally twist and misinterpret much that is said to them and often only hear what they want to. It seems to me, therefore, that an essential part of therapy—particularly when one is working with two people as in a marriage, a parent-child relationship, or some form of partnership—is to aid individuals to say clearly what they mean and to learn to listen openly in order to hear accurately what the other person is attempting to say.

I ask couples seen in joint therapy sessions, to use the "feedback" technique repeatedly to facilitate understanding each other and to get their messages across.

"We're going to try an experiment," I told the Rogers. "Obviously, the two of you aren't getting anywhere the way you're going at talking, and I have found a method that really proves helpful to people. I imagine that most of the talking at home between the two of you is just like you were doing here a minute ago, right?"

Both people nodded vigorously. "Oh, yes," Mary said. "Why even last night . . ." her eyes started to fill with tears, and I could tell we were in for another angry tirade.

"Hold it," I said firmly. "Continuing to blame each other for faults and shortcomings is, as we've discussed before, the opposite of rationally accepting the things other people say and do, even when what they do is admittedly poor. We don't have to *like* what people do, but we do have to accept what they do and say because that's reality. Then we can go ahead and try to change some of the ways that other people act, to see if we can get the world to be more the way we'd like it. But the way the two of you are trying to change each other doesn't seem to me to be bringing you the kinds of results that you both have repeatedly told me you want. So let's try something new, OK?"

I went on then to outline the ground rules for the "feedback" technique. First, one spouse could say anything he or she wanted—bring up a problem, "bitch" about something, etc. I instructed them to try to keep it fairly brief; during the time one person was talking the other was not allowed to interrupt or say anything. When the first person had had his say, then the other person was to say back to him the gist of what had been communicated. He did not have to use exactly the same words or terms, but what was important was to try to say back the *meaning* of what the first person had said. The original speaker was then either to agree (yes, that was what he had been trying to say) or disagree (no, that was not quite what he really had meant, or even that was *definitely* not the correct interpretation). If the second person did not "feed back" what had been said to the satisfaction of the first person, then the first party was instructed to repeat his message. The second person was told that he or she was to refrain from making faces or emoting in any negative way (a deep sigh at the right time can get across beautifully the message that you think someone is a real jackass); the listener was to try to listen and interpret as carefully as he could.

When the first person had repeated his message, the second person was to try again to feed back what had been said. The first person was also instructed to refrain from any negative criticism of what the second person was saying (since a well-timed "Dummy!" can again frustrate opening channels of communication).

This "stop-repeat-go" technique was to continue until the first person agreed that the feedback did, indeed, say what he had been trying to say. Only when the first person was relatively satisfied was the second person permitted to answer the statement of the first person.

It has been my experience that when the first person is given uninterrupted freedom to make a statement, he seems to be more *willing* to try to really say what he means and is more likely to be *able* to do so because of a lessening of frustration and anxiety (he knows he is not going to be interrupted). Also, the establishment of ground rules and getting a commitment from the two people that they will try to follow those rules "forces" the second party to focus on *what* is being said and not on his *reaction* to it. As a result this technique tends to short-circuit the usual prejudicial comeback that many people think up and have ready to fire when the first person stops to draw a breath. Patients later tell me in check-up sessions that they feel a responsibility to get accurately the message of the first person, and that occasionally an aspect of their neurosis is working, in that they know that I, too, am listening carefully for them to "say back."

That is the real message I am trying to get him to learn. Even if the person goes on and tells himself the typical, irrational sentences that he uses to disturb himself and create the negative sustained emotions and philosophies that constitute his neurosis (Ard, 1966; Harper, 1959; Ellis, 1961), I feel that he is now doing the correct thing (trying to listen carefully) though possibly for the wrong reason.

Since I too believe that it can be helpful at times to use the person's neurosis against itself (Seabury, 1968), I do not mind too much if he listens carefully to his wife partly because he is afraid of my disapproval. At least he is listening. I would hope that later, with practice and sustained effort, I could get him to do the correct thing for the appropriate reason (that is, to listen because he really wants to communicate with his wife).

Now it's the second person's turn to talk. Usually what happens is that he answers back, hostilely, to the original "charges," giving facts and history to prove or disprove certain points. (I instruct the second person, too, to try to keep it fairly brief so that we can apply the feedback technique. If a statement is too long, we easily forget what was said, and confusion once again reigns.) When the second person has had his short say, I instruct the first person to feed back what was said. Again, he need not use the same terms the other person has used, but only try to explain the gist of what was said. If the second person agrees right off, "Yes, that's pretty much what I meant," then the first person has his turn to speak again.

In practice, this rarely happens (unless the second person, in hostilely trying to get the first person to upset himself, says, "You are a rat"; here the first person may be able to ferret out the exact meaning of what the second person said, and *is* able to accurately feed back the meaning: "You really think I *am* a rat!"). Most of the time there will be a slow interchange between people: the second person's having his say over and over again, the first person's attempting to feed back what he had said, and the second person's repeating it over and over. But usually, with persistence, the second party finally says, "Yes, that's what I'm trying to tell you."

By now, a half hour may have elapsed, and everyone present (including the therapist) can feel the strain of belaboring each point. There is certainly some feeling of frustration on the part of the people involved, but I usually find a marked reduction in anger and hostility, a sort of "caught-up-in-the-process" feeling; and because I am constantly interrupting and reminding them of the rules, they agree to follow. Doing this often in a humorous fashion, I find that by this point in the session there may be a few smiles or even laughs as the couple begins to communicate with each other—maybe for the first time in years.

In a single therapy session, we may not cover more than one or two points. But this, as I explain to them, is not significant. As they learn to communicate more accurately, they can speed up the process. What we are now interested in is *quality* of communication, not quantity. Then I often assign them homework—to continue where we left off in the office; to keep talking, first one, followed by feedback, then the other, followed by feedback, on and on. (Homework assignments are an integral part of the rational-emotive psychotherapeutic technique: see Ard, 1966, Ellis, 1962, Harper, 1959.)

Granted, there are times when patients "need" to ventilate. But I have found that usually when they are allowed to talk on and on, they simply repeat themselves, continue to reindoctrinate themselves with nonsensical sentences, and feel more and more sorry for themselves, concretizing their poor self concepts. If I feel that a patient needs to talk at length, I do not encourage joint sessions.

Now, back to the Rogers. After the instructions were laid out and questions of procedure carefully answered, Jack Rogers again stated what he had first said at the start of their session—namely, that he liked sex with his wife, but that he felt he could possibly like it even more and get greater satisfaction, as he hoped she would, too. He said he wasn't demanding anything of her, but just preferred her to be more open, experimental, less inhibited, and more sexy.

Immediately, when Jack had stopped talking—in fact even before he had finished—his life had begun to cloud up, and her first words were, "Damn—he and his sex . . ."

I interrupted her in a loud voice, "Illegitimate! Illegal! No just answering how you feel. You are to feed back what Jack is trying to say to you. Now please go ahead and try."

She gave me a look that made it appear she had doubts about the legality of my parent's marriage, thought a minute, and said to Jack in a disgusted voice, "You just want more oral sex."

I asked Jack, "Is that what you are trying to say?"

"No, he replied, it wasn't."

"Try it again," I said. "Tell Mary again."

Jack repeated, in essence, what he had already stated twice before. As they tried to talk, his wife would either give him an irrelevant answer or say he was blaming her for all their failures; occasionally, as they progressed, she would touch on a point he had made and get part of it.

Jack was having his difficulties, too, since he was repeatedly getting frustrated, found it hard to sit and listen to his wife be hostile, sarcastic, and self-pitying, and was quite humanly getting tired of repeating himself over and over.

To avoid giving a verbatim account of the long, detailed interchange that followed, let me simply state that by the end of the session, after much crying and display of hostility on the wife's part, accompanied by some, though less, hostility on her husband's part, the talking gradually changed in its tone and content. At one point, Mary said to Jack, "Well, I guess what you're trying to say is that you'd like me to question some of the ideas I have about sex, and maybe if I were freer, I could enjoy it more and so could you."

Jack gave both her and me a huge grin. "Yah, damn, that's exactly what I'm saying—at least in part. Hey, how about that, we finally did really talk to each other!"

Our time was up. I encouraged each of them to keep on trying, to use the method at home, and to pick out some more areas to discuss. Next week we would do the same thing again—in fact for weeks and weeks to come, until they had really learned how to listen, interpret, and talk. As the Rogers left, I jotted a note in my notebook that I felt there had occurred a marked reduction in the level of hostility that they had shown to one another when they had come in for that particular session, and I had high hopes that this feedback method would be even more helpful to them in the future.

REFERENCES

Ard, B. N., Jr. (Ed.). *Counseling and psychotherapy*. Palo Alto, Calif.: Science and Behavior Books, 1966.

Ellis, A. *Reason and emotion in psychotherapy*. New York: Lyle Stuart, 1962.

Ellis, A., & Harper, R. A. *Creative marriage*. New York: Lyle Stuart, 1961. (a)

Ellis, A., & Harper, R. A. *A guide to rational living*. Englewood Cliffs, N. J.: Prentice-Hall, 1961. (b)

Harper, R. A. *Psychoanalysis and psychotherapy: 36 systems.*. (Paperback) Englewood Cliffs, N. J.: Prentice-Hall, 1959.

Seabury, D. *The art of selfishness*. (Paperback) New York: Cornerstone Library, 1968.

Counseling Regarding
Sexual Problems

> *I regard sex as the central problem of life. And now that the problem of religion has practically been settled, and that the problem of labor has at least been placed on a practical foundation, the question of sex—with the racial questions that rest on it—stands before the coming generations as the chief problem for solution.*
>
> HAVELOCK ELLIS

As Havelock Ellis noted in the quote introducing this section, sex may be seen as the central problem of life. But even if sex is not viewed as that important, it is certainly a central problem for most of the clients who consult marriage counselors and therefore deserves a separate section in a handbook on marriage counseling.

In Chapter 35, Albert Ellis, one of the outstanding sexologists in the United States, reports on the kinds of sexual problems which existed in one hundred consecutive cases seen in his marriage counseling practice, and raises the basic question as to whether sex is really an important factor in marital incompatibility.

In Chapter 36, psychiatrist Walter B. Stokes deals with inadequate female orgasm as a problem in marriage counseling. Just how important is it? Dr. Stokes also raises two further questions: Is the current image of Miss America actually much improvement over her grandmother? And where did Miss America get her narcissistic, unloving view of sex? Dr. Stokes discusses just what can be done about the problem of inadequacy of female orgasm and gives specific suggestions that will be of help to marriage counselors as well as interested husbands and wives.

The whole subject of orgasm has received considerable attention in the literature of late. With emancipation women are demanding more equality in sexual relations, including equal orgasms. Sometimes the marriage manuals have contributed to the problems in this area by over-selling "simultaneous orgasm." The professional literature may have helped cause some problems regarding orgasm by raising the question of vaginal versus clitoral orgasm. For some recent discussions of this matter, the interested reader may consult Albert Ellis, "Is the Vaginal Orgasm a Myth?" (in

A. P. Pillay and A. Ellis, Eds. *Sex, Society and the Individual*. Bombay, India: International Journal of Sexology, 1953); W. H. Masters and V. E. Johnson's *Human Sexual Response* (1966, pp. 66–67); and J. L. McCary's *Human Sexuality* (1967, pp. 318–319).

Alfred Stern, a gynecologist, discusses in Chapter 37 the diagnostic pitfalls encountered by the gynecologist which might be applicable to marriage counseling. Specifically, Dr. Stern discusses the distorting twists in the appearance of cases which can result from the patient's psychosomatic productions, ambivalent sabotage, manipulation of the therapist, selective emphasis, and semantic haziness. The professional marriage counselor will find many helpful suggestions on things to look for in the therapist-client communication.

In Chapter 38, Albert Ellis gives some practical, down-to-earth suggestions on how to increase sexual enjoyment in marriage. In typical Ellis style (i.e., very plain English), specific suggestions are made which might be called "uncommon rules of marital sex," along with some more common ones. Some of these suggestions are provocative, some might be considered controversial, but all are worthy of serious consideration. This is the sort of material which the counselor might want to have reproduced in order to distribute to his clients (after securing the proper permissions, of course).

For additional material the counselor may consult Ben Ard's, "Seven Ways to Enjoy Sex More," *Sexology* 35:508–510; 1969. The counselor may also wish to write some material himself to be mimeographed for distribution to clients who consult him about sexual problems.

CHAPTER 35

Sex Problems of Couples Seen
for Marriage Counseling

Albert Ellis

There has been much discussion in the recent literature on marriage and divorce as to whether sex is an important factor in marital incompatibility. Many cases are cited to show that sexual problems exist between couples who contemplate or actually go for divorce; and many cases are cited to demonstrate that it is nonsexual rather than sexual difficulties that lead to marital disagreement. To shed a little objective light on this subject, it was decided to study one hundred couples who were seen for marital counseling to discover how many and what kind of sex problems existed between these couples.

Accordingly, one hundred consecutive cases seen by the author in his marriage counseling practice in New York City were investigated. These couples were routinely questioned, in the course of being counseled, to discover exactly what kinds of sex problems were felt to exist by either the husband, the wife, or both partners to the marriage. The obtained results are listed in Table 1.

From the data in Table 1, it can be seen that in only six of the hundred couples who came for marriage counseling did it appear that no sex problem whatever existed between the mates. In the other 94 instances distinct sex problems existed; and, all told, 155 such problems were found, or an average close to two problems per couple.

Of the sex problems that were found, the majority were of such a nature that they could be deemed female rather than male problems. That is to say, about twice as many females as males tended to have relatively low sex desires, to be seriously inhibited, and to have difficulties in satisfactorily completing coitus. The only two areas in which the males seemed to have a distinctly greater number of sex problems were (*a*) in the area of having sexual obsessions or fixations and (*b*) in the area of not being sufficiently romantic in the course of their relations with their wives.

The general picture one receives, then, of the sexual problems of these husbands and wives is that the males were significantly more interested in

Reprinted, with the permission of the author and the publisher, from the *Journal of Family Welfare*, 1957, *3*, 81–84.

TABLE 1

SEX PROBLEMS OF 100 COUPLES SEEN FOR MARRIAGE COUNSELING

PROBLEM	N
Wife less sexually interested than husband	37
Husband less sexually interested than wife	17
Wife seriously sexually inhibited	20
Husband seriously sexually inhibited	5
Wife unable to achieve orgasm in any manner	15
Husband has serious impotence problems	8
Wife has serious homosexual problems	1
Husband has serious homosexual problems	8
Wife has sexual obsessions or fixations	1
Husband has sexual obsessions or fixations	7
Wife complains of husband's poor sex technique	8
Husband complains of wife's poor sex technique	15
Wife complains that husband is not romantic or loving during sex act	10
Husband complains that wife is not romantic or loving during sex act	1
Wife complains that husband takes too long to reach an orgasm	3
Husband complains that wife takes too long to reach an orgasm	5
Total	155*
Number of cases in which neither the wife nor the husband appears to have any sexual problem	6

*Total problems more than 100 because some couples reported multiple problems.

sex satisfaction than were the females. This difference theoretically could have resulted from (a) genetic differences or (b) socially learned differences. As the marriage counseling sessions progressed, it became apparent that in most instances the differences were not entirely genetic or constitutional. As these husbands and wives were instructed in better methods of sexual technique, and as they were helped to overcome their emotional disturbances, their sex relations usually improved considerably and their number of complaints significantly decreased. In some instances, however, even though the general marital difficulties cleared up, some of the serious sex differences remained, tending to indicate that constitutional factors in sexual incompatibility can by no means be entirely ignored.

Assuming that many of the sex problems involved in these marriages were of a nonconstitutional nature, the question arises as to whether the sex difficulties caused or were an outcome of the nonsexual incompatibilities of the couples investigated. No clearcut answer could be given to this question in many of the cases seen, as it was exceptionally difficult, especially by the time they came for counseling, to determine whether the sexual or nonsexual disturbances came first. The impression usually was gained that the process went something like this: (a) For a variety of reasons, one or both partners to the marriage were distinctly neurotic or psychotic prior to the wedding. (b) The difficulties of achieving a sound interpersonal relationship in marriage added to the original emotional disturbance. (c) Because of the original disturbance, as well as because of simple ignorance of sexual processes, considerable sexual disturbance existed in one or both of the mates prior to marriage. (d) This sexual disturbance also tended to increase because of the difficulties of adjusting to the other mate. (e) Once the general emotional disturbance became severe, it led to greater sexual disturbance; and once the sexual problems became severe, they led to greater emotional problems. (f) In the final analysis, by the time the couple came for marriage counseling, severe emotional and sexual problems usually existed, and the marital difficulties could only be solved by forthrightly tackling both these interacting sets of problems with active psychotherapeutic techniques, which included considerable direct sex education.

The findings of this study would seem to indicate, therefore, that two seemingly divergent views of sexual incompatibility in marriage are both largely correct. On the one hand, sexual problems of a serious nature do seem to exist in many or most couples who get into marital difficulties; and these sexual problems have a pernicious effect on their marriages. But at the same time, nonsexual problems of a serious nature also seem to exist in many or most cases of marital incompatibility; and these nonsexual emotional problems have a pernicious effect on sexual adjustment. Whether the chicken or the egg comes first in these cases seems to be unimportant. *Both* sexual and nonsexual sources of marital difficulty must be energetically tackled if effective marriage counseling is to be done.

CHAPTER 36

Inadequacy of Female Orgasm as a Problem in Marriage Counseling

Walter R. Stokes

At the outset it seems appropriate to have a look at the question: Just how important, in the course of marriage counseling, is the attainment of orgastic response by the wife? I am aware that there is considerable diversity of opinion among us on this issue. Some tend to minimize the importance of mutual sex enjoyment or to feel that adjustment will automatically follow if the overall interpersonal relationship can be improved. A few even go so far as to question whether orgastic capacity in the wife is really of much importance to the success of a marriage. Others see a high rate of passionate sex activity and orgastic response as utterly essential to a good marriage and view it as the touchstone to satisfactory married life.

It is well to acknowledge that there exists among therapists and counselors a marked difference of opinion as to which comes first: poor sex adjustment (often involving inadequate female response) or poor interpersonal adjustment at nonerotic levels.

Before moving into closer examination of the questions I have raised, it is necessary to set a few things straight. Living in a culture such as ours we are enormously handicapped in our efforts to understand and to develop the best potential of either sex. We simply do not have much of a store of reliable information or experience about the expression of female sexuality at its guiltless, happy optimum. In a great measure this must be attributed to the unfortunate cultural heritage of sex mores in our society. I wish to document this briefly, particularly as it relates to women and female orgastic response.

Our sex mores are heavily influenced by the doctrines of Hebraic-Christian morality. In this mystical system there is a basic assumption that enjoyment of sex is sinful, nothing better than bait in the Devil's cruel trap. It is conceded in the Book of Genesis story that Eve was a natural, curious, sex-enjoying creature but for following her inclinations she is pictured as turning loose all the misfortunes of mankind. In a considerable sense she represents both the first and the last sexually responsive woman.

Reprinted with permission of the author and the publisher from the *Journal of Sex Research*, 1968, 4, 225–233.

All her female descendants are supposed to be so terrified by the results of Eve's bad judgment that they are to regard erotic emotion with horror and aversion. This ideal reaches its full flower in the Christian myth of the Immaculate Conception and the character of the Virgin Mary. Her awesome, desexualized, icily frigid personality is the female image every little girl must emulate if she wishes to become a "lady" in the Christian sense. Therefore girls find themselves under enormous pressure to deny their instinctual erotic feelings or to express them only in sublimated, symbolic, or furtive ways. The effect of this upon the development of orgastic capacity in intercourse is painfully obvious. It is strikingly summarized in a couple of stories told me early in my practice by a cultured, elderly woman who had been reared in the strictest Victorian tradition, as a member of one of the First Families of Virginia.

She commented that up to the time of her marriage her mother had never directly mentioned sex in any way. But as her wedding approached the mother took her aside and grimly instructed "You are about to be married and must be thinking of having children. To do this a woman must submit to revolting physical contact with her husband. She must summon all her courage and endure this, as she does childbirth. It is said that there are women who enjoy sexual contact with a man, but this has never been known in the history of our family. I am sure you will not enjoy the sex act but if you should, never let your husband know, for no decent man can respect a woman who does."

The second story told by this daughter of Victorianism had to do with a visit she made to a burlesque show with one of her early boy friends. They went there for a daring lark. But when the lewd jokes of the comedians began to register the boy was humiliated and apologetically begged her to leave at once. She drew herself up and replied acidly "No! Do you think I would permit these ruffians the satisfaction of knowing that I understand their vile jokes?"

It may appear that I am belaboring a dead horse in these references to the past. Someone may justifiably point to the recent progress made by all three of our major religious faiths in moving away from the old sex puritanism. In so far as this is really true I rejoice over the change and am happy to see religious morality letting up on sex. But I raise two serious questions about the change that is taking place.

First, is the current image of Miss America actually much improvement over her grandmother? When I observe Miss America's superficial, empty glamour values; her cultivated narcissism; her seductive use of phoney sex appeal to win prestige and material rewards; and her poor record in marriage, I wonder whether she is a great deal closer to appreciating and expressing sex in a sound, functional way than was her grandmother.

This brings me to my second question: Where did Miss America get her narcissistic, unloving view of sex? Why did not her family and others give her a biologically and socially sound conception of sex? My suspicion, backed by much clinical observation, is that, just as in the old days, the family and society of today are still pretty much taken in by the ancient myths and are still feebly capable of giving children rational, humanly understanding support in the realm of sex development.

I would not wish to imply that there has been no progress in this century. But I suggest that much of the so-called progress is in the empty, unloving directions of glamour sex, thrill sex, and pornography rather than coming more in tune with affectionate human relatedness or operating as the magnificent creative and social force which I believe it should be.

I am much disturbed by the role of television and all forms of commercial advertising in cementing the false image of female sexuality which I have ascribed to Miss America. Also I am distressed by the fact that television and Madison Avenue advertising are peculiarly dominated by the voices of censors who can not tolerate sex as a warm, functional human reality. To put it bluntly, a glamorized image of the Virgin Mary is still being held before our children.

Here I shall return to the question "Just how important is orgastic enjoyment in the personal and marital life of a woman?" Judging from the testimony of the relatively few women of excellent orgastic capacity with whom I have explored this critically and carefully I surmise that it is of overwhelming importance if a woman is to know the fullness of life and the peculiar joys and satisfactions that are experienced in affectionately sharing her erotic emotions with a man of like capacity. I am not denying that a woman may find a good deal of pleasure and meaning in life without orgastic enjoyment. But I am led to believe that no other experience gives her so much happiness when enjoyed in an affectionate, genuinely mutual relationship.

It seems significant to note that my personal observations are derived from thirty-five years of private practice in the field of marriage and family counseling. Last Spring, upon my retirement from clinical work, I found, in the course of sorting and destroying case records, that there were nearly 9,000 of them, involving almost as large a number of other persons, mostly spouses and children. I have saved for study 1,500 records of cases on which I have extensive information, many with prolonged follow-up ranging from 10 to 35 years.

Throughout this considerable clinical experience, devoted to premarital preparation, marriage counseling, child guidance, and psychotherapy, I have been constantly alert to the significance of female orgasm as a factor relevant both to a woman's personal happiness and the general state of her family life. It is my carefully weighed conclusion that although some women may endure marriage without orgastic satisfaction such a marriage is, at best, of poor quality compared with those in which the wife is erotically alive and regularly reaches orgasm in intercourse with her husband. I am convinced that for a woman to function at her best as either wife or mother she must have the rich emotional experience of guiltless capability to enjoy orgasm in intercourse. However, as a clinician experienced in our culture, I wish emphatically to stress that I do not consider it wise for a marriage counselor to set this goal for all clients. Some are incapable of attaining it because of unfavorable early life conditioning while others face the reality of a hopelessly inadequate husband who refuses to seek help or cannot respond to it. Thus if some marriages are to continue (and it may be, for many reasons, necessary that they should) the wise counselor will not always make too much of female orgastic attainment. Nevertheless I feel deeply certain that a marriage of high quality and enduring satisfaction is not possible without orgastic response on the part of the wife.

Some clinical highlights bearing upon this come to mind. I think of the countless times that women who could not reach orgasm have sought my help, desperate and fed-up over pretending a good erotic relationship with the husband; I recall the large number of women with impotent husbands who have achieved satisfaction in extramarital relations and the transforming happiness (as well as conflict) it has brought them; and I am impressed by the capability of sexually responsive women to give their children a superior kind of support and guidance in all that relates to sexual development. The latter observation stems from much long-term observation of families, particularly the many instances in which I have given premarital preparation to the mother and years later to her daughter also.

I find something deeply significant in the fact that during all of my clinical experience I encountered only two instances in which a woman who regularly achieved orgasm with her husband came to me contemplating divorce. In each case there was a staggering discrepancy in the cultural backgrounds of the spouses and the husband was unable to provide enough financial security to undertake the responsibility of children. When divorce was finally decided upon, in each of these marriages the spouses wept bitterly and parted with reluctance. I am glad to report that it was not long before each entered a new and more suitable marriage. Against these two cases I have seen many hundreds of marriages break up in the face of poor sex response by the wife, even though in most instances the cultural backgrounds of the spouses were reasonably compatible.

In order to be sure of what we are talking about it seems essential to offer definitions of both adequate and inadequate orgastic response. I choose to define adequate female orgasm as regular or frequent attainment, during intravaginal intercourse, of a high degree of erotic excitement culminating in a spasmodic pelvic and generalized reaction attended by intense sensation of pleasure and followed by feelings of fulfillment and a state of relaxation.

I exclude from my definition of satisfactory orgasm that which can be attained only by means of manual or oral stimulation of the clitoris or other parts of the body. I flatly reject the widely known dictum of my esteemed colleague and friend, the late Dr. Robert L. Dickinson, that "orgasm is orgasm, however won." I have encountered convincing evidence that female orgastic experience is fully satisfactory only when there is enthusiastic, unrestrained acceptance of intravaginal intercourse. Even then it may not be satisfactory if accompanied by a compulsion to draw upon morbid fantasies.

The common clinical forms of inadequate female response may be summarized and defined as follows.

1. Fearful early marriage response based upon ignorance and inexperience and sometimes coupled with actual physical pain.

2. Chronic aversion to any kind of genital stimulation.

3. Passive acceptance of intercourse without erotic arousal or with insufficient arousal to reach orgasm.

4. Compulsive preference for various kinds of clitoral or breast stimulation, linked with rejection of intravaginal participation.

5. Ability to reach orgasm in intercourse only through mental detachment from the partner and substitution of morbid fantasies, usually pornographic and sado-masochistic in nature.

6. Mention must be made of inadequate female response due directly to chronic inadequacy in the male.

In addition to my attempt at defining adequate orgastic response I would like to add something about degrees of inadequacy. I suggest the following gradations.

1. The situation where the wife has a generally good relationship with the husband and experiences some erotic arousal but can not gain orgasm during intercourse. This is probably the complaint most often heard. I have observed that in cases of this kind, especially when seen early in marriage, the difficulty tends to disappear spontaneously with continued marital experience. However, improvement may usually be hastened by counseling and reassurance, involving both husband and wife. This is the mildest form of our problem.

2. The frequently seen cases in which the wife has orgastic response on some occasions but where the husband's sex need is much more active than hers, resulting in a degree of sexual incompatibility that induces mutual hostility. Here is a situation that often lends itself to successful counseling, employing techniques of education, reeducation, mutual discussion and sensible compromise.

3. The case where intercourse is attended by little or no erotic arousal and the general personal adjustment with the husband is poor. Usually such a woman is unconsciously rejecting a sound female role and the problem is a grave one, unlikely to respond to the counseling approach. Deep-level psychotherapy is indicated as soon as a firm diagnostic opinion can be formed. The prognosis is variable. Sometimes excellent results are attained but often a patch-work of improvement is the best that can be done. In some of these cases, with more severe personality disturbance, both counseling and psychotherapy may fail or achieve meagerly limited success.

4. A situation, either with or without erotic response, in which there is chaotic personality disturbance, as in severe obsessive-compulsive neurosis, prepsychotic states, chronic alcoholism, and psychosis. Some of these cases are readily identifiable while others must be observed for some time before a diagnosis can be made. Counseling is quite ineffective. Psychiatric referral is generally advisable. These women have suffered the severest kinds of early traumata in both basic human relatedness and sex related-

ness. The female role is either rejected or accepted only in a false, unrealistic, unworkable form. Even under the best of contemporary psychotherapy it is often difficult to correct the major pathology fully. Notwithstanding, it is a rare case in which some stabilization can not be achieved if the therapist is geared to the realities of the situation and can make appropriate compromise with his preferred goals. I have treated a few persons of each sex, psychotically disturbed, who have learned to enjoy sex relations under limited circumstances but have come to recognize and accept it that they were not stable enough to handle the responsibilities of marriage and parenthood.

Those whose training is largely in counseling and limited in regard to psychotherapy are likely, when dealing with the more complicated types of inadequate female sex response, to consider referring the client to a psychotherapist, perhaps a psychiatrist. Judgment about this must derive from training and experience and take into account the referral resources that are available. If such a referral is to be made I caution against overselling to the client the results to be expected. It is best to make a modest, guarded estimate about the probable benefits of deep-level psychotherapy. Often the client solicits extravagant reassurances of magical results but it is in the interest of all concerned to give a sober, factual appraisal of what lies ahead.

It is prudent for nonmedical counselors, when confronted by a problem of inadequate female sex response, to require a gynecological consultation or to get an opinion from a physician who has already given the client a pelvic examination. This is a routine step that protects the interests of both client and counselor. In a vast majority of cases nothing will be found that is relevant to the sex response problem but certainly there are anatomical or disease conditions that might account for all the difficulty or contribute heavily to it. Obviously there are situations in which failure to insist upon a pelvic examination could result in a suit for malpractice.

Now I wish to take a close look at the proposition "Which comes first, good sex response or a good generally affectionate relationship?" Much as I value the experience of good sex, I hold that the mutually trusting, affectionate relationship comes first and that without it sex is reduced to an unsatisfactory caricature.

The strength of my feeling about this has grown with the years of personal and clinical experience. As I have dealt with people in great sexual difficulties: the neurotic, the compulsive sex deviant, the juvenile delinquent, the criminal, and the psychotic I have been impressed by the failure of all of them to achieve a basis for trusting, affectionate human relatedness in early life. Also for most of them their early sex interests were associated with their worst experiences of rejection and guilt. Thus I am persuaded that first there must be an adequate degree of trusting, affectionately toned human relatedness and that erotic relatedness must be successfully superimposed upon this without creation of serious emotional trauma.

This concept has support in the work of Harry Harlow and associates on affectional responses and sex behavior of our cousin, the rhesus monkey. In essence Harlow's work demonstrates that unless the young monkey is able, at a critical early age, to experience affectionate relatedness to others of his kind he will grow up incapable of normal social adjustment, including incapability to follow an adequate pattern of sex interest and behavior.

The plight of many young human beings is worse than that of Harlow's deprived monkeys for they suffer not only affectional deprivation but are also subjected to a barrage of terrifying interpretations regarding any display of erotic emotion. Small wonder that they seek refuge in the phony world of romantic glamour sex or its opposite number, the world of pornography and sado-masochism. Here appears to be the genesis of schizophrenic process: a deep defect in trusting human relatedness coupled with desperate grasping at weird ideals that can never integrate with basic emotional needs. Under such circumstances the best adjustment that can be hoped for is a kind of anxious pseudo-mutuality that dooms any human being to failure as a spouse and as a parent. Such a person, as a parent, will try desperately to administer his false values to his child but the harder he tries the more confused and unloving the child becomes, even though on the surface a deceptive semblance of stability is presented to the world.

As I see it, we are reaching a point in our cultural evolution where we are rapidly gaining insight into the morbidities that afflict our emotional lives and which are manifested as defects in both general human relatedness and sex relatedness in particular. I believe, however, that some of us are groping in the right direction. I believe, too, that as we are able to discard our traditional irrationalities more and more of us will do better and better at understanding the inescapable emotional needs of children and will meet them with increasing affection and greater skill. It is only through such a process of slow cultural evolution that I am able to visualize substantial solution of the plague of inadequate sex response in both sexes.

Meanwhile, as counselors and therapists, we are confronted with the daily problem of what to do about the complaints of female unresponsiveness that are pouring in in increasing volume. I suggest that the first thing a counselor should do is to feel and to display genuine concern and not to brush the problem aside or minimize it unduly, which some have a tendency to do. Next, in taking a comprehensive life history of the client, sexual aspects should be explored as completely as the sensibilities of the client will permit at the time. If possible, the husband should be interviewed in the same thorough manner, with equal attention to sex attitudes and behavior. Out of these interviews relatively simple and successful remedial measures may emerge. In other instances it may seem best to do some tentative experimenting through educational and conjoint interview techniques.

I trust that we shall never overlook how very much the sex response of one spouse is likely to be affected by that of the other. Since the heterosexual relationship involves two people any examination of their sex difficulties must take each into account in a deeply inquiring and emphatic way. If there is to be understanding and satisfaction between men and women concerning sex it can be achieved only through mutual concern and respect.

CHAPTER 37

Diagnostic Pitfalls Encountered by the Gynecologist

Alfred Stern

Physician and counselor are building a great part of their diagnoses on the client's story. They are often misled. Certain phenomena of the disease itself and some actions by the patient, together with his selective perception and presentation, combine often to disguise the problem. Camouflage is so much a part of the fabric of many a medical and social illness, that distinct patterns of its working can be identified. The field of gynecology gives ample opportunity to do so. A demonstration of typical challenges to gynecological history-taking may be of interest to the counselor too.

Distorting twists in the appearance of the case can result from the patient's: (*a*) psychosomatic productions, (*b*) ambivalent sabotage, (*c*) manipulation of the therapist, (*d*) selective emphasis, or (*e*) semantic haziness.

PSYCHOSOMATIC PRODUCTIONS

False pregnancy, "pseudo cyesis" or "grossesse nerveuse" is a common occurrence in gynecological practice. The patient misses her period, her abdomen feels heavy, her breasts become larger, she is nauseated, she notices even fetal movements. No negative examination will stand against the impact of her own observation, no negative pregnancy test will shake her conviction. Some cases have been carried through the extreme of nine months' duration, exploding on the 280th day with "labor pains" and the production of the patient's first period again instead of the baby for which everything was stubbornly prepared. It is to be noticed that these signs and symptoms are true: measurements have been increasing without the patient's doing anything about it; the periods really have been absent due to cessation of ovulation. Such tangible functional and material changes occur in women who are overly involved in the desire to become or not to become pregnant. Wish and fear, separately or combined, set in motion actions which result in somatic effects.

Spasms at intercourse ("vaginism") or prohibitive dryness are bodily disturbances which interfere with copulation. They are, however, misunderstood when they are regarded as the *cause* of the dysfunction instead of as *means* of dysfunction. They can be overcome with finality only when the overt or hidden wish for dysfunction is diagnostically and therapeutically attended to. Local treatment of the vaginal cramp or the introital dryness gives relief, but it will not cure the complex disturbance of which the bodily symptoms are merely a disguised expression. In a less obvious manner than in gynecology, this mechanism can run its disturbing course in any system (circulatory, digestive, etc.). If the emotional, goal-directed origin is unrecognized, it may become autonomous: the endocrine menstrual regulation may remain upset after the pregnancy has been credibly disproven, or the arrhythmic heartbeats continue long after the conditioning death fear or death wish have faded.

The marriage counselor's client will frequently point out how illness has initiated, aggravated, or perpetuated marital difficulties or, in turn, how marital conflict has produced illness. The counselor's first obligation is to obtain competent medical advice whether the roots of the sickness are plainly somatic or psychosomatic. Secondly, he has to encourage medical treatment regardless of the source of the illness because in either case the sickness is real. In the case of psychosomatic origin, the counselor has a third—the most difficult—task, namely to see to it that the symptomatic treatment is not used by the patient to procrastinate or to avoid the attempt of attacking the underlying problem. Proposals such as "Let the doctor first cure my cramps, and then we shall see how my husband and I straighten out our problems" should meet with the counselor's firm rejection. A patient to whom illness serves as a weapon of defense or aggression will not readily part with his armament. In fact, he cannot unless the source has been cleared. This is the counselor-therapist's great assignment.

AMBIVALENT SABOTAGE

The physician who sees a great number of cases of sterility will find among them a sizeable sector where husband and wife are anatomically and physiologically healthy and their interactions normal. They are ready to submit to any type of operation which might be necessary and to accept any kind of medication which may be indicated to correct their childlessness. Often they have already tried, without success, several procedures meant to eliminate existing or suspected defects. The physician who habitually asks the sterility patient whether she takes vaginal douches, will get an impressively large number of affirmative answers. He will find many women who apply vaginal irrigations regularly once or even more frequently during twenty-four hours. He will be more startled to learn on further questioning that these douches are taken "naturally after intercourse." It is obvious that this practice is apt to defeat the purpose of conception.

This self-evident contradiction between proclaimed goal and adopted procedure ought to have been visible to a thoroughly truthful and sufficiently intelligent adult as most of these women are. However, the illogic did not occur to them. This selective blindness points toward a deeper dichotomy.

The douching habit is more widely spread in our civilization than one would assume. It has been handed down to the young girl by her mother or by nonprofessional or professional advisors, all of them anxious to impress her with the virtues of cleanliness. The more impressed the girl has become with the idea of cleanliness, the more orthodoxly will she, as a woman, adhere to the douching habit. Compulsive reactions lead her to stay away from any "contamination," or if this is not feasible at least to undo them. Truly, she wants a child; but she would like to avoid becoming pregnant. She believes in the emotional, moral, and social values of marital and family life; but she is in some way incapable of giving up her chastity. Puritanism is one of the deep roots of American culture. An extraneous technical development lately has given to this ethical maxim a scientific rationalization: our modern cellophane-wrapped, chlorinated civilization is obsessed with sterility. Under the influence of these religious and secular forces a considerable number of women entertain consciously or subconsciously an emotional barrier against contact and apply primitive contraceptive methods though they would like to have a child. They are not fully aware of their rejection of contact and they do not clearly appreciate the meaning and effect of their douching.

Some patients can easily be made to recognize their ambivalent feelings concerning conception. They will realize and admit them when pointed out. They will make up their minds and either discontinue prevention or stop asking for sterility treatment. Other patients whose resentment of conception is more covered up and of a more neurotic nature will have greater difficulties in changing their attitudes—if they ever succeed at all. Some may make the apparent concession of giving up douching altogether or at least douching after intercourse, but they may show other mechanisms of defense.

The example of ambivalence as an obstacle to conception, often unknown to both patient and doctor, illustrates the active impact of the patient's innermost desire on his condition and curability. It also shows the obscuring effect of ambivalence on history presentation. In the twilight of the client's ambivalence, merely the facts which cause the consultation are presented, but not the essential ones which caused the trouble. To give another illustration: the rational user of the contraceptive pill who, however, deeply yearns for motherhood (or who wants to tie her man to herself through pregnancy) will tell the doctor that she has missed her period; she will ask for correction of her "abnormal endocrine function" or will complain about "the unreliability of the pill," but she will not volunteer the information nor possibly grasp the fact that she has missed taking the contraceptive regularly.

Physicians and counselors have to take into consideration the possibility of their patient's sabotaging actions and sabotaging slips and their tendency to suppress this part of their story.

MANIPULATION OF THE THERAPIST

More misleading than the suppression of facts can be the misdirecting tendency of the patient in the presentation of her case.

With the greater safety of surgery and consequently its wider application, the physician sees increasing numbers of people with a history of previous operations, and with pointed complaints suggesting the performance of another one. An old evil has been eliminated surgically; it is necessary now to remove the present one. The physician who follows this line of thought and action will find little resistance by his patient, he will not be lacking eager cooperation and early praise for his removal of a real imperfection. There were, in fact, bodily changes (not a psychosomatic production); the operation was not without indication. But the surgeon will probably soon be a link merely in a continuous chain of various operators. Patients who carry a multitude of scars of appendectomy, cholecystectomy, ovarian cyst excision, Caesarian section, freeing of adhesions in one combination or another, and who now offer their somewhat afflicted uterus for hysterectomy, should be viewed with greatest care and reserve. An unending history of unending sufferings and failings may well indicate that the patient suffers more from her desire for suffering than from her existing local abnormality.

The counselor's client shows stigmata less visible than surgical scars, but they are recognizable just the same. Masochistic compulsion to self-punishment is often at the root of the patient's ready plunge into the hospital or into analytic counseling and its agonizing introspection. The compulsion will not be cured by yielding to the demand. Retaliative or sadistic infliction of worry and inconvenience and expenses upon the partner is another motive for the all-too-ready submission to perpetuous and ostentatious therapy. The wish to postpone decisions by time-consuming pseudo-action may also induce the patient or counselee to seek multiple and protracted "cures." The therapist becomes easily the unknowing instrument of his client's weakness. He will even be praised for his circumscribed service by the patient who wants more of it, and he will be willingly paid for his limited therapeutic achievements by the client who uses the friendly occasion of a well-terminated procedure to escape further investigation by gracefully ending the relationship. The healer—doctor or counselor—who incorporates these "successes" into his roster of triumphs must arrive at questionable conclusions and statistics.

The therapist has to be critically careful that his actions will not subtly serve the unsound tendencies of his patient who endeavors to misdirect and to squander his skills on nonpertinent issues. The good diagnostician will sense this danger at the first encounter.

SELECTIVE EMPHASIS

The significance of real pathology can be misjudged when seen out of context.

The gynecologist is often approached by patients or by referring general practitioners to remove by surgery a tumor long known to have existed. He does so competently. The patient is thankful and blossoms during the ensuing recovery and vacation period. The findings confirm the previous diagnosis that the condition was old, benign and causing the discomfort which has been now happily eliminated. In some cases however, the patient returns with very similar or almost identical complaints or she complains about the absence of the organ which carried the tumor or she continues with new and different complaints. The short honeymoon of postoperative relief is over. What has gone wrong? Certainly, the existing pathology has been removed; obviously, the purpose of the procedure has *not* been met. The disappointing discovery is that the tumor and the discomfort, though having a potentially causative relationship, were in fact coincidental. This raises the question why a patient who has been consistently aware of an untoward condition suddenly at a certain moment subjects herself to surgery. The answer may be that other conditions prevailed which became so unmanageable as to propel her into a dramatic act that provided for a break in her tense situation. The break could have most likely been provided by lesser means and risks than by irreversible surgery. Instead, a big operation has been put on stage which was understood to be the complete cure. The let-down is inevitable, because with all this effort merely a short-circuit has been mended. The high voltage remains unattended, ready to blow another fuse sooner or later.

The temptation to do an immediate conspicuous professional healing job and the client's desire to have done just that, threatens the counselor in the same measure as the physician. He too has to ask himself over and over again: Is the specific disturbance within the family relationship which is demonstrated at the time of the request for counseling, sufficiently or primarily or at all responsible for the marital discord? A couple who has managed together to squeeze through years of living on a shoe-string does not falter suddenly because of wrong budgeting, even if they claim so. "Operating" on their finances is expedient, but it is short-lived as marital therapy. The husband, who after years of family building, gets suddenly upset by his wife's chronic frigidity, or the wife who comes to the counselor complaining because she has never in her life reached a "real" orgasm, are rarely helped by teaching them various cohabitational techniques in response to their chief complaints. Even the more disconcerting occurrence of a third party within a marriage should be viewed as an *expression* possibly, instead of the *origin*, of trouble. The counselor may do a spectacular but basically insufficient job of removing the object out of the picture. His operative success will be as short-lived as the surgeon's curative result was.

It is human to see the part rather than the whole. The more bewildering and embarrassing a situation is, the more does one seem inclined to simplification. The counselee and the patient, in their job description to the counselor and physician, tend to make their story simple and selective. The therapist is in danger to accept the "evidence."

No case is completely analyzed unless the timing of the patient's quest for counsel is included in the evaluation. By taking a snapshot merely of the present condition, dramatic as it may be, one may stare only at the straw that breaks the camel's back.

SEMANTIC HAZINESS

All of the preceding illustrations have in common that the information given by the patient was, for one reason or the other, incomplete or misleading and the case therefore easily misunderstood. Much harder to identify are the cases in which the conversation between physician and patient remains meaningless though the patient does not feel any compunction to tell her complete story. The fault for these failures of communication lies with the indulgence, by both parties, in operating with nondescriptive words and hazy ideas.

A not uncommon gynecological complaint is the "lack of getting satisfaction out of intercourse" or the "failure to reach the climax." After elimination of all cases with bodily or emotional hindrances, a sizeable group of unafflicted women remains who are perturbed by their lack of achievement. Under these circumstances the examiner will have to question the validity of the complaint. He will often find that these complaints don't stand scrutiny. "Satisfaction" is subjective and not measurable. "Climax," like the summit within a mountain range, can be recognized as the peak only against the patient's whole range of experiences and expectations. As long as she imagines a still higher one, she will not consider it as supreme. The patient's dissatisfaction depicts nothing objective; it reflects her opinion that her actions and reactions are inferior to what they should be. The interrogating physician therefore had better learn something about her measures and standards. They may be rather unrealistic, taken from dreams, movies, magazines, or the boasting tales of her classmates and friends.

People who are unsure of themselves take their values and laws from outside sources. Fearful lest they do things wrong and in need of guidance at every enterprise, they stifle any immediate experience of their own and doubt its validity. Convinced that they have not lived up to the textbook, they then ask the expert for the cure. The worst service one can give to such patients is to correct minor imperfections which are barely related to the issue; this would prove to her that she is really not as she "ought to be." The best service one can give her is to free her thinking from the tyranny of words which are disturbing as long as they are not clarified, and of ideas which will not be her own as long as they have not been challenged.

It is not merely the client who accepts and passes on semantic semblances as currency. While the gynecologist is in danger to handle "climax" and "satisfaction" as measurable indices of health and sickness, the psychological counselor may find himself in a similar situation when he takes up the signal words "love" and "happiness" as used by his client without questioning their meaning. The counselee who complains of the partner's lack of love should better be asked to make quite clear what is meant by "love." The need for clarification may change the picture of the case completely. The client who deplores the absence of happiness should better be asked to specify "happiness." It may turn out to be embarrassingly trivial or foolishly unrealistic. The Declaration of Independence lists among our unalienable rights "the pursuit of happiness," but it refrains wisely from identifying or postulating or promising happiness. The counselor should not name nor define nor promise it either.

Many a doctor and counselor-patient and counselee relationship remains fruitless because ideas and words are used and exchanged without clarification of what their meaning is, whether they have the same meaning for both participants in the conversation, or whether they have any meaning at all.

Many more pitfalls for therapist-client communication can be enumerated. Their various patterns are jointly shaped by the patient's intrinsic make-up and by the external circumstances. Prominent among these and decisive for the handling of the case is the therapist's personality. He has to be ever vigilant not to be prone himself to any of the unconscious manipulations which beset the patient's story. This is his best protection from falling for them and from resenting them. Neither attitude would be helpful.

CHAPTER 38

How to Increase Sexual Enjoyment in Marriage

Albert Ellis

Whenever I think of the ways in which one can increase sexual enjoyment in marriage, several usual and a few unusual methods come to mind. Here, as a sort of reminder list, are some of the usual ways, many of which may be found, in more detail, in some of the standard marriage manuals that I and other authors have written in recent years. A little later on in this article, I shall mention some of the more unusual techniques.

If you would enhance sexual enjoyment in your own marital relationship, you can—

1. Look upon your mate not as a statistic or an average individual, but as a unique person who has his (or her) own personal physical and emotional likes and dislikes.

2. Closely observe your partner's reactions and responses to your sexual overtures; and don't hesitate to ask, in plain damned English, what he (or she) finds most exciting, satisfying, and orgasm-producing.

3. Stop expecting your mate to be spontaneously aroused on many occasions, particularly after you have been married for a long period of time. As a husband, be prepared to woo your wife actively in lots of instances, before she becomes intensely interested in sex; and, as a wife, don't be surprised if your husband frequently has to be actively seduced and physically handled before he really takes fire.

4. Experiment! Try all kinds of positions, pathways, and portals that you think, in your wildest imagination, might prove to be enjoyable to you and your spouse. And try new methods several times, in an unprejudiced manner, before you conclude that they are not your cup of sex.

5. Be considerate and loving. Be kind to your mate nonsexually during the day if you expect him or her to be in the mood to have great sex with you at night. Go out of your way, coitally or noncoitally, to see that he or she is fully aroused and satisfied before you finish having sex.

6. Try innovation and novelty. Having intercourse in one particular manner that both of you maximally enjoy is fine; but most sex partners also want some amount of variety from time to time: such as having sex in new ways and under somewhat unusual conditions (such as on the living room floor or on a deserted beach).

7. Be informed. Sex relations do not just come naturally, but also have to be learned. Find out, from books, from talks with friends, from experience with other partners before marriage, and from other sources, what are the likely sources of sex satisfaction for you and your mate, and discover which of the ideas you thereby gather really work for the both of you.

8. If necessary, use suitable aids to arousal and fulfillment. If you or your spouse have any difficulty becoming excited or reaching climax, don't hesitate to try sexually stimulating writings, photographic material, or recordings; orgasm-retarding devices, such as nupercaine ointment or condoms; electric vibrators; lubricating jelly; sexually arousing clothing; or various other devices which work well, in your individual cases, to speed up or slow down orgasm.

9. Try, at times, multiple sex stimulation. As a husband, you can stimulate your wife's clitoral region at the same time you are having intercourse with her; as a wife, you can kiss your husband passionately on the lips while you are massaging his penis.

10. Get rid of all ideas that certain kinds of sex acts between spouses are evil or perverted. Open-mindedly try all kinds of oral, anal, caressive, and other noncoital activities that you and your mate happen to enjoy, as long as they are physically harmless; and do not hesitate to continue some of these acts up to and including orgasm, if that is what both of you prefer.

The unprejudiced and experimental use of the foregoing ideas is now quite common today and has unquestionably enhanced the sex lives of innumerable couples. A few less usual methods which you may also try are as follows:

1. Accept the fact that sex pleasure often requires considerable work. This is not so strange as it may at first sound: since pleasure and competence at innumerable other sports—such as golf and tennis—also require much work and practice. Anyway, sex enjoyment with your mate will often be considerably increased if you persistently *work* at thinking up new delightful ideas, trying procedures that you never dared to try previously, getting rid of your sexual hangups, and persisting at certain acts and positions until your movements become semiautomatic and awkwardness is replaced by smooth performance.

2. Force yourself at times to have sex with your spouse, even when you seem to be totally indifferent or even averse to having it. Innumerable human acts—including eating, walking, and writing a story or essay— appear to be positively loathesome when we think about doing them. But when we force ourselves to eat, to go for a walk, or to sit down at the typewriter and write, we frequently become intensely involved in what we are doing, and after perhaps a few minutes of indifferent, or aversive efforts, throw ourselves, on some occasions, into the "undesired" activity; and you will often be surprised how, once started, it catches on, and you sometimes end up by having one of the greatest times you ever had in bed.

3. Think! Sex arousal and satisfaction is hardly only a matter of proper physical stimulation and readiness. It is largely mediated by the

cerebral cortex, by focused thinking on specifically "sexy" things. If, therefore, you are having trouble getting aroused or coming to climax, think as hard as you can of the kind of things that you personally find exciting: of the curve of your mate's breasts, for example, or the softness of her thighs, or the way she firmly clasps your back at the height of her passion. If you find that thinking of your partner is not in itself sufficiently arousing, then you can think of anything else that you do find stimulating: of sexual or nonsexual fantasies that enkindle your desires. If your mate is amenable, you can sometimes even openly discuss your fantasies with him or her, and engage in them mutually. But if this is not feasible, you can always think whatever you wish to think in your own mind—as long as you thereby do not withdraw entirely into yourself, and pull yourself away from relating to your spouse in the process.

4. Make a real effort to enjoy sex to the utmost. Intense enjoyment is largely a matter of willful focusing. You can go to a concert or a play and let yourself be distracted by thoughts of business, what your children are doing, or almost anything else, and you will hardly enjoy the music or the acting very much. But if you make an effort to focus on the sounds and the action on stage, and meaningfully throw your thoughts, senses, and feelings into them, you will be much more likely to enjoy the performance to the hilt. So, again, with sex. If you deliberately concentrate on heightening your sensations and feelings while you are going through love play, coitus, and after-play with your mate, you will usually be able to find pleasures that you were hardly aware existed. Rather than just *letting* sex joy occur, you can often *make* it occur—if you really try to feel it and enhance it.

5. Dare to be selfish about your sexual enjoyment. Be, as previously noted in this article, duly considerate of your mate, and do your best to see that he or she gets full satisfaction. But at the same time make sure that you do your very best to have a ball yourself. For although your spouse may be very willing to help you enjoy yourself sexually, only you can determine exactly what is most satisfying to you and how you can do it with her. Consequently, you'd better self-interestedly keep asking yourself, "What do *I* really want sexually, and how can I best obtain it?" If, for example, you find after considerable experience with your mate that coming to orgasm by noncoital methods is usually more satisfying to you than achieving climax through intercourse, honestly and fully acknowledge that fact to yourself—and then unashamedly communicate it to him or her. Even if you also find that your mate prefers intercourse, you can still insist that in many or most cases, you be satisfied in the way that you want. Then, either before or after you achieve orgasm in your preferred manner, you can do your best to satisfy your spouse during coitus. Thus, you could, if you are a male, have intercourse with your wife, bring her to orgasm in that manner while holding off your own climax, and then induce her to give you your orgasm by some other noncoital means. And if you are a female, you could also first satisfy your husband with intercourse and then have him satisfy you noncoitally. In any event, don't *only* see that your mate is fully gratified while rarely or never inducing him or

her to engage in the type of sex that you really want. Be largely true to yourself—and then you will normally be much more willing and eager to cooperate fully in pleasing your mate as well. Conversely, if you rarely get what you most desire in your conjugal relations, you will tend to become hostile toward your mate, sexually turned off, and much less cooperative.

By following the foregoing uncommon rules of marital sex, as well as by seriously considering the more common ones listed at the beginning of this article, you and your spouse may not achieve the greatest connubial pleasure ever attained in human history, but you will most probably considerably increase your sexual enjoyment.

Professional Issues and Ethics in Marriage Counseling

One of the principal reasons which makes the eradication of quackery forever impossible is to be found in the fact which finds expression in the proverb "Stupidity is a hardy perennial."

WILHELM EBSTEIN

In the field of marriage counseling there are many professional issues and ethical problems which deserve underscoring and discussion, if professionally qualified marriage counselors are to supplant "quacks" in the field. These issues must be explicitly dealt with and clarified for the sake of the profession and the public who uses these professional services.

Professional marriage counseling has finally "come of age," as it were. The American Association of Marriage Counselors was founded in 1942, so the profession might be said to be, in this sense, over twenty-five years old. In order to gain some historical perspective on this growing profession, Emily Mudd has presented in Chapter 39 a brief history of the first twenty-five years of the national organization.

In Chapter 40 Richard K. Kerckhoff discusses the profession of marriage counseling as viewed by members of four allied professions: clergymen, physicians, social workers, and attorneys. In this study in the sociology of occupations, Dr. Kerckhoff deals with several related questions: What do members of these professions think about marriage counseling? What relationship do they see between marriage counseling and their own professions? In what ways do they react as members of interest groups? One finding was that members of each of these professions chose their own profession as best equipped to do marriage counseling.

The American Association of Marriage Counselors' Code of Ethics is presented in Chapter 41. Any profession needs to have an explicit code of ethics, and both members of the profession and the public need to be aware that such a code exists. It states the goals—the ideals—and the limits of the profession.

In Chapter 42, Ben N. Ard, Jr. and Constance C. Ard discuss laws regarding marriage counseling in several states. A comparison of these state laws with the ideals of the profession, as stated in the previous chapter, is well worth study.

Charles Dickerson, coordinator of the Marriage Counseling Section, Professional and Vocational Standards, State of California, raises in Chapter 43 the basic question: are marriage counselor laws adequate? He discusses the protection of the public, where we stand at this time, complaints, and suggestions for changes in the law.

Finally, in Chapter 44, the membership categories in the American Association of Marriage Counselors are spelled out in detail so that counselors considering joining this organization will know its standards.

CHAPTER 39

AAMC: The First Twenty-five Years, 1942–1967

Emily H. Mudd

This short summary will describe the origin, growth, and functioning over a twenty-five year period of a relatively new national, clinically-oriented organization—The American Association of Marriage Counselors. The purpose of the Association is to foster the exchange of pertinent information, and promote and maintain standards at a professional level in a new field of clinical specialization. Its special focus is upon the interpersonal relationships between men and women, and how these may be constructive, mutually supportive, and a source of strength to the family group. This approach is useful within the practice of the recognized "helping" professions: medicine, psychology, social work, law, the ministry, and teaching.

Sources of information consist of the written records of committee and annual meetings, correspondence, and the recorded recollections of the charter members. Many of these documents were utilized in the statement entitled "The American Association of Marriage Counselors," prepared in 1957 by Lester Dearborn and others, which serves as an appendix to the volume *Marriage Counseling, A Casebook* (Association Press, 1958). These materials, together with subsequent annual reports and documents prepared by Dr. and Mrs. David Mace, executive directors of the association during the years 1960–67, have provided the base on which this survey rests.

The experience of studying this material quickened the writer's appreciation of the gap between the written reports, calmly recording what is now a *fait accompli*, and the emotionally laden interchanges so familiar to all A.A.M.C. members that often accompanied its evolution. But after all, what other kind of interchange could realistically be expected of strong-minded individualists, in an interdisciplinary association dedicated to new and pioneering approaches to old problems?

The reader unfamiliar with this story cannot hope to catch these subtle nuances. But for those who have been part of the story's unfolding,

Reprinted with permission of the author and the publisher from *American Association of Marriage Counselors: The First 25 Years*. Dallas: American Association of Marriage Counselors, 1967.

as for the writer, memories will be reactivated and the voices of friends and associates, audible now only to the inner ear, will restore the rich overtones and undertones, rounding out the inevitable shortcomings of this necessarily brief factual record.

MATTERS OF FACT—THE WAY AND THE HOW

The American Association of Marriage Counselors developed out of the confluence of at least two streams of activity and interest.

One was a committee organized by Dr. Robert L. Dickinson on "Socio-Sexual Relations of Men and Women," which met irregularly in New York City to exchange data and information. It had a strong core of medical members but included others, such as Mrs. Marion Bassett, who was a particularly active member of it.

Concurrently with the exploration of this group, some members of the Groves Conference (originated by Dr. Ernest Groves) were also moving toward action. As early as 1934 and again in 1939, Mr. Lester Dearborn had discussed with Mrs. Stuart (now Dr. Emily) Mudd and Dr. Abraham Stone the formation of a group "for the purpose of establishing standards, exchanging information, and helping in the development of interest in marriage counseling." In 1939, as a step in this direction, Dr. Groves appointed a Committee on the Protection of Professional Standards.

Dr. Robert W. Laidlaw and Mr. Dearborn, members of both groups, invited the following persons to meet with them in New York on June 20, 1942: Dr. Robert L. Dickinson, Dr. and Mrs. Ernest R. Groves, Mrs. Stuart Mudd, Dr. Valeria Parker, and Dr. Abraham Stone. A second meeting was held with a small, carefully expanded invitation list in October of that year. On April 30, 1943, the first clinical session of the group took place.

For two years, up to the spring of 1945, Mr. Lester Dearborn chaired the group. In April, 1945, the following officers were elected: president, Dr. Ernest Groves; first vice-president, Mr. Lester Dearborn; second vice-president, Mrs. Stuart Mudd; secretary-treasurer, Dr. Robert W. Laidlaw.

It is worth noting that out of this small group of professional persons, who had become so deeply interested in the problems of sex and marriage, no less than fifty percent came primarily from the medical specialties, while the rest represented such fields as social work, psychology, and sociology. The group was at first informally organized, its purposes being almost exclusively to exchange clinical experiences, to aid in the development of counseling techniques, and to study the results of their use.

By 1943 the group had become more organized, aware of the need to define membership requirements more closely and to produce a formal statement of purpose. Of particular importance to the thirty-one dues-paying members in 1944 was the sense of mutual support and challenge gained through their shared professional interest. The association was formally incorporated in 1947.

Those who have served as presidents of the association have been, in order: Dr. Ernest R. Groves (from November, 1945), Dr. S. Bernard Wortis (November, 1946), Dr. Abraham Stone (November, 1947), Dr. Robert Laidlaw (May, 1950), Dr. Emily Mudd (May, 1952), Dr. Lewis Sharp (April, 1954), Mr. Lester Dearborn (May, 1956), Dr. Lawrence Crawley (May, 1958), Dr. Robert Harper (May, 1960), Dr. Sophia Kleegman (acting president from January, 1962), Dr. Aaron Rutledge (May, 1962), Mrs. Ethel Nash (October, 1965), Dr. Gerald Leslie (November, 1966), Dr. James Peterson (October, 1967), and Dr. Gerhard Neubeck (1968).

PHASES OF DEVELOPMENT

History is made by plans which are first projected, then carried into effect. But these plans may be accomplished, or frustrated, by the impact and impetus of divergent views and experience, emerging from the biases of individual attitudes and feelings—the unpredictable variations of human personality. Plans are also greatly conditioned by the hard-core reality of available financial resources—a factor which inevitably sets the stage upon which creative and basic pioneer work plays out its richly divergent roles.

A careful review of this twenty-five year period suggests to the writer five major phases in the development and activities of the association. These may be described as: the Beginning Years, 1942–47; the Golden Years, 1948–55; the Years of Anxiety, 1956–60; the Years of Consolidation, 1960–63; the Years of National Expansion, 1963–67.

The Beginning Years, 1942–47

According to a statement by its formally elected secretary and later president, Robert W. Laidlaw, M.D., "The American Association of Marriage Counselors is a professional organization which concentrates its work specifically on marriage counseling. It has this stated purpose in the by-laws: to establish and maintain professional standards in marriage counseling. This purpose shall be furthered by meetings, clinical sessions, publications, and research. Membership in it is open to those who meet its detailed requirements for clinicians in the field or for affiliates whose work in this or related fields is outstanding, and for associates whose background, training, and beginning practice are sufficiently advanced to enable them to gain professionally by meeting with the more experienced counselors." Under the influence of the second president, Dr. Samuel Wortis, in 1947, the association first discussed certification, courses on marriage education, bibliotherapy, and even mass education. Financially, those were carefree days. There was a budget of $1,427.00 and a balance at year's end of $30.00!

The Golden Years, 1948–55

The second phase was ushered in by the leadership of Dr. Abraham Stone, president, and Dr. Robert Laidlaw, secretary. As a team they exhibited enthusiasm, mutual respect, and dedication. They believed that marriage counseling was important to the healthy development of our society and that dignified, intelligent means would be found for its successful launching.

The association's announced concern for establishing and maintaining professional standards was implemented by two special projects during this period. In 1948, together with the marriage counseling section of the National Council on Family Relations, the A.A.M.C. released a joint statement of standards for acceptable and recognized marriage counselors. These were presented in terms of (1) academic training, (2) professional experience and qualifications, (3) personal qualifications.

Later, in 1954, at its annual meeting in Philadelphia, the association formally accepted the report of the Committee on Criteria for Marriage Counseling Centers. This report made specific recommendations for minimum standards to apply to organizations which, either exclusively or as a specialized part of their total service, offered marriage counseling. The recommendations dealt with matters relating to organization and structure, qualifications of professional staff, provision for staff case-conferences, supervision, consultation, and referral. They also dealt with the question of confidentiality of records, and with that of fees. An appropriate committee was appointed to explore ways and means of implementing these recommendations.

Earlier, in 1949, a Legal Committee had been appointed and had cooperated with a committee from the NCFR to explore possibilities of licensing counselors and marriage counseling clinics. Active in this investigation was Mrs. Harriet Pilpel, a distinguished member of the legal profession. Mrs. Pilpel has served continuously since, with enthusiasm and great helpfulness, as legal counsel to the association, which owes a great deal to her keen insight, clarity, and vision.

At this time, too, there was increasing interest in the national aspect of A.A.M.C. responsibility, and a Committee on Regional Groups was established. Meanwhile, an association member, Dr. Janet Nelson, registered for a year of in-service supervised training at the Marriage Council of Philadelphia, and by doing so initiated the concept of specialized advanced training in the field.

With the association's activities thus rapidly multiplying, the officers and Executive Committee could no longer handle the organizational details from their own offices. Part-time help was employed and paid for by generous contributions from individual members. But diminishing resources both of energy and of pocketbooks would undoubtedly have curbed enthusiasm if Dr. Robert Laidlaw had not communicated to a patient some of his own enthusiasm for the work and goals of the A.A.M.C. This kind lady most generously left to the association its first and, to date, its only legacy.

The advent of this sizeable source of income served as a powerful and practical catalyst to action. The beginning groundwork of ideas and possibilities had already been laid. An office and a paid administrative officer were now acquired. Funds were allocated to the making of a systematic survey of the then functioning marriage counseling services. By 1954, as a result of the field trips made by Dr. Janet Nelson, it was possible to obtain an objective picture of the services currently available in the United States in this specialized field and to compare it with the criteria already established and accepted by the association. These investigations laid the groundwork for national expansion and served as a stimulus to local agencies to improve their services. Because of the wide divergences in actual standards, there was no attempt at that time to undertake the accreditation of clinics, although this possibility was explored with related national associations.

As early as 1950, the association had accepted the idea of publishing a casebook, and a contract had been signed with the Association Press by 1952. This project, supported with necessary funds allocated from the treasury, involved the officers, the Casebook Committee, and many of the members in close communication and effort for seven years until the manuscript went to press in 1958 under the title *Marriage Counseling—A Casebook*. A decade later, the volume is still in demand.

During this period the Executive Committee had been meeting regularly, and its members were elected, by design, from different geographic regions. Expenses of travel were available to encourage full attendance without undue personal deprivation. Budgets naturally increased with expanding activity. The legacy, Dr. Laidlaw had declared, "was given to be spent wisely."

The board accepted Dr. Laidlaw's stated philosophy, and during 1952–54 with Emily Mudd, president, and Janet Nelson, secretary, the work of the existing committees was extended and intensified. In addition a Committee on Training was appointed. One of its primary tasks was to seek ways and means to provide in-service supervised training, which was now increasingly in demand by young professional men and women who wished to supplement their basic skills in order to specialize in marriage counseling. The Fellowship Committee, under the able guidance of Evelyn Duvall, and later of Dr. Luther Woodward, drew up criteria, processed applications, and investigated services with good training potential. Twelve or more fellowships were conferred, amounting in all to approximately twelve thousand dollars of A.A.M.C. legacy funds.

It was also during 1952–54 that the A.A.M.C. subsidized a section devoted to articles on marriage counseling, in the journal *Marriage and Family Living*. The subsidy ran to $750.00 per issue, and these articles appeared in some six or seven issues of the journal, until the arrangement unhappily terminated in a disagreement about editorial authority.

A definition of marriage counseling generally acceptable to association members at that time was presented by the Criteria Committee in the 1950's. This may still seem appropriate to many members in 1967. Marriage counseling was considered a specialized field of family counseling, primarily concerned with the interpersonal relations of husband and wife, wherein the clients are aided to reach a self-determined resolution of their problems. A further distinction was made in 1955 by one of the officers (Mudd) who wrote:

"... the focus of the counselor's approach is the relationship between the two people in marriage rather than, as in psychiatric therapy, the reorganization of the personality structure of the individual."

Without attempting to resolve the complicated area of the relationship between psychotherapy and counseling, the association made it clear at that time that psychotherapy and counseling were not considered synonymous. Members of the A.A.M.C. might do psychotherapy—many of them did—but this was not essential to their work in marriage counseling. This activity derived from their own individual basic training and qualifications. The marriage counselor *per se* was not considered to be a psychotherapist. This issue was of special importance in relation to the question of the private practice of non-medical counselors. With these differences in mind, in 1955, the association appointed a Private Practice Committee to study and explore this controversial subject.

A Program and Development Committee, chaired by Dr. Abraham Stone in 1953–54, sought to relate program potential to the association's available financial resources. In 1955 Dr. Lewis Sharp, president, and Dr. Janet Nelson, secretary, encouraged an assortment of existing committees to continue active work, and new committees were added: on grievances, on ways and means, and on fund raising.

The Years of Anxiety, 1956–60

When Mr. Lester Dearborn became president in May of 1956, the work of the association was rapidly expanding. For example, the Committee on Training and Standards had embarked upon a survey of three of the then-existing training centers—those at the Marriage Council of Philadelphia; at the Menninger Foundation in Topeka, Kansas; and at the Merrill-Palmer Institute in Detroit. Data were obtained by means of a prepared questionnaire, administered during an official site visit by Dr. Janet Nelson. After study of the results of this investigation, the training programs at these centers were officially approved.

However, the association was beginning to face problems inevitable to its extended program. The funds provided by the earlier legacy were running out. Financial resources available from dues were quite inadequate to meet the growing demands. Marriage counseling was arousing increasing interest, on the part of both the public and members of the helping professions. The New York office was swamped with requests for counseling help and inquiries of many kinds, and the time of the administrative office was being consumed in meeting these demands. The available resources of the A.A.M.C. were clearly becoming over-extended.

By early 1960 Dr. Lawrence Crawley, who was then president, was faced with a crisis following the resignation of the administrative officer. He appointed a special committee to formulate plans for the future of the A.A.M.C. The approved plan recommended inviting Dr. and Mrs. David Mace, who has successfully built up a national organization in this field in England, to honor the A.A.M.C. by becoming joint executive directors. Their acceptance moved our association from near annihilation to a more optimistic consolidation.

The Years of Consolidation, 1960–63

Dr. Robert Harper assumed the presidency at a time of drastic transition. He strongly supported bold new policies. The New York office was closed, and the Maces transferred the national headquarters of the association to their home community in New Jersey, with a dramatic reduction in costs. An attempt to augment membership by requiring less clinical experience, which had been adopted by constitutional amendment, was terminated. As the years passed, the trend was decisively in the direction of tightening membership standards. Dues were, with the loyal support of the members, substantially increased. A three year grant totaling $24,000.00 was procured from the Pathfinder Fund by an A.A.M.C. board member to supplement the budget, while financial aid for special projects was provided by the Mary Duke Biddle Foundation.

These and other promising developments were achieved with the continued support of Dr. Harper, and later of Dr. Sophia Kleegman, who filled out the unexpired term during which he was unable to continue to serve. A Code of Ethics for Marriage Counselors, initiated earlier by Dr. Maurice Karpf, was at this time developed by Dr. Walter Stokes, and given formal acceptance at the annual business meeting of 1962. A general overhaul of the association's entire administrative structure resulted in the framing of the new constitution and by-laws, which were approved at the annual business meeting of 1963. Both of these documents are printed in the annual directory of members.

The Years of National Expansion, 1963–67

The steady guidance of presidents Aaron Rutledge (1962–65), Mrs. Ethel Nash (1965–66), and Dr. Gerald Leslie (1966–67), and the vitality, imagination, and able organization and leadership of David and Vera Mace, have proved a revitalizing dynamic for the association.

No marriage counseling service *per se* functions under A.A.M.C. auspices, nor does the association perform any certifying procedures. However, a directory of members listed alphabetically and geographically is now published yearly and is available at $2.00 per copy from the headquarters office. A nationwide mail referral service is also operated. The association makes referrals only to its clinical members or to agencies of high repute.

Since its inception, the association has taken consistent interest in the definition and redefinition of membership standards. These have now been firmly established for some years. There are three categories of "clinical" members: *fellow*, *member*, and *associate member*. In addition, there are the categories of *affiliate* and *associate-in-training*.

The composition of the A.A.M.C. membership reflects the interdisciplinary character of marriage counseling. In 1955, an investigation of clinical members indicated that the medical profession was in the majority, representing 31 percent (gynecology, 12 percent; general medicine, 9 percent; psychiatry, 9 percent; urology, 1 percent). In addition, 18 percent were ministers, 16 percent, social workers; 13 percent, psychologists; 11 percent, educators; 11 percent, sociologists. (The indicated profession refers to the academic field in which initial training and advanced degrees were obtained.) However, in 1966 the structure of the clinical membership showed a decisive shift. According to the directory, "in rough percentages psychology claims 26 percent; social work, 25 percent; ministry, 15 percent; education, 8 percent; medicine, 8 percent; sociology, 5 percent; law, 1 percent." The remaining 12 percent could not be identified exclusively with one specific discipline. Some were qualified in as many as three separate fields.

Although in no way offering "accredited" standing, membership in the association is meaningful insofar as it represents a screening in terms of training, experience, and personal qualifications. According to a statement made by Dr. David Mace in July, 1967, ". . . membership of the A.A.M.C. has now come to mean, for all practical purposes, the possession of the only recognized credential in the field of professional marriage counseling, a kind of guarantee of dependable service to the general public." Training and experience initially stem from the original disciplines in which the member is qualified. In addition, there is a common body of knowledge, techniques, and qualifications that cross-cuts the professions involved.

To provide in-service training which supplements existing skills and is focused on marriage counseling is the responsibility of the Committee on Training and Standards, which has continued its work since 1952. There are currently eight training centers in North America which have met the A.A.M.C. standards. Others are likely to emerge in the future.

The association owes a great deal to the strenuous and time-consuming toil of its Admissions Committee, which thoroughly investigates all new applications for the various categories of membership. There has in recent years been encouraging regional development. Some of the now eleven regional associations function with spirit and efficiency, others with less vitality. The newsletters regularly circulated by the executive directors have proved invaluable as a means of communication between members and with outside groups.

Before their retirement as executive directors in October, 1967, David and Vera Mace listed the special needs of the association, in addition to the maintenance of the basic present services, as follows:

1. To develop all possible ways and means of increasing A.A.M.C. membership, without endangering the high standards of clinical competence which have built up respect for our organization.

2. To coordinate more closely the work of our training programs, and to encourage and develop further training programs (the National Institute for Mental Health, which already gives grants to two of the programs, might be persuaded to subsidize others); and to provide all possible means, in the form of workshops and arrangement for approved supervision, to enable professional persons already clinically qualified to get the additional orientation and training needed to give them the specialized competence to meet our membership requirements.

3. To explore fully the promising idea of closer cooperation, and even possible merger, with the Family Therapy movement, and in the process to secure for the A.A.M.C. the professional journal it so badly needs.

4. To explore actively possible sources of financial support which will put the A.A.M.C. operation thoroughly on its feet, and enable the association to do the work and exert the influence that will further its goals at this time of great opportunity.

SUMMARY

In summary we have seen something of the vision that brings a new organization into being. We have surveyed the why and the how of the A.A.M.C. We have followed the excitement of infancy, the joys of childhood, and the struggle of adolescence. We have seen the door opening into adulthood.

What in an overall sense has been accomplished? With no apologies we can claim the advent of a new specialization of use to all the helping professions—medicine, psychiatry, the ministry, teaching, social work, the law, and community mental health. We have united together in membership individuals within these professions who focus a substantial part of their clinical work on the interpersonal relations of marriage.

Minimum standards in professional preparation and practice, necessary to qualify for membership and to protect adequate practice, have been agreed upon and publicized, as have standards for adequately functioning marriage counseling services and for accredited training in this specialization. A few fellowships have been available to approved persons desiring training. Certain training centers have been officially approved, others disapproved, and still others are under investigation. A casebook based on the actual clinical work of association members has been published, and is widely used for teaching. Regional groups representing wide areas of the United States are active in sharing with the national headquarters the continuing process of education of members and would-be members through meetings, conferences, and publications. Consultation is offered to individuals and groups wishing to develop resources in the field. The association has participated actively in assisting states in the difficult task of regulating marriage counseling by encouraging adequately trained marriage counselors and excluding persons practicing in the field who do not meet minimum standards and who are hazards to the public.

And finally, a *full time* paid executive director, Dr. Edward Rydman, has accepted the challenging task of serving this young adult association. This task involves assisting in the continuation of those activities of proved value to the association and of initiating new approaches which, hopefully, will uphold and extend those high professional standards of membership, of office performance, and of community relationships of which the association, as it now reaches the quarter-century mark and looks back, can be justly proud.

REFERENCES

Dearborn, L. The American Association of Marriage Counselors. In *Marriage counseling: A casebook*. New York: Association Press, 1958.

Mace, D. Annual report, Association of Marriage Counselors, 1960 through 1967.

Mudd, E. H. Psychiatry and marital problems. *Eugenics Quarterly*, 1955, 2, 110–117.

CHAPTER 40

The Profession of Marriage Counseling as Viewed by Members of Four Allied Professions

Richard K. Kerckhoff

Within the last twenty years, marriage counseling has been assuming some of the characteristics usually associated with a new profession. Previously, the only marriage counseling done by professional people was that practiced as an unofficial side-line by clergymen, physicians, teachers, attorneys, and others. Since these latter groups, along with social workers, psychologists, and psychiatrists, still give most of the marriage counsel that is given in a professional setting, a question arises about their reaction to the emergence of a specialized profession of marriage counseling. Also, since the new profession of marriage counseling is still not very strongly established as a separate profession, it might be assumed that the reaction of the more established professions, as expressed through their organized "pressure groups," will be an important factor in the future structure, function, and status of the new profession.

That assumption was made in this study. It was hypothesized that there are areas of ignorance and antipathy concerning marriage counseling and the marriage counseling profession among members of four of these allied professions: clergymen, physicians, social workers, and attorneys. An attempt was made to discover what members of these professions think about counseling, what they think it is and should be. What relationship do they see between marriage counseling and their own professions? In what ways do they react like members of interest groups?

The main instruments used in this study to test the hypothesis and answer the questions were personal interviews with professional people in the four chosen occupations and a 77-item questionnaire. Prior to the building of the final questionnaire, hundreds of interviews and open-end statements were gathered and two trial questionnaires were tested. One thousand and ten copies of the final questionnaire were mailed to random samples drawn from membership lists of organized bodies of the four

Reprinted with permission of the author and the publisher from *Marriage and Family Living*, 1953, *15*, 340–344.

professional groups in Detroit, Michigan. When a return of 120 social worker questionnaires and 80 of each of the other three professions had been received, the sampling was "closed" and these 360 questionnaires were analyzed. The statistical analysis was composed of percentages for the various responses and critical ratio analysis to determine the statistical significance of the differences between percentages.

An estimate of the probable differences between those who replied to the questionnaire and those who did not was made, although in this study there was special interest in people who have strong opinions and who might feel like expressing them via the questionnaire. The study includes an analysis of "first wave" and "second wave" questionnaires compared with each other and with replies to a short, three-item questionnaire filled out by persons who refused to fill out the large questionnaire. It was also possible to make a telephone study of thirty attorneys who failed to return any questionnaire and to compare the results of these interviews with the responses made by those attorneys who did return questionnaires. Although differences are found in these various comparisons, they are not clear-cut unidirectional differences. In general, however, they lead one to believe that people who returned the questionnaire differed from people who did not largely because of the *intensity* of their acceptance or rejection of marriage counseling, rather than because they were as a group either more likely to be accepting or more likely to be rejecting.

Although no well-established measuring device could be found with which to compare the questionnaire to test its validity, it was possible to note comparisons on specific areas of the questionnaire with other studies and with the author's professional experience as a marriage counselor as well as with the personal interview results. Some confidence in the validity of the instrument was gained through these "tests." The reliability of the instrument was tested by test-retest, comparison of responses to similar items within the questionnaire, comparison of responses to certain items which appeared on both the final questionnaire and on the earlier questionnaire, and by split-sample tests of responses to specific items on the final questionnaire. In the last-mentioned test both odd and even samples made responses within one standard error of the responses of the total sample; for example, while 45 percent (S. E. of 2.6) of the 360 respondents said they knew where to find a good marriage counselor, 43 percent of the 180 odd-numbered respondents said so and 47 percent of the even-numbered ones agreed.

It was found that a third of the 360 respondents claimed to have made referrals to a marriage counselor in the past; this ranged from 10 percent of the attorneys to almost half of the clergy. About 17 percent claimed to have heard of a national organization of marriage counselors. Almost all of the respondents said that they came into contact with cases of marital difficulties in their professional work, and half the social workers and more than nine-tenths of the three other professional groups claimed to have done some marriage counseling during the past year. Twenty-eight percent, mostly clergymen and social workers, replied that they had had some formal training in marriage counseling; 23 percent considered themselves marriage counselors. Only 16 percent of the questionnaire respondents would say that marriage counseling today is a profession; 42 percent believed it is becoming a profession, and 16 percent said it would be a mistake to professionalize marriage counseling. More than four-fifths of the clergy, social workers, and physicians claimed that marriage counseling today is either "worthwhile" or "very worthwhile," and two-thirds of the attorneys agreed. Nine percent of the total respondents felt that marriage counseling is "of little or no worth," and two percent said it is "harmful or dangerous." Fifty-eight percent said they would refer cases to a marriage counselor if a capable one opened an office nearby. Very few (usually less than 10 percent) of the respondents said marriage counseling is quackery or pseudo-science or strictly "advice to the lovelorn" material for newspapers. The specific objections to counseling were more often based on ignorance that counseling of a professional nature exists or confidence that the respondents themselves could do adequate marriage counseling. The personal interviews also discovered a vague feeling that marriage counseling is too "loose," not organized, not really a profession, and so, not acceptable for referral relations. In items wherein the respondents' conceptions of the relationship between counseling and their own professions were examined, it was definitely found that most opposition to a separate profession of marriage counseling centered in that area where the new profession might compete with, or infringe upon, the established professions' prerogatives. However, very few respondents except some of the lawyers actually claimed marriage counseling is a threat to their profession. When asked which professional group today—including the separate profession of marriage counselors—is best equipped to do marriage counseling, each of the four sub-samples chose its own profession as best equipped. All four groups chose "full-time marriage counselors" as second best, however, and a great deal of interest in, and desire to know more about, this newer professional group was expressed. All of the above ideas about counseling are amplified by various other questionnaire responses and by the personal interview material which is quoted in the study.

To become a professional body, the questionnaire respondents claimed, marriage counselors must do a better public relations job, create better relations with other professional groups, become better organized, establish more rigid professional standards, and license practitioners. They tended to expect future marriage counseling to be practiced both by a separate group of counselors and by members of the "allied" professions. They said that a person who practices marriage counseling should have a great many personal virtues not usually demanded in most occupations; both personality traits and social characteristics such as marital status and religious affiliations were included in their specifications. As for the training of counselors, the respondents almost all agreed that a graduate or professional degree is needed for this work. Psychology, theory and techniques of counseling, social work, sociology, human biology, theology, and medicine were chosen as the most important subject matter fields for the counselor trainee; and again each professional group considered its own academic preparation as most important for marriage counseling.

The respondents tended to choose "mental hygiene" goals as most important for marriage counseling rather than "traditional" goals. Most frequently chosen from a 13-point checklist were: "To help the couples understand and appreciate each other's personality, to safeguard the welfare of children, to help the counselee grow in emotional maturity, to help people enjoy their marriages more, to help the counselee understand himself." The clergy leaned more strongly toward "traditional" goals, such as "to prevent divorces, to impress the counselee with the seriousness of his marriage vows, and to help make marriage the sacred institution it once was." In stating their views on the functions a counselor should and should not perform, the respondents showed considerable agreement with the professional literature on marriage counseling. In general, the social workers were more in agreement with the views of professional counselors as expressed in the literature than were the other three groups. As for the method of counseling, 31 percent of the 360 respondents chose a response which indicated that they favored a "directive" role on the part of the counselor, 20 percent chose a "non-directive" role, and 42 percent chose a middle-of-the-road course; the clergy split almost evenly on the three courses but leaned toward the two extremes, the physicians favored the middle-of-the-road and the directive relationship, especially the latter, and the attorneys were mostly "directive."

In personal interviews, as well as in numerous other questionnaire items not mentioned herein, it was found that the professional groups being tested had many other specifications for the profession of marriage counseling. Defining goals and eliminating publicity-seeking quacks in the field were often suggested by social workers; attorneys most often suggested licensing or other legal controls on the new profession; and the clergy were most interested in the adequacy of the marriage counselor's spiritual or religious views.

In comparing the replies made to the questionnaire by the four professional groups, the conclusion was made that the clergy were the most enthusiastic about marriage counseling but were also most suspicious of the counseling done by persons not closely associated with organized religion; they tended to see counseling as religious work. The Catholic clergy failed to reply to the questionnaire to such an extent that the clergy sample is almost entirely Protestant (the Jewish sample was small to begin with). Of all the clergy, however, the Catholic respondents were most confident that the counseling being done by their church is adequate.

The social workers tended throughout the study to "talk the same language" as that used by marriage counselors. However, few social workers would make referrals to the average marriage counselor who is not himself a social worker or psychiatrist, since most of these social workers expressed a preference for family case workers. Some interesting data were discovered by examining the social worker responses closely enough to compare case workers with group workers, and psychiatric social workers with medical social workers.

The physicians in this study showed some traditional conservatism about the new marriage counseling profession and tended to view marital problems in medical terms. Few of them had any formal training in counseling and almost all of them do counseling in their work. General practitioners were compared with obstetrician-gynecologists in this study.

The attorneys were the most outspoken of the four groups against the new profession of marriage counseling; they, along with the physicians, were least well acquainted with counselors or with where to find a marriage counselor. The attorney sample was analyzed in terms of those who had handled the most divorce cases compared with those who had handled the least, to see if significant differences appeared in their questionnaire responses.

The data were also examined to see what relationship certain views of marriage counseling had with personal characteristics such as age, sex, marital status, length of professional practice, religion, and income. Some interesting differences were noted when these categories were subdivided, but the resulting samples were so small that relatively few statistically significant differences were found.

In conclusion, a good deal of ignorance and some antipathy to the new profession were found among people who are in a good position to know about marriage counseling and to influence its future as a profession. Very little concrete opposition to the newer profession was found, but a large amount of distrust was expressed. The author's general impression is that this distrust, along with the normal vested interests of the older professions, and the present inadequacies in the field of marriage counseling itself, will tend to be a deterrent to the future growth of the profession of marriage counseling.

CHAPTER 41

AAMC: Code of Professional Ethics

This Code was drawn up by a specially-appointed Committee of the A.A.M.C. during 1960–61. It was then studied by the Board of Directors and sent out to the entire clinical membership for further suggestions. After these suggestions had been examined by the Board of Directors the final revision of the code was approved at the Annual Business Meeting on May 19, 1962.

All clinical members of the A.A.M.C.—fellows, members, and associate members—are under obligation to abide by the rules set out in this code.

Section 1. It shall be the duty of each member to safeguard high standards of ethical practice, particularly as defined in the following sections. Should a fellow member appear to violate this code he may be cautioned, through friendly remonstance, or formal complaint against him may be made in accordance with the following procedure:

a. Complaint of unethical practice shall be made in writing to the Standing Committee on Ethics and Professional Practices. A copy of the complaint shall be furnished simultaneously to the person or persons against whom it is directed.

b. The Standing Committee on Ethics and Professional Practices shall decide whether the complaint warrants investigation. If investigation is indicated, the Standing Committee on Ethics shall constitute itself an Investigating Committee and shall include in its membership at least one member of the Board and at least two members from the local area involved. This Investigating Committee shall make one or more local visits of investigation of the complaint. After full investigation the Committee shall report its findings and recommendations to the Board, upon which the Board shall take appropriate action.

c. The defendant shall have free access to all charges and evidence cited against him. He shall have full freedom to defend himself before the Investigating Committee and before the Board, including the right to legal counsel.

d. Recommendations to be made by the committee shall include advice that the charges are unfounded; recommendation of specified admonishment; reprimand; and dismissal from membership.

e. In accepting membership in the Association each member binds

Reprinted with permission of the publisher from the *American Association of Marriage Counselors Directory, 1968–69*. Dallas: American Association of Marriage Counselors, Inc., 1968. Pp. 99–103.

himself to accept the judgment of his fellow members as to standards of professional ethics, subject to the safeguards provided in this section. Acceptance of membership involves explicit agreement to abide by the acts of discipline herein set forth. Should a member be finally expelled from the Association, he shall at once surrender his membership diploma to the Board of Directors. Failure to do so may be countered by such action as legal counsel may recommend.

Section 2. Should a member of this Association be expelled from another professional group for unethical conduct, the Standing Committee on Ethics shall investigate the matter and act in the manner provided in Section 1 respecting charges of unethical conduct.

Section 3. Advertising of professional services is prohibited, except as to simple professional signs and brief telephone listings, devoid of all claims about service, and the indirect advertising involved in professional communications and participation in community projects relating to marriage and family life. In the course of public speaking and writing, care should be exercised to avoid emphasis upon one's personal professional competence.

Section 4. Affiliates and associates-in-training shall not represent themselves as having membership status in the Association.

Section 5. When expressing professional opinions or points of view, no officer or member shall make it appear, directly or indirectly, that he speaks in behalf of the Association or represents its official position, except as authorized by the Board of Directors.

Section 6. The affiliation of members with professional groups, clinics, or agencies operating in the marriage and family life field is encouraged and advised. Similarly, interdisciplinary contact and cooperation are encouraged.

Section 7. The counselor should be cautious in his initial prognosis. He should avoid unwarranted optimism, while offering dignified and reasonable support.

Section 8. Financial arrangements should always be discussed at the start and handled in a business-like manner, including the rendering of periodic statements, unless some other procedure is agreed upon. In establishing fees, the client's ability to pay should be taken into consideration.

Section 9. Receipt or payment of a commission for referral of a client is prohibited. *You've got to be kidding*

Section 10. Referrals generally should be acknowledged. Significant information in aid of the referral process usually should be sought from the referral source.

Section 11. Records indicative of the problems and the scope of service shall be kept for each client and shall be stored in a space assuring security and confidentiality.

Section 12. Except by written permission, all communications from clients shall be treated in complete confidence and never revealed to anyone. When a client is referred to in a professional case report, his identity shall be thoroughly disguised, and the report shall so state.

Section 13. The counselor should always bear in mind that he may meet clients with whose problems he is not fully qualified to deal. In such case he should make appropriate referral.

Section 14. While the marriage counselor will feel satisfaction in the strengthening of a marriage, he should not feel obligated to urge that the married partners continue to live together at all costs. There are situations in which all resources fail and in which continued living together may be severely damaging to one or several persons. In such event it is the duty of the counselor to assess the facts as he sees them. However, the actual decision concerning separation or divorce is a responsibility that must be assumed by the client, and this should be made clear to him. If separation or divorce is decided upon, it is the continuing responsibility of the counselor to give further support and counsel during a period of readjustment, if that appears to be wanted and needed, as it often is.

Section 15. The counselor should recognize that the religious convictions of a client may have powerful emotional significance and should be approached with caution and sensitivity. If there are problems in this area, consideration should be given to the desirability of consultation with a clergyman of the client's faith.

Section 16. Disparagement of a colleague to a client should be avoided; to do otherwise is unprofessional.

Section 17. It is desirable for the counselor to seek opportunities for community leadership and public education in matters relating to marriage and the family and to cooperate with others so engaged.

Section 18. The counselor has an obligation to continue postgraduate education and professional growth in all possible ways, including active participation in the meetings and affairs of the Association.

ADDENDA TO CODE OF PROFESSIONAL ETHICS

One-Counselor Agencies
It shall be unethical for a member to represent to the public that a marriage counseling clinic, agency, or center is being operated if in fact the member is engaged in independent individual practice. Legal incorporation shall not in itself be satisfactory evidence of existence of a *de facto* clinic. There must be actual association of three or more qualified professional persons working together at least half-time as a clinical team at the same location. The advertising of a clinic shall be subject to the same restrictions as apply to individual members.

Telephone Listings

For listing in the yellow pages of the telephone directory: Nothing in the listing should make one individual or firm's listing stand out from other listings in the directory. Bold-face type, or other than ordinary type size, should be avoided. Space should not be enclosed in a lined box nor exceed that needed to contain the information; generally no more than five lines should be used. The listing may consist of the person's name; highest earned degree; A.A.M.C. clinical membership category; state certification, if obtained (e.g., Certified Psychologist); diplomate status, if attained (e.g., Diplomate of the American Board of Examiners in Professional Psychology); address; and telephone number. If a person wishes, he may list an additional address and telephone number, but his name should be listed only once. Office hours (or the statement "by appointment only") may be listed if permitted by the local telephone company. Whereas joint practice is not to be discouraged, a title such as "Family Institute" or "Marriage and Family Relations Clinic" is an acceptable telephone listing only if the joint venture is truly a clinic of three or more professional people. Titles utilizing the name of a city, county, or state imply the group to be a community agency. If such a listing is used, it should be clearly evident in the listing that the clinic or group is a private group and not community sponsored. Three or more A.A.M.C. members in a given community may list themselves together under the A.A.M.C. heading and may use the A.A.M.C. insignia. In this case only, a lined box may be used.

For listing in the white pages of the general telephone directory: Listing may include, in addition to name, address, and telephone number, the words, "Marriage Counselor" or "Marriage and Family Counselor" in small light type, thus:

JONES, JOHN B. MARRIAGE COUNSELOR
500 WEST 38 STREET   462-4537
RES. 111 PARK RD.   462-4828

CHAPTER 42

Laws Regarding Marriage Counseling

Ben N. Ard, Jr., and Constance C. Ard

Despite the fact that marriage counselors have had a national organization (the American Association of Marriage Counselors, Inc.) since 1942, laws in the states were much later in coming. The first state law regulating marriage counselors was passed in California in 1963, and went into effect January 1, 1964.

The California law reads as follows:

MARRIAGE, FAMILY, AND CHILD COUNSELOR LICENSING LAW
(Business and Professions Code Sections 17800 to 17847, inclusive)
ARTICLE 1. REGULATION

Section 17800. After January 1, 1964, no person who engages in the business of marriage, family, or child counseling shall advertise himself as being, or performing the services of, a marriage, family, child, domestic, or marital consultant or adviser, nor in any way use these or similar titles to imply that he performs these services without a license as provided by this chapter. Nothing in this chapter shall be construed to restrict, limit, or withdraw provisions of the Social Work Licensing Law, Medical Practices Act, or Psychology Certification Act.

The provisions of this chapter shall not apply to any priest, rabbi or minister of the gospel of any religious denomination, nor to any person who is licensed to practice medicine or admitted to practice law in this state, nor to any organization which is both a nonprofit and a charitable organization.

Section 17801. A person engages in the business of marriage, family, or child counseling who performs or offers to perform or holds himself out as able to perform such a service.

Section 17802. "Advertise," as used in this chapter, includes but not by way of limitation, the issuance of any card, sign, or device to any person, or the causing, permitting, or allowing of any sign or marking on or in any building or structure, or in any newspaper or magazine or in any directory, with or without any limiting qualification. Signs within church buildings and notices in church bulletins mailed to a congregation shall not be construed as advertising within the meaning of this chapter.

Section 17803. A person desiring to advertise the performance of marriage, family, or child counseling services shall apply to the Director of Professional and Vocational Standards for a license and pay the license fee required by this chapter.

Section 17804. To qualify for a license an applicant shall have all the following qualifications:

(*a*) At least a master's degree in marriage counseling, in social work or in one of the behavioral sciences, including, but not limited to, sociology or psychology, obtained from a college or university accredited by the Western College Association, the Northwest Association of Secondary and Higher Schools, or an essentially equivalent accrediting agency as determined by the department.

(*b*) At least two years' experience, of a character approved by the director, under the direction of a person who holds the degree specified in subdivision (*a*) or at least two years' experience of a type which in the discretion of the director is equivalent to that obtained under the direction of such a person.

Section 17805. The director shall issue an appropriate license within the fields referred to in Section 17801 in such form as the director may deem appropriate to every applicant who qualifies under the chapter.

Section 17806. The director may adopt such rules and regulations as may be necessary to enable him to carry into effect the provisions of this chapter. Such rules and regulations shall be adopted in accordance with Chapter 4.5 (commencing with Section 11371) or Part 1 of Division 3 of Title 2 of the Government Code.

Section 17807. The director may employ whatever additional personnel is necessary to carry out the provisions of this chapter.

Section 17808. The director may grant waivers, biennially, to institutions which are both nonprofitable and charitable and to educational institutions which meet the accrediting requirements contained in Section 17804. Institutions applying for such waivers shall demonstrate (*a*) adequate supervision of nonlicensed counseling personnel, and (*b*) community need or (*c*) a training need.

Section 17809. The director may issue a license to any person who, at the time of application, holds a valid license issued by a board of marriage counselor examiners or corresponding authority of any state, provided, in the opinion of the board, the requirements for such licensure are substantially equivalent of the requirements of this chapter, and upon payment of the fees specified.

Section 17810. An advisory committee to the Director of Professional and Vocational Standards may be created. It shall be named the Advisory Committee on Marriage, Family, and Child Counselors and shall be composed of five members to be appointed by the Governor for terms of four years. No member shall serve more than two consecutive terms. There shall be a public member, a psychologist certified in California, a registered social worker, a minister who meets the requirements of the American Association of Pastoral Counselors, and a sociologist. Excluding the public member, each member of the board shall be licensed as a marriage, family, and child counselor.

ARTICLE 2. DENIAL, SUSPENSION AND REVOCATION

Section 17820. The director may refuse to issue a license, or may suspend or revoke the license of any licensee if he has been guilty of unprofessional conduct which had endangered or is likely to endanger the health, welfare, or safety of the public. Such unprofessional conduct shall include:

(*a*) Conviction of a felony, or of any offense involving moral turpitude, the record of conviction being conclusive evidence thereof.

(*b*) Securing a license by fraud or deceit practiced on the director.

(*c*) Using any narcotic as defined in Division 10 (commencing with Section 1100) of the Health and Safety Code or any hypnotic drug or alcoholic beverage to an extent or in a manner dangerous to himself, or to any other person, or to the public and to an extent that such action impairs his ability to perform his work as a marriage, family, or child counselor with safety to the public.

(*d*) Improper advertising.

(*e*) Violating or conspiring to violate the terms of this chapter.

(*f*) Committing a dishonest or fraudulent act as a marriage, family, or child counselor resulting in substantial injury to another.

Section 17821. In addition to the grounds contained in Section 17820 the director shall revoke the license of any person, other than a physician and surgeon, who uses or offers to use hypnosis or drugs, or a certified psychologist who uses or offers to use hypnosis, in the course of performing marriage, family, or child counseling services.

Section 17822. A plea or verdict of guilty to a charge of a felony or of any offense involving moral turpitude is deemed to be a conviction within the meaning of this article. The director shall order the license suspended or revoked, or shall decline to issue a license, when the time for appeal has elapsed, or the judgment of conviction has been affirmed on appeal or when an order granting probation is made suspending the imposition of sentence.

Section 17823. The proceedings conducted under this article shall be held in accordance with Chapter 5 (commencing with Section 11500) of Part 1 of Division 3 of Title 2 of the Government Code.

The California law also has an Article 3 on penalties and an Article 4 on revenue which are not reprinted here.

This original California law has since been amended or changed to combine two boards previously kept separate, that is, the board of social workers and the board of marriage counselors have been combined into one overall board of social workers and marriage counselors. This would seem to be, in effect, putting marriage counselors under the social workers category. Since psychologists have a separate board, as do many other professions, one would wonder if it would not be better to keep marriage counselors under their own separate board. The overall board would have an over-representation of social workers, it would seem. The board is made up of two members who shall be state-certified social workers, two shall be state-registered social workers, two shall be state-licensed marriage, family, and child counselors, and three shall be public members.

If marriage counselors are to be recognized as a profession, then it would seem they need a separate board, as they had under the original law.

We are indebted to Aaron Rutledge, of the Merrill-Palmer Institute in Detroit, and former President of the American Association of Marriage Counselors, for sending us the new Michigan law on marriage counseling. Dr. Rutledge informs us that a major error occurred as people were drafting the bill (possibly through a typographical error in copying from another document) wherein the words "or marriage or pastoral counseling" were inserted in Section 6(c). It is our understanding that it is the intent of the local professionals in Michigan to get the law amended whereby this phrase will be struck from the law at the earliest opportunity. The educational qualifications would then be: a doctorate (plus experience) or a master's degree in social work (plus experience).

The State of Michigan Act Number 292, Public Acts of 1966, as amended, Act 69, Public Acts of 1967, is known as the "Marriage Counseling Certification Act." Section 6 states, "Any person wishing to apply for certification as a marriage counselor shall meet the following qualifications and submit proof satisfactory to the board that

(a) he is of good moral character.

(b) he is a resident of the state.

(c) he meets the following educational qualifications: a doctorate in psychology, sociology, psychiatry, marriage or pastoral counseling, or another equivalent doctorate together with 5 years' professional experience including 1 year specialization in marriage counseling under the direct supervision of a certified marriage counselor; or a master's degree in social work *or marriage or pastoral counseling** from an institution approved by the board together with 5 years' professional experience."

Section 13 provides that "any communication between the marriage counselor and the person or persons counseled is confidential. Its secrecy shall always be preserved. This privilege is not subject to waiver, except where the counselor is a party defendant to a civil, criminal or disciplinary action arising from such counseling in which case the waiver is limited to that action. Notwithstanding any other law to the contrary, if cases are counseled upon court referral, the marriage counselor may submit to the appropriate court a written evaluation of the prospects or prognosis of a particular marriage without divulging facts or revealing confidential disclosures. Attorneys representing spouses who are the subject of such an evaluation shall have the right to receive a copy of the report."

The state of New Jersey is one of the latest states to have introduced proposed legislation regulating marriage counseling. We are indebted to Thomas McGinnis, Ed.D., president of the New Jersey Association of Marriage Counselors, for sending us a copy of the proposed New Jersey law.

Some aspects of this proposed law deserve comment. It states, "The practice of marriage counseling consists of the application of principles, methods and techniques of counseling and psychotherapy for the purpose of resolving psychological conflict, modifying perception and behavior, altering old attitudes and establishing new ones in the area of marriage and family life." This avoids the old dilemma of whether marriage counseling and psychotherapy are distinct, different practices by including them both under the law.

---

*Italics added for editorial emphasis.

The educational requirements are: at least a master's degree in social work, marriage or pastoral counseling, psychology, sociology of the family, family life education, or another field of study, or some closely allied field to medicine, in which it is established by the applicant's transcripts that an appropriate course of study has been successfully completed; the degree to have been obtained from an accredited institution so recognized at the time of granting of such degrees.

Experience requirements are three years of full-time counseling experience, or its equivalent, of a character approved by the board, two years of which must have been in marriage counseling.

Another section deals with confidentiality and states that any communication between a marriage counselor and the person or persons counseled shall be confidential and its secrecy preserved. This privilege shall not be subject to waiver, except where the marriage counselor is a party defendant to a civil, criminal, or disciplinary action arising from such counseling, in which case the waiver shall be limited to that action.

We are indebted to Esther Oshiver Fisher, a marriage counselor in New York City, for sending us a copy of the new domestic relations law in the state of New York, which sets up a Conciliation Bureau. The provisions of this new law became effective on September 1, 1967. Amendments have been passed which became effective on September 1, 1968.

The law creates and establishes a state conciliation bureau in each judicial district of the Supreme Court. All parties to an action for divorce shall be required to attend at least one conciliation conference, or may, upon good cause shown and in the discretion of the commissioner, secure a certificate of no necessity for a conference and conciliation procedures shall be at an end. The conciliation commissioner (an attorney) may refer the parties to a counselor.

In conducting a conciliation conference, a counselor shall do such acts as he feels necessary to effect a reconciliation of the spouses or an adjustment or settlement of the issues of the matrimonial action.

The whole idea of having conciliation counselors or commissioners meet with couples considering divorce should get a good, extensive trial run in the state of New York. Perhaps we will get some evidence from this experience as to how effective such marriage counseling can be.

CHAPTER 43

Marriage Counselor Laws:
Are They Adequate?

Charles H. Dickinson

To judge the adequacy of our California law, we must first review the reasons why we have such a statute in the first place. Why did the legislature, in 1963, determine that a law was necessary to protect the public?

Unlike many state-licensed or -certified professional or vocational groups, the pressure did not come from those to be licensed, but from the public and the state legislature.

In 1962 members of the state assembly received complaints of unscrupulous practitioners, of outright frauds and irregularities in the ill-defined profession loosely termed "marriage, family, and child counseling." The Assembly Interim Committee on Governmental Efficiency and Economy staged an exhaustive study of the situation. Reputable professional practitioners in this and closely related fields, as well as those about whom complaints had been made, were asked—or subpoenaed—to testify. The hearing in Los Angeles hit the headlines with lurid accounts of some of the practices. The *Saturday Evening Post* ran an eight-page spread on the subject.

A bipartisan bill was introduced by Assemblyman Don Mulford of Alameda County and the chairman of the committee, Assemblyman Lester A. McMillan of Los Angeles. The bill was backed by the reputable practitioners in the state—practically all of whom would have to come under the licensing requirements.

PROTECTION OF THE PUBLIC

Why did this come about? The legislature is interested in protecting the public. This is the basic reason—and should be—for all such laws. How does the marriage, family, and child counselor statute protect the public? (1) By assuring that all who hold the license must meet certain basic minimums in education and experience; (2) by bringing marriage counselors under the professional discipline and legal code of behavior en-

Reprinted with permission of the author and the publisher from *Marriage Counseling Quarterly*, 1968, *3*, 1–5.

forced by state statutes; (3) by providing for a policing machinery to control fraud and malpractice.

There is, however, something more to a state licensing program than establishing standards and qualifying people for a particular license or certificate, more than exercising police powers and correcting or punishing violations of a particular act.

Implicit in each law is protection of the public by encouraging higher standards of individuals in their dealings with the public, recruiting into the professional fields more qualified persons and individuals with more potential, providing the service of informing the public of those certified or licensed, making it easier to obtain names of qualified professional persons.

The licensed person is more likely to be competent because he has completed certain formal education and training, and has had experience. We can also guarantee that he is under some control. He is known to the state. Sooner or later he will run into trouble if he persists in questionable practices or irregular conduct.

Since he is under a professional licensing law, a fair assumption can be made that he will tend to be more concerned with "professional" ethics and with guarding his professional reputation. Just the fact that one is licensed will mean that this is his profession—his life's work. Certainly we can expect exceptions to this—and we have already had them, but we have found the vast majority are conscientiously and sincerely trying to provide the public with a much-needed and competent service.

From the situations that have come to our attention, the public is learning to ask, before undertaking counseling, as to whether or not the practitioner is licensed by the state. This does provide protection. We can say, then, that the licensing act is meeting a real need.

Actually, one of the most important aspects of "protection of the public" has come from the marriage counselors themselves and their organizations as they have grown and become more closely identified with this profession. A feature of the history of the marriage, family, and child counselor licensing program is the fact that the professional associations, particularly the California State Marriage Counseling Association and the older Southern California Association of Marriage Counselors (affiliated with the American Association of Marriage Counselors), as well as the associations of the older concerned groups, such as the National Association of Social Workers, the affiliates of the National Psychological Association, etc. have expressed their interest, concern, and support of a separate marriage, family, and child counselor licensing law. They have been very much concerned with the fact that unqualified persons were doing marriage counseling, in that it has cast a reflection on the entire professional group, whatever the particular type of educational background and training. Numerous expressions have been received from members of related professional associations that they are very much interested in obtaining the marriage counselor license even though it may duplicate their certification from other state regulating bodies.

In general, marriage counselors recognize that they have thus received professional identification, recognition, and status, but they have, along with these, inherited responsibility. They have in a measure the responsibility for policing their own profession. They have a responsibility to attain high standards.

WHERE WE STAND AT THIS TIME

The administration of the law was made the responsibility of the Director of the Department of Professional and Vocational Standards, and the program thus became one of the more than thirty-five boards, bureaus, commissions, and sections of that department. The department provides all necessary administrative services. The marriage counselors have thus become established as one of the family of professions and vocations licensed, certified, or registered by the state. The section is completely self-supporting from the fees of the license holders set up in a special fund, which is used only for the necessary expenses of the program.

At present there are 1,800 licenses in effect. In all, 2,187 applications have been filed, of which 1,945 have been issued.

COMPLAINTS

We have received a number of complaints, but most have been found, upon even a cursory inspection, to have little basis. Some have been explored more fully but have proven, upon inspection, to have little grounds for action. Efforts are always made to remove or ameliorate the cause of the complaint before pressing for more stringent legal action.

Most of the applicants have been clearly eligible. We have had some borderline cases, but these borderline cases have not been the ones which caused the fraudulent situations and the uproar which led to the passage of the bill in the first place. The ones the legislators were worried about were the outright charlatans and frauds who were utterly unqualified and who pretended to be something they were not. Some sported self-awarded degrees, including Ph.D.'s, Doctors of Divinity, and other doctors' degrees, as well as a string of initials of no value and of no meaning, or degrees awarded by fly-by-night, now nonexistent diploma mills. We have come across degrees awarded by highly titled colleges, the diplomas for which were apparently run off in the back rooms of bars. Even some doctors' degrees were awarded to less than high school graduates for the writing of a composition by the individual on his philosophy of life—and, of course, for the payment of a fee.

Although, of course, we have no way of actually assessing how many of these have discontinued their operations, we do know, for instance, of some who have changed to other fields, or have left the state. Investigators from the department have called upon some and found that suspected individuals have suddenly left for parts unknown. We have had cases where the person advertising has completely changed his advertising. He may still imply that he is a doctor of something or other, but he now no longer advertises that he is a "marriage counselor." Now he may be a "personal counselor" or perhaps even a "spiritual counselor." At least he is no longer claiming to be a member of an extremely valuable, honorable, ethical profession.

SUGGESTIONS FOR CHANGES IN THE LAW

As we have proceeded with administration of this program in accordance with the responsibility placed upon the director of our department and his staff, we have encountered certain difficulties which have suggested to us ways in which the law could be improved to make it more effective. Legislative and governmental committees have also made suggestions. In line with our responsibilities we have called these to the attention of the legislature and will do so in the future.

From my experience here are some changes which could be most profitably made in the law to improve its effectiveness:

Definition of practice needed: The statutes should contain a sharper definition, and licensing should be based on what is actually done, rather than the title used. At present, unless the individual presents himself to the public and advertises himself to the public specifically as a marriage counselor, he does not need to come under the licensing act. We recognize that it would be practically impossible to engage in such an endeavor profitably without some form of professional advertising, but a good workable definition in simple, concrete terms is needed.

Removal of, or limitations on, exemptions: A major difficulty seems to be in the weakening effect on the statutes of the section on exemptions (Sec. 17800). Although we had sought to have the exemptions removed so that all practicing marriage counselors would come under the licensing provisions, this was not acceptable to the legislature and the exemptions were reinstated. We had felt that ministers, for instance, would not be advertising in the usual sense of the word and would not be affected. There was objection to this, however, and the very touchy subject of church and state entered here. A difficulty is that there is no definition of what a minister is in the first place. The government has always been extremely leery of any laws which seem to restrict or limit the practice of religion. As a result, self-ordained or disillusioned ministers who have either given up their churches or who have been expelled, have, in some instances, apparently turned to marriage counseling as a livelihood. The absolute nature of this exemption means that completely unqualified, self-ordained ministers can take fees from clients under the pretense that they are assisting them with marital problems. Although lawyers and doctors are also exempted, apparently very few, if any, are engaged in marriage counseling outside of their professional activities.

I would think that either the section providing for the exemptions should be eliminated entirely, or it should be changed to read: "The provisions of this chapter shall not apply to any priest, rabbi, or minister of the gospel of any religious denomination when performing counseling services as part of his pastoral or professional duties in connection with a specific church or synagogue of any religious denomination; nor to any person who is licensed to practice medicine or admitted to practice law in this state when providing help or counseling services as part of his professional practice."

Privileged communication: The suggestion has been made that the statute provide for privileged communication for marriage counselors by adding a paragraph similar to that in the medical and psychologists' acts, which could read perhaps as follows: "For the purpose of this chapter the confidential relations and communications between counselor and client shall be placed upon the same basis as is provided by law between attorney and client and nothing contained in this chapter shall be construed to require any privileged communication to be disclosed."

I agree that this would provide a much-needed protection to the professional counselors and should be proposed to the legislature.

Reasons for denial or suspension: The bill in the 1965 legislature changed the section on denial, suspension, and revocation (section 17820), and in general this was a great improvement. There might be some disagreement with this, but I believe it would meet some of the needs of administering the program if a paragraph were added to read, as a reason for disciplinary action: "Committing an act or acts which demonstrate the individual is not of good moral character."

A paragraph should also be added under this section to provide for action in cases of mental illness. I believe that it should read somewhat as follows: "The director may suspend the license of any licensee upon a determination by the director, based upon competent authority, that such licensee is incapable of performing his duties as a marriage, family, or child counselor because of mental illness. The director shall not restore such license to good standing until he is satisfied with due regard for the public interest that such person's license may be safely restored."

CHAPTER 44

Membership Categories in the American Association of Marriage Counselors

Edward J. Rydman [*]

The classes of A.A.M.C. membership and the requirements are as follows:

Fellow. A minimum of five years in good standing as a *member* of the association and significant contributions to the field of marriage counseling.

Member. Recognized professional training for, and at least five years' experience in, clinical marriage counseling, in accordance with accepted ethical standards.

Associate Member. Recognized professional training for, and at least two years of experience in, clinical marriage counseling, in accordance with accepted ethical standards.

Associate-in-Training. This category is open to any person who is currently receiving, or has recently successfully completed, training on an internship basis in a training program approved by the association, or who is receiving approved supervision by arrangement with the Admissions Committee.

It will be seen that the membership categories move upward in a series of steps. The beginner, in an approved internship program, may become an associate-in-training. As soon as he has completed a total of two years (or its equivalent spaced over a longer period) of acceptable experience in marriage counseling, he may apply to become an associate member. After a further three years of acceptable experience, making a total of five in all, he may apply to become a member. Five years after that, he could be eligible, if he met other requirements, to be nominated and elected to the status of fellow.

Of course, a person already appropriately qualified and with sufficient experience may apply directly for the status of associate member or member. Fellows are designated directly by the Board of Directors. Applications for the other three categories are processed by the admissions committee.

In making its evaluation of an applicant, the Admissions Committee looks for the following:

---

[*] Dr. Rydman is Executive Director of the A.A.M.C.

1. *Possession of whatever graduate degree is necessary for the practice of a recognized profession.* At the present time, one of the following degrees from a fully accredited institution is required: an M.D. in medicine; a doctor's degree in psychology, sociology, education, or a closely related field; a master's degree in social work; a three-year B.D. in religion, or other recognized three-year graduate degree from a theological seminary, plus an adequate clinical orientation; an LL.B. in law, plus clinical orientation. However, where a high level of clinical competence in marriage counseling has been clearly demonstrated, an applicant may be accepted who possesses a fully accredited master's degree in any recognized professional discipline.

2. *At least three years of practice in a recognized profession* subsequent to obtaining the appropriate graduate degree.

3. *Adequate training in marriage counseling*, viewed as an advanced specialty in the wider fields of counseling and psychotherapy. The training programs currently approved by the A.A.M.C. require an academic year of supervised clinical internship. Other internship considered to be fully equivalent to this may be submitted to the Admissions Committee for evaluation.

4. *Sufficient experience in the practice of marriage counseling* to have familiarized the applicant with a variety of types of marital disharmony. For associate member status, the applicant should have been actively engaged in marriage counseling for about half of his professional time during a two-year period; for member status, for a five-year period. Less concentrated experience would have to be extended for longer periods to provide adequate equivalents. The applicant may be required to submit case material for evaluation and to undergo an oral examination in order to establish his clinical competence.

5. *Personal maturity and integrity.* The Admissions Committee may carry out whatever investigation is deemed necessary to secure satisfactory evidence of this.

All members of the association are bound by its Code of Professional Ethics, a copy of which is sent upon request.

The annual dues are: fellows, $40; members, $35; associate members, $30; associates-in-training, $10. All classes of membership may attend all regular meetings and clinical sessions of the association. All except associates-in-training are entitled to vote. Associate members are not eligible for major office but have one representative on the Board of Directors. Fellows, members, and associate members receive a diploma suitable for framing.

The status of member and associate member can be awarded only when the names and addresses of those concerned have been mailed to the entire membership and no objections have been sustained.

The appropriate forms for membership application may be obtained from the Executive Director. A processing fee of $25 is required from applicants for associate member or member status.

Applicants for A.A.M.C. membership should understand clearly that *the standards of the association are high and its investigations thorough.*

Counseling Regarding Divorce

> *The land of marriage has this peculiarity, that strangers are*
> *desirous of inhabiting it, whilst its natural inhabitants would*
> *willingly be banished from thence.*
>
> MONTAIGNE

The question of whether or not to get a divorce is one of the most crucial questions which clients bring to marriage counselors. The professional marriage counselor has to have some perspective on divorce in our society in order to be of help to clients considering whether or not to dissolve their marriage. As Max Lerner has said in his discussion of *America as a Civilization*:

> There are no people in the world who make greater demands upon marriage than Americans do, since they lay greater exactions upon it and also expect greater psychic satisfaction from it. They do not make the necessarily right demands, but whether right or wrong, they don't settle easily for a small fraction [1957, p. 595].

American attitudes toward divorce are shifting, as Lerner has also shown, with a more experimental attitude developing which might be described as no longer seeing divorce as a final disaster but as a temporary setback in a continuing quest.

In Chapter 45, Ben N. Ard, Jr., and Constance C. Ard, marriage counselors in private practice in San Francisco, discuss the question: What should the marriage counselor's stance be regarding divorce? On this crucial issue authorities in the field have differed. A sampling of some of the opinions are offered in this chapter, but each reader will have to decide for himself which position he will take with regard to divorce. What position he takes will, of course, determine what sort of counseling regarding divorce he will provide.

Another husband-wife team, John W. Hudson and Dorothy J. Hudson, collaborate in Chapter 46 to discuss counseling with children involved in the divorce situation—a rarely discussed topic in the field.

CHAPTER 45

Counseling Regarding Divorce

Ben N. Ard, Jr., and Constance C. Ard

What should the marriage counselor's stance be regarding divorce? Opinions among authorities in the field have varied over the years. Kingsley Davis (1963) has stated:

> Presumably a marriage counselor would attempt to remain neutral, simply trying to give the couple insight into their own motives and some knowledge concerning the possible psychological and social effects of their actions. But since people who do marriage counseling are usually sponsored by religious, social work, or government agencies, their moral evaluation with reference to divorce is likely to be somewhat conservative and hence not strictly neutral [p. 461].

But Davis went on to say that "the literature on marriage counseling suggests a conservative attitude toward divorce, but a more professional, or disinterested, attitude is emerging. It is recognized that the goal of making a marriage work does not preclude the possibility that divorce itself may be desirable [p. 472]" (cf. Mudd, 1951, Chapters 1, 9, 10).

In an extensive discussion of the field of marriage counseling, a past president of the American Association of Marriage Counselors, Gerald R. Leslie (1964), has said:

> A common misconception among laymen and some professional persons is that marriage counseling has the promotion and preservation of marriages as its primary goal. Such persons view marriage counseling as directed toward buttressing traditional, conservative standards of family life and being generally opposed to solutions involving unconventional personal behavior, separation, and divorce. The value position assumed by most professional marriage counselors is, in fact, quite different. . . . marriage counseling more often than not exerts its influence toward the development, maintenance, and restoration of marriages. But in some instances, marriage counselors aid clients to dissolve unsatisfactory marriages and either to live without partners or to develop new and healthier relationships [p. 915].

Some clients come to the marriage counselor with their minds pretty well made up to get a divorce but with some need to check this decision out with a professional person not emotionally involved in the situation. As Kingsley Davis (1963) has said, "Once the decision to obtain a divorce has been made by one or both parties, the chief role of the marriage counselor refers no longer to marital adjustment but rather to divorce adjustment [p. 462]." An earlier analysis of the problem of conflicting ends in marriage counseling may be found in another article by Davis (1936), dealing with the application of science to personal relations.

Some "family courts" have attempted reconciliation of marital partners in conflict after they have filed for divorce, or at least when they first come to the attention of the court (Bridgman, 1959). But agreement in the field is not found even on this point. "Those who believe that the incidence of divorce can be greatly reduced through the counseling of couples after they have already sought divorce are probably mistaken. By that time marital discord or ennui has usually grown too deep to be banished by verbal discussion [Davis, 1963, p. 462]."

William Kephart (1964) notes that "with regard to marriage counseling, for instance, there are no figures which would tell what percentage of the litigants in divorce actions are reconciled (or of those reconciled, what proportion remains reconciled) as compared to parallel figures in a regular divorce court which has no counseling service [p. 956]."

Attitudes toward divorce have traditionally been of a negative sort in our society. Sometimes, among the slightly more sophisticated groups, who would not resort to the traditional arguments against divorce, "psychiatric" or "psychological" arguments are raised.

> Occasionally there is a tendency to regard divorce itself as a mental disorder or at least as an evidence of such a disorder. This, however, is merely a sly way of condemning divorce. . . . Divorces are in fact so much a part of American folkways and mores that they cannot be regarded as abnormal [Davis, 1963, pp. 470–471].

Because of these negative attitudes toward divorce in our culture, the marriage counselor needs to help those of his clients who get divorced to make the best possible adjustment. He can help, not only through good counseling (perhaps followed through the troubled times after the divorce has been granted), but also through referring clients to community organizations such as Parents Without Partners, which are available in many large cities.

When considering a divorce, after separation, when going through the process of getting a divorce, and particularly after getting a divorce, many clients can benefit from some contact with Parents Without Partners. It performs a unique function in that the members, divorced themselves, can because of their own experiences give perspective and enlightened support to those facing marital breakup.

This organization conducts a community service program called "SOS—Focus on Divorce," which is designed to help those who are approaching or undergoing divorce. The main objectives of the program are (1) to give people deciding about divorce a more objective understanding of the causes of their own marital conflicts and a realistic look at all aspects of the future, so that whether their decision is to remain married or to divorce, they can carry it out more sanely; (2) to alleviate the feelings of aloneness, guilt, and failure common to all who experience marital trouble and divorce; and (3) to help the children of a troubled marriage by improving the attitude and behavior of their parents through the development of their personal growth and maturity.

One of the arguments still frequently used against divorce is that couples should stay together "for the childen's sake." Yet, as Ellen Key (1911) pointed out so long ago, "If the young are accustomed to see their elders content with false and ugly relations, they will learn to be so likewise [p. 295]." This is still devastatingly true.

J. L. Despert (1953), in a study of children of divorce, has concluded, "Divorce is not the costliest experience possible to a child. Unhappy marriage without divorce—what we shall call emotional divorce—can be far more destructive to him than divorce [p. 18]."

William J. Goode (1956) concurs in his book *After Divorce*: "In all likelihood, almost every serious researcher in American family behavior has suggested that the effects of continued home conflict might be more serious for the children than the divorce itself [p. 309]."

The marriage counselor does not have to become a lawyer to be of effective help to his clients, but he may wish to familiarize himself with several books which are of practical help both to the counselor and the client. For example, the counselor may profitably consult Pilpel and Zavin's book, *Your Marriage and the Law* (1952); Haussamen and Guitar's *The Divorce Handbook* (1960); or Kling's paperback, *The Complete Guide to Divorce* (1967). These books may be mentioned to the client who is considering divorce, also.

The laws are indeed complex and can even be said to be stupid, in so far as they are so blatantly self-defeating for so many human beings in our culture. Divorce reform, or more specifically, reform of our divorce laws, is urgently needed. Why has something so obviously needed not come about? Henry Foster (1967) has suggested that probably one of the biggest reasons is because such reform must come through the state legislatures.

> . . . historically, the clergy all too often has placed religious dogma or principle above human interests and salvation above legitimate human needs. It is the intransigence of the clergy, not the stupidity of lawyers, that accounts for most of the anomalies of our divorce law. . . . Divorce reform is no easy matter. In many if not most states, organized religion and powerful churchmen, who may or may not reflect the actual beliefs of their parishioners, usually succeed in blocking any substantive reform of the divorce laws. . . . Proponents of divorce reform and a therapeutic approach to family problems must overcome the entrenched opposition of some moralists and some churchmen who enjoy inordinate prestige with legislators [pp. 180, 182, 184].

REFERENCES

Bridgman, R. P. Marriage conciliation. Pp. 672–684 In Ellis and Abarbanel (Eds.) *The Encyclopedia of sexual behavior*. Vol. 2. New York: Hawthorn, 1961.

Davis, K. The application of science to personal relations. *American Sociological Review*, April, 1936, *1*, 236–251.

Davis, K. Divorce. Pp. 461–474 In Fishbein and Burgess (Eds.) *Successful marriage*. Rev. ed. Garden City, N. Y.: Doubleday, 1963.

Despert, J. L. *Children of divorce*. Garden City, N. Y.: Doubleday, 1953.

Foster, H. H., Jr. The institutions of divorce. Pp. 177–188 In H. L. Silverman (Ed.) *Marital counseling*. Springfield, Ill.: Charles C. Thomas, 1967.

Goode, W. J. *After divorce*. Glencoe, Ill.: Free Press, 1956.

Haussamen, F. and Guitar, M. A. *The divorce handbook*. New York: Putnam, 1960.

Kephart, W. M. Legal and procedural aspects of marriage and divorce. Pp. 944–968 In H. T. Christensen (Ed.) *Handbook of marriage and the family*. Chicago: Rand McNally, 1964.

Key, E. *Love and marriage*. New York: Putnam, 1911.

Kling, S. G. *The complete guide to divorce*. New York: Simon and Schuster, 1967.

Leslie, G. R. The field of marriage counseling. Pp. 912–943 In H. T. Christensen (Ed.) *Handbook of marriage and the family*. Chicago: Rand McNally, 1964.

Pilpel, H., and Zavin, T. *Your marriage and the law*. New York: Rinehart, 1952.

CHAPTER 46

The Marriage Counselor, the Child, and Marital Conflict

John W. Hudson and Dorothy J. Hudson

One does not have to be in the practice of marriage counseling very long before being confronted with the realization that there are going to be marriages, which, despite the best clinical ability and efforts, will terminate in divorce. In those relationships where there are no children involved, the adults are the major concern of the counselor. But with couples who have children, the counselor has a responsibility to use his skills to help the children with their adjustments. A review of the literature on marriage counseling fails to reveal articles dealing with the role of the marriage counselor in assisting children in adjusting to their parents' divorce. This is particularly unfortunate because studies done on children from divorced and broken homes indicate there is an increased possibility that these children's marriages will be terminated by separation or divorce. "It has become one of the most thoroughly accepted tenets of marital prediction analysis that children of unhappy marriages are poor marital risks themselves [Udry, 1966, p. 506]." However, it is the quality of the childhood experience, not the mere fact of divorce, that is the crucial element. Studies also indicate that children who come from broken homes have a higher rate of deviant behavior than children from unbroken homes.

> Even when the class position of parents is held constant, the delinquency rate of children is higher for broken than for unbroken homes. Similarly, the rate of delinquency among boys and girls is higher for those whose parents are separated or divorced than it is for those who have lost a parent by death [Goode, 1966, p. 549].

Children living in the presence of marital conflict often show behavioral problems of their own. Following a divorce children are often confused and angry and fail to understand their new relationship to their parents. The role of the divorced adult in our society is poorly defined. The role of the child in the family and community when his parents are seeking a divorce, is similarly ambiguous. The child's relationship with his peers is altered. The children's problems are further complicated when one or both of the parents remarry and the child is faced with stepparents, and not infrequently, stepbrothers and/or sisters. The purpose of this paper is to outline some of the problems and conflict areas of the child whose parents are in marital conflict or seeking divorce, and to suggest counseling approaches which will help alleviate the stress in this transitional period.

Whether the marriage counselor assists directly in the adjustments of the children involved in a divorce or whether he counsels indirectly through the parents depends on a number of factors: (1) the ages of the children, (2) with whom the children are living at the time, (3) the amount of hostility between the adults seeking the divorce, (4) whether the counselor is seeing one or both of the couple, and (5) how clearly the parents perceive the divorce affecting their children. The marriage counselor has an important and sometimes neglected role in working with parents and children of marriages where severe marital conflict is present. Hope for the young child's future can most effectively be achieved by counseling first with the parent. It is important for the counselor to allow the parent to express his feelings of frustration and guilt about his marriage and children. This in itself, though, is not sufficient. Many counselors fail to provide explicit and direct advice on how to cope with reality problems omnipresent in severe marital conflict. In our experience some parents will arrive at effective solutions to the problems related to their children in time, but a direct approach will bring stability more rapidly into the situation.

Where there has not been open hostility between two adults they tend to believe that their children are unaware of the pending marital crisis. This is usually not the case. Most young children are sensitive to the emotional moods of their parents. Although they may not be consciously aware of the disorganization in the marriage, they are aware that something is amiss. The parent needs to be informed early in the counseling that it is an error to believe he can protect the child against the reality of the marital conflict. The parent should be told that he can play a significant role in helping the child adjust to the situation. It is probably true that some children (most likely adolescents), because of involvement in their own activities, are unaware of the tensions between their parents. First we will discuss the young child's awareness of marital conflict, his responses, frustrations, and behaviors, and some suggestions the counselor can make to the parent in ways to relate to his child.

Many couples will resist telling the child anything is wrong in the marriage, because they do not wish to face either their own emotional conflict over the faltering marriage or the child's questioning. During a marital crisis, it is wise to advise the parent to tell the child that Mom and Dad are not getting along but that it has nothing to do with him. The counselor should warn the parent that the reaction from the child when receiving this information is likely to be strong, frequently grief, followed by unending questions, total indifference, or else rejection of the whole idea.

The variety of problems that manifest themselves in children who know their parents are in conflict include all the normal behavior of each developmental stage plus the individual child's response to the stress situation. It is important that a distinction be made for the parent between these two sets of behavior. Normal behavior is apt to be viewed as problem behavior by one or both parents who are under emotional stress. When the level of tension within the family is elevated over a long period of time, the child may begin to act out his own emotional insecurity. The child's vague awareness that something is wrong may crystallize initially at the point of the parents' separation. For the first time he may experience disorganization in his world. The young child may express his insecurity in a variety of ways. His feelings are open and revealed through hitting, shoving, biting, kicking, pushing, tripping and/or incessant whining and crying. In such instances the parent needs to be reminded by the counselor that the child finds himself in a situation for which he has few defenses. The child may struggle with guilt, thinking that he is responsible for the situation. The more anxious a child is, the less able he is to ask questions. In such a case the counselor should remind the parent that a child may be thinking to himself, "What will happen to me?" The child may be afraid of being left alone or being abandoned. Often changes occur in the child's eating and sleeping behavior. He sometimes returns to bed-wetting, behaving in a generally negative manner, clinging to the parent, and showing little or no interest in his regular play activities. The parent of the young child frequently responds to the named behaviors with both frustration and guilt. The frustration elicits feelings of hostility toward the child or the spouse, which result in further exacerbating the problems. The parent who feels guilty about his hostility toward his child will often overcompensate. The child quickly learns to play upon his parent's guilt and may use this as a weapon to manipulate the parent.

The parents need to have concrete suggestions regarding methods of handling the child's questions and behavior. Since most adults going through serious marital conflict are emotionally disturbed and disorganized, it is imperative that the counselor be clear and decisive in his recommendations. The counselor should caution the parents to be careful when talking in the presence of the child. The parents should avoid discussions pertaining to the cost of child support, the difficulties of bringing up a child alone, of arranging for his future, or any other aspect of the parents' problems which may reinforce the child's anxiety and set up the very patterns which the parents are trying to avoid!

Probably the most difficult and yet one of the most essential tasks for the parent to accomplish is to avoid criticizing the estranged spouse in the presence of the child. The most serious mistake a parent can make is to put the child in the position where he must choose sides. The result of such actions produces a child who feels guilty, resentful, disloyal, and frightened. The counselor should emphasize to the parent the importance of informing the child of the marital conflict with the repeated assurance that he is not responsible for the problems in the marriage. The counselor should remind the parent that he must spell out in simple language to the child that nearly all children have to learn to face some adverse circumstances, to accept them, and to go on from there. It is important for the parents to stress to the child that parents are human beings who have made mistakes.

When a parent commits himself to a date or activity with the child, the parent has the responsibility to make every effort to keep his promise. When the parent breaks his promise, the child comes to distrust the adult world and may interpret the broken promise as evidence of his unacceptability as a person.

Visitations with the separated parent should be as relaxed as possible. The counselor should caution the parent not to make these visits overwhelmingly special events. Showers of presents and sensational activities can be used by the child either as a weapon against the parent he is living with or as a vehicle for indulging his fantasy life.

Visitations provide an excellent method for the parents to express their hostility toward one another via the child. Not having the child ready on time for the visit or unnecessary delay in returning the child at the appointed time are sometimes used as weapons. Arguments over the frequency of visits, where and with whom visits can occur, all provide ammunition for the hostile parents' guns. Ideally, visits should not be too frequent. Every three or at most two weeks is usually often enough. However, any visiting arrangement should be flexible and subject to change with circumstances.

If the counselor is seeing only one of the spouses, a great deal can be done in helping him interpret fairly to the child the behavior of the estranged spouse. It is imperative that the counselor help the parent to be uncritical and nonhostile in his explanations to the child.

A child returning home following a date or visit with the absent parent provides fertile ground for one of the most common and detrimental acts of the neurotic spouse. Under the thinly masked guise of a child's pleasure or welfare, a parent may pump the child for information. The "who's, where's, why's and what's" erode the child's experience and violate his rights to his own private relationship with the absent parent. The counselor should be emphatic in pointing out that questioning can lead only to alienation of the child; it encourages lying and builds strong feelings of resentment and hostility toward his interrogator. The counselor can reassure the questioning parent that the significant aspects of the visit will be forthcoming if he will learn to practice self-discipline and patience. The parent who persists in nagging, harrassing, and threatening the child for detailed information contributes to a breakdown in communication. The counselor can point out to the parent in charge the value of recognizing and accepting the meaning these visits have to the child, supporting and reinforcing the pleasure and satisfaction the child may derive from them.

There are children (usually older ones) who may resist or refuse to visit the absent parent, despite the encouragement of the parent in charge. In these cases the parent should not insist that the child visit the absent parent. When a child refuses to visit the absent parent, a conference between the counselor and child may be beneficial.

Just as money produces an arena for conflict within marriage, it provides one of the most destructive tools for conflict in separation and divorce. The counselor who can prevent the child from becoming the pawn in the battle for economic justice has accomplished an important task. The mother may restrict the child's contact with the father in an effort to pressure for child support. In turn the father may withhold child support as a means of manipulating or punishing the mother. No matter what the motivations are, the child is the victim. The child may conclude that he is not being treated as a person of worth in his own right. It does not require a high level of sophistication for the child to realize that a price has been placed on his head, thus contributing to the child's feelings of worthlessness.

The stabilizing influence of the home and the neighborhood on a child is clearly recognized. Children who are experiencing the dissolution of their parent's marriage can reap untold benefits if home and neighborhood factors can be held constant. Many adults in the throes of a marital crisis wish to break with their environment because of painful memories and experiences. The counselor should urge the parent wherever possible to maintain continuity in the life space of the child. This can be facilitated by living in the same house, attending the same school, playing with the same friends, and following familiar routines. The shock of marital crisis can be softened significantly by keeping the child's routine as nearly like his former life as possible.

In most states small children are almost automatically placed with the mother. Where the children are in their teens, the decision with whom to live may be more complicated. Separating children and having them live with one parent six months and the other parent another six months adds to their confusion and feeling of not belonging anywhere. Rather, living with one parent most of the time and the other parent on weekends and/or vacations is a more desirable solution.

The adolescent, like the young child and preadolescent, needs continual reassurance. The same rules that apply to young and preadolescent children generally apply to an adolescent. Instead of an adolescent's saying, "I'll never marry," he may develop attitudes which will later cause him to fear any sexual experience or else to be promiscuous about it, to be afraid of giving and receiving love, to run from any kind of permanent attachment, or to be cynical about marriage. The adolescent can act out his reactions to the marital conflict in a manner which can bring him into serious conflict with other adults, his peers, and the civil authorities.

The marriage counselor is in a unique position to help the adolescent whose parents are having severe marital problems. If the counselor is to be effective in helping the adolescent, he may need to have a series of counseling interviews with the child and/or his parents. The first and most difficult problem in counseling with an adolescent is to gain his confidence. There is no reason why he should trust a counselor, and particularly a marriage counselor. If a divorce is pending, the marriage counselor may already be defined as a failure by the adolescent.

With adolescents it is especially necessary for the counselor to be honest, firm, and decisive. The adolescent who feels his world is falling apart can benefit from the counselor's reassurance. Although the marriage is dissolving, parenthood is not. The counselor can assure the adolescent that we cannot know everything about another person, his motives, his unhappiness, etc. The adolescent should be told that his father or mother may have acted unwisely in some instance, but that no one is perfect. The adolescent should be informed when one or both of his parents is seriously disturbed. The counselor should provide the adolescent with an adequate understanding of the illness. Whenever possible the adolescent should be instructed in how to avoid becoming involved in his parents' problems.

The adolescent who experiences teasing and tormenting from his peers needs help from the counselor in understanding the reasons behind his friends' cruelty. The counselor needs to explain that teen-agers may tease because they are perhaps not sure all is well with them in their own families. The adolescents' hostility may take the form of smugness which is often a cover for their own underlying feelings of doubt and insecurity.

It is important that the counselor guide the adolescent to interpret actions not as "good" or "bad," "black" or "white," but as the outward signs of complex and often conflicting inner drives. It is incumbent on the counselor that he not teach the adolescent to condone inappropriate behavior, but rather to understand the unreasoning and uncontrollable forces which drive people to behave badly to one another. The adolescent's parent can benefit from the counselor's explanation of the difficulties that adolescents experience as the result of separation or divorce. Particular attention needs to be directed to helping the parents understand the intense feelings of rejection and hostility toward them that the teen-ager may manifest at the time of the divorce.

Just as the child looks to his parent for support and reassurance, many parents going through marital conflict look to their children for comfort and solace. The counselor should caution the parent against putting the child into the position of feeling that it is his responsibility to meet the companionship or affectional needs of the parent.

The parent who finds himself with the responsibility of the daily care for the child frequently attempts to play both mother and father roles. The counselor needs to point out that the consequences result in neither role's being performed effectively. A child can benefit from a clearly defined male or female role but is confused by an attempt on the part of the parent to play both roles.

The process of marital disorganization is extremely complex. It is rare to find parents with sufficient emotional maturity to preclude their working out at least a portion of their own frustrations on their children. Persons going through marital conflict have few resources available to support the emotional needs of others. Lines of loyalty are drawn quickly among family and friends.

The adversary procedure of the divorce courts frequently compounds the problem. Since its inception the profession of marriage counseling has recognized the value of working with a couple toward a more sane and rational divorce. It has been recognized that divorced persons benefit markedly from marriage counseling. If the marriage counselor will work with the children as well as the parents, it is our contention that all members of the family will benefit. Effective counseling can minimize the conflict, guilt, and hostility for both parents and children.

> Men and women must, of course, go to the law for their decree of divorce. But when settlements involving children are concerned, when custody and visitation, maintenance and the division of parental authority are to be decided, let them not bring these questions unresolved to court! [Despert, 1962, p. 190].

The personnel of the courts do not have the time or the training to deal effectively with the emotional problems of parents and children. In many instances the marriage counselor has the key to determine what the long-range impact of marital conflict will be for the child. Where divorce is inevitable, why not make it a learning experience? Finally, the counselor can aid parents in realizing that a basic desire of every child is to have a mother and father who are in fundamental agreement. But if his parents cannot remain together, then at the very least the child must still be allowed to continue to believe in both.

REFERENCES

Despert, J. L. *Children of divorce*. New York, N. Y.: Doubleday, 1962.

Goode, W. J. Family disorganization, In R. K. Merton and R. A. Nisbet (Eds.), *Contemporary social problems*. New York, N. Y.: Harcourt, Brace & World, 1966.

Gordon, I. J. *Children's views of themselves*. Washington, D. C.: Association for Childhood Education International, 1959.

Ilg, F. L. & Ames, L. B. *Child behavior*. New York, N. Y.: Dell Publishing Co., 1962.

Pollack, J. H. Seven mistakes divorced parents make. *Parents Magazine*, 1967, March, p. 48+.

Udry, J. R. *The social context of marriage*. New York, N. Y.: J. B. Lippincott, 1966.

Technical Assistance for the Marriage Counselor

There is nothing, Sir, too little for so little a creature as man. It is by studying little things that we attain the great art of having as little misery and as much happiness as possible.

SAMUEL JOHNSON

In previous sections we have been studying deep and complex matters. In this section we move to what may seem at first glance to be little things, relatively speaking. But the busy marriage counselor needs to know about several matters of a technical and practical nature in order to be able to function efficiently in his profession.

The "tools of the trade" (forms, inventories, etc.) are matters rarely discussed in the more formal papers in the literature. In Chapter 47 Constance C. Ard examines the initial interview, intake interview forms, marriage counseling inventories, sex knowledge inventories, marriage prediction schedules, release forms, and other practical matters which may prove a valuable introduction for the beginning counselor as well as a review of available aids for the experienced counselor.

In Chapter 48 Mrs. Ard discusses information-gathering techniques in marriage counseling: note-taking, ways of safeguarding confidentiality, tape-recording, video tape, one-way screens, and written communication.

Bibliotherapy is a technique used in marriage counseling as well as in other forms of psychotherapy, and many books on marriage are available as possible choices. In Chapter 49, Albert Ellis, who has written many books in this field, gives in his usual forthright manner his opinions regarding various books that have been used in bibliotherapy. Which are to be recommended out of the literally hundreds of marriage manuals that exist? Ultimately, each reader will have to decide for himself, but Dr. Ellis gives frank, straightforward reasons for choosing his favorites. The article may serve to stimulate the counselor, student, or layman to read several of the recommended (and unrecommended) books in the field. All the books discussed in Chapter 49 are essentially books that the counselor might consider recommending to his clients.

In the final offering in the section, Chapter 50, Ben N. Ard, Jr., discusses basic professional books for the marriage counselor. This whole handbook makes constant referrals to various books in the field. This last chapter attempts to pull together the professional books which the beginning marriage counselor will want to become familiar with, and which would help the more experienced counselor keep up to date or extend his knowledge in special areas. The books referred to in this last chapter are all listed in the annotated bibliography which follows immediately in Appendix A.

CHAPTER 47

The Tools of the Trade

Constance C. Ard

In marriage counseling, as in most professions, there are certain "tools of the trade," such as inventories, forms, etc. which it behooves the practitioner to be aware of so that he can make the professional judgment as to when and *whether* to use them. This chapter will discuss some of the available materials which might be of value in marriage counseling and related problems. Space will not allow for a detailed illustration of each available form or inventory, but several examples will be presented for consideration.

Helpful though they are, the use of these "tools" should not become routine, or be expected to take the place of effective counseling, which is still the most basic tool of the trade.

INITIAL INTERVIEW

Available literature on the function and type of information secured in the initial interview is rather meager. A great deal of the material pertaining to the initial interview which could present some possible resource information for marriage counselors is discussed under headings such as "the psychiatric examination," "the diagnostic study," or "the case study."

The function of the initial interview is to provide an understanding of what the problem is, as the client views it. It marks the beginning of a unique interpersonal relationship for the client as well as the marriage counselor.

The marriage counselor may well benefit from being aware of his social manners and the nonverbal reactions or responses of his new client[*] (cf. Ard 1969; Beier, 1966; Ekman, 1965; Dittman, 1961; Fretz, 1966). After he invites his client to be seated, he may begin the discussion by clarifying available data—such as the client's phone call stating the reason for coming for marriage counseling, or the referral of the client by another professional. This provides an opportunity for both counselor and the client to revise any incorrect data.

---

[*]Throughout this chapter the term "client" may refer to the *couple* that has sought counseling, as well as to either husband or wife individually.

Initial stages of rapport will, hopefully, begin to develop. If the counselor and client seem incompatible, this could be discussed. Such things as amount of fee, and how payment of the fee will be made, need to be discussed. Also a general overview of what the client wants to gain from marriage counseling would help to determine the extent of motivation for counseling and the reasons for coming to see a marriage counselor. Other ground rules, such as making and canceling of appointments, can be discussed. Perhaps these ground rules could be typed and presented to each client to keep.

Certain pertinent identifying information can be included in an intake interview form, similar to this one:

INTAKE INTERVIEW FORM

Interviewer: (if in clinic situation)

Name: Sex: Age: Military Status: Date:

Address: Home Phone Number:

Occupation: How Long: Business Phone Number:

Amount of Income: Education:

Source of Income, If Not Employed:

Marital Status: How Long Married: Age of Spouse:

Education of Spouse: Occupation of Spouse:

        Amount of Income of Spouse:

Number and Ages of Children:

Any Previous Marriages:

Previous Therapy with:

Where: Length:

Reasons For Coming to Marriage Counseling:

How Long Has Problem(s) Existed:

How Has This Affected Relationship to Job, Family,
Self, Friends, etc.:

Another form listing a number of physical and psychological symptoms could also be given to the client to fill out. He would check the terms which best describe how he is feeling and/or his current situation. If both spouses are present, each fills out a form independently.

CHECKLIST OF PROBLEMS AND FEELINGS*

Tension	Digestive symptoms
Depression	Sexual problem
Suicidal ideas	Impotency
Severe anxiety	Homosexuality
Hallucinations	Phobias
Delusions	Compulsions
Dangerous	Excessive use of sedatives
Excited	Insomnia
Physical symptoms	Nightmares
Fatigue	Stomach trouble
Headaches	No appetite
Dizziness	Obsessions
Unable to relax	Always worried about something
Unable to have a good time	Don't like weekends or vacations
Overambitious	Shy with people
Can't make friends	Can't make decisions
Can't keep a job	Inferiority feelings
Home conditions bad	Financial problems

No communication with spouse or children

Description (elaboration) of those checked:

MARRIAGE COUNSELING INVENTORIES

A brief discussion of the value and purposes of marriage counseling inventories and some examples of those available may prove helpful for the counselor. Before deciding which to use, if any, he may wish to familiarize himself with critical essays by Bernard (1933), Ellis (1948), Kelly (1941), and Terman & Wallin (1949).

The *Psychotherapy Inventory*, formally known as the *Individual and Marriage Counseling Inventory* (1967), was prepared by Aaron L. Rutledge. It consists of three sections: "Personal Data," "Your Parental Family," and "The Personal Relations in My Family." Examples of the questions asked are:

*Adapted from Wolberg, 1954, pp. 814 and 833.

Personal Data

Sex, birth date, age, height, weight?
Religious preference?
Present marital status?
Any previous marriages?
Do you feel that you have lived a happy life?
List sources from which you received most of your sex information.
List problems or subjects, in order of their importance to you, which you
    would like to discuss with the counselor.

Your Parental Family

Your parents' ages at marriage?
Nationality background?
Do parents live together? If separated or divorced, your age then?
Do you feel closest to your father or mother?
Rate your parents' marriage.
If you are married, did your parents approve of your marriage?

The Personal Relations in Your Family

Write several paragraphs about the following—
    1. your father as an individual, including personality changes.
    2. your mother as an individual, including personality changes.
    3. your parents' relationship to each other.
    4. your brothers and sisters.
    5. both constructive and destructive influences upon yourself and upon
       the remainder of the family from both the short-range and long-term
       points of view.

The *Marriage Personality Inventory* (Form IV. Marriage), was constructed by Karl V. Schultz, Ph.D., and is published by the Psychological
Services Press, 364 Fourteenth Street, Oakland, California 94612.

Dr. Schultz has constructed an inventory which provides a means of
describing oneself, one's parents, one's mate and one's marriage. This
inventory consists of 200 questions (accompanied by an answer sheet)
covering the following areas: Marriage rating; Growing-up years—childhood, teenage; Parents—background, personality; Personality; Health;
Vocation; Money and finance; Love, marriage, divorce; Sex; Child rearing;
Interests; Communication and decision making; Religion; Philosophy of
life.

The client is to mark the available rating space which best describes
the *degree of similarity or difference* between him and his mate. In the
second column space is available to rate these same questions as to the
effect on marriage—negative, neutral, or positive. Examples of statements
presented are:

Growing-up years
Unpleasant and unhappy
Pleasant and happy
Did not feel close to relatives
Felt close to relatives

Parents
   Family income below average
   Family income above average
   Forced or sarcastic, cutting sense of humor
   Easy, pleasant, relaxed sense of humor
Personality
   Changes personality depending on whom with
   Has distinct personality of own
   Blames self when things go wrong
   Blames others when things go wrong
Health
   Has important health-physical limitations
   Excellent physical health
Vocation
   Pay more important than personal satisfaction
   Personal satisfaction from job more important than pay
Money and finance
   Unconcerned about material things
   Ambitious for financial, material success
Love, marriage, divorce
   Love is something that is there or not—can't make it grow or die
   Love grows or dies depending on how much put into it
   Person shows love by giving, being, or doing what pleases mate
   Person shows love by being (him-/her-) self—and encouraging mate to be
      (him-/her-) self
Sex
   Sex is most important need-drive of life
   Sex is only one of the important need-drives of life
Child rearing
   Chances for good marriage better without children
   Having children important for a successful marriage
Interests
   Little interest in home upkeep and improvement projects
   Enjoys home upkeep and improvement projects
Communication and decision-making
   When senses disagreement, gets angry and blows
   Easy give and take in working out problems-differences
Religion
   Person should follow guidance of church and its leaders
   Up to each person to work out his own religion
Philosophy of life
   Environment, culture, religion, etc. makes people very different
   Underneath, people are very much same—wherever they are

SEX KNOWLEDGE INVENTORIES

One *Sex Knowledge Inventory* (Form X, Experimental Edition, for Marriage Counseling, 1950), was developed by Gelolo McHugh. It is published by the Family Life Publications, Inc., P. O. Box 6725, College Station, Durham, North Carolina.

The intended purpose of this sex knowledge inventory is to help the taker better understand the constructive part of sex in life. This inventory is a measure of what individuals know about sex. The Sex Knowledge Inventory consists of 80 questions and includes a glossary of unfamiliar terms (*cervix, circumcision*, etc.).

Some of the questions asked are:

What is the relation between sex attraction and love?

What kinds of sex play may be used by a couple before or during sex relations?

What should a couple do about sex relations on the first night of marriage?

How long should each act of sex relations last?

When a woman is sexually excited, which of her sex organs is usually enlarged and quite firm?

What position should be used for sex relations?

How much of the unsatisfactory sex relations in marriage is caused by differences in size of the male and female sex organs?

How do large differences in sex drive affect the possibility of a satisfactory sexual adjustment in marriage?

What should a man do if he consistently has premature ejaculations?

What do physicians say about the effects of modern birth control methods?

What is the effect of circumcision during infancy or childhood on sex relations of the adult?

What changes usually occur in menstruation after marriage?

What does the size of the female sex organs indicate?

What is the effect of eating foods such as oysters, raw eggs, olives, celery, etc., on sex desire?

What is the usual effect of masturbation on ability to become a parent?

A second *Sex Knowledge Inventory*, also developed by Gelolo McHugh, concerns itself with the vocabulary and anatomy related to sex. This too can be obtained through the Family Life Publications, Inc.

Part I asks for the identification of the proper names for male and female sex parts—organ or structure. Diagrams accompany it. Part II seeks the inventory-taker's knowledge regarding the male and female sex parts without knowing their names. For example: "What covers and protects the male reproductive glands?" Part III calls for matching of words that best fit the available definitions.

DATING, COURTSHIP, AND MARRIAGE PREDICTION SCHEDULES

The Family Life Publications, Inc., also make available a *Courtship Analysis* and a *Dating Problems Checklist* accompanied by a Counselor's and Teacher's Guide. These checklists, too, were developed by Gelolo McHugh. The intended purpose of the Dating Problems Checklist is to help those couples who are contemplating becoming engaged. This checklist may also be utilized as a communications device for couples who want to know each other better and who want to understand their needs for a good courtship and a successful marriage.

It has been suggested that after couples have completed the Courtship Analysis, they should openly and frankly discuss their responses. This seemingly would provide an excellent opportunity for a couple to communicate about traits, behaviors, etc., that might help or hinder an acceptance of each other or a long-term relationship.

A *Marriage Prediction Schedule*, constructed by Ernest W. Burgess (University of Chicago), was prepared for those persons who are seriously contemplating marriage. It was designed for engaged couples, but could be of interest to anyone who would like to better understand his probability of success in marriage. This prediction schedule consists of five parts with a total of 74 questions.

This is not a complete representation of the available inventories or schedules available to the marriage counselor, but a mere sample. For further reference, the interested counselor may consult Locke (1951), Burgess and Cottrell (1939), and Terman et al (1938). It is hoped these aids will remain as aids and not be relied on so routinely or so heavily as to take the place of the more valuable direct confrontation between the marriage counselor and those who are in need of premarital or marital counseling!

The authorization of the client's release of interview data, tapes, etc. needs to be mentioned. This is of great importance in maintaining professional ethics and confidentiality. Two suggested forms are as follows:

AUTHORIZATION FOR THE CLIENT'S RELEASE OF INTERVIEW DATA AND TAPES

Third Party Release

TO:
ADDRESS:

I would appreciate your releasing to
all interview data and tapes regarding my marriage counseling. I herewith grant permission for this release.

(Signature of client)

WITNESS:
DATE:

Direct Release to Counselor

I hereby permit   to utilize any case
(Marriage Counselor)
material or tape recordings in any professional manner desired. I understand that all personal, indentifying information will be eliminated.

(Signature of client)

DATE:

REFERENCES

Ard, C. Nonverbal communication in marriage counseling, *Marriage Counseling Quarterly*, 1969.
Beier, E. G. *The silent language of psychotherapy*. Chicago: Aldine, 1966.
Bernard, J. An instrument for measurement of success in marriage. *Publications of the American Sociological Society*, 1933, *27*, 94–106.
Burgess, E. W. & Cottrell, L. S. *Predicting success or failure in marriage*. Englewood Cliffs, N. J.: Prentice-Hall, 1939.
Dittman, A. T., & Wynne, L. C. Linguistic techniques and the analysis of emotionality in interviews. *Journal of Abnormal Psychology*, 1961, *63*, 201–204.
Ekman, P. Communication through nonverbal behavior: A source of information about an interpersonal relationship. In S. S. Tomkins & C. E. Izard (Eds.). *Affect, cognition and personality*. New York: Springer Press, 1965. Pp. 390–442.
Ellis, A. The value of marriage prediction tests. *American Sociological Review*, 1948, *13*, 710–718.
Fretz, B. Postural movements in a counseling dyad. *Journal of Counseling Psychology*, 1966, *13*, No. 3.
Kelly, L. E. Marital compatibility as related to personality traits of husband and wife as rated by self and spouse. *Journal of Social Psychology*, 1941, *13*, 193–198.
Locke, H. J., & Klausner, W. J. Marital adjustment of divorced persons in subsequent marriage. *Sociology and Social Research*, 1948, *33*, 97–101.
Locke, H. J. *Predicting adjustment in marriage*. New York: Holt, 1951.
McHugh, G. *A courtship analysis*. Durham, N. C.: Family Life, 1966.
McHugh, G. *Dating problems checklist*. Durham, N. C.: Family Life.
McHugh, G. *Sex knowledge inventory*. Durham, N. C.: Family Life, 1950.
Terman, L. M., & Wallin, P. The validity of marriage prediction and marital adjustment tests. *American Sociological Review*, 1949, *14*, 497–505.
Terman, L. M., *et al. Psychological factors in marriage happiness*. New York: McGraw-Hill, 1938.
Wolberg, L. R. *The technique of psychotherapy*. New York: Grune & Stratton, 1954.

CHAPTER 48

Information-Gathering Techniques in Marriage Counseling

Constance C. Ard

If marriage counseling is to develop and progress as a scientific profession, the counselor needs to be familiar with techniques of gathering objective information on what happens in marriage counseling. Several techniques are of value—note-taking, tape-recording, the use of the video tape, one-way screens, and written communication. The initial interview data, questionnaires, and inventories, discussed in Chapter 45, "Tools of the Trade," are also useful.

NOTE-TAKING

Perhaps the most common information-gathering technique—and the least threatening, not only to clients but also to the marriage counselor—is note-taking. One advantage is that it can be continued throughout the session if it does not interfere with the therapist's active participation.

Sigmund Freud waited until the end of each day to write up his notes on the various patients he had seen during the day. Authorities who object to taking notes during therapeutic sessions might feel this is the only feasible way to make a record of their cases. However, there are obvious flaws in making notes at the end of the day—the possibility of distortions, the blurring of details, and simply the failure to remember accurately due to the time lapse between the occurrence and the recording. Other professionals (e.g., Sullivan, 1954) have suggested it is better to make notes immediately after each therapeutic session, but there is still the danger of leaving out important data.

The notes can be recorded on a specific note-taking form or ordinary paper. This would vary, presumably, according to personal taste or perhaps professional setting. The most important factor involved in the recording of personal and private information is *confidentiality*. Therefore, if notes are filed by client name, they should be kept in a locked file cabinet. As an alternative they might be filed under a coded system, with only an identifying number on the file folder and a separate card file to record number and corresponding name. The latter system might be advisable in an agency setting where other personnel have access to the files.

There is a difference between note-taking and interview summaries. Some marriage counseling clinics require that each counselor turn in a *summary* of every client seen. The information called for varies, but it usually consists of name, number of the visit, and several general statements describing the interview contents. Note-taking, in comparison, is a more detailed "log" of important ideas, feelings, growth, etc., which is kept in a *confidential* file of the counselor.

Confidentiality, respect for the integrity of each person seen, and guarding the welfare of those persons can hardly be overemphasized. Section 12 in the American Association of Marriage Counselors (1967) Code of Ethics states:

> "Except by written permission, all communications from clients shall be treated in complete confidence and never revealed to anyone. When a client is referred to in a professional case report, his identity shall be thoroughly disguised and the report shall so state [p. 84]."

Traditionally, both the client and society are of importance to the marriage counselor. For example, Wrenn (1966, p. 179) suggests as a principle that the counselor is primarily responsible to the client and ultimately to society. (This does not imply that the marriage counselor is out to "save" marriages for society's sake.) Wrenn (Ard, 1966) poses several interesting questions: What is confidential and what is not? How do you record information considered confidential? Under what conditions can the counselor be legally required to disclose information given him while in a counseling relationship?

The marriage counselor's legal position needs to be "checked out" according to the laws of the state where he practices, as there may be more legal leeway than is recognized.

> "For example, he does not have to release any personal or counseling records merely upon the request of an officer or a court, a state, or the federal government. In fact he probably should *not*, for the client can sue the counselor for failing to protect his interests. A warrant for the release of the records is necessary. Furthermore, the counselor may keep confidential notes on his clients in the form of personal memoranda and since these do not become part of the official records of the institution (or clinic) or of his office they do not have to be released when the personal records of an individual are taken into custody [Wrenn, in Ard, 1966, p. 174]."

Another point of interest regarding information supplied by the client is that it is almost always "hearsay" evidence and therefore not admissible in court [Wrenn, p. 175].

TAPE RECORDING

The tape recorder appears to be at present the most practical and helpful means of recording data. It leaves the marriage counselor free to observe more of the nonverbal as well as the verbal interaction and to take a more active role in the counseling session; furthermore, the tape is available for him to analyze more thoroughly at a later time.

Valuable use of the recorded sessions could also be made by the married partners themselves. For couples who do not think much progress or growth has occurred in counseling, an available tape may provide evidence of positive change and growth. Again, the counselor might ask the couple to listen to a specific tape at home as a "homework assignment," providing "listening proof" of how they speak to each other and what they are really communicating. They may even find in it clues to why they react as they do to some of their spouse's comments. As additional "homework," the couple could write (or perhaps tape-record) their reactions to the recorded session. If a couple wants to keep a particularly significant tape, they could purchase it at cost.

Tape recording of interviews can also be an excellent self-improvement device for marriage counselors. Many counselors may have the tendency not to grow in their interviewing skills. One way of checking up on oneself is by listening to one's own work critically. For even greater professional stimulation, perhaps a tape could be sent to a colleague; or interested professionals might have a monthly meeting to discuss one another's tapes and related problem areas in counseling. Tape recordings are also of great value as training aids.

Harper and Hudson (1952) suggest that perhaps counselors are more frightened of possible deleterious effects of tape recording interviews than are clients, and that some clients may feel *more* secure in knowing that the marriage counselor has an accurate record of their discussion.

Like other material from counseling sessions, recorded tapes must be treated with complete confidentiality, except upon signed release by the client. (See page 433.) The tapes, too, should be housed under lock and key. Information such as speed of recording, date, number of interview, and a coded identification of the client should be placed on the tape box. Numbers, "blind" identifying labels such as "The Case of the Girl in the Red Coat," or simply initials might provide a code to fit a particular professional environment.

VIDEO TAPE

The newest and most intriguing form of information-gathering device is the video tape. It not only records verbal output but also the very important *nonverbal* interaction of each participant. The size, quality, and quantity of equipment needed varies among manufacturers. Unfortunately, however, all video equipment is still probably too expensive for most individual counselors in private practice.

Video equipment can be utilized effectively in both individual sessions and in groups. It can "zero in" on the individual speaker showing a close-up of facial expressions and body position. Or, if a husband is expressing a specific problem area, the focus can switch for a few moments to his wife's nonverbal reaction, then back to the husband.

The video tape appears to be a valuable and stimulating device when working with couples. It helps one spouse become more aware of what the other spouse is saying, both verbally and nonverbally. "A woman commented, 'I can see how smug I look when you are talking to me. You must feel like hitting me' [Alger & Hogan, 1967, p. 1426]." If one person does something nonverbally that his partner interprets as negative when the tape is replayed, the counselor can have him "check it out" verbally by asking what was meant by the action. In short, video tape can help both clients become more congruent in action and speech.

By the instant replay of video tapes, the counselor can present the "fresh" experience or interaction for discussion and observation, rerunning it as many times as necessary. As suggested by Alger and Hogan (1967), the video technique helps the client become more aware of his own and others' behavior and feelings, and he tends to remember the new insight.

The video tape seems to offer practically endless possibilities for stimulating professional growth. For instance: (1) The counselor may observe how he relates to the client, or how the client relates to him; he can no longer remain in his safe realm of "objectivity." (2) He may also observe his reactions to interaction between clients. (3) Video tapes could replace demonstrations of marriage counseling techniques at professional meetings, thus increasing the authenticity and avoiding the effects on clients of possible distractions, disturbances, or viewer reactions. Another advantage of the video tape is that it can be used regardless of the theoretical orientation of the therapists.

The research possibilities of video tape seem to be largely untapped as yet. Some research has been reported by Ekman (1964), Ekman & Friesen (1967), Alger & Hogan (1967), Krumboltz, Varenhorst and Thoresen (in press), Dittman (1962), Kagan, Krathwohl, & Miller (1963), Stoller (in press), Walz & Johnson (1963), and Rogers (1968).

ONE-WAY SCREENS

One-way screens provide a variety of uses. Fulweiler (1968, p. 187), for example views the family interaction of his clients from behind a one-way mirror and enters the consulting room only to make an intervention or interpretation. (As a variation, the therapist might make his interpretations via an intercom.) Also, because the participants are unable to see observers, interested professionals who are not personally involved in the session can observe the interaction of the participants.

This also provides an excellent learning device, in that students and beginning counselors may observe experienced counselors demonstrate various marriage counseling techniques.

WRITTEN COMMUNICATION

Visotsky (1965) maintains that a great deal of written material is usually presented by the client to the therapist. Instead of laying aside this information, why not encourage the client to write more? An individual or couple sees the counselor perhaps once a week for fifty minutes. It seems evident that more than fifty minutes per week is needed to change deep-lying values, attitudes, behavior, etc. By written communication the client may spend up to an hour or two every day thinking and doing something about his problems.

Burton (1965) agrees that "written production" may help to immerse the client into therapy. If a client finds it difficult to talk about a problem, the counselor may suggest that it be written out. Of course this may not necessarily continue as a standard procedure—perhaps should not—because it could offer the client a way to escape direct confrontation.

Burton (1965) has also used the keeping of diaries in marriage counseling. Frequently, the first interviews of a married couple are full of expressed hostility. If each of the partners keeps a separate diary, feelings and thoughts about the spouse and problem areas can be looked at more rationally outside the interview setting.

Ellis (1965) asks his clients to do some type of "homework assignment" throughout the week. This frequently consists of writing down some of the significant happenings of the week or some of the "mental sentences" the client has been telling himself.

Once again, with written communication, confidentiality should be maintained, and all identifying material should be coded or erased.

REFERENCES

American Association of Marriage Counselors, Inc., *Directory of Members*. Dallas: A.A.M.C., 1967.

Alger, I. & Hogan, P., The use of video tape recordings in conjoint marital therapy. *American Journal of Psychiatry*, 1967, 73, 1425–1430.

Burton, A. The use of written productions in psychotherapy. In L. Pearson (Ed.), *The use of written communications in psychotherapy*. Springfield, Ill.: Charles C Thomas, 1965.

Dittman, A. T. The relationship between body movements and moods in interviews. *Journal of Consulting Psychology*, 1962, 26, 480.

Ekman, P. Body position, facial expression, and verbal behavior during interviews. *Journal of Abnormal and Social Psychology*, 1964, 68, 295–301.

Ekman, P. & Friesen, W. V. Nonverbal behavior in psychotherapy research. *Research on Psychotherapy*, 1967, Vol. 3 (A.P.A.).

Ellis, A. The use of printed, written and recorded words in psychotherapy. In L. Pearson (Ed.), *The use of written communications in psychotherapy*. Springfield, Ill.: Charles C Thomas, 1965.

Fulweiler, C. Personal communication. Cited in D. D. Jackson (Ed.), *Therapy, communication, and change*. Palo Alto: Science and Behavior Books, 1968.

Harper, R. A., & Hudson, J. W. The use of recordings in marriage counseling. *Marriage and Family Living*, 1952, 14, 332–334.

Kagan, N., Krathwohl, D. R., & Miller, R. Stimulated recall in therapy using video tape: A case study. *Journal of Counseling Psychology*, 1963, 10, 237–243.

Krumboltz, J. D., Varenhorst, B. B., & Thoresen, C. E., Nonverbal factors in the effectiveness of models in counseling. *Journal of Counseling Psychology* (in press).

Rogers, A. H. Video tape feedback in group psychotherapy. *Psychotherapy: Theory, Research and Practice*, 1968, 5, 37–39.

Stoller, F. Focused feedback with video tape: Extending the group's functions. In F. M. Gazda (Ed.), *Basic innovations in group psychotherapy and counseling*. Springfield, Ill.: Charles C Thomas (in press).

Sullivan, H. S. *The psychiatric interview*. New York: W. W. Norton, 1954.

Visotsky, H. M. Foreword. In L. Pearson (Ed.), *The use of written communication in psychotherapy*. Springfield, Ill.: Charles C Thomas, 1965.

Walz, G. R. & Johnson, J. A. Counselors look at themselves on video tape. *Journal of Counseling Psychology*, 1963, 10, 232–236.

Wrenn, G. The ethics of counseling. In B. N. Ard, Jr. (Ed.), *Counseling and psychotherapy*. Palo Alto: Science and Behavior Books, 1966.

CHAPTER 49

Bibliotherapy:
Books on Marriage for Clients

Albert Ellis

Many patients come to psychotherapy or to marriage and family counseling with specific sex, love, and marriage problems; and most therapists and counselors find it advisable, from time to time, to recommend supplementary reading material to these patients, particularly in regard to sex technique. The problem is: *Which* books, out of the literally hundreds of marriage manuals that exist, are to be recommended? I have a decidedly biased response to this question, as I have for many years found practically all the extant works sadly lacking. This is the main reason that I have written so many sex-marriage books myself, so that I could have texts for my own patients which I could unqualifiedly endorse. Let me forthrightly enunciate some of my prejudices.

First: Does the old, classical literature on sex—such as the works of Richard von Krafft-Ebing, Havelock Ellis, Iwan Bloch, August Forel, and Magnus Hirschfeld—have much usefulness today? No, not for most patients and counselees. Although this material is interesting for professionals and students of sex, and was very useful in its day, it is largely antiquated and misleading, and can do as much harm as good. Havelock Ellis's one-volume *Psychology of Sex* is not too bad today; but even its range of information leaves much to be desired.

How about the oriental classics, such as K. Malla's *Ananga Ranga*, Mohammed Nefzawi's *Perfumed Garden*, and Vatsyayana's *Kama Sutra*? Again, no. A few decades ago, these works were far ahead of their day and made interesting reading for inhibited westerners. But they are full of mysticism, religious fanaticism, and antiscientism, and are only safe in the hands of highly sophisticated, selective readers who will not take whole sections of them very seriously.

What can be said for the work of Freud and his disciples, such as Karl Abraham, Edmund Bergler, Helen Deutsch, Sandor Ferenczi, J. C. Flugel, Ernest Jones, Theodor Reik, and Wilhelm Stekel? Very little. The libido theory of personality growth and development is almost unadulterated

Reprinted with permission of the author and the publisher from *Voices*, 1966, 2, 83–85.

hogwash; the Freudian views of pregenitality and later fixation and regression are brilliant fantasies for which there seems to be no scientific verification; the psychoanalytic notions of love and hate are highly speculative and still unsubstantiated; and the Freudian dogma on female sexuality is a holy horror. One of the most execrable marriage manuals of our time, Marie Robinson's *The Power of Sexual Surrender*, typically emphasizes the pernicious Freudian view that women must have a so-called vaginal orgasm in order to be sexually well-adjusted; and innumerable other psychoanalytically-inspired works (including Wilhelm Reich's semi-psychotic *Function of the Orgasm*) uncritically accept this position, which has probably had more to do with sabotaging the sex life of innumerable couples than any other doctrine in recent times. A psychotherapist who recommends any sex-marriage book to his patients which has even a moderate flavor of Freudianism does so to their great peril.

How about the standard marriage manuals of the last thirty years, some of which have sold millions of copies? Of the older manuals of this sort, a few, such as W. F. Robie's *The Art of Love*, were unusually frank for their day and are still usable, though a little outdated. The most popular one of the lot, T. H. Van de Velde's *Ideal Marriage*, is great in regard to its description of intercourse positions, but it is romantically puritanical in many respects, and takes the unscientific position that sexual relations have to be finished off with penile-vaginal copulation leading to orgasm if they are to be considered normal and natural. Its (and many other sex manuals') deification of the glories of simultaneous orgasm has done enormous harm to the sex-love life of untold numbers of couples during the last several decades; and for all its good points, it nonetheless serves as a monument of sexual stupidity. Abraham and Hannah Stone's *A Marriage Manual*, which has also been fabulously popular for many years, is not as puritanical as *Ideal Marriage*, but it omits many salient, down-to-earth attitudes and much information, and is definitely on the namby-pamby side.

Several recent sex-marriage manuals are much better than the older books, in that they less inhibitedly delineate ideas and facts that the former omitted and pretty fully accept the point that sex *relations* are much broader and more inclusive than sex *intercourse*. They show sex partners how to achieve *some* forms of satisfaction that are individually tailored for *themselves*, and that are not necessarily "normal" or "natural" to *all* couples. They also face the fact that orgasm is orgasm, however achieved, and that there is nothing sacred about penile-vaginal copulation. These books acknowledge the scientific findings of modern researchers, such as Alfred C. Kinsey and his associates, and William H. Masters and Virginia E. Johnston. Included in this category are Inge and Sten Hegeler's *An ABZ of Love*, Phyllis and Eberhard Kronhausen's *The Sexually Responsive Woman*, G. Lombard Kelly's *Sex Manual*, and Robert Street's *Modern Sex Techniques*. The most popular of the up-to-date marriage manuals is my own *The Art and Science of Love*, which I wrote because of the deficiencies of most of the other works in the field, and which has helped hundreds of my own patients to achieve far better sex-love lives.

Because sex is hardly the only part of a love or marital relationship, the question also arises: What books can be recommended for a couple who want to thoughtfully consider the emotional aspects of marriage? Years ago, I recommended John Levy and Ruth Munroe's *The Happy Family*, but this book has been out of print for some time now. Most of the other books in the field I view dimly, since they tend to be psychoanalytically oriented and/or basically puritanical. Two books that I can largely accept are Rudolf Dreikurs' *Challenge of Marriage* and Richard Robertiello's *Sexual Fulfillment and Self-Affirmation*. For the most part, I have had to write my own books to use with my patients in this respect—especially, *The American Sexual Tragedy* and (in collaboration with Robert A. Harper) *Creative Marriage* (published in paperback form as *The Marriage Bed*). Even more important, I have found that in the area of love relations people do much better with each other when they understand themselves and others in general psychological ways, and when they realize what nonsense they are telling themselves to interfere with their love relationships and to create needless hatred and dissension. To this end, I have found my books *How to Live with a Neurotic* and (again in collaboration with Robert A. Harper) *A Guide to Rational Living* most helpful in helping save many love relationships that otherwise seemed to be going on the rocks.

I have often been asked whether I use any kind of anatomy atlas or other special visual aids to teach techniques of intercourse. The answer is no, although I sometimes draw a sketchy diagram for my patients to show them where the female clitoris is, as distinct from the vaginal opening. No book that I know of has adequate pictures of sex positions, though Dr. Sha Kokken's recent volume published in Japan, *A Happier Sex Life*, has some interesting illustrations of puppets in different poses (and also has much puritanical nonsense in its accompanying text). I find that if couples read the details of sex positions and then open-mindedly experiment with their own variations, that is all that is necessary for their achieving proficiency.

More to the point, I think that bibliotherapy can be used to help males and females loosen up in their sex attitudes, so that they are then willing and eager to try anything in and out of the books that may be useful in their own sex-love relations. To this end, I often recommend fictional works, such as John Cleland's *Fanny Hill*, Marquis de Sade's *Complete Justine and Other Writings*, and the novels of Henry Miller. On the nonfictional side, I especially find that Rey Anthony's *Housewife's Guide to Selective Promiscuity* is a useful book for inhibited females to read. Although the edition of this book published by Ralph Ginzburg has been banned from the mails, the original manuscript edition can still be obtained (for five dollars) from Seymour Press, Box 12035, Tucson, Arizona 85711.

Other nonfictional works which I find very helpful in undermining the puritanical blockings of patients which prevent them from having a full sex-love life include Rene Guyon's *The Ethics of Sexual Acts*, Hugh Hefner's *Playboy Philosophy*, Alfred C. Kinsey's *Sexual Behavior in the*

Human Female, Lawrence Lipton's *The Erotic Revolution*, Lars Ullerstam's *Erotic Minorities*, and Wayland Young's *Eros Denied*. I have made quite a contribution to the field of sexual liberalism myself, and among my own books which I find most helpful in getting patients to loosen up in this respect are *Sex Without Guilt, The American Sexual Tragedy, If This Be Sexual Heresy. . . , The Case for Sexual Liberty, The Search for Sexual Enjoyment*, and (edited in collaboration with Albert Abarbanel) *The Encyclopedia of Sexual Behavior*.

A final word on bibliotherapy and nonmarital sex relations. Up until quite recently there were virtually no good books for unmarried individuals who wanted sexual guidance, since the extant literature was firmly preoccupied with the sex lives of married couples. Ira S. Wile edited a pioneering book on the *Sex Life of the Unmarried Adult* in 1934; but this has long been out of print. A few years ago Helen Gurley Brown made quite a stir with her *Sex and the Single Girl*—a fairly wishy-washy text, but one which at least fully espoused premarital sex relations for women. Since that time, several other books dealing with the problems of single people have appeared, most of them ultra-sensationalistic or else, like Evelyn M. Duvall's *Why Wait Till Marriage*, incredibly naive and puritanical for today's world. Seeing that nothing to my own liking existed, I wrote *Sex and the Single Man* and *The Intelligent Woman's Guide to Man-Hunting*, both of which, I am happy to say, have helped thousands of unmarried individuals to achieve a higher degree of sex-love fulfillment.

To sum up: Innumerable books exist which purport to be helpful to single and married individuals who desire to enhance their sex, love, and marital relationships. Most of them are puritanical, over-romantic, or sensationalistic, and may do their readers more harm than good. A few of them are objective and liberal, and can be selectively used by psychotherapists and marriage and family counselors with their patients and clients. This article gives a highly personal view of some of the wheat and chaff in the field.

CHAPTER 50

Basic Books for the
Marriage Counselor

Ben N. Ard, Jr.

The professional marriage counselor is one, presumably, who has made a special study of the problems and interpersonal relationships of marriage and family life—in brief, the stresses and strains involved in membership in a marriage and family, and the psychosocial factors and influences of such membership on the personality, according to the American Association of Marriage Counselors (Mudd *et al*, 1958). Marriage counseling may be regarded as a specialized field of family counseling which centers largely on the interpersonal relationship between husband and wife. As Reevy (1967) has pointed out, marriage counseling involves many disciplines and is interprofessional (or interdisciplinary) in character. Those who wish to enter the field require a common body of scientific knowledge, techniques, and qualifications. The AAMC standards require (whatever the field of major emphasis) accredited training in: psychology of personality development; elements of psychiatry; human biology, including the fundamentals of sex anatomy, physiology, and genetics; the sociology of marriage and the family; legal aspects of marriage and the family; and counseling techniques.

This chapter is intended to provide an introduction to some of the major, basic books in these areas which would be of benefit to the professional marriage counselor. Obviously the fields covered are much too large to include all of the possible books in each area; therefore, some selection is necessary and inevitable. No doubt someone's favorite book will most certainly be left out. But the start of a professional library is indicated here; hopefully any professional marriage counselor would continue to add to his professional library as knowledge in the field grows. Where possible, an attempt has been made to select books of a scientific nature that are still in print. All of the books discussed can be found in Appendix A.

One additional comment might be worthy of attention: for this "professional library" as for any other, a bookplate might well be put in each of the books stating: "Possession does not imply approval"—certainly not of everything which appears in these books. All books should be read with a critical, inquiring mind, and the material checked out against further evidence. With that disclaimer, let us proceed to the books that might prove basically helpful to the professional marriage counselor.

Several classified bibliographies of articles, books, and pamphlets on sex, love, marriage, and family relations have appeared in the literature, for example, those of Ellis and Doorbar (1951, 1952) as well as previous efforts by Ard (1955, 1961). Aldous and Hill (1967) have published an *International Bibliography of Research in Marriage and the Family, 1900–1964*. Collections of papers on marriage counseling may be found in Silverman's *Marital Counseling* (1967); Klemer's *Counseling in Marital and Sexual Problems* (1965); Greene's *The Psychotherapies of Marital Disharmony* (1965); Fishbein and Burgess's *Successful Marriage* (1963); Mudd et al, *Marriage Counseling: A Casebook* (1958); Nash et al, *Marriage Counseling in Medical Practice* (1964); and Mudd and Krich's *Man and Woman* (1956).

For the psychology of personality development, several books may serve, e.g., Hall and Lindzey's now standard *Theories of Personality* (1957); Gordon's more experimentally- or research-oriented *Personality and Behavior* (1963); McCary's collection of six modern approaches to the *Psychology of Personality* (1956); Witmer and Kotinsky's fact-finding report, *Personality in the Making* (1952); and Sahakian's collection of readings, *Psychology of Personality: Readings in Theory* (1965). For a practical, down-to-earth book which can be given to clients as bibliotherapy, Albert Ellis has written *How to Live with a Neurotic* (1957).

For the elements of psychiatry, the marriage counselor may find the following books profitable: Arieti's two-volume *American Handbook of Psychiatry* (1959); Freedman and Kaplan's *Comprehensive Textbook of Psychiatry* (1967); Sullivan's *The Psychiatric Interview* (1954); Ruesch and Bateson's book which discusses the social matrix of psychiatry, *Communication* (1951); and an excellent recent study of *Depression* by Beck (1967).

For the legal aspects of marriage and the family, one may profitably consult Pilpel and Zavin's book, *Your Marriage and the Law* (1952); Haussamen and Guitar's *The Divorce Handbook* (1960); Kling's very practical paperback, *The Complete Guide to Divorce* (1963); or finally, Slovenko's comprehensive book, *Sexual Behavior and the Law* (1965). Farber and Wilson have published a symposium on *Teenage Marriage and Divorce* (1967). Goode has shown what happens *After Divorce* (1956).

For the sociology of marriage and the family, some of the information needed may be gleaned from Christensen's monumental *Handbook of Marriage and the Family* (1964); Sussman's *Source-book in Marriage and the Family* (1963); or Stephens' collection of *Reflections on Marriage* (1968), which represents a wide range of approaches, viewpoints, and areas of professional competence, e.g., men like Albert Ellis, Eric Berne, David Riesman, and William H. Whyte, Jr. Two good collections of readings are Schur's *The Family and the Sexual Revolution* (1964) and Bell and Vogel's *A Modern Introduction to the Family* (1960). Winch et al have published a collection of *Selected Studies in the Family* (1962). Two standard texts widely used in the field are Blood's *Marriage* (1962) and Robert Bell's *Marriage and Family Interaction* (1963). A new text is Saxton's *The Individual, Marriage, and The Family* (1968). Whyte, in his

The Organization Man (1956), has provided a sociological study of a way of life that many Americans are now leading. Blood and Wolf have provided a sociological study of different classes and ethnic groups in their book *Husbands and Wives* (1960). Cuber and Harroff have contributed a study of sexual behavior among the affluent in their book *The Significant Americans* (1965). Komarovsky has described *Blue-Collar Marriage* (1962). Bernard has described *Marriage and Family among Negroes* (1966). Albert Ellis, in his book *The Folklore of Sex* (1951), has documented the conflicting views held in America.

For human biology, including the fundamentals of sex anatomy, physiology, and genetics, there are a wide variety of books available. For sex anatomy, Dickinson's *Atlas of Human Sex Anatomy* (1949) is still probably the definitive book. Hastings, in his book *A Doctor Speaks on Sexual Expression in Marriage* (1966), discusses sexual anatomy and physiology, and also includes some of Dickinson's drawings of sexual anatomy. LeMon Clark has edited a very practical *Illustrated Sex Atlas* (1963) in paperback. Of course, every marriage counselor should be familiar with Masters and Johnson's *Human Sexual Response* (1966). Oliven has recently revised a manual on *Sexual Hygiene and Pathology* (1965). Allen, in England, has published *A Textbook of Psychosexual Disorder* (1962).

Sexual problems and sexual behavior form a large part of the day-to-day concerns the marriage counselor faces in his profession. Unfortunately, the publications in this area are quite uneven, with many books of questionable scientific value. Among some of the better references available in this particular area are the two monumental volumes edited by Ellis and Abarbanel, *The Encyclopedia of Sexual Behavior* (1961). De Martino has edited an excellent anthology dealing with *Sexual Behavior and Personality Characteristics* (1963). Brown and Kempton's *Sex Questions and Answers* (1950) is a good reference book because, among other things, it is in question and answer form. Stone and Stone's *A Marriage Manual* (1952) also follows the question-and-answer format. Albert Ellis's *The Art and Science of Love* (1960) is a very straightforward, down-to-earth book of the "marriage manual" sort, with emphasis on the sexual aspects. Another book which can be given to clients is Ellis's *Sex Without Guilt* (1965). McCary, in his book *Human Sexuality* (1967), has provided an objective and comprehensive reference as well as a contemporary marriage manual. Wahl has edited a book on *Sexual Problems* (1967), which deals with diagnosis and treatment in medical practice, with contributions from eighteen authorities.

A knowledge of the Kinsey volumes (1948, 1953) would seem to be virtually a necessity for marriage counselors. Gebhard et al (1958, 1965) have continued the investigations started by Kinsey. (See Appendix A for titles.)

Information about birth control should be available to every marriage counselor if he is to discuss such matters intelligently with his clients, even though the actual instruction in birth-control techniques is a function of the specially trained physician. Guttmacher's paperback, *A Complete Book of Birth Control* (1969), is an excellent, brief book, including discussion of the pill. Dickinson's *Techniques of Conception Control* (1950) has a professional, brief, but well-illustrated description of various birth-control methods (not including the pill). Rainwater and Weinstein have provided an excellent discussion of sex, contraception, and family planning in their book *And the Poor Get Children* (1960). Tietze (1960) has edited a *Selected Bibliography of Contraception: 1940–1960* for the National Committee on Maternal Health (2 East 103rd Street, New York, New York 10029) and it is available for only one dollar.

Some historical, cross-cultural perspective is needed on the subject of sex, if the marriage counselor is to rise above the limitations of the narrower aspects of attitudes toward sex in our culture. Several books can help him gain this needed perspective, including Ditzion's historical *Marriage, Morals, and Sex* (1953); Young's *Eros Denied* (1964); Lipton's description of the *Erotic Revolution* (1965); Bassett's fictional discussion of *A New Sex Ethics and Marriage Structure* (1961); English anthropologist Dingwall's critical look at *The American Woman* (1956); Ellis's *The American Sexual Tragedy* (1962); Taylor's *Sex in History* (1954); Comfort's *Sexual Behavior in Society* (1950); Lewinsohn's *A History of Sexual Customs* (1958); Ford and Beach's *Patterns of Sexual Behavior* (1951); Bernard's *The Sex Game* (1968); and Packard's *The Sexual Wilderness* (1968).

To do an effective job in premarital counseling the marriage counselor today needs to have considerable background in scientific knowledge about dating behavior, including premarital sexual behavior. For this sort of scientific knowledge, he can turn to Ehrmann's *Premarital Dating Behavior* (1959); Bell's *Premarital Sex in a Changing Society* (1966); Reiss's *Premarital Sexual Standards in America* (1960) and *The Social Context of Premarital Sexual Permissiveness* (1967); as well as Kirkendall's *Premarital Intercourse and Interpersonal Relationships* (1961). A book on *Premarital Counseling* has been written by Rutledge (1966). For books of practical help to the single person, two books by Albert Ellis are written especially for the single person: *Sex and the Single Man* (1963) and *The Intelligent Woman's Guide to Man-Hunting* (1963). Albert Gordon has presented a study of *Intermarriage* (1964), which is relevant in premarital counseling, as is Locke's *Predicting Adjustment in Marriage* (1951).

Counseling techniques may be said to be one of the most important areas where marriage counselors need to be up to date. There are several general books on marriage counseling, such as Mudd et al, *Marriage Counseling: A Casebook* (1958); Eisenstein's *Neurotic Interaction in Marriage* (1956); Johnson's *Marriage Counseling: Theory and Practice* (1961); Silverman's *Marital Counseling* (1967); Klemer's *Counseling in Marital and Sexual Problems* (1965); Taylor's *Marriage Counseling* (1965); Cuber's *Marriage Counseling Practice* (1948); Herbert and Jervis's *A Modern Approach to Marriage Counseling* (1959); Wallis and Booker's *Marriage*

Counseling (1958); Mudd's *The Practice of Marriage Counseling* (1952); Mudd and Krich's *Man and Wife* (1956); and Skidmore, Garret, and Skidmore's *Marriage Counseling* (1956).

The marriage counselor will find that more general books on different theoretical approaches to psychotherapy and counseling can prove helpful in working with marital and premarital problems. Some such books are those by Harper on *Psychoanalysis and Psychotherapy: 36 Systems* (1959), which is an excellent brief summary in a compact paperback; Ard's *Counseling and Psychotherapy* (1966), which includes many classics on theories and issues by various authorities; Frank's comparative study of psychotherapy, *Persuasion and Healing* (1963); Wolberg's two volumes on *The Technique of Psychotherapy* (1967); Patterson's *Theories of Counseling and Psychotherapy* (1966); Stein's *Contemporary Psychotherapies* (1961); Greenwald's excellent anthology of *Active Psychotherapies* (1967); Brammer and Shostrom's text on *Therapeutic Psychology* (1968); Stefflre's book on *Theories of Counseling* (1965), which includes four widely used theories; Watzlawick et al., *Pragmatics of Human Communication* (1967); McCary's *Six Approaches to Psychotherapy* (1955); Ford and Urban's comparative study of *Ten Systems of Psychotherapy* (1963); Mahrer's excellent book on *The Goals of Psychotherapy* (1967), which allows the reader to compare some of the leading theorists; and Greene's book on *The Psychotherapies of Marital Disharmony* (1965), wherein twelve contributors discuss varying views.

Books which deal with specialized techniques or particular theoretical approaches are those by Rogers, on *Client-Centered Therapy* (1951); Herzberg, on *Active Psychotherapy* (1945); Ellis, on *Reason and Emotion in Psychotherapy* (1962); Satir, on *Conjoint Family Therapy* (1964); Jackson's two volumes, one on *Communication, Family, and Marriage* (1968), and one on *Therapy, Communication, and Change* (1968); Ackerman, on *The Psychodynamics of Family Life* (1958); Rosenbaum and Alger's psychoanalytic perspective of *The Marriage Relationship* (1968); Wolpe, Salter, and Reyna's anthology of twelve contributors who discuss the challenge of *The Conditioning Therapies* (1964); Wolpe and Lazarus' guide to treatment through *Behavior Therapy Techniques* (1966); Riesman et al. *Mental Health of the Poor* (1964), a book of readings on new treatment approaches for low income people; Grier and Cobbs, two black psychiatrists, who discussed the inner dimensions of black men and women's life in America; Goldstein et al., who have applied nonclinical research findings to psychotherapy, both individual and group, in their book *Psychotherapy and the Psychology of Behavior Change* (1966); Bellak and Small's description of *Emergency Psychotherapy and Brief Psychotherapy* (1965), Phillips et al., *Short-Term Psychotherapy and Structured Behavior Change* (1966); Wolberg's *Short-Term Psychotherapy* (1965); Eysenck's *Experiments in Behavior Therapy* (1964), which consists of readings in modern methods of treatment derived from learning theory; Holland's *Fundamentals of Psychotherapy* (1965), which utilizes the explanatory and descriptive concepts of general psychology; Stieper and Wiener's *Dimensions of Psychotherapy* (1965), which discusses the major parameters of psychotherapy; Beier's discussion of *The Silent Language of Psychotherapy* (1966); and Pearson's *The Use of Written Communication in Psychotherapy* (1965).

Bibliotherapy, or suggesting particular books for clients to read, is a technique the marriage counselor may wish to consider. Many of the books previously discussed might be recommended to particular clients. Some books have been specifically written for use with clients, such as Ellis and Harper's *Creative Marriage* (1961), as well as their more general book, *A Guide to Rational Living* (1961). Lederer and Jackson's book, *The Mirages of Marriage* (1968), might also be considered.

The foregoing books will give the beginning marriage counselor some idea of the knowledge in the field which is relevant to his needs. The older, more experienced counselor may check over the familiar items and move on to some of the newer books to bring himself up to date. All counselors need to keep reading critically so that they may stay abreast of the constantly changing field called marriage counseling.

REFERENCES

Ard, B. N., Jr. Sex knowledge for the marriage counselor. *Merrill-Palmer Quarterly*, Winter 1955, *1*, 74-82.

Ard, B. N., Jr. Basic books on sex for family life educators. *The Family Life Coordinator*, July 1961, *10*, 63-68.

*Ellis, A., & Doorbar, R. R. Classified bibliography of articles, books, and pamphlets on sex, love, marriage, and family relations published during 1950. *Marriage and Family Living*, Spring 1951, *13*, 71-86.

Ellis, A., & Doorbar, R. R. Recent trends in sex, marriage and family research. *Marriage and Family Living*, November 1952, *14*, 338-340.

Mudd, E. H., et al. (Eds.) *Marriage counseling: A casebook.* New York: Association Press, 1958.

Reevy, W. R. Educational and professional training of the marital counselor. In Silverman, H. S. (Ed.), *Marital Counseling.* Springfield, Ill.: Thomas, 1967. Pp. 5-21.

---

* The various books referred to in the foregoing article may all be found in the annotated bibliography.

Appendices

Appendix A

ANNOTATED BIBLIOGRAPHY

Ackerman, N. W. *The psychodynamics of family life.* New York: Basic Books, 1958.

Aldous, J., & Hill, R. L. *International bibliography of research in marriage and the family, 1900–1964.* Minneapolis: University of Minnesota Press, 1967.

Allen, C. E. *A textbook of psychosexual disorders.* London: Oxford University Press, 1962.
[A standard text by an English psychiatrist.]

Ard, B. N., Jr. (Ed.) *Counseling and psychotherapy: classics on theories and issues.* Palo Alto: Science and Behavior Books, 1966.
[Articles by Branden, Browning, Callis, Ellis, Glasser, Maslow, Mowrer, Peters, Rogers, Samler, Thorne, Tyler, Williamson, and Wrenn.]

Arieti, S. (Ed.) *American handbook of psychiatry.* New York: Basic Books, 1959.
[A monumental two volumes; a standard in the field.]

Bassett, M. *A new sex ethics and marriage structure.* New York: Philosophical Library, 1961.
[A fictitious pair of college teachers, Adam and Eve, discuss a new sex ethic and marriage pattern.]

Beck, A. T. *Depression.* New York: Harper & Row, 1967.
[Clinical, experimental, and theoretical aspects of depression.]

Beier, E. G. *The silent language of psychotherapy.* Chicago: Aldine, 1966.
[A comprehensive, documented study of the crucial role of covert communication, persuasion, and social reinforcement in psychotherapy.]

Bell, N. W., & Vogel, E. F. (Eds.) *A modern introduction to the family.* New York: Free Press of Glencoe, 1960.

Bell, R. R. *Marriage and family interaction.* Homewood, Ill.: Dorsey Press, 1963.

Bell, R. R. *Premarital sex in a changing society.* Englewood Cliffs, N. J.: Prentice-Hall, 1966.
[A paperback Spectrum book which analyzes sociologically the changing nature of premarital sex in American society.]

Bellak, L. & Small, L. *Emergency psychotherapy and brief psychotherapy.* New York: Grune & Stratton, 1965.

[Experiences of the Trouble-Shooting Clinic in Queens, N. Y., which provided 24-hour emotional first-aid station.]

Bernard, J. *Marriage and family among Negroes.* Englewood Cliffs, N. J.: Prentice-Hall, 1966.
[A woman sociologist looks at Negro families.]

Bernard, J. *The sex game.* Englewood Cliffs, N. J.: Prentice-Hall, 1968.
[A sociologist discusses communication between the sexes—with words and without.]

Blood, R. O., Jr. *Marriage.* New York: Free Press of Glencoe, 1962.
[One of the standard texts in the field.]

Blood, R. O., Jr., & Wolfe, D. M. *Husbands and wives.* Glencoe, Ill.: Free Press, 1960.
[The dynamics of married living; a sociological study of different classes and ethnic groups in Detroit; comparisons with farm families.]

Brammer, L. M., & Shostrom, E. L. *Therapeutic psychology.* 2d ed. Englewood Cliffs, N. J.: Prentice-Hall, 1968.
[A comprehensive introduction to the field of psychological counseling and psychotherapy.]

Brown, F., & Kempton, R. T. *Sex questions and answers.* New York: McGraw-Hill, 1950.
[A guide to happy marriage; simple, direct, and authoritative answers to the sex questions most frequently asked.]

Christensen, H. T. (Ed.) *Handbook of marriage and the family.* Chicago: Rand McNally, 1964.
[A team approach of twenty-four leading authorities, providing an extensive treatment of theory and research in the field of marriage and the family.]

Clark, L. (Ed.) *Illustrated sex atlas.* New York: Heath Publications, 1963.
[A very practical paperback book with 287 illustrations. Includes a glossary of sex terms and a complete index.]

Comfort, A. *Sexual behavior in society.* New York: Viking, 1950.
[A bold, serious discussion by a rational humanist from England.]

Cuber, J. F. *Marriage counseling practice.* New York: Appleton-Century-Crofts, 1948.

Cuber, J. F., & Harroff, P. B. *The significant*

Americans. New York: Appleton-Century, 1965.
[A study of sexual behavior among the affluent by two sociologists.]

De Martino, M. F. (Ed.) *Sexual behavior and personality characteristics.* New York: Citadel Press, 1963.
[Twenty-four contributors discuss a wide variety of topics.]

Dickinson, R. L. *Atlas of human sex anatomy.* Baltimore: Williams & Wilkins, 1949.
[The definitive book on the subject.]

Dickinson, R. L. *Techniques of conception control.* Baltimore: Williams & Wilkins, 1950.
[Includes various methods but not the pill; also includes fifty excellent illustrations.]

Dingwall, E. J. *The American woman.* New York: Rinehart, 1956.
[An English anthropologist takes a controversial look at American women; a historical study.]

Ditzion, S. *Marriage, morals and sex.* New York: Bookman Associates, 1953.
[Dr. Ditzion, a librarian, has provided a history of ideas from colonial times to the era of the Kinsey report.]

Ehrmann, W. *Premarital dating behavior.* New York: Holt, 1959.
[This is a study of the premarital sexual activities in dating as reported by 1,000 male and female college students on written schedules and by 100 of these subjects in personal interviews.]

Eisenstein, V. W. (Ed.) *Neurotic interaction in marriage.* New York: Basic Books, 1956.
[An authoritative study of the problem areas in modern marriage by twenty-five specialists in psychoanalysis, psychology, anthropology, and social work.]

Ellis, A. *The folklore of sex.* New York: Charles Boni, 1951.
[An analysis of the conflicting attitudes toward sex as expressed in magazines, radio, TV, plays, novels, songs, and movies.]

Ellis, A. *How to live with a neurotic.* New York: Crown, 1957.
[Practical, rational advice on how to live with a neurotic, at home or at work.]

Ellis, A. *The art and science of love.* New York: Dell paperback, 1960.
[An objective, practical, honest, modern marriage manual dealing forthrightly with sex.]

Ellis, A. *The American sexual tragedy.* 2nd ed. New York: Lyle Stuart, 1962.
[An unflinching account of the difficulties that result from our sexual mores.]

Ellis, A. *Reason and emotion in psychotherapy.* New York: Lyle Stuart, 1962.
[The most comprehensive statement of rational-emotive psychotherapy.]

Ellis, A. *The intelligent woman's guide to man-hunting.* New York: Lyle Stuart, 1963.
[A very blunt, outspoken book which pulls no punches. Intended for the woman who wants to attack rationally the problem of man-hunting.]

Ellis, A. *Sex and the single man.* New York: Lyle Stuart, 1963.
[A practical, down-to-earth book, written in plain English for the single man who wants to integrate sex into his life in a rational manner.]

Ellis, A. *Sex without guilt.* Rev. ed. New York: Grove Press paperback, 1965.
[The frank and candid views one expects from this famous sexologist.]

Ellis, A., & Abarbanel, A. B. *The encyclopedia of sexual behavior.* New York: Hawthorn, 1961.
[Two volumes with contributions by ninety-eight authorities. The most extensive work of its kind.]

Ellis, A., & Harper, R. A. *A guide to rational living.* Hollywood: Wilshire Book Co., 1961.
[A good book for bibliotherapy. Practical, down-to-earth, written in plain English for the layman.]

Ellis, A., & Harper, R. A. *Creative marriage.* New York: Lyle Stuart, 1961 (also available as a Tower paperback, retitled *The marriage bed*).
[A discussion of the problems of marriage and advice on how to handle them by rational psychotherapy.]

Eysenck, H. J. (Ed.) *Experiments in behavior therapy.* New York: Macmillan, 1964.
[Readings in modern methods of treatment of mental disorders derived from learning theory.]

Farber, S. M., & Wilson, R. H. L. (Eds.) *Teenage marriage and divorce.* Berkeley: Diablo Press paperback, 1967.
[A symposium with papers by fourteen contributors from various disciplines and a panel of teenagers who discussed why they "didn't wait."]

Fishbein, M., & Burgess, E. W. (Eds.) *Successful marriage.* Revised ed. Garden City, N. Y.: Doubleday, 1963.
[Thirty-eight contributors discuss various aspects of marriage.]

Ford, C. S., & Beach, F. A. *Patterns of sexual behavior.* New York: Harper, 1951.
[The most comprehensive study yet made of 190 different societies.]

Ford, D. H., & Urban, H. B. *Systems of psychotherapy.* New York: Wiley, 1963.
[A comparative study of ten systems: Freud, the ego analysts, Dollard and Miller, Wolpe, Adler, Rank, Rogers, existential analysis, Horney, and Sullivan.]

Frank, J. D. *Persuasion and healing*. New York: Schocken Books, 1963.
[A comparative study of the various schools of modern psychotherapy.]

Freedman, A. M., & Kaplan, H. I. (Eds.) *Comprehensive textbook of psychiatry*. Baltimore: Williams & Wilkins, 1967.
[An eclectic, multidisciplinary, comprehensive textbook.]

Gebhard, P. H., *et al. Pregnancy, Birth and Abortion*. New York: Harper, 1958.
[A study of approximately seven thousand women by the Institute for Sex Research (founded by Kinsey).]

Gebhard, P. H., *et al. Sex offenders*. New York: Harper & Row, 1965.
[The results of the study by the Institute for Sex Research of 1,500 sex offenders.]

Goldstein, A. P., *et al. Psychotherapy and the psychology of behavior change*. New York: Wiley, 1966.
[Applies nonclinical research findings to psychotherapy, both individual and group.]

Goode, W. J. *After divorce*. Glencoe, Ill.: Free Press, 1956.
[What happens to mothers who divorce.]

Gordon, A. I. *Intermarriage: Interfaith, interracial, interethnic*. Boston: Beacon, 1964.
[Presents statistical and case data on a variety of intermarriages. Views of 5,000 students.]

Gordon, J. E. *Personality and behavior*. New York: Macmillan, 1963.
[An integrated presentation of personality against a background of experimental research.]

Greene, B. L. (Ed.) *The psychotherapies of marital disharmony*. New York: Free Press, 1965.
[Twelve contributors, mostly psychiatrists and social workers, discuss these topics originally presented in a panel in Chicago on March 20, 1964, for the American Orthopsychiatric Association.]

Greenwald, H. (Ed.) *Active psychotherapies*. New York: Atherton, 1967.
[Includes a wide variety of theorists on various approaches; e.g., psychoanalysis, behavioral therapy, interactional analysis, reciprocal inhibition, rational therapy, implosive therapy, and others.]

Grier, W. H., & Cobbs, P. M. *Black rage*. New York: Basic Books, 1968.
[Two black psychiatrists discuss the inner dimensions of black men and women's life in America.]

Guttmacher, A. F. *The complete book of birth control*. New York: Ballentine Books paperback, 1961.
[Medical techniques, the new pills, contraceptive products, and popular myths are discussed by the Chairman of the Medical Committee of the Planned Parenthood Federation of America.]

Hall, C. S., & Lindzey, G. *Theories of personality*. New York: Wiley, 1957.
[A variety of approaches to personality are described, with brief biographies of the men associated with each approach. A standard text.]

Harper, R. A. *Psychoanalysis and psychotherapy: 36 systems*. Englewood Cliffs, N. J.: Prentice-Hall, 1959.
[An excellent brief summary of thirty-six different systems of psychotherapy in a compact paperback.]

Hastings, D. W. *A doctor speaks on sexual expression in marriage*. Boston: Little, Brown, 1966.
[The chairman of the Department of Psychiatry and Neurology at the Medical School of the University of Minnesota writes from the modern point of view, not the moralistic. Includes the well-known drawings of Dr. R. L. Dickinson.]

Haussamen, F., & Guitar, M. A. *The divorce handbook*. New York: Putnam's Sons, 1960.
[A good handbook for reference in the marriage counselor's library.]

Herbert, W. L., & Jervis, F. V. *A modern approach to marriage counseling*. London: Methuen, 1959.
[An English team's approach to marriage counseling.]

Herzberg, A. *Active psychotherapy*. London: Research Books, 1945.
[An unusual approach, using "tasks" assigned by the therapist.]

Holland, G. A. *Fundamentals of psychotherapy*. New York: Holt, Rinehart & Winston, 1965.
[An approach to psychotherapy utilizing the explanatory and descriptive concepts of general psychology.]

Jackson, D. D. (Ed.) *Communication, family, and marriage. Human communication*, Volume 1. Palo Alto: Science and Behavior Books, 1968.
[Papers by Jackson, Bateson, Fry, Haley, Kantor, Riskin, Satir, Watzlawick, and Weakland on generalizations from clinical observation; the double bind theory; communication, systems and pathology; and research approaches and methods.]

Jackson, D. D. (Ed.) *Therapy, communication, and change. Human communication*, Volume 2. Palo Alto: Science and Behavior Books, 1968.
[Papers by Jackson, Bateson, Fry, Haley, Satir, Watzlawick, Weakland, Weblin, and Yalom on psychotic behavior and its interactional contexts; the interactional contexts of

other behavior; interactional views and reviews of psychotherapy; conjoint family therapy.]

Johnson, D. *Marriage counseling: Theory and practice.* Englewood Cliffs, N. J.: Prentice-Hall, 1961.
[A text by a counselor formerly on the staff at the Menninger Clinic.]

Kinsey, A. C., *et al. Sexual behavior in the human male.* Philadelphia: Saunders, 1948.
[The most extensive research on the subject ever completed; results of interviews with 5,300 males across the U. S.]

Kinsey, A. C., *et al. Sexual behavior in the human female.* Philadelphia: Saunders, 1953.
[The results of interviews with nearly eight thousand women across the U. S.]

Kirkendall, L. A. *Premarital intercourse and interpersonal relationships.* New York: Julian Press, 1961.
[A research study of interpersonal relationships based on case histories of 668 premarital intercourse experiences reported by 200 college-level males.]

Klemer, R. H. (Ed.) *Counseling in marital and sexual problems.* Baltimore: Williams & Wilkins, 1965.
[A physician's handbook with chapters by twenty different specialists.]

Kling, S. G. *The complete guide to divorce.* New York: Simon & Schuster, 1963.
[A practical paperback in question-and-answer form. Includes a dictionary of legal terms, a directory of legal-aid services, a directory of lawyers' referral services.]

Komarovsky, M. *Blue-collar marriage.* New York: Random House, 1962.
[A portrayal of working-class existence, of value to the marriage counselor.]

Lederer, W. J., & Jackson, D. D. *The mirages of marriage.* New York: Norton, 1968.
[This book covers the false assumptions of marriage and discusses how to make a marriage work.]

Lewinsohn, R. *A history of sexual customs.* New York: Harper, 1958.
[A cross-cultural examination in objective terms.]

Lipton, L. *The erotic revolution.* Los Angeles: Sherbourne Press, 1965.
[An affirmative view of the new morality.]

Locke, H. J. *Predicting adjustment in marriage.* New York: Holt, 1951.
[A comparison of a divorced and a happily married group, a total of 929 persons (a general population sample).]

Mahrer, A. R. (Ed.) *The goals of psychotherapy.* New York: Appleton-Century-Crofts, 1967.
[The goals of psychotherapy, as seen by leading theorists such as Wolberg, Saul, White-born, Fine, Rosen, Raimy, Wolpe, Van Kaam, Gendlin, Ellis, Dreikurs, Kelly, and others.]

Masters, W. H., & Johnson, V. E. *Human sexual responses.* Boston: Little, Brown, 1966.
[A pioneer study; a research of eleven years into the anatomy and physiology of human sexual response in 382 women and 312 men.]

McGinnis, T. *Your first year of marriage.* Garden City, N. Y.: Doubleday, 1967.
[A frank and practical guide for the newly married.]

Mudd, E. H. *The practice of marriage counseling.* New York: Association Press, 1952.
[A text by one of the early leaders in the field.]

Mudd, E. H., *et al,* (Eds.) *Marriage counseling: A casebook.* New York: Association Press, 1958.
[This casebook was edited for the American Association of Marriage Counselors and includes 41 typical cases adapted from the files of 38 leading marriage counselors.]

Mudd, E. H., & Krich, A. (Eds.) *Man and wife.* New York: Norton, 1956.
[An anthology with contributions from several different authorities.]

McCary, J. L., & Scheer, D. E. (Eds.) *Six approaches to psychotherapy.* New York: Dryden Press, 1955.
[A symposium of the views of Hobbs, Wolberg, Slavson, Reider, Thorne, and Moreno.]

McCary, J. L. (Ed.) *Psychology of personality.* New York: Grove, 1956.
[Six modern approaches by six different authorities: Leopold Bellak, Raymond Cattell, George Klein, Margaret Mead, Nevitt Sanford, and David McClelland.]

McCary, J. L. *Human sexuality.* Princeton: Van Nostrand, 1967.
[A contemporary marriage manual. An objective and comprehensive reference source for personal, premarital, and marriage counseling.]

Nash, E. M., *et al.* (Eds.) *Marriage counseling in medical practice.* Chapel Hill: University of North Carolina Press, 1964.
[A symposium with twenty-two contributors, mostly physicians, written primarily for physicians, covering marriage counseling by the physician; premarital medical counseling; concepts of marital diagnosis and therapy; and marriage counseling instruction in the medical school curriculum.]

Oliven, J. F. *Sexual hygiene and pathology.* (2d ed.) Philadelphia: Lippincott, 1965.
[A manual for the physician and the professions.]

Packard, V. *The sexual wilderness.* New York: McKay, 1968.
[The contemporary upheaval in male-female relationships.]

Patterson, C. H. *Theories of counseling and psychotherapy*. New York: Harper & Row, 1966.
[Presents a variety of viewpoints.]

Pearson, L. (Ed.) *The use of written communications in psychotherapy*. Springfield, Ill.: Thomas, 1965.
[Contributions by Arthur Burton, Albert Ellis, Molly Harrower, and Victor Raimy.]

Phillips, E. L., & Wiener, D. N. *Short-term psychotherapy and structured behavior change*. New York: McGraw-Hill, 1966.
[A theory of psychotherapy closely tied to direct, observable behavior.]

Pilpel, H., & Zavin, T. *Your marriage and the law*. New York: Holt, Rinehart & Winston, 1952.
[A practical, helpful book for the lay person and the marriage counselor.]

Rainwater, L., & Weinstein, K. K. *And the poor get children*. Chicago: Quadrangle Books, 1960.
[An excellent discussion of sex, contraception, and family planning among the poor.]

Reiss, I. L. *Premarital sexual standards in America*. Glencoe, Ill.: Free Press, 1960.
[A sociological investigation of the relative social and cultural integration of American sexual standards.]

Reiss, I. L. *The social context of premarital sexual permissiveness*. New York: Holt, Rinehart & Winston, 1967.
[The first sociological study of a national probability sample in the area of premarital sexual attitudes.]

Riessman, F., *et al*. (Eds.) *Mental health of the poor*. New York: Free Press of Glencoe, 1964.
[Readings on new treatment approaches for low-income people.]

Rogers, C. R. *Client-centered therapy*. Boston: Houghton Mifflin, 1951.
[The spokesman for client-centered therapy presents perhaps the definitive book on the approach.]

Rosenbaum, S. & Alger, I. (Eds.) *The marriage relationship*. New York: Basic Books, 1968.
[Some twenty-five members of the Society of Medical Psychoanalysts provide psychoanalytic perspectives of the marriage relationship.]

Ruesch, J., & Bateson, G. *Communication: The social matrix of psychiatry*. New York: Norton, 1951.
[One of the early contributions which introduced a theoretical approach which has greatly influenced family therapy.]

Rutledge, A. L. *Pre-marital counseling*. Cambridge, Mass.: Schenkman, 1966.
[Deals with wide-ranging information of value to the marriage counselor.]

Sahakian, W. S. (Ed.) *Psychology of personality: Readings in theory*. Chicago: Rand McNally, 1965.
[Selections from twenty-one prominent psychologists, with biographical material by the editor.]

Satir, V. *Conjoint family therapy*. Palo Alto: Science and Behavior Books, 1967.
[A guide to theory and technique; family theory; communication theory; theory and practice of therapy.]

Saxton, L. *The individual, marriage, and the family*. Belmont, Calif.: Wadsworth, 1968.
[An excellent new text with a good glossary.]

Schur, E. M. (Ed.) *The family and the sexual revolution*. Bloomington: Indiana University Press, 1964.
[Selected readings by a variety of contributors focusing on sex standards, premarital intercourse, the social roles of women, and birth control.]

Silverman H. S. (Ed.) *Marital counseling*. Springfield, Ill.: Thomas, 1967.
[A large volume presenting thirty-six nationally known specialists on a variety of topics.]

Skidmore, R., Garrett, H. V. S., & Skidmore, C. J. *Marriage counseling*. New York: Harper, 1956.
[A standard text in the field.]

Slovenko, R. (Ed.) *Sexual behavior and the law*. Springfield, Ill.: Thomas, 1965.
[A comprehensive book with forty-seven contributors.]

Stefflre, B. (Ed.) *Theories of counseling*. New York: McGraw-Hill, 1965.
[Presents four widely used theories by four different experts.]

Stein, M. I. (Ed.) *Contemporary psychotherapies*. New York: Free Press of Glencoe, 1961.
[Ten leading psychotherapists discuss the theoretical orientations of the major therapies. Each theorist contributed a paper dealing with theory and one on a case discussion or research.]

Stephens, W. N. (Ed.) *Reflections on marriage*. New York: Crowell, 1968.
[Represents a wide range of approaches, viewpoints, and areas of professional competence; e.g., men like Albert Ellis, Eric Berne, David Riesman, and William H. Whyte, Jr.]

Stieper, D. R., & Wiener, D. N. *Dimensions of psychotherapy*. Chicago: Aldine, 1965.
[An experimental and clinical approach, discussing research on the major parameters of psychotherapy.]

Stone, H., & Stone, A. *A marriage manual*. (Rev. ed.) New York: Simon & Schuster, 1952.
[One of the widely accepted marriage manuals, in question-and-answer form.]

455

Sullivan, H. S. *The psychiatric interview*. New York: Norton, 1954.
[This book is concerned with any kind of interviewing which aims at clarifying certain patterns of living, to the end that benefit may accrue to the person being interviewed.]

Sussman, M. B. *Sourcebook in marriage and the family*. (2d ed.) Boston: Houghton Mifflin, 1963.
[Seventy-five articles on marriage and the family.]

Taylor, D. L. *Marriage counseling*. Springfield, Ill.: Thomas, 1965.
[A brief introduction to nondirective marriage counseling, with emphasis on communication and feelings. No footnotes, no bibliography, no references.]

Taylor, G. R. *Sex in history*. New York: Vanguard, 1954.
[An objective look at sex throughout history.]

Tietze, C. (Ed.) *Selected bibliography of contraception 1940–1960*. New York: National Committee on Maternal Health, 1960.

Wahl, C. W. (Ed.) *Sexual problems*. New York: Free Press, 1967.
[Diagnosis and treatment in medical practice; contributions from eighteen authorities.]

Wallis, H. J., & Booker, H. S. *Marriage counseling*. London: Routledge, Kegan Paul, 1958.

Watzlawick, P., Beavin, J. H., & Jackson, D. D. *Pragmatics of human communication*. New York: Norton, 1967.
[A study of interactional patterns, pathologies, and paradoxes of human communication with special attention to behavior disorders.]

Whyte, W. H., Jr. *The organization man*. New York: Doubleday, 1956.
[A sociological study of a way of life that many Americans are now leading, and that many more are likely to lead.]

Winch, R. F., *et al.* (Eds.) *Selected studies in the family*. New York: Holt, Rinehart & Winston, 1962.
[One of the standard books of readings in the field.]

Witmer, H. L., & Kotinsky, R. (Eds.) *Personality in the making*. New York: Harper, 1952.
[The fact-finding report of the Midcentury White House Conference on Children and Youth.]

Wolberg, L. R. (Ed.) *Short-term psychotherapy*. New York: Grune & Stratton, 1965.
[Nine theorists join Wolberg in discussing various aspects of brief or short-term psychotherapy.]

Wolberg, L. R. *The technique of psychotherapy*. (2d. ed.) New York: Grune & Stratton, 1967. 2 vols.
[A comprehensive textbook with many practical suggestions. Several good appendices.]

Wolpe, J., & Lazarus, A. C. *Behavior therapy techniques*. London: Pergamon Press, 1966.
[A guide to the treatment of neuroses from the behaviorist approach.]

Wolpe, J., Salter, A., & Reyna, L. J. (Eds.) *The conditioning therapies*. New York: Holt, Rinehart and Winston, 1964.
[Twelve contributors discuss the challenge of conditioning therapies in psychotherapy.]

Young, W. *Eros denied*. New York: Grove, 1964.
[Sex in Western society is discussed by an English scholar in a frank, open manner.] .

Appendix B
FILMS FOR MARRIAGE AND FAMILY COUNSELORS

Are You Ready for Marriage? 15 minutes; distributed by Craig Corporation. Larry and Sue, a young couple, consult a marriage counselor after Sue's parents express concern about the marital plans of their daughter. Through productive questioning, the counselor points out important considerations regarding courtship, engagement, and marriage. A practical checklist is presented. (1952)

Choosing for Happiness. 14 minutes; distributed by McGraw-Hill Book Company. Is he right for me? is the question asked each time the central character meets a new boy. All have something she wants, but when she tries to change them, they drift away leaving her puzzled and hurt. She discovers that she must first examine herself and be willing to change before she can demand that other individuals change.

Eye of the Beholder. 30 minutes; distributed by Stuart-Reynolds Productions. An excellent film expressing various individual's reactions, perceptions, and opinions regarding a young man throughout a series of events which are happening to, and affecting, him. It later photographs the young man in his reality and what the true events were that took place. (1956)

How Do You Know It's Love? 13 minutes; distributed by Craig Corporation. For a happy marriage, a feeling of attraction is not enough. Mature love, as this movie explains, can be judged by certain factors. Young persons need a basis for understanding, discussion, insight, and judgment of this problem— how do you know when it is love? (1953)

How Much Affection? 20 minutes; distributed by McGraw-Hill Book Company. A high-school boy and girl struggle with conflicting forces which develop from their love toward each other. The problem of what is right behavior is discussed. (1958)

Is This Love? 14 minutes; distributed by McGraw-Hill Book Company. This movie contrasts two girls' romances (college roommates) and their ideas regarding love and what constitutes a successful marriage. (1958)

Marriage Is a Partnership. 17 minutes; distributed by Craig Corporation. Via the utilization of the flashback technique, topics such as marital loyalties, responsibilities, and the making of other decisions during early years of marriage is shown. Other related problems discussed are: in-laws, personal adjustment, and budgeting. (1953)

Parents Are People, Too. 15 minutes; distributed by McGraw-Hill Book Company. A high-school teacher helps teen-age students (through a "gripe session") begin to understand the views held by their parents. Group discussions can prove to be helpful in evaluating and summarizing of ideas. (1955)

Social-Sex Attitudes in Adolescence. 22 minutes; distributed by McGraw-Hill Book Company. Shows the important experiences of a teenage boy and girl as they mature and understand their sexual development. (1953)

This Charming Couple. 19 minutes; distributed by McGraw-Hill Book Company. This film follows the courtship of two young people who are in love with love and not with each other. They refuse to evaluate the good qualities and shortcomings of each other. (1956)

Appendix C
AGENCIES FOR REFERRALS

The agencies listed below are only a few of the many responsible places where one may secure information about professional assistance for marriage counseling. Most cities of any size have a directory which lists local agencies (frequently available through the United Fund, Community Chest, or Red Feather offices). Colleges or universities sometimes are also good resources for referrals to clinics or training centers.

American Association of Marriage Counselors, Inc., 3603 Lemmon Avenue, Dallas, Texas 75219. [A *Directory of Members* is available, including regional associations.]

American Institute of Family Relations, 5287 Sunset Boulevard, Los Angeles, California 90027.

American Personnel and Guidance Association, 1607 New Hampshire Avenue, N. W., Washington, D. C. 20009. [Publishes a *Directory of Approved Counseling Agencies*, some of which provide marriage counseling.]

Family Service Association of America, 215 Fourth Avenue, New York, New York 10003.

Institute for Rational Living, Inc., 45 East 65th Street, New York, New York 10021.

Merrill-Palmer Institute, 71 East Ferry Avenue, Detroit, Michigan 48202.

National Association for Mental Health, Inc., 10 Columbus Circle, New York, New York, 10019.

Planned Parenthood Federation of America, Inc., 501 Madison Avenue, New York, New York 10022.

Reproductive Biology Research Foundation, 4910 Forest Park Boulevard, St. Louis, Missouri 63108.

Appendix D
PROFESSIONAL ORGANIZATIONS

The following professional organizations are a few of the ones that might prove particularly helpful for marriage counselors:

Academy of Psychologists in Marital Counseling, William R. Reevy, Ph.D., President, c/o Department of Psychology, New Mexico Institute of Mining and Technology, Socorro, New Mexico 87801.

American Association of Marriage Counselors, Inc., 3603 Lemmon Avenue, Dallas, Texas 75219.

American Orthopsychiatric Association, 1790 Broadway, New York, New York 10019.

California State Marriage Counseling Association, 9172 Vons Drive, Garden Grove, California 92641.

National Association for Mental Health, Inc., 10 Columbus Circle, New York, New York 10019.

National Council on Family Relations, 1219 University Avenue, S. E., Minneapolis, Minnesota 55414.

Planned Parenthood Foundation of America, Inc., 501 Madison Avenue, New York, New York 10022.

SIECUS (Sex Information and Education Council of the United States), 1855 Broadway, New York, New York 10023.

Society for the Scientific Study of Sex, 12 East 41st Street (Suite 1104), New York, New York 10028.

Appendix E

PSYCHOTHERAPY INVENTORY

AARON L. RUTLEDGE

Director of Psychotherapy Program, The Merrill-Palmer Institute

Confidential information for the use of your psychotherapist. For pre-marital or marriage counseling, each of the couple should fill out an Inventory.

Published by

THE MERRILL-PALMER INSTITUTE, 71 East Ferry Avenue, Detroit, Michigan 48202

© Aaron L. Rutledge 1967; revision of "Individual and Marriage Counseling Inventory" © 1956

The "Psychotherapy Inventory" is reproduced here by permission of the author and publisher.

A. PERSONAL DATA

Date today_____ Referred by:_____

                                                Name   Position   Address

1. List problems, in order of their importance to you, which you would like to discuss:_____

2. INDIVIDUAL DATA:
   Sex_____ Date of birth_____ Age_____ Height_____ Weight_____
   Education completed (grades, degrees or courses)_____
   Further study plans_____
   Religious preference (denomination): In childhood_____ Now_____
   Military service: (branches and dates)_____
   Describe your life: Very happy_____ Happy_____ Average_____ Unhappy_____ Very unhappy_____
   List sources from which sex information was received_____

3. OCCUPATIONAL DATA:
   Type of employment and position or duties_____

   Previous employment_____
   Annual income *before* deductions: Your income_____ Mate's income_____ Total_____

4. PHYSICAL HEALTH DATA:
   Very good_____ Good_____ Average_____ Poor_____. List present illnesses, symptoms, including allergies

   List childhood and other illnesses, surgery, handicaps, etc., underlining any which caused serious difficulty_____

   When was last medical check-up?_____. Reason for this, and findings_____

   List or describe purpose of *medication* of any kind now being taken_____

   Your Physician_____
                                        Name   Telephone
                   Address

5. EMOTIONAL HEALTH DATA:
   Ever had serious mental disturbance or a "nervous breakdown"?_____ When?_____
   Treated by_____
   Hospitalized?_____ How long ill?_____
   List all previous psychotherapy, counseling, or other treatment for personal and/or marital problems:

Dates	Type of Problem	Name of Professional or Agency

   Type of health insurance carried_____
   (Does it cover emotional or mental problems?)_____

6. MARITAL AND FAMILY STATUS:
   Single_____ Going Steady_____ Engaged_____ How long_____ Number previous engagements_____
   Married_____ Date Married_____ How long dating mate_____ How long engaged_____
   Mate's age_____ Occupation_____ Education_____ Religion_____
   Children by present marriage:

Name	Age	Comments (residence, custody, support, etc.)

   Separated_____ When separated_____; Widowed_____ When widowed_____
   Divorced_____ When divorced_____ Divorce applied for_____ By whom_____
   Previous marriages: How many_____ How terminated_____ Date_____
   Children by *previous* marriages:

Name	Age	Comments (residence, custody, support, etc.)

B. YOUR PARENTAL FAMILY

Your Father   *Your Mother*

1. Age now if living_____ _____
   Age at death and date_____ _____
2. Nationality background_____ _____
3. Education completed (Circle)

   Grammar School   5   6   7   8   5   6   7   8

   High School   9   10   11   12   9   10   11   12

   College   1   2   3   4   1   2   3   4

   Graduate   1   2   3   4   1   2   3   4

4. Occupation_____ _____

   (Father—major and minor:

   Mother—before and after marriage)_____ _____

5. Religious (denominational) preference

   Present_____ _____

   In Childhood_____ _____

6. Age at Marriage_____ _____

7. Rate your parents' marriage

   Very happy_____ Happy_____ Average_____ Unhappy_____ Very unhappy_____

8. Do parents live together? Yes_____ No_____ Separated_____ Your age then_____ Divorced_____ Your age then_____

9. Remarried? Mother_____ Your age then_____; Father_____ Your age then_____

10. Do you feel closest to your father?_____; Your mother?_____

11. If you are married, did your parents approve? Father: Before_____ Later_____. Mother: Before_____ Later_____

12. Data about your brothers and sisters in order of birth:

Age	Sex	Living (yes, no)	Education	Occupation	Health	Marital Status	Marital Adjustment (very happy, happy, average, unhappy, very unhappy)	Number Children

13. Describe other persons who lived in your parental home and their relationship to you_____
_____
_____
_____

Code No._____

Your name_____

Street address_____

City_____ State_____ Zip Code_____

Telephone: Residence:_____ Office:_____

Code No._____

C. THE PERSONAL RELATIONS IN MY PARENTAL FAMILY

For use *only* if specifically assigned; even then, if this portion of the Inventory causes undue anxiety, delay completing it until you have discussed the material with your psychotherapist.

Write several paragraphs about each of the following:

1. My father as an individual, including personality changes
2. My relationship to him through the years
3. My mother as an individual, including personality changes
4. My relationship to her through the years
5. My parents' relationship to each other:
   1) Which was dominant? By choice or by necessity?
   2) Which was submissive? By choice or by necessity?
   3) Describe what you know about their relationship:
      a) As two personalities
      b) As financial team, or otherwise
      c) As members of their community
      d) In handling problems
      e) In dealing with children
      f) Their affectional life, including sex relations
6. Discuss your brothers and sisters:
   1) Their reaction to parents
   2) Their reaction to each other
   3) Your relationship to them individually and collectively
7. Evaluate both constructive and destructive influences upon yourself and upon the remainder of the family from both the short range and long term points of view.

Do not write below this line

Code No._____; Psychotherapist_____; Fee_____

Dates Seen		Presenting Problems:

Diagnosis and Revealed Problems:

Outcome:

A SIMPLIFIED RECORD SYSTEM FOR COUNSELORS

Aaron L. Rutledge

The bulk of individual counseling on any high school, college, or university campus is accomplished by professors and other staff members as an activity over and above their regular duties. Particularly active as part-time counselors are the deans, house managers, personnel directors, chaplains, and professors of family life, home economics, sociology, and psychology. Only a few of the larger universities have services in conjunction with a health center or psychology department which provide psychotherapy for staff and students. In increasing number, colleges and universities are establishing counseling centers, but intensive service tends to be limited by lack of trained staff to the most disturbed individuals.

Whether a full or part-time activity, one of the basic requisites to intelligent handling of a problem by clinical counseling is a confidential record of interview material. The record serves as a basis for the counselor in subsequent contact, as material for critical self-study of his technique and effectiveness, and as a source of reliable information in referral or in collaboration with other professional persons. If some uniformity of records could be established among counselors, they would provide an invaluable resource for investigation of types of problems handled and methods and techniques used toward their resolution. Of course, such use necessarily would be contingent upon having a carefully selected research team and the clients' permissions.

Broad experience in counseling family members, of all ages and presenting varying problems, has resulted in the development of an effective method of keeping records of pertinent information. It requires a minimum of effort when only brief notes are possible and provides for a most complete record system when adequate secretarial assistance is available.

Two auxiliary needs are basic to an adequate record system; secretarial help and anonymity of the counselee in the handling of the records. Secretarial assistance may be inadequate for typing interview notes; in fact, for part-time counselors it may be limited to a student available for part-time secretarial help, or nonexistent. The personality or level of development of a secretary may contraindicate exposing her to information obtained in counseling. With student help a counselor may feel that it is unfair to burden her with the responsibility of keeping confidences, and many students would not want fellow students to have access to material about them. Colleges and agencies are beginning to realize that adequate secretarial-receptionist staff is secondary in significance only to the qualifications of counselors in counseling and guidance programs.

Lock filing cabinets, or a safe, are essential, and should be kept in a room which is securely locked when authorized personnel are not in it. Keys must not be available to very many people, and locks must be changed when a key is lost. Each incoming secretary must be instructed thoroughly in the proper record procedure, the significance of individual personalities, and the importance of their confidences remaining inviolate. Better, by far, to be meticulous and methodical about the record system than to be careless and then spend time worrying. Records are not likely to be stolen, although it has occurred, but precautions bring peace of mind to the counselor who feels responsible to the trust of people, and it is reassuring to clients—to college and university students, especially—to know that their confidences are handled profes-

---

Reprinted by permission of author and publisher.

sionally. Every person involved with counseling should understand that information about an individual, including whether he has been or is being seen, is not to be given to *anyone* (even relatives or professional persons) without the specific permission of the client, and then only by the counselor in charge. The only exceptions would be professional consultants used by the counselor, and a code system eliminates the necessity of disclosing names to them.

A code system is an added guarantee of confidentiality, since it prevents clients' names from appearing in conjunction with any statements about them. A code book or card file containing the names of the clients, their code numbers, and perhaps the interview dates, should be available only to those actually doing counseling. It is best that even the location of the code key be confidential in a relatively uncontrolled environment. At the first interview, a number is assigned to the client by the counselor or, in a setting which warrants it, by the secretary. The name and number go into the code key file; only the number appears with all information. Of course the client does not know his number; only that the records are coded.

Coding methods are limited only by ingenuity, but the simpler the better. Records may be numbered chronologically as persons appear for counseling. All members of the same family may have the same number: the letters M and F may be attached to denote sex; children who are seen become MC and FC; if more than one child of the same family and sex are seen, numbers are added in parentheses to indicate them in the order of birth. For instance, since Mrs. X is the fiftieth person to request counseling her number is 50F. Her husband is interviewed and becomes 50M. They have three girls but only the one born second is seen; she becomes 50FC(2). Simply by clipping together the information about each person, the record of the family may be kept together.

With or without adequate secretarial help, a workable record system is essential to clinical counseling, whether in a counseling center or by a part-time counselor. When the counselor compiles his own records they must be brief. As an aid to counseling and as a means of collecting uniform data conducive to research, the author developed the *Individual and Marriage Counseling Inventory.** This is a four-page, printed folder which can be filled out by the individual immediately before the initial interview. Part A provides space for "personal data," which enables the person to depict his educational, marital, occupational, financial, religious, cultural, and health statuses, as well as to state the major problems with which he wishes help. Part B is devoted to "family data," which gives vital information about the parental family of the person. Part C is a guide for the individual to use in discussing the personal relationships in his family as an aid to discovering some of the most dynamic factors in counseling preparatory to marriage. It should never be used with a disturbed client except in a controlled situation. Therefore, for general office use the inventory should be folded inside out and stapled so as to conceal Part C. The final one-half page of the folder provides space for the counselor to record dates of interviews, presenting problems, further difficulties revealed in counseling, and the outcome.

The folder is printed upon paper almost as heavy as the "manila folders" commonly used for filing. Filed with the folded edge down, the code number is on the left upper corner. Interview notes and other papers may be filed within the folder, eliminating the necessity of purchasing and preparing a "file folder." Placed in a standard manila folder the *Inventory* does not protrude but, because over all it is 9 x 11 inches,

---

*The current edition has been retitled *Psychotherapy Inventory*. It is available on a nonprofit basis through the Counseling Service, Merrill-Palmer School, 71 East Ferry Avenue, Detroit, Michigan. Price: 20 forms, $1.00; 50 forms, $2.00.

it is readily found among 8-1/2 x 11 inch papers. Page 2 of the *Inventory* provides space for the name and address of the individual, arranged so that it can be removed with scissors as a card 3 x 5 inches and filed as the code card. Identical numbers are placed on both the *Inventory* folder and the code card. The inventory forms simplify establishing and maintaining a record system and make unnecessary the puchase of either manila folders or file cards.

Name Index

Abarbanel, Albert, 263, 443, 446, 452
Ackerman, Nathaan W., 141, 168, 172, 175, 180, 221–224, 228, 230, 448, 451
Adler, Alfred, 92, 106, 114, 452
Adler, K. A., 106, 114
Aiken, H. D., 55–56, 59
Albert, G., 64, 7
Aldous, J., 445, 451
Alger, I., 132, 137, 438–439, 448, 455
Allen, C. E., 446, 451
Allport, G., 128, 137
Ames, L. B., 423
Ard, Ben N., Jr., 1, 10–14, 32, 50–60, 92, 115–119, 169, 213–219, 351–353, 356, 379, 399–403, 411, 413–416, 426, 436, 439, 451
Ard, Constance C., 92, 128–138, 379, 399–403, 411, 413–416, 425, 427–439
Arieti, S., 445, 451
Aurelius, Marcus, 117
Axline, Virginia, 134, 137

Bach, George R., 301, 313–321
Ballard, R. G., 99, 105
Barbara, D. A., 128, 137
Basamania, B. W., 221, 230
Bassett, M., 447, 451
Bateson, G., 141, 144, 169, 213–214, 218–219, 445, 453, 455
Beach, F. A., 447, 452
Beavin, J. H., 213, 219, 456
Beck, A. T., 445, 451
Beckman, D. R., 129–130, 137
Bedford, Stewart, 32, 83–87
Beier, E. G., 134–135, 137, 427, 434, 449, 451
Bell, C., 128, 137
Bell, J. E., 142, 168, 220–221, 225, 228, 230
Bell, N. W., 445, 451
Bell, Robert R., 263, 445, 447, 451
Bellak, L., 448, 451
Bergler, Edmund, 440
Berkowitz, L., 55, 59
Berlien, I. C., 220, 230
Bernard, Jessie, 263, 429, 434, 446–447, 451
Berne, E., 246, 445
Bird, H. W., 221, 230
Bird, W., 180
Birdwhistell, R., 128, 137, 144, 168
Blinder, Martin G., 231, 233–246
Blood, Robert O., Jr., 302, 329–341, 445–446, 451
Bloy, Myron B., Jr., 277–278
Booker, H. S., 447, 456
Bowen, Murray, 92, 139–168, 172, 180, 220, 224, 228, 230
Bowman, H. A., 332, 341
Brammer, L. M., 448, 451

Branden, Nathaniel, 58–59, 218–219, 451
Bridgman, Ralph P., 414, 416
Broderick, Carlfred, 263
Brody, W. M., 228, 230
Brooks, S., 130, 137
Brown, F., 446, 451
Brown, Helen Gurley, 443
Browning, R. L., 219, 451
Bruner, Jerome, 129
Burgess, E. W., 37, 40, 332, 341, 433–434, 445, 452
Burtness, James H., 274, 278
Burton, A., 439

Caen, Herb, 54
Calderone, Mary, 267, 278
Callis, Robert, 451
Carroll, E. J., 222–224, 230
Chagall, M., 130
Chance, E., 224, 228, 230
Chesser, E., 299
Christensen, H. T., 94, 105, 263, 445, 451
Clark, LeMon, 446, 451
Cleland, John, 442
Cobbs, P. M., 448, 453
Collier, J. L., 274, 278
Comfort, A., 447, 451
Cornelison, A., 168
Cottrell, L. S., 40, 433–434
Crawley, Lawrence, 383, 386
Cuber, J. F., 11, 14, 61–62, 71, 446–447, 451

Davis, Kingsley, 37, 40, 413–414, 416
Davitz, F., 128, 137
Davitz, J. L., 128, 137
Day, Donald, 54, 59
Dearborn, Lester, 381–383, 386, 389
Delaney, D. J., 130, 137
De Martino, M. F., 446, 452
de Sade, Marquis, 442
Despert, J. L., 415–416, 423
Deutsch, Danica, 106, 114
Deutsch, Helen, 440
Dickerson, Charles H., 31, 380, 404–408
Dickinson, Robert L., 363, 382, 446–447, 452
Dingwall, E. J., 447, 452
Dittman, A. T., 128, 137, 427, 434, 438–439
Ditzion, S., 447, 452
Dollard, J., 452
Donne, John, 231
Doorbar, R. R., 445, 449
Dreikurs, Rudolf, 442, 454
Duvall, Evelyn, 385, 443
Dysinger, R., 144, 168

Ebstein, Wilhelm, 379
Ehrlich, D., 71

467

Subject Index